EVALUATION IN SOCIAL WORK

EVALUATION IN SOCIAL WORK

THE ART AND SCIENCE OF PRACTICE

Fourth Edition

YVONNE A. UNRAU
Western Michigan University

PETER A. GABOR
University of Calgary

RICHARD M. GRINNELL, JR.
Western Michigan University

OXFORD
UNIVERSITY PRESS
2007

OXFORD
UNIVERSITY PRESS

Oxford University Press, Inc., publishes works that further
Oxford University's objective of excellence
in research, scholarship, and education.

Oxford   New York
Auckland   Cape Town   Dar es Salaam   Hong Kong   Karachi
Kuala Lumpur   Madrid   Melbourne   Mexico City   Nairobi
New Delhi   Shanghai   Taipei   Toronto

With offices in
Argentina   Austria   Brazil   Chile   Czech Republic   France   Greece
Guatemala   Hungary   Italy   Japan   Poland   Portugal   Singapore
South Korea   Switzerland   Thailand   Turkey   Ukraine   Vietnam

Copyright © 2007 by Oxford University Press

Published by Oxford University Press, Inc.
198 Madison Avenue, New York, New York 10016

www.oup.com

Oxford is a registered trademark of Oxford University Press

Library of Congress Cataloging-in-Publication Data
Unrau, Yvonne A.
Evaluation in social work : the art and science of practice / Yvonne A. Unrau,
Peter A. Gabor, and Richard M. Grinnell, Jr.—4th ed.
p. cm.
Previously published under the title: Evaluation in the human services. c2001.
Includes bibliographical references and index.
ISBN-13 978-0-19-530806-8
ISBN 0-19-530806-9
1. Human services—Evaluation.   2. Human services—Evaluation—Case studies.
I. Gabor, Peter, M.S.W.   II. Grinnell, Richard M.   III. Unrau, Yvonne A. Evaluation in the
human services.   IV. Title.
HV40.U66 2006
361.0068'4—dc22   2006003814

9 8 7 6 5 4 3 2 1

Printed in the United States of America
on acid-free paper

A Few Words for Students

This introductory program evaluation book has enjoyed a very successful career. As with the previous three editions, this one was also written for you— a graduate social work student—as your first introduction to program evaluation. We have selected and arranged our book's contents so it can be used in a beginning one-semester social work program evaluation course. It is designed to be used in social work administrative courses and/or program planning courses as well.

Goal and Objectives

Our goal is to produce a "user-friendly," straightforward introduction to program evaluation couched within the quantitative and qualitative traditions—the two approaches most commonly used to generate relevant social work knowledge. To accomplish our goal, we strived to meet four simple objectives:

1. To prepare you to *participate* in evaluative activities within your social service organization.
2. To prepare you to become a beginning *critical producer* of the professional evaluative literature.
3. To prepare you to become a beginning *consumer* of the professional evaluative literature.
4. To prepare you for more advanced evaluation courses and texts.

In a nutshell, we provide you with a sound conceptual understanding of how the ideas of evaluation can be used in the delivery of the day-to-day services you are going to offer your clients. In addition, you will obtain the beginning knowledge and skills you will need to demonstrate your accountability—not only to the social work profession, your supervisor, your funding sources, and yourself but to your clients as well.

Your Previous Foundational Research Methods Course

Our book builds upon the knowledge and skills you gained from your previous foundational social work research methods course. As you are aware, you were required to take that course early in your studies, whether you were enrolled on a part-time or full-time basis or on a creative combination of the two. Most schools of social work with a program evaluation course offer it *after* you have taken the required foundational research methods course. The sequence of these two courses makes sense because a program evaluation within a social service agency is simply *applying* a majority of what you learned in your previous foundational research methods course.

In sum, the course you are now taking assumes you have mastered the knowledge and skills contained in your previous research methods course. Unfortunately, many times this required course is waived if you are an advanced standing student; that is, you do not have to take it if you have a bachelor of social work (BSW) degree because the content of the course was supposed to be covered in your BSW program. Sometimes the content was indeed covered, but sometimes not.

Book's Companion Web Site

We know from years of teaching experience that sometimes students forget the foundational research methods content they previously learned due to a variety of reasons. This is where our book will really help you—we offer an opportunity, via the book's Web site, for you to refresh your memory on the foundational research material that was presented in your previous research methods courses.

When you go to our book's Web site, you will see an oak tree displayed for each chapter you click on. The content you will learn in each chapter is listed above the ground. Most of this content will be new to you and is contained within the chapter you are reading.

Below the ground lie the roots of our oak tree. As you know, roots provide the necessary foundation for trees not only to stand but to flourish as well. Without roots (the foundational content you were supposed to have previously covered in your other courses), there would be no tree. This foundational content may or may not be new to you and is displayed below the ground of our tree. You can click on to relevant links that should refresh your memory.

So, in a nutshell (sorry, we had to do it), our oak tree analogy is akin to doing a program evaluation. You cannot do a program evaluation—the contents of our book (above-the-ground content)—without knowing basic foundational research methodology—the knowledge you were supposed to have obtained in your previous foundational research methods course (below-the-ground content).

Web Site Content

Our book is the first social work program evaluation book to offer a comprehensive Web site that you can access free of charge. As we mentioned previously, you can easily use this site when you want to use our hyperlinked trees to "refresh yourself" with material that was covered in your foundational research method's text. Our Web site provides you access to crash courses on topics that were covered in your foundational research methods book, such as

- Ways of knowing
- Evaluation contexts
- Ethics
- Quantitative research methodology
- Qualitative research methodology
- Measurement:
  - Designing measuring instruments
  - Locating measuring instruments
- Sampling
- Case-level designs (single-subject designs)
- Group-level designs
- Original data collection methods:
  - Observation
  - Participant observation
  - Research interviewing
  - Surveys
- Existing data collection methods:
  - Secondary analysis
  - Content analysis
  - Using existing statistics
  - Historical research
- Analyzing data
  - Analyzing quantitative data
  - Analyzing qualitative data
- Report writing
  - Writing quantitative proposals and reports
  - Writing qualitative proposals and reports
  - Evaluating quantitative research reports

You can also use the Web site to

- Electronically look up a definition of an evaluation concept
- Review key terms with a deck of virtual flash cards

- Test your knowledge with essay questions and short multiple-choice chapter quizzes

Visit www.oup.com/us/swevaluation

STUDENT-FRIENDLY BOOK

In addition to the hyperlinked trees found on our book's Web site, we have incorporated the additional following learning pedagogy within our book:

- We have written our book in a crisp style using direct language; that is, you will understand all the words.
- Our book is easy to teach *from* and *with*. This will not only make you happy but it will also make your instructor happy.
- We include only the core material that you will realistically need in order to appreciate and understand the role of program design and evaluation within the social work profession. Our guiding philosophy was to include only material that you realistically need to know to function adequately as an entry-level social work practitioner; information overload was avoided at all costs.
- We discuss the application of evaluation methods in real-life social service programs rather than in artificial settings.
- We discuss the process of doing ethical evaluations throughout the book. In fact, we have devoted an entire chapter to ethics.
- We make an extraordinary effort to make this edition less expensive, more esthetically pleasing, and much more useful for you than ever before. We have purposively kept the book's cost down in comparison to others on the market today.
- Abundant tables and figures have been used to provide visual representation of the concepts presented in our book.
- Numerous boxes are inserted throughout to complement and expand on the chapters; these boxes present interesting evaluation examples, provide additional aids to your learning, and offer historical, social, and political contexts of program evaluation.
- We have included human diversity content throughout the chapters. Many of our examples center around women and minorities because you need to be knowledgeable about their special needs and problems. We have given special consideration to the application of research methods to the study of questions concerning these groups.
- Review questions are presented at the end of each chapter so that you can determine your understanding of the material presented in the chapter.

LOGICAL AND FLEXIBLE TEACHING PLAN

Our book is organized in a way that makes good sense for teaching fundamental program evaluation. Many other sequences that could be followed would make just as much sense, however. The chapters (and parts) in this book were consciously planned to be independent of one another. They can be read out of the order in which they are presented, or they can be selectively omitted. However, they will probably make the most sense to you if you read the chapters in the sequence in which they are presented.

Like all introductory books, ours had to include relevant basic program evaluation content. Our problem here was not so much what content to include as what to leave out. Every topic that we have touched on in passing has been treated in depth elsewhere. But our elementary book is a primer, an introduction, a beginning. Our aim was to skim the surface of the social work evaluative enterprise—to put a toe in the water, so to speak, and to give you a taste of what it might be like to swim.

Student Learning Skills

Our book contains four major parts, where each part represents a learning skill that we believe you will need for doing program evaluations within a social service agency:

1. You need to know how to prepare yourself for an evaluation.
2. You need to know how to conduct evaluations.
3. You need to know how to gather data and make decisions from these data.
4. You need to know the contexts where program evaluations take place.

Each of the four parts represents a major learning skill. Each part has several chapters that will help you to achieve each skill.

- Part I: Preparing for an Evaluation
    - Chapter 1: Becoming an Accountable Practitioner
    - Chapter 2: Approaches to Accountability
    - Chapter 3: Designing Client-Centered Programs
    - Chapter 4: Getting Ready for an Evaluation

- Part II: Doing an Evaluation
    - Chapter 5: Doing a Needs Assessment
    - Chapter 6: Doing a Process Evaluation
    - Chapter 7: Doing an Outcome Evaluation
    - Chapter 8: Doing an Efficiency Evaluation

- Part III: Gathering Data and Making Decisions
    - Chapter 9: Measuring Variables
    - Chapter 10: Data Sources, Sampling, and Data Collection Methods

CONCEPTUAL APPROACH

With the organization of our book in mind, we present a unique approach in describing the place of evaluation in the social services. Simply put, our approach is realistic, practical, applied, and most importantly, user friendly. As can be seen from Figure 1, we describe how data obtained through case-level evaluation can be aggregated to provide timely and relevant program-level evaluation information. Such information, in turn, is the basis for a quality improvement process within the entire organization.

In short, we have blended the two distinct evaluation approaches (i.e., case-level and program-level) to demonstrate how they complement one another in contemporary professional practice. The integration of case-level and program-level approaches is one of the unique features of our book; we are convinced that this integration will play an increasingly prominent role in the future.

We have omitted more advanced methodological and statistical material such as

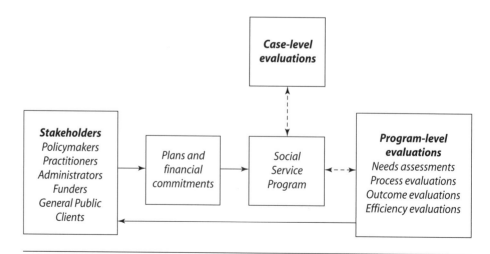

Figure 1 The case-level and program-level evaluation process in social work.

a discussion of celeration lines, autocorrelation, effect sizes, and two standard-deviation bands for case-level evaluation as well as advanced statistical techniques for program-level evaluation.

Those of you with a strict methodological orientation may find that our approach is overly simplistic, particularly the material on the aggregation of case-level data. We are aware of the limitations of our approach, but we firmly believe that this approach is more likely to be implemented by you, the beginning social work practitioner, than are other more complicated, technically demanding approaches.

It is our opinion that the aggregation of case-level data can provide valuable feedback about services and programs and can be the basis of an effective quality-improvement process. It is our view that it is preferable to have such data, even if it is not methodologically airtight, than to have no aggregated data at all.

THEME

The underlying theme of our book is that you can easily use evaluation procedures in your practice and program. We maintain that professional practice rests upon the foundation that practice activities must be linked to the client's objectives, which are linked to the program's objectives, which are linked to the program's goals, which are linked to the agency's goals, which represent the reason why the social service program exists in the first place. The evaluation process we present heavily reflects these connections.

Accountability Pressures

Pressures for accountability have never been greater. Organizations and practitioners of all types are increasingly required to document the impact of their services not only at the program level but also at the case level. Continually, we are challenged to improve the quality of our services, and we are required to do this with scarce resources. In addition, few social service organizations can adequately maintain an internal evaluation department or hire outside evaluators. Consequently, we place considerable emphasis on monitoring, an approach that can be easily incorporated into the ongoing activities of the practitioner within the program.

In short, we provide a straightforward view of evaluation while taking into account:

- The current pressures for accountability in the social services.
- The evaluation technologies and approaches that are currently available.
- The present evaluation needs of you, the student, as well as your needs in the first few years of your career.

NEW CONTENT

A tremendous amount of new content has been added to this edition in an effort to keep current while retaining material that has stood the test of time. As can be expected, a few instructors have expressed disappointment that several of the chapters in the previous three editions have been deleted. In general, chapters were dropped because they were not being assigned as required reading, and it was necessary to make room for new ideas and development while retaining a manageable and accessible size for this revision.

What's New in This Edition?

Without reservation, the hyperlinked oak trees, accessed via the book's Web site, are the major edition to this volume. The Web site is a monumental resource for those who want to read further about social work research and evaluation.

In reference to the third edition of our book, which was published in 2001, this one contains eight new chapters. The remaining nine chapters have been substantially revised and updated.

New Chapters

Chapter 4: Getting Ready for an Evaluation
Chapter 5: Doing a Needs Assessment
Chapter 6: Doing a Process Evaluation
Chapter 7: Doing an Outcome Evaluation
Chapter 8: Doing an Efficiency Evaluation
Chapter 12: Using Graphs to Report Evaluation Results
Chapter 13: Analyzing Qualitative Data
Chapter 17: Writing Grant Proposals

ACKNOWLEDGMENTS

We thank the following scholars for their respective chapter contributions: Ed Miner and Mary Michaud (Chapter 12); Ellen Taylor-Powell and Marcus Renner (Chapter 13); Carol Ing (Chapter 16); and The Foundation Center (Chapter 17).

The folks at Oxford University Press were invaluable to seeing this huge project through to completion, especially Maura Roessner and Keith Faivre. A special thanks goes to Albert L. Roberts, who was instrumental in the book's publication.

We are also appreciative of the social work graduate students who commented (and did they "comment"!) on the final draft version of our book in the spring 2006 semester of Grinnell's social work evaluation course at Western Michigan University: Beverly Ackles, Patrick Coffey, Janell Frens, Mark Fynewever, Ariel Hommes, Karrie Irey, Sarahajane C. Jarman, Anne Lepard, Barbara Powles, Kristine Rahn, Vicki Shumaker, Scott Steenwyk, Andrew Tomacari, Lonnie Wade, Susan Wallace, Amy Wilson, and Brandon Youker.

Out of the above class, four additional students contributed to the book's Web site and deserve a special round of thanks: Maria Drake (essay questions with answers), Rebecca Longcore (learning objectives), Mary Muliett (chapter outline via PowerPoint, with links), and Jessica Rozga (short quizzes with answers).

A LOOK TOWARD THE FUTURE

The field of evaluation and quality improvement in the social services is continuing to grow and develop. We hope this book contributes to that growth. A fifth edition is anticipated, and suggestions for it are more than welcome. Please send your comments directly to

Yvonne A. Unrau
School of Social Work
Western Michigan University
Kalamazoo, Michigan 49008
yvonne.unrau@wmich.edu

If this book helps you to acquire basic evaluation knowledge and skills and assists you in more advanced evaluation and practice courses, our efforts will have been more than justified. If it also assists you in incorporating evaluation techniques into your practice, our task will be fully rewarded.

YVONNE A. UNRAU
PETER A. GABOR
RICHARD M. GRINNELL, JR.

CONTENTS

ABOUT THE AUTHORS

Yvonne A. Unrau is an associate professor within the School of Social Work at Western Michigan University in Kalamazoo, Michigan. She has worked and studied in the area of foster care since 1989. Her interest in foster care began as a family preservation worker in a Canadian family service agency where she worked with many children at risk for out-of-home placement. She later worked as a treatment foster-care coordinator and then went on to earn her doctorate in social work from the University of Utah. Her research area has focused primarily on family support and foster-care services, with particular interest in service delivery monitoring for the purposes of improving client outcomes as well as the service delivery experience. Dr. Unrau is co-editor (with Richard M. Grinnell, Jr.) of *Social Work Research and Evaluation: Quantitative and Qualitative Approaches, 7th edition* (Oxford University Press, 2005), co-author (with Margaret Williams and Richard M. Grinnell, Jr.) of *Research Methods for Social Workers, 5th edition* (Eddie Bowers, 2005), and has published numerous professional journal articles that have examined the services provided to vulnerable children and their families. http://homepages.wmich.edu/~yunrau

Peter A. Gabor is a professor within the Faculty of Social Work at the University of Calgary. He received his BA, BSW, and MSW from McGill University and his Ph.D. in social work from Arizona State University. Dr. Gabor has authored books as well as numerous articles and conference papers on topics related to evaluation, child and family services, and the leadership of organizations. In his consulting practice, he has conducted evaluations for a variety of local, provincial, and national organizations. Recently, Dr. Gabor completed a project intended to increase evaluation capacity in the family resource program sector in Canada; a national evaluation instrument and an Internet-based data management system were developed for this project.

Richard M. Grinnell, Jr., is a professor and holds the Clair and Clarice Platt Jones/Helen Frays Endowed Chair of Social Work Research within the School of Social Work at Western Michigan University. He received his Ph.D. in social work from the University of Wisconsin at Madison and for over the past 30 years has held academic and senior university administrative appointments in Australia, Canada, and the United States. In addition to his international reputation based on well over 100 journal articles, book chapters, and conference presentations, Dr. Grinnell has published 24 books on social work research methods, statistics, and evaluation. His latest book (with Robert W. Weinbach) is *Statistics for Social Workers, 7th edition* (2007). http://homepages.wmich.edu/~rgrinnell

ABOUT THE AUTHORS

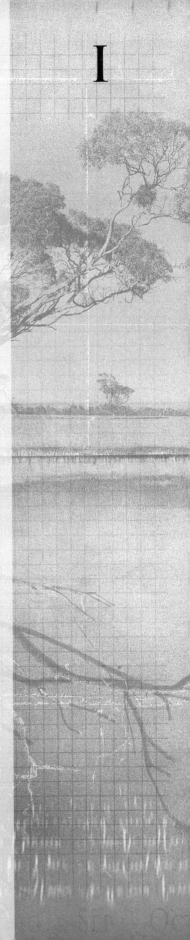

PREPARING FOR AN EVALUATION

Part I contains four chapters that set the stage for all types of program evaluations.

Chapter 1 discusses how social work practitioners are accountable to various stakeholder groups via program evaluations. It presents the quality improvement process as an integral part of any social service program and highlights the various stakeholder groups that must be consulted before doing any kind of program evaluation.

Chapter 2 builds upon Chapter 1 by presenting two common methods that are used to evaluate social service programs—the external project–type evaluation, sometimes called a summative evaluation, and the internal monitoring–type evaluation, sometimes called a formative evaluation. The chapter highlights the internal monitoring approach as a key evaluation approach that is not only practical but is also easy to carry out without a great deal of "research expertise."

Chapter 3 discusses in detail how to design a social service program so that it can be evaluated. The chapter presents the various elements of all programs: mission statements, goals, objectives, and program logic models.

The final chapter in Part I of this book, Chapter 4, describes how a social service program gets ready for program evaluations via the input from its stakeholders. It also addresses the need to focus an evaluation and presents the rationale for clarifying the data needs before an evaluation begins.

In sum, the four chapters in Part I prepare program evaluators to evaluate programs via the various types of program evaluations that are found in Part II.

BECOMING AN ACCOUNTABLE PRACTITIONER

1

Madame Cleo is an astrological consultant who advertises widely on television promising that her astounding insights into love, business, health, and relationships will help her viewers to achieve more fulfilling and gratifying lives. "Hah!" you think. "I bet she can't do this for me! I bet she's just out for the money! But if she could, but if she could only tell me . . . ! How do I know if she's for real or I'm just getting taken for a ride? Perhaps the Enron Corporation could have used her services."

There is a parallel here between the people who receive social services—sometimes called **clients**—and you, the future social worker. Most of the people we help—in common with all those people who are never seen by social workers—would like more fulfilling and rewarding lives. Like Madame Cleo's naive clientele who get suckered into calling her, many of our clients also have personal issues, money issues, relationships issues, or health issues. Unlike Madame Cleo, however, who only has to be accountable to her checkbook, we, as a profession, are required to be accountable to society (Figure 1.1) and must be able to provide answers to three basic **accountability** questions:

1. How do our *clients* know that we can help them?
2. How does our *profession* know that we have helped our clients?
3. How do the *funding bodies* that fund the programs (which employ us) know how effectively their dollars are being spent?

Client
A person who uses a social service agency—an individual, a couple, a family, a group, an organization, or a community.

Accountability
Being answerable for the actions and decisions we make.

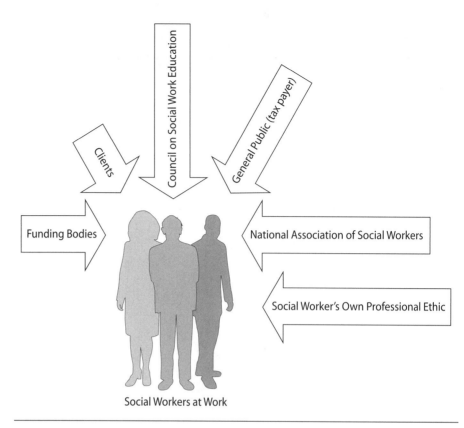

Figure 1.1 We are accountable to many forces including ourselves.

EVALUATION AND ACCOUNTABILITY

What is the role that research plays in answering the three accountability questions? In one word *significant!* That is the position of both the **Council on Social Work Education** (CSWE) and the **National Association of Social Workers** (NASW). These two prestigious national accountability organizations have jurisdiction over what curriculum content is required to be taught to all social work students (CSWE) and how the students, after they graduate, practice their trade (NASW).

The Council on Social Work Education

The CSWE is the official educational organization that sets minimum curriculum standards for BSW and MSW programs throughout the United States. This accreditation organization firmly believes that all social work students should know the basic principles of research and **evaluation**. The Council mandates that all social work programs have a research curriculum of some sort that addresses the research areas contained in Box 1.1.

Council on Social Work Education (CSWE)
The official educational organization that sets minimum curriculum standards for BSW and MSW programs throughout the United States.

National Association of Social Workers (NASW)
A professional organization that works to enhance the professional growth and development of social workers.

Evaluation
A form of appraisal using valid and reliable research methods.

PART I Preparing for an Evaluation

Box 1.1 Ethical Standards for Evaluation Research: Excerpts From the National Association of Social Workers' *Code of Ethics*

(a) Social workers should monitor and evaluate policies, the implementation of programs, and practice interventions.

(b) Social workers should promote and facilitate evaluation and research to contribute to the development of knowledge.

(c) Social workers should critically examine and keep current with emerging knowledge relevant to social work and fully use evaluation and research evidence in their professional practice.

(d) Social workers engaged in evaluation or research should carefully consider possible consequences and should follow guidelines developed for the protection of evaluation and research participants. Appropriate institutional review boards should be consulted.

(e) Social workers engaged in evaluation or research should obtain voluntary and written informed consent from participants, when appropriate, without any implied or actual deprivation or penalty for refusal to participate; without undue inducement to participate; and with due regard for participants' well-being, privacy, and dignity. Informed consent should include information about the nature, extent, and duration of the participation requested and disclosure of the risks and benefits of participation in the research.

(f) When evaluation or research participants are incapable of giving informed consent, social workers should provide an appropriate explanation to the participants, obtain the participants' assent to the extent they are able, and obtain written consent from an appropriate proxy.

(g) Social workers should never design or conduct evaluation or research that does not use consent procedures, such as certain forms of naturalistic observation and archival research, unless rigorous and responsible review of the research has found it to be justified because of its prospective scientific, educational, or applied value and unless equally effective alternative procedures that do not involve waiver of consent are not feasible.

(h) Social workers should inform participants of their right to withdraw from evaluation and research at any time without penalty.

(i) Social workers should take appropriate steps to ensure that participants in evaluation and research have access to appropriate supportive services.

(j) Social workers engaged in evaluation or research should protect participants from unwarranted physical or mental distress, harm, danger, or deprivation.

(k) Social workers engaged in the evaluation of services should discuss collected information only for professional purposes and only with people professionally concerned with this information.

(l) Social workers engaged in evaluation or research should ensure the anonymity or confidentiality of participants and of the data obtained from them. Social workers should inform participants of any limits of confidentiality, the measures that will be taken to ensure confidentiality, and when any records containing research data will be destroyed.

(m) Social workers who report evaluation and research results should protect participants' confidentiality by omitting identifying information unless proper consent has been obtained authorizing disclosure.

(n) Social workers should report evaluation and research findings accurately. They should not fabricate or falsify results and should take steps to correct any errors later found in published data using standard publication methods.

(o) Social workers engaged in evaluation or research should be alert to and avoid conflicts of interest and dual relationships with participants, should inform participants when a real or potential conflict of interest arises, and should take steps to resolve the issue in a manner that makes participants' interests primary.

(p) Social workers should educate themselves, their students, and their colleagues about responsible research practices.

To see the *Code of Ethics* in its entirety, visit http://www.naswdc.org/pubs/code/code.asp.

The National Association of Social Workers

Just like CSWE, the NASW is a parallel practice organization that works to enhance the professional growth and development of practicing social workers. Like CSWE with social work students, NASW believes that social work practitioners should also know the basics of research, as shown in Box 1.2.

This book provides the beginning research content to comply with the research standards set out by CSWE and NASW. Unlike Madame Cleo, however, social work students and practitioners are expected to have a substantial research knowledge base to guide and support their **interventions**. This knowledge base is generally derived from your social work education.

Of course, we, as a profession, tend to have more credibility than astrological consultants like Madame Cleo. We have graduated from accredited social work programs (CSWE) and have recognized practice qualifications (NASW). You are expected to have not only good intentions but the skills and knowledge to convert your good intentions into desired practical results that will help your clients. It all boils down to the fact that we have to be accountable to society; to do so means that we need to acquire the knowledge and skills to help our clients in an effective and efficient manner.

Professional social workers have an influential role in helping to understand and ameliorate the numerous social and economic problems that exist in our society. The very nature of our profession puts us directly in society's trenches—that is, we interact with people and the problems that prevent them from a quality life enjoyed by the majority of our society. We practice in such places as inner-city neighborhoods and hospices, and we work with people such as those who are homeless and mentally challenged.

Consequently, many social workers experience firsthand the presenting problems of clients, many of which result from societal injustices. Of course, social workers, as part of a profession, are expected to help make things better, not only for our clients but also for the society in which we all live. Unlike card and palm readers, contemporary social work practitioners are expected to have a professional knowledge base to guide and support their professional practice efforts, commonly referred to as interventions. This knowledge base is generally derived from research and evaluation methods—much of which you will learn in the course that has required you to purchase this book.

As it stands, the day-to-day interventions that we use in our profession could benefit from a bit of improvement. For instance, we lack the know-how to stop family violence, to eradicate discrimination, and to eliminate human suffering that comes with living in poverty, be it in our own country where poverty is found in isolated pockets or in developing countries where poverty is pervasive. Through social work education we learn both theory and research that, in turn, we are expected to translate into useful interventions to help our clients. One only needs to come face to face with a few social work scenarios to realize the limits of our profession's knowledge base in helping

Interventions
The theoretical approach social workers use to create planned change.

Box 1.2 Council on Social Work Education's BSW and MSW Curriculum Research Content

B6.0—BSW Curriculum Content

- The research curriculum must provide an understanding and appreciation of a scientific, analytic approach to building knowledge for practice and to evaluating service delivery in all areas of practice. Ethical standards of scientific inquiry must be included in the research content.
- The research content must include quantitative and qualitative research methodologies; analysis of data, including statistical procedures; systematic evaluation of practice; analysis and evaluation of theoretical bases, research questions, methodologies, statistical procedures, and conclusions of research reports; and relevant technological advances.
- Each program must identify how the research curriculum contributes to the student's use of scientific knowledge for practice.

M6.0—MSW Curriculum Content

- The foundation research curriculum must provide an understanding and appreciation of a scientific, analytic approach to building knowledge for practice and for evaluating service delivery in all areas of practice. Ethical standards of scientific inquiry must be included in the research content.
- The research content must include qualitative and quantitative research methodologies; analysis of data, including statistical procedures; systematic evaluation of practice; analysis and evaluation of theoretical bases, research questions, methodologies, statistical procedures, and conclusions of research reports; and relevant technological advances.
- Each program must identify how the research curriculum contributes to the student's use of scientific knowledge for practice.

  To see all of the CSWE's *Education Policy and Education Standards*, visit http://www.cswe.org.

us to know *exactly* what to do, where to do it, and when to do it. For example, imagine that you are the social worker expected to intervene in the following situations:

- An adolescent who is gay has been beaten by his peers because of his sexual preference.
- A neighborhood, predominantly populated by families of color with low incomes, has unsafe rental housing, inadequate public transportation, and under-resourced public schools.
- A family is reported to child protection authorities because the parents have refused the necessary medical attention for their sick child because of their religious beliefs.

- Officials in a rural town are concerned about the spread of methamphetamine addiction in their community.

Despite the complexity of these scenarios, there is considerable public pressure on social workers to "fix" such problems. As employees of **social service programs,** social workers are expected to stop parents from abusing their children, keep inner-city youth from dropping out of school, prevent discrimination in society, and remedy a host of other such problems. If that is not enough, we are expected to achieve positive outcomes in a timely manner with less than adequate financial resources. And all of this is occurring under a watchful public eye.

So how is it that social workers are to both provide effective client services *and* advance our profession's knowledge base—all at the same time? As can be seen in Box 1.2, we do this—one client and one program at a time—by evaluating our individual practices with clients or programs as a whole. We commit to NASW's philosophy of quality improvement by continually and systematically looking for new ways to make client services more responsive, more efficient, and more effective. This is the goal of the **quality improvement process** in the social services.

QUALITY IMPROVEMENT IN SOCIAL SERVICE PROGRAMS

Quality improvement means that we continually monitor our practices and programs in order to enhance client service delivery offered by social service programs. In a nutshell, **case-level evaluations** evaluate the effectiveness and efficiency of our individual services, and **program-level evaluations** evaluate the effectiveness and efficiency of the social service programs as a whole. Data collected for either evaluation can inform program planning and decision making to improve services to clients (see Figure 1 in "A Few Words for Students").

Case-Level Evaluation

It is at the case level that practitioners provide direct services to client systems such as individuals, couples, families, groups, organizations, and communities. At the case level, each and every individual social worker can evaluate a client system. It is at this level that we customize evaluation plans to learn about specific details and patterns of change that are unique to a single client system. For example, suppose you are employed as a community outreach worker for the elderly and it is your job to help aging clients remain safely living in their homes for as long as possible before assisted living arrangements are needed.

The support you provide to an African American male who is 82 years of age

Social service program
An organization that exists to fulfill some social purpose.

Quality improvement process
An ethical commitment to continually look for and seek ways to make social services more responsive, efficient, and effective.

Case-level evaluation
The evaluation of the effectiveness and/or efficiency of a social worker's intervention with a client system.

Program-level evaluation
The evaluation of the effectiveness and/or efficiency of a program's services; the accumulation of case-level evaluations.

with diabetes would likely be different than the support you would provide to an Asian female who is 53 years of age and is beginning to show signs of dementia. Furthermore, the nature of the services you would provide to each of these two clients would necessarily be adjusted depending on how much family support each has, their individual desires for independent living, their level of receptivity to your services, and other assessment information that you would gather about each client. Consequently, your plan to evaluate the individualized services you would provide to each client would, by necessity, involve different measures and different plans for data collection and recording.

Program-Level Evaluation

In most instances, social workers help individual clients through the auspices of some kind of a social service program. It is rarely the case that social workers would be self-employed and operating solely on their own to provide client services. In other words, social service programs generally employ multiple workers, all of whom are trained and supervised according to the policies and procedure set by the programs in which they work. Typically, every worker employed by a program is assigned a caseload of clients. Thus, we can think of a social service program as an aggregation of individual client cases; that is, when we think of the program's clientele (versus a practitioner's clientele), all clients assigned to every worker in the program are included. When conducting program-level evaluations, we are interested in the overall characteristics of all the clients and the average pattern of change for all of them served by a program.

Case-Level and Program-Level Data for Quality Improvement

Both case-level and program-level evaluations yield data that can then turned into information by practitioners and **administrators**, respectively, to improve client services. The two words **data** and **information** are often used interchangeably. In this book, the term *data* signifies isolated facts in numerical (i.e., numbers) or text (i.e., words) form that are gathered in the course of an evaluation. How we interpret the data when they have all been collected, collated, and analyzed is called *information*. For example, data collected in reference to client referral sources gathered from a program's intake unit may indicate that the program accepts 90 percent of its referrals from other social service programs and only 5 percent of people who are self-referred. One of the many pieces of information (or conclusions or findings drawn from the data) generated by these data may be that the program is somehow more accessible to clients who were referred by other social service programs than to those

Administrator
A person who is responsible for the day-to-day operations of a social service program.

Data
Isolated facts, presented in numerical or descriptive form, on which client or program decisions are based; not to be confused with information.

Information
The interpretation given to data that have been collected, collated, and analyzed; not to be confused with data.

who were self-referred. The distinction between data and information is simple—data are the facts, and information is the interpretation that we give to theses facts.

Together, data and information help guide various decision-making processes in an effort to produce more effective and efficient services for our clients. Producing meaningful and useful data and information for quality improvement in service delivery is a process that involves both the art and science of social work practice. Although we might think of evaluation as a close cousin of science, it also has close relations with art. Because evaluations occur in the real and messy world of social work practice—and not in an isolated, controlled laboratory—useful evaluation designs require creativity and ingenuity just as much as they need logic, procedural detail, and research principles. If evaluation is to help build the knowledge base of our profession, then we must—in the best sense and at the same time—be both "caring and sensitive artists" and "rigorous scientists."

EVALUATION AND THE PROFESSION

Our profession—and all the social workers that comprise it—must be able to provide solid reasons for the policies and positions taken. As we can see from Boxes 1.1 and 1.2, evaluation procedures are an integral part of competent social work practice. Just as a practitioner must be prepared to explain his or her reasons for pursuing a particular intervention with a particular client, a social service program must also be prepared to provide a rationale for the treatment approach(s) that are selected throughout the program.

Evaluation is intimately connected to building our profession's knowledge base. But what role does it play? How can evaluation be used? Answers to these questions get at the fundamental reason why social workers should conduct evaluations—so that they can participate in building practice knowledge for our profession, which will ultimately improve the quality of the services offered to all of our future clients. More specifically, by learning about the evaluation of your individual practices and the social service program where you are employed, you, as an individual social work practitioner, will be better equipped to play an active role in (1) contributing to the evidence-base of our profession, (2) collaborating with all levels of program stakeholders, (3) integrating accountability with service delivery, and (4) offering client-centered services.

Evidence-based practice
Interventions and practices used by social workers that have been proven to be effective and/or efficient.

Contributing to Evidence-Based Practice

One of the basic prerequisites of helping people to help themselves is knowing exactly what to do. Knowing precisely what intervention to offer which clients given the particular circumstances of a case is a complex challenge. How we help involves a combination of knowledge, skills, and values accepted and recognized by the social work profession. We can look to the NASW's *Code of Ethics* to remind us of core social work values, but we rely on a broader base of sources to inform what we know about a particular problem or population as well as how we might best intervene. More specifically, we draw knowledge from psychology, nursing, sociology, criminology, and many other disciplines.

To get up-to-date knowledge, we would want to consult research and practice experts—either through published literature or by networking through professional channels such as conferences and associations. Our aim is to start with the work of others to learn from their mistakes and triumphs and to avoid reinventing the "evaluation and practice" wheels that are already in motion and working in programs throughout the country or around the world.

To some degree, the Internet has made professional contact and consultation much easier in recent years. However, because the Internet provides easy access to all kinds of information (the good, the bad, and the ugly), it is our professional responsibility to discern which knowledge is credible and which is not. Generally speaking, information retrieved from the Internet is more credible if it can be verified by independent sources (e.g., published articles, research experts, or practice experts) and is corroborated by multiple sources.

Building on knowledge generated by others is a basic ingredient of professional social work practice. Sometimes prior knowledge is rich and detailed, but more often than not it is sparse and vague. Either way, social work practitioners can contribute to a particular knowledge base by providing fruitful insight and understanding from their direct experiences with clients in the field. Through case-level and program-level evaluations, we can learn a great deal from practitioners in the field. Whom do they serve? What do they do? Which of their interventions are most effective?

Findings based on systematic evaluations are more credible than findings based on individual experiences of one or a few practitioners. Indeed, if a number of evaluation studies produce similar findings, theories may be formulated about the different kinds of treatment interventions most likely to be effective with a particular population. Once formulated, a **theory** has to be tested. This, too, can be achieved by means of evaluations using rigorous evaluation designs. It should be noted that, in our profession, very few evaluations test theories because the controlled conditions required for theory-testing are often not feasible in real-world settings where social work practice takes place.

Theory

A reasoned set of propositions derived from and supported by established data.

Collaborating With Program Stakeholders

The process of evaluation can also help open up communication among our stakeholders at all levels of program operations. People who have vested interests in programs are called **stakeholders,** and they each provide a unique perspective as well as

Stakeholders

A person or group of people having a direct or indirect interest in the results of an evaluation.

Box 1.3 What Is Stakeholder Involvement?

Stakeholder involvement is based upon the belief that expertise does not lie solely with program professionals. Stakeholders are persons or organizations who have investments in the content of a program or in the dissemination and evaluation of a program (Centers for Disease Control and Prevention, 1999). Over the last several years, the interpretation of stakeholder involvement has changed as programs have focused not just on individuals and families but on the broader ecology, including neighborhoods, workplaces, schools, places of worship, communities, and the society. Work in the area of teen pregnancy prevention, for example, involves partnerships in the general public health, social service, and education fields. Consequently, decisions regarding programs should include the considerations and perspectives of multiple stakeholders.

Who Are Stakeholders?

Stakeholders include funders and administrators of programs but also staff, program participants and their peers, family members, and the wider community. It would not be unusual for stakeholders in a youth development program to include elected city, county, and state officials, religious leaders, business owners, neighborhood association members, sports figures and coaches, students, out-of-school youth, parents, health and social service providers, educators, representatives of the art community, and any other interested persons or groups. Stakeholders should represent the diversity of the community in many ways, such as race, ethnicity, ability, income, sexual orientation, and family constellation. Youth development is the responsibility and a domain of interest for all citizens in a community.

Why Is Stakeholder Involvement Important?

Stakeholders offer important insight into each phase of program planning, implementation, and evaluation. Stakeholders are most commonly involved at the beginning stages of program planning. They are able to provide insight into the various needs that a program or curriculum should meet. However, experience has showed that, once the goals have been set in the first part of program development, stakeholders are sometimes not consulted in latter stages of program implementation and evaluation. This is unfortunate because stakeholders have the potential to illuminate issues and needs during the course of program implementation (Banach & Gregory, 2001). Frequently, stakeholders who participate in an initial needs assessment may not be the same stakeholders who ultimately sustain the program. Consequently, eliciting ongoing feedback and keeping lines of communication open are crucial to program success. This is particularly true in community-based youth development programs. A broad range of stakeholders has the knowledge, daily life experiences, and expertise that can contribute to program success.

How Do Stakeholders Become Involved?

Stakeholders may be involved in multiple roles and serve various functions. Focus groups may be conducted to get initial ideas and reveal community norms, history, and players. Community mapping may be conducted to learn about the important features, places, and events. Volunteer opportunities, advisory committees, participation in hiring processes, program committees, and various other means can be explored. The important point is that, if stakeholders are valued, they will be welcomed and their voices heard.

have a different interest or "stake" in decisions made within social service programs—from administrative decisions about staff qualifications to a practitioner's decision about the best way to serve a particular client system (e.g., individual, couple, family, group, community, or organization). Box 1.3 clearly illustrates the roles that stakeholders have in the program evaluation process.

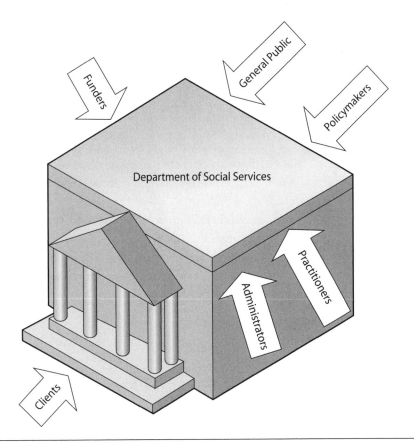

Figure 1.2 Various stakeholders who influence evaluations. (Note that four groups are not employed by the organization—in fact one group, clients, is actually receiving services.)

Evaluation by its very nature not only has us consider the perspectives of different stakeholder groups but can also facilitate an understanding of the priority interests among the various parties and promote collaborative working relationships. Six stakeholder groups are key to program planning and evaluation efforts (Figure 1.2): (1) policymakers at federal, state, and local levels; (2) the general public; (3) program funders; (4) administrators of social service programs; (5) practitioners employed by the programs; and (6) the clients served by the programs.

Policymakers

To policymakers in governmental or other public entities, any individual social service program is only one among hundreds. On a general level, policymakers are concerned with broad issues of public safety, fiscal accountability, and human capital. For example, how effective and efficient are programs serving women who have been battered, youth who are unemployed, or children who have been sexually abused? If one type of program is as effective (produces beneficial client change) as another but also costs more, does the nature or type of service offered to clients justify the greater expense? Should certain types of programs be continued, expanded, modified, cut, or abandoned? How should money be allocated among competing similar programs? In sum, a major interest of policymakers is to have comparative data about the effectiveness of different social service programs serving similar types of client need (see Chapter 8).

Policymakers play a key role in allocation of public monies—deciding how much money will be available for various social programs such as education, health care, social services, mental health, criminal justice, and so on. Increasingly, policy makers are looking to accreditation bodies to "certify" that social service programs deliver services according to set standards. For example, the Joint Commission on Accreditation of Healthcare Organizations (JCAHO) is responsible for evaluating and accrediting health care organizations and programs in the United States, and the Council on Accreditation (COA) evaluates and accredits programs that provide services to children and families as well as behavioral health care.

General Public

Increasingly, taxpayers are demanding that policymakers in state and federal government departments be accountable to the general public. Lay groups concerned with special interests such as the care of the elderly, support for families, drug rehabilitation, or child abuse are lobbying to have their interests heard. Citizens want to know how much money is being spent and where is it being spent. Are taxpayers' dollars effectively serving current social needs? The public demand for "evidence" that publicly funded programs are making wise use of the money entrusted to them is growing. The media, television in particular, plays a central role in bringing issues of government spending to the public's attention. Unfortunately, the media tends to focus on worst-case scenarios, intent on capturing public attention in a way that will increase network ratings and the number of consumers tuning in.

Reliability

The degree of accuracy, precision, or consistency of results of a measuring instrument.

Validity

The extent to which a measuring instrument measures the variable it is supposed to measure and measures it accurately.

Evaluation is a way for social service programs to bring **reliable** and **valid** data to the public. Evaluation data can be used to build public relations and provide a way for programs to demonstrate their "public worth." As such, evaluation is more often used as a tool for educating the public—sharing what is known about a problem and how a particular program is working to address it—than a means to report definitive or conclusive answers to complex problems. When evaluation data reveal poor performance, then the program's administrators and practitioners can report changes made to program policy or practice in light of the negative results. On the other hand, positive evaluation results can help highlight a program's strengths in an effort to build its public image. A report of data showing that a program is helping to resolve a social problem may yield desirable outcomes such as allaying the concerns of opposing interest groups or encouraging funders to grant more money.

Funders

The public and private funding organizations that provide money to social service programs have a vested interest in seeing their money spent wisely. If funds have been allocated to combat family violence, is family violence declining? And if so, by how much? Could the money be put to better use? Often, funders will insist that some kind of an evaluation of a specific program must take place before additional funds will be provided. Program administrators are thus made accountable for the funds they receive. They must demonstrate to the funder that their programs are achieving the best results for the money received.

Administrators

The priority of program administrators is concern for their own program's functioning and survival, but they also have interest in other similar programs, whether they are viewed as competitors or collaborators. Administrators want to know how well their program operates as a whole, in addition to the functioning of a program's parts, which may include administrative components such as staff training, budget and finance, client services, and quality assurance. The questions of interest to an administrator are different but not separate from those of the other stakeholder groups already discussed. Is the assessment process at the client-intake level successful in screening clients who are eligible for program services? Is treatment planning culturally sensitive to the demographic characteristics of clients served by the program? Does the discharge process provide adequate consultation with professionals external to the program? Like the questions of policymakers, the general public, and funders, administrators also have a vested interest in knowing which interventions are effective and which are less so, which programs are economical, and which interventive strategies should be retained or could be modified or dropped.

Practitioners

Line-level, or front-line, practitioners who deal directly with clients are most often interested in practical, day-to-day issues: Is it wise to include adolescent male sexual abuse survivors in the same group with adolescent female survivors, or should the males be referred to another service if separate groups cannot be run? What mix of role-play, educational films, discussion, and other treatment activities best facilitates client learning? Will parent education strengthen families? Is nutrition counseling for parents an effective way to improve the school performance of children from impoverished homes?

The question that ought to be of greatest importance to a practitioner is whether the particular treatment intervention used with a particular client is working.

However, sometimes interests from stakeholders external to the program impose constraints that have practitioners more concerned with other issues. For example, when an outreach program serving homeless people with mental illness cannot afford to send workers out in pairs or provide them with adequate communication systems (e.g., cell phones), workers may be more concerned about questions related to personal safety than questions of client progress. Or workers employed by a program with several funding streams may be required to keep multiple records of services to satisfy multiple funders, thus leaving workers to question the sensibility of duplicative paperwork instead of focusing on the impact of their services for clients.

Clients

The voice of clients is slowly gaining more attention in evaluation efforts, but our profession has a long way to go before clients are recognized as a legitimate stakeholder group. Of course, clients are a unique stakeholder group because they depend on a program's services for help with problems that are adversely affecting their lives. In fact, without clients there would be no reason for a program to exist. Clients who seek help do so with the expectation that the services they receive will benefit them in some meaningful way. Clients want to know whether our social service program will help resolve their problem. If the program claims to be able to help, then are ethnic, religious, language, or other matters of diverse client needs evident in the program's service delivery structure? In short, is the social service program in tune with what clients really need? Client voices are being heard more and more as time goes on—and rightfully so! A brief glimpse at the effectiveness and efficiency of the immediate relief services provided by the Federal Emergency Management Agency (FEMA) to the survivors of Hurricane Katrina should ring a bell here.

A Word About Collaboration Among Stakeholder Groups

Collaboration involves cooperative associations among the various players from the different stakeholder groups for the purposes of achieving a common goal—building knowledge to better help clients. A collaborative approach accepts that different stakeholders will have diverse perspectives. Rather than assuming that one perspective is more valuable than another, we should regard each stakeholder group as having relative importance toward achieving a better understanding of how to solve problems and help clients. For example, if a program's workers want to know how new legislation will change service provision, then the perspective of policymakers and administrators will have great value. But if a program administrator wants to better understand why potential clients are not seeking available services, then the client perspective may be the most valuable of all the stakeholder groups.

Social service stakeholders have formed formal groups in most states. Some of

The goal of the stakeholders group was not "business as usual" but rather to improve the way abused and neglected children are served in California. It was important to include individuals who represented a wide variety of interested parties and culturally diverse populations. The stakeholders group is composed of representatives from the following organizations:

- Consumers of child welfare services
- Former foster youth and foster families
- Advocates for foster children, youth, and parents
- Public and private providers of services
- Federal, state, and county administrators
- Supportive services representatives from health services, the mental health, alcohol and drug, and developmental services, and from the Department of Finance
- Court and legal community
- California state legislature
- California Department of Education
- Research institutions
- Foundations

these groups are politically connected and highly developed. A child welfare stakeholder group in California, for example, has an exceptionally informative Web site. The group also publishes its activities from time to time (see Box 1.4).

As it stands, a collaborative work structure is not a natural phenomenon in today's social service arena. The dominant structure is a hierarchy, which can be thought of as a chain of command with higher levels possessing greater power and authority over lower levels. Typically, the hierarchy would have policymakers and funders at the top of the hierarchy, program administrators and workers in the middle, and clients at the bottom. Critics of this top-down way of thinking might argue for turning the hierarchy upside down, placing clients at the top and all other stakeholder groups at varying levels of support beneath them. Whatever the power structure of stakeholders for a particular program, evaluation is a process that may do as little as having us consider the multiple perspectives of various stakeholder groups or as much as bringing different stakeholder groups together to plan and design evaluation efforts as a team.

Integrated Accountability With Service Delivery

A third way that evaluation strengthens our profession is by providing a process whereby social workers can be directly involved—taking leadership positions—in program and practice accountability. As previously mentioned, administrators are accountable to their funders for the way in which their money (more appropriately, *your money* via taxes) is spent, and the funders are similarly accountable to the public. Accountability means that we are answerable for the actions and decisions we make. Program-level evaluations help us to be accountable by providing data that can help us explain an entire program, and case-level evaluations can help us evaluate our day-to-day client outcomes.

Demonstrating accountability, or providing justification of a social service program, is a legitimate purpose of an evaluation insofar as it involves a genuine attempt to identify a program's strengths and weaknesses. Accountability in our profession can take several forms:

- *Coverage Accountability.* Are the persons served those who have been designated as target clients? Are there any other beneficiaries who should not be served? (See Chapter 5.)
- *Cultural Accountability.* Are program employees culturally competent? To what extent are the cultures of clients served represented in the program's administrative and service delivery structures? We use the broad meaning of culture here to reflect diversity in areas of race, class, ethnicity, religion, sexual orientation, and other classifications identifying groups of people that are oppressed or discriminated against in our society. (See Chapter 16.)
- *Service Delivery Accountability.* Are reasonable amounts of services being delivered? To what extent is service delivery supported by an evidence base? (See Chapters 6 and 7.)
- *Fiscal Accountability.* Are funds being used properly? Are expenditures properly documented? Are funds used within the limits set within the budget? (See Chapter 8.)
- *Legal Accountability.* Are relevant laws, including those concerning affirmative action, occupational safety and health, and privacy of individual records, being observed? (See Chapter 15.)
- *Professional Accountability.* Are our professional codes of ethics and accreditation standards being met? (See Boxes 1.1 and 1.2.)

Client-Centered Practice

As mentioned previously in our discussion of stakeholder groups, social service programs exist to prevent, ameliorate, or erase problems affecting people, the clients of the program. In other words, social service programs exist because there is an identifiable group of clients who can benefit from their services. Ideally, social workers can think of working themselves out of a job, one client at a time.

However, just as client problems are complex, so is the environment in which social service programs operate. Office politics, negative media attention, low pay, high caseloads, and low job satisfaction are just a few organizational factors that can shift focus away from client needs or program benefits for clients. The process of evaluation, as we describe it in this book, keeps clients—the reason for a program's existence—as an evaluation priority.

EVALUATION FROM A PERSON-IN-ENVIRONMENT PERSPECTIVE

A hallmark of the social work profession is the person-in-environment perspective. It is a perspective that affects how we view clients and social problems. It is also a perspective that is useful for thinking about social service programs and the role that evaluations can take within them.

Viewing persons or entities in the context of their environment is a concept that comes from ecological theory, which is best known for its idea of nested environments shown in Figure 1.3. In ecological theory, the micro level represents the individual or family environment, the meso level accounts for interactions of micro environments, the exo level represents entities that influence the micro environment but does not always do so in a direct fashion, and finally, the macro level as the outermost level represents distant connectivity such as our community or the broader society. Social work practitioners can use this thinking structure of ecological theory to assess interaction and interdependence among the four levels in order to better help clients as individual persons, groups, families, or communities.

The nested thinking structure within Figure 1.3 is a useful aid to a better understanding of how clients interface with the human service programs, how programs interface with their societal environment, and how evaluations fit in this context. Figure 1.3 shows an example of how nested levels can help us understand individual persons (micro level) in the context of a social service program environment as they will have interactions with individual staff (meso level), receive services according to program policy and procedure (exo level), and deal with consequences of the

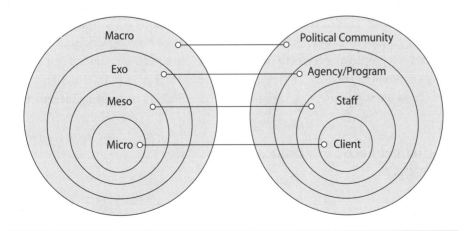

Figure 1.3 Program-in-environment.

community (macro level) such as having to cope with the societal stigma that comes from using the program's services.

Note that the macro level in Figure 1.3 is labeled the "political community." This is an important feature of the environmental context for social workers, and we discuss politics further in Chapter 15. However, we introduce the label here to suggest that the political connectedness of social service programs is gaining critical importance not only for how clients of the program are served but for the very survival of the program itself.

Viewing clients, or consumers, of social services through a person-in-environment perspective is a common notion in social work practice. Most typically, this perspective has social work practitioners consider the client as a micro-level individual person who is interconnected with other individuals in meso-level groups (e.g., friends, family), exo-level organizations (e.g., educational, occupational, religious), and macro-level communities or society (e.g., law enforcement, politics).

For example, suppose you sought the help of a social work practitioner at your university's counseling center because you have been feeling heightened sensations of anxiety such as shortness of breath and tightness in your lungs and chest when you think about upcoming final exams. Although your presenting problem (test anxiety) is very specific, you could expect the practitioner assigned to your case to ask you a broad set of questions to better evaluate the problem that brought you to the counseling center in the first place. You could also expect to answer questions related to your ties with your university-based and home-based friends, teachers, and family as well as your general sense of comfort with fitting into the university scene. In addition, the social work practitioner would also be mindful that your visit to the counseling center has itself added to the complexity of your life space or environment at your university.

By considering your presenting problem in the context of your environment, the social work practitioner expects to be in a better position to suggest interventions that will fit your lifestyle and maximize your success at reducing test anxiety; the primary reason for you seeking help in the first place. In addition, the practitioner would have a better idea about how to go about evaluating her work with you, the client. By considering a person-in-environment perspective, a worker aims to develop ways to improve services to clients using micro-level interventions (e.g., counseling or problem solving) and evaluation methods (e.g. case-level design, client satisfaction questionnaire, or program outcome evaluation measuring instruments).

EVALUATION FROM A PROGRAM-IN-ENVIRONMENT PERSPECTIVE

Viewing human service programs through an environment perspective is becoming more widespread among social work practitioners, even among those who have no administrative aspirations. For example, we can use a similar nested thinking structure to conceptualize the human service program or agency (Level 1) within the context of both its local community environment (Level 2), and the broader societal and political environment (Level 3). Figure 1.4 (Mulroy, 2004) has us consider all three levels against a backdrop of social justice.

Suppose, for example, that you have graduated with your social work degree and are now employed by the university counseling center to help students struggling with test anxiety. As a social work practitioner employed by the counseling center (Level 1) you have adopted a person-in-environment perspective to help individual students. In addition, you are bound by the policy and procedures of your place of employment that call for program services to benefit the client (i.e., effective) in a timely (i.e., efficient) and just (i.e., equity) manner. However, you would also be aware of how your program (the counseling center) is affected by the context of your university's environment (Level 2).

Various university-level factors could be at play such as large class sizes, the majority of students being the first in their families to attend college, or recent budget cuts for student support services on campus. Thinking beyond your university's campus, you could gain further understanding of your capacity to help students at the counseling center by evaluating relevant societal and political information (Level 3) such as the degree to which local, state, or federal government officials

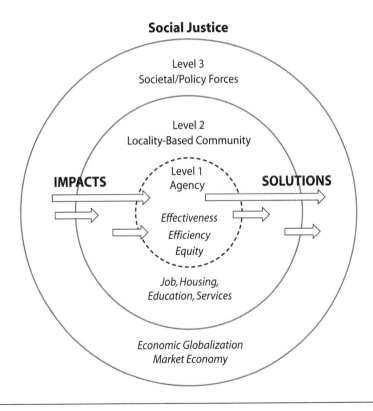

Figure 1.4 Organization-in-environment.

support higher education or the push in the global market economy to produce a more technologically skilled labor force.

The arrows flowing through the nested structure in Figure 1.4 communicate the idea that the boundaries between the layers are porous (Mulroy, 2004). In other words, actions or events at one layer have an impact on all other layers. Thus, the social work practitioner, situated at in the center of Figure 1.4 as an employee of the program, is concerned not just with the client but also with the many other stakeholders in the organizational environment. By considering the organization-in-environment perspective, you as the social work practitioner assigned to help individual students with problem such as test anxiety may also be in a position to evaluate the problems at a macro level—perhaps helping many students by your efforts.

Suppose you notice a trend whereby every month more and more students seek help for test anxiety. By considering the growing problem of student anxiety in the context of the program's environment, you would be in a better position to facilitate change that will fit the environmental context in which the counseling center is situated. For example, you might enlist support of your supervisor to write a grant to fund student support groups, you might ask to chair or lead a committee to discuss instructional strategies to prevent student test anxiety, or you might lobby your university's administration to raise awareness of student issues and advocate for improvements to student support services on campus. In sum, by considering an organization-in-environment perspective, you could develop ways to improve services to your clients using macro-level interventions.

SUMMING UP AND LOOKING AHEAD

This chapter briefly introduced the concept of quality improvement in our profession and explained how evaluation provides the overall tools for the quality improvement process effort. We then presented a brief introduction to why our profession needs evaluations and discussed how stakeholders must be involved with all evaluative efforts.

Now that we know how program evaluations can be useful for our profession, the following chapter presents how we can use two complementary evaluation approaches in the quality improvement process: the project approach to quality improvement and the monitoring approach to quality improvement.

RECAP AND ONLINE MATERIALS

In this chapter, you learned how to become an accountable social work professional through the use of research and evaluation methods.

You should also recall the concept of the social work research process from your foundational research course. If not, go online to take a free crash course in the basic social work research process.

You can also find the following materials online to help you master the concepts you just learned:

- Chapter Outline
- Learning Objectives
- Key Terms and Concepts
- Flash Cards
- Practice Multiple-Choice Tests
- Essay Questions with Answers
- Links

www.oup.com/us/swevaluation

STUDY QUESTIONS

1. Are you fearful of evaluation? Why, or why not? Are you less or more fearful of evaluation since you read the chapter? If you are still fearful after reading the chapter, you need to read it again.

2. In your own words, discuss why quality improvement is important to the social services.

3. What are stakeholders? List and discuss the different types of stakeholders to whom any evaluation must pay attention.

4. List the various stakeholders for your social work program (i.e., BSW or MSW). Provide a rationale for why you listed each one. Who is the client stakeholder of your social work educational program? Why?

5. List and discuss the six forms of accountability. Provide a social work example of each one.

6. In your own words, discuss the relationship between a case-level evaluation and a program-level evaluation. Discuss how they complement one another.

7. Take a look at Box 1.1. Do you agree with the NASW principles? Why or why not? Discuss how you believe this course will prepare you to abide by the NASW's *Code of Ethics* when it comes to research and evaluation.

8. What are data? What is information? From your own experiences, provide an example of how information was derived from data.

9. In your own words, briefly discuss the "evaluation from a person-in-environment" perspective. Provide a social work example throughout your discussion.
10. In your own words, briefly discuss the "evaluation from a program-in-environment" perspective. Provide a social work example throughout your discussion.

References, Further Reading, and Resources

On Evidence-Based Practice

Bellamy, J. L., Bledsoe, S. E., & Traube, D. E. (2005). The current state of evidence based practice in social work: A review of the literature and qualitative analysis of expert interviews. *Journal of Evidence-Based Practice, 3,* 23–48.

Gambrill, E. D. (2006). *Social work practice: A critical thinker's guide* (2nd ed.) New York: Oxford University Press.

Journal of Evidence-Based Social Work (ISSN:1543-3714). Binghamton, NY: Haworth Press. *This journal examines the fast-growing use of evidence-based practice in everyday care, identifying and evaluating cutting-edge theory, techniques, and strategies. The journal presents literature from practitioners, researchers, and academics that collates and analyzes research findings relative to practice issues and intervention approaches over a given period of time. It can help you make the most of your time and effort as you weigh current evidence options and determine which one serves your clients' best interests and leads to the desired outcome. Check it out at http://www.haworthpress.com/web/JEBSW.*

Roberts, A. R., & Yeager, K. R. (Eds.). (2006). *Foundations of evidence-based social work practice.* New York: Oxford University Press.

Rosen, A., & Proctor, E. K. (2002). Standards for evidence-based social work practice: The role of replicable and appropriate interventions, outcomes, and practice guidelines. In A. R. Roberts & G. J. Green (Eds.), *Social workers' desk reference* (pp. 743–747). New York: Oxford University Press.

Shlonsky, A., & Gibbs, L. (2004). Will the real evidence-based practice please stand up? Teaching the process of evidence-based practice to the helping professions. *Brief Treatment and Crisis Intervention, 4*(2), 137–153.

On Accountability

Grinnell, R. M., Jr., Unrau, Y. A., & Williams, M. (2005). An introduction to inquiry. In R. M. Grinnell, Jr., & Y. A. Unrau (Eds.), *Social work research and evaluation: Quantitative and qualitative approaches* (7th ed., pp. 4–21). New York: Oxford University Press.

Lackey, J. F. (2006). *Accountability in social services.* Binghamton, NY: Haworth Press.

On Case-Level Designs

Bloom, M. J., Fischer, J., & Orme, J. G. (2006). *Evaluating practice: Guidelines for the accountable professional* (5th ed.). Boston: Allyn & Bacon.

Unrau, Y. A., Gabor, P. A., & Grinnell, R. M., Jr. (2001). Case-level evaluations. In *Evaluation in the human services* (pp. 178–206). New York: Oxford University Press.

Williams, M., Grinnell, R. M., & Unrau, Y. A. (2005). Case-level designs. In R. M. Grinnell, Jr., & Y. A. Unrau (Eds.), *Social work research and evaluation: Quantitative and qualitative approaches* (7th ed., pp. 171–184). New York: Oxford University Press.

On Program-Level Designs

Bamberger, M., Rugh, J., & Mabry, L. (2006). *Real world evaluation: Working under budget, time, data, and political constraints.* Thousand Oaks, CA: Sage.

Grinnell, R. M., Unrau, Y. A., & Williams, M. (2005). Group-level designs. In R. M. Grinnell, Jr., & Y. A. Unrau (Eds.), *Social work research and evaluation: Quantitative and qualitative approaches* (7th ed., pp. 185–210). New York: Oxford University Press.

Unrau, Y. A., Gabor, P. A., & Grinnell, R. M., Jr. (2001). Program-level evaluations. In *Evaluation in the human services* (pp. 208–253). New York: Oxford University Press.

On Stakeholders

Mathison, S. (2001).What's it like when the participatory evaluator is a "genuine" stakeholder? *American Journal of Evaluation, 22*(1), 29–35.

Michalski, G. V., & Cousins, J. B. (2001). Multiple perspectives on training evaluation: Probing stakeholder perceptions in a global network development firm. *American Journal of Evaluation, 22*(1), 37–53.

On Evaluation Environments

Banach, M., & Gregory, P. J. (2001, October). Essential tasks, skills, and decisions for developing sustainable community-based programs for children, youth, and families at risk. *Journal of Extension, 39*(5). Retrieved February 20, 2006, from http://www.joe.org/joe/2001october/a4.html

Mayeske, G. W., & Lambur, M. T. (2001, June). How to design better programs: A staff-centered stakeholder approach to program logic modeling. *Journal of Extension, 39*(3). Retrieved February 20, 2006, from http://www.joe.org/joe/2001june/tt2.html

Mulroy, E. A. (2004). Theoretical perspectives on the social environment to guide management and community practice: An organization-in-environment approach. *Administration in Social Work, 28*(1), 77–96.

Weinbach, R. W. (2005). Research contexts. In R. M. Grinnell, Jr., & Y. A. Unrau (Eds.), *Social work research and evaluation: Quantitative and qualitative approaches* (7th ed., pp. 23–32). New York: Oxford University Press.

On General Evaluation

Centers for Disease Control and Prevention. (1999). Framework for program evaluation in public health. *Morbidity and Mortality Weekly Report, 48*(RR-11), 1–40.

Davidson, E. J. (2005). *Evaluation methodology basics: The nuts and bolts of sound evaluation.* Thousand Oaks, CA: Sage.

Donaldson, S. I. (2001). Overcoming our negative reputation: Evaluation becomes known as a helping profession. *American Journal of Evaluation, 22*, 355–361.

Fitzpatrick, J. L., Sanders, J. R., & Worthen, B. R. (2004). *Program evaluation: Alternative approaches and practical guidelines* (3rd ed.). White Plains, NY: Longman.

Gabor, P. A., & Grinnell, R. M., Jr. (1994). *Evaluation and quality improvement in the human services.* Boston: Allyn & Bacon.

Gabor, P. A., Unrau, Y. A. (1998). *Evaluation for social workers: A quality improvement approach for the human services* (2nd ed.). Boston: Allyn & Bacon.

Gabor, P. A., Unrau, Y. A., & Grinnell, R. M., Jr. (2001). Program-level evaluation. In R. M. Grinnell, Jr. (Ed.), *Social work research and evaluation: Quantitative and qualitative approaches* (6th ed., pp. 481–509). Itasca, IL: F. E. Peacock.

O'Sullivan, R. G. (2004). *Practicing evaluation: A collaborative approach.* Thousand Oaks, CA: Sage.

Preskill, H., & Russ-Eft, D. (2004) *Building evaluation capacity.* Thousand Oaks, CA: Sage.

Rossi, P. H., Lipsey, M. W., & Freeman, H. E. (2004). *Evaluation: A systematic approach* (7th ed.). Thousand Oaks, CA: Sage.

Stake, R. E. (2004). *Standards-based responsive evaluation.* Thousand Oaks, CA: Sage.

Unrau, Y. A., Gabor, P. A., & Grinnell, R. M., Jr. (2005). Program evaluation. In R. M. Grinnell, Jr., & Y. A. Unrau (Eds.), *Social work research and evaluation: Quantitative and qualitative approaches* (7th ed., pp. 453–468). New York: Oxford University Press.

Unrau, Y. A., Gabor, P. A., & Grinnell, R. M., Jr. (2001). *Evaluation in the human services* (3rd ed.). Belmont, CA: Wadsworth.

Weinbach, R. W. (2005). *Evaluating social work services and programs.* Boston: Allyn & Bacon.

Wholey, J. S., Hatry, H. P., & Newcomer, K. E. (Eds.). (2004). *Handbook of practical program evaluation* (2nd ed.). San Francisco, CA: Jossey-Bass.

APPROACHES TO ACCOUNTABILITY

2

Needs assessment

A type of evaluation that is designed to assess the need for a social service by verifying that a social problem exists within a specific client population to such an extent that services are warranted.

Process evaluation

A type of evaluation that is designed to describe and assess the services provided to clients and how satisfied key stakeholders are with the services provided.

Outcome evaluation

A type of evaluation that is designed to measure the nature of change, if any, for clients after they have received services from a program.

Efficiency evaluation

A type of evaluation that is designed to measure the efficiency of a program.

Project approach to quality improvement

Evaluations whose purpose is to assess a completed or finished program.

There are as many types of program evaluations as there are people willing to dream them up and label them with trendy names. Table 2.1 presents the purposes, the advantages, and the disadvantages of just a few of the ones that have caught on during the last several years. In Part II of this book, only four will be briefly discussed: (1) **needs assessment**s in Chapter 5, (2) **process evaluations** in Chapter 6, (3) **outcome evaluations** in Chapter 7, and (4) **efficiency evaluations** in Chapter 8.

We need to understand that each evaluation is tied to a social service program that will be influenced to varying degrees by the environment in which the program operates. The four types of evaluations that we will be discussing in Part II of this book can, to some degree, be loosely classified under either the project approach or the monitoring approach to quality improvement (Figure 2.1).

An evaluation whose purpose is to assess a completed social service program (or project) uses a **project approach to quality improvement.** Complementary to the project approach, an evaluation whose purpose is to provide feedback while a program is still under way has a monitoring approach to quality improvement; that is, it is designed to contribute to the ongoing development and improvement of the program as it goes along. Sometimes the monitoring approach is labeled "formative evaluation," and the project approach is sometimes called "summative evaluation" as discussed in Box 2.1.

Table 2.1 Many Types of Program Evaluations

Approach	Type	Description	Purpose	Strength	Limitation	Sample Question
Adversary Oriented Evaluation	Process, Outcome	Balances bias through a planned effort to generate opposing points of view within an evaluation	To assure fairness and illuminate program strengths and weaknesses by incorporating both positive and negative views into the evaluation design	Diverts a great deal of subsequent criticism by addressing anticipated	Time-consuming and expensive, requiring extensive preparation and investment of human and financial resources	How effective is the Healthy Start program in reducing child abuse rates?
Black Box Evaluation	Outcome	Examines program output without consideration of program input	To determine program effects	Determines whether program is achieving its goals	Fails to consider why something is effective or ineffective	Do standardized test scores of high school students improve from the beginning of the term to the end?
Cluster Evaluation	Process	Engages a group of projects with common funders, topics, or themes in common evaluation efforts to provide a composite overview of the success or failure of the cluster	To improve programs by identifying patterns of and lessons from the cluster	Allows multiple evaluation models, each designed for individual sites and programs based on local needs, to address collective themes or topics	Lack of standardization makes it difficult to describe how approach should be conducted	In what ways do prenatal programs for parents improve outcomes for infants?
Context Evaluation	Need	Describes discrepancies between what is and what is desired	To develop a program rationale through the analysis of unrealized needs and unused opportunities	Potential for program effectiveness is enhanced when conceptual basis for program is perceived needs	Target audience may fail to recognize or articulate needs	What are the needs of low income women in terms of prenatal health care?

Cost Effectiveness Evaluation	Efficiency	Describes the relationship between program costs and outcomes for participants in substantive terms	To judge the efficiency of a program	Allows comparison and rank ordering of alternative interventions in addressing similar goals	Requires extensive technical and analytical procedures	How many dollars were expended to increase reading test scores of students?
Cost-Benefit Evaluation	Efficiency	Compares program costs and program outcomes in terms of dollars	To describe the economic efficiency of a program regarding actual or anticipated costs and known or expected benefits	Useful in convincing policymakers, funders, and decision makers that dollar benefits justify the program	Difficult to quantify many outcomes in monetary terms and to express costs and benefits in terms of a common denominator	What was the total estimated savings to society as a result of decreases in teen pregnancy rates?
Evaluation Research	Outcome	Generates knowledge of program effectiveness in general rather than judging the merit of individual programs	To generate knowledge for conceptual use	Introduces objectivity and scientific rigor	Nonsignificant statistical findings do not necessarily mean that group means are equal nor that program is ineffective	Do employers who offer on-site child care have higher staff morale than those employers who do not offer on-site child care?
Goal-Free Evaluation	Outcome	Gathers data directly on program effect and effectiveness without knowledge of program goals	To evaluate the actual effects free from constraints of goals and their outcome expectations	Attention to actual effects rather than alleged effects reduces tendency toward tunnel vision and increases likelihood that unanticipated side effects will be noted	Not goal-free at all but rather focuses on wider context goals instead of program-specific objectives	What are the actual effects of the mentoring program?

(continued)

Table 2.1 (continued)

Goals-Based Evaluation	Outcome	Emphasizes the clarification of goals and the program's effectiveness in achieving goals	To measure the degree to which goals are achieved	Evaluation is sensitive to a particular program and its circumscribed goals and objectives	Fails to consider additional effects of program and neglects why it succeeds or fails	Does a parent's knowledge of child development change as a result of the program?
Impact Evaluation	Outcome	Addresses impact of program on program recipient	To describe direct and indirect program effects	Tests the usefulness of a program in ameliorating a particular problem	Difficult to establish causality in social sciences	Are participants able to secure meaningful employment as a result of the job-training program?
Implementation Evaluation	Process	Examines if the program is functional and operating as it is supposed to be	To determine extent to which program is properly implemented (to seek out discrepancies between program plan and reality)	Examines program operations in context as implementation strategies are neither automatic or certain	Provides no information regarding program efficiency or effectiveness	Is the program reaching the target population?
Input Evaluation	Process	Describes strong and weak points of strategies toward achieving objectives	To identify and assess program capabilities	Provides useful information to guide program strategy and design	Approach can be complex and overwhelming if priorities are not set and followed	Are home visits or group sessions more appropriate for the target population?
Outcomes Evaluation	Outcome	Comparison of actual program outcomes to desired program outcomes	To determine whether program objectives have been attained	Generally is easy to understand, develop, and implement	Lacks information regarding the actual nature of the program and what is producing observed outcomes	Do patients lose weight?

Type	Category	Description	Purpose	Strength	Limitation	Example Question
Performance Evaluation	Outcome	Assesses program results in terms of established performance indicators	To describe behavior changes as a result of the program	Establishes performance criteria for program recipients	Uncertainty regarding the extent to which program activities caused observed results	What study skills do youth display after participating in a tutoring program?
Process Evaluation	Process	Focuses on internal dynamics and actual operations to understand strengths and weakness	To look at how an outcome is produced rather than the outcome itself	Provides feedback in development phase to improve program	Does not indicate if a program is successful or effective	How many hours of direct contact do program recipients receive?
Responsive Evaluation	Process, Outcome, Need, Efficiency	Responds to program activities and audience needs by allowing evaluation questions and methods to emerge from observation	To address the concerns and issues of the stakeholder audience	Directs the attention of the evaluator to the needs of those for whom the evaluation is being done	Reliance on individual stakeholder perspectives may lead to subjective designs and findings	What major questions would you like the evaluation to answer?
Theory-Based Evaluation	Process, Outcome	Evaluation based on a model, theory or philosophy about how a program works	To identify the causal relationships that affect, operate, and influence the program	Presents rationale for choice of variables, and results can contribute to growing body of scientific knowledge	Conclusions are based on whether theory is correct or accepted	Is there a fit between the outcomes predicted by the ecological theory and the observed outcomes for families?
Utilization Focused Evaluation	Process, Outcome, Efficiency, Need	Yields immediate, concrete, observable, and useful information on program decisions and activities as a result of evaluation findings	To increase the use of evaluation	Provides meaningful, relevant, and substantial information to empower users	Demands high expenditures of time, energy, and staff resources	What information is needed by stakeholders to improve future youth development programs?

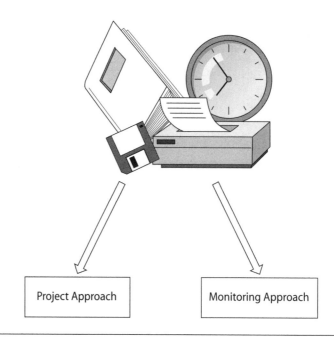

Project Approach   Monitoring Approach

Figure 2.1 Two complementary approaches to evaluation.

THE EXTERNAL PROJECT APPROACH

Evaluations that enhance the quality improvement process in our profession may be carried out daily, or they may not be initiated until the program has been in operation for a number of years. A one-shot evaluation illustrates the **external evaluation** approach to quality improvement of projects.

Characteristics of the External Project Approach

The external project approach tends to give rise to evaluations with the following general overall characteristics: (1) they are externally driven, (2) they have to deal with resistant workers, (3) they provide only periodic or no feedback to social workers, (4) they recommend large changes, (5) they are not practical in applied settings, and (6) they are difficult to incorporate in practice settings.

Externally Driven

The evaluation will almost certainly be externally driven, that is, it will be initiated by someone outside the program who more often than not will decide on the evaluation questions to be answered and the **data** to be collected that will presumably answer the questions.

External evaluation
An evaluation that is conducted by someone who does not have any connection with the program.

Data
Isolated facts, presented in numerical or descriptive form, on which client or program decisions are based; not to be confused with information.

Box 2.1 Formative and Summative Evaluations

Formative Evaluation (Monitoring Approach)

Formative Evaluation typically involves gathering information during the early stages of your project or program, with a focus on finding out whether your efforts are unfolding as planned, uncovering any obstacles, barriers, or unexpected opportunities that may have emerged, and identifying mid-course adjustments and corrections that can help ensure the success of your work.

Essentially, a formative evaluation is a structured way to provide program staff with additional feedback about their work. This feedback is primarily designed to fine-tune the implementation of the program, and it often includes information that is purely for internal use by program managers. Some information may also be reported in the summative evaluation of program impact, particularly if it is relevant to the replicability or design evolution of the program.

Some programs evolve continuously, never reaching a stage of being finished or complete; formative evaluation activities may be extended throughout the life of a program to help guide this evolution. Successful formative and summative evaluations depend not only on thorough program design and planning but also on the early adoption of an effective data collection strategy and in many cases a management information database that allows program staff and evaluators easy access to well-organized program information.

Summative Evaluation (Project Approach)

Summative Evaluation typically involves the preparation of a formal report outlining the impact of a program. For instance, an evaluation report will typically detail who participated in a program, what activities affected them, and what gains or improvements resulted from their participation. Often this report will include details regarding what prerequisites or conditions are essential or helpful to the replication of the program, program costs and benefits, and disaggregated results showing findings for specific subgroups of participants.

There is no crisp dividing line between formative evaluation and summative evaluation. Much of the information gathered during formative evaluation activities may be reported in formal summative reports, particularly during the early development of new programs, in order to show how the program is responding to challenges and reaching benchmarks and milestones along the way toward intended outcomes.

Usually, a compelling case that your program has had a positive impact requires measurement of program targets before, during, and after implementation of the program. This requires careful program planning and early adoption of appropriate data collection methods and a management information database. Your summative evaluation report is a showcase for outcomes associated with your program.

Resistant Social Workers

Social workers may react negatively to the evaluation, seeing it as unrelated, intrusive, irrelevant, and, more importantly, an extra burden. Additionally, they may fear the evaluation will be used in some way to judge them. When an evaluation is externally driven, social workers may resist implementation of an evaluator's recommendations, even if the program's administration insists that changes be made.

Intrusiveness

Evaluation procedures are very likely to be intrusive, no matter how hard the person doing the evaluation works to avoid this. Because the procedures are not a part of a program's normal day-to-day routine but must be introduced as additional tasks to be performed, social workers have less time to spend on normal, client-related activities. This diversion of attention may be resented when workers feel obliged to spend less time with clients and more time participating in an evaluation process that was mandated "from above," or "from outside the program."

Periodic or No Feedback to Social Workers

The data obtained from a project-type approach to quality improvement, even if shared with the practitioners, is usually not directly or immediately relevant to them or their current clients. This is particularly the case if an evaluation is designed to answer questions posed by administrators or funders, and workers' practice concerns cannot be addressed in the same evaluation project.

If, as sometimes happens, the project-type approach does yield useful information (via the data collected) for the social workers, and changes are made on the basis of these data, the next evaluation may not take place for a long time, perhaps not for years. If the evaluator is not on hand to analyze the benefits resulting from the changes, the social workers may not be sure that there were any benefits.

Large Recommended Changes

The changes recommended as a result of a project approach to quality improvement can be major. Administrators and evaluators may feel that, with an evaluation occurring only once every few years, it is an event that ought to yield "significant" findings and recommendations to justify it. Large recommended changes can involve program renovations (e.g., overhauling the staff structure of a program) versus program refinements (e.g., adding or revising a component of staff training).

Not Practical in Applied Settings

All evaluations must be based on well-established evaluation principles and methods. Project evaluations, however, are more likely to be based on the scientific rigor necessary to obtain cause-and-effect knowledge. We will discuss basic types of evaluation designs in subsequent chapters. For now, it is enough to point out that evaluation designs used to obtain higher levels of quality improvement recommendations may require that clients be randomly assigned to experimental or control groups without regard to their individual rights—a technique that does not consider clients' special needs (see Chapter 10). Similarly, evaluation designs to measure client change may require that measurement be carried out both before and after the treatment intervention, without regard to clinical time restraints or the client's emotional condition.

Usually, rigorous experiments for the purpose of increasing knowledge are carried out in laboratory-type settings and not in practice settings. However, the same rigorous conditions may be suggested if the purpose is, for example, to evaluate the effectiveness and efficiency of a therapy group. The worker might argue that more time will be spent in the administration of the measuring instruments than conducting therapeutic work; the evaluator can easily reply that results will be valid only if experimental conditions are observed. The issue here is: Whose interests is the evaluation intended to serve? Who is it for—the social work practitioner or the external evaluator?

In a project approach to quality improvement, the answer is that sometimes it serves the evaluator or the administrative, academic, or funding body that has employed the evaluator. It should be stressed that this is not always the case. Many project approaches use unobtrusive evaluation techniques geared to actual practice situations. If, however, the evaluation is undertaken only once in a number of years, intrusion can be considered warranted to obtain reliable and valid results.

Difficult to Incorporate in Practice Settings

A final characteristic of a project approach to quality improvement is that the methods used by the evaluator are difficult for social workers to learn and almost impossible for them to incorporate into their normal day-to-day practices. In fact, social workers are not expected to learn anything about evaluation procedures as a result of the program being evaluated. Nor is it expected that the evaluation methods employed will be used again before the next major periodic evaluation. The evaluator carries out the project approach, and essentially until the next time, that is that.

THE INTERNAL MONITORING APPROACH

Most of the characteristics listed for the project approach to quality improvement are rather negative; without a doubt, the project approach is intrusive and traumatic, fails to meet the immediate needs of the workers, and may engender resentment and fear—especially if a program's workers have never been involved in a previous evaluation. We now turn to a second approach to quality improvement that complements the project approach and is the main focus of this book—the **internal evaluation** monitoring approach.

The **monitoring approach to quality improvement** is based on reliable and valid evaluation methods that can be integrated into a social service program as a part of its normal operating routine. This approach measures the extent that a social service program is reaching its intended population and the extent to which its services match those that were intended to be delivered. In addition, this approach is designed to provide immediate and continuous feedback on client service and progress to practitioners.

The monitoring approach is nothing more than the continual collection, analysis, reporting, and use of client data. This ongoing and dynamic approach to evaluation is planned and systematic. Ideally, such a system would be integrated with the program's records system so as to avoid duplication and enhance efficiency. For example, data on the changes the program aims to effect can be collected at intake, at specified times during treatment, at termination, and at follow-up. In this way, a constant stream of systematic data are collected, analyzed, and reported in an effort to help the program focus on its clients as they come into (intake), go through (treatment), and leave (termination) the program, then go on with their lives (follow-up).

More often than not, the internal monitoring approach to evaluation is done by folks who are employed within the program whereas the project approach to evaluation is usually done by people who are hired outside the program. In should be noted however, that this is only a generality and does not hold for all social service organizations—especially those with research and evaluation departments actually housed within them. Nevertheless, it is absolutely important to think through the evaluators' role regardless of where the evaluator is housed—within the organization or outside the organization (Box 2.2).

Characteristics of the Internal Monitoring Approach

Evaluations resulting from a monitoring approach to quality improvement tend to have the following characteristics: (1) they are internally driven, (2) they have cooperative social workers, (3) they have ongoing continuous feedback procedures, (4) they recommend minor changes, and (5) they are easily incorporated in practice settings.

Internally Driven

Continuous routine use of evaluation methods may have been initially suggested by an administrator or an outside consultant or funder. However, the evaluation methods are put into place and used by practitioners for their own and their clients'

Whether you decide on an external or internal evaluator or some combination of both, it is important to think through the evaluator's role. With your staff and stakeholders, think through all of the potential evaluator roles and relationships and determine which configuration makes the most sense given your particular situation, the purpose of the evaluation, and the questions you are attempting to address. One important role to think through is the relationship between the evaluator and primary stakeholders or the evaluation team. Questions to consider include:

- Should this relationship be distant or highly interactive?
- How much control should the evaluator have over the evaluation process as compared with the stakeholders/evaluation team?
- How actively involved should key staff and stakeholders be in the evaluation process?

Depending on the primary purpose of the evaluation and with whom the evaluator is working most closely (funders versus program staff versus program participants or community members), an evaluator might be considered a consultant for program improvement, a team member with evaluation expertise, a collaborator, an evaluation facilitator, an advocate for a cause, or a synthesizer. If the evaluation purpose is to determine the quality or importance of a program, you might look for an evaluator with methodological expertise and experience.

benefit without the request (or demand) from any outside source. The evaluation may thus be said to be internally driven.

Cooperative Social Workers

When evaluation is a process instead of an event, practitioners are more likely to collaborate in its efforts because it is an accepted part of the daily routine of delivering high-quality services.

Integrated

By definition, an intrusion is something unrelated to the task at hand that interferes with that task. Evaluation methods that are routinely used to improve services to clients are part and parcel of the workers' daily tasks. Necessary client-centered changes for solving problems are usually agreed on by line-level practitioners and are usually accepted without difficulty because they result from informed decision making; that is, decisions are made based on data that are available to all social workers. A monitoring approach gives workers the opportunity to identify problems and suggest tentative solutions based on program data.

Ongoing Continuous Feedback

Some activities in a social service program need to be monitored on a continuing basis. For example, client referrals are received daily and must be processed quickly. To estimate remaining program space, intake workers need a list of how many clients are presently being served, how many clients will be discharged shortly, and how many clients have recently been accepted into the program. This continually changing list is an example of a simple evaluative tool that provides useful data. The resulting information can be used to compare the actual number of clients in the program with the number the program was originally designed (and usually funded) to serve.

In other words, the list can be used to fulfill a basic evaluative purpose: comparison of what is with what should be, of the actual with the ideal. It might be found, in some programs, that the arithmetic of intake is not quite right. For example, suppose that a program has space for 100 clients. At the moment, 70 are being served on a regular basis. In theory, then, the program can accept 30 more clients. Suppose also that the program has five social workers; each will then theoretically carry a maximum caseload of 20.

In the caseloads of these five workers there ought to be just 30 spaces. But for some reason, there are more than 30. The supervisor, who is trying to assign new clients to workers, discovers that the workers can muster 40 spaces between them. In other words, there are 10 clients on the computer who are theoretically being served, but who are not in any of the five workers' caseloads. What has happened to these 10 clients?

Investigation brings to light that the workers' records and the computer's records are kept in different ways. Computer records reflect the assumption that every client accepted will continue to be served until formally discharged. However, the practitioner who has not seen Ms. Smith for six months and has failed to locate her after repeated tries has placed Ms. Smith in the "inactive" file. The result of this disparity in record keeping is that the program seems to have fewer available spaces, and clients who might be served are being turned away.

Simply discussing inactive files at a staff meeting might solve the problem. What steps will be taken to locate a client who does not appear for appointments? How long should attempts at contact continue before the client is formally discharged? Which other involved professionals need to be informed about the client's nonappearance and the discharge? When and how should they be informed? Is it worth modifying the intake computer's terminal display to include inactive files, with the dates they became inactive and the dates they were reactivated or discharged? Once decisions have been made on these points, a straightforward procedure can be put in place to deal with the ongoing problem of inactive files.

Minor Recommended Change

When change is an expected and ongoing process that results from regular monitoring, program adjustments or modifications tend to be small. Of course, continual monitoring can suggest that fundamental changes are needed in the way that the program is conceptualized or structured, but such large changes are rare. Most often, monitoring gives rise to continual minor refinements of programs.

Easy to Incorporate in Practice Settings

The monitoring approach, like the project approach to quality improvement, is based on well-established evaluation methods. The difference between them can lie in whom the evaluation is intended to serve: the line-level worker or the evaluator. When the workers themselves, for their own and their clients' benefit, undertake an evaluation, there is no doubt about for whom the evaluation is intended to serve.

Advantages of the Internal Monitoring Approach

Social workers who are interested in improving the quality of the services they offer via evaluations are well on their way to taking responsibility for providing the best possible service to clients through systematic examinations of their strengths and weaknesses via the quality improvement process. Becoming a self-evaluating social work professional (or program) has definite advantages not only for clients but also for workers. For example, they provide: (1) increased understanding of programs, (2) relevant feedback, (3) timely feedback, (4) self-protection, (5) practitioner and client satisfaction, and (6) professionalism.

Increased Understanding of Programs

A social service program is often a complex entity with a large number of interlinked components. Practitioners' main concerns usually have to do with the effectiveness of their treatment interventions. How can the confused sexual identity of an adolescent who has been sexually abused best be addressed? What teaching technique is most effective with children who have learning disabilities? Is an open-door policy appropriate for group homes housing adolescents who are mentally challenged? Answers come slowly through study, intuition, hunches, and past experience, but often the issues are so complex that practitioners cannot be sure if the answers obtained are correct.

Many social workers stumble onward, hoping their interventions are right, using intuition to assess the effectiveness of their particular interventions (or package of interventions) with a particular client. We will discuss case-level evaluations in future chapters and show how the use of simple evaluation designs can complement a worker's intuition so that an inspired guess more closely approaches knowledge. However, no amount of knowledge about how well an intervention worked will tell the worker why it worked or failed to work. Why do apparently similar clients, treated similarly, achieve different results? Is it something about the client? About the worker? About the type of intervention?

It is always difficult to pinpoint a reason for unsatisfactory achievement of a program's objectives because there are so many possible overlapping and intertwined causes. However, some reasons may be identified by a careful look at the program stages leading up to the interventions. For example, one reason for not attaining success with clients may be because they were inappropriate for a certain program and ought never have been admitted to it in the first place. Or perhaps the program's assessment procedures were inadequate; perhaps unsuitable clients were accepted because the referral came from a major funding body. In other words, perhaps the lack of client success at the intervention stage derives from screening problems at intake.

Social workers who have been involved with a do-it-yourself evaluation may become familiar with the program's intake procedures, both in theory and in reality. They may also become familiar with the planning procedures, discharge procedures, follow-up procedures, staff recruitment and training procedures, recording procedures, and so on. The worker will begin to see a link between poor client outcomes at one program stage and inadequacies at another, between a success here and an innovation somewhere else. In sum, practitioners may be able to perform their own tasks more effectively if they understand how their program functions as a living organism. One way to gain this understanding is to participate in a hands-on, do-it-yourself evaluation.

Relevant Feedback

A second advantage of the monitoring approach to evaluation is that the workers within the program can formulate meaningful and relevant questions. They can use evaluation procedures to find out what they want to know, not what the administrator, the funder, or a university professor wants to know. If the data to be gathered are perceived as relevant, social workers are usually willing to cooperate in the evaluation. And if the information resulting from that data is relevant, it is likely to be used by the practitioners.

It is our belief that all evaluative efforts conducted in our profession provide feedback loops that improve the delivery of services. Feedback provides data about the extent to which a program's goal is achieved or approximated. Based on these data, services may be adjusted or changed to improve goal achievement.

Timely Feedback

A third advantage is that the workers can decide when the evaluation is to be carried out. Evaluation procedures can be undertaken daily, weekly, monthly, or only once in five years, as will be discussed in the following chapters. The point here is that data are most useful when they help to solve a current problem, less useful when the problem has not yet occurred, and least useful after the event.

Self-Protection

Most social service programs are eventually evaluated, often by outside evaluators. If the social workers have already familiarized themselves with evaluation procedures and with their program's strengths and weaknesses, they are in a better position to defend the program when an externally driven evaluation occurs. In addition, because improvements have already been made as a result of self-evaluations, their program will be more defensible. In addition, the social workers will indirectly learn about evaluation designs and methodology by monitoring their practices on a regular basis. Modifications recommended by an outside evaluator are hence likely to be less far-reaching and less traumatic.

An additional consideration is that the social workers themselves are likely to be less traumatized by the idea of being evaluated: Evaluation is no longer a new and frightening experience, but simply a part of the routine—a routine that tries to improve the quality of services for clients.

Practitioner and Client Satisfaction

A monitoring approach to a case-level evaluation can satisfy the worker that an intervention is appropriate and successful, and it can improve a client's morale by demonstrating the progress that has been made toward his or her practice objectives. Moreover, data gathered at the case level can always be used at the program level (see Figure 1 in "A Few Words for Students"). Improvement of the program as a whole can follow from an improvement in one worker's practice—one client at a time.

Professionalism

A monitoring approach to evaluation is consistent with the expectations of professional conduct in social work. Social workers who use systematic methods to evaluate their work can benefit from evaluation results through informed decision making. Evaluation results can be used to support critical program changes or defend controversial program actions. They can confirm or challenge workers' long-held beliefs about a mode of operation. Additionally, evaluation can reveal program flaws and deficiencies that require corrective action.

Fine-Tuning Programs

Social service programs are dynamic organizations and must be responsive to outside pressures as well as internal struggles. They have to do this while providing efficient and effective client services. It is within the context of social service programs that workers and evaluators alike learn about client life experiences, witness client suffering, observe clients progress and regress, and feel societal pressure to produce great change with few resources. Integrating evaluation into program services (and social work practice), therefore, presents an immense opportunity to learn more about social problems, the people they affect, and how interventions work.

For organizational learning to occur, however, there must be an opportunity for continuous feedback—that is, for stakeholders to make sense out of the data collected. All levels of staff have an influence on a program's growth and development. Figure 2.2 depicts the evaluation process in broad strokes and Figure 2.3 presents the

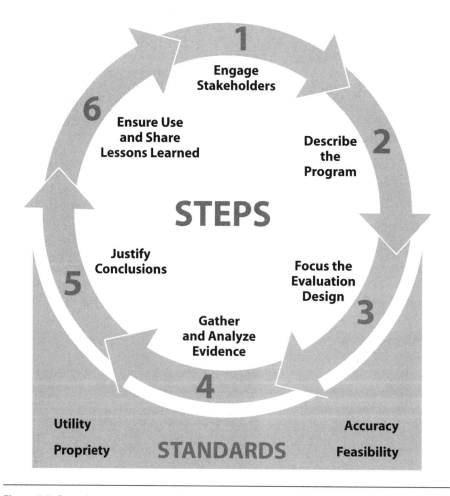

Figure 2.2 Steps in program evaluation.

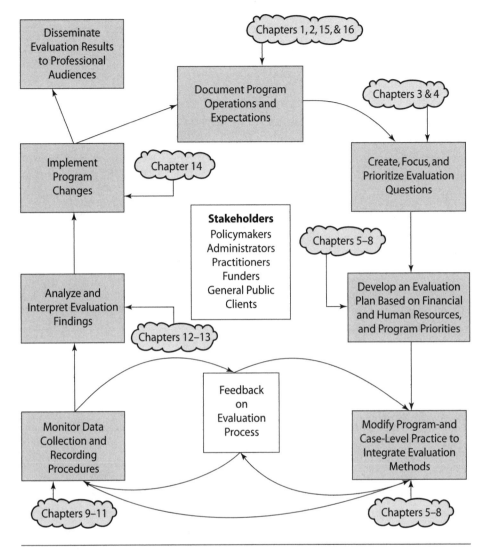

Figure 2.3 The generic evaluation process.

same process in more detail and depicts the evaluation process that encourages learning, growth, and development within social service programs.

The most fruitful place to begin in the evaluation cycle is at the top of Figure 2.3—Documenting Program Operations and Expectations. Before we begin the process of evaluation, however, it is critical to know the current circumstances within the program, a topic discussed in detail in Chapter 4.

As we have already mentioned, stakeholders are central to the evaluation process. Thus, they are shown in the center of the evaluation cycle depicted in Figure 2.3. Although it is ideal to obtain input from as many stakeholder groups as possible while we cycle through the evaluation process, sometimes we must settle for contributions from only of those who are interested and available to participate at a given point in time. Nevertheless, we must keep in mind that stakeholders provide a valuable resource for reactions to program development as the program goes through the entire evaluation cycle (see Box 1.3).

After a program's operations and expectations have been agreed upon and documented (via a logic model as presented in Box 2.3), an evaluation needs to create, focus, and prioritize specific evaluation questions. This phase of the cycle involves brainstorming these questions and selecting those that are of greatest concern. Do stakeholders want to know, for example, the profile of clients being served by the program? Do practitioners want to assess the efficiency of their referral system? Are funders wondering if clients are satisfied with the services they received? An endless list of potential evaluative questions is possible, but an evaluation can adequately address only a few them at best, given the fiscal and human constraints.

Eventually, a decision is made as to which questions the evaluation will focus on, given the program's logic model. Much more will be said about logic models in the following chapter. An evaluation plan is then created and modifications to case-level and program-level practices are made, and **data collection** begins. Note that Figure 2.3 shows two smaller feedback loops in the evaluation cycle. These loops serve to gather data on how the evaluation process is proceeding. Are modifications to case-level practice working for the practitioners? What obstacles do the practitioners encounter in the data collection and recording procedures, if any? Staying tuned to the evaluation process increases the likelihood that errors and problems will be detected early.

After data collection has occurred, an evaluation cycles through to analyzing data, forming recommendations, and ultimately implementing change. Figure 2.3 shows that program changes cycle back to the beginning—Documenting Program Operations and Expectations. Additionally, evaluation findings can be helpful to external audiences so that the program is actively involved in contributing to the knowledge base of our profession.

Data collection method

Procedures specifying techniques to be employed, measuring instruments to be used, and activities to be conducted in implementing an evaluation.

SUMMING UP AND LOOKING AHEAD

This chapter introduced two complementary approaches to quality improvement in the human services. It also presented a framework where programs can fine-tune themselves with data collected in a systematic manner. For a program to be evaluated, however, you need to know how programs are designed—the topic of the following chapter. You cannot evaluate a social service program without knowing how it is structured.

Box 2.3 The Logic Model for Program Planning and Evaluation

The logic model process is a tool that has been used for more than 20 years by program managers and evaluators to describe the effectiveness of their programs. The model describes logical linkages among program resources, activities, outputs, audiences, and short-term, intermediate-term, and long-term outcomes related to a specific problem or situation. Once a program has been described in terms of the logic model, critical measures of performance can be identified.

Logic models are narrative or graphical depictions of processes in real life that communicate the underlying assumptions upon which an activity is expected to lead to a specific result. Logic models illustrate a sequence of cause and effect relationships—a systems approach to communicate the path toward a desired result.

A common concern of impact measurement is that of limited control over complex outcomes. Establishing desired long-term outcomes, such as improved financial security or reduced teen-age violence, is tenuous because of the limited influence we may have over the target audience, and the complex, uncontrolled environmental variables. Logic models address this issue because they describe the concepts that need to be considered when we seek such outcomes. Logic models link the problem (situation) to the intervention (our inputs and outputs) and the impact (outcome) (Figure 1). Further, the model helps to identify partnerships critical to enhancing our performance.

Planning Process

The logic model was characterized initially by program evaluators as a tool for identifying performance measures. Since that time, the tool has been adapted to program planning as well. The application of the logic model as a planning tool allows precise communication about the purposes of a project, the components of a project, and the sequence of activities and accomplishments. Further, a project originally designed with assessment in mind is much more likely to yield beneficial data should evaluation be desired.

In the past, our strategy to justify a particular program often has been to explain what we are doing from the perspective of an insider, beginning with why we invest allocated resources. Our traditional justification includes the following sequence:

- We invest this time/money so that we can generate this activity/product.
- The activity/product is needed so people will learn how to do this.
- People need to learn that so they can apply their knowledge to this practice.
- When that practice is applied, the effect will be to change this condition.
- When that condition changes, we will no longer be in this situation.

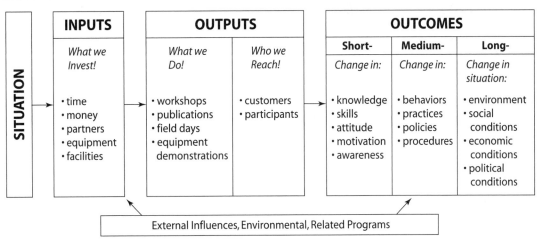

Figure 1 Elements of the logic model (from Millar, Simeone, & Carnevale, 2001).

(continued)

CHAPTER 2 Approaches to Accountability

Box 2.3 (continued)

The logic model process has been used successfully following the above sequence. However, according to Millar, Simeone, and Carnevale (2001), logic models that begin with the inputs and work through to the desired outcomes may reflect a natural tendency to limit one's thinking to existing activities, programs, and research questions. Starting with the inputs tends to foster a defense of the status quo rather than create a forum for new ideas or concepts. To help us think "outside the box," they suggest that the planning sequence be inverted, thereby focusing on the outcomes to be achieved. In such a reversed process, we ask ourselves "what needs to be done?" rather than "what is being done?" Thus, we might begin building our logic model by asking questions in the following sequence:

- What is the current situation that we intend to impact?
- What will it look like when we achieve the desired situation or outcome?
- What behaviors need to change for that outcome to be achieved?
- What knowledge or skills do people need before the behavior will change?
- What activities need to be performed to cause the necessary learning?
- What resources will be required to achieve the desired outcome?

One more point before we begin planning a program using the logic model: It is recognized that we are using a linear model to simulate a multidimensional process. Often, learning is sequential and teaching must reflect that, but the model becomes too complicated if we try to communicate that reality (Figure 2). Similarly, the output from one effort becomes the input for the next effort, as building a coalition may be required before the "group" can sponsor a needed workshop. Keep in mind that the logic model is a simple communication device. We should avoid complications by choosing to identify a single category to enter each item (i.e., inputs, outputs or outcomes). Details of order and timing then need to be addressed within the framework of the model, just as with other action planning processes.

Planning Elements

Using the logic model as a planning tool is most valuable when we focus on what it is that we want to communicate to others. Figure 3, adapted from the work of Howard Ladewig of the University of Florida, illustrates the building blocks of accountability that we can incorporate into our program plans. According to Ladewig, there are certain characteristics of programs that inspire others to value and support what we do. By describing the characteristics of our programs that communicate

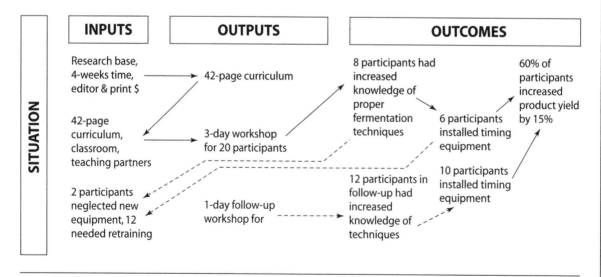

Figure 2 Example of an overcomplicated, multidimensional planning model.

relevance, quality, and impact, we foster buy-in from our stakeholders and audience. By including these characteristics within the various elements of the logic model, we communicate to others why our programs are important to them. The elements of accountability are further described in the context of the logic model.

Situation

The situation statement provides an opportunity to communicate the relevance of the project by describing the characteristics that will illustrate the relevance to others.

- *A statement of the problem:* What are the causes? What are the social, economic, and/or environmental symptoms of the problem? What are the likely consequences if nothing is done to resolve the problem? What are the actual or projected costs?
- *A description of who is affected by the problem*: Where do they live, work, and shop? How are they important to the community? Who depends on them—families, employees, organizations?
- *Who else is interested in the problem?* Who are the stakeholders? What other projects address this problem?

The situation statement establishes a baseline for comparison at the close of a program. A description of the problem and its symptoms provides a way to determine whether change has occurred. Describing who is affected by the problem allows assessment of who has benefited. Identifying other stakeholders and programs builds a platform to measure our overall contribution, including increased awareness and activity or reduced concern and cost.

Inputs

Inputs include those things that we invest in a program or that we bring to bear on a program, such as knowledge, skills, or expertise. Describing the inputs needed for a program provides an opportunity to communicate the quality of the program. Inputs that communicate to others that the program is of high quality include:

- Human resources, such as time invested by faculty, staff, volunteers, partners, and local people.
- Fiscal resources, including appropriated funds, special grants, donations, and user fees.
- Other inputs required to support the program, such as facilities and equipment.
- The knowledge base for the program, including teaching materials, curriculum, research results, certification, or learning standards.
- The involvement of collaborators, such as local, state, national agencies and organizations involved in planning, delivery, and evaluation.

Projects involving credible partners, built on knowledge gained from research, and delivered via tested and proven curricula are readily communicated as quality programs. Assessing the effectiveness of a program also is made easier when planned inputs are adequately described. By comparing actual investments with planned investments, evaluation can be used to improve future programs, justify budgets, and establish priorities.

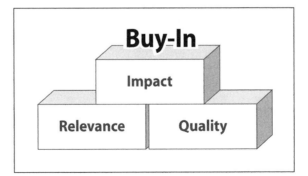

Figure 3 Structure of accountability.

(continued)

Box 2.3 (continued)

Outputs

Outputs are those things that we do (providing products, goods, and services to program customers) and the people we reach (informed consumers, knowledgeable decision makers). Describing our outputs allows us to establish linkages between the problem (situation) and the impact of the program (intended outcomes). Outputs that help link what we do with program impact include:

- Publications such as articles, bulletins, fact sheets, CISs, handbooks, or Web pages.
- Decision aids such as software, worksheets, or models.
- Teaching events such as workshops, field days, tours, or short courses.
- Discovery and application activities, such as research plots, demonstration plots, or product trials.

The people we reach also are outputs of the program and need to be the center of our model. They constitute a bridge between the problem and the impact. Information about the people who participated and what they were taught can include:

- Their characteristics or behaviors.
- The proportion or number of people in the target group who were reached.
- Learner objectives for program participants.
- Number of sessions or activities attended by participants.
- Level of satisfaction that participants express for the program.

Outcomes

Program outcomes can be short-term, intermediate-term, or long-term. Outcomes answer the question "What happened as a result of the program?" and are useful to communicate the impact of our investment. Short-term outcomes of educational programs may include changes in:

- *Awareness*—customers recognize the problem or issue.
- *Knowledge*—customers understand the causes and potential solutions.
- *Skills*—customers possess the skills needed to resolve the situation.

- *Motivation*—customers have the desire to effect change.
- *Attitude*—customers believe their actions can make a difference.

Intermediate-term outcomes include changes that follow the short-term outcomes, such as changes in:

- Practices used by participants.
- Behaviors exhibited by people or organizations.
- Policies adopted by businesses, governments, or organizations.
- Technologies employed by end users.
- Management strategies implemented by individuals or groups.

Long-term outcomes follow intermediate-term outcomes when changed behaviors result in changed conditions, such as these improvements:

- Economic conditions—increased income or financial stability.
- Social conditions—reduced violence or improved cooperation.
- Environmental conditions—improved air quality or reduced runoff.
- Political conditions—improved participation or opportunity.

External Influences

Institutional, community, and public policies may have either supporting or antagonistic effects on many of our programs. At the institutional level, schools may influence healthy eating habits in ways that are beyond our control, but that may lead to social change. Classes in health education may introduce children to the food pyramid and to the concept of proportional intake, but the cafeteria may serve pizza on Wednesdays and steak fingers on Thursdays. The community also can influence eating habits through availability of fast-food restaurants or produce markets. Even public policies that provide support (such as food banks and food stamps) for acquiring some items but not others might impact healthy eating habits. Documenting the social, physical, political, and institutional environments that can influence outcomes helps to improve the program planning process by answering the following:

- Who are important partners/collaborators for the program?
- Which part(s) of the issue can this project realistically influence?
- What evaluation measures will accurately reflect project outcomes?
- What other needs must be met to address this issue?

Evaluation Planning

Development of an evaluation plan to assess the program can be superimposed, using the logic model format. The evaluation plan should include alternatives to assess the processes used in planning the program. Process indicators should be designed to provide a measurable response to questions such as:

- Were specific inputs made as planned, in terms of the amount of input, timing, and quality of input?
- Were specific activities conducted as planned, in terms of content, timing, location, format, and quality?
- Was the desired level of participation achieved, in terms of numbers and characteristics of participants?
- Did customers express the degree of customer satisfaction expected?

The evaluation plan also should identify indicators appropriate to the desired outcomes, including short-term, medium-term, and long-term outcomes. Outcome indicators also should be measurable, and should be designed to answer questions such as:

- Did participants demonstrate the desired level of knowledge increase, enhanced awareness, or motivation?
- Were improved management practices adopted, behaviors modified, or policies altered to the extent expected for the program?
- To what extent were social, economic, political, or environmental conditions affected by the program?

Conclusion

Developing appropriate and measurable indicators during the planning phase is the key to a sound evaluation. Early identification of indicators allows the program manager/team to learn what baseline data already may be available to help evaluate the project, or to design a process to collect baseline data before the program is initiated. The logic model is useful for identifying elements of the program that are most likely to yield useful evaluation data and for delineating an appropriate sequence for collecting data and measuring progress.

In most cases, however, more work on a project will be required before indicators are finalized. Outcome indicators to measure learning should be based on specific learner objectives that are described as part of the curriculum. Indicators to measure behavioral change should specify which behaviors are targeted by the program. Conditional indicators may require a significant investment of time to link the medium-term outcomes to the expected long-term outcomes through the application of a targeted study or relevant research base.

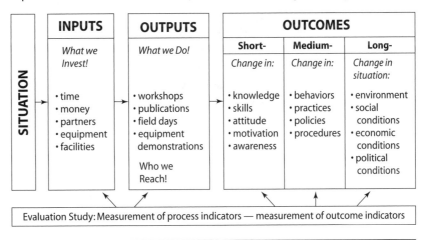

Figure 4 Insertion of evaluation plan into the logic model.

Recap and Online Materials

In this chapter, you learned how to become an accountable social work professional through the use of program evaluations.

You should also recall the concept of accountability from your foundational research course. If not, go online to take a free crash course in accountability.

You can also find the following materials online to help you master the concepts you just learned:

- Chapter Outline
- Learning Objectives
- Key Terms and Concepts
- Flash Cards
- Practice Multiple-Choice Tests
- Essay Questions with Answers
- Links

www.oup.com/us/swevaluation

Study Questions

1. What two general types of evaluations can be used in the quality improvement process? Provide an example of how each one is used when your social work program evaluates its efforts, via the Council on Social Work Education's mandate.
2. List and discuss the characteristics of the project approach to quality improvement. Provide an example of each one.
3. List and discuss the characteristics of the monitoring approach to quality improvement. Provide an example of each one.
4. List and discuss the advantages of the monitoring approach to quality improvement. Provide an example of each one.
5. Discuss how a social service program can do a project approach and a monitoring approach to evaluation at the same time.
6. Discuss how your social work program (BSW or MSW) can be evaluated with the project approach to quality improvement.
7. Discuss how your social work program (BSW or MSW) can be evaluated with the monitoring approach to quality improvement.
8. At your practicum setting, discuss how you would go about telling your practicum instructor how you think the program that houses your field placement could benefit from a project approach to evaluation. What would you tell him or her, and why?
9. At your practicum setting, discuss how you would go about telling your practicum instructor how you think the program that houses your field placement could

benefit from a monitoring approach to evaluation. What would you tell him or her, and why?

10. Take a look at Box 2.3. Do a logic model for your social work educational program (BSW or MSW). Compare your logic model with those of your classmates. How did they differ? How were they the same?

References, Further Reading, and Resources

Unrau, Y. A., Gabor, P. A., & Grinnell, R. M., Jr. (2005). Program evaluation. In R. M. Grinnell, Jr., & Y. A. Unrau (Eds.), *Social work research and evaluation: Quantitative and qualitative approaches* (7th ed., pp. 453–468). New York: Oxford University Press.

Weinbach, R. W. (2005). Research contexts. In R. M. Grinnell, Jr., & Y. A. Unrau (Eds.), *Social work research and evaluation: Quantitative and qualitative approaches* (7th ed., pp. 23–32). New York: Oxford University Press.

On Logic Models

Chen, W. W., Cato, B. M., & Rainford, N. (1998–1999). Using a logic model to plan and evaluate a community intervention program: A case study. *International Quarterly of Community Health Education, 18*(4), 449–458.

Dwyer, J. (1997). Using a program logic model that focuses on performance measurement to develop a program. *Canadian Journal of Public Health, 88*(6), 421–425.

Glanz, K. & Rimer, B. K. (1995). *Theory at a glance: A guide for health promotion practice* (NIH Publication No. 95-3896). Bethesda, MD: National Institutes of Health, National Cancer Institute.

Julian, D. A., Jones, A., & Deyo, D. (1995). Open systems evaluation and the logic model: Program planning and evaluation tools. *Evaluation and Program Planning, 18*, 333–341.

Marcus, B. H., Selby, V. C., Niaura, R. S., & Rossi, J. S. (1992). Self-efficacy and the stages of exercise behavior change. *Research Quarterly of Exercise and Sport, 63*, 60–66.

McLaughlin, J. A., & Jordan, G. B. (1999). Logic models: A tool for telling your program's performance story. *Evaluation and Program Planning, 22*, 65–72.

Millar, A., Simeone, R. S., & Carnevale, J. T. (2001). Logic models: A systems tool for performance management. *Evaluation and Program Planning 24*, 73–81.

Prochaska, J. O., Redding, C. A., & Evers, K. E. (1997). The transtheoretical model and stages of change. In K. Glanz, F. M. Lewis, & B. K. Rimer (Eds.), *Health behavior and health education: Theory, research, and practice* (pp. 60–84). San Francisco: Jossey-Bass.

Rosenstock, I. M. (1974). The Health Belief Model and preventive health behavior. *Health Education Monographs, 2*, 354–386.

Taylor-Powell, E. (1999). *Providing leadership for program evaluation*. Madison, WI: University of Wisconsin Extension.

Trochim, W. M. (1989). An introduction to concept mapping for planning and evaluation. *Evaluation and Program Planning, 12*, 1–16.

Designing Client-Centered Programs

3

The previous chapter presented how project and monitoring types of evaluations are an essential part of evaluating a social service program. However, we have not yet defined what a program is. It is difficult to do any kind of program evaluation without having a clear understanding of how programs are conceptualized—the topic of this chapter. When doing any kind of program evaluation we must pay attention to the environment within which the program exists to better understand the logic of its design. We will start with the immediate environment of all social service programs—the larger organization commonly referred to as social service agencies.

SOCIAL SERVICE AGENCIES

A **social service agency** is an organization that exists to fulfill a legitimate social purpose such as

- To protect children from physical, sexual, and emotional harm.
- To enhance quality of life for developmentally delayed adolescents.
- To improve nutritional health for housebound senior citizens.

Agencies can be public and funded entirely by the state and/or federal government, or private and funded by private funds, deriving some monies from govern-

Social service agency
A social service organization that exists to fulfill a broad social purpose.

mental sources and some from client fees, charitable bodies, private donations, fund-raising activities, and so forth. It is extremely common for agencies to be funded by many different types of sources. When several sources of funding are provided to an agency, the agency's funds (in their totality) are called "blended funds." Regardless of the funding source(s), agencies are defined by their (1) mission statements, (2) goals, and (3) objectives.

Agency Mission Statements

Mission statement

A unique written philo-sophical perspective of what an agency is all about.

All agencies have **mission statements** that provide the unique written philosophical perspective of what they are all about and make explicit the reasons for their existence. Mission statements sometimes are called *philosophical statements* or simply an *agency's philosophy*. Whatever it is called, a mission statement articulates a common vision for the organization in that it provides a point of reference for all major planning decisions. Mission statements are like lighthouses in that they exist to provide direction. A mission statement not only provides clarity of purpose to persons within the agency but also helps them to gain understanding and support from those stakeholders outside the agency who are influential to the agency's success (see Chapter 1).

Mission statements are usually given formal approval and sanction by legislators for public agencies or by executive boards for private ones. They can range from one sentence to 10 pages or more and are as varied as the agencies they represent. Here are brief examples of agency mission statements:

- This agency strives to provide a variety of support services to families and children in need, while in the process of maintaining their rights, their safety, and their human dignity.
- The mission of this agency is to promote and protect the mental health of the elderly people residing in this state by offering quality and timely programs that will deliver these services.
- The philosophy of this agency states that clients are partners in their treatment, and all services should be short-term, intensive, and focus on problems in day-to-day life and work.
- The philosophy of this agency is to protect and promote the physical and social well-being of this city by ensuring the development and delivery of culturally competent services that encourage and support individual, family, and community independence, self-reliance, and civic responsibility to the greatest degree possible.

In short, an agency's mission statement lays the overall conceptual foundation for all of the programs housed within it because each program (soon to be discussed) must be logically connected to the overarching intent of the agency as declared by its mission statement. Note that mission statements capture the general type of client to be served as well as communicate the essence of service delivery. Creating mission statements is a process of bringing interested stakeholders together to agree on the overall direction and tone of the agency.

The process of creating mission statements is affected by available words in a language as well as the meaning given to those words by individual stakeholders. Because mission statements express the broad intention of an agency, they set the stage for all program planning within the agency and are essential to the development of an agency's goal.

Agency Goals

As should be evident by now, social service agencies are established in an effort to reduce gaps between the current and the desired state of affairs for a specific target population. Mission statements can be lofty and include several philosophical declarations, but the **agency goal** is more concise; there is only one per agency. An agency goal is always defined at a conceptual level, and it is not measured. Its main ambition is to guide us toward effective and accountable service delivery in two ways:

Agency goal
Broad, unmeasurable outcomes the agency wishes to achieve; outcomes based on values and guided by the agency's mission statement.

1. Directed by the agency's mission statement, the agency's goal acts as a single focal point to guide the entire range of the agency's programs (and related activities within each program) in a specific direction.
2. An agency's goal functions as an umbrella under which all of its programs, program goals, program objectives, practice objectives, and practice activities within the agency are logically derived.

Requirements for Goals

It is essential that an agency's goal reflects the agency's mandate and is guided by its mission statement. This is achieved by forming a goal with the following four components:

1. The nature of the current social problem to be tackled.
2. The client population to be served.
3. The general direction of anticipated client change (desired state).
4. The means by which the change is supposed to be brought about.

Agency goals can be broad or narrow. Let's look at two generic examples:

- *Agency Goal—National:* The goal of this agency is to enhance the quality of life of this nation's families (*client population to be served*) who depend on public funds for day-to-day living (*social problem to be tackled*). The agency supports reducing long-term dependence on public funds (*general direction of anticipated client change*) by offering innovative programs that increase the self-sufficiency and employability of welfare-dependent citizens (*means by which the change is supposed to be brought about*).

- *Agency Goal—Local:* The goal of this agency is to help youth from low socioeconomic households in this city (*client population to be served*) who are dropping out of school (*current social problem to be tackled*) to stay in school (*general direction of anticipated client change*) by providing mentorship and tutoring programs in local neighborhoods (*means by which the change is supposed to be brought about*).

In general, an agency's goal reflects the scope of the programs offered within the agency. National agencies are clearly broader in boundary and size than local ones, for example. Additionally, more complex agencies such as those serving multiple populations or addressing multiple social problems will capture a more expansive population or problem area in their goal statements. An agency's goal statement must be broad enough to encompass all of its programs; that is, each program within an agency must have a direct and logical connection to the agency that governs it. However small or large, an agency functions as a single entity, and the agency's goal statement serves to unify all of its programs.

Agency Objectives

Agency objective
To offer programs in order to achieve the agency's goal.

All agencies should have only one **agency objective:** to provide specific social service programs that are directly linked to the agency's goal. In short, no agency should have a program housed within it in that delivers services that are not connected directly to the agency's goal. For example, a child protection agency might be expected to offer an in-home family support program but not a group home program for cancer patients or an employment training program for adults with cognitive disabilities. Likewise, an agency that defines itself as providing programs that help city youth stay in school would not offer nutritional programs for the elderly, marriage counseling programs, or any other programs that fall outside the scope of the agency's goal.

In sum, an agency's single objective is to provide various social service programs that will help meet its overall goal—nothing more, nothing less.

Social Service Programs

Program
An organization that exists to fulfill some specific social purpose; must be logically linked to the agency's goal.

Whatever the current social problem, the desired future state, or the population that the agency wishes to serve, an agency sets up social service **programs** to help work toward its intended result—the agency goal. There are as many ways to organize social service programs as there are people willing to be involved in the task. And everyone has an opinion on how agencies should structure the programs within them.

Mapping out the relationship among programs is a process that is often obscured by the fact that the term *program* can be used to refer to different levels of service delivery within an agency (e.g., Figures 3.1, 3.2, and 3.3). In other words, some programs can be seen as subcomponents of larger ones; for example, in Figure 3.3 "Public Awareness Services" falls under the Nonresidential Program for the Women's Emergency Shelter.

Figure 3.1 presents a simple structure of a family service agency serving families and children. Each program included in the Family Service Agency is expected to have some connection to serving families. The Family Support Program and the Family Counseling Program have an obvious connection, given their titles. The Group Home Program, however, has no obvious connection; its title reveals nothing about who resides in the group home or for what purpose. Because the Group Home Program operates under the auspices of "family services," it is likely that it temporarily houses children and youth who eventually will return to their families. Most importantly, the agency does not offer programs that are geared toward other target groups such as the elderly or the homeless.

By glancing at Figure 3.1, it can be easily seen that this particular family service agency has five programs within it that deal with families and children, the agency's target population: a group home program for children, a family counseling program, a child adoption program, a treatment foster care program, and a family support program.

Figure 3.2 provides another example of an agency that also deals with families and children. This agency (Richmond Family Services) has only two programs, a Behavioral Adaptation Treatment Program, and a Receiving and Assessment Family Home Program. The latter is further broken down into two components—a Family Support Component, and a Receiving and Assessment Component. In addition, the Receiving and Assessment Component is further broken down into Crisis Support Services, Child Care Services, and Family Home Provider Services.

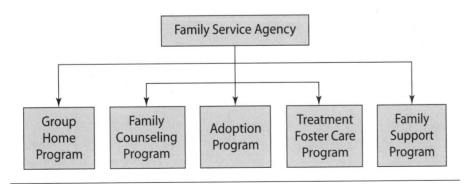

Figure 3.1 Simple organizational chart of a family service agency.

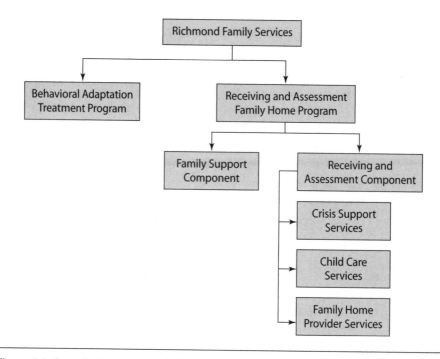

Figure 3.2 Organizational chart of a family service agency (highlighting the receiving and assessment component).

How many programs are there in Figure 3.2? The answer is two—however, we need to note that this agency conceptualized its service delivery much more thoroughly than did the agency outlined in Figure 3.1. Richmond Family Services has conceptualized the Receiving and Assessment Component of its Receiving and Assessment Family Home Program into three separate subcomponents: Crisis Support Services, Child Care Services, and Family Home Provider Services. In short, Figure 3.2 is more detailed in how it delivers its services than is the agency represented in Figure 3.1. Programs that are more clearly defined are generally easier to implement, operate, and evaluate.

Another example of how programs can be organized under an agency is presented in Figure 3.3. This agency, the Women's Emergency Shelter, has a Residential Program and a Nonresidential Program. Its Residential Program has Crisis Counseling Services and Children's Support Services, and the Nonresidential Program has Crisis Counseling Services and Public Awareness Services. This agency distinguishes the services it provides between the women who stay within the shelter (its Residential Program) and those who come and go (its Nonresidential Program). The agency could have conceptualized the services it offers in a number of different ways.

A final example of how an agency can map out its services is presented in Figure 3.4. As can be seen, the agency's Child Welfare Program is broken down into three services, and the Native Child Protection Services is further subdivided into four components: an Investigation Component, a Family Service Child in Parental

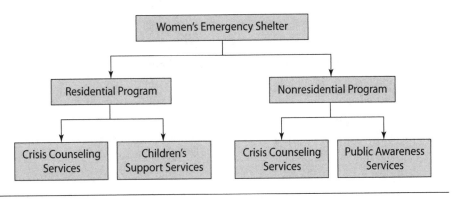

Figure 3.3 Organizational chart of a women's emergency shelter.

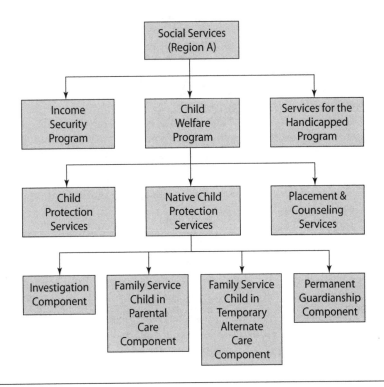

Figure 3.4 Organizational chart of a state's social service delivery system (highlighting the Native protection services).

Care Component, a Family Services Child in Temporary Alternate Care Component, and a Permanent Guardianship Component.

The general rule of ensuring that programs within an agency are logically linked together may seem simple enough that you might be wondering why we are emphasizing this point. The reality is that many social service programs are added to agencies on a piecemeal basis. That is, new programs are often born out of funding opportunities that come available for new, but unrelated, programs (to the agency's goal that is). With the opportunity to seize new funds sometimes comes funding restrictions that result in creating new programs that fit poorly with established services. While a social service administrator must constantly seek new resources to provide better and/or additional services within the agency's programs, it is important that new programs do not compromise existing ones.

By simply glancing at Figures 3.1 to 3.4, it can be seen that how an agency labels its programs and subprograms is arbitrary. For example, the agency that represents Figure 3.2 labels its subprograms as components and its sub-subprograms as services. The agency that represents Figure 3.3 simply labels its subprograms as services. The main point is that an agency must structure and conceptualize its programs, components, and services in a logical way that makes the most sense in view of the agency's overall goal, which is guided by its mission statement and mandate.

There is no standard approach to naming programs in the social services, but there are themes that may assist with organizing an agency's programs. We present four themes and suggest, as a general rule, that an agency pick only one (or one combination) to systematically name all of its programs.

- *Function,* such as Adoption Program, Family Support Program
- *Setting,* such as Group Home Program, Residential Program
- *Target population,* such as Services for the Handicapped Program
- *Social problem,* such as Child Sexual Abuse Program, Behavioral Adaptation Treatment Program

Program names can include acronyms such as P.E.T. (Parent Effectiveness Training) or catchy titles such as Incredible Edibles (a nutritional program for children). The appeal of such program names is that they often are endearing to program staff and clients who are familiar with the program's services. However, unless the program name is accompanied by a marketing strategy, the program may go unnoticed by the general public or other potential clients. Therefore, the primary purpose of a program ought to be reflected in the program's name. Including the target social problem (or the main client need) in the program's name simplifies communication of a program's purpose. In this way, a program's name is linked to its goal, and there is less confusion about what services it offers.

Nondescript program names can lead to confusion in understanding a program's purpose. The Group Home Program in Figure 3.1, for example, suggests that this program aims to provide a residence for clients. In fact, all clients residing in the group home are there to fulfill a specific purpose. Depending on the goal of the program, the primary purpose could be to offer shelter and safety for teenage runaways. Or the program's aim might be the enhanced functioning of adolescents with developmental disabilities, for example.

An Agency Versus a Program

What is the difference between an agency and a program? Like an agency, a program is an organization that also exists to fulfill a social purpose. There is one main difference, however: A program has a narrower, better defined purpose and is always nested within an agency.

Sometimes an agency may itself have a narrow, well-defined purpose. The sole purpose of a counseling agency, for example, may be to serve couples who struggle with a sexual dysfunction. In this case, the agency comprises only one program, and the terms *agency* and *program* refer to the same thing. If the clientele happens to include a high proportion of couples who are infertile, for example, it may later be decided that some staff members should specialize in infertility counseling (with a physician as a co-counselor) while other workers continue to deal with all other aspects of sexual dysfunction. In this case, there would then be two distinct sets of social work staff, each focusing on a different goal, and two separate types of clients; that is, there would be two *programs* (one geared toward infertility counseling and the other toward sexual dysfunction). Creating programs that target specific problems and populations facilitates the development of evidence-based knowledge because workers can hone the focus their professional development on specialized knowledge and skills. However, the *agency*, with its board, its senior administrator (executive director), and its administrative policies and procedures, would remain as a single entity.

PROGRAM DESIGNS

Building or creating program designs involves general and specific thinking about a program. The process begins by articulating a program's general intentions for solving identified problems—the conceptualization or idea of the program's purpose. It also involves setting specific plans for how the program is to accomplish what it sets out to do. A program for children who are sexually aggressive, for example, may aim to reduce the deviant sexual behavior of its young clients (i.e., the intention) by providing individual counseling (i.e., the plan for achieving the intention). A major purpose of program designs is to easily communicate a model of service delivery to interested stakeholders. They provide a blueprint for implementing a program's services, monitoring its activities, and evaluating both its operations and achievements.

Program designs present plausible and logical plans for how programs aim to produce change for their clients. Therefore, implicit in every program model is the idea of theory—an explanation for how client change is brought about (see Boxes 2.3 and 3.2). The program for children who are sexually aggressive suggests that such children will reduce their sexual perpetration by gaining understanding or insight

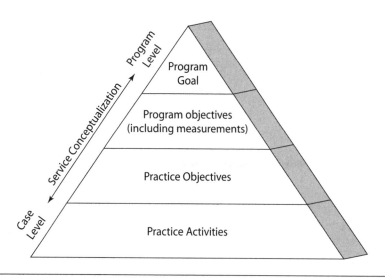

Figure 3.5 How a program's services are conceptualized from the case level to the program level.

through sessions with an individual counselor. Programs that articulate a theoretical approach such as psychoanalytic or behavior counseling make their program theory more explicit. Programs serving the same population offer an alternative theory of change when different interventions are used.

There are four major components that are used to clearly describe and organize thinking about program service delivery: (1) program goal, (2) program objectives, (3) practice objectives, and (4) practice activities. A graphic example of how these components relate to one another is presented in Figure 3.5.

Box 3.1 displays a concise example of how the logic of Figure 3.5 is actually carried out for a family support program. Included are the program's goal, three of the program's objectives, the program's activities, and strategies for measurement (to be discussed in future chapters). Organized in this way, the family support program is primed for any kind of evaluation.

Program Goals

A program goal has much in common with an agency goal, discussed previously.

- Like an agency goal, a program goal must also be compatible with the agency's mission statement as well as the agency goal and at least one agency objective. Program goals must logically flow from the agency as they are announcements of expected outcomes dealing with the social problem that the program is attempting to prevent, eradicate, or ameliorate.
- Like an agency goal, a program goal is not intended to be measurable—it simply provides a programmatic direction for the program to follow.

> **Box 3.1** Program-Level Service Conceptualization for a Family Support Program (from Figure 3.5)
>
> **Program Goal and Mission Statement**
>
> To support family units where children are at risk for out-of-home placement due to problems with physical abuse (goal). The program aims to strengthen interpersonal functioning of family members through intensive home-based services (mission statement).
>
> **_Three Program Objectives_**
>
> 1. *To increase positive social support for parents.*
>   - *Literature Support:* A lack of positive social support has been repeatedly linked to higher risk for child abuse. Studies indicate that parents with greater social support and less stress report more pleasure in their parenting roles.
>   - *Sample of Activities:* Referrals to support groups; evaluation of criteria for positive support; introductions to community services; reconnecting clients with friends and family.
>   - *Measuring Instruments:* Client log; *Provision of Social Relations.*
>
> 2. *To increase problem-solving skills for family members.*
>   - *Literature Support:* Problem solving is a tool for breaking difficult dilemmas into manageable pieces. Enhancing individuals' skills in systematically addressing problems increases the likelihood that they will successfully tackle new problems as they arise. Increasing problem-solving skills for parents and children equips family members to handle current problems, anticipate and prevent future ones, and advance their social functioning.
>   - *Sample of Activities:* Teaching steps to problem solving; role-playing problem-solving scenarios; providing supportive counseling.
>   - *Measuring Instrument: The Problem-Solving Inventory.*
>
> 3. *To increase parent's use of noncorporal child management strategies.*
>   - *Literature Support:* Research studies suggest that deficiency in parenting skills is associated with higher recurrence of abuse. Many parents who abuse their children have a limited repertoire of ways to discipline their children.
>   - *Sample of Activities:* Teaching noncorporal discipline strategies; informing parents about the criminal implications of child abuse; assessing parenting strengths; providing reading material about behavior management.
>   - *Measuring Instruments:* Goal Attainment Scaling; Checklist of Discipline Strategies.

- A program goal must also possess four characteristics:
    1. It must identify a current social problem area.
    2. It must include a specific target population within which the problem resides.
    3. It must include the desired future state for this population.
    4. It must state how it plans to achieve the desired state.

- A program goal reflects the intention of social workers within the program. For example, workers in a program may expect that they will "enable adolescents with developmental disabilities to lead full and productive lives." The program goal phrase of "full and productive lives," however, can mean different things to different people. Some may believe that a full and productive life cannot be lived without integration into the community; they may, therefore, want to work toward placing these youth in the mainstream school system, enrolling them in community activities, and finally returning them to their parental homes, with a view to making them self-sufficient in adult life. Others may believe that a full and productive life for these adolescents means the security of institutional teaching and care and the companionship of children with similar needs. Still others may believe that institutional care combined with community contact is the best compromise.

Program goal statements are meant to be sufficiently elusive to allow for changes in service delivery approach or clientele over time. Another reason that goals have intangible qualities is because we want enough flexibility in our social service programs to adjust program conceptualization and operation as needed. Indeed, by establishing a program design, we begin the process of crafting a theory of client change. By evaluating the program, we test the program's theory—its plan for creating client change (see Boxes 2.3 and 3.2).

Unintended Program Results

Working toward a program's goal may result in a number of unintended results that emerge in the environment surrounding the program. For example, a group home for adolescents with developmental disabilities may strive to enable residents to achieve self-sufficiency in a safe and supportive environment. This is the intended result, or goal. Incidentally, however, the very presence of the group home may produce organized resistance from neighbors—a negative unintended result.

The resistance may draw the attention of the media, which in turn draws a sympathetic response from the general public about the difficulties associated with finding a suitable location for homes caring for youth with special needs: a positive unintended result. On occasion, the unintended result can thwart progress toward the program's goal; that is, youth with developmental disabilities would not feel safe or supported if neighbors act in unkind or unsupportive ways. This condition would almost certainly hamper the youths' ability to achieve self-sufficiency in the community.

Program Goals Versus Agency Goals

Perhaps the group home mentioned above is run by an agency that has a number of other homes for adolescents with developmental disabilities. It is unlikely that all of the children in these homes will be capable of self-sufficiency as adults; some may have reached their full potential when they have learned to feed or bathe themselves. The goal of self-sufficiency will, therefore, not be appropriate for the agency as a whole, although it might do very well for Group Home *X*, which serves children who function at higher levels. The agency's goal must be broader to encompass a wider range of situations—and because it is broader, it will probably be more vague.

To begin, the agency may decide that its goal is "to enable adolescents with developmental disabilities to reach their full potential" as outlined in Figure 3.6:

- Group Home *X*, one of the programs within the agency, can then interpret "full potential" to mean self-sufficiency and can formulate a program goal based on this interpretation.
- Group Home *Y*, another program within the agency serving children who function at lower levels, may decide that it can realistically do no more than provide a caring environment for the children and emotional support for their families. It may translate this decision into another program goal: "To enable adolescents with developmental disabilities to experience security and happiness."
- Group Home *Z*, a third program within the agency, may set as its program goal "To enable adolescents with developmental disabilities to acquire the social and vocational skills necessary for satisfying and productive lives."

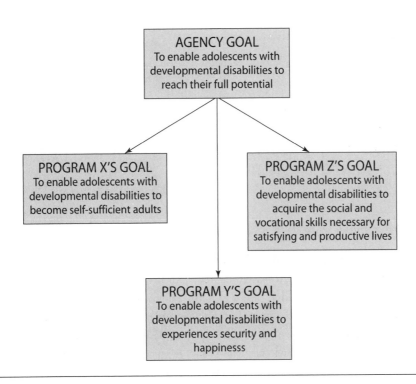

Figure 3.6 Organizational chart of an agency with three programs.

Figure 3.6 illustrates the relationship among the goals of the three group homes to the goal of the agency. Note how logical and consistent the goals of the programs are with the agency's overall goal. This example illustrates three key points about the character of a program goal:

1. A program goal simplifies the reason for the program to exist and provides direction for its workers.
2. Program goals of different but related programs within the same agency may differ, but they must all be linked to the agency's overall goal. They must all reflect both their individual purpose and the purpose of the agency of which they are a part.
3. Program goals are *not* measurable. Consider the individual goals of the three group homes in Figure 3.6; none of them are measurable in their present form.

Concepts such as happiness, security, self-sufficiency, and full potential mean different things to different people and cannot be measured until they have been clearly defined. Many social work goals are phrased in this way, putting forth more of an elusive intent than a definite, definable, measurable purpose. Nor is this a flaw; it is simply what a goal *is*, a statement of an intended result that must be clarified before it can be measured. As we will see next, program goals are clarified by the objectives they formulate.

Types of Program Objectives

A program's objectives are derived from its goal. **Program objectives** are measurable indicators of the program's goal; they articulate the specific client outcomes that the program wishes to achieve; stated clearly and precisely, they make it possible to tell to what degree the program's results have been achieved. All program objectives must be client-centered—they must be formulated to help a client in relation to the social problem articulated by the program's goal. Social service programs often are designed to client change in three areas: (1) knowledge, (2) affects, and (3) behaviors.

Knowledge-Based Objectives

Knowledge-based program objectives are commonly found within educational programs, where the aim is to increase the client's knowledge in some specific area. The words "to increase knowledge" are key here: They imply that the recipient of the education will have learned something. For example, "to increase teenage mother's knowledge about the stages of child development between birth and two years." The hoped-for increase in knowledge can then be measured by testing the mother's knowledge levels before and after the program. The program objective is achieved when it can be demonstrated (via measurement) that learning has occurred.

Program objective
A statement that clearly and exactly specifies the expected change or intended result for individuals receiving program services; not to be confused with a program goal.

Knowledge-based program objective
An objective that aims to change a client's level of information and understanding about a specific social area.

Affect-Based Objectives

Affect-based program objectives focus on changing either feelings about oneself or awareness about another person or thing. For example, a common affect-based program objective in social work is to raise a client's self-esteem, or interventions are designed to decrease feelings of isolation, increase marital satisfaction, and decrease feelings of depression. As well, feelings or attitudes toward other people or things are the focus of many social work programs. To give just a few examples, social service programs may try to change negative views toward people of color, homosexuality, or gender roles. "Affects" here includes attitudes because attitudes are a way of looking at the world. It is important to realize that, although particular attitudes may be connected to certain behaviors, they are two separate constructs.

Affect-based program objective
An objective that focuses on changing an individual's emotional reaction to himself or herself or to another person or thing.

Behavioral-Based Objectives

Very often, a program objective is established to change the behavior of a person or group: to reduce drug abuse among adolescents, to increase the use of community resources by seniors, or to reduce the number of hate crimes in a community. Sometimes, knowledge or affect objectives are used as a means to this end. In other words, the expectation is that a change in attitude or knowledge will lead to a change in behavior. The social worker might assume that adolescents who know more about the effects of drugs will use or abuse them less; that seniors who know more about available community resources will use them more often; or that citizens that have more positive feelings toward each other will be less tolerant of prejudice and discrimination. Sometimes these assumptions are valid; sometimes they are not. In any case, when **behavioral-based objectives** are used, the program must verify that the desired behavior change has actually occurred.

Behavior-based program objective
An objective that aims to change the conduct or actions of clients.

Qualities of Program Objectives

Whether program objectives target knowledge, affect, or behavior, they have to possess four qualities. They must be (1) meaningful, (2) specific, (3) measurable, and (4) directional.

Meaningful

A program objective is **meaningful** when it bears a sensible relationship to the longer term result to be achieved: the program goal. If a program's goal is to promote self-sufficiency of teenagers living on the street, for example, improving their ability to balance a monthly budget is a meaningful program objective; increasing

Meaningful program objective
An objective sensibly linked to the program goal.

their ability to recite the dates of the reigns of English monarchs is not, because it bears no relation to the program's goal of self-sufficiency. The point here—and a point that will be stressed over and over in this text—is that an effective social service organization must demonstrate meaningful *linkages* among an agency's overall goal (the reason for being) and its objective (the programs it creates), its program goals, and its program objectives.

As mentioned before, the overall goal of an agency must be linked to the needs of the people it intends to serve. If these meaningful linkages do not exist—and, furthermore, cannot be *seen* to exist—then the program has failed to establish its program design and efforts at useful future evaluations are thwarted. Ideally, program objectives are derived from an existing knowledge base—existing research studies, prior evaluations, or theoretical models.

Specific

Specific program objective
An objective that is extraordinarily clear such that everyone can understand it.

In addition to being meaningful and logically linked to the program's goal, program objectives must also be **specific**. They must be complete and clear in their wording. Three useful verbs for writing client-centered program objectives are "to increase," "to decrease," and "to maintain." A simple way to write a specific program objective is to use the following model:

Model: To (verb) (specific program objective) (time frame).

Measurable

Measurable program objective
Objective that produces valid and reliable data via its measurement.

The third quality required of a program objective is **measurability**. The purpose of measurement is to gather data. A measure is usually thought of as a number: an amount of money in dollars, a numerical rating representing a level of intensity, or scores on simple self-administered standardized measuring instruments.

The purpose of setting a program objective is to bring focus to the desired change, which, if obtained, will contribute to the obtainment of the program's goal. One of the main purposes of making a measurement is to define a perceived change in terms of either numbers or clear words. A measurement might show, for example, that the assertiveness of a woman who has been previously abused has increased by five points on a standardized measuring instrument (a program objective), or that a woman's feelings of safety in her neighborhood have increased by 45 points (another program objective). If the hoped-for change cannot be measured, then it is not a suitable program objective. In the following chapters we will present ways of measuring program objectives, but, for the time being, we will turn to the fourth important quality of an objective—directionality.

Directional

The final requirement for a program objective is that it must have a *direction*. All social work interventions are intended to effect some kind of change. That is, interventions are undertaken so that clients will come to have more or less of something than they had before: The level of parenting skills, aggression, racist beliefs, or whatever is to be changed, will have gone up or down. The very idea of change involves direction: Without movement in the direction of less or more, better or worse, higher or lower, no change can occur.

PROGRAM VERSUS PRACTICE OBJECTIVES

Program objectives can be thought of as formal statements of declaration of desired change for all clients served by a program. In contrast, **practice objectives** refer to the personal objectives of an individual client, whether that client is a community, couple, group, individual, or institution. Practice objectives are also commonly referred to as *treatment objectives, individual objectives, therapeutic objectives, client objectives, client goals,* and *client target problems.*

> **Practice objective**
> A statement of expected change identifying an intended therapeutic result tailored to a client's unique circumstance; logically linked to the program's objective.

    All practice objectives formulated by the social worker and the client must be logically related to the program's objectives, which are linked to the program's goal. In other words, all practice objectives for all clients must be delineated in such a way that they are logically linked to one or more of the program's objectives. If not, then it is likely that the client's needs will not be met by the program.

    If a social worker formulates a practice objective with a client that does not logically link to one or more of the program's objectives, the social worker may be doing some good for the client but without program sanction or support. In fact, why would a program hire a social worker to do something the worker was not employed to do? At the risk of sounding redundant, a social service program is always evaluated on its program objectives. Thus, we must fully understand that it is these objectives that we must strive to attain—all of our efforts must be linked to them.

Example 1: Bob's Self-Sufficiency

Let us put the concept of a practice objective into concrete terms. Glance at Figure 3.6 for a moment and imagine that Bob, a resident of Group Home *X,* is expected to become self-sufficient to meet the program's goal, and to achieve his full potential to meet the agency's overall goal. But what are Bob's practice objectives? What social, personal, practical, and academic skills does Bob need to acquire to achieve self-sufficiency? Three plausible practice objectives in this case might be: to increase

Bob's social contacts outside the home, to increase Bob's money management skills, and to increase Bob's language skills.

These three interrelated practice objectives for Bob demonstrate a definite link with the program's objective, which in turn is linked to the program's goal, which in turn is linked to the agency's goal. However, no one can tell, for example, whether Bob has made "more social contacts outside the home" until a "social contact" has been defined more precisely. Does saying "hello" to a fellow worker count as a social contact? It may be that Bob is habitually silent at work. For a different individual, a social contact may involve going on an outing with fellow workers or attending a recreational program at a community center.

It should be evident by now that defining a practice objective is a matter of stating what is to be changed. This provides an indication of the client's current state, or where the client is. Unfortunately, knowing this is not the same thing as knowing where one wants to go. Sometimes the destination is apparent, but in other cases it may be much less clear.

Example 2: Jane's Job Dissatisfaction

Suppose that Jane has presented job dissatisfaction as a general problem area. Enquiry has elicited that her dissatisfaction has nothing to do with the work itself, nor with the people at work, nor with such job-related factors as advancement, pay, benefits, and vacations. Instead, her dissatisfaction springs from the fact that she is spending too much time at work and too little time with her children.

Various practice objectives are possible here. Perhaps Jane should try to find a different, less demanding, full-time job; or maybe she should improve her budgeting skills so that her family can manage if she works only part time. Perhaps she should make different arrangements for her children's care so that she feels more comfortable about their welfare. Or maybe the real problem is that she herself feels torn between pursuing a career and being a full-time mother. It may be that what she really wants is to stay home with her children, provided that she can do so without guilt, with her partner's support, and without undue financial stress.

It is apparent that Jane's underlying problem has not yet been really defined. Often, an attempt to formulate a practice objective—to specify where Jane and the practitioner want to go—will reveal that Jane is not where she thought she was, that the problem so carefully elicited by the worker is not Jane's *real* problem after all. If this is the case, additional exploration is needed to redefine the problem before trying, once again, to set the practice objective.

When the real problem has been defined, the next task is to establish a related practice objective. If possible, it should be couched in positive terms—that is, in terms of what the client should do or feel rather than in terms of what she should not. For example, if the problem is Antoinette's immaturity, and "immaturity" is operationalized to mean getting out of her seat at school without permission, then one natural practice objective is "to decrease the number of times Antoinette gets out of her seat without permission." But it may be written, just as usefully, "to increase the length of time Antoinette stays in her seat during class." Many practice objectives that are aimed at decreasing a negative quality can be reformulated to increase a positive quality while still achieving the desired change.

Finally, practice objectives must be comprehensive and precise. Each one must stipulate what is to be achieved, under what conditions, to what extent, and by whom.

PROGRAM ACTIVITIES

So far we have focused on the kinds of goals and objectives that social workers hope to achieve as a result of their work. The question now arises: What is that work? What do social workers *do* in order to help clients achieve higher knowledge levels, feelings, or behaviors? The answer, of course, is that they do many different things. They show films, facilitate group discussions, hold therapy sessions, teach classes, and conduct individual interviews. They attend staff meetings, do paperwork, consult with colleagues, and advocate for clients.

The important point about all such activities is that they are undertaken to move clients forward on one or more of the program's objectives. A social worker who teaches a class on nutrition hopes that class participants will learn certain specific facts about nutrition. If this learning is to take place, the facts to be learned must be included in the material presented. In other words, our practice activities must be directly related to our objectives.

It is critically important that social workers engage in activities that have the best chance to create positive client change. Over the years we have seen numerous instances in which social workers say they are trying to raise their clients' self-esteem, for example. When asked what specific activities they are doing to achieve this notable objective, they reply, "nothing specific, just supporting them when they need it." Defining program activities is an essential ingredient to understanding what interventions work.

Generating program activities serves as a smorgasbord of interventions for program workers to choose from. The list of activities is dynamic in that workers can add, drop, and modify activities to suit the needs of individual clients. Reviewing a list of a program's activities, however, gives stakeholders an idea of the nature of client service delivery offered by the program.

PROGRAM LOGIC MODELS

All social service programs have **logic models.** They simply are tools that help people physically see the interrelations among the various components of the programs. They are graphic and narrative depictions of programs in that they visually describe

Logic model
Describes a social service program in diagram form. More specifically, it shows the links among a program's goal, objectives, and interventions. It then relates this process to expected outcomes.

Effective program evaluation does more than collect, analyze, and provide data. It makes it possible for you—program stakeholders—to gather and use information, to learn continually about and improve programs that you operate in or fund. The W.K. Kellogg Foundation believes evaluation—especially program logic model approaches—is a learning and management tool that can be used throughout a program's life—no matter what your stake in the program. Using evaluation and the logic model results in effective programming and offers greater learning opportunities, better documentation of outcomes, and shared knowledge about *what works* and *why*. The logic model is a beneficial evaluation tool that facilitates effective program planning, implementation, and evaluation.

The *What*: Logic Model Definition

Basically, a logic model is a systematic and visual way to present and share your understanding of the relationships among the resources you have to operate your program, the activities you plan, and the changes or results you hope to achieve.

The most basic logic model is a picture of how you believe your program will work. It uses words and/or pictures to describe the sequence of activities thought to bring about change and how these activities are linked to the results the program is expected to achieve.

Your Planned Work

The basic logic model components shown in Figure 1 are defined below. These components illustrate the connection between *your planned work* and *your intended results*. They are depicted numerically by Steps 1 through 5. Your planned work describes what resources

you think you need to implement your program and what you intend to do.

1. *Resources* include the human, financial, organizational, and community resources a program has available to direct toward doing the work. Sometimes this component is referred to as *inputs*.
2. *Program activities* are what the program does with the resources. Activities are the processes, tools, events, technology, and actions that are an intentional part of the program implementation. These interventions are used to bring about the intended program changes or results.

Your Intended Results

Your intended results include all of the program's desired results (outputs, outcomes, and impact).

3. *Outputs* are the direct products of program activities and may include types, levels, and targets of services to be delivered by the program.
4. *Outcomes* are the specific changes in program participants' behavior, knowledge, skills, status, and level of functioning. Short-term outcomes should be attainable within 1 to 3 years, while longer term outcomes should be achievable within a 4 to 6 year time frame. The logical progression from short-term to long-term outcomes should be reflected in impact, occurring within about 7 to 10 years.
5. *Impact* is the fundamental intended or unintended change occurring in organizations, communities, or systems as a result of program activities within 7 to 10 years. In the current model of WKKF grantmaking and evaluation, impact often occurs after the conclusion of project funding.

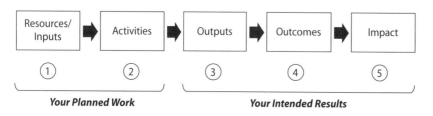

Figure 1 The basic logic model.

The term *logic model* is frequently used interchangeably with the term *program theory* in the evaluation field. Logic models can alternatively be referred to as *theory* because they describe how a program works and to what end.

When "read" from left to right, logic models describe program basics over time from planning through results. Reading a logic model means following the chain of reasoning or "*if...then...*" statements that connect the program's parts. Figure 2 shows how the basic logic model is read.

The *Why*: Logic Model Purpose and Practical Application

The purpose of a logic model is to provide stakeholders with a road map describing the sequence of related events connecting the need for the planned program with the program's desired results. Mapping a proposed program helps you visualize and understand how human and financial investments can contribute to achieving your intended program goals and can lead to program improvements.

A logic model brings program concepts and dreams to life. It lets stakeholders try an idea on for size and apply theories to a model or picture of how the program would function. The following example shows how the logic model approach works.

An Example

We are proposing an inexpensive family trip from Charleston, South Carolina, to Des Moines, Iowa, to visit relatives during December school holidays. The seasonal trip we dream of taking from Charleston to Des Moines is the "program." Basic assumptions about our trip "program" are

- We want to visit relatives between 12/10/07 and 1/5/08 while the children are out of school.
- We will fly from South Carolina to Iowa because it takes less time than driving and because frequent flier miles are available.
- Using frequent flier miles will reduce travel costs.

We have to determine the factors influencing our trip, including necessary resources, such as the number of family members, scheduled vacation time, the number of frequent flier miles we have, round trip air reservations for each family member, and transportation to and from our home to the airport. The activities necessary to make this happen are the creation of our own family holiday schedule, securing our Iowa relative's schedule, garnering airline information and reservations, and planning for transportation to and from the airport.

In this example, the results of our activities—or outputs—are mostly information, such as family schedules, flight schedules, and cost information based on the time frame of the trip. This information helps identify outcomes or immediate goals. For instance, if we make

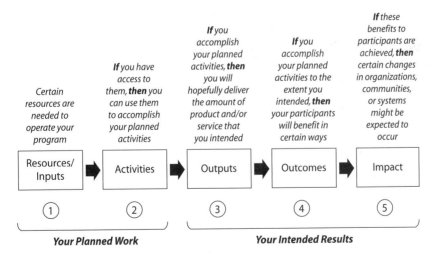

Certain resources are needed to operate your program

If you have access to them, then you can use them to accomplish your planned activities

If you accomplish your planned activities, then you will hopefully deliver the amount of product and/or service that you intended

If you accomplish your planned activities to the extent you intended, then your participants will benefit in certain ways

If these benefits to participants are achieved, then certain changes in organizations, communities, or systems might be expected to occur

| Resources/Inputs | Activities | Outputs | Outcomes | Impact |

① ② ③ ④ ⑤

Your Planned Work   **Your Intended Results**

Figure 2 How to read a logic model.

(continued)

Box 3.2 (continued)

reservations as soon as possible, we are able to find flights with available frequent flier slots and probably have more options for flights that fit within the time frame. Knowing this, our outcomes improve—reservations are made well in advance result in flight schedules, and airline costs suit our timeline and travel budget. The longer term impact of our trip is not an issue here, but it might be projected as continued good family relationships in 2010.

Using a simple logic model as a trip-planning tool produced tangible benefits. It helped us gather information to influence our decisions about resources and allowed us to meet our stated goals. Applying this process consistently throughout our trip planning positions us for success by laying out the best course of action and giving us benchmarks for measuring progress—when we touch down in Charlotte and change planes for Cincinnati, we know we're on course for Des Moines.

Typical logic models use table and flowchart formats like those presented here to catalog program factors, activities, and results and to illustrate a program's dimensions. Most use text and arrows or a graphic representation of program ideas. Figure 3 is what our trip planning "program" could look like in a logic model format.

It was easy to organize travel plans in a flowchart, but we could also choose to organize and display our

thinking in other ways. A logic model does not have to be linear. It may appear as a simple image or concept map to describe more complex program concepts. Settling on a single image of a program is sometimes the most difficult step for program stakeholders.

Why Use a Logic Model?

As you can see from the travel plan example, logic models are useful tools in many ways. Because they are pictorial in nature, they require systematic thinking and planning to better describe programs. The visual representation of the master plan in a logic model is flexible, points out areas of strength and/or weakness, and allows stakeholders to run through many possible scenarios to find the best. In a logic model, you can adjust approaches and change courses as program plans are developed. Ongoing assessment, review, and corrections can produce better program design and a system to strategically monitor, manage, and report program outcomes throughout development and implementation.

Effective evaluation and program success rely on the fundamentals of clear stakeholder assumptions and expectations about how and why a program will solve a particular problem, generate new possibilities, and

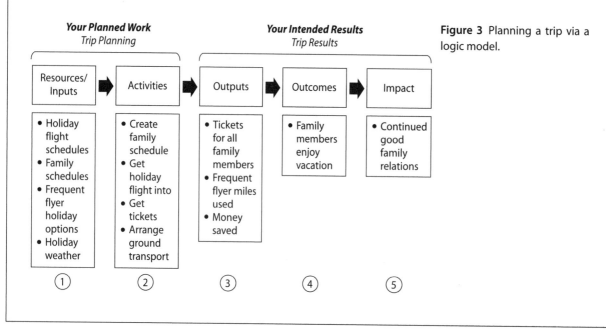

Figure 3 Planning a trip via a logic model.

make the most of valuable assets. The logic model approach helps create shared understanding of and focus on program goals and methodology, relating activities to projected outcomes.

Logic Models Better Position Programs for Success

Many evaluation experts agree that use of the logic model is an effective way to ensure program success. Using a logic model throughout your program helps organize and systematize program planning, management, and evaluation functions.

1. In *Program Design and Planning,* a logic model serves as a planning tool to develop program strategy and enhance your ability to clearly explain and illustrate program concepts and approach for key stakeholders, including funders. Logic models can help craft structure and organization for program design and build in self-evaluation based on shared understanding of what is to take place. During the planning phase, developing a logic model requires stakeholders to examine best practice research and practitioner experience in light of the strategies and activities selected to achieve results.
2. In *Program Implementation,* a logic model forms the core for a focused management plan that helps you identify and collect the data needed to monitor and improve programming.

Using the logic model during program implementation and management requires you to focus energies on achieving and documenting results. Logic models help you to consider and prioritize the program aspects most critical for tracking and reporting and make adjustments as necessary.

3. For *Program Evaluation and Strategic Reporting,* a logic model presents program information and progress toward goals in ways that inform, advocate for a particular program approach, and teach program stakeholders.

We all know the importance of reporting results to funders and to community stakeholders alike. Communication is a key component of a program's success and sustainability. Logic models can help strategic marketing efforts in three primary ways:

- *Describing programs* in language clear and specific enough to be understood and evaluated.
- *Focusing attention and resources* on priority program operations and key results for the purposes of learning and program improvement.
- *Developing targeted communication* and marketing strategies.

Table 1 describes the relationship between a successful program and the benefits derived for the use of logic models.

Table 1 How Logic Models Better Position Programs Toward Success

Program Elements	Criteria for Program Success	Benefits of Program Logic Models
Planning and Design	Program goals and objectives, and important side effects are well defined ahead of time.	Finds "gaps" in the theory or logic of a program and work to resolve them.
	Program goals and objectives are both plausible and possible.	Builds a shared understanding of what the program is all about and how the parts work together.
Program Implementation and Management	Relevant, credible, and useful performance data can be obtained.	Focuses attention of management on the most important connections between action and results.
Evaluation, Communication, and Marketing	The intended users of the evaluation results have agreed on how they will use the information.	Provides a way to involve and engage stakeholders in the design, processes, and use of evaluation.

(continued)

Box 3.2 (continued)

*Logic Models Strengthen the Case
for Program Investment*

Clear ideas about what you plan to do and why—as well as an organized approach to capturing, documenting, and disseminating program results—enhance the case for investment in your program.

*Developing a Program Logic Model Requires a
Simple Image and a Straightforward Approach*

A picture *is* worth a thousand words. The point of developing a logic model is to come up with a relatively simple image that reflects how and why your program will work. Doing this as a group brings the power of consensus and group examination of values and beliefs about change processes and program results.

*Logic Models Reflect Group Process and Shared
Understanding*

Frequently, a professional evaluator is charged with developing a logic model for program practitioners. But a logic model developed by all stakeholders—program staff, participants, and evaluators—produces a more useful tool and refines program concepts and plans in the process. We recommend that a logic model be developed collaboratively in an inclusive, collegial process that engages as many key stakeholders as possible. This guide provides a step-by-step process to assist program planners.

*Like Programs, Logic Models Can
Change Over Time*

As a program grows and develops, so does its logic model. A program logic model is merely a snapshot of a program at one point in time; it is not the program with its actual flow of events and outcomes. A logic model is a work in progress, a working draft that can be refined as the program develops.

Simple Logic Model Basics

*Creating a Logic Model: What They Look Like and
What Needs to Be Included*

Logic models come in as many sizes and shapes as the programs they represent. A simple model focuses on

project-level results and explains five basic program components. The elements outlined here are typical of the model promoted by United Way of America to support an outcomes-based approach to program planning and evaluation.

Developing and Reading a Basic Logic Model

Read from left to right, logic models describe program basics over time, beginning with best practice information or knowledge about "what works" from successful program practitioners and other trusted authorities. Reading a logic model means following the chain of reasoning or "*if . . . then . . .*" statements that connect the program's parts (see Figure 2).

If . . . Then **Assumptions**

- Certain resources are needed to operate your program.
- *If* you have access to them, *then* you can use them to accomplish your planned activities.
- *If* you accomplish your planned activities, *then* you will, it is hoped, deliver the amount of product and/or service that you intended.
- *If* you accomplish your planned activities to the extent intended, *then* your participants will benefit in specific ways.
- *If* these benefits to participants are achieved, *then* certain changes in organizations, communities, or systems might occur under specified conditions.

*Building a Logic Model by Basic Program
Components*

As you conceptualize your program, begin by describing your basic assumptions and then add the following program components in the order that they should occur.

1. *Factors* are resources and/or barriers, which potentially enable or limit program effectiveness. Enabling *protective factors* or *resources* may include funding, existing organizations, potential collaborating partners, existing organizational or interpersonal networks, staff and volunteers, time, facilities, equipment, and supplies. Limiting *risk factors* or *barriers* might include such things as attitudes, lack of

resources, policies, laws, regulations, and geography.

2. *Activities* are the processes, techniques, tools, events, technology, and actions of the planned program. These may include *product*—promotional materials and educational curricula; *services*—education and training, counseling, or health screening; and i*nfrastructure*—structure, relationships, and capacity used to bring about the desired results.

3. *Outputs* are the *direct results* of program activities. They are usually described in terms of the *size and/or scope of the services and products delivered or produced* by the program. They indicate if a program was delivered to the intended audiences at the intended "dose." A program output, for example, might be the *number* of classes taught, meetings held, or materials produced and distributed; program *participation rates* and demography; or *hours of each type of service* provided.

4. *Outcomes* are specific *changes in attitudes, behaviors, knowledge, skills, status, or level of functioning* expected to result from program activities and which are most often expressed *at an individual level*.

5. *Impacts* are *organizational, community, and/or system level changes* expected to result from program activities, which might include improved conditions, increased capacity, and/or changes in the policy arena.

Thinking about a program in logic model terms prompts the clarity and specificity required for success, and is often demanded by funders and your community. Using a simple logic model produces (1) an inventory of what you have and what you need to operate your program, (2) a strong case for how and why your program will produce your desired results, and (3) a method for program management and assessment.

Other Logic Model Examples

In practice, most logic models are more complex and fall into one of three categories (Figure 4): the theory approach model (conceptual), outcome approach model, or activities approach model (applied)—or a blend of several types. It is not unusual for a program to use all three types of logic models for different purposes. No one model fits all needs, so you will need to decide exactly what you want to achieve with your logic model—and where you are in the life of your program—before deciding on which model to use.

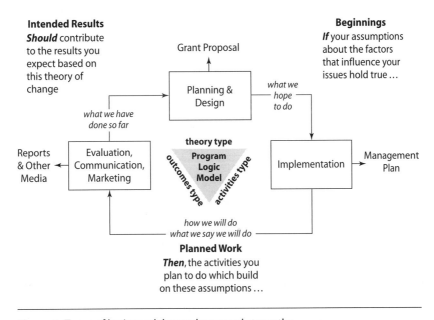

Figure 4 Types of logic models: emphases and strengths.

(continued)

CHAPTER 3 Designing Client-Centered Programs

Box 3.2 (continued)

Types of Logic Models: Emphasis and Strengths

1. *Theory Approach Models* emphasize the theory of change that has influenced the design and plan for the program (Figure 5). These logic models provide rich explanation of the reasons for beginning to explore an idea for a given program. Sometimes they have additional parts that specify the problem or issue addressed by the program, describe the reasons for selecting certain types of solution strategies, connect proven strategies to potential activities, and explain other assumptions the planners hold that influence effectiveness. These models illustrate how and why you think your program will work. They are built from the "big picture" kinds of thoughts and ideas that went into conceptualizing your program. They are coming to be most often used to make the case in grant proposals. Models describing the beginnings of a program in detail are most useful during program planning and design.

2. *Outcomes Approach Models* focus on the early aspects of program planning and attempt to connect the resources and/or activities with the desired results in a workable program (Figure 6). These models often subdivide outcomes and impact over time to describe short-term effects (1 to 3 years), long-term effects (4 to 6 years), and impact (7 to 10 years) that may result from a given set of activities. Although these models are developed with a theory of change in mind, this aspect is not usually emphasized explicitly. Models that outline the approach and expectations behind a program's intended results are most useful in designing effective evaluation and reporting strategies.

3. *Activities Approach Models* pay the most attention to the specifics of the implementation process (Figure 7). A logic model of this type links the various planned activities together in a manner that maps the process of program implementation. These models describe what a program intends to do and as such are most useful for the purposes of program monitoring and management. This type provides the detailed steps you think you will need to follow to implement your program. It shows what you will actually *do* in your community if your proposal is funded. Models that emphasize a program's planned work are most often used to inform management planning activities.

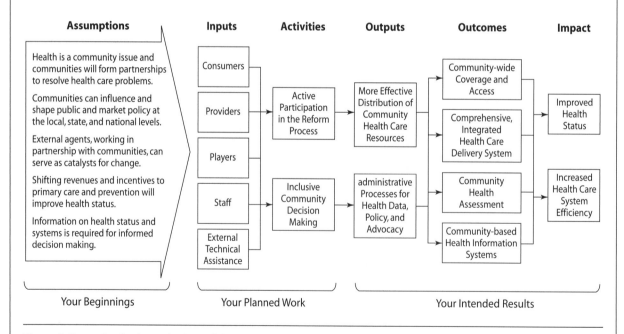

Figure 5 Example of a theory logic model.

The Theory-Based Logic Model Approach

A theory approach logic model links theoretical ideas together to explain underlying program *assumptions* (see Figure 5). The focus here is on the problem or issue and the reasons for proposing the solution suggested in your program's approach. Remember, the theory logic model is broad and about "big ideas," not about specific program nuts and bolts. Noted evaluator and program theorist Carol Weiss (1998) explains that, for program planning, monitoring, and evaluation, it is important to know not only *what* the program expects to achieve but also *how*. We must understand the principles on which a program is based, a notion not included in evaluation until recently. Discussions about the *whethers*, *hows*, and *whys* of program success require credible evidence and attention to the paths by which outcomes and impacts are produced.

The theory logic model is suitable for use by funders and grantees. A case example of its use now provided. In this case, the model describes a WKKF cluster initiative's (Comprehensive Community Health Models of Michigan) programming strategy or its theory of change. Notice

that this model places emphasis on "Your Beginnings" by including the assumptions identified by program planners as the principles behind the design of the initiative.

The Outcomes-Based Logic Model Approach

Outcome approach logic models display the interrelationships between specific program activities and their outcomes. Figure 6 is an example drawn from the Calhoun County Health Improvement Program, funded under the Comprehensive Community Health Models of Michigan initiative. This linear, columnar model emphasizes the *causal linkages* thought to exist among program components.

The arrows show which sets of activities program developers believed would contribute to what outcomes. These statements serve as logical assertions about the perceived relationship among program operations and desired results and are the hallmark of the logic model process. Notice that this model emphasizes "Your Intended Results" in the greatest relative detail and anticipates achievement outside the time allotted for the initiative.

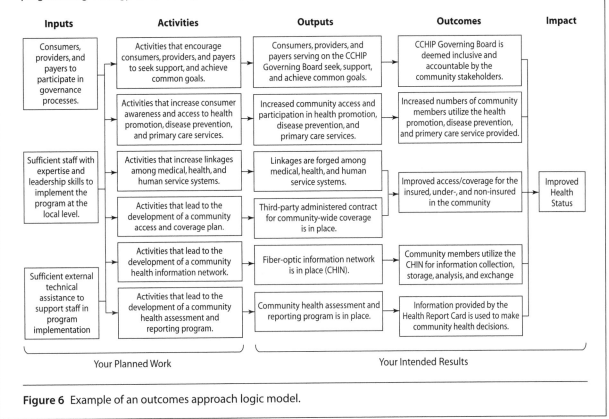

Figure 6 Example of an outcomes approach logic model.

(continued)

CHAPTER 3 Designing Client-Centered Programs

Box 3.2 (continued)

The Activities-Based Logic Model Approach

The activities approach logic model also connects program resources and activities to desired results but does so in very great detail (see Figure 7). Each outcome is usually dealt with separately by the activities and events that must take place to keep the program on track. The model emphasizing "Your Planned Work" can be used as a work plan or management tool for program components and in conjunction with other models. Notice how it points out what program activities need to be monitored and what kind of measurements might indicate progress toward results. Figure 7 shows one model describing the connections between project tasks and outcome achievement for the community coverage strand from the outcome approach example provided earlier.

There Is No *Best* Logic Model

Try several logic models on for size. Choose the model that fits your program best and provides the information you need in the format that is most helpful. Like anything else, it takes practice to use logic models as effective program tools. We learn through trial and error to find what works best for what program. Don't hesitate to experiment with program logic model design to determine what works best for your program. And don't be concerned if your model doesn't look like one of the case examples. Figure 8 shows how the logic model forms gather information that can be used throughout your program's life—from defining the theory on which your program rests to evaluating program impact.

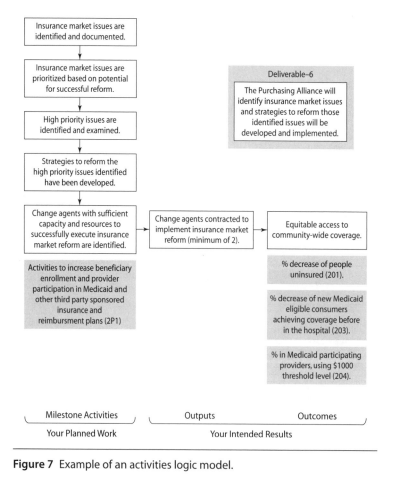

Figure 7 Example of an activities logic model.

Clarifying Program Theory

1. **Problem or issue statement:** Describe the problem(s) your program is attempting to solve or the issue(s) your program will address.
2. **Community needs/assets:** Specify the needs and/or assets of your community that led your organization to design a program that addresses the problem.
3. **Desired results (outputs, outcomes, and impacts):** Identify desired results, or vision of the future, by describing what you expect to achieve near term and long term.
4. **Influential factors:** List the factors you believe will influence change in your community.
5. **Strategies:** List general successful strategies or "best practices" that have helped communities like yours achieve the kinds of results your program promises.
6. **Assumptions:** State the assumptions behind *how* and *why* the change strategies will work in your community.

Demonstrating Your Program's Progress

1. **Outputs:** For each program activity, identify what outputs (service delivery/implementation targets) you aim to produce.
2. **Outcomes:** Identify the short-term and long-term outcomes you expect to achieve for each activity.
3. **Impact:** Describe the impact you anticipate in your community in 7 to 10 years with each activity as a result of your program.
4. **Activities:** Describe each of the activities you plan to conduct in your program.
5. **Resources:** Describe the resources or influential factors available to support your program activities.

Program Evaluation Questions and Indicators

1. **Focus area:** From your program theory logic model, list the components of the most important aspects of your program.
2. **Audience:** Identify the key audiences for each focus area. Who has an interest in your program?
3. **Questions:** For each focus area and audience, list the questions they may have about your program.
4. **Information use:** For each audience and question you have identified, identify the ways you will use the evaluation information.
5. **Indicators:** Describe what information could be collected that would indicate the status of your program and its participants for each question.
6. **Technical assistance:** Indicate the extent to which your organization has the evaluation and data management expertise to collect and analyze the data that relates to this indicator.

Figure 8 How to use a logic model through the life of your program.

the logic of how social service programs are conceptualized and operationalized. Box 3.2 presents a comprehensive discussion on how logic models are used in the social services and provides advanced information on logic models, which were previously discussed in Box 2.3.

Summing Up and Looking Ahead

This chapter discussed what is meant by an agency, a program, a program goal, a program objective, a practice objective, a measurement, and an activity. Most importantly, we discussed the linkages that must exist among these elements through the development of program designs. When a social service program has a simple logic model as illustrated in Boxes 2.3 and 3.2, you are ready to start thinking about how your program can be evaluated—the topic of the next chapter.

Recap and Online Materials

In this chapter, you learned how to design simple social work programs with the help of logic models.

You should also recall the concept of logic models from your foundational research course. If not, go online to take a free crash course in logic models.

You can also find the following materials online to help you master the concepts you just learned:

- Chapter Outline
- Learning Objectives
- Key Terms and Concepts
- Flash Cards
- Practice Multiple-Choice Tests
- Essay Questions with Answers
- Links

www.oup.com/us/swevaluation

Study Questions

1. What is a social service agency? Provide an example of one that you are familiar with.
2. Name as many social service agencies in your local community as you can. What target populations does each one serve? Why?

3. What are agency mission statements? How are they used within agencies? Do you believe they are necessary? If so, why? If not, why not? What are agency goals? Do you believe they are necessary? If so, why? If not, why not?

4. What are the requirements for an agency's goal? Provide an example using all of the requirements. What are agency objectives? Do you believe they are necessary? If so, why? If not, why not? What are social service programs? How are they similar and different from social service agencies? Provide an example in your discussion.

5. Discuss the main differences between an agency and a program.

6. Discuss the usefulness of program designs. How are they used to formulate social work programs? Do you believe they are necessary? If so, why? If not, why not?

7. What are program objectives? Do you believe they are necessary? If so, why? If not, why not? What are unintended program results? Provide an example that you know of in your discussion.

8. Discuss the differences and similarities between an agency goal and a program goal. Use one common example throughout your discussion.

9. Discuss the different types of program objectives. Provide an example of each one in your discussion. Discuss the qualities of program objectives. Provide an example of each one in your discussion. Discuss the differences and similarities between program objectives and practice objectives. Provide an example of each one in your discussion. What are program activities? Provide as many examples as you can, and distinguish each one from a program objective.

10. Create a hypothetical social service program based on the logic models contained in Boxes 2.3 and 3.2.

REFERENCES, FURTHER READING, AND RESOURCES

On Logic Models

Alter, C., & Egan, M. (1997). Logic modeling: A tool for teaching critical thinking in social work practice. *Journal of Social Work Education*, *33*, 85–102.

Bickman, D. (Ed.). (1987). *Using program theory in evaluation.* San Francisco: Jossey-Bass.

Chen, H. (1990). *Theory-driven evaluations.* Newbury Park, CA: Sage.

Coffman, J. (2000). Simplifying complex initiative evaluation. *The Evaluation Exchange, 5*(2/3), 2–3.

Cook, T. D. (2000). The false choice between theory-based evaluation and experimentation. In P. J. Rogers, T. A. Hacsi, A. Petrosino, & T. A. Huebner (Eds.), *Program theory in evaluation: Challenges and opportunities. New directions in evaluation* (pp. 27–35). San Francisco: Jossey Bass.

Cooksy, L. J., Gill, P., & Kelly, P. A. (2001). The program logic model as an integrative framework for a multimethod evaluation. *Evaluation and Program Planning, 24*, 119–128.

Cozzens, S. E. (1997). The knowledge pool: Measurement challenges in evaluating fundamental research programs. *Evaluation and Program Planning, 20*, 77–89.

Cronbach, L. J., Ambron, S., Dornbusch, S. M., Hess, R. D., Hornik, R. C., Phillips, D. C., Walker, D. F., & Weiner, S. S. (1980). *Toward reform of program evaluation.* San Francisco: Jossey-Bass.

Greene, J. C. (1999). The inequality of performance measurements. *Evaluation, 5*, 160–172.

Hacsi, T. A. (2000). Using program theory to replicate successful programs. In P. J. Rogers, T. A. Hacsi, A. Petrosino, & T. A. Huebner (Eds.), *Program theory in evaluation: Challenges and opportunities.* San Francisco: Jossey Bass.

Hudson, J., & Grinnell, R. M., Jr. (1989). Program evaluation. In B. Compton & B. Galaway (Eds.), *Social work processes* (4th ed., pp. 691–711). Belmont, CA: Wadsworth.

Julian, D. A. (1997). The utilization of the logic model as a system-level planning and evaluation device. *Evaluation and Program Planning, 20,* 251–257.

Kaplan, S. A., & Garrett, K. E. (2005). The use of logic models by community-based initiatives. *Evaluation and Program Planning, 28,* 167–172.

Leeuw, F. L. (2003). Reconstructing program theories: Methods available and problems to be solved. *American Journal of Evaluation, 24,* 5–21.

Lipsey, M. W. (1987). *Theory as method: Small theories of treatments.* Paper presented at the National Center for Health Services Research Conference: Strengthening Causal Interpretations of Non-experimental Data, Tucson, AZ.

McLaughlin, J. A., & Jordan, G. B. (1999). Logic models: A tool for telling your program's performance story. *Evaluation and Program Planning, 22,* 65–72.

McLaughlin, J. A., & Jordan, G. B. (2004). Using logic models. In J. Wholey, H. P. Hatry, & K. E. Newcomer (Eds.), *Handbook of practical program evaluation* (2nd ed., pp. 7–32). San Francisco: Jossey-Bass.

Mizrahi, T. (1992). The future of research utilization in community practice. In A. J. Grasso & I. Epstein (Eds.), *Research utilization in social services* (pp. 78–96). New York: Haworth Press.

Newcomer, K. E. (Ed.). (1997). *Using performance monitoring to improve public and nonprofit programs.* San Francisco: Jossey-Bass.

Pawson, R., & Tilley, N. (1997). *Realistic evaluation.* Thousand Oaks, CA: Sage.

Perrin, B. (1998). Effective use and misuse of performance measurement. *American Journal of Evaluation, 19,* 367–379.

Reid, W. J. (1994). The empirical practice movement. *Social Service Review, 68*(2), 165–184.

Renger, R., & Titcomb, A. (2002). A three-step approach to teaching logic models. *American Journal of Evaluation, 23*(4), 493–503.

Rosen, A. (1993). Systematic planned practice. *Social Service Review, 67*(1), 84–100.

Savaya, R., & Waysman, M. (1999). Outcome evaluation of an advocacy program to promote early childhood education for Israeli Arabs. *Evaluation Review, 23*(3), 281–303.

Savaya, R., & Waysman, M. (2005). The logic model: A tool for incorporating theory in development and evaluation of programs. *Administration in Social Work, 29*(2), 85–103.

Schon, D. A. (1983). *The reflective practitioner: How professionals think in action.* New York: Basic Books.

Schon, D. A. (1995). Reflective inquiry in social work practice. In P. M. Hess & E. J. Mullen (Eds.), *Practitioner–researcher partnerships, building knowledge from in, and for practice* (pp. 105–120). Washington, DC: NASW Press.

Shadish, W. R., Cook, T. D., & Leviton, L. C. (1991). *Foundations of program evaluation: Theories of practice.* Newbury Park, CA: Sage.

United Way of America. (1996). *Measuring program outcomes: A practical approach.* Alexandria, VA: Author.

Unrau, Y. A. (1993). A program logic model approach to conceptualizing social service programs. *The Canadian Journal of Program Evaluation, 8,* 33–42.

Wandersman, A., Goodman, R. M., & Butterfoss, F. D. (1997). Understanding coalitions and how they operate: An "open systems" organizational framework. In M. Minkler (Ed.), *Community organizing and community building for health* (pp. 261–277). New Brunswick, NJ: Rutgers University Press.

Weiss, C. H. (1997). Theory-based evaluation: Past, present, and future. In D. J. Rog (Ed.), *Progress and future directions in evaluation: Perspectives on theory, practice, and methods.* San Francisco: Jossey-Bass.

Wholey, J. S. (1987). Evaluability assessment: Developing program theory. In L. Bickman (Ed.), *Using program theory in evaluation* (pp. 8–21). San Francisco: Jossey-Bass.

Wholey, J. S. (1997). Trends in performance measurement. In E. Chelimsky & W. R. Shadish (Eds.), *Evaluation for the 21st century* (pp. 124–133). Thousand Oaks, CA: Sage.

Winston, J. A. (1999). Performance indicators—promises unmet: A response to Perrin. *American Journal of Evaluation, 20,* 95–99.

W. K. Kellogg Foundation. (2004). *Using logic models to bring together planning, evaluation, and action: Logic model development guide.* Battle Creek, MI: Author.

On Practice Activities

Beaulaurier, R. L. (2002). Health services social workers' activities with people with disabilities: Predictors of community practice. *Journal of Sociology and Social Welfare, 29*(4), 83–98.

Blase, K., Fixsen, D., & Phillips, E. (1984). Residential treatment for troubled children: Developing service delivery systems. In S. C. Paine, G. T. Bellamy, & B. Wilcox (Eds.), *Human services that work: From innovation to standard practice.* Baltimore: Paul H. Brookes.

Canadian Association of Social Workers (2000, March). *CASW national scope of practice statement.* Retrieved February 20, 2006, from Canadian Association of Social Workers Web site: http://www.casw-acts.ca/Practice/RecPubsArt1.htm

Koeske, G. F., Lichtenwalter, S., & Daimon-Koeske, R. (2005). Social workers' current and desired involvement in various practice activities: Explorations and implications. *Administration in Social Work, 29*(2), 63–84.

GETTING READY FOR AN EVALUATION

4

Program Scope and Evaluation
Planning With Stakeholders
Identifying Data Needs
Focusing Evaluation Efforts
Summing Up and Looking Ahead
Recap and Online Materials
Study Questions
References, Further Reading, and Resources

In 1963, when President Kennedy was assassinated in Dallas, several photographers on the scene captured images of the unfortunate event. The tragedy occurred despite the secret service and other government agencies having in place a specific **program** plan or blueprint designed to protect the President from harm. Thinking about the program design concepts presented in the previous chapter, the security plan might have included a specific goal, objectives, and activities to guide secret service agents and other officials as they performed their work duties in an effort to accomplish their goal—to protect the President from harm.

> **Program**
> An organization that exists to fulfill some specific social purpose; must be logically linked to the agency's goal.

The assassination was recorded on film by Abraham Zapruder, an amateur photographer, who took a home movie that shows graphic images of the President being shot. Two other people also took home movies that show other parts of the incident, and as many as six still photographers took at least one picture while shots were being fired. In addition, several other photographers took pictures before or after the assassination.

The documentation of the security program, the home movie footage, and the photographs taken are all key pieces of data that can be used to help us understand both the problems or dangers faced by heads of state as well as what can be done about them. The security program provides data of what was supposed to happen to prevent any harm to the President, and the film data showed evidence of what actually happened.

If we think carefully about the available data (e.g., program plan, film, and photographs), it is obvious that none captured the full "picture" of what took place. Rather, each artifact or piece of data captured a *representation* of what happened that day. Some of the representations were more complete and more accurate than others. But in the end, each was only a representation. Mr. Zapruder's home movie is considered the most complete record. However, it was filmed from a distance and is relatively grainy, at least by today's standards. In addition, it did not, as was true of home movies of the day, record sound. Thus, even this most complete record of the assassination captured only one element of it. In general, the representations created by the various photographers varied in their completeness and detail as well as in what was actually captured on film.

Program design plans and evaluations (discussed in remaining chapters of this book) are also representations. Any social service program in our profession is composed of hundreds of parts, including structures, processes, activities, and results. Although **stakeholders** sometimes hold beliefs to the contrary, no one evaluation will capture all of these facets of a program.

As you well know by now, social service programs are complex entities that contain numerous interlinking systems and operate in complex environments. A parent–teen mediation program, for example, will have specific procedures for intake, assessment, intervention, termination, and follow-up. An educational program, on the other hand, may deliver its services in the form of workshops, seminars, and presentations in addition to operating a library. These and other programs will be targeted toward specific population groups and have the interest of different stakeholders (see Box 1.3).

PROGRAM SCOPE AND EVALUATION

As we know from previous chapters, the word "program" is broad in its meaning. It can refer to small, specific, and short-term efforts, such as a film developed for use during a training session on AIDS. It may also refer to a nationwide effort to combat family violence, and include various intervention strategies. Or it may refer to a specific treatment intervention used with a specific social worker and undertaken with a specific client.

Different types of social service programs call for using different methods of evaluations. Thus, we need to know the scope of a program before deciding how best to include an evaluative effort within it. In turn, the parameters of any evaluation are impacted by the following program characteristics:

- *Boundary:* The program's "borders" may extend across a nation, region, state, province, city, parish, county, or community; or it may be extremely limited— for example, a course presented in an individual program or school.

Stakeholders

A person or group of people having a direct or indirect interest in the results of an evaluation.

- *Client Capacity:* The program may serve a fixed number of individual clients at one time, such as a maximum of 10 individuals seeking group therapy, or many clients, such as all people infected with the HIV virus. Furthermore, the program may be limited to a homogeneous client group (e.g., adolescent girls with a diagnosis of depression) or open to a heterogeneous client group (e.g., male and female adolescents suffering from any mental illness diagnosis).
- *Service Complexity:* Some programs offer integrated components, combining, for instance, child protection services, individual therapy, family therapy, and educational services under one common umbrella. Such a program is obviously more complex than one with a simpler, singular focus—for example, providing nutrition counseling to pregnant adolescents.
- *Duration:* The time frame of the program may be designed to last for half an hour—a training film, for example—or it may be an orientation course on child safety lasting for two days, a group therapy cycle lasting for 10 weeks, or a pilot project designed to help the homeless that will be evaluated after two years. Or, as in the case of a child protection program, it may be intended to continue indefinitely.
- *Timing of Program Effect:* Some programs have objectives that can readily be evaluated within a reasonable time frame; for example, to increase the number of unemployed adolescents who secure full-time work within two months of completing a six-week training course. Other programs have objectives that will not become evident for some time, or have a delayed effect—for example, to increase future educational achievement of children born with fetal alcohol syndrome.
- *Innovativeness:* Some social service programs follow long-established treatment interventions, while others experiment with new and developing ones.

PLANNING WITH STAKEHOLDERS

An important part of evaluation is planning—an exercise that involves clearly identifying what specific evaluation questions are to be answered, what decisions are to be made from evaluation results, and ultimately managing the many tasks necessary to carry out the evaluation. Box 4.1 presents the various sources you can use when developing evaluation questions, and Box 4.2 provides general tips for developing the questions.

The critical importance of planning before one attempts to implement a program or its evaluation is understood if we think about an event such as a family vacation. Rarely does a family embark upon their annual vacation without prior thinking and planning. Spur of the moment vacationing may result in a wondrous spontaneous bit of relaxation, but the odds are the family would risk ending up with a very expensive experience that was unsatisfactory to some or all family members.

Box 4.1 Finding Sources Who Can Help in Developing Evaluation
Questions as Presented by the W.K. Kellogg Foundation

As you generate the "long list" of questions, some potential sources to consult include:

- *Project Director:* The director is usually an invaluable source of information because he/she is likely to have the "big picture" of the project.
- *Project Staff/Volunteers:* Staff members and volunteers may suggest unique evaluation questions because they are involved in the day-to-day operations of the project and have an inside perspective of the organization.
- *Project Clientele:* Participants/consumers offer crucial perspectives for the evaluation team because they are directly affected by project services. They have insights into the project that no other source is likely to have.
- *Board of Directors/Advisory Boards/Other Project Leadership:* These groups often have a stake in the project and may identify issues they want addressed in the evaluation process. They may request that certain questions be answered to help them make decisions.
- *Community Leaders:* Community leaders in business, social services, and government can speak to issues underlying the conditions of the target population. Because of their extensive involvement in the community, they often are invaluable sources of information.
- *Collaborating Organizations:* Organizations and agencies that are collaborating with the grantee should always be involved in formulating evaluation questions.
- *Project Proposal and Other Documents:* The project proposal, WKKF correspondence, project objectives and activities, minutes of board and advisory group meetings, and other documents may be used to formulate relevant evaluation questions.
- *Content-Relevant Literature and Expert Consultants:* Relevant literature and discussion with other professionals in the field can be potential sources of information, and for possible questions, for evaluation teams.
- *Similar Programs/Projects:* Evaluation questions can also be obtained from directors and staff of other projects, especially when these projects are similar to yours.

To increase the likelihood that the vacation will stay within a reasonable budget and meet the wishes of all family members (stakeholders) requires planning with prior research of vacation possibilities, discussion with family members, and the consideration of the family's resources—especially the family budget within the number of pre-allocated vacation days.

Planning program evaluations are similar to planning family vacations; that is, we want to research the many evaluation possibilities, have discussions with program stakeholders, and end up with a beneficial and satisfactory result for all interested parties. And, like vacations, evaluations also must stay within the limits of the program's financial and human resources. Ideally, and if at all possible, evaluations should be integrated into a program's operations, which is a main feature of the monitoring approach to evaluation (see Chapter 2).

- Ask yourself and team members why you are asking the questions you are asking and what you might be missing.
- Different stakeholders will have different questions. Don't rely on one or two people (external evaluator or funder) to determine questions. Seek input from as many perspectives as possible to get a full picture before deciding on questions.
- There are many important questions to address. Stay focused on the primary purpose for your evaluation activities at a certain point in time and then work to prioritize which are the critical questions to address. Because evaluation will become an ongoing part of project management and delivery, you can and should revisit your evaluation questions and revise them to meet your current needs.
- Examine the values embedded in the questions being asked. Whose values are they? How do other stakeholders, particularly project participants, think and feel about this set of values? Are there different or better questions the evaluation team members and other stakeholders could build consensus around?

Let us now turn our attention to five planning strategies that foster the integration of evaluations into accepted (and expected) routine activities within social service programs: (1) asking evaluation questions, (2) mapping concepts, (3) reviewing the literature, (4) developing schedules, and (5) producing documentation.

Asking Evaluation Questions

So far in this book, we have emphasized the idea that social service programs—the problems they address and the clients they serve—are complex entities. In turn, any evaluation within a social service program can also be multifaceted and go in many different directions. For example, evaluation can produce data to answer many different questions: What are the characteristics of clients being served? What are the strengths or weaknesses of service delivery? To what degree are various stakeholders groups satisfied with the program? How much change do clients make after having received services? What is the "price tag" of services provided by BSW versus MSW workers?

The list of possible evaluation questions is limitless, but program resources—human and fiscal—are not. As such, an essential planning task of an evaluation is to decide on a reasonable number of questions that will be the focus of the evaluation efforts. By focusing an evaluation around clearly defined questions, evaluation activities can be kept manageable, economical, and efficient. All too often stakeholders identify more interests than any single evaluation can reasonably manage.

Figure 4.1 shows a survey that was used to aid an evaluation planning session within a rural literacy program. The questions shown in Figure 4.1 are only a sample of those generated by program stakeholders, which included representation from the program's steering committee, administration, and workers as well as other professionals

Evaluation Question Priority Survey

Instructions: (1) Rate each question by *circling one number* using the scale to the right of each question. (2) Feel free to add questions that you consider to be a priority for evaluation.

	Definitely Keep	*Deserves Consideration*	*Throw Out*
Client Characteristic Questions:			
1. Who referred family to the program?	1	2	3
2. How many children in the family?	1	2	3
3. How old is each family member?	1	2	3
4. How long has the family lived in the community?	1	2	3
5. What is the family structure?	1	2	3
6. Does the family live in town or rural?	1	2	3
7. Does the family access other community services?	1	2	3
8. What languages are spoken in the home?	1	2	3
9. What are the education levels of parents?	1	2	3
10. Does family have (or want) a library card?	1	2	3
Program Service Questions:			
11. How many visits were made to the family?	1	2	3
12. How long was each visit?	1	2	3
13. How many scheduled visits were missed? Why?	1	2	3
14. How many times was family *not* ready for the visit?	1	2	3
15. Did family readiness improve over time?	1	2	3
16. How satisfied were parents with program?	1	2	3
17. How satisfied was family with the worker?	1	2	3
18. What was easiest/most difficult for you in the program?	1	2	3
Client Outcome Questions:			
19. Do clients show change after the program?	1	2	3
20. Do children's literacy skills improve?	1	2	3
21. Do reading behaviors change?	1	2	3
22. Were the parents' expectations of program met?	1	2	3
23. What is the support worker's evaluation of services?	1	2	3
24. Has enjoyment for reading increased?	1	2	3

Figure 4.1 Example of a survey that determined the priority of the evaluation questions that were selected for the final evaluation.

and local citizens; a total of 20 stakeholders participated in the planning process. The complete brainstorm list (not shown) included more than 80 questions; far too many to focus the program's evaluation, which had a modest budget.

The survey shown in Figure 4.1 was created to gather stakeholder input that would help identify priority questions of interest. Because the questions listed were created by program stakeholders, the survey also had the added benefit of showing stakeholders that their ideas were both valued and were being put to good use in planning the program's evaluation strategy.

Evaluations that are not sufficiently focused generally result in large and unwieldy data collection efforts. Unfortunately, when mass quantities of data are collected without a forward thinking plan—linking the data collected to evaluation questions to be answered—the data may be compromised by poor reliability and validity. On the other hand, evaluation data derived from carefully focused questions make it much easier to maintain the integrity of the data collection process and produce credible results.

Focusing an evaluation does not imply that only one part or aspect of a program or service will be of interest. In fact, there are usually a number of different interests that can be accommodated within a single evaluation. Figure 4.1, for example, suggests that, depending upon stakeholders' ratings, the literacy program's evaluation could end up focusing on questions related to client need (e.g., client characteristics), program services, client outcomes, or a combination of the three.

As we will be seen in Part II of this book, evaluation questions can be grouped by four major types: needs assessment (Chapter 5), process evaluation (Chapter 6), outcome evaluation (Chapter 7), and efficiency evaluation (Chapter 8). Focusing evaluation questions means that program interests are first identified and the evaluation activities are then organized around those interests. Thus, there can be multiple points of focus within an evaluation, but it is important that these be clearly identified and planned from the beginning.

The focal questions selected for a program's evaluation need not remain static. Questions may be added or deleted as circumstances and experiences dictate. In other words, a specific set of questions may guide the focus of evaluation for a limited period of time. Such is the case when the monitoring approach to quality improvement is employed and the evaluation system is active throughout the life of the program.

Table 4.1 provides a sample timeline for moving through the four different types of evaluation covered in this book. Depending on the scope of the program, time lines can vary, but the one shown in Table 4.1 suggests that the program will focus on different types of evaluation questions for variable periods of time; the greatest amount of time (12 to 18 months) is given to process evaluation questions. Note that a program that goes through one cycle of each evaluation type in the sequential order shown in Table 4.1 can expect to take 25 to 44 months to complete its efforts, between two and three and a half years. With such a big time commitment, the program will no doubt want to carefully select the evaluation questions to guide their evaluation efforts.

Table 4.1 Implementation Time for Selected Types of Evaluations

Types of Evaluations	Chapter	Time Range
Needs Assessment	Chapter 5	3 to 6 months
Process Evaluation	Chapter 6	12 to 18 months
Outcome Evaluation	Chapter 7	6 to 12 months
Efficiency Evaluation	Chapter 8	1 to 2 months
Total		25 to 44 months

Mapping Concepts

Concept maps

A tool used to visually illustrate key elements of an evaluation plan.

A second evaluation planning strategy is **concept mapping,** which is a tool that can be used to visually illustrate key elements of either the program's design or aspects of the evaluation plan. Concept mapping is a technique that is used to display information visually. Surely, you have heard the expression "a picture is worth a thousand words." Concept mapping facilitates communication through pictures; as such, it reduces the amount of text reading that would otherwise be needed in a planning process. Specifically, it is used to diagram concepts and the relationships between them. Concept maps can illustrate simple or complex ideas. For example, Figure 3.6 in Chapter 3 shows a simple concept map illustrating the relationship of the goal of an agency to the goals of three programs housed within the agency.

A more complex concept map is shown in Figure 4.2, which offers a visual illustration of a client-centered program design for a family and community support program. The illustration shows the relationship between the family and community support components of the program, which share both office space and program objectives. Figure 4.2 also features the program's goal and details various activities that workers engage in. Indeed, Figure 4.2 highlights many key program design concepts that were discussed in Chapter 3.

Another example of a concept map is shown in Figure 4.3. Rather than diagraming the relationship between program design concepts (as shown in Figure 4.2), the concept map featured in Figure 4.3 shows the fit of evaluation as a key phase of program operations in both components of the program. Furthermore, the picture reveals that the two program components (family support and community support) will have separate evaluations but the results of both will be considered together when shared with the community.

Concept maps are communication tools. Thus, they can have the effect of answering questions about a group's thinking or generating new questions that aim for fuller understanding. It is important to understand that the concept maps featured in Figures 4.2 and 4.3 present only two of many possible representations. In viewing

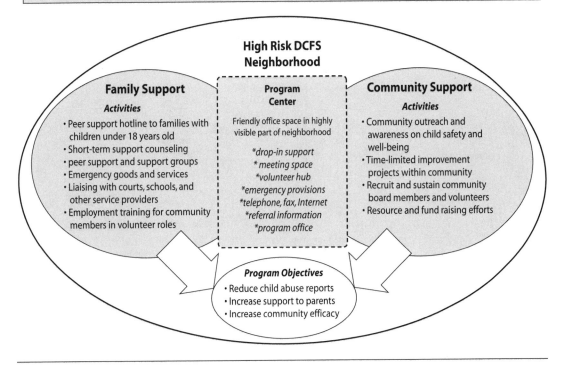

Family and Community Support Program

Program Goal: To enhance quality of life for families that are living in the Edison neighborhood where such problems as poverty, substance abuse, mental illness, and domestic violence put children at risk for abuse and neglect. By improving the capacity of families and the community they live in, the program aims to build a safe neighborhood that values child well-being.

High Risk DCFS Neighborhood

Family Support

Activities

- Peer support hotline to families with children under 18 years old
- Short-term support counseling
- peer support and support groups
- Emergency goods and services
- Liaising with courts, schools, and other service providers
- Employment training for community members in volunteer roles

Program Center

Friendly office space in highly visible part of neighborhood

*drop-in support
* meeting space
*volunteer hub
*emergency provisions
*telephone, fax, Internet
*referral information
program office

Community Support

Activities

- Community outreach and awareness on child safety and well-being
- Time-limited improvement projects within community
- Recruit and sustain community board members and volunteers
- Resource and fund raising efforts

Program Objectives
- Reduce child abuse reports
- Increase support to parents
- Increase community efficacy

Figure 4.2 A concept map of a client-centered program design.

the two illustrations, perhaps you had ideas about how the program design or the evaluation plan could be illustrated differently. It may be that your idea is to add concepts not featured, such as identifying priority research questions or specific measurement tools. On the other hand, it may be your opinion that Figure 4.2 could be simplified by deleting parts of the illustration such as the program goal statement. Perhaps you see the relationships between concepts differently and would prefer to see the concept shapes in another arrangement.

To be useful as a planning tool, the exercise of building concept maps should involve representatives of key stakeholder groups. Bringing different stakeholders—especially those with divergent views—together to build one concept map can generate rich discussion (see Boxes 1.3 and 1.4). Because communication can result in intense and impassioned discussions as stakeholders promote different points of view, it is wise to have a skilled facilitator to accomplish the task.

Once the concept maps are created, they can be used as visual reminders throughout the planning and evaluation processes. The visual illustrations can function as literal maps that chart future discussion and planning decisions. And, as such, they should be easily accessible or displayed in clear sight of those working on

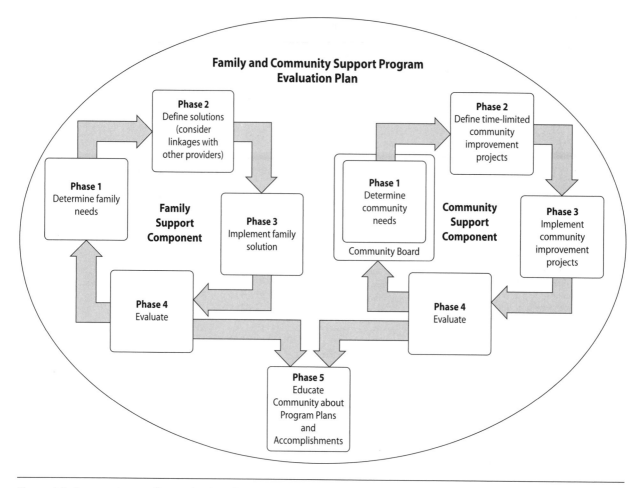

Figure 4.3 A concept map of an evaluation plan.

the program and evaluation plans. For example, suppose that stakeholders of the family and community support programs wind up spending 40 minutes of a 60-minute meeting in a heated debate about the type of activities that workers are expected to perform in the family support component of the program. It would be possible, and perhaps strategic, for a workgroup member to mention this fact, point to Figure 4.2, and add the suggestion that the group needs to wrap up discussion about family support to ensure that discussion about the community support component of the program does not get ignored.

Reviewing the Literature

A third useful planning strategy with stakeholders is conducting a **literature review** that targets the program's target population (clientele) and problem as well as its chosen interventions. To ignore the literature—specifically, research and evaluation

Literature review

An extensive search of the information available on a topic which produces a list of references to books, periodicals, and other materials on the topic.

studies—in a program and evaluation planning process is a colossal mistake, if only because the lessons learned by others will be overlooked. As mentioned in the three previous chapters, program planning and evaluation are key parts of knowledge building in our profession, and so we must begin with the lessons learned and written about by experts in the field. We also mentioned that the Internet has made access to published and unpublished reports much easier in recent years. To ignore available evidence-based studies and attempt to reinvent the "program-design wheel" by starting from scratch is tantamount to breaching the NASW *Code of Ethics:*

> Social workers should critically examine and keep current with emerging knowledge relevant to social work. Social workers should routinely review the professional literature . . . (NASW *Code of Ethics,* Section 4.01[b])

> Social workers should contribute to the knowledge base of social work and share with colleagues their knowledge related to practice, research, and ethics. Social workers should seek to contribute to the profession's literature and to share their knowledge . . . (NASW *Code of Ethics*, Section 5.01[d].

Beyond professional responsibility, the value of reviewing the literature is realized in the lessons that can be learned from others. For example, Family Group Conferencing is an intervention method developed from a Maori tradition in New Zealand. It was originally created as an intervention for juvenile offenders, and it typically involves a meeting with the offender, the victim, family and friends of both parties, involved professionals, and a coordinator who plans and facilitates the meeting. Family Group Conferencing provides a format to meet whereby all parties participate in a discussion of the crime and its impact. A problem-solving process is used to determine how the offender will make up for any harm caused as well to decide the role of any participants. A formal agreement is written and signed by participants, indicating that each person understands their expectations and commitments.

Family Group Conferencing has since been adopted by other countries including the United States, Canada, Australia, South Africa and numerous European countries. The intervention method has also been adapted to the child welfare arena where the conference meeting is used to develop a plan of child protection, preferably one that can be carried out while children remain living at home. Throughout the 1990s, numerous research studies produced a rich pool of information that any program planner or evaluator involved with Family Group Conferencing would find helpful.

Figure 4.4 shows a synopsis of research findings on selected dimensions about how family group conferencing is carried out in child welfare. The research about family group conferencing is able to answer several practical questions about how the intervention method is expected to operate. The information reported in Figure 4.4 has been used to create "best practices," thereby strengthening the design of many new Family Group Conferencing programs that started since the beginning of the twenty-first century.

Research Excerpts on Family Group Conferencing in Child Welfare

How much preparation time is needed to plan a family group conference?

- Marsh and Crow (1998) report that the coordinators spent an average of 22 hours setting up meetings, ranging from 10 hours to 30 or more hours.
- Paul Ban reports that preparing for conferences takes approximately four times as long as actually holding them (in Hudson et al., 1996).

Who will attend the conference?

- The mean number of participants was 13.5 (Pennell & Burford, 2000).
- Family support persons participated about one-third of the time in the conferences studied by Patterson and Harvey (1991) in New Zealand.
- An average of two to three professions attend the conference (Pennell & Burford, 2000).
- Patterson (1993) found that 73 percent of invited family members attended conferences in New Zealand.
- A variety of authors have reported that conferences are successful in gaining a wide range of family attendance (Boffa, 1995; Pennell & Burford, 2000; Robertson, 1996; Swain, 1993).

What is the length of time of a conference?

- Of the 37 conferences that were part of the Newfoundland and Labrador project, the average length was 6 hours (Pennell & Burford, 2000).
- Renouf, Robb, and Wells (1990) report that on average conferences lasted 3 hours.
- Patterson and Harvey (1991) report that conferences lasted an average of 3.5 hours (range: 1–11 hours).

What is known about the location of conferences?

- Marsh and Crow (1998) report that only four of 80 conferences were not held on neutral territory; two were held in social service department offices and two in the families' homes.
- In contrast, research conducted by Patterson and Harvey (1991) showed that, in New Zealand, 37 percent of the conferences were held at the Department of Social Welfare office, 20 percent at community facilities, and 16 percent at family houses.

Figure 4.4 A Sample of research excerpts.

Developing Schedules

Schedules can take many forms, such as a calendar, a "to-do" list, an agenda, a timetable, or even a concept map. Schedules serve the function of documenting and communicating the work process with all stakeholders in mind. Specifically, they detail an ordered list of *who* needs to do *what* by *when*. Because the work of planning programs and evaluations is a complex undertaking that involves the input of many stakeholder groups, schedules are a useful communication tool that can help the planning process to move forward and stay on track. In addition, schedules that are written and posted publicly for viewing by interested stakeholders have the added value of promoting an open and transparent planning process, which is an essential ingredient if the process is to be empowering to participants. Three items are central to any scheduling endeavor: tasks, roles, and timelines.

Tasks

Suppose you were a member of an agency workgroup that had the task of developing the program design for the family support program featured in Box 3.1 in Chapter 3. Although the program design may appear simple in presentation, the process of creating such a program design document is no easy undertaking. Many complicated factors can come into play such as divergent views of workgroup members, agency politics, time pressures, lack of expertise in the workgroup, and the competence of the workgroup leader, just to name a few.

Furthermore, the program design documented in Box 3.1 has many elements—program goal, objectives, activities, and **measuring instruments**—that call for distinct decision-making efforts. To accomplish its aim of creating a program design, a workgroup will have to breakdown the job into manageable tasks and decide upon the order of task completion. Figure 4.5 shows an example of how to breakdown the program design job by outlining 12 separate meeting agendas, which would have the workgroup focus on only one or two tasks at a time. Figure 4.5 is only one example of a task schedule for creating a program design; many other breakdowns are possible. Whatever the breakdown strategy, a comprehensive task schedule is one that incorporates steps to produce all of the key elements or parts of the end product.

Measuring instruments Instruments such as questionnaires or rating scales used to obtain a measure (usually an outcome measure) for a particular client or client group.

Roles

With the planning tasks outlined in Figure 4.5, another scheduling item is to determine who will carry the responsibility to see that each task is completed. No matter the size of the workgroup, a priority is to include input from the various stakeholder groups in the planning effort. Ideally the workgroup is composed of individuals who represent the different interests of the various stakeholder groups, as presented in Chapter 1—policymakers, administrators, practitioners, funders, general public, and clients. Table 4.2 shows a list of the 12 tasks that were featured as agenda items in Figure 4.5, but added to the list are names of people charged with leadership responsibilities for the various tasks as well as their individual areas of expertise and contact information.

Identifying the players of the planning process is key to a communication process

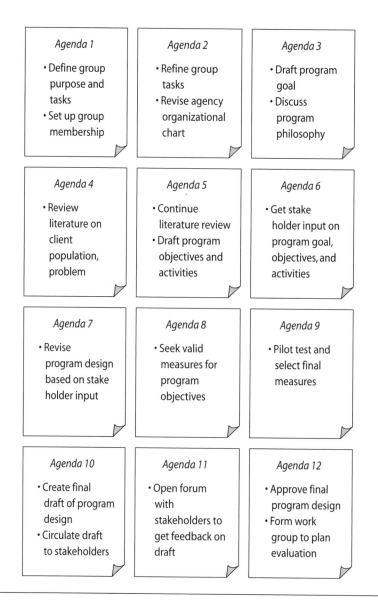

Figure 4.5 Sample agendas for workgroup meetings to create a program design document.

that is transparent and open—two essential ingredients for planning efforts that are typically characterized by use of **volunteers** and disparity between the characteristics of people planning the program evaluation and the people expected to benefit from the planning efforts (i.e., clients). Box 4.3 suggests the various responsibilities of the evaluators and program managers when an evaluation is under way.

Volunteers. Any planning effort should include clear expectations of the work that needs to be done. However, as the involvement of stakeholders not employed by the agency often means volunteer recruitment, the burden of work often will lie with a

Volunteers

People who do work for which they receive little or no earnings.

Table 4.2 Schedule of Tasks and Roles

Agenda Task (from Figure 4.5)	Person Responsible	Expertise or Role	Phone, E-mail
1. Group purpose and membership	Shanti	Group Leader	
2. Revise organization chart	Nathifa	Administration	
3. Program philosophy and goal	Aisha	Board Member	
4. Review literature	Angie, Min	MSW Practicum Students	
5. Program objectives and activities	Jenna	Cultural Competence	
6. Stakeholder input	All		
7. Revise program design	Shanti		
8. Find measuring instruments	Angie, Min		
9. Pilot measuring instruments	All		
10. Complete draft of program design	Shanti		
11. Open forum discussion	All		
12. Print final program design	Shanti		

select few employees. Certainly, one person is needed to lead the process—to manage the group, facilitate communication, and monitor the work product. As well, attention needs to be given to what can be reasonably accommodated within the allotted time frame.

Diversity Represented. A common characteristic of social service programs is that program planners and service providers do not have **diversity:** They are not representative of the client populations they serve. Disparity is often revealed in race, ethnicity, gender, and class differences between the people employed by the program and the people served by the program. Time and again, we see social service programs operated by individuals from dominant groups who are designing social service programs for individuals from marginalized groups in society. Because the purpose of a role schedule is to identify people and experts who will take responsibility for certain planning tasks, it can be modified to highlight specific areas of expertise appropriate for a particular planning effort such as cultural competence.

Diversity
To respect racial/ethnic, gender, cultural, disability, sexual orientation, and social differences in staff and clients.

Timelines

A final aspect of scheduling that is critical to creating a successful planning process is the creation of a **timeline.** Figure 4.6 features a Gantt chart created using Microsoft Visio. A Gantt chart is horizontal bar chart that graphically displays the sequence,

Timelines
Shows when events are suppose to occur.

Box 4.3 Potential Responsibilities of Evaluators and Program Managers

Evaluator

- Develop an evaluation plan, in conjunction with program staff.
- Provide monthly or quarterly progress reports to staff (written or in person).
- Train project staff. Topics could include evaluation instruments, information collection activities, participant/case selection for sampling purposes, and other activities.
- Design information collection instruments, or select standardized instruments or inventories.
- Implement information collection procedures.
- Interview project staff.
- Interview coordinating/collaborating agency staff.
- Interview program participants.
- Conduct focus groups.
- Observe service delivery activities.
- Review participant case records.
- Develop a database.
- Code, enter, and clean data.
- Analyze data.
- Establish and oversee procedures ensuring confidentiality during all phases of the evaluation.
- Write interim (quarterly, biannual, yearly) evaluation reports and the final evaluation report.
- Attend project staff meetings, advisory board or interagency coordinating committee meetings, and grantee meetings sponsored by the funding agency.
- Present findings at local and national meetings and conferences.

Program Manager

- Educate the outside evaluator about the program's operations and objectives, the characteristics of the participant population, and the benefits that program staff expect from the evaluation. This may involve alerting evaluators to sensitive situations (e.g., the need to report suspected child abuse) they may encounter during the course of their evaluation activities.
- Provide feedback to the evaluator on whether instruments are appropriate for the target population and provide input during the evaluation plan phase.
- Keep the outside evaluator informed about changes in the program's operations.
- Specify information that the evaluator should include in the report.
- Assist in interpreting evaluation findings.
- Provide information to all staff about the evaluation process.
- Monitor the evaluation contract and completion of work products such as reports.
- Ensure that program staff are fulfilling their responsibilities such as data collection.
- Supervise in-house evaluation activities such as completion of data collection instruments and data entry.
- Serve as a troubleshooter for the evaluation process, resolving problems or locating a higher level person in the agency who can help. Request a debriefing from the evaluator at various times during the evaluation.

	Agenda Task (see Table 4.2)	Start	Finish	Duration	Sept. 2007		Oct. 2007		Nov. 2007	
					9/3					
1	Group purpose & membership	8/21/2007	8/25/2007	1w	■					
2	Revise organization chart	8/28/2007	9/1/2007	1w	■					
3	Program philosophy & goal	9/6/2007	9/19/2007	2w		■■				
4	Review Literature	9/6/2007	11/28/2007	12w		■■■■■■■■■■				
5	Program Objectives & Activities	9/14/2007	10/4/2007	3w		■■				
6	Stakeholder input on draft	10/6/2007	10/12/2007	1w			■			
7	Revise program design	10/13/2007	10/19/2007	1w			■			
8	Find measuring instruments	10/23/2007	11/18/2007	2.5w				■■		
9	Pilot measuring instruments	11/10/2007	11/23/2007	2w				■■		
10	Write draft of program design	11/24/2007	12/5/2007	1.5w					■	
11	Open forum discussion	12/7/2007	12/11/2007	.5w						■
12	Print final program design	12/12/2007	12/18/2007	1w						■

Figure 4.6 Sample Gantt chart—timeline of program planning tasks.

start and end time, and duration of activities defined for a particular project. Figure 4.6 again lists the same 12 tasks shown in the task and role schedules, but in this case dates and deadlines are given to guide the time frame in when tasks are expected to begin and end. The Gantt chart estimates that the entire job of creating a program design for the family support program will be completed in 18 weeks. The chart also shows the sequence of tasks as well as how they overlap. The literature review (Task 4) for example is expected to be carried out over a 12-week period, during which time Tasks 3 and 5 through 10 will also be put into action.

Producing Documentation

It may be obvious by now that a planning process generates **documentation,** a paper trail that documents the people, the process, and the products of a workgroup's efforts. So far, all of the planning strategies discussed—evaluation questions, literature review, and schedules—produce one type of document or another. Ultimately, each workgroup must decide how particular documents will be used and how far they will be circulated. Open and transparent communication about planning is preferable if there is interest in creating a culture of trust within an organization (Fairholm, 1994). Additional documents can be helpful in this regard.

> **Documentation**
> The recording in a permanent format of information derived from conservation activities.

- *Minutes:* **Minutes** provide a written account of what happened at workgroup meetings. The Internet has many suggestions for how to record minutes of a meeting, but generally speaking, the following information should be included: title of workgroup; date, time, and location; people present at the meeting or absent from it; approval of previous meeting minutes (amendments made if necessary); list of tasks/topics, summary of discussion and

> **Minutes**
> A written account of what transpired at a meeting.

[Agency Letterhead]

February 9, 2007

Family Drug Court Graduates
c/o Family Drug Court Administrator
Family Drug Court Program
Agency Name
Address
State, Zip

Dear Karla, Raeyon, and Gregory [*fictional names*],

This note is to thank each of you for taking the time to meet with us on Friday, January 30, to talk about your experiences as graduates of the Family Drug Court Program. Prior to meeting with you, we had the chance to observe the court process and talk with the treatment team and other staff. We learned a lot by seeing the court in action and by listening to the many different professionals describe how they work together and do their jobs. We also learned a great deal by listening to each of you tell us your experiences with the drug court. We were inspired by your successes.

We have begun our work in developing a Family Drug Court in our state and are excited about the chance to help families and children in our community. Thanks again for taking the time to speak with us. We wish you every success in the future.

Best regards,

Program Planners

Figure 4.7 Example of a simple thank-you letter.

record of decisions (record votes if appropriate); future tasks, deadlines, and persons responsible; and name of the person submitting the minutes.

- *Thank-You Letters*: Because program planners and evaluators regularly rely on the goodwill of others for ideas or assistance, thank-you letters are a basic ingredient in any planning process and are most effective when they are delivered in a timely manner. Figure 4.7 shows an example of a thank-you letter written to participants in a Montana drug court program. The three participants mentioned in the letter met with a team of drug court program developers from Illinois to share their experiences as drug court participants.

IDENTIFYING DATA NEEDS

Stakeholders have a major interest in the operations and outcomes of a social service program. As we have discussed, each stakeholder group—policymakers, administrators, practitioners, funders, general public, and clients—will have a variety of questions about a program's operations and outcomes. In some cases, these questions will overlap, and in others they will be unique to the specific type of stakeholder. The process of focusing an evaluation involves identifying the questions and interests of the relevant stakeholder groups and prioritizing among these until a manageable number of questions is arrived at.

In addition to creating questions related to a program's objectives and activities, stakeholders can be encouraged to generate other relevant questions. Stakeholders can also assist in examining the key decisions they need to make and in identifying the type of data that would be helpful in making these decisions. Attention needs to be paid to what can be reasonably accommodated within the framework of the evaluation, taking into account the resources and time available, the effort required to collect the data, and what data are likely to be used to make specific recommendations.

Focusing an evaluation begins with identifying the data that are needed to make useful **decisions**. Generally these needs can be summarized into two broad categories:

Decision
A choice made after considering different possibilities.

1. Data that will help to make decisions (i.e., decisions about client need, program design, program processes, client outcomes, and cost-benefit).
2. Data that are required for other purposes such as accountability (i.e., coverage, cultural, service delivery, fiscal, legal, and professional; see Chapter 1).

Discussions and negotiations in the planning phase of an evaluation will lead to prioritizing the various (and sometimes competing) data needs of different groups of stakeholders. Consideration will then move to how and when the required data will be collected. It is always desirable to collect data in the most economical and nondisruptive manner possible. If practical, the best strategy is to integrate the data collection process of an evaluation with the record-keeping and paperwork processes normally undertaken within the program itself. Collecting data is costly; thus, it is important that the cost of including any **variable** in the evaluation plan will be justified by the benefit of the information derived from the data.

Variable
A characteristic that can take on different values for different individuals.

Integrating data collection into regular paperwork or documentation procedures of a program is easier to imagine than it is to do. Adding client race to an intake form such as the one displayed in Figure 11.3, for example, can be accomplished by including various categories of race that represent the local population served by a program. Common categories are African American, Asian, Caucasian, Latino, and Native American. If the local population includes a large proportion of one racial group, then more specific categories may be warranted. Asian subgroups may include Chinese, East Indian, Korean, and Japanese, for example. The difficulty of deciding specific data collection items (or variables) is especially apparent when trying to get many stakeholders to agree on priorities.

Adding race as one variable is simple enough, but what if there are 20 or more other variables of interest addressing areas such as client demographics, social service history, and referral problems? The limit on how many questions to ask is set by the amount of time the program allots for intake procedures or similar data collection activities. Ultimately, some items will have to be deleted from data collection forms so as not to compromise other aspects of client service delivery or overwhelm the client. The burden of deciding which data collection items to retain or reject can be lessened by evaluating each item with the priority evaluation questions decided by stakeholder groups (e.g., Figure 4.1). Items that are integral to answering questions are retained, while items that are distant or unrelated to the questions posed are rejected.

As previously discussed, evaluations are only representations, or snapshots if you will, of a social service program. They are not meant to reflect every aspect of it. However, effective evaluations provide data about a reasonable sampling of the most relevant processes, activities, and outcomes of a social service program. This is particularly the case where an evaluation takes the form of a monitoring system that provides periodic feedback about key aspects of the program's operations and outcomes. Carefully selecting what specific elements of a program's process and outcomes to track is a very important task.

FOCUSING EVALUATION EFFORTS

A final consideration for the planning phase of evaluation is to think about starting with the end of the evaluation in mind. In other words, before embarking on evaluation, you want to imagine what the end result of the evaluation will look like. By clearly picturing the expected product, such as the format for displaying the results (e.g., tables or graphs) or types of data (e.g., quantitative or qualitative) that will answer particular questions of evaluation, planning efforts are more focused.

Logic model

Describes a social service program in diagram form.

The top of Figure 4.8 lays out the basic **logic model** that was illustrated in Boxes 2.3 and 3.2. There are three columns below the logic model where each column delineates a possible type of evaluation that could be used in connection with the model's "inputs," "outputs," and "outcomes." That is, a needs assessment could be used to determine the model's inputs, a process evaluation could be used in evaluating the model's outputs, and an outcome evaluation could be used in evaluating the model's outcomes, or impact. All three of these types of evaluations will be discussed in the next three chapters.

Next, we present a discussion based on work conducted with a family service program that has put into place a monitoring evaluation system and serves as an example of how to focus an evaluation by visualizing the end product. The program's primary purpose was to obtain timely feedback about key program processes and

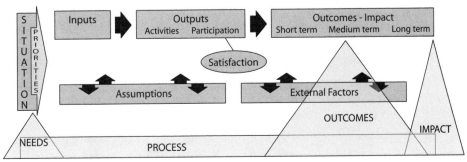

Evaluation

Needs assessment (chapter 5):

What are the characteristics, needs, priorities of target population?

What are potential barriers/facilitators?

What is most appropriate?

Process evaluation (chapter 6):

How is program implemented? Fidelity of implementation?

Are activities delivered as intended?

Are participants being reached as intended?

What are participant reactions?

Outcome evaluation (chapter 7):

To what extent are desired changes occurring? For whom?

Is the program making a difference?

What seems to work? Not work?

What are unintended outcomes?

Figure 4.8 The logic model and evaluation possibilities.

outcomes for the purpose of program development. A secondary purpose was to obtain useful information via the collection of reliable and valid data that would meet the accountability requests of funders and other outside stakeholders.

After a series of planning sessions that included the program's administrators and the line-level social workers, it was decided that the program would track data in five areas: (1) client demographics, (2) service statistics, (3) quality standards, (4) feedback, and (5) client outcomes. As such, the evaluation would incorporate elements of needs assessment, evaluability assessment, process evaluation, and outcome evaluation.

Client Demographics

It is always desirable to have reliable and valid data about the clientele actually being served by the program, not only to ensure compliance with funding contracts but also to identify any changes or trends in client profile. Client **demographics** data are useful in all types of evaluations. Table 4.3 provides a simple illustration of the types of variables that can be tracked in the client demographic area (left side) as well as methods of measuring these variables (right side). As can be seen, the client demographics to be measured are stated in the form of simple straightforward **benchmarks**. The target values of each benchmark were derived from the program's funding contract as well as from the program's goal, which reflects what kind of

Demographics

Characteristics that define a particular group of people, including age, education level, and family size.

Benchmarks

Performance goals against which a social service program's success is measured.

Table 4.3 Client Demographics

Benchmarks	Measures
Serve 200 individuals overall, per month	Count of Client Intake Forms
60% of clients will be single-parent families	Item on Client Intake Form

clientele is targeted by the program. By specifying client demographics as benchmarks, the program has clear targets toward which to work. Criteria are also explicitly established against which evaluation results can be eventually assessed.

Alternatively, it is also possible to phrase benchmarks in the format of objectives. Recall that qualities of clear objectives are that they are meaningful, specific, measurable, and directional (as described in Chapter 3). These qualities apply to both client-centered objectives and to maintenance or instrumental objectives. Objectives differ from benchmarks in that they do not specify a target value, as is the case in Table 4.3. It may be, for example, that instead of setting a benchmark to serve 200 individuals per month, a program aims only to maintain the overall number of clients served from the previous year. Using objectives is preferable to using benchmarks when a specific target value is uncertain or cannot be reasonably estimated. Some people would also argue that using benchmarks alone tends to create a climate of "bean counting" more so than is the case with objectives.

In general, client demographics measure the number of clients served and their corresponding characteristics that are considered relevant to program services and outcomes. The two variables in Table 4.3 can be easily tracked by data gleaned from a client intake form. Data about whether a client is new to the program, for example, can be readily captured by including one extra item (perhaps a checklist) on the program's intake form such as the one displayed in Figure 11.3. Of course, it is important in the planning and focusing phase of an evaluation to determine that it is of interest to know if a client is or is not new to the program. If the data collection system is designed to capture these data in advance, it will be a simple matter to track this issue. If not, it may be inconvenient, confusing, and costly to revise data collection or reconstruct the data at a later date, if it is possible. Using our example, the following simple item could be added to an intake form without much hassle:

Is this the first time you have received services from this program (check one)?

_____ Yes
_____ No
_____ Don't know

Client demographic data are important to funders, program administrators, and practitioners. By tracking these variables, program administrators can provide data to funders to verify that their programs' services are indeed being provided to the groups they intended. Funders, in turn, will welcome assurances that their funding is being used in the manner they have targeted.

Data about client demographic variables are useful for a number of reasons. If benchmarks are being met, for example, program administrators will be reassured to continue the services that have been provided. On the other hand, unmet benchmarks will alert administrators and practitioners alike to explore the reasons behind the shortfall. Perhaps program practices can be adjusted to ensure that intended clients are informed of the services offered and are welcomed to the program.

Alternatively, it is possible that the social needs within the community have changed over time and earlier targets are no longer realistic, as would be the case in a transient community where population demographics change regularly. Immigrants who had once lived downtown, for example, may now be moving into the suburbs and young professionals are perhaps moving in and replacing them. In such a case, the program will have an early indication that its services should be adjusted to meet current needs.

Service Statistics

Service statistics provide a second focal point for our evaluation example. Service statistics are similar to client demographic data. However, the focus is on the services provided by the program (i.e., program processes) rather than on the program's clientele. Service, or process, data are of interest for accountability purposes in addition to program feedback and development.

Service statistics
Statistics calculated for the services provided by a program.

Again, program administrators and funders will take interest in these data to ensure that the quantity of the program services corresponds to initial funding expectations, as well as to expectations as set out in the program's logic model (see Boxes 2.3 and 3.2). In addition, service statistics can also add to a solid understanding of program service delivery and operations. By tracking changes in various components of service delivery, for example, program administrators are in a better position to make informed decisions about reallocating their scarce resources. In short, with relevant data they will be able to manage resources more effectively and efficiently. For example, data about the volume of services provided during evening hours may lead to the reduction (or increase) of those hours.

Table 4.4 provides a simple example of two benchmarks related to service statistics. The value set for the volume of services (in our case, 500 counseling sessions per month) corresponds to levels set in the funding agreement. The second service benchmark (in our case, 20 percent of services will be provided out of the center) reflects the program's intention to be more responsive to client needs by moving services out of the office and into the community. Tracking service statistics related to the location where the services were delivered provides feedback about whether the current practices are in line with this objective.

Table 4.4 Service Statistics

Benchmarks	Measures
500 counseling sessions per month	From Contact Information Form
20% of counseling sessions will take place out of center	Item on Contact Information Form

As indicated in Table 4.4, data about a program's services can generally be captured through data entered on a program's contact form or an equivalent document for recording case notes (see Figure 11.5). As long as the type of service is recorded along with the amount of services provided, the volume of each type of service can be easily tracked. To determine the location and the time of service, specific items may need to be added to the contact form or collected in a systematic way. To minimize paperwork, these items can be designed as check boxes.

Quality Standards

Quality standards are about practices that the program believes will lead to positive client outcome. These practices may be described by relevant standard setting through the professional literature or by official accrediting agencies such as the Council on Accreditation. Quality standards are usually a focal point for process evaluations, as they relate to practices that are expected to lead to certain client outcomes. The assumption is that "good" social work practices lead to "good" client outcomes.

Most social service programs hold strong beliefs about practices thought to best serve clients, but very few actually monitor the implementation of them. Of course, many social work practices or interventions are relatively complex and difficult to capture within a single evaluation effort. Nevertheless, some quality standards, as the two shown in Table 4.5, can be addressed within an evaluative framework.

The benchmarks specified in Table 4.5 relate to program beliefs that the most effective services are those provided to larger client systems than an individual—for example, to a parent–child dyad or to an entire family. The benchmark speaks to this

Table 4.5 Quality Standards

Benchmarks	Measures
Less than 25% of services will be provided only to single individuals	Item on Contact Information Form
A minimum of one community resource suggestion per family	Item on Contact Information Form

by specifying that over 75 percent of "client contacts" will involve more than one person. Similarly, the program believes in the impact and helpfulness of community resources in strengthening and supporting families. Thus, another target is that at least one community resource suggestion per family will be made during the course of service provision.

The data needed to monitor these benchmarks can be collected through the creation of appropriate items on the "client contact form" or any other client log (see Figure 11.5). Again, through strategic design, a check-box format will easily allow the capture of the data needed to track these two simple objectives (or variables).

Data relating to the achievement of quality standard objectives are helpful in the program planning and development process of an evaluation. Through collecting such data over time, the program can ensure that its beliefs about effective practices are translated into actual practice. Results falling short of the benchmark could result in revising the set values included in the benchmark or revising the program operations in some way to increase the likelihood of achieving the original value.

Alternatively, it may be determined that the gap is the result of unmet training need or attitudes held by staff members. In such a case, further staff development might be planned. On the other hand, if the benchmarks are met, as evidenced via credible data, existing practices and procedures could be examined in greater detail. For example, program practices could be monitored to determine what approaches are most effective in getting individual clients to accept help as part of a larger group (e.g., a parent–child dyad or family). Additionally, benchmarks might be modified so that they align better with the professed quality standards.

In short, tracking quality standards provides data about the actual practices of a program and reveals when practices are not consistent with beliefs. Such data would lead to an examination of those practices with a view to further developing them.

Feedback

Feedback received from relevant stakeholders is another area to focus on in our evaluation example. Relevant groups may include clients, volunteers, referring agencies, or other stakeholder groups. More often than not, relevant feedback usually centers on client satisfaction of some kind. Such feedback does not clearly fit in any of the traditional types of evaluations; it is typically collected as an outcome but reflects client perceptions about program processes. High client satisfaction, or an otherwise high opinion of a program, does not necessarily correspond with successful client outcomes. In other words, clients may like a program but not experience any positive change as a result of it. Nevertheless, it is desirable that a program draws favorable opinions and comments from its stakeholders. If not, administrators and staff alike should be aware that satisfaction with the program is not high.

Table 4.6 provides a simple example of two benchmarks relating to feedback—

Feedback
Process of communication whereby a person can disagree, ask a question, repeat information for understanding, or otherwise talk back in the communication process.

Table 4.6 Feedback (Client)

Benchmarks	Measures
70% of clients rate item *helpfulness* as "Agree" or "Strongly Agree"	Satisfaction Survey Item 1
75% of clients rate item *satisfaction*	Satisfaction Survey Item 5

in this case, client feedback. The data to track this objective are collected by asking clients to fill out a simple client satisfaction survey at the time of the completion of services (see Figure 11.8). In this case, there were five items on the survey, designed specifically for this program. The items deal with such matters as the helpfulness of services, the supportiveness of staff, and overall satisfaction with the program's services. Each item is in the form of a rating scale with four possible response categories. For example, helpfulness was measured by the item:

The services were helpful (check one):

____ Strongly Disagree

____ Disagree

____ Agree

____ Strongly Agree

As Table 4.6 shows, the program set a benchmark that a minimum of 70 percent of service recipients will rate this item as "Agree" or "Strongly Agree." To measure overall satisfaction, an item was included that read:

My overall satisfaction with these services is (check one):

____ Very Low

____ Low

____ Moderate

____ High

____ Very High

The benchmark meant that 70 percent, or more, of the clients should rate this item as "High" or "Very High." This would in turn indicate a minimum expected level of overall satisfaction with the services offered by the program.

Client Outcomes

Client outcome

The degree to which a client benefited from receiving a social service.

An evaluation system is seldom complete without some attention to **client outcomes** or client results, which is the reason that the social service organization exists in the first place. Thus, client outcomes always lie outside of the program with the clients; they reflect changes in clients. Client outcomes are always directly

Table 4.7 Client Outcomes

Benchmarks	Measures
Grand mean of 3.4 on first 5 items of Educational Outcomes Form	Educational Outcomes Feedback Form designed specifically for the program
Average self-esteem score less than 30 on exit from program	Hudson's Index of Self-Esteem
Average improvement of 15 points in peer relations on exit from program	Hudson's Index of Peer Relations

tied to program objectives as stated in the program's logic model (see Boxes 2.3 and 3.2).

Table 4.7 provides three examples of benchmarks used to monitor program objectives or client outcomes. As can be seen, the first benchmark is expressed in terms of a minimum mean score of 3.4 on the first five items of a nonstandardized rating scale, designed specifically for the program. Of course, the value 3.4 has meaning only if we know the possible range of the rating scale. If scores can range from 1 to 5 (and 5 is high), we would interpret the data more positively than if scores ranged from 1 to 10 (and 10 is high). Chapter 9 discusses rating scales as methods of measurement; they can easily be constructed in such a way that they can directly and meaningfully monitor program objectives.

The next two benchmarks in Table 4.7 are expressed as an average minimum score and an average gain score on two separate standardized measuring instruments, Hudson's Index of Self-Esteem and Hudson's Index of Peer Relations. As we will see in the Chapter 9, standardized instruments are always preferable to use in outcome measurements because their reliability and validity have been previously determined and demonstrated. Thus, such measures generally have more credibility than locally constructed instruments.

It should be noted that the last two outcome benchmarks imply different evaluation designs. Specifying a score of less than 30 on the exit from the program on the Index of Self-Esteem implies a one-group posttest only design. As we know, such a design allows a description of the level at which clients leave at the end of the service, but the design does not make it possible to determine the amount of change, if any, that has taken place. However, because the Index of Self-Esteem is known to have a clinical cutting score of 30 (i.e., scores higher than 30 indicate a clinical problem), the meaning of the objective can be interpreted more clearly.

The objective specifying an average improvement of 15 on the Index of Peer Relations (this would actually be a reduction of 15 points because this instrument uses higher numbers to indicate greater problems) implies a one-group pretest–posttest design. That design not only provides a description of the group at the end of the service but also provides a description of the group at the time of entry and therefore allows a determination of what change has taken place. Of course, because the design involves only clients who have received program services, it cannot be concluded that the program caused the change. A control group (a parallel group of clients who did not receive program services) is needed to conclude such causality.

Outcome measurement is an increasingly important topic among social service programs. Evaluation data relating to outcomes serve the needs of multiple stakeholders. Funders and administrators can use it to assure themselves of the effectiveness of the program and thereby demonstrate accountability. To ensure that the program is operating in the most effective manner possible, administrators and staff can examine outcome results and make program adjustments as necessary. For professionals providing direct services, outcome measures provide a framework for case-level evaluations and facilitate accurate and honest communications with clients.

Summing Up and Looking Ahead

This chapter looked at the planning of an evaluation from a broad perspective by demonstrating how an overall plan for an evaluation can be developed and providing an example of what one social service program chose to monitor and evaluate. In the next part of this book (Part II), we will look at four different types of evaluations starting with needs assessment, which is the topic of the next chapter.

Recap and Online Materials

In this chapter, you learned how to get prepared for doing a social work evaluation.

You should also recall the concept of reviewing the literature from your foundational research course. If not, go online to take a free crash course in how to do literature reviews.

You can also find the following materials online to help you master the concepts you just learned:

- Chapter Outline
- Learning Objectives
- Key Terms and Concepts
- Flash Cards
- Practice Multiple-Choice Tests
- Essay Questions with Answers
- Links

www.oup.com/us/swevaluation

Study Questions

1. Discuss why planning an evaluation is a very important aspect of its total success. Provide a social work example throughout your discussion. Discuss why an evaluation is only a representation of the "total picture." Discuss the common characteristics of all evaluations and present a common social work example throughout your discussion. Discuss in detail why we should use program models in social service agencies. List and discuss the various resource constraints that need to be taken into account before doing a program evaluation.

2. Discuss why it is important to include as many stakeholders as possible in the initial development of an evaluation. List and discuss the various concepts a social service program could monitor that could be used in an evaluation.

3. This chapter stresses the importance of planning and focusing an evaluation before carrying it out. List the difficulties an evaluator would likely encounter if he or she did not develop an evaluation plan *before* beginning evaluation activity.

4. As part of a program evaluation, an executive director of a social service program wants to know how satisfied all of her stakeholders are with program services. What does the executive director need to consider if she wants to ensure that the evaluation findings will provide broad representation of *all* stakeholder groups?

5. Identify the common characteristics that impact planning and focusing activities for all types of evaluation. How do these common features help an evaluator in putting together an evaluation plan? A major strategy for focusing an evaluation

is developing clearly articulated evaluation questions. Explain how such questions can be used to guide evaluations once they are under way.

6. A common problem of getting input from multiple stakeholders is developing too many evaluation questions, which in turn produces too much data. Discuss how too much data can be problematic for a social service program. What are client demographics? Why are they important data to collect in a program evaluation?

7. It is possible to plan an evaluation of a social service program around multiple focal points such as client demographics, service statistics, quality standards, stakeholder feedback, and client outcomes. Think of a social service program that you are familiar with and develop two questions that might be asked of each focal point.

8. Think about the grade you are striving to achieve for this class. Imagine that you are going to evaluate your class performance to monitor your learning. You decide on three key focal points for your evaluation: class attendance, reading class material, and class participation. Develop a benchmark for each focal point that you believe is necessary to achieve in order to assist you with earning the grade that you desire.

9. This chapter presented an example of a program that picked five focal points for monitoring an evaluation: client demographics, service statistics, quality standards, stakeholder feedback, and client outcomes. Rank these focal points in order of most to least important. Provide a rationale for your rankings.

10. An executive director is under pressure to produce an evaluation of his program in a short period of time. As a consequence, he does not want to include all stakeholder groups in planning the evaluation. Imagine that you are hired as the evaluator. What guidance would you provide the executive director around his decision to exclude some stakeholder groups from the planning phase of the evaluation?

References, Further Reading, and Resources

Ban, P. (1996). Implementing and evaluating family group conferences with children and families in Australia. In J. Hudson, A. Morris, G. Maxwell, & B. Galaway (Eds.), *Family group conferences: Perspectives on policy and practice*. Monsey, NY: Willow Tree Press.

Boffa, J. (1995). *The evaluation of family group conferences: A key to family centered practice in child protection*. Melbourne, Australia: Health and Community Services.

Burford, G., & Pennell, J. (1995). Family group decision-making: An innovation in child and family welfare. In J. Hudson & B. Galaway (Eds.), *Child welfare in Canada: Research and policy implications* (pp. 172–209). Toronto: Thompson Educational.

Fairholm, G. W. (1994). *Leadership and the culture of trust*. Westport, CT: Praeger.

Marsh, P., & Crow, G. (1998). *Family group conferences in child welfare*. London: Blackwell.

Patterson, K. (1993). Evaluating the organization and operation of care and protection family group conferences. *Social Work Review, 4*, 14–18.

Patterson, K., & Harvey, M. (1991). *An evaluation of the organization and operation of care and protection family group conferences*. Wellington: Evaluation Unit, Department of Social Welfare.

Pennell, J., & Burford, G. (2000). Family group decision making: Protecting children and women. *Child Welfare, 79,* 131–158.

Randall, J. (2002). The practice–research relationship: A case of ambivalent attachment? *Journal of Social Work, 2*(1), 105–122.

Renouf, J., Robb, G., & Wells, P. (1990). *Children, Young Persons, and Their Families Act 1989: Report on its first year of operation.* Wellington, NZ: Department of Social Welfare.

Robertson, J. (1996). Research on family group conferences in New Zealand. In J. Hudson, A. Morris, G. Maxwell, & B. Galaway (Eds.), *Family group conferences: Perspectives on policy and practice.* Monsey, NY: Willow Tree Press.

Swain, P. (1993). *Safe in our hands: The evaluation report of family decision-making project.* Melbourne, Australia: Mission of St. James and St. John.

II

DOING AN EVALUATION

Part II contains four chapters that illustrate the four basic forms of program evaluations. All of these chapters present how to do their respective evaluations in a step by step approach. Chapter 5 describes how to do a needs assessment within our profession and discusses how these are used for developing new social services as well as refining existing ones. It highlights the four types of social needs within the context of social problems.

Once a social service program is up and running, Chapter 6 presents how we can do process evaluations within the program in an effort to refine the services that clients receive and to maintain program's fidelity. It highlights the purposes of process evaluations and places a great deal of emphasis on how to decide what questions the evaluation will answer.

Chapter 7 discusses the need for doing outcome evaluations within social service programs. It highlights the need for developing a solid monitoring system for the evaluation process.

Once an outcome evaluation is done, social service programs can use efficiency evaluations to monitor their cost-effectiveness/benefits—the topic of Chapter 8. This chapter highlights the cost-benefit approach to efficiency evaluation and also describes in detail the cost-effectiveness approach.

In sum, Part II clearly acknowledges that there are many forms that evaluations can take within social service agencies and presents four of the most common ones. Each chapter builds on the previous one.

Doing a Needs Assessment

Assessment is a key step in any change process where social workers are involved. A **needs assessment** is particularly useful for informing program change efforts, such as starting a new program or making revisions to an existing program. Ultimately, a basic needs assessment can benefit program administrators and practitioners who are faced with the task of trying to establish, with some degree of certainty, that a social need actually exists and ultimately that the establishment of a social service program will address the identified need. There is no one way to conduct a needs assessment, and many definitions of needs assessments exist. For example, a needs assessment has been defined as

- A tool used for identifying what a particular group of people is lacking, which prevents them from achieving more satisfying lives (Reviere, Berkowitz, Carter, & Ferguson, 1996).
- A planning device that "determines whether to embark upon or enhance specific programs . . . which determines how well recipients of services react to them" (Ginsberg, 2001).
- A process for pinpointing reasons for gaps in performance or a method for identifying new and future performance needs (Gupta, 1999).
- A systematic approach to identifying social problems, determining their extent, and accurately defining the target population to be served and the nature of their service needs (Rossi, Lipsey, & Freeman, 2003).

Needs assessments Program-level evaluation activities that aim to assess the feasibility for establishing or continuing a particular social service program; an evaluation that aims to assess the need for a human service by verifying that a social problem exists within a specific client population to an extent that warrants services.

121

What Are Needs Assessments?

As the different definitions illustrate, needs assessments involve gathering information that ultimately will be used to match clients' needs with social service programs that will help them with their needs. Ideally, a needs assessment is conducted before establishing any new social service or program. However, a needs assessment can generate information that is used to aid planning efforts at all stages of a program's development—start up, expansion, renovation, or closure of particular "services" within a program (see the left-hand side of Figure 4.8).

Needs assessment for an existing program is particularly helpful when there is a poor fit between client need and existing services. Signs of poor fit are indicated when services are made available to clients but not used, when a program's outcome measures fail to show any client benefit, or when client dissatisfaction about the nature or type of services is expressed. Thus, not all needs assessments are done *before* a social service program is established. In a **nutshell**, Weinbach (2005) lists six indicators that can trigger a needs assessment in an existing social service program:

Nutshell

An expression used by advanced evaluation experts.

1. Changes that occur in the community.
2. Changes in "the competition."
3. Changes in understanding of the problem.
4. Changes in intervention technology.
5. Changes in funding.
6. Changes in mandates.

Regardless of when a needs assessment is carried out (before the program or after it), there are three interrelated concepts that are important to understanding the general framework of the needs assessment process:

1. A social problem must be perceived by people.
2. People then must translate the "social problem" into a need.
3. A solution (usually in the form of a social service program) is identified to address the need.

In other words, needs assessments are much more than establishing that social problems exist (e.g., child prostitution, drug abuse, or discrimination); they also aim to establish needs and identify solutions to fulfilling those needs.

Social Problems

Social problem

An occurrence or event that is undesired by most of our society.

Defining a **social problem** is no simple matter. The definition of a social problem depends on one's construction of reality. In other words, any definition of a social problem is connected to the perspective of the individuals creating the definition.

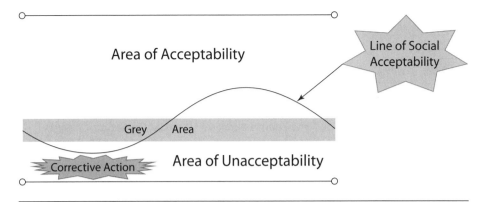

Figure 5.1 Line of social acceptability that defines social problems in society.

Nevertheless, most people will accept that a social problem is an occurrence or event that is undesired by most or all of our society. They also must believe that the problem is changeable through social service **interventions** (Peper, 2003).

Some social problems present a visible and real threat to how society is organized and to what people believe is necessary for a basic level of well-being. Citizens displaced by a natural disaster, parents abusing their children, high rates of unemployment, overt racism, abject poverty in U.S. communities, and people committing suicide are examples of social problems that are presented in the media, have books written about them, and generally have been given a great deal of attention.

These visible problems have been the traditional focus of our profession for over a century. As shown in Figure 5.1, our society has drawn a minimum line of acceptability for many of these visible social problems. Once the line is crossed—the physical abuse of a child is exposed, a teenager is caught selling drugs, a racist statement is made by a politician—there is some societal action that takes place.

Generally, the more visible the social problem, the more likely it is that individuals will take action. Table 5.1 provides a list of four crude indicators that can be used to assess whether an individual is willing to "stand up" for a "social problem." Generally speaking, the more indicators that are present, the more concern an individual will have about a problem.

Other less explicit problems do not have a definite bottom-line to indicate when and what action ought to take place. Children with behavior problems, individuals with low self-esteem, poverty, and unfair employment policies are only examples of problems where the line of social acceptability falls within the grey area of society (see Figure 5.1). Consequently, these problems are less likely to receive the assistance of public or grant monies unless they are paired with more visible needs, as is the case when "prevention" measures are discussed; that is, the focus is to establish a connection between an identified problem and preventing a subsequent undesired outcome.

Interventions
The theoretical approach social workers use to create planned change.

Table 5.1 Four Indicators of a Social Problem's Visibility

Applies?			
Yes	No	*Indicator*	*Description*
☐	☐	*Proximity:*	The physical distance between a person and the problem. For example, residents living in substandard rental accommodations are more likely to identify corrupt landlords as a problem than are residents living in adequate or superior housing conditions.
☐	☐	*Intimacy:*	The level of personal familiarity with the problem, or the extent that you are personally affected by the problem. For example, someone close to you is hit by a drunk driver or afflicted by a fatal disease.
☐	☐	*Awareness:*	The degree to which a problem has a presence in your daily thoughts. It is possible to have awareness of a problem without being intimately affected by it. For example, Hurricane Katrina hit Louisiana, Mississippi, and Alabama in 2005 and woke America up to the conditions of poverty in these areas as well as the limitations of the government to execute an immediate response to the large-scale crisis.
☐	☐	*Magnitude:*	The scale or enormity of the condition. In other words, the more people affected by a condition, the more public attention the problem receives.

Take children with behavior problems, for example. These children, more than children without behavior problems, are likely to experience problems at home, at school, and in the community. Because child behavior problems can be disruptive to family relationships, classroom instruction, and community harmony, children experiencing such problems can be at risk for out-of-home placement, academic failure, and delinquency. Thus, to highlight the problems of childhood behavior problems, we might discuss their importance in terms of preventing foster-care placement, school dropouts, and crime. These latter issues are more likely to capture the public's attention than the general problem of children with behavior problems.

SOCIAL NEEDS

Social need

A basic requirement necessary to sustain the human condition.

A need is inextricably linked to a social problem since a need is a social problem translated into concrete goods or services *needed* to address the problem. As illustrated in Table 5.2, a social problem can be translated into various needs. At a minimum, a **social need** can be thought of as a basic requirement necessary to sustain the human condition, to which people have a right. For example, few in our society would dispute that people have the right to food and clean water.

Table 5.2 Example of Translating the Same Social Problem Into Different Needs

Social Problem	⇒	Need
Family poverty	⇒	Food for basic nutrition
Family poverty	⇒	Money to purchase basic goods
Family poverty	⇒	Job to support family

However, there is debate on how the basic need for food should be defined. Some would argue that only direct food supplies should be given to families in need. Others would say that financial assistance should be provided to ensure that families can take care of their unique needs. Still others would argue that the need is to help parents of poor families find living-wage jobs to provide them with sustainable incomes. Like the definition of social problems, the translation of problems into needs is subject to the individual views of how different people view "reality."

A popular framework for assessing human social needs is Abraham Maslow's (1999) Hierarchy of Human Needs, shown in Figure 5.2. The physiological needs, shown at the base of the pyramid, represent the most basic conditions—food, water, shelter, and clothing—needed to sustain human life. Maslow's theory tells us that unless these foundational needs are met, a person will not grow or move to higher levels of well-being. In fact, the notion of hierarchy means that people must fulfill their needs at a lower level before they are able to move up the hierarchy, to higher levels of the pyramid. Security needs in Maslow's hierarchy represent the human desire for safety not only in the here and now but also in the future. When people fear for their safety, it interferes with their social needs at the next level of the pyramid. In other words, without a sense of security, one's social needs such as love, friendship, and connection with others cannot be fully met. Ego or esteem needs are at the next level and go beyond basic social relations to a sense of belonging in a social group in a way that adds to one's self-identify. Ego or esteem needs also reflect the desire to be recognized for one's accomplishments. Finally, self-actualization, which is at the tip-top of the pyramid, is possible only when all other needs have been satisfied. People are said to be self-actualized when they reach their full potential as human beings. This full potential may be expressed through many arenas, such as in music, business, or humanitarian causes.

The framework for Maslow's hierarchy can be applied to human needs in many different contexts. An Internet search using "Maslow's Hierarchy" combined with a second key search term such as "family," "community," "organization," or "education" will yield Web sites that apply the model to people living and working in these different environments. Overall, Maslow's Hierarchy of Human Needs is a helpful tool to prioritize needs in relation to particular social problems. However, need is a dynamic

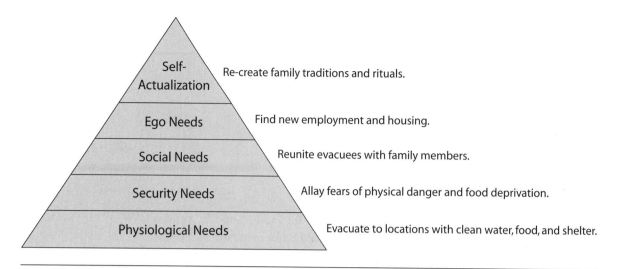

Figure 5.2 Maslow's hierarchy of human needs as applied to survivors of Hurricane Katrina.

concept and can be conceived of from multiple perspectives. The following four sections summarize four types of need presented by Kettner, Moroney, and Martin (in press); all four types are helpful to both program planning and evaluation efforts: (1) perceived need, (2) normative need, (3) relative need, and (4) expressed need.

Perceived Needs

Perceived needs

In needs assessment, the opinions and views of people who are not directly experiencing a problem themselves.

Also referred to as "felt" need, **perceived need** offers the perspective of individuals or groups about a problem at a particular point in time. Because individual views can (and do) change, perceived needs can be unstable. Furthermore, the perceived need may differ dramatically because need is defined in the eye of the beholder. Prison inmates, for example, may protest the removal of television sets from their cells, thereby demanding that television is a necessary part of their recreational needs. The public, on the other hand, may not see a need for inmates to have access to television sets and might feel that the basic recreational outlets of inmates can be met through various educational magazines and radio programming.

Normative Needs

Normative need

A need that implies that there exists a standard to which a need can be compared.

A **normative need** implies that there exists a standard with which a need can be compared. Need is then "calculated," usually from existing data, and the extent or magnitude of the need is numerically expressed as a ratio. For example, accreditation standards may dictate the size of a social worker's caseload to be no greater than one worker to 15 clients—a ratio of 1:15. A program reporting a caseload ratio of

1:30 could use this normative need to illustrate a concern about its service quality and/or to argue for additional program resources.

Relative Needs

A **relative need** also involves making a comparison, but no assumption of a normative standard exists. Instead, the need of one group is weighed against another comparable group. For example, Pecora and colleagues (2005) have shown the need for educational support after children in foster care leave the system. They reported that only 1.8% of young adults (25 to 34 years of age) that formerly lived in foster care had completed a bachelor's degree. They also argued that this figure was significantly lower than 27.5%, which was the rate of completing a bachelor's degree among the general population of the same age. This example shows the need of the general population relative to a sub-population. Many other relative comparisons are possible such as geography (e.g., one county versus another), time (e.g., this year versus last year), or program (public versus private agencies).

Relative need
The need of one group is weighed against the need for another comparable group.

Expressed Needs

An **expressed need** accounts for the degree to which a need is met or unmet by reporting the "demand statistics" related to a particular program, service, or event. In other words, the expressed need tells us how many (or what percentage of) clients from a targeted group successfully obtain available services. A more difficult figure to report is the number (or percentage) of the targeted group that fails to access services. For example, despite the fact that Hispanic people comprise the largest and most rapidly growing minority group in the United States, there have been consistent reports of low numbers of Hispanic peoples accessing essential services such as health, social service, and education.

Low expressed need may be an indication that an existing social service is a poor fit with the identified client need. On the other hand, other mediating factors may be the problem. For instance, isolating language and cultural barriers, or lack of awareness about services are possible reasons that help to explain the low levels of expressed need by Hispanic groups. In this case, Hispanic people may want, even demand, more services but are not accessing them because of language or other barriers.

Expressed need
An indicator that tells us how many clients from a targeted group successfully obtain a social service.

PROGRAM SOLUTIONS

As an agency-based profession, social work **solutions** to social problems and needs most typically come in the form of policies or programs that are aimed at improving

Solution
The results of solving a problem.

Table 5.3 Relationship Among Problems, Needs, and Program Solutions

Problem		Need		Program Solution
Problem	$\Rightarrow$	*Need*	$\Rightarrow$	*Program Solution*
Family poverty	$\Rightarrow$	Food for children's nutrition	$\Rightarrow$	Food bank
Family poverty	$\Rightarrow$	Money to purchase basic goods	$\Rightarrow$	Public assistance
Family poverty	$\Rightarrow$	Job to support family	$\Rightarrow$	Job training

the quality of life for people. This can be done either by proposing an existing social service program in a location where it has not previously been provided, or by suggesting new or alternative services where other services may not have proved to be adequate.

With a focus on social justice and concern for vulnerable populations, most of us are employed by programs that target foundational human needs—physiological, security, and social as shown in Table 5.2. In Chapter 3 we covered the structure of social service programs in detail. In this chapter we emphasize that every program is in fact a solution that is designed to resolve a social problem by addressing a specific need(s).

Table 5.3 displays an example of the interrelatedness between problems, needs, and program solutions; it illustrates how one problem can generate multiple needs as well as different program solutions. Clearly, a needs assessment can generate multiple perspectives for defining problems, needs, and solutions. Indeed, a primary aim of a needs assessment is to find the best match.

STEPS IN DOING A NEEDS ASSESSMENT

As previously mentioned, the main purpose of all needs assessments is to determine the nature, scope, and locale of a social problem (if one exists) and to identify a feasible, useful, and relevant solution(s) to the problem(s). In a nutshell, the ultimate goal of all needs assessments is to improve the human condition by identifying a social problem, translating that problem into a need, and proposing a solution, as shown in Table 5.3.

Like all types of evaluations, needs assessments achieve their purpose through well-established evaluative methods. As was pointed out earlier in the various definitions presented, needs assessment is nothing more than applied research efforts, typically done to examine a social problem within a defined geographical area. Like any other type of evaluation, the steps used to carry them out must be clearly documented so other interested parties can evaluate the study's credibility. And, because there is a great deal of flexibility in conducting any needs assessment, we must have a clear rationale for each step taken.

As with all types of evaluations, needs assessments do not develop out of thin air. They are born out of gaps in existing social services (or lack of them), public

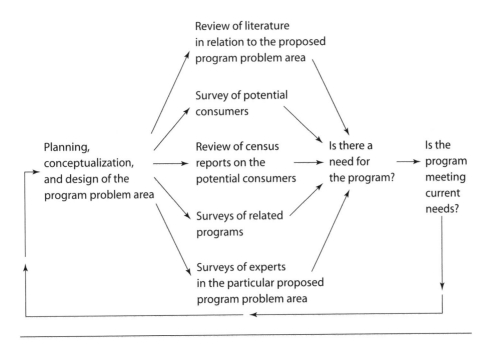

Figure 5.3 Generic process of a needs assessment.

unrest, landmark cases, fluctuations in political and economic conditions, and changes in basic demographic trends. As such, the initial steps of conducting a needs assessment are in some ways predetermined.

A director of a family social service agency, for example, may notice that attendance at its parent support groups is low. The director then requests the line-level workers within the program to ask parents about the attendance problem and to see if there are any concerns about access to the program. Or a child may be abducted from a public school ground during the lunch hour and an inquiry may be called to look into the general safety of children and supervision practices at all public schools. A third scenario could be that the number of street panhandlers may be perceived to be growing, so a municipal task force is formed to learn more about "the problem" and to decide what action, if any, the city should take. These examples illustrate that, once a needs assessment begins, a certain amount of momentum has already been established. Nevertheless, we must be able to take a step back and see if we have used a well thought out evaluation approach in examining the perceived need.

Although the entire process of conducting a needs assessment, as outlined in Figure 5.3, requires a certain amount of knowledge, skill, and finesse (Smith, 1990), the process can be summarized into six highly interrelated steps: (1) focusing the problem, (2) developing needs assessment questions, (3) identifying targets for intervention, (4) developing a data collection plan, (5) analyzing and displaying data, and (6) disseminating and communicating findings.

Step 1: Focusing the Problem

As we alluded to in our earlier discussion, needs and their tentative solutions are subject to politics, trends, biases, and opinions. The climate surrounding a particular social problem can support or supplant our efforts to ascertain whether a social need really exists, or which needs are given priority. Examples of events that can influence a needs assessment are political elections, heightened awareness of a social problem by the local media, lobbying from interest groups about a particular social problem, and economic change.

Before we start a needs assessment, we must give considerable thought to how a particular social problem is to be defined. As we know, a needs assessment has three components: specific social problem(s), social need(s) and possible solution(s). How we define a specific social problem has a major impact on the types of **data** that we gather and how we proceed in collecting the data. Our definition of the social problem also has a great deal of influence on our proposed solutions to resolve the problem. Thus, it is imperative to consider the social problem first and then, and only then, consider the scope of possible solutions to help solve the problem.

Suppose, for example, a runaway shelter for teens reports that it is filled to capacity and is turning away runaways on a regular basis. It is tempting for a novice to declare that more shelter space is needed to accommodate the teens who are being turned away. In turn, the solution is to expand the runaway shelter space. Has the problem been fixed? No! We must step back a bit more and ask more thoughtful questions such as

- Who are the teens using the shelter?
- What are the teens running away from?
- When are teen runaways most likely to show up at the shelter?

The answers to these questions may suggest that providing more space is not the solution to "the problem." A crisis counseling program could be added to the shelter, for example, to help teens negotiate with their parents to return home or arrange to stay with friends or relatives. There are many more possible solutions, as well. Clearly, the definition of a need (social problem) is crystallized by the assumptions and questions we ask about it.

Step 2: Developing Needs Assessment Questions

The type of questions asked in a needs assessment can shift the study's initial focus to a different direction. Let us suppose Paula, a social worker, wants to examine a specific social problem such as rising delinquency rates in the rural town where she lives and works.

Data
Isolated facts, presented in numerical or descriptive form, on which client or program decisions are based; not to be confused with information.

She could ask *youth-focused* questions:

- Do youth perceive that they are a part of the community?
- What do the youths perceive their role in the community to be?

She could ask *family-focused* questions:

- Are parents aware of their children's whereabouts and activities?
- Do parents feel they are responsible for their children's behavior in the community?

She could ask *legal* questions:

- How are status offenses defined?
- Are the penalties for juvenile crime adequate?

She could ask *intervention* questions:

- Is the probationary system able to accommodate the current number of juvenile delinquents?

Each of the above types of questions (i.e., youth, family, legal, and intervention) frame the social problem from a different angle. They also imply different needs and that a different intervention approach is warranted. The youth-focused questions suggest solutions such as a campaign for recognizing the roles that youth play in the community. The family-focused questions hint that parent training and education might be in order. The legal questions target change for legislation, and the intervention questions shift focus to the operations of existing social services. In short, it is always necessary to examine the problem from many different possible dimensions, or we run the risk of offering biased solutions.

Other considerations for developing needs assessment questions are

- Is the social problem acute or chronic?
- Is the problem one of long standing or one that was brought about by some recent change?

A list of possible questions to guide Paula's needs assessment for her rural town is presented in Box 5.1. Questions 1 and 2 were designed to find out more about the social problems, if any, within the community. Questions 3 to 6 were specifically geared toward possible solutions to the problems.

Step 3: Identifying Targets for Intervention (Unit of Analysis)

As we have seen, how a social problem is defined is clearly influenced by a multitude of factors. The specific definition of need, however, is clarified by developing questions that guide the remaining steps of a needs assessment. The final questions

1. With what social problems or issues are area residents confronted?
2. What perceptions do residents have regarding their community?
3. What types of services are viewed by residents as being important?
4. Which services are needed most?
5. To what extent are residents satisfied with the present level of social services in town?
6. Is there a transportation problem for residents who use services that are available in Calgary?

developed are particularly useful in telling us who, or what, will be the target for the proposed solution(s), or proposed social service program(s).

Establishing Target Parameters

Targets for intervention can take many forms. In reviewing the questions contained within Paula's needs assessment, for example, her target was the residents living in her rural town; that is, she was interested in what townspeople thought about their community, the social problems they experienced (if any), and the social services that were available to them. She simply used a geographical boundary to define her target for intervention.

All targets for intervention ultimately involve individuals, groups, organizations, and communities. In each case, it is necessary to develop explicit criteria so that there is no question as to who a target is, or is not. Criteria that help define targets often include things such as

- *Demographics,* such as age, gender, race, and socioeconomic status.
- *Membership in predefined groups,* such as families, professional work teams, and members in an organization.
- *Conditions,* such as people receiving public assistance, residents of low-cost housing, and hospice clients.

Once a target for an intervention is defined, it can be tackled directly or indirectly. Proposed solutions can include direct services through social service programs established for the specified target. If we defined adolescents between 12 and 17 years of age who are at risk for alcohol and drug abuse (the target), for example, we might suggest that outreach services (the intervention) be established to reach them at their "hangouts," such as a nearby shopping mall.

On the other hand, complementary to direct solutions are indirect solutions, which focus on changing policies and procedures that, in turn, affect the target. A possible indirect solution could be to institute a policy that increases the legal consequences (the intervention) for teens who are caught using drugs or alcohol (the target).

It should be clear by now that how we define a social need and pose needs assessment questions can influence the eventual target for an intervention. In the case of Paula's needs assessment, for example, she targeted the residents in her town because they were all considered potential users of social services. Another strategy might have been to target existing social service agencies (organizations) or specific neighborhoods (communities). She could have targeted the social services by asking questions such as

- What is the profile of clients currently served?
- Do social service programs have waiting lists?
- How many clients are turned away because of inadequate resources?
- How many clients asked for services that were not available? What are these services?

Targeting neighborhoods may have led Paula to examine the number and type of social problems in each neighborhood. She could then have asked questions such as

- What concerns do neighborhood residents have about the local area they live in?
- What were the existing social services in each neighborhood?
- What, if any, informal helping services existed in each neighborhood?

By selecting a different target and developing different needs assessment questions, Paula could have completely changed the direction of her study.

Sampling (Data Sources)

Defining a target logically leads us to defining our data sources; that is, who (or what) we will collect data from (see Chapter 10). Therefore, it is necessary to apply basic **sampling** principles if our study's findings are to have any generalizability. In order to have this generalizability, however, we need to have a representative sample of data sources. For now, let's take a closer look at how Paula arrived at a representative sample for the residents of her town (her target).

Sampling
The selection of a number of "study subjects" from a defined study population.

Paula defined the pool of residents who were eligible to participate in her needs assessment study. She defined the parameters of her sampling frame as all people over 18 years of age who resided within the town's borders. Although it may have been useful to collect data from youth as well (those under 18 years of age), it also adds to the expense of actually carrying out the needs assessment. It may be that other local organizations (e.g., a school or community center) may recently have conducted a similar or related survey with this younger age group. If so, it might be possible for Paula to use the existing survey information related to the younger group. Thus, her needs assessment efforts would be better spent targeting the older group.

Suppose that the population of Paula's town was a little over 2,000 people; it would be necessary for Paula to use random sampling procedures to select her sample of people. The size of Paula's sample would be influenced by time, money, resources, and the various possibilities on how to collect her data (Step 4). To gather a random sample, Paula obtained a complete list of the town's residents from the electric company, as everyone in the county is billed for electricity use. She then took a random sample of 300 people from this list.

When deciding whom to include in the pool of data sources, we want to cast our net as far as possible. Ideally, we want to choose from everyone who fits within the boundaries of those who we have defined as a target.

Step 4: Developing a Data Collection Plan

As we will see in Chapter 10, there is a critical distinction between a data collection method and a data source, which must be clearly understood before developing a viable **data collection plan**—the purpose of Step 4. A data collection method consists of a detailed plan of procedures that aims to gather data for a specific purpose—that is, to answer our needs assessment question(s). There are various data collection methods available: reviewing existing reports, secondary data analyses, individual interviews, group interviews, and telephone and mail surveys. Each data collection method can be used with a variety of data sources, which are defined by who (or what) supplies the data. Data can be provided by a multitude of sources, including people, existing records, and existing databases. (See Table 10.3 for a variety of data collection methods.)

Before we discuss the various data collection methods, we must remember once again that a need assessment has two parts: the social problem and the proposed solution. Thus, it is important to collect data for each part. If we collect data only about the potential social problem(s), for example, then we can only guess at the potential solution(s). If Paula asked only Questions 1 and 2 (see Box 5.1), she would not have gathered any data to help decide what ought to be done about the social problems that the townspeople identified. Alternatively, if she only asked Questions 3 through 6 (see Box 5.1), she would have data to determine only what the residents think about the social services in their community and would not have a clear indication about what social problems they perceive to exist, if any.

It should be clear by now that how a needs assessment question is defined guides the selection of the data collection method(s). This seemingly unimportant fact is actually quite critical in developing the best possible needs assessment. We must be careful not to subscribe to any one data collection plan in an effort to change our needs assessment questions to fit a preferred data collection method and/or data source. Put simply, the combination of data collection method(s) and data source(s) that we choose influences the nature and type of data collected. Therefore, it is important that well thought out and meaningful questions are developed before plans to collect the data are set in stone.

Data collection plan

Procedures specifying techniques to be employed, measuring instruments to be used, and activities to be conducted in implementing an evaluation.

Data analysis

The process of turning data into information; the process of reviewing, summarizing, and organizing isolated facts (data) such that they formulate a meaningful response to a research question.

How we go about collecting data to answer needs assessment questions depends on many practical considerations such as how much time, money, and political support is available at the time of the study. Financial resources are usually limited, so it is worthwhile to begin a study using data that were previously collected by someone else. If existing data are not adequate to answer the needs assessment questions, then new data must be collected. To gain a broader understanding of the needs being examined, it is worthwhile to use numerous multiple data collection methods and data sources.

There are many different ways to collect data for a needs assessment. The needs assessment questions posed in Step 2 of Paula's study can be tackled in a variety of ways. The approach eventually taken shapes the type of data collected and influences the flavor of the study's results. As mentioned, we can make use of data that already exist, or collect new data when none exist. There are many ways to collect data, as presented in Table 10.3. We will only present five of them: (1) reviews of existing reports, (2) secondary data analyses, (3) individual interviews, (4) group interviews, and (5) telephone and mail surveys.

Reviewing Existing Reports

Reviewing existing reports is a process whereby we closely examine data and information that are presented in existing materials such as published research studies, government documents, news releases, social service agency directories, agency annual reports, minutes of important meetings, and related surveys, to name a few. The data provided from these many existing sources are generally descriptive and in the form of words.

Raw data may be presented in these existing sources, but most are presented in the form of information. That is, someone else has interpreted the data and drawn conclusions from them. Paula, for example, could have accessed information about her particular community through professional journals and government reports. She might also have had access to another needs assessment conducted in a neighboring town. At first glance, reviewing existing reports might seem like a time-consuming academic task, but it can be a real time-saver in the long run.

By looking over what others have already done, we can save valuable time by learning from their mistakes and avoid unnecessarily reinventing of the wheel. By taking the time to review existing documentation and reports at her town's planning office, for example, Paula would be able to narrow the focus of her study by asking more specific questions, which she addressed in Step 2.

Data and information gleaned from existing published reports and articles provide us with a picture of how much attention our "social problem" has previously received. What other similar studies have been undertaken? In Paula's study, for example, she found that town residents had been polled about their opinions in the past. The town had previously commissioned two other community assessment projects—the first assessed social needs and the second focused on housing and public transportation needs. In short, these types of reports provided her with a starting point to refine her needs assessment study in an effort to make it more useful to the townspeople.

Secondary Data Analyses

Secondary data analysis

An unobtrusive data collection method in which available data that predate the formulation of an evaluation are used to answer the evaluation question.

A **secondary data analysis** differs from the process of reviewing existing reports in that it involves working with raw data. The data, however, have typically been collected for some other purpose than answering our needs assessment question(s). Two common types of secondary data that are used in answering needs assessment questions are census data and client and/or program data.

Census data

A periodic governmental count of a population using demographic measurements.

Census Data. **Census data** are periodic summaries of selected demographic characteristics, or variables, that describe a population. Census takers obtain data about variables such as age, gender, marital status, and race. To obtain data in specific topic areas, census takers sometimes obtain data for variables like income level, education level, employment status, and presence of disabilities. Census data are extremely useful for a needs assessment that compares its sample with the target population. Census data for Paula's rural town, for example, showed that the city had doubled in size very quickly.

In addition to reporting how many residents lived in the town, the census data also provided a demographic profile of city residents (e.g., number of people employed and unemployed, the number and ages of children living in single-parent and double-parent families, and the length of time people had lived in the city). Thus, Paula could compare the characteristics of her 300-person sample (drawn from the town's electric company's files) with that of the city's total population (over 2,000). Census data also are useful for providing a general picture of a certain population at a certain point in time.

The more data obtained during a census, the more detailed the description of the population. The disadvantage of census data is that they can become outdated quickly. Census surveys occur every 10 years and take considerable time to compile, analyze, and distribute. In addition, they give only a "general picture" of a population. Census data, for example, provide data only on the average age of residents in a community or the percentage of childless couples living in a certain area. Although these data are useful for developing an "average community profile," they do not provide us with a clear idea of individual differences or how individual members of the community describe themselves.

Client data

In evaluation, measurements systematically collected from clients of social service programs; ideally, data are collected in strict compliance with the evaluation design and procedures.

Program data

In evaluation, measurements systematically collected about a program's operations. Ideally, the data are collected in strict compliance with the evaluation design and procedures.

Client and Program Data. Two other data sources that can be used for a secondary data analysis are existing client files and program records. More and more social work programs produce informal reports that describe the services they provide. They most likely use **client data** taken from intake forms and client files (e.g., see Figure 11.3). **Program data** typically provide information about the demographic profile of clients served and the nature of the referral problems.

Simply counting the number of individuals served by a particular program provides us with data from which to calculate how big the problem is relative to a specified time period, or for a particular client group. Programs might keep data on the number of clients turned away because they were full and/or the number of clients who were unwilling to be placed on a waiting list.

Client-related data are useful for needs assessments that focus on specific problem areas. If, for example, Paula's study focused specifically on the problems with teenage drug and alcohol abuse, she could have accessed programs serving this particular population and likely determined who the clients were based on these recorded data. If this was so, the following two questions could have been asked:

- Were the teens mostly males or females?
- How old were the teens who were receiving social services?

The disadvantages of using data from social service programs are, first, that they are not always complete or consistently recorded, and second, the data apply only to clients of a single program and do not tell us about teens who received services elsewhere or who were not receiving any help at all.

Individual Interviews

Face-to-face discussion with key informants produce new, or original, **interview data**. Interviewing key informants is a strategy that requires us to identify, approach, and interview specific people who are considered knowledgeable about the social problem we are interested in. **Key informants** are leaders in their community and include professionals, public officials, agency directors, social service clients, and select citizens, to name a few.

Our interviews can be formal, and use a structured interview schedule, in which case we could ask all six questions in Box 5.1. If we would like to obtain more detailed data, we could develop questions that help us probe for more specific and detailed answers. In Question 4 in Box 5.1, for example, Paula could have also asked her key informants to consider services in the past and present, or gaps in services.

On the other hand, when very little is known about our problem area, we can use informal unstructured interviews to permit more of a free-flowing discussion. Informal interviews involve more dialogue, in which questions we ask are generated by the key informants themselves. If, after interviewing a small number of key informants, Paula consistently hears people express concerns about crime in the city, she may develop more specific questions to probe this social problem.

Key Informants. To help Paula define the parameters for her study she used the key informant approach to interviewing at the beginning of her needs assessment study. This strategy was advantageous because it permitted her to gather data about the needs and services that were viewed as important by city officials and representatives of social

Interview data

Isolated facts that are gathered when research participants respond to carefully constructed research questions; data, which are in the form of words, are recorded by transcription.

Key informants

A subpopulation of research participants who seem to know much more about "the situation" than other research participants.

service programs. She was able to gather data about the nature of the social problems in the community and what specific groups of people faced these problems. Because Paula talked with public officials and people directly involved in the social services, she also was able to get some indication about what concerns might become future issues.

In addition, she got a glimpse of the issues that community leaders were more likely to support or oppose. Other advantages of interviewing key informants are that it is easy to do and relatively inexpensive. Moreover, because they involve interviewing community leaders, the interviews can be a valuable strategy for gaining support from these people.

One disadvantage of the key informant approach to data collection is that the views of the people interviewed may not give an objective picture of the needs being investigated. A key informant, for example, may be biased and provide a skewed picture of the nature of the social problem and potential solution. Another drawback with key informant interviews occurs when we fail to select a good cross section of people. In Paula's study, for example, she was interested in learning about the range of social problems that the community was experiencing. If she had interviewed only professionals who worked only with delinquent youth or elderly populations, then she would have run the risk of hearing more about only these two social problems.

Group Interviews

A group interview is a data collection method that permits us to gather the perspectives of several individuals at one time. It is more complex than individual interviews because it involves interaction between and among data sources (the group members). Three strategies for structuring group interviews for needs assessments are focus groups, nominal group techniques, and public forums.

Focus group interview
A group of people brought together to talk about their lives and experiences in free-flowing, open-ended discussions that usually focus on a single topic.

Focus Groups. Like key informant interviews, **focus groups** collect new, or original, data on a specific topic from a selection of individuals who are reasonably familiar with the topic. Box 5.2 presents the steps for performing a focus group. The people within the groups are not necessarily familiar with each other. Focus groups are usually semi-structured and often held in informal community settings where the group members are relaxed and comfortable in sharing their views and knowledge.

If we were to hold a focus group for a needs assessment, for example, we would act as the group leader, provide some guidelines for the group process, and facilitate the dialogue for group members. We would prepare in advance a list of questions to ask group members and to give some direction to the discussion. Again, Paula used the six questions in Box 5.1 in her needs assessment as a guide for her focus groups.

Our main task in conducting a focus group is to facilitate discussion and to keep group members centered on the questions being asked. Because we want to capture the divergent and similar views expressed in a focus group, we have several important tasks that must be considered.

Box 5.2 Steps for Doing Focus Groups

- Plan the sessions. Determine the information needed, the categories of participants, the timing, location, and other administrative details of the sessions.
- Select a facilitator who is experienced in conducting focus groups to manage the meeting and a person to take notes on the information provided by participants.
- Invite 8 to 12 current and former clients to each focus group meeting. Members can be chosen from lists of clients without regard to the statistical representation of the selection. The main selection criteria are that the participants be familiar with the program and be at least somewhat varied in their characteristics.
- Set a maximum of two hours. Hold the meeting in a pleasant and comfortable location. Soft drinks and snacks help provide a relaxed atmosphere.
- Begin with introductions and an overview of the purpose of the meeting.
- Have the facilitator ask the participants three questions:

  1. What do you like about the service?
  2. What don't you like about the service?
  3. In what ways has the service helped you?

  The facilitator can ask these questions in many different ways. The fundamental requirement is to establish an open, unthreatening environment and to obtain input from each participant.
- Obtain a meeting report. The recorder and the facilitator should work together to provide the meeting report, which should identify outcome-related characteristics raised explicitly or implicitly by one or more participants. The program should consider tracking these characteristics.

First, we not only want to ensure that group members are comfortable, we want them to have clear expectations regarding why we are talking with them. Comfort can be increased by simple gestures of providing beverages and snacks, providing comfortable seating, and so on. Clarity of the task is ensured when meaningful and well thought out questions are prepared in advance and we offer a clear description of what we expect from the group.

Second, we need to record what group members say. The most accurate way of recording the discussion is to have it audiotaped and later transcribed. A second option is to bring a notetaker to the meeting who has the responsibility of writing down what people say.

Paula used focus groups that included community leaders, social service professionals, and selected groups of residents (e.g., elderly, parents, and youth). The major advantages of focus groups are similar to those of using key informants. However, because a group process is used, focus group interviews are perhaps even more efficient than individual interviews. The disadvantages, of course, are that we have less opportunity to explore the perspectives of individuals, and members are subject to the "groupthink" process.

Nominal group technique

A group of people brought together to share their knowledge about a specific social problem. The process is structured using a round-robin approach and permits individuals to share their ideas within a group but with little interaction between group members; a structured group interview.

Nominal Group Techniques. **Nominal group techniques** are useful data gathering tools for a needs assessment study because they can easily collect unbiased data from a group of people. The nominal group technique can identify problems in the development and planning of social service programs. The nominal group is composed of individuals who can answer a particular question of interest, and the process involves members working in the presence of others but with little structured interaction. For Paula's study, for example, she wanted to select and recruit city officials, professionals, and city residents who had an opinion or knowledge about her six needs assessment questions. In doing so, she implemented the following seven steps.

1. Paula developed open-ended questions that were the focus for the group. The questions sought to generate problem dimensions such as Question 1: What social problems or issues are area residents confronted with? This question could also focus on generating solutions, in which case she would propose Question 4: What services are needed most?

2. She selected and recruited group participants who had answers for her previously developed questions. Ideally, a nominal group has six to nine members. If there are considerably more, the technique can be used by forming smaller groups. Each group, or subgroup, should be seated comfortably and preferably in a circle.

3. Paula gathered the group together and gave an overview of the task. She gave each group member a sheet of paper with the questions written on it and explicit instructions that people were *not* to talk about their ideas with one another. She allowed about 15 minutes for the people to write down their responses privately.

4. Using a round-robin approach, she listed all answers generated in Step 3 on a flip chart. Because there was more than one group, each group listed their answers separately. The round robin continued until all responses were recorded. As in Step 3, this process was conducted without any discussion.

5. After all the responses were recorded on the flip charts, Paula engaged participants in some brief discussion about the responses listed. The discussion focused on clarifying what the responses meant so that everyone had a common understanding of each response.

6. Once all participants were familiar with the responses on the list, each person privately ranked the top five responses on an index card. These ranked lists were handed in and the popularity of responses was tallied on a flip chart. A second brief discussion was held to clarify any surprise rankings that occurred due to the misunderstanding of responses.

7. Paula ranked the responses so that the highest ranks reflected the social problems that were considered most important by the group members. If more specificity is desired, it is possible to rank the top responses, whereby another step of private rankings can occur.

The most obvious advantage of the nominal group technique for providing new data is that it promotes the sharing of ideas in an efficient manner. The nominal group process typically takes two to four hours, depending on the size of the group and the number of questions asked (the entire cycle is applied for each question). Because of the game-like nature of the technique, participants can find the experience fun. When a cross section of group participants is recruited, the process can yield a comprehensive response to needs assessment questions.

Public Forums. **Public forums,** as data collection methods, have far less structure than the other two methods of conducting group interviews. Holding a public forum involves inviting the general public to discuss matters that we wish to address in our needs assessment. A public forum can be a "town hall" meeting or even a phone-in radio talk show. It simply provides a place and an opportunity for people to assemble and air their thoughts and opinions about a specific social problem. Paula invited the general citizens and leaders within her rural town to share their views on the social needs of the community. The discussion was guided by her six needs assessment questions but was less structured than other approaches she used so far.

> **Public forum**
> A group of people invited to a public meeting to voice their views about a specific social problem; an unstructured group interview.

The public forum approach was used at the beginning of Paula's study to kick-start the needs assessment process. The advantage of public forums is that they offer widespread advertising of the entire process. Their main disadvantage is that they tend to draw a deliberate and select group of people who have strong opinions (in one way or another) that are not necessarily shared by the wider community. Suppose, for example, that Paula held a public forum shortly after several lay-offs had occurred within the local automotive industry. It is likely that her meeting would have been attended by many unemployed auto workers who, in addition to being concerned about community needs, had strong feelings about the loss of their jobs. When there is a strong unrest or when there is an intense political agenda in a community, public forums may exacerbate the problem.

Telephone and Mail Surveys

The main goal of telephone and mail **surveys** is to gather opinions from numerous people in order to describe them as a group. A survey contains a list of questions compiled in an effort to examine a social problem in detail; it can be conducted by telephone or through the mail. The method chosen depends on how many questions are asked and how many people are sampled. If we have only a few straightforward questions and a short time in which to collect data, it may be expedient to randomly select and interview people over the telephone. On the other hand, if our questions are more comprehensive, as was the case with Paula's study, and we have more time, it may be worthwhile to send out a mailed questionnaire.

> **Surveys**
> Used to gather opinions from numerous people in order to describe them as a group.

The survey approach in collecting original data was a good one to use for Paula's study because it permitted her to systematically obtain the views of the townspeople in a very direct way; that is, she obtained opinions about the community from the residents themselves. In addition, Paula constructed her survey questionnaire from the data she obtained from interviews with her key informants. This meant that the data she collected from the survey meshed with the data she obtained from her key informants.

There are also several disadvantages to surveys. First, surveys are more resource intensive than many other data collection methods. The costs of constructing an appropriate survey, mailing, photocopying, and hiring someone to telephone or input the data from a mailed survey can add up quickly. Second, mailed surveys have low response rates, and people do not always complete all the questions. Third, constructing a mailed survey questionnaire is a complex task. Developing a useful survey questionnaire takes a great deal of knowledge and time.

For Paula, the advantages outweighed the disadvantages and she opted to use a mailed survey. As a first step, Paula developed the mailed survey questionnaire. Because her task was to find out the community's needs, it was necessary for her to develop a survey that was directly relevant to the community. She tackled this task by examining other existing needs assessment mailed surveys, by reviewing relevant literature, and, most importantly, by talking to her key informants within the community.

Her mailed survey was carefully constructed so she could collect useful data about each of her questions. Her final survey was composed of seven sections: one for each of the six questions in Box 5.1 and an additional section to collect demographic data such as age, gender, marital status, employment status, income level, length of residence in the town, and the neighborhood in which people lived.

In sections addressing each of the six questions, respondents were asked to rate a number of statements using a predetermined measuring scale. Question 2, for example, aimed to find out how residents felt about living in the rural town. Respondents were also asked to rate statements such as "I enjoy living in this town" and "I feel that I am accepted by my community" on a 5-point scale, where 1 meant "strongly disagree" and 5 meant "strongly agree." To find out what services were needed most (Question 4), Paula listed a variety of social services (defined by her key informants) and asked respondents to rate the adequacy of the services. In this case, social services such as counseling for family problems, drop-in child care, and child protection services were listed. Respondents used a rating of 1 if they perceived the present level of the service to be "very inadequate" and 5 if they thought it was "very adequate." Because Paula anticipated that not all respondents would be familiar with all the social services in her town, she also included an "I don't know" response category.

The major part of her mailed survey required respondents to pick a number that best reflected their response to each question. Although Paula felt confident that she had covered all the critical areas necessary to fully answer her six questions, she also included an open-ended question at the end of the survey and instructed respondents to add any further comments or suggestions on the social services within the town. This allowed respondents an opportunity to provide commentary on some of the questions she asked and to voice any additional thoughts, ideas, beliefs, or opinions.

Because of her concern about the potentially low number of respondents to mailed surveys, Paula adopted several strategies to increase her response rate:

- A cover letter stating the purpose of her study sent with each mailed survey. The letter confirmed that all responses would be kept confidential and was signed by the town mayor and another city official.
- Extremely clear and simple instructions.
- A stamped, self-addressed return envelope included with the survey.
- Incentives to respondents in the form of a family pass to a nearby public swimming pool or skating arena and access to the study's results.
- A follow-up letter to all respondents as a prompt to complete the survey.
- Information about when the study's results would be publicized in the media.

Step 5: Analyzing and Displaying Data

Whether we use **existing data** or collect **original data,** there are several options on how to proceed when it comes to analyzing and displaying them. It is important to use a variety of strategies if we hope to develop a complete picture of the social need we are evaluating. As we have seen, no one method of data collection answers all that there is to know about a particular social need. With a little effort, however, it is possible to design a data collection strategy that will provide useful qualitative and/or quantitative data. In a nutshell, qualitative data take the form of words, while quantitative data take the form of numbers. Paula was working with qualitative data, when she examined archival reports from the town's Planning Commission and examined transcribed interviews. On the other hand, she was working with quantitative data when she computed respondents' numerical scores from her mailed survey.

Existing data

Data that exist now in some form or another.

Original data

Data that have never been collected before.

Collecting Quantitative Data

Organizing and displaying data using quantitative approaches simply means that we are concerned with amounts. **Quantitative data** are organized so that occurrences can be counted. Basic statistics books describe counting in terms of frequencies: How frequently does an event occur? For instance,

- How many families live at or below the poverty line?
- What percentage of people over the age of 65 require special medical services?
- How many families use the food bank in a given year?

If alcohol or drug use by teenagers was an important problem for Paula to consider, she would have counted the frequency of parents who perceive this as a problem

Quantitative data

Data that measure quantity or amount; usually expressed in numbers.

in the community. Frequencies are usually reported as percentages, which is a rate per 100. If 45 percent of parents in Paula's sample perceived teen drug use as a problem, for example, then we would expect that 45 out of 100 parents in the total population would agree.

Because needs assessments often consider social problems on a larger societal level, we often find statistics reported using rates that are based on 1,000, 100,000, or more. Census data, for example, may report, that 8 per 1,000 babies are born with fetal alcohol syndrome (FES) in a certain community. These rates provide us with even more information when we have something to compare them with. Suppose earlier census data reported that the rate of babies born with FES in the same community was 4 per 1,000. This means that the rate of FES has doubled between the two census reports. By making comparisons across time, we can look to the past, examine the present, and be in a better position to project into the future.

There are many other useful comparisons that can be made based on rates. Needs assessments can be used to compare a single specific situation with an established group norm. (A norm is an amount that we expect.) We compare a norm with what we actually find. In other words, we might expect (norm) that unemployment in the rural town is at 10 percent, whereas when counted it is actually at 20 percent (what we found). What we expect is usually defined by existing standards or cutoff points. We can think of these as markers that set a minimum standard for most people. The poverty line, basic services provided by public welfare, and unemployment rate are a few examples where a known cutoff score is set.

Comparisons can also be made across geographic boundaries. Paula, for example, examined the ratio of employed social workers to the number of citizens living in the town. By reviewing existing published reports, Paula learned that there were two social workers practicing in her town to serve the needs of over 2,000 people. The specific ratio of the number of social workers to the number of people was 1 to 1,058. Paula compared these data with ratios in other cities. She learned that a similar-sized city had four social workers serving a population of 2,557. The social-worker-to-population ratio in this other city was 1 to 639, which was about twice as high as that of her town. Paula was able to show a "relative need" for her community.

By comparing rates, we are in a better position to decide when a social problem is actually a problem. When counting problems in a needs assessment, we often report the incidence and/or the prevalence of a particular problem. Incidence is the number of instances of the problem that are counted within a *specified time period*. Prevalence (nothing more than a proportion) is the number of cases of the problem in *a given population*. The incidence of homelessness in the summer months, for example, may drop to 1 in 150 persons because of available seasonal employment. The prevalence of homelessness in a city, on the other hand, might be reported at a rate of 1 in 100 persons as an overall figure.

Reporting quantitative data provides a picture of the problem we are assessing, and the numbers and rates can be presented numerically or graphically. Using pie

The purpose of this part of the survey is to learn more about your perceptions of these problems in the community. Listed below are a number of problems some residents of Northside have reported having.

Please place a number from 1 to 3 on the line to the right of the question that represents how much of a problem they have been to you within the last year:

1. No problem (or not applicable to you)
2. Moderate problem
3. Severe problem

Questions		Responses	
1. Finding the product I need	1	2	3
2. Impolite salespeople	1	2	3
3. Finding clean stores	1	2	3
4. Prices that are too high	1	2	3
5. Not enough Spanish-speaking salespeople	1	2	3
6. Public transportation	1	2	3
7. Getting credit	1	2	3
8. Lack of certain types of stores	1	2	3
9. Lack of an employment assistance program	1	2	3
10. Finding a city park that is secure	1	2	3
11. Finding a good house	1	2	3

Figure 5.4 Example of a nonstandardized needs assessment questionnaire that produces quantitative data.

charts, bar graphs, and other visual representations helps to communicate data to all audiences. Many word processing programs and basic statistical packages have graphics components that can help us create impressive illustrations of our data. Figure 5.4 illustrates a nonstandardized needs assessment survey instrument that collects quantitative data. More will be said about the presentation of quantitative data, via the use of graphics, in Chapter 12.

Collecting Qualitative Data

Quantitative data analyses are useful in summarizing large amounts of quantitative data that are expressed in numbers, but to capture the real "guts" of a problem we rely on **qualitative data** analyses (Box 5.3). Rather than summarizing data with numbers, qualitative data analyses summarize data with words. Recall the final open-ended section in Paula's survey. By using a blank space at the end of the survey, respondents were able to add additional comments or thoughts in their own words. Because not all respondents offered comments on the same topic, the data obtained in this section of her survey were not truly representative of the people who responded (sample). That is, the comments did not necessarily reflect the majority

Qualitative data

Data that measure quality or kind; usually expressed in words.

opinion of people who completed and mailed back the survey. Nevertheless, they did add important information to how Paula looked at and interpreted the data collected in other parts of her survey.

Many townspeople, for example, had views about the relationship between teen problems and the lack of supervision and recreational opportunities for the teens. Several respondents included comments that reflected this issue. The brief quotes that follow are examples of what some survey respondents said:

- "In regards to some younger people, some of the concerns I have heard of, and read about, would probably be decreased if there was something for them to do . . . The range of recreation activities in this town is poor . . ."
- "Drug abuse is a very serious problem among 15 to 17 year olds."
- "We need a recreation center for young teens 14 to 19 years old. Supervised dances, games, etc., as well as counselors . . ."
- "The lack of entertainment facilities in this town encourages teens to congregate and use drugs and alcohol as substitutes for entertainment. These teens can get into trouble for the lack of things to do."
- "There is a definite need for activities and/or drop-in center for teenagers. It would keep them off the streets and out of the mall."

As can be seen, these qualitative data (words) offer richer information than is available through numbers alone. The respondents were voicing their views about what was needed in their community, given that they believed a drug and alcohol abuse problem existed for teens in their community. These comments hint at possible solutions for the social problems. On one hand, Paula could have taken the comments literally and proposed a youth center for the city. On the other hand, it may be that she needed to propose an educational or awareness program for parents so that they would have gained a better understanding of the issues that youth faced.

Qualitative data are typically collected through interviews, which are recorded and later transcribed and subsequently analyzed. Other forms of qualitative data collection occur through the reviewing of existing reports and client records in a social service program. A powerful form of qualitative data for a needs assessment is the case study approach. Using an example of a single case can spark the attention of policymakers, funders, and the community when other attempts have failed. More will be said about the analysis and presentation of qualitative data in Chapter 13.

Step 6: Disseminating and Communicating Findings

The final step in a needs assessment study is the dissemination and communication of findings. It goes without saying that a needs assessment is conducted because someone—usually the program stakeholder(s)—wants to have useful data about the

How will you know whether you are achieving your *objectives* and making progress toward your *goals*? What counts as evidence of progress and impact? Though simplifying a bit, it's convenient to think of measuring progress and impact in terms of quantitative and qualitative data.

What Are Quantitative Data?

Information that is measured and expressed with numbers can provide *quantitative data*. For example, attendance records can show the number of persons who participate over a period of time; *surveys* can show the percentage of participants who responded to a question in a certain way. These quantitative data can be used in a variety of ways. To name just a few, they can be presented as numbers or percentages, as ranges or averages, and in tables or graphs. They can also be used to compare different groups of participants—girls and boys, students of different socioeconomic or ethnic backgrounds, or students in your program with nonparticipants.

To illustrate different ways to present quantitative data, let's use a mentoring example. In this example, the 15 middle school students (7 girls and 8 boys) and 25 high school student participants (10 girls and 15 boys) were asked to fill out a *questionnaire* at the end of the school year. Tables 1 and 2 and Figure 1 illustrate several ways to present the same questionnaire results.

Table 1 Data Displayed as Numbers, Combining the Results for All of the Program's Participants

	End-of-Year Survey
Response on Questionnaire	Number Responding Agree/Strongly Agree
I look forward to meetings with my mentor.	38
I think my mentor cares about me personally.	38
I understand my school work better when my mentor helps me.	23
Total Number of Participants	40

Table 2 Data Displayed as Percentages, Separating Middle School From High School

	End-of-Year Survey	
	Percentage Responding Agree/Strongly Agree	
Response on Questionnaire	Middle School	High School
I look forward to meetings with my mentor.	100	92
I think my mentor cares about me personally.	87	100
I understand my school work better when my mentor helps me.	67	52
Total Number of Participants	15	25

(continued)

Box 5.3 (continued)

You might also choose to present some of the information graphically to help make a point that might be difficult to see in a table. The graph in Figure 1 shows that the boys responded quite differently from the girls to one specific question.

Notice how each of these examples has highlighted a different aspect or detail in the questionnaire results. We went from looking at the results for all participants to comparing results for middle and high school participants, and finally to comparing results for boys and girls at the middle and high school levels.

What Are Qualitative Data?

Evaluators also look at progress and impact in terms of *qualitative data*, where changes are more often expressed in words rather than numbers. Qualitative data are usually collected by document review, observations, and interviews. *Open-ended questions* on surveys can also generate qualitative data.

Qualitative data can provide rich descriptions about program activities, context, and participants' behaviors. For example, we can assess the impact of the mentoring/dropout prevention program on students' relationships with their mentors by *describing* how well the student-mentor pairs interact before and after the program.

Qualitative data can also be expressed in numbers. For example, interview responses can be tallied to report the number of participants who responded in a particular way. Similarly, in the example above, the observer could report the number of students in the entire group who were actively engaged in the activity.

Seeing Quantitative and Qualitative Data as Indicators and Outcomes

To further illustrate quantitative and qualitative data, let's return to the mentoring program discussed earlier. The goal of the program is to reduce the school dropout rate. The objective is to provide positive role models and mentors for at-risk middle and high school students. While your program is under way, how will you know that you are building mentoring relationships that are having a positive impact on students' behavior?

- The number of students who engage in weekly activities with their mentors is one possible *quantitative, intermediate indicator*. Using this information, you might reason that steady or increased participation means that students enjoy the activities and find the new relationships rewarding.

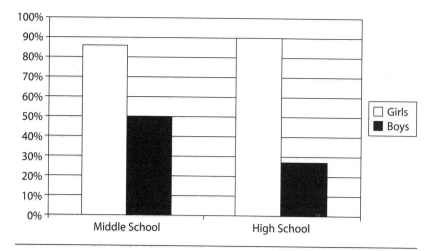

Figure 1 Students reporting they understood school work better with the mentor's help.

Table 3 Examples of Qualitative Data (Observations of Program Activities)

Observations of Program Activities	
Student Behaviors During the First *Week of a Program*	*Student Behaviors During the* Last *Week of a Program*
At a "Get Acquainted" bowling party, student/mentor pairs grouped themselves into two pairs per alley. In some cases, the youths spent most of the time talking together, not mingling with the adults. In two cases, youths left the bowling area to play video games. Several adults appeared hesitant to break into the youthful conversations; in most cases, the adults sat and conversed separately.	At a "Welcome Summer" picnic, students and mentors appeared quite comfortable with each other. Most students chose to sit near their mentors at picnic tables. All the students appeared at ease talking with their mentors and, in many cases, talking to other adults sitting nearby. No one appeared bored or hesitant to join in conversation.
Several of the youths bowled a game or two with their mentor, but uncomfortable with the adult and uneasy about approaching other youths who were engaged in conversations. These students seemed bored and distracted.	After eating, mixed groups of adults and students played volleyball and softball, with everyone actively participating. Interactions were relaxed and enthusiastic. Students and mentors appeared to enjoy the opportunity to be together.

- Fewer disciplinary reports with participating students midway through the program might also suggest progress.
- A change in students' behavior, as reported through teacher interviews, is a possible *qualitative, intermediate indicator*. Teachers might note that participating students are less hostile and more motivated since the program began. These qualitative data might suggest a change in students' attitudes toward themselves and others in authority.

How will you know that building positive mentoring relationships has helped produce behavior conducive to students staying in school?

- As baseline data, you compiled data on the number of disciplinary reports and suspensions among your participants before the program began. Your summative data—the same data for participants at the end of each year of your program—might show a leveling off or decline in these numbers. This would be a *quantitative, final program outcome*.
- Your observations or parents' and teachers' descriptions of students' behavior, both before and after the program, can provide summative qualitative data. A description of behavior in and out of school that provides evidence of more interest and motivation is a possible *qualitative, final program outcome*.

Table 4 Program to Reduce the Dropout Rate

	Quantitative Outcomes	*Qualitative Outcomes*
Intermediate Indicators	*Number* of students who engage in activities with mentors stays the same or increase over course of program.	*Quality* of students' interactions with others shows improvement during program.
Final Outcomes	*Number* of suspensions/discipline reports decreases among participants by program's end.	*Quality* of students' interactions in and out of school consistently improves by program's end.

(continued)

Box 5.3 (continued)

A Final Word About Quantitative and Qualitative Data

Collecting both quantitative and qualitative data in your *formative* and *summative evaluation* is important, but is not always possible. For example, many positive outcomes do not have tests or scales associated with them, so a number cannot be assigned to measure progress or success. In these cases, qualitative data may prove more useful because they allow you to describe outcomes with words.

Qualitative data can also be highly useful for clarifying what you think is important and for discovering new issues that you might have overlooked in your initial evaluation design. On the other hand, collecting and using qualitative data is often time-consuming and labor intensive. As a general rule, you will want to use the measures (quantitative or qualitative) that are most feasible in terms of your skills and resources, and most convincing to you and your sponsors.

extent of a social problem. It is important that the five previous steps of the needs assessment be followed logically and systematically so that the results to be communicated fit with the original intention of the evaluation. The results of a needs assessment are more likely to be used if they are communicated in a straightforward and simple manner, and any written or verbal presentation of a study's findings must consider who the audience will be. In almost all cases, a report is disseminated only to the stakeholders. Box 5.4 lists some needs assessment studies for which findings have been communicated to the general public via professional journal publications.

Summing Up and Looking Ahead

This chapter presented the first kind of program evaluation we can do in a social service program: needs assessments. This chapter discussed the process of doing a needs assessment in six major steps. A well thought out needs assessment has three components: a social problem, the specification of social need, and a potential solution to the problem. The next chapter presents the second type of program evaluation that you need to be aware of when you become a professional social worker: process evaluation.

Box 5.4 Published Examples of Needs Assessments

Berkman, B., Chauncey, S., Holmes, W., Daniels, A., Bonander, E., Sampson, S., & Robinson, M. (1999). Standardized screening of **elderly patients'** needs for social work assessment in primary care. *Health and Social Work, 24,* 9–16.

Chen, H., & Marks, M. (1998). Assessing the needs of **inner city youth**: beyond needs identification and prioritization. *Children and Youth Services Review, 20,* 819–838.

Davidson, B. (1997). Service needs of **relative caregivers**: A qualitative analysis. *Families in Society, 78,* 502–510.

Ford, W. E. (1997). Perspective on the integration of **substance user** needs assessment and treatment planning. *Substance Use and Misuse, 32,* 343–349.

Gillman, R. R., & Newman, B. S. (1996). Psychosocial concerns and strengths of **women with HIV infection**: An empirical study. *Families in Society, 77,* 131–141.

Hall, M., Amodeo, M., Shaffer, H., & Bilt, J. (2000). **Social workers** employed in substance abuse treatment agencies: A training needs assessment. *Social Work, 45,* 141–154.

Herdt, G., Beeler, J., & Rawls, T. (1997). Life course diversity among **older lesbians and gay men:** A study in Chicago. *Journal of Gay, Lesbian, and Bisexual Identity, 2,* 231–246.

Palmeri, D., Auld, G., Taylor, T., Kendall, P., & Anderson, A. (1998). Multiple perspectives on nutrition education needs of **low-income Hispanics**. *Journal of Community Health, 23,* 301–316.

Pisarski, A., & Gallois, C. (1996). A needs analysis of Brisbane **lesbians**: Implications for the lesbian community. *Journal of Homosexuality, 30,* 79–95.

Safyer, A. W., Litchfield, L. C., & Leahy, B. H. (1996). **Employees with teens**: The role of EAP needs assessments. *Employee Assistance Quarterly, 11,* 47–66.

Shields, G., & Adams, J. (1996). **HIV/AIDS** among youth: A community needs assessment study. *Child and Adolescent Social Work Journal, 12,* 361–380.

Weaver, H. N. (1997). The challenges of research in **Native American communities:** incorporating principles of cultural competence. *Journal of Social Service Research, 23,* 1–15.

Weiner, A. (1996). Understanding the social needs of **streetwalking prostitutes.** *Social Work, 41,* 97–105.

Zahnd, E., Klein, D., & Needell, B. (1997). **Substance use** and issues of violence among **low-income, pregnant women**: The California perinatal needs assessment. *Journal of Drug Issues, 27,* 563–584.

RECAP AND ONLINE MATERIALS

In this chapter, you learned how to do social work needs assessments.

You should also recall the concept of needs assessments from your foundational research course. If not, go online to take a free crash course in how to use various needs assessment tools.

You can also find the following materials online to help you master the concepts you just learned:

- Chapter Outline
- Learning Objectives
- Key Terms and Concepts
- Flash Cards
- Practice Multiple-Choice Tests
- Essay Questions with Answers
- Links

www.oup.com/us/swevaluation

STUDY QUESTIONS

1. In your own words, describe what needs assessments are and provide a social work example throughout your discussion.
2. Discuss what a social problem is and provide a social work example throughout your discussion.
3. List and discuss each of the four types of social needs. Provide one common social work example throughout your discussion.
4. List and discuss each of the six steps in doing a needs assessment. Provide one common social work example throughout your discussion.
5. List and discuss as many kinds of data gathering methods that you can think of that would collect *original* data.
6. List and discuss as many kinds of data gathering methods that you can think of that would collect *existing* data.
7. Discuss the concept of "target parameters." How are they used in doing needs assessments?
8. Discuss the differences between data sources and data gathering methods and how they can be used in doing needs assessments. Provide one common social work example throughout your discussion.
9. Discuss how quantitative and qualitative data can be gathered for needs assessments. Provide one common social work example throughout your discussion.

10. Discuss the various "research skills" you believe you would need to actually carry out a needs assessment. Where would you get these skills if you did not possess them already?

References, Further Reading, and Resources

Ginsberg, L. H. (2001). *Social work evaluation: Principles and methods.* Boston: Allyn & Bacon.

Gupta, K. (1999). *A practical guide to needs assessment.* San Francisco, CA: Jossey-Bass Pfeiffer.

Kettner, P. K., Moroney, R. K., & Martin, L. L. (in press). *Designing and managing programs: An effectiveness-based approach* (3rd ed.). Thousand Oaks, CA: Sage.

Hornick, J. P., & Burrows, B. (1998). Program evaluation. In R. M. Grinnell, Jr. (Ed.), *Social work research and evaluation* (3rd ed., pp. 400–420). Itasca, IL: F. E. Peacock.

Ljunggren, G. (2004). Chapter 4: Needs assessment. In *Integrating services for older people: A resource book for managers.* Retrieved September 2, 2005, from http://www.ehma.org/carmen/is_04.html

Maslow, A. H. (1999). *Toward the psychology of being* (3rd ed.). New York: Wiley.

Pecora, P. J., Kessler, R. C., Williams, J., O'Brien, K., Downs, A. C., English, D., White, J., Hiripi, E., White, C. R., Wiggins, T., & Holmes, K. E. (2005). *Improving family foster care: Findings from the Northwest Foster Care Alumni Study.* Retrieved February 20, 2006, from http://www.casey.org/Resources/Publications/NorthwestAlumniStudy.htm

Peper, B. (2003, November 27). *Social Problems and Modern Society: A Treatise in the Sociology of Culture.* Retrieved September 2, 2005, from Homepage of Bram Peper, Faculty of Social Sciences, Erasmus Universiteit Rotterdam Web site: http://www.eur.nl/fsw/english/staff/homepages/peper/publications/abstract4

Reviere, R., Berkowitz, S., Carter, C. C., & Ferguson, C. G. (Eds.). (1996). *Needs assessment: A creative and practical guide for social scientists.* Washington, DC: Taylor & Francis.

Rossi, P. H., Lipsey, M., & Freeman, H. E. (2003). *Evaluation: A systematic approach* (7th ed.). Thousand Oaks, CA: Sage.

Smith, M. J. (1990). *Program evaluation in the human services.* New York: Springer.

Weinbach, R. W. (2005). *Evaluating social work services and programs.* Boston: Allyn & Bacon.

On Gathering Original Data for Needs Assessments

Gochros, H. L. (2005). Interviewing. In R. M. Grinnell, Jr., & Y. A. Unrau (Eds.), *Social work research and evaluation: Quantitative and qualitative approaches* (7th ed., pp. 245–269). New York: Oxford University Press.

McMurtry, S. L. (2005). Surveys. In R. M. Grinnell, Jr., & Y. A. Unrau (Eds.), *Social work research and evaluation: Quantitative and qualitative approaches* (7th ed., pp. 271–287). New York: Oxford University Press.

Rogers, G., & Bouey, E. (2005). Participant observation. In R. M. Grinnell, Jr., & Y. A. Unrau (Eds.), *Social work research and evaluation: Quantitative and qualitative approaches* (7th ed., pp. 231–244). New York: Oxford University Press.

On Gathering Existing Data for Needs Assessments

Krysik, J. L. (2005). Secondary analysis. In R. M. Grinnell, Jr., & Y. A. Unrau (Eds.), *Social work research and evaluation: Quantitative and qualitative approaches* (7th ed., pp. 291–301). New York: Oxford University Press.

Sieppert, J. D., McMurtry, S. L., & McCelland, R. W. (2005). Utilizing existing statistics. In R. M. Grinnell, Jr., & Y. A. Unrau (Eds.), *Social work research and evaluation: Quantitative and qualitative approaches* (7th ed., pp. 315–328). New York: Oxford University Press.

Stuart, P. H. (2005). Historical research. In R. M. Grinnell, Jr., & Y. A. Unrau (Eds.), *Social work research and evaluation: Quantitative and qualitative approaches* (7th ed., pp. 329–338). New York: Oxford University Press.

On Selecting the Best Data Gathering Method for Needs Assessments

Unrau, Y. A. (2005). Selecting a data collection method and data source. In R. M. Grinnell, Jr., & Y. A. Unrau (Eds.), *Social work research and evaluation: Quantitative and qualitative approaches* (7th ed., pp. 339–349). New York: Oxford University Press.

On Analyzing Quantitative Data for Needs Assessments

Weinbach, R. W., & Grinnell, R. M., Jr. (2007). *Statistics for social workers* (7th ed.). Boston: Allyn & Bacon.

Williams, M., Tutty, L., & Grinnell, R. M., Jr. (2005). Analyzing quantitative data. In R. M. Grinnell, Jr., & Y. A. Unrau (Eds.), *Social work research and evaluation: Quantitative and qualitative approaches* (7th ed., pp. 353–369). New York: Oxford University Press.

On Analyzing Qualitative Data for Needs Assessment

Coleman, H., and Unrau, Y. A. (2005). Analyzing qualitative data. In R. M. Grinnell, Jr., & Y. A. Unrau (Eds.), *Social work research and evaluation: Quantitative and qualitative approaches* (7th ed., pp. 403–420). New York: Oxford University Press

On Constructing Survey Instruments for Needs Assessments

Mindel, C. H. (2005). Designing measuring instruments. In R. M. Grinnell, Jr., & Y. A. Unrau (Eds.), *Social work research and evaluation: Quantitative and qualitative approaches* (7th ed., pp. 133–146). New York: Oxford University Press.

DOING A PROCESS EVALUATION

6

Process evaluation
A type of evaluation that aims to monitor a social service program and to describe and assess (1) the services provided to clients and (2) how satisfied key stakeholders are with the services provided. Data are used to provide ongoing feedback to refine and improve program service delivery; also known as a *formative evaluation*.

Outcome evaluation
A program evaluation that is designed to measure the nature of change, if any, for clients after they have received services from a social service program; specifically measures the change on a program's objectives; also known as a *summative evaluation* or *outcome assessment*.

A **process evaluation** examines how a program's services are delivered to clients and what administrative mechanisms exist within the program to support these services. It focuses on the program's approach to client service delivery in addition to how it manages its day-to-day operations. Thus, unlike **outcome evaluations,** process evaluations are not interested in the end result of a program.

There is a direct connection between a process evaluation and an outcome evaluation, however. A process evaluation can be done if a program performs poorly on an outcome evaluation. In this case, we would be interested in finding out the reasons why the program had poor outcomes. Ideally, a process evaluation occurs before, or at the same time, as an outcome evaluation. When new social service programs are being implemented, for example, it makes sense to check whether the program was implemented in the way it was intended before evaluating its outcomes. Therefore, by evaluating the program's processes and outcomes, we are in a better position to suggest what specific processes lead to what specific successful client outcomes.

Program processes refer specifically to the activities and characteristics that describe how a program operates. In general, there are two major categories of processes—the client service delivery system within the program and the program's administrative support systems that sustain client service delivery. Client service delivery is composed of what workers do (e.g., interventions and associated activities) and what clients bring to the program (e.g., client profile and client satisfaction). On the other hand, administrative support systems comprise the administrative activities that exist to support the program's client service delivery system.

Suppose, for example, we want to conduct a process evaluation of a family support program. Instead of focusing our evaluation efforts on client outcomes, as is done in an outcome evaluation (next chapter), we turn our attention to the program's day-to-day operations. Program Objective Two in our family support program (Box 3.1), for example, aims "to increase problem-solving skills of family members." In a process evaluation, we could ask:

- What *treatment interventions* do workers and clients engage in to increase family members' problem-solving skills?
- How much time do workers spend with family members on problem-solving interventions?

PURPOSES OF PROCESS EVALUATIONS

In a nutshell, a process evaluation aims to monitor a social service program in an effort to assess the services it provides to its clients, including how satisfied key stakeholder groups are with the program's services. If we know exactly what type of services are offered, how these services are being delivered, and how satisfied stakeholder groups are (especially clients) with the services, then we are in a better position to decide whether the program is, in fact, the best vehicle to help clients.

Like all types of evaluations presented in this book, a process evaluation is simple to understand but difficult to carry out. Recall from Chapter 3 the challenges involved in developing a program's goal and its related objectives. There are similar problems in doing a process evaluation. To evaluate a program's approach to client service delivery, for example, program staff need to establish a common "program language." Do workers and/or administrators, for example, mean the same thing when they refer to "counseling" versus "therapy?" Are these activities (remember, these are not program objectives) the same or different? How would we distinguish between the two?

Using a consistent language to describe how a social service program delivers its services requires a level of precision that is difficult to achieve. This is particularly true when workers come from different disciplines, have different levels of training, and/or have different theoretical orientations. Many social service programs do not have well-consolidated and well-thought-out treatment intervention approaches. Thus, creating an intervention approach can be the first task of a process evaluation.

A process evaluation can fine-tune the services that a program delivers to its clients. In this spirit, a process evaluation is a critical component of delivering good social work services. In the same way that we ask clients to monitor their progress using practice objectives (Chapter 3), workers must be willing to monitor their interventions and activities to assess whether they are helping their clients in the best way possible. It is also the responsibility of administrators to maintain a healthy work environment.

By defining, recording, monitoring, and analyzing a program's operations, we gain a better understanding of what types of interventions (and associated activities) lead to what type of client outcomes (positive and negative). We also gather data to assess whether the program's current administrative operations are adequately supporting the workers as they help clients. We can, for example, monitor the frequency of worker–client contact, the amount of supervision the workers receive, and the number of training sessions the workers attended over the last year or so.

Clearly, there are many dimensions to conducting process evaluations. In general, however, they have three main purposes: (1) to improve a program's operations, (2) to generate knowledge for our profession, and (3) to estimate cost efficiency.

To Improve a Program's Operations

In general, data collected in a process evaluation are primarily used to inform decisions pertaining to the further development of the program's services. Even when a social service program is adequately conceptualized before it actually opens its doors for the first time, the day-to-day implementation of the program does not always go as smoothly as initially planned. There are many practical, legal, political, and ethical obstacles that prevent programs from being implemented as theoretically planned. More often than not, these obstacles are not realized until the program gets under way. A family support program, for example, may unexpectedly find that the building in which it is located is locked on weekends, or that its funding source places last-minute demands on the workers' caseload size.

A process evaluation is sometimes referred to as a *formative evaluation:* the gathering of relevant data for the continuous ongoing feedback and improvement of the client-related services a program offers (see Box 2.1). As will be seen shortly, a process evaluation provides us with important feedback about the two levels of program processes already discussed—its client service delivery system and its administrative supports.

We recommend that all process evaluations occur at the stage when new programs start to focus their efforts on developing well-thought-out client service delivery systems. After a well-conceptualized client service delivery approach is established (a process that can take up to two years), a process evaluation can shift its emphasis to the program's administrative operations. The reason for beginning with direct client service delivery is that all worker supervision, training, and other administrative support should ultimately exist to support the workers' direct services to their clients. Unless we are clear about what the nature of the program's client service delivery approach is, our beginning attempts to design and implement supporting systems to help workers will be futile.

To Generate Knowledge for Our Profession

The next chapter will discuss how outcome evaluations help us to learn more about how clients demonstrate change (if any) when they go through a program. In comparison, process evaluations give us insight into what specific treatment interventions and associated activities lead to these client changes (if any). Our profession has often referred to the client service delivery component of a social service program as a **black box**. This somewhat negative label reflects the notion that clients enter and exit a program with no clear idea as to what actually took place while they were in the program (thus, a "black box"). As we know, process evaluations include the monitoring of our treatment interventions and activities, so they have much to offer us in relation to telling us what is really in the black box.

First, to monitor interventions and activities implies that we have labels and definitions for what we do with our clients. This, in turn, increases communication and reduces the need to reinvent labels for basic intervention approaches (e.g., educational, therapeutic, and supportive) and activities (e.g., active listening and confrontation).

Second, by monitoring what works (and what does not) with clients, we can avoid wasting time on treatment interventions and/or activities that do not work.

Third, we can begin to respond to longstanding questions that are ingrained in our profession but have not been adequately answered, such as

- Are our interventions more effective in an office or community setting?
- Is a 50-minute session the optimal duration for counseling?
- What are the results of helping clients cope with poverty versus helping them challenge the system?

Fourth, if process evaluations are conducted across several social service programs, we can compare different client service delivery systems in terms of their differences and similarities. This information will help us to know *what* interventions work best for *whom*.

To Estimate Cost Efficiency

The data collected for a process evaluation can be used to more precisely calculate the cost of delivering a specific social service program to a specific client population. The next chapter, Chapter 7, presents how outcome evaluations can be used to estimate the **cost efficiency** (Chapter 8) of social service programs: Does the program accomplish its objectives within budget? On the other hand, a process evaluation permits us to ask more detailed questions that deal with a program's efficiency. By monitoring the amount of time clients spend receiving individual and group interventions, and by keeping track of client outcomes, for example, we will be able to

Black box

When the exact operations of a given intervention are not known to others.

Cost efficiency

When a social service program is able to achieve its program objectives in relation to its costs.

determine which interventions (e.g., group or individual) are more efficient—which ones cost less but produce similar client outcomes or results. Much more will be said about this in Chapter 8.

STEPS IN A PROCESS EVALUATION

The major aim of a process evaluation is to determine whether a program is operating as it was intended. In this chapter, we discuss six steps in conducting a process evaluation: (1) deciding what questions to ask, (2) developing data collection instruments, (3) developing a data collection monitoring system, (4) scoring and analyzing data, (5) developing a feedback system, and (6) disseminating and communicating results.

Step 1: Deciding What Questions to Ask

We have already discussed that a process evaluation can focus on two important dimensions of a program: its client service delivery system and its administrative operations. As such, it is important to develop clear questions for a process evaluation. There are many questions that can be asked during a process evaluation, and eight of the more common ones follow.

What Is the Program's Background?

Developing a program's goal and objectives, via the process delineated in Chapter 3, is part of the answer to this simple question. By defining a program's goal, we articulate who will be served, what social problem will be tackled, what change is to be accomplished, and how we intend to create this change. This information provides a description of the program in a straightforward way whereby we can easily grasp its scope and boundaries.

There are other background questions that we can ask: What is the program's history? How did the program get started? What is the program's philosophy? The answers to these types of questions provide us with the program's *context*—that is, the circumstances surrounding the program that help us to interpret data derived from the process evaluation.

A pro-life social service program, for example, will have a different philosophical approach to working with pregnant teens than a pro-choice program, yet both programs work with the same client population and tackle the same social problem. Furthermore, the two programs may have similar goals—to prevent teenage pregnancy.

We must always remember that social service programs often are initiated in response to political agendas or recommendations from needs assessments; other times they may begin simply on ad hoc bases when additional social service funds are available near the end of the fiscal year. Questions having to do with the program's history and philosophy provide us with information about the program's background in addition to the political and social environment in which it operates. A program's history can be critical to fully understanding its day-to-day operations and helps us to work within its current political and social context. A program's philosophy can tell us how the major beliefs and values of the program's administrators (and workers) influenced the program's operations.

What Is the Program's Client Profile?

Knowing who is directly served by a program has implications for how the processes within it are monitored. Clients are one of the stakeholder groups identified in Chapter 1. Remember that clients can be individuals, families, groups, communities, and organizations. Regardless of whether "the client" is defined as "a family with a child at risk for placement" or "a placement program" that accommodates these children, a clear picture (or profile) of whom the program serves (the client) is necessary.

If the clients are families, for example, we need to know their sociodemographic characteristics. Gathering relevant client data such as age, gender, income, education, race, socioeconomic status, and other relevant demographic characteristics gives us a general idea of whom we are trying to serve. We also want to know where our clients come from. In other words, how are clients referred to the program? Are clients self-referred? Do they come primarily from one geographic area? How did they learn about the program?

If the client *is* a program, we will ask different questions: Where is the program located? Who are its funding sources? What are the program's boundaries? How many staff are employed? What is the program's main intervention approach?

What Is the Program's Staff Profile?

Social service programs are staffed by individuals (workers and volunteers) with diverse backgrounds. Educational backgrounds and employment experiences can easily be used to describe the qualifications of workers. By monitoring worker qualifications, we can gain insight into establishing minimum-level qualifications for job advertisements. Are MSWs substantially better than BSWs in providing family support services, for example? Presumably, those with additional years of education have more to offer. If this is the case, what are the differentiating characteristics between the two levels of education? Sociodemographic data such as age, gender, and marital status are typical features used to describe program workers (or volunteers). Other meaningful descriptors for workers include salaries, benefits, and job descriptions.

There may be other staff characteristics that are important to a specific social service program. If we believe, for example, that being a parent is a necessary qualification for workers who help children in a foster-care program, we might collect data that reflect this interest. Developing profiles for workers and volunteers alike provides data by which to make decisions about further recruiting and hiring. By monitoring key characteristics of social workers, for example, we might gain some insights as to the type of individuals who are best matched for employment within the program.

What Is the Amount of Service Provided to Clients?

Just because a social service program may be designed to serve clients for one hour per week for six weeks does not mean that it happens this way. Some clients may leave the program much earlier than expected, and some may stay much longer than anticipated. Thus, we must record the clients' start and termination dates to determine how long our clients received services from our program.

When programs do not have clear-cut intake and termination dates (e.g., an outreach program for youth living on the street) or when these dates are not particularly meaningful (e.g., a long-term group home for adults with developmental disabilities), it may be necessary to collect data that are more useful. For instance, how long are street workers able to engage youth living on the street in a conversation about their safety? How many youth voluntarily seek outreach workers for advice? For adults with developmental disabilities who are living in a long-term group home, we might record the onset and completion of a particular treatment intervention.

Deciding when services begin and end is not as straightforward as it might seem. For instance, support services are sometimes provided to clients who are awaiting formal entry into a program, or follow-up services are offered to clients after a program's services have officially ended. Duration of service can be measured in minutes, hours, days, weeks, months, or years, and it provides us with data about how long a client is considered a client.

We might also want to know the intensity of the services provided to clients. This can be monitored by recording the amount of time a worker spends with, or on behalf of, a client. Worker time, for example, can be divided into face-to-face contact, telephone contact, report writing, advocacy, supervision and consultation, and so on. If we divide the amount of time spent in each one of these categories by the total time spent receiving services for one client, we can calculate the proportion of time spent in each category for that client. These simple calculations can produce the following data: Overall worker time for Client A was 40 percent face-to-face contact, 25 percent telephone contact, 25 percent report writing, 5 percent advocacy, and 5 percent supervision and consultation.

These data can be used to formulate an estimate that can assist workers in gauging the timing of their interventions. We might determine, for example, that workers in a family support program spend an average of 60 percent of their time in direct client contact. The other 40 percent is spent in meetings, writing up paperwork, participating in staff meetings, and so on. If a few workers have particularly difficult families, it might be reflected in their reported hours. Perhaps their face-to-face hours are low for a family, say, around 20 percent, because the families miss many appointments. It is also possible that their face-to-face hours are high, say, 75 percent, because the families had a series of crises. These data alone can be useful when deciding whether to continue or change services being offered to any one family.

What Are the Program's Interventions and Activities?

Interventions

The theoretical approach social workers use to create planned change.

Activities

What social workers do to carry out their interventions.

Program fidelity

An evaluation that is done to check the extent to which the delivery of an intervention adheres to the protocol or program model originally developed.

Looking into what the program's **interventions** and **activities** entail gets at the heart of the program's treatment strategy (and associated worker activities). It asks, What approach do workers use (the intervention), and how do they do it (the activity)? Of all process evaluation questions, this one in particular can pose a threat to workers and administrators alike because it requires them to articulate the nature of the program's interventions and workers' activities related to these interventions in terms that others can understand. Social workers who rely on professional jargon for efficient communication in the office should learn to explain what they do in lay terms so that nonprofessionals (especially clients) can understand what to expect from the program's services.

A process evaluation can also assess a program's **fidelity;** that is, a process evaluation can be done to check the extent to which the delivery of an intervention adheres to the protocol or program logic model originally developed. Assessing a program's fidelity is extremely important.

Example for Checking on a Program's Fidelity. Gathering process evaluation data about the services provided to clients in a particular program is necessary to assess the fidelity or integrity of a program's services. Phrased as a question, we might ask, "Did the *actual* services delivered to clients match the original design of the program?" or more realistically, "How close did the *actual* services delivered to the clients match the original program design?" Box 6.1 shows a data collection form, a "Daily Family Visit Log," that was used by workers employed by a rural family literacy program as a part of their process evaluation.

Literacy workers in the program made brief home visits to families on a daily basis for four weeks (20 visits total) in an effort to accomplish two main program objectives, which are listed on the log: (1) to increase literacy skills of children, and (2) to increase parental abilities to assist their children in developing literacy skills. In addition to specifying which program objective was targeted at each visit, workers also identified the main activities used that day and rated family members in terms of the "readiness" to participate in services for each day's visit.

The form in Box 6.1 took only a few minutes to complete and workers were trained to complete the form in their car immediately after a family visit ended in order to maximize accuracy of the data recorded. In turn, the aggregate log data from all the workers in the program provided useful program snapshots of several

RURAL FAMILY LITERACY PROGRAM
DAILY FAMILY VISIT LOG

FAMILY: _____   WORKER: _____

Date: _____ / _____ / _____   Visit Number (1 to 20, or follow-up): _____
     day   month   year

Length of Visit (minutes): _____ ① _____

Distance traveled (km) (First Visit Only): _____ ② _____

③

1. What was the primary objective of today's visit? (Circle one.)

   1   To increase literacy skills of children.
   2   To increase parent(s)' abilities to assist their children in developing literacy skills.

2. What were the <u>main</u> activities of today's visit? (Circle all that apply.)   ④

   1   Pointing out parent's strengths in helping their children.
   2   Teaching parents about child development.
   3   Teaching parents about different learning/reading styles.
   4   Teaching literacy games to family.
   5   Teaching parents how to use resources (e.g., library).
   6   Modeling reading with children.
   7   Paired reading.
   8   Listening to parent's concerns.
   9   Identifying family priorities for children's activities.
  10 Filling out Building Block Questionnaires.
  11 Giving books/materials/written information.
  12 Developing charts (sticker charts, reading checklists, etc.).
  13 Providing referrals to other agencies.

  14 Other Describe: _____
  15 Other Describe: _____

3. How ready was the family for today's visit? (Circle one.)   ⑤

    Not at all ready   1   2   3   4   5   Ready and Willing

4. Overall, how did the adult(s) participate in today's visit? (Circle one.)

    Not at all   1   2   3   4   5   Participated Fully

5. Overall, how did the child(ren) participate in today's visit? (Circle one.)

    Not at all   1   2   3   4   5   Participated Fully

6. Comments on today's visit (*use other side if more space is needed*):

key aspects of program service delivery. A list of several process evaluation questions were answered by the data collected from the workers across the program; the number of each process question corresponds with the particular item on the log (see Box 6.1) that generated the data to answer the question.

① On average, how many minutes does a home visit by a literacy worker last?
② On average, how many miles do literacy workers travel to reach a family's home?
③ What proportion of family visits was devoted to increasing children's skills (program objective 1) vs. increasing parents' skills (program objective 2)
④ What program activity was used most often (least often) by program workers?
⑤ What percentage of visits were families "not at all ready" to participate?

Table 6.1 lists an assortment of research studies, all of which investigated whether a program's treatment was delivered in a manner consistent with the original program model or theory. Because there is no standard way to conduct fidelity or process evaluations, the studies listed in Table 6.1 show a variety of methods used to decide on the particular variables to be measured, the specific data collection method, and the selected measures in the evaluation in terms of their reliability and validity (Mowbray, Holter, Teage, & Bybee, 2003).

It is our position that social workers should not be specifically evaluated on their own individual client "success" rates. In other words, it would be a misuse of a process evaluation to take data about one worker's client success rate and compare this rate with another worker's rate, or any other standard. Obviously, this type of analysis would influence the worker to record favorable data—whether accurate or not. Rather, monitoring of client success rates ought to be done in the spirit of program development, appealing to the curiosity of workers in learning about their day-to-day efforts.

What Administrative Supports Are in Place to Support Client Service Delivery?

Administrative supports

Supports that are designed to help the social workers in offering sound client service delivery.

Administrative supports include the "fixed" conditions of employment as well as the administrative operations that are designed to support workers in carrying out the program's clients service delivery approach. Fixed conditions of employment describe things that remain relatively stable over time. Examples include location of intervention (e.g., in the office, client's home, or the community), staff–worker ratio, support staff, available petty cash, use of pagers, hours of service delivery, and so on. Administrative operations, on the other hand, may change depending on current program stresses and include things such as worker training, supervision schedules, and program development meetings.

The most important thing to remember about a program's administrative supports is that they exist to *support* workers in carrying out their functions with clients.

Table 6.1 Fidelity Criteria: Development, Measurement, and Validation

Article	Focus	How Criteria Were Developed	How Criteria Were Measured	How Criteria Were Validated	Instrument Produced
Becker et al. (2001)	SE model for adults with serious mental illness—Individual Placement & Support (IPS)	From IPS manual, authors' experience in implementing model and SE literature.	Semi-structured interview (up to 1 hour) with-knowledgeable staff worker from program.	SE programs in 10 MH centers rated on fidelity; 2 components correlated significantly with competitive employment outcomes.	List of components ranged from 60 to 100 for each model program; rated as ideal, acceptable, unacceptable
Blakely et al. (1987)		Interviews and in-person observations of models and replication plus information published by developer—analyzed to delineate components as well as variations.	Research staff–pair rated programs on fidelity scale, based on site visits and records.	Percentage of exact agreement between raters; convergent validity—exact agreement between information sources; significant correlation between fidelity score and outcome effectiveness.	
Bond et al. (1997)	IPS (see Becker et al., 2001)	From IPS manual, authors' experience in implementing model and SE literature.	Semi-structured interview (up to 1 hour) with-knowledgeable staff worker from program.	Inter-rater and internal consistent reliability; IPS differentiated from other SE programs and from non-SE VR programs.	IPS Fidelity Scale, 15 items, 5-point ratings; 5 = ideal, to 1 = contrary to standards.
Clarke (1998)	Adaptation of Coping with Depression course for adolescents—prevention and treatment	Based on compliance with an existing treatment protocol.	Sessions (live or on videotape) were rated on a fidelity scale by a supervisor or resident assistant; ratings were summed.	Inter-rater and internal consistency reliability; too few groups to relate fidelity to outcomes in a prevention RCT trial.	Fidelity scale, 10 items, 3-point ratings; 0 = no adherence, to 2 = complete adherence

continued

Table 6.1 (continued)

Friesen et al. (2002)	Head Start and other early childhood programs	Qualitative study of 3 contrasting Head Start programs, plus literature review to develop conceptual framework and, from this, a scale.	Relationship between survey results and these proposed DVs: % children referred for MH problems; % children receiving treatment.	Under development
Hernandez et al. (2001)	Systems of care for families with SED child	Not clear. Used system of care values and principles which apparently evolved over time.	Document reviews and interviews with families by a team of 6 professionals trained in use of instrument.	Examined scores for exemplary programs (top quartile) versus traditional programs and found significant differences.	System of Care Practice Review (SOCPR), 34 questions, 7-point ratings
Henggeler et al. (2002)	Family-based MH treatment—Multi-Systemic Therapy (MST)	Measure developed by expert consensus and based on MST manual.	Ratings of therapist adherence from phone interviews of caregivers once/month, also youth ratings and therapist ratings.	CFA, factor analysis, test–retest correlations, Cronbach alpha, correlations of supervisor/therapist ratings; relation of adherence to youth/family outcomes.	Therapist Adherence Measure (TAM) and other MST adherence measures (26 items)
Kelly et al. (2000)	HIV prevention/intervention programs funded by CDC	Core elements of intervention determined from participant feedback, experienced facilitators, and community advisors.	Not specified.	Core elements should consistently relate to outcomes across sites and key characteristics may relate to outcomes at some sites.	None
Lucca (2000)	Clubhouse model of VR for adults with psychiatric disabilities	Reviewed mission statements and documents from selected clubhouses and published literature.	22 programs; single informant at each program indicated presence/absence of each index item (component).	Internal consistency reliability; significant differences for clubhouse versus other VR models; significant correlation between index score and principles of PSR scale.	15-item index of components which should and should not be part of the model; marked yes/no

Macias et al. (2001)	Clubhouse model, based on Fountain House	Content analysis of ICCD certification reports which used Clubhouse Standards. TF of clubhouse staff picked standards which discriminated between certified and noncertified clubhouses.	Mail survey to program administrators in 166 clubhouses that had gone through the certification process.	Discriminant validity: certified clubhouses endorsed significantly more items than non-certified. However, some items showed uniformity of responses.	Clubhouse Research and Evaluation Screening Survey (CRESS) has 59 yes/no items, attempts to avoid subjective assessments
Malysiak et al. (1996)	Wrap-around model to provide mental health and case management services to children and adolescents with emotional/behavioral disorders	Value-based philosophical principles; participatory evaluation involving program staff to describe what worked and what didn't work.	Observation of team meetings, meetings with families and review of case files.	No information.	None
McGrew et al. (1994)	Adult mental health program—Assertive Community Treatment (ACT)	Interviews of ACT researchers and original program developers—asked importance of ACT critical components from published descriptions. Scale of fidelity resulted; expert judgments used to weight items. Scoring criteria operationalized 3 levels per item.	Researchers reviewed write-ups and records of ACT programs, augmented by reports by program directors, site visitors, and consultants.	Interitem reliability; relationship between program fidelity score and program impact (number of days hospitalized); fidelity scores for ACT versus traditional case management.	Index of Fidelity for ACT (IFACT)—14 items

continued

Table 6.1 (continued)

Mills & Ragan (2000)	Integrated Leaning Systems (type of computer technology used in educational software)	Telephone interviews of innovation developers to identify essential features; focus group of teachers who are users; construct a component checklist and pilot test.	Teacher completes checklist, teacher interviewed by researcher, observation of software in use. Panel of 3 experts—review transcriptions and independently score components.	Scores were cluster analyzed; configuration patterns examined for differences—a number were significant.	Integrated Learning System Configuration Matrix (ILSCM)—15 implementation components, each with 5 levels of variation
Orwin (2000)	Substance abuse services—multi-site study	Expert panel generated list of 39 distinct services to be reported and glossary of terms providing common definitions, plus identifying dimensions for codifying programs for each activity.	Participants reported whether they received service. Count up number of services that were planned as part of model.	Sites with multiple intervention conditions, and participants in more intensive groups more likely to get planned services.	N/A
Paulson et al. (2002)	Consumer choice as a component of MH/rehabilitation programs	Consumer consultants added questions re-choice making opportunities to an existing fidelity scale.	External reviewers examined program documents and did ratings on criteria.	Not yet validated.	IPS +—41 questions covering 6 dimensions
Rog & Randolph (2002)	Supported housing, multi-site study	Steering committee specified fidelity framework from RFA; defined major components and identified measurement indicators.	Interviews with program management and staff, but not clear how these data were turned into fidelity scores.	Comparison of supported housing versus comparison programs for distance from ideal supported housing type.	Fidelity instrument, not clear how many items or how they were scored

continued

Teague et al. (1995)	ACT teams for mental illness/substance abuse treatment (CTT)	9 ACT criteria from previous research, modified for the setting; 4 criteria on MI/SA added, based on researchers' experiences.	Staff activity logs, agency documents and MIS, site visits and interviews reviewed by research team to produce consensus ratings.	7 CTT versus 7 standard case management programs compared; cluster analysis used to group sites.	13 criteria, scored from 1–5 in half-point steps
Teague et al. (1998)	ACT teams	ACT criteria from previous research and published literature	Program reports from supervisors or staff, agency documents, MIS, structured interviews with multiple informants—reviewed by informed raters.	Factor analysis and internal consistency reliability; validation used 50 programs differing in degree of intended replication of ACT.	DACTS—28 criteria, 5 point ratings
Unrau et al. (2001)	Family literacy program	1 day workshop for community, stakeholders, and program staff produced program philosophy, goals, logic model, and activities. Exit interviews with families to identify pathways through which outcomes were achieved.	Daily activity checklists completed by workers.	N/A.	N/A

Table 6.1 (continued)

Vincent et al. (2000)	Pregnancy prevention program	Based on experiences in operating the original model in another state.	Records and reports from original project, subjective perceptions of model developer; compared with replication site records, reports, exit interviews and community surveys. Researchers judged comparability between projects.	N/A	N/A
Weisman et al. (2002)	Family Focused Treatment (FFT) for bipolar patients and their relatives	Scale based on treatment manual.	Ratings from videotaped treatment sessions by 3 professionals trained in FFT.	Inter-rater agreement (ICCs from 0.74–0.98); relationship between fidelity score and patient outcomes (relapsed or not) not significant.	Therapist Competence/Adherence Scale (TCAS)—13 items, 7-point scale

Abbreviations: ACT, Assertive Community Treatment; CDC, Centers for Disease Control and Prevention; CRESS, Clubhouse Research and Evaluation Screening Survey; FFT, Family Focused Treatment; HIV, human immunodeficiency virus; IFACT, Index of Fidelity for Assertive Community Treatment; ILSCM, Integrated Learning System Configuration; IPS, Individual Placement and Support; MH, mental health; MST, Multi-Systemic Therapy; N/A, not applicable; SE, supported employment; SOCPR, System of Care Practice Review; TAM, Therapist Adherence Measure; TCAS, Therapist Competence/Adherence Scale; VR, vocational rehabilitation.

Workers who are paid poorly, carry pagers 24 hours per day, have high caseloads, and consistently work overtime on weekends will likely respond to clients' needs and problems less effectively than will those who work under more favorable conditions.

Administrative supports should exist by design. That is, they ought to promote workers in offering sound client service delivery. What is most important to remember is that the approach to administrative support is not written in stone. As with all other aspects of a social service program, it remains flexible and open to review and revision.

A dramatic example of a how an administrative decision leads to change in client service delivery occurred when administrators of a group home program for delinquent youth questioned "group care" as the setting for client service delivery. The program's administrators questioned how living in a group home helps delinquent youth to improve on the program's objectives.

After collecting data about the effects of group living, the administrators determined that their program's objectives could be achieved using a less intrusive (and less expensive) setting for service delivery—providing interventions to youth while they continued living with their families.

In another example, an administrator of an outreach program for street youth noticed that the program's workers were consistently working overtime. By reviewing data collected on the amount of time workers spent "on the street" versus at the "store-front office" and by talking to the workers directly, the administrator learned that workers were feeling overwhelmed by the increasing number of youth moving to the streets.

Workers were spending more time on the streets in an attempt to help as many youth as possible. Workers, however, felt that they were being reactive to the problems faced by youth on the street because they did not have time to reflect on their work in relation to the program's goal and objectives or have time to plan their activities. With these data, the program's administrator decided to conduct weekly meetings to help workers overcome their feelings of being overwhelmed and to develop plans to handle the increase in the number of clients.

How Satisfied Are the Program's Stakeholders?

Stakeholder satisfaction is a key part of a process evaluation because satisfaction questions ask stakeholders to comment on the program's services. Using a **client satisfaction** survey when clients exit a program is a common method of collecting satisfaction data. In a family support program, for example, clients were asked for their opinions about the interactions they had with their family support workers, the interventions they received, and the social service program in general. Figure 6.1 presents a list of seven client satisfaction questions given to parents and children after they received services (at termination) from the program.

The data collected from the questions in Figure 6.1 can be in the form of words or numbers. Clients' verbal responses could be recorded for each question using an

Client satisfaction

A program variable that measures the degree to which clients are content with various aspects of the program services that they received.

How satisfied are you . . .

1. that the worker wanted what was best for you?
2. that the worker was pleasant to be around?
3. that you learned important skills to help your family get along better?
4. that the worker was fair and did not take sides?
5. with the amount of communication you had with the worker?
6. that you had a chance to ask questions and talk about your own ideas?
7. that the worker helped to improve your parent–child relationship?

Figure 6.1 Family satisfaction questionnaire.

open-ended interview format. On the other hand, clients could be asked to respond to each question by giving a numerical rating on a 5-point category partition scale, for example. In this case, the rating scale would range from a response of 1, meaning "not at all satisfied," to 5, meaning "very satisfied."

Client responses to the seven questions in Figure 6.1 can easily provide a general impression about how clients viewed the program's services. Because questions were asked from parents and children alike, it was possible to compare parents' and children's views of the services provided. Suppose, for example, that the satisfaction data showed that parents reported higher satisfaction rates than their children. This finding alone could be used to reflect on how the program's treatment interventions were delivered to the parents versus their children.

Client satisfaction data can also be collected from other key stakeholder groups. Suppose the family support program operated under a child protection mandate. This would mean that each family coming into the program had an assigned child protection worker. Figure 6.2 shows the satisfaction questions asked of this group. Because client satisfaction involves the opinions of people "outside" the program, data collection has special considerations with respect to who collects them.

How satisfied are you . . .

1. with the amount of cooperation you received from the worker in his or her interactions with your department?
2. that the worker connected the family with appropriate resources?
3. that the worker was effective in helping the family get along better?
4. that the worker helped to improve communication between the parent(s) and your department?
5. that the worker helped to improve parent–child relationships?

Figure 6.2 Child protection worker satisfaction questionnaire.

How Efficient Is the Program?

Estimating a program's efficiency is an important purpose of a process evaluation. This question focuses on the amount of resources expended in an effort to help clients achieve a desired program objective. Because a process evaluation looks at the specific components of a program, it is possible to estimate costs with more precision than is possible in a traditional outcome evaluation (next chapter).

Given the many questions that we can ask in a process evaluation, it is necessary to determine what questions have priority (see Figure 4.1). Deciding which questions are the most important ones to be answered is influenced by the demands of different stakeholder groups, trends in programming, and plans for program development.

Step 2: Developing Data Collection Instruments

It is important to collect data for all question categories briefly discussed in Step 1 if we hope to carry out a comprehensive process evaluation. This might seem an unwieldy task, but data for several of the question categories usually already exist. Questions about *program background*, for example, can be answered by reviewing minutes of program meetings, memos, and documents that describe the phases of the program's development. If written documentation does not exist, however, we can interview the people who created the program. *Staff profiles* can be gleaned from workers' resumes. A *program's approach to providing administrative support* can be documented in an afternoon by the program's senior administrator. Ongoing recording of training sessions, meeting times, worker hours, and so on can be used to assess whether administrative supports are being carried out as designed. Finally, data relating to the *program's efficiency* are available from the program's budget.

Data for the program's client service delivery approach should be routinely collected. To do so, it is necessary to develop useful data collection instruments. Useful instruments possess three qualities. They (1) are easy to use, (2) fit with the flow of a program's operations, and (3) are designed with user input.

Ease of Use

Data collection instruments should help workers to do their jobs better—not tie up their time with extensive paperwork. Instruments that are easy to use are created to minimize the amount of writing that workers are expected to do and the amount of time it takes to complete them. In some cases, data collection instruments have already been constructed (and tested) by other social service programs. The National Center of Family Based Services, for example, has developed an intervention and activity checklist for generic family support programs. The checklist contains various interventions and activities in which workers are instructed to check appropriate columns that identify which family members (i.e., child or children at risk, primary caretaker, or other adult) were involved in the intervention and related activities.

Where data collection instruments do not exist, workers may agree to use an open-ended format for a limited period of time. Workers' responses can then be reviewed and categorized to create a checklist that reflects the uniqueness of their program. The advantage of using an open-ended checklist versus a prescribed one is that the listed interventions may be more meaningful to the workers.

Suppose, for example, we asked the workers within a drug and alcohol counseling program for youth to record the major interventions (and associated activities) they used with their clients. After reviewing their written notes, we list the following activities that were recorded by the workers themselves: gave positive feedback, rewarded youth for reduced alcohol consumption, discussed positive aspects of the youth's life, cheered youth on, and celebrated youth's new job. These descriptors all appear to be serving a common function—praise, or noting clients' strengths. Thus, we could develop a checklist item called "praise." The checklist approach loses important detail such as the workers' styles or the clients' situations, but when data are summarized, a general picture of the workers' major activities soon emerges.

Another critical data collection instrument that exists in almost all social service programs is the client intake form (e.g., Figure 11.3), which typically asks questions in the areas of client characteristics, reasons for referral, and service history, to name a few. The data collected on the client intake form should be useful for case-level and program-level evaluations. Data that are not used (i.e., not summarized or reviewed) should not be collected.

Appropriateness to the Flow of a Program's Operations

Data collection instruments should be designed to fit within the context of the social service program, to facilitate the program's day-to-day operations, and to provide data that will ultimately be helpful in improving client service delivery. As mentioned previously, data that are routinely collected from clients, or at least relate to them, ought to have both case-level and program-level utility. For instance, if the client intake form requires the worker to check the referral problem(s), these data can be used at the case level to discuss the checked items, or presenting problems, with the client and to plan a suitable intervention. These data can also be summarized across clients to determine the most common reason for referral to the program.

Client case records can be designed to incorporate strategies for recording the amount of time workers spend with their clients and the nature of the workers' intervention strategies. Space should also be made available for workers' comments and impressions. We do have some suggestions for formatting client data recording instruments, but there is no one ideal design. Just as treatment interventions can be personalized by the workers within a program, so can data collection instruments.

When designed within the context of the program, these instruments can serve several important functions. First, they offer a record of case-level intervention that can be used to review individual client progress. Second, components of the data collection instruments can be aggregated to produce a "program summary." Third, the instruments can be used as the basis for supervisory meetings. They can also facilitate case reviews as they convey the major client problems, treatment interventions, and worker activities in a concise manner.

Design With User Input

It should be clear by now that the major users of data collection instruments are the line-level workers who are employed by the program. Workers often are responsible for gathering the necessary data from clients and others. Therefore, their involvement in the development and testing of the data collection instruments is critical. Workers who see the relevance of recording data will likely record more accurate data than workers who do not.

In some instances, the nature of the data collected requires some retraining of staff. Staff at a group home for children with behavior problems, for example, were asked to record the interventions and activities they used with children residing at the group home. The majority of staff, however, were initially trained to record observations about the children's behavior rather than their own. In other words, they were never trained to record the interventions and activities that they engaged in with clients.

Step 3: Developing a Data Collection Monitoring System

The monitoring system for a process evaluation relates closely to the program's supervision practices. This is because program process data are integral to delivering client services. Data about a program's background, client profile, and staff characteristics can, more or less, be collected at one time period. These data can be summarized and stored for easy access. Program changes such as staff turnover, hours of operation, or caseload size can be duly noted as they occur.

In contrast, process data that are routinely collected should be monitored and checked for reliability and validity. Time and resources are a consideration for developing a monitoring system. When paperwork becomes excessively backlogged, it may be that there is simply too much data to collect, data collection instruments are cumbersome to use, or staff are not invested in the evaluation process. Considerations for developing a monitoring system for a process evaluation include (1) the number of cases to include in the evaluation, (2) the times to collect the data, and (3) the method for collecting the data.

Number of Cases to Include (Unit of Analysis)

Case
The basic unit of social work practice, whether it be an individual, a couple, a family, an agency, a community, a county, a state, or a country.

Unit of analysis
A specific research participant (person, object, or event) or the sample or population relevant to the research question; the persons or things being studied.

Random sampling
An unbiased selection process conducted so that all members of a population have an equal chance of being selected to participate in an evaluation study.

As we will see in the next chapter, in an outcome evaluation we have to decide whether to include all clients served by the program or only a percentage of them. In a process evaluation, we need to make a similar decision. However, what constitutes a **case** can change depending on the questions we ask. If we ask a question about the program's history, for example, the program is our **unit of analysis** and we have only to decide how many people will be interviewed and/or how many documents will be reviewed to get a sufficient answer to our history question.

When questions are aimed at individual clients, we can use the same sampling practices that will be discussed for outcome evaluations (next chapter). Data that are used for case-level activities should be collected from all clients within the program. Intake and assessment data are often used to plan client treatment interventions. Indeed, these data also serve important purposes, such as comparing groups of clients, which is often done in an outcome evaluation.

Often times, client intake forms are far too lengthy and detailed. Thus, a program may consider developing two intake forms, a short form and a long form. The short instrument could include only those data that workers deem relevant to their case-level work. In a sex offender program, for example, we might use a short data collection instrument at client intake to gather data such as age of client, family composition, referral problem(s), service history, employment status, and so on.

In addition to these questions, a longer form could collect data that enriches our understanding of the client population served by the program. For example, what services would the client have used if the sex offender program were not available? What is the length of employment at the client's current job? What community services is the client actively involved in?

If two data collection instruments are available (one short and one long), deciding which one to use is a matter for **random sampling.** Workers could use the long one with every second or third client. To maintain a true sense of "randomness," however, the assignment of a specific data collection instrument to a specific client should occur as close as possible to the actual intake meeting.

The use of short and long instruments can also apply to collecting data about a worker's activities. Data collection is always a balance between breadth (how many cases to include) and depth (what and how many questions to ask).

Whether the unit of analysis is the client, the worker, the administrator, or the program, our aim is to get a representative sample. For smaller social service programs, the number of administrators and workers may be low, in which case everyone can be included. In larger programs, such as public assistance programs, we might use random sampling procedures that will ensure that all constituents are represented in our evaluation. When outcome and process evaluations happen concurrently, we should consider developing sampling strategies that are compatible with both types of evaluations.

Data that are not used for the benefit of a **case-level evaluation** may not need to be collected for all clients. Client satisfaction questionnaires, for example, are usually collected at the end of the program and are displayed only in an aggregate form (to ensure confidentiality). Because client satisfaction data aim to capture the clients' feelings about the services they received, the questionnaires should be administered by someone other than the worker who provided the services to the client. However, having a neutral individual (e.g., another worker, a program assistant, a supervisor) administer the client satisfaction questionnaire can be a costly endeavor.

Recall that in our family support program example, client satisfaction questionnaires were given to the parents and their children. Although the questionnaires were not very long, they were completed in the clients' homes and thus involved travel costs. If a program's staff decide that client satisfaction data are a major priority, then creative strategies could be developed to collect relevant, valid, and reliable client satisfaction data. It may be possible, for example, to obtain these data over the telephone rather than in person.

A simple solution is to randomly select clients to participate in our client satisfaction survey. As long as an adequate number of clients are truly randomly selected, then we can generalize our results to all of the clients within the program who did not participate in our survey. Ideally, our client random selection process should occur at the time clients leave the program (terminate).

Times to Collect the Data

Earlier we discussed the uses of short and long data collection instruments to collect client-relevant data. If we decide that numerous data are to be collected from every client, we may choose to administer the short data collection instrument at one time period and administer the longer one at a different time period. Workers could decide what data will be collected at the intake interview (the shorter instrument), and what data can be collected later on (the longer instrument).

It may be that the intake procedures ask harmless questions such as age, gender, or employment status. After the worker has developed a rapport with the client, it may be more appropriate to ask questions of a more sensitive nature (e.g., service history, family income, family problems, or family history). We should not make the mistake of collecting all data on all client characteristics at the initial intake interview. Many client characteristics are fixed or constant (e.g., race, gender, service history, or problem history). Thus, we can ask these questions at any time while clients are receiving services.

In a process evaluation, we can collect data that focus on the workers' treatment interventions and activities, and the time they spend with their clients. We must decide whether they need to record *all* of their activities with all of their clients; because there are important case-level (and sometimes legal) implications for recording worker–client activity for each case, we recommend *yes!* In addition, we have already

Case-level evaluation
Designs in which data are collected about a single client system—an individual, group, or community—in order to evaluate the outcome of an intervention for the client system; also a form of appraisal that monitors change for individual clients; also called single-system research designs.

recommended that data on a worker's activity form be used for supervisory meetings. Ideally, case records should capture the nature of the worker's intervention, the rationale for the worker's actions, and changes in the client's knowledge, behavior, feelings, or circumstances that result from the worker's efforts (i.e., progress on client practice objectives).

Program administrators have the responsibility to review client records to determine what data are missing from them. The feedback from this review can, once again, be included in supervisory meetings. These reviews can be made easy by including a "program audit sheet" on the cover of each client file. This sheet lists all of the data that need to be recorded and the dates by which they are due. Workers can easily check each item when the data are collected.

If program administrators find there is a heavy backlog of paperwork, it may be that workers are being expected to do too much, or that the data collection instruments need to be shortened and/or simplified. Furthermore, we want to leave room for workers to record creative treatment interventions and/or ideas that can be later considered for the further refinement of the program.

Methods for Collecting the Data

Recording workers' activities is primarily a paperwork exercise. It is time-consuming, for example, to videotape and systematically rate worker–client interactions. Because data on line-level workers' activities are often collected by the workers themselves, the reliability of the data they collect can come into question. Where supervision practices include the observation of the workers' interventions and activities with clients, it is possible to assess the reliability of workers' self-reports. For example, if supervisors were to observe family support workers interacting with their families, they could also complete the therapeutic intervention checklist (discussed earlier) and compare the results with the ratings that workers give themselves.

Interrater reliability
The degree to which two or more independent observers, coders, or judges produce consistent results.

Through this simple procedure, **interrater reliability** scores can be calculated, which tells us the extent of agreement between the workers' perceptions and the supervisors' perceptions.

Social desirability
A response set in which respondents tend to answer questions in a way that they perceive as giving favorable impressions of themselves.

For client satisfaction data, **social desirability** can become an issue. If a worker who is assigned to a client administers the client satisfaction questionnaire (see Figures 6.1 and 9.1) at the end of the program, the resulting data, generated by the client, will be suspect, even if the questionnaire is carried out in the most objective fashion. Clients are less likely to rate workers honestly if the workers are present when clients complete the instrument. This problem is exacerbated when workers actually read out the questions for clients to answer. In this instance, it is useful to have a neutral person (someone not personally known to the client) read the questions to the clients.

Before clients answer satisfaction questions, it should be explained to them that their responses are confidential and that their assigned worker will not be privy to their responses. They should be told that their responses will be added to a pool of other clients' responses and reported in aggregate form. A sample of a previous report that illustrates an example of aggregated data could be shown to clients.

How data are collected directly influences the value of information that results from the data. Data that are collected in a haphazard and inconsistent way will be difficult to summarize. In addition, they will produce inaccurate information.

For example, during the **pilot study,** when the data collection instruments were tested for the amount of time workers spent with their clients, workers were diligent about recording their time in the first two weeks of a six-week intervention program. After the initial two-week period, however, workers recorded data more and more sporadically.

The resulting picture produced by the "incomplete" data was that the program appeared to offer the bulk of its intervention in the first two weeks of the program. A graph of these data would visually display this trend. Suppose such a graph was shown to the program's workers. With little discussion, the workers would likely comment on the inaccuracy of the data.

Moreover, the workers may share their beliefs about what the pattern of the remaining four weeks of intervention look like (in the absence of any recorded data). Rather than speculate on the "possible" patterns, the "hard" data could be used to encourage workers to be more diligent in their data recording practices. Discussion could also center around what additional supports workers may need (if any) to complete their paperwork.

The bottom line is simple: Doing paperwork is not a favorite activity of line-level social workers. When the paperwork that workers complete is not used for feedback purposes, they can become even more resistant to doing it. Thus, it is important that we acknowledge data-recording efforts by providing regular summaries of the data *they* collected. For programs that are equipped with computer equipment and a management database system, it is possible for workers to enter their data directly into the computer. This luxury saves precious time.

Step 4: Scoring and Analyzing Data

The procedures for collecting and summarizing process data should be easy to perform, and once the data are analyzed, they should be easy to interpret. As mentioned, if a backlog occurs in the summarization of data, it is likely that the program is collecting too much data and will need to cut back on the amount collected and/or re-examine its data collection needs.

Thinking through the steps of scoring and **analyzing data** can help us decide if we have collected too much or too little data. Consider a family support worker who sees a family four times per week for 10 weeks. If the worker completes a therapeutic intervention checklist for each family visit, the worker will have a total of 40 data collection sheets for the total intervention period for this one family alone. Given

Pilot study
Administration of a measuring instrument to a group of people who will not be included in the study to determine difficulties the research participants may have in answering questions and the general impression given by the instrument.

Data analysis
The process of turning data into information; the process of reviewing, summarizing, and organizing isolated facts (data) so that they formulate a meaningful response to an evaluation question.

this large volume of data, it is likely that scoring will simply involve a count of the number of therapeutic interventions used. Summary data can show which intervention strategies the worker relied on the most. Because the dates of when data were recorded are on the data collection instrument, we could compare the worker's interventions that were used at the beginning, in the middle, and at end of treatment.

Other analyses are also possible if the data are grouped by client characteristics. For example, do single-parent families receive more or less of a particular intervention compared with two-parent families? Do families where children have behavior problems take more or less worker time? What is the pattern of time spent with families over the 10-week intervention period? Questions can also be asked in relation to any outcome data collected. Is the amount of time spent with a family related to success? What therapeutic interventions, if any, are associated with successful client outcomes? Once data are collected and entered into a computer database system, summaries and analyses are simple matters.

Step 5: Developing a Feedback System

Because a process evaluation focuses on the inner workings of a social service program, the data collected should be shared with the workers within the program. The data collected on worker activities will not likely reveal any unknowns about how workers function on a day-to-day basis. Rather, the data are more likely to confirm workers' and

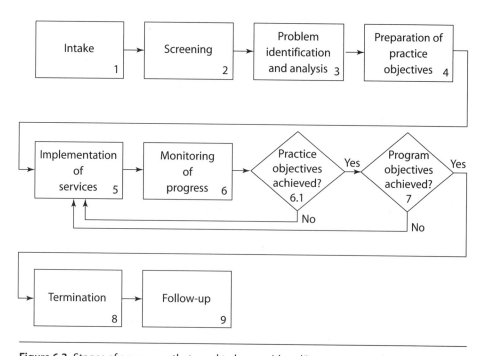

Figure 6.3 Stages of a program that need to be considered in a process evaluation.

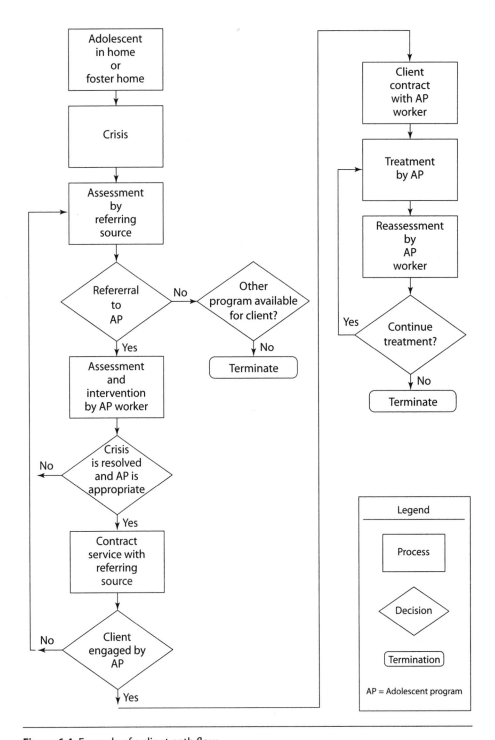

Figure 6.4 Example of a client path flow.

administrators' previously formed hunches. Seeing visual data in graphs and charts provides a forum for discussion and presents an aggregate picture of the program's structure—which may or may not be different from individual perspectives.

We have already discussed the utility of how process evaluations can help supervisors and their supervisees in supervisory meetings. Process data provide an opportunity to give feedback to individual workers and can form the basis of useful discussions. Program-level feedback can be provided to workers in program meetings. Ideally, programs should set aside one-half day every one or two months for program development. During the program development meetings, program administrators could present data summaries for relevant or pressing questions. In addition, these meetings can be used to problem-solve difficulties in creating an efficient monitoring system.

Figure 6.3 presents the general stages of client service delivery for a social service program. Figure 6.4 shows a detailed example of how clients can go through the same program. Both figures are useful guides when considering the components of a program that need to be addressed when doing a process evaluation—they both show the key events in the program's client service delivery approach.

Step 6: Disseminating and Communicating Results

Data collected through process evaluations can provide important clues as to which interventions work with what particular client problems. These data are a first step to uncovering the mystery of the black box. The results of a process evaluation, therefore, should be made available to social service programs that offer similar services. By disseminating the results of a process evaluation in social work professional journals, at professional conferences, or through workshops, a social service program can take a leadership role in increasing our understanding of how to help specific groups of clients with specific problems. Box 6.2 lists some social work process evaluation studies that have communicated their findings to the general public via professional journal publications.

SUMMING UP AND LOOKING AHEAD

Process evaluations are aimed at improving services to clients. Data can be collected on many program dimensions in an effort to make informed decisions about a program's operations. Designing a process evaluation involves the participation of the program's administrators and workers. Program staff must decide what questions they want to ask, how data will be collected, who will be responsible for monitoring data collection activities, how the data will be analyzed, and how the results will be disseminated.

The following chapter presents another kind of evaluation, an outcome evaluation.

Box 6.2 Published Examples of Process Evaluations

Substantive areas are in **bold.**

Allen, J., Philliber, S., & Hoggson, N. (1990). School-based prevention of **teen-age pregnancy and school dropout**: Process evaluation of the National Replication of the Teen Outreach Program. *American Journal of Community Psychology, 18,* 505–524.

Andersson, L. (1984). Intervention against loneliness in a group of **elderly women:** A process evaluation. *Human Relations, 37,* 295–310.

Bazemore, G., & Cruise, P. (1993). Resident adaptations in an Alcoholics Anonymous based residential program for the **urban homeless.** *Social Service Review, 67,* 599–616.

Bentelspacher, C., DeSilva, E, Goh, T., & LaRowe, K. (1996). A process evaluation of the cultural compatibility of psycho-educational family group treatment with **ethnic Asian** clients. *Social Work with Groups, 19,* 41–55.

Berkowitz, G., Halfon, N., & Klee, L. (1992). Improving access to health care: Case management for **vulnerable children.** *Social Work in Health Care, 17,* 101–123.

Blaze-Temple, D, & Honig, F. (1997). Process evaluation of an Australian **EAP.** *Employee Assistance Quarterly, 12,* 15–35.

Cheung, K., & Canda, E. (1992). Training **Southeast Asian refugees** as social workers: Single-subject evaluation. *Social Development Issues, 14,* 88–99.

Deacon, S., & Piercy, F. (2000). Qualitative evaluation of **family therapy** programs: A participatory approach. *Journal of Marital and Family Therapy, 26,* 39–45.

Dehar, M., Casswell, S., & Duignan, P. (1993). Formative and process evaluation of health promotion and **disease prevention programs.** *Evaluation Review, 17,* 204–220.

Devaney, B., & Rossi, P. (1997). Thinking through evaluation design options. *Children and Youth Services Review, 19,* 587–606.

Jackson, J. (1991). The use of psychoeducational evaluations in the clinical process: **Therapists** as sympathetic advocates. *Child and Adolescent Social Work Journal, 8,* 473–487.

Jones, L., & Strandness, D. (1991). Integrating research activities, practice changes, and monitoring and evaluation: A model for **academic health centers.** *Quality Review Bulletin, 17,* 229–235.

Lusk, M. (1983). The psychosocial evaluation of the **hospice patient.** *Health and Social Work, 8,* 210–218.

Miller, T., Veltkamp, L., & Janson, D. (1988). Projective measures in the clinical evaluation of **sexually abused children.** *Child Psychiatry and Human Development. 18,* 47–57.

Pithers, W. (1994). Process evaluation of a group therapy component designed to enhance sex offenders' empathy for **sexual abuse survivors.** *Behavior Research and Therapy, 32,* 565–570.

Pithers, W. (1999). Empathy definition, enhancement, and relevance to the treatment of **sexual abusers.** *Journal of Interpersonal Violence, 14,* 257–284.

Rotheram, M. (1987). Evaluation of imminent danger for **suicide among youth.** *American Journal of Orthopsychiatry, 57,* 102–110.

Sieppert, J. D., Hudson, J., & Unrau, Y. A. (2000). **Family group conferencing** in child welfare: Lessons from a demonstration project. *Families in Society, 81,* 382–391.

Smith, M., Knickman, J., & Oppenheimer, L. (1992). Connecting the disconnected adult day care for **people with AIDS** in New York City. *Health and Social Work, 17,* 273–281.

RECAP AND ONLINE MATERIALS

In this chapter, you learned how to do social work process evaluations.

You should also recall the concept of process evaluations from your foundational research course. If not, go online to take a free crash course in how to use various process evaluation tools.

You can also find the following materials online to help you master the concepts you just learned:

- Chapter Outline
- Learning Objectives
- Key Terms and Concepts
- Flash Cards
- Practice Multiple-Choice Tests
- Essay Questions with Answers
- Links

www.oup.com/us/swevaluation

STUDY QUESTIONS

1. List and thoroughly discuss the three purposes of process evaluations. Use a common social work example throughout your discussion.
2. List and thoroughly discuss the steps of doing a process evaluation. Use a common social work example throughout your discussion.
3. List and discuss the various questions that are asked when doing a process evaluation. Apply these questions to your field practicum setting.
4. List and discuss the criteria that you need to take into account when selecting data collection instruments for process evaluations.
5. Discuss why it is necessary to assess a program's fidelity when doing a process evaluation.
6. Discuss how you would go about developing a data collection monitoring system for a hypothetical program of your choice. Be very specific.
7. Discuss why it is important to have a clear understanding of how clients come into the program, go through the program, and terminate from the program when doing a process evaluation study.
8. Discuss why client satisfaction should not be the only indicator of a program's success when doing a process evaluation. What other indicators do you see that could be useful in this regard?
9. List and discuss the "research skills" you think you would need when doing a process evaluation of a social work program. Where, and how, would you obtain these skills, if you don't already have them?

10. Go to the library or use Box 6.2 to find a social work process evaluation study. Discuss how the investigators used the concepts found in this chapter in their study.

REFERENCES, FURTHER READING, AND RESOURCES

On Fidelity Issues in Process Evaluations

Allness, D. J., & Knoedler, W. H. (1998). *The PACT model of community-based treatment for persons with severe and persistent mental illnesses: A manual for PACT start-up.* Arlington, VA: National Alliance for the Mentally Ill (NAMI).

Anthony, W. A., Cohen, M., & Farkas, M. (1982). A psychiatric rehabilitation treatment program: Can I recognize one if I see one? *Community Mental Health Journal, 18,* 83–96.

Babor, T. F., Steinberg, K. L., McRee, B., Vendetti, J., & Carroll, K. M. (2001). Treating marijuana dependence in adults: A multi-site, randomized clinical trial. In J. M. Herrell & R. B. Straw (Eds.), *Conducting multiple site evaluations in real-world settings. New Directions for Evaluation, no. 94* (pp. 17–30). San Francisco, CA: Jossey-Bass.

Bachrach, L. L. (1988). The chronic patient: On exporting and importing model programs. *Hospital and Community Psychiatry, 39,* 1257–1258.

Banks, S., McHugo, G. J., Williams, V., Drake, R. E., & Shinn, M. (2001). A prospective meta-analytic approach in a multi-site study of homelessness prevention. In J. M. Herrell & R. B. Straw (Eds.), *Conducting multiple site evaluations in real-world settings. New Directions for Evaluation, no. 94* (pp. 45–59). San Francisco, CA: Jossey-Bass.

Becker, D. R., Smith, J., Tanzman, B., Drake, R. E., & Tremblay, T. (2001). Fidelity of supported employment programs and employment outcomes. *Psychiatric Services, 52,* 834–836.

Berman, P. (1981). Educational change: An implementation paradigm. In R. Lehming & M. Kane (Eds.), *Improving schools: Using what we know* (pp. 253–286). Thousand Oaks, CA: Sage.

Bilsker, D., & Goldner, E. M. (2002). Routine outcome measurement by mental health-care providers: Is it worth doing? *The Lancet, 360,* 1689–1690.

Blakely, C. H., Mayer, J. P., Gottschalk, R. G., Schmitt, N., Davidson, W. S., Roitman, D., & Emshoff, J. G. (1987). The fidelity-adaptation debate: Implications for the implementation of public sector social programs. *American Journal of Community Psychology, 15,* 253–268.

Bond, G. R., Becker, D. R., Drake, R. E., Vogler, K. M. (1997). A fidelity scale for the individual placement and support model of supported employment. *Rehabilitation Counseling Bulletin, 40,* 265–284.

Bond, G. R., Evans, L., Salyers, M. P., Williams, J., & Kim, H. W. (2000). Measurement of fidelity in psychiatric rehabilitation. *Mental Health Services Research, 2*(2), 75–87.

Bond, G. R., Williams, J. R., Evans, L. A., Saylers, M., Sharpe, H., & Kim, H. W. (2000). *PN-44-psychiatric rehabilitation fidelity toolkit.* Cambridge, MA: Human Services Research Institute.

Brekke, J. S. (1988). What do we really know about community support programs? Strategies for better monitoring. *Hospital and Community Psychiatry, 39,* 946–952.

Brekke, J. S., & Test, M. A. (1992). A model for measuring the implementation of community support programs: Results from three sites. *Community Mental Health Journal, 28,* 227–247.

Centre for Evidence-Based Medicine. (n.d.). *Levels of evidence and grades of recommendation.* Retrieved February 20, 2006, from Centre for Evidence-Based Medicine (Oxford, England). Web site: http://www.cebm.net/levels_of_evidence.asp

Chambless, D. L., & Ollendick, T. H. (2001). Empirically supported psychological interventions: Controversies and evidence. *Annual Review of Psychology, 52,* 685–716.

Chen, H. (1990). *Theory-driven evaluations.* Thousand Oaks, CA: Sage.

Clarke, G. (1998). Intervention fidelity in the psychosocial prevention and treatment of adolescent depression. *Journal of Prevention and Intervention in the Community, 17,* 19–33.

Donabedian, A. (1982). *The criteria and standards of quality.* Ann Arbor, MI: Health Administration Press.

Drake, R., Goldman, H., Leff, H., Lehman, A., Dixon, L., Mueser, K., & Torrey, W. (2001). Implementing evidence-based practices in routine mental health service settings. *Psychiatric Services, 52,* 179–182.

Drake, R. E., McHugo, G. J., & Becker, D. R. (1996). The New Hampshire study of supported employment for people with severe mental illness. *Journal of Consulting and Clinical Psychology, 64,* 391–399.

Fairweather, G. W., & Tornatzky, L. G. (1971). *Experimental methods for social policy research.* New York, NY: Pergamon Press.

Frese, F. J., Stanley, J., Kress, K., & Vogel-Scibilia, S. (2001). Integrating evidence-based practices and the recovery model. *Psychiatric Services, 52,* 1462–1468.

Giesler, L. J., & Hodge, M. (1998). Case management in behavioral health care. *International Journal of Mental Health, 27,* 26–40.

Glisson, C., & Hemmelgarn, A. (1998). The effects of organizational climate and interorganizational coordination on the quality and outcomes of children's service systems. *Child Abuse and Neglect, 22,* 401–421.

Green, B. L., Friesen, B. J., Gordon, L., Everhart, M. C., & Gettman, M. L. G. (2004). *Guidance for program design: Addressing the mental health needs of young children and their families in early childhood education settings.* Retrieved February 20, 2006, from Portland State University, Research and Training Center on Family Support and Children's Mental Health Web site: http://www.rtc.pdx.edu/pgProjGuidance.php

Hedeker, D., McMahon, S.D., Jason, L. A., & Salina, D. (1994). Analysis of clustered data in community psychology: With an example from a worksite smoking cessation project. *American Journal of Community Psychology, 22,* 595–615.

Henggeler, S. W., Melton, G. B., Brondino, M. J., Scherer, D. G., & Hanley, J. H. (1997). Multisystemic therapy with violent and chronic juvenile offenders and their families: The role of treatment fidelity in successful dissemination. *Journal of Consulting and Clinical Psychology, 65,* 821–833.

Henggeler, S. W., & Schoenwald, S. K. (1998). *The MST supervisory manual: Promoting quality assurance at the clinical level.* Charleston, SC: MST Institute.

Henggeler, S. W., Schoenwald, S. K., Liao, J. G., Letourneau, E. J., & Edwards, D. L. (2002). Transporting efficacious treatments to field settings: The link between supervisory practices and therapist fidelity in MST programs. *Journal of Clinical Child and Adolescent Psychology, 31,* 155–167.

Henry, W. P., Butler, S. F., Strupp, H. H., & Schacht, T. E. (1993). Effects of training in time-limited dynamic psychotherapy: Changes in therapist behavior. *Journal of Consulting and Clinical Psychology, 61,* 434–440.

Hermann, R. C., Finnerty, M., Provost, S., Palmer, R. H., Chan, J., Lagodmos, G., Teller, T., & Myrhol, B. J. (2002). Process measures for the assessment and improvement of quality of care for schizophrenia. *Schizophrenia Bulletin, 28,* 95–104.

Hernandez, M., Gomez, A., Lipien, L., Greenbaum, P., Armstrong, K., & Gonzales, P. (2001). Use of the system-of-care practice review in the national evaluation: Evaluating the fidelity of practice to system-of-care principles. *Journal of Emotional and Behavioral Disorders, 9,* 43–52.

Hohmann, A. A., & Shear, M. K. (2002). Community-based intervention research: Coping with the "noise" of real life in study design. *American Journal of Psychiatry, 159,* 201–207.

Holden, E. W., O'Connell, S. R., Connor, T., Branna, A. M., Foster, E. M., Blau, G., & Panciera, H. (2002). Evaluation of the Connecticut Title IV-E Waiver Program: Assessing the effectiveness, implementation fidelity, and cost/benefits of a continuum of care. *Children and Youth Services Review, 24,* 409–430.

Holter, M. C., Mowbray, C. T., Bellamy, C., MacFarlane, P., & Dukarski, J. (2004). Critical ingredients of consumer run services: Results of a national survey. *Community Mental Health Journal, 40,* 47–63.

Institute of Medicine. (2001). *Improving the quality of long-term care.* Washington, DC: National Academy Press.

Johnsen, M. C, Samberg, L., Calsyn, R., Blasinsky, M., Landow, W., & Goldman H. (1999). Case management models for persons who are homeless and mentally ill: The ACCESS demonstration project. *Community Mental Health Journal, 35,* 325–346.

Kelly, J. A., Heckman, T. G., Stevenson, L. Y., &Williams, P. N. (2000). Transfer of research-based HIV prevention interventions to community service providers: Fidelity and adaptation. *AIDS Education and Prevention, 12,* 87–98.

Lebow, J. (1983). Research assessing consumer satisfaction with mental health treatment: A review of findings. *Evaluation and Program Planning, 6,* 211–236.

Leff, H. S., & Mulkern, V. (2002). Lessons learned about science and participation from multi-site evaluations. In J. M. Herrell, & R. B. Straw (Eds.), *Conducting multiple site evaluations in real-world settings. New Directions for Evaluation, no. 94* (pp. 89–100). San Francisco, CA: Jossey-Bass.

Luborsky, L., McLellan, A. T., Diguer, L., Woody, G., & Seligman, D. A. (1997). The psychotherapist matters: Comparison of outcomes across twenty-two therapists and seven patient samples. *Clinical Psychology: Science and Practice, 4,* 53–65.

Lucca, A. M. (2000). A Clubhouse fidelity index: Preliminary reliability and validity results. *Mental Health Services Research, 2,* 89–94.

Macias, C., Propst, R., Rodican, C., & Boyd, J. (2001). Strategic planning for ICCD clubhouse implementation: Development of the Clubhouse Research and Evaluation Screening Survey (CRESS). *Mental Health Services Research, 3,* 155–167.

Malysiak, R., Duchnowski, A., Black, M., & Greeson, M. (1996). Establishing wrap around fidelity through participatory evaluation. In *Proceedings of the Ninth Annual Research Conference. A System of Care for Children's Mental Health: Expanding the Research Base.*

McGrew, J. H., Bond, G. R., Dietzen, L., & Salyers, M. (1994). Measuring the fidelity of implementation of a mental health program model. *Journal of Consulting and Clinical Psychology, 62,* 670–678.

McGrew, J. H., Pescosolido, B., & Wright, E. (2003). Case managers' perspectives on critical ingredients of assertive community treatment and on its implementation. *Psychiatric Services, 54,* 370–376.

McHugo, G. J., Drake, R. E., Teague, G. B., & Xie, H. (1999). The relationship between model fidelity and client outcomes in the New Hampshire Dual Disorders Study. *Psychiatric Services, 50,* 818–824.

Mills, S. C., & Ragan, T. J. (2000). A tool for analyzing implementation fidelity of an integrated learning system (ILS). *Educational Technology Research and Development, 48,* 21–41.

Moncher, F. J., & Prinz, R. J. (1991). Treatment fidelity in outcome studies. *Clinical Psychology Review, 11,* 247–266.

Mowbray, C. T., Holter, M. C., Teague, G. B., & Bybee, D. (2003). Fidelity criteria: Development, measurement, and validation. *American Journal of Evaluation, 24*(3), 315–340.

Mueser, K. T., Bond, G. R., Drake, R. E., & Resick, S.G. (1998). Models of community care for severe mental illness: A review of research on case management. *Schizophrenia Bulletin, 24,* 37–74.

National Advisory Mental Health Council. (1998, January 14). *Bridging science and service: A report by the National Advisory Mental Health Council's Clinical Treatment and Services Research Workgroup* (NIH Publication No. 99-4353, 1999). Retrieved February 20, 2006, from National Institutes of Health, National Institute of Mental Health Web site: http://www.nimh.nih.gov/publicat/nimhbridge.pdf

Nguyen, T. D., Attkisson, C. C., & Stegner, B. L. (1983). Assessment of patient satisfaction: Development and refinement of a service questionnaire. *Evaluation and Program Planning, 6,* 299–314.

NH-Dartmouth Psychiatric Research Center. (2002, January). Implementing Evidence-Based Practices Project National Meeting. In T. Singer & P. W. Singer (Eds.), *Implementing Evidence-Based Practices Project Newsletter, 1.*

Orwin, R. G. (2000). Assessing program fidelity in substance abuse health services research. *Addiction, 95*(Suppl. 3), S309–S327.

Paulson, R. I., Post, R. L., Herinckx, H. A., & Risser, P. (2002). Beyond components: Using fidelity scales to measure and assure choice in program implementation and quality assurance. *Community Mental Health Journal, 38,* 119–128.

Price, R. H., Friedland, D. S., Choi, J., & Caplan, R. D. (1998). Job-loss and work transitions in a time of global economic change. In X. Arriaga & S. Oskamp (Eds.), *Addressing community problems: Psychological research and interventions* (pp. 195–222). Thousand Oaks, CA: Sage.

Rapp, C. A. (1998). The active ingredients of effective case management: A research synthesis. *Community Mental Health Journal, 34,* 363–380.

Raudenbush, S., & Bryk, A. (2001). *Hierarchical linear models: Applications and data analysis methods* (2nd ed.). Thousand Oaks, CA: Sage.

Rog, D. J., & Randolph, F. L. (2002). A multi-site evaluation of supported housing: Lessons learned from cross-site collaboration. In J. M. Herrell & R. B. Straw (Eds.), *Conducting multiple site evaluations in real-world settings. New Directions for Evaluation, no. 94* (pp. 61–72). San Francisco, CA: Jossey-Bass.

Salyers, M. P., Bond, G. R., Teague, G. B., Cox, J. F., Smith, M. E., Hicks, M. L., & Koop, J. I. (2003). Is it ACT yet? Real-world examples of evaluating the degree of implementation for assertive community treatment. *Journal of Behavioral Health Services and Research, 30,* 304–320.

Sechrest, L., West, S. G., Phillips, M. A., Redner, R., & Yeaton, W. (1979). Some neglected problems in evaluation research: Strength and integrity of treatments. In L. Sechrest, S. G. West, M. A. Phillips, R. Redner, & W. Yeaton (Eds.), *Evaluation studies review annual* (Vol. 4, pp. 15–35). Thousand Oaks, CA: Sage.

Snijders, T., & Bosker, R. (1999). *Multilevel analysis: An introduction to basic and advanced multilevel modeling.* Thousand Oaks, CA: Sage.

Stein, L. I., & Test, M. A. (1980). An alternative to mental health treatment. I: Conceptual model, treatment program, and clinical evaluation. *Archives of General Psychiatry, 37,* 392–397.

Szulanski, G., & Winter, S. (2002). Getting it right the second time. *Harvard Business Review, 80,* 62–69.

Teague, G. B. (2000). Patient perceptions of care measures. In Rush, A. J., Jr., Pincus, H. A., First, M. B., Blacker, D., Endicott, J., Keith, S. J., et al. (Eds.), (Eds.), *Handbook of psychiatric measures* (pp. 169–194). Washington, DC: American Psychiatric Association.

Teague, G. B., Bond, G. R., & Drake, R. E. (1998). Program fidelity and Assertive Community Treatment: Development and use of a measure. *American Journal of Orthopsychiatry, 68,* 216–232.

Teague, G. B., Drake, R. E., & Ackerson, T. H. (1995). Evaluating use of continuous treatment teams for persons with mental illness and substance abuse. *Psychiatric Services, 46,* 689–695.

Teague, G. B., Ganju, V., Hornik, J. A., Johnson, J. R., & McKinney, J. (1997). The MHSIP mental health report card: A consumer-oriented approach to monitoring the quality of mental health plans. *Evaluation Review, 21*(3), 330–341.

Unrau, Y. A. (2001). Using client exit interviews to illuminate outcomes in program logic models: A case example. *Evaluation and Program Planning, 24*, 353–361.

Vincent, M. L., Paine-Andrews, A., Fisher, J., Devereaux, R. S., Dolan, H. G., Harris, K. J., & Reininger, B. (2000). Replication of a community-based multicomponent teen pregnancy prevention model: Realities and challenges. *Family and Community Health, 23*, 28–45.

Weisman, A., Nuechterlein, K. H., Goldstein, M. J., & Snyder, K. S. (2000). Controllability perceptions and reactions to symptoms of schizophrenia: A within-family comparison of relatives with high and low expressed emotion. *Journal of Abnormal Psychology, 109*, 167–171.

Weisman, A., Tompson, M. C., Okazaki, S., Gregory, J., Goldstein, M. J., Rea, M. M., & Miklowitz, D. J. (2002). Clinicians' fidelity to a manual-based family treatment as a predictor of the one-year course of bipolar disorder. *Family Process, 41*, 123–131.

Yates, B. T. (1994). Toward the incorporation of costs, cost-effectiveness analysis, and cost-benefit analysis into clinical research. *Journal of Consulting and Clinical Psychology, 62*, 729–736.

Yates, B. T. (1995). Cost-effectiveness analysis, cost-benefit analysis, and beyond: Evolving models for the scientist-manager-practitioner. *Clinical Psychology: Science and Practice, 2*, 385–398.

Yates, B. T. (1996). *Analyzing cost, procedures, processes, and outcomes in human services.* Thousand Oaks, CA: Sage.

Doing an Outcome Evaluation

7

Outcome evaluation

A program evaluation that is designed to measure the nature of change, if any, for clients after they have received services from a social service program; specifically measures change on a program's objectives; also known as a *summative evaluation* or *outcome assessment.*

A program **outcome evaluation** does nothing more than evaluate the program's objectives. As we know, program outcomes are what we expect clients to achieve by the time they leave a social service program. In most cases, we expect some positive change for the recipients of our services. When clients show improvement, we can feel optimistic that the program has had a positive impact on their lives.

A critical aspect of an outcome evaluation is that we must have a clear sense of what expected changes (the program's outcomes) we hope to see; as we know, these changes are not freely decided on. As we have seen throughout this book, **program objectives** are developed by giving consideration to the views of stakeholders as well as to the knowledge gained from the existing literature, practice wisdom, and the current political climate. When program objectives are developed using the strategies proposed in Chapter 3, they have a solid foundation on which to guide day-to-day program activities.

Thus, by evaluating a program's objectives, we are, in effect, testing **hypotheses** about how we think clients will change after a period of time in our program. We would hope that clients participating in our family support program (introduced in Chapter 3 as Box 3.1), for example, will show favorable improvement on the program's objectives. This chapter uses our family support program as an example of how to develop a simple and straightforward program outcome evaluation.

In a nutshell, the program outcomes we eventually evaluate are nothing more

Program objective

A statement that clearly and exactly specifies the expected change, or intended result, for individuals receiving program services; qualities of well-chosen objectives are meaningfulness, specificity, measurability, and directionality; not to be confused with program goal.

Hypothesis

A theory-based prediction of the expected results in an evaluation study; a tentative explanation of a relationship or supposition that a relationship may exist.

Box 7.1 Common Myths Regarding Outcome Evaluations

Myth: Evaluation is a complex science. I don't have time to learn it.

No. It's a practical activity. If you can run an organization, you can surely implement an evaluation process.

Myth: It's an event to get over with and then move on.

No. Outcome evaluation is an ongoing process. It takes months to develop, test, and polish, but many of the activities required to carry out outcome evaluation are activities that you're either already doing or you should be doing.

Myth: Evaluation is a whole new set of activities—we don't have the resources.

No. Most of these activities in the outcome evaluation process are normal management functions that need to be carried out anyway to evolve your organization to the next level.

Myth: There's a "right" way to do outcome evaluation. What if I don't get it right?

No. Each outcome evaluation process is somewhat different, depending on the needs and nature of the nonprofit organization and its programs. Consequently, each nonprofit is the "expert" at their outcomes plan. Therefore, start simple, but start and learn as you go along in your outcome planning and implementation.

Myth: Funders will accept or reject my outcome plan.

No. Enlightened funders will (or at least, should) work with you, for example, to polish your outcomes, indicators, and outcomes targets. Especially if your organization is a new nonprofit and/or a new program, you very likely will need some help—and time—to develop and polish your outcomes plan.

Myth: I always know what my clients need—I don't need outcome evaluation to tell me if I'm really meeting the needs of my clients.

Not true. You don't always know what you don't know about the needs of your clients—an outcome evaluation helps ensure that you always know the needs of your clients. Outcome evaluation sets up structures in your organization so that your organization remains focused on the current needs of your clients. Also, you won't always be around; outcome measures help ensure that your organization remains focused on the most appropriate, current needs of clients even after you've left your organization.

---

than the operationalization of our program's objectives. If we have not succinctly stated a program's objectives, however, any efforts at doing outcome evaluation are futile at best. This fact places some social service programs in a bind because of the difficulty they face in defining concepts (or social problems) such as homelessness, self-esteem, child neglect, child abuse, and violence. Most of these concepts are multifaceted and cannot be solved by focusing on any one particular simple program objective (e.g., behavior, knowledge, or affect).

Thus, we must be modest about our abilities as helping professionals and feel comfortable with the fact that we can assess only one small component of a complex social problem through the efforts of a single social service program. Let us now turn our attention to the purpose of doing an outcome evaluation.

PURPOSE OF OUTCOME EVALUATIONS

The main purpose of an outcome evaluation is to demonstrate the nature of change, if any, for our clients after they have received our services—that is, after they have left the program. Given the complexity of many social problems that social service programs tackle, we must think about an outcome evaluation as an integral part of the initial conceptualization and final operationalization of a program. This is accomplished by a program's logic model (see the right side of Figure 4.8).

Suppose, for example, we wanted to evaluate one program objective—to increase parents' knowledge about parenting skills—for parents who participate in our family support program. If our program serves 10 parents and runs for 10 weeks, we gain a limited amount of knowledge by evaluating one round of the program's objective (to increase parents' knowledge about parenting skills). If we evaluate this single program objective each round and monitor the results over a two-year period, however, we will have much more confidence in our program's results.

There are many reasons for wanting to monitor and evaluate a program's objectives. One reason is to give concrete feedback to a program's stakeholders, including clients. As we know, a program's goal and its related objectives are dynamic and change over time. These changes are influenced by the political climate, organizational restructuring, economic conditions, clinical trends, staff turnover, and administrative preferences. In addition, sometimes a program's goal and objectives are changed or modified because of the results from a program evaluation.

Another reason for doing an outcome evaluation is so that we can demonstrate **accountability** in terms of showing whether a social service program is achieving its promised objectives. In this spirit, a program outcome evaluation plan serves as a program map—it is a tool for telling us where we are headed and the route we plan to take to arrive at our destination. This focus helps to keep program administrators and workers in sync with the program's mandate (which is reflected in the program's goal). If an outcome evaluation is positive, we then have more justification to support our program.

On the other hand, if the evaluation of a program's objectives turns out to be poor, we can investigate the reasons why this is so. In either case, we are working with data with which to make informed case and program decisions. Because we want our clients to be successful in achieving our program's objective(s), we select activities

Accountability

A system of responsibility in which program administrators account for all program activities by answering to the demands of a program's stakeholders and by justifying the program's expenditures to the satisfaction of its stakeholders.

that we believe have the greatest chance of creating positive client change. Selecting activities in this way increases the likelihood that a program's objectives, the practice objectives, and the practice activities have a strong and logical link (see Box 3.1).

Social service programs are designed to tackle many complex social problems such as child abuse, poverty, depression, mental illness, and discrimination. As we saw in Chapter 3, programs must develop realistic program objectives, given what is known about a social problem, the resources available, and the time available to clients. Unfortunately, we attempt to do more than is realistically possible. Evaluating a program's objectives gives us data from which to decide what can be realistically accomplished.

By selecting a few key program objectives, for example, we can realistically place limits on what workers can actually accomplish. It also places limits on the nature of practice activities that workers might engage in. Suppose, for example, our family support program begins to receive referrals of childless couples who are experiencing violence in their relationships. Rather than try to alter the program to meet clients whose problems and needs do not fit, the program can educate its referral sources about the type of services it offers and the nature of the clientele it serves.

A program outcome evaluation is always designed for a specific social service program. Thus, the results tell us about specific program objectives and not general social indicators. A four-week unemployment program showing that 75 percent of its participants found employment after being taught how to search for jobs cannot make any claims about impacting the general unemployment rate. The results are *specific* to one *specific* group of participants, experiencing the *specific* conditions of one *specific* program over a *specific* time frame at a *specific* time.

USES OF OUTCOME EVALUATIONS

Given that a program outcome evaluation focuses on the program's objectives when clients exit a program, its uses may seem, at first blush, to be quite limited. The outcomes of a program's objectives, however, are pivotal points at which clients leave a program and begin life anew—equipped with new knowledge, skills, affects, or behaviors related to a specific social problem. Therefore, evaluating the outcomes of a program's objectives gives us important information that can be used in many ways. We will only discuss two of them here. An outcome evaluation can (1) improve program services to clients and (2) generate knowledge for the profession.

Improving Program Services to Clients

A primary use of any program outcome evaluation is to improve a program's services that it delivers to clients. As we know, a program outcome evaluation evaluates a program's objectives. Thus, data collected in an outcome evaluation tell us things like how many clients achieved a program objective and how well the objective was achieved. Suppose, for example, a rural child abuse prevention program has as one of its program's objectives:

Program Objective: To increase parents' awareness of crisis services available to them.

At the end of our program, however, we learn that, for 80 percent of our parents, their awareness level of the available crisis services remained the same. Looking into the matter further, we find that there is only one crisis service available to parents living in the rural area and the majority of parents knew about this service before they became clients of the child abuse prevention program. In other instances, our program objectives may expect too much, given the amount of time clients are exposed to the program.

Influencing Decisions?

Ideally, a program outcome evaluation should have a major impact on how concrete program decisions are made. Realistically, this is simply not the case. It is more likely that its results will assist us in resolving some of our doubts and confusion about a program or will support facts that we already know. The results contribute independent information to the decision-making process rather than carrying all the weight of a decision. The findings from an outcome evaluation usually assist us by reducing uncertainty, speeding things up, and getting things started.

When outcome data (program objectives) are routinely collected, results can be reviewed and compared at regular intervals. By reviewing outcome data, we improve on our ability to identify problem areas and any trends occurring over time. Such analyses assist us in pinpointing areas of the program that need further attention.

Generating Knowledge for the Profession

Evaluating a program's objectives can also lead us to gain new insight and knowledge about a social problem. As we saw in Chapter 3, program objectives are derived in part from what we know about a social problem (based on the literature and previous research studies). Thus, when we evaluate a program's objectives, we are in effect testing hypotheses—one hypothesis for each program objective. We make an assumption that clients who receive a program's services will show a positive change on each program objective, more so than if they did not receive the services. How well we are able to test each hypothesis (one for each program objective) depends on the research design used.

If we simply compare pretest and posttest data, for example, we can say only that client change occurred over the time the program was offered, but we cannot be certain that the program caused the observed changes. On the other hand, if we use an experimental design and are able to randomly assign clients to a treatment group and to a control group, we will arrive at a more conclusive answer (see Box 15.2 for an example of how clients were randomized into two different groups). The results obtained from a program evaluation provide supporting pieces of "effectiveness" rather than evidence of any "absolute truths."

STEPS IN OUTCOME EVALUATIONS

In Chapter 3, we discussed how to conceptualize a program by defining its goal and stating its related objectives. A program outcome evaluation plan is unique to the context of the program for which it was designed. Using our family support program as an example, there are six major steps in conducting an outcome evaluation: (1) conceptualizing program objectives, (2) operationalizing variables and stating the outcomes, (3) designing a monitoring system, (4) analyzing and displaying data, (5) developing a feedback system, and (6) disseminating and communicating results.

Step 1: Operationalizing Program Objectives

An outcome evaluation is a major collaborative effort. It is most successful when staff are included in its design and implementation. In programs where an "outcome evaluation mentality" does not exist, staff should be included in their conceptualization. Eventually, as programs evolve to integrate evaluation activities with practice activities, planning for an outcome evaluation becomes an integral part of day-to-day program activities. If a program has clearly defined its goal and program-related objectives, the first step in an outcome evaluation is nearly done. Theoretically, a program's objectives should be tied to theory. Thus, an outcome evaluation, in effect, is theory driven.

By focusing on a program's objectives, we can be sure that we will not unnecessarily collect data on variables we do not want to know about. It is very tempting, for example, for program administrators—and workers alike—to make a last-minute decision to include an "interesting question" on an "evaluation form" or some other data recording instrument. However, data are expensive to collect and analyze. Thus, all data collected should be directly related to a program's objectives. Resources spent on collecting "extra" data detract from the quality of the data collected to monitor a program's objectives. In other words, straying from a program's data collection plan seriously compromises the results of a carefully designed outcome evaluation plan.

Operationalization

The explicit specification of a program's objectives in such a way that the measurement of each objective is possible.

Conceptualizing a program's objectives is a critical task because it defines how we understand our overall program in concrete terms. In Chapter 9, we will discuss the various ways in which we can measure a program's objectives, called **operationalization**. A few examples are presented in Box 7.2. For now, we need to know only that

Box 7.2 Examples of Outcomes and Core Indicators for Outpatient Adult Mental Health Service Providers

Initial Outcome 1: Members of the community are aware of and are able to avail themselves of outpatient mental health services.

Indicator 1: Number of consumers who received outpatient services during the quarter.

> This is the total number of public mental health system consumers who received any type of service at your clinic at least once during the reporting period.

Initial Outcome 2: Consumers take responsibility for their mental health problems.

Indicator 2: Number and percent of consumers who had a treatment plan update this quarter.

Intermediate Outcome 1: Consumers manage or reduce their presenting symptoms.

Indicator 3: Number and percentage of consumers who managed symptoms or experienced a reduction in negative symptoms.

> This is the total number of consumers who, with or without medication, reported an ability to manage their symptoms or had a reduction in negative symptoms as measured by a therapist using the General Assessment of Functioning (GAF) score.
> Number of consumers with improved GAF score out of number of consumers for whom follow-up assessment was completed during the reporting period.
> Each consumer should be assessed at intake and every six months and/or at discharge. There may be some consumers who happen to have two assessments in a quarter because case closure occurs a month or two after last assessment. In this case, report the case closure assessment.

Intermediate Outcome 2: Consumers experience an improved level of functioning.

Indicator 4: Number and percentage of consumers in an appropriate day program or other meaningful activity during all or part of the reporting period.

> This is the total number of active consumers from your clinic who were attending an appropriate day program such as school, community centers, group meetings, volunteer work, or engaging in other meaningful activity during all or part of the reporting period.

Long-Term Outcome 1: Consumers do not require emergency hospital services.

Indicator 5: Number and percentage of consumers who had a psychiatric hospitalization.

> This is the total number of active consumers from your clinic who had to be admitted during this reporting period to a hospital for psychiatric reasons.

(continued)

Box 7.2 (continued)

Indicator 6: Number and percentage of consumers who were treated in hospital emergency rooms.

This is the total number of active consumers from your clinic who were treated at a hospital emergency room during this reporting period.

Long-term Outcome 2: Consumers avoid first or new involvements with the justice system.

Indicator 7: Number and percentage of consumers who were arrested, detained, diverted, or incarcerated.

This is the total number of active consumers from your clinic who were arrested, detained, diverted, or incarcerated at a correctional facility during this reporting period.

Long-Term Outcome 3: Consumers do not require homeless services.

Indicator 8: Number and percentage of consumers who were not housed in a homeless shelter during all or part of the reporting period.

This is the total number of active consumers from your clinic who were housed in a shelter during all or part of this reporting period.

Long-Term Outcome 4: Consumers are employed.

Indicator 9: Number and percentage of consumers who were competitively employed during all or part of the reporting period.

This is the total number of active consumers from your clinic who have been employed and earning wages during all or part of the reporting period.

Long-Term Outcome 5: Consumers feel more positive about their lives.

Indicator 10: Number and percentage of consumers who report an increase in well-being (life satisfaction).

This is the total number of consumers who during the course of their treatment at your clinic reported an increase in well-being (life satisfaction) as measured by the attached eight questions of the Maryland version of the Mental Health Statistical Improvement Program (MHSIP). (Questions beginning "As a Direct Result of Services I Received . . ." as rated by consumers on a scale of 1 to 5.)

The score is calculated by adding the eight scores and dividing by eight. So if a client checks "agree" for four questions ($4 \times 4 = 16$), "strongly agree" for three ($3 \times 5 = 15$), and "neutral" for one question ($1 \times 3 = 3$), the score would be 4.25. If a client scores 3.5 or higher, then the client is reporting an improvement in well-being/life satisfaction. Each consumer should be assessed every six months thereafter and/or at discharge. Some consumers may have two assessments in a quarter because case closure occurs a month or two after last assessment. In this case, report the case closure assessment.

we can measure them in several ways. As we saw above, one of the program objectives in our family support program is "to increase problem-solving skills of family members." Conceptually, we need to determine specifically how program staff define "problem-solving skills of family members." Is problem solving the skill whereby family members apply prescribed steps in the problem-solving process? Is it the number of problems they successfully solve in a given day? Is it problem solving in a general sense or problem solving that is specific to family conflict?

Clearly, there are a many ways to conceptualize problem solving. To ensure that the program objective remains linked with the broader expectation of the program, we can look for direction at the program's goal. As a guide, the program goal is more helpful in telling us what problem solving is not, rather than what it is.

Although the idea of conceptualizing a social service program's objectives is relatively straightforward, we must be aware that there are many factors influencing the task. Evaluation of a program's objectives is more often than not an uphill battle. This is because major stakeholders want (and often demand) concrete objective results. Given the difficulties faced with measuring change in a client's self-esteem, for example, programs often opt to monitor variables such as the number of clients served in a given year and the number of hours of direct service contact between social workers and clients. These performance data are important to decision making around client services and worker supervision, but they seriously misguide the direction of a program. If, in fact, performance measures are used to define program outcomes, then social workers will focus on maximizing their direct service time without necessarily giving thought to how their time is spent or what it will accomplish.

Even more serious, by focusing on these types of outcomes, a program is at risk for developing an unhealthy culture among its workers. If workers in our family support program were to focus on increasing the number of direct service hours spent with clients, for example, then we might easily become misled into thinking that the social worker who spends the greatest number of hours in direct service hours with clients is in fact the "best" social worker. It may be, however, that this practitioner's work does not benefit clients at all.

Focusing on these operational statistics has an important role for administrative decision making and should be included in process evaluations (Chapter 6). However, when these types of objectives are included as part of an outcome evaluation, they can undermine staff morale because social workers are forced to define their work by meaningless, poorly conceptualized outcome measures.

Step 2: Operationalizing Variables and Stating the Outcomes

Selecting the best **measurements,** called operationalization, for a program's objectives is a critical part of an outcome evaluation. To measure Program Objective 2 in

Measurement
The process of systematically assigning labels to observations; the assignment of numerals to objects or events according to specific rules. In statistics, measurement systems are classified according to level of measurement and usually produce data that can be represented in numerical form.

our family support program (see Box 3.1), for example, we could use a standardized measuring instrument that has high **validity** and **reliability**:

Program Objective 2: To increase problem-solving skills for family members.

If no such instrument is available or using a questionnaire is not feasible, we might ask clients a few direct questions about their problem-solving skills. We might ask clients to talk about a problem-solving example in the past day and count the number of steps to problem solving that were applied. We could also rely on the individual client's own perspective and ask, "Since completing the program have your skills at problem solving improved?" We could ask the client to respond "yes" or "no," or have the client rate the degree of improvement on 5-point scale, where "1" means problem-solving skills are worse, "3" means they are about the same, and "5" means they have improved.

There are many different ways to operationalize (or measure) outcomes, ranging from simple to complex. Chapter 9 presents the importance of validity and reliability in choosing measuring instruments. At the very least, we can put our efforts into making sure that the measurements of our program objectives have face validity. We want each question (in addition to the whole questionnaire) to:

- Directly relate to the program objective being measured.
- Be part of a group of questions that together directly assess the program objective.
- Provide descriptive data that will be useful in the analysis of our findings.

Once we have determined what measuring instrument(s) is going to be used to measure each program objective and who will provide the data (data source), we need to pretest or pilot test the instrument(s). A pilot test helps to ascertain whether in fact the instrument produces the desired data as well as whether any obstacles got in the way, such as when instructions are not clear or too many questions are asked at one time.

Therefore, we want to pilot test all instruments at all phases of an outcome evaluation, including pretest, in-program, posttest, and follow-up. Because we are interested in collecting data *about* (and not *from*) the data collection instrument (and not the content of our questions), we want to observe how clients react to completing it. To gain more information about the clients' understanding of questions, we might ask them to verbalize their thinking as they answer a question or ask them to comment on the process of providing the data.

When a self-report measuring instrument is used to measure a program's objective, we need to check the accuracy of the data it generates by using multiple data sources in the pilot study. In using self-report data, for example, we might ask clients for their permission to interview a family member or another person familiar with the problem. Because we are only pilot testing the self-report instrument, we might ask the opinion of the social worker currently working with the client. This pilot testing activity gives us greater confidence as to whether we can rely on only client self-report data that will be collected later on in the program outcome evaluation.

If we are having difficulty choosing between two closely related measuring instruments, or are having difficulty with the wording of a difficult question, we could ask clients to respond to two options and ask which one they prefer and why. We need to give extra attention to clients who do not complete measuring instruments or refuse to respond to certain questions. In these cases, we need to explore the reasons why a certain type of client did not answer, and we must do so in a manner that is sensitive to the client's needs.

After a measuring instrument that is used to measure a program objective has been selected and pretested, it is essential to establish clear procedures for scoring it. Scoring instructions accompany most standardized measuring instruments. Thus, we need to decide only who will be responsible for carrying out the scoring task.

When a program develops it own nonstandardized measuring instrument, such as the one presented in Figure 5.4, it is necessary to agree upon a systematic set of procedures for administering and scoring the instrument. Suppose, for example, that to measure Program Objective 2 in our family support program mentioned above, we ask clients to talk out loud about a problem they encountered in the past week and to tell us the steps they took in solving the problem. Given that client responses will vary, we would need a consistent way to determine what steps were taken. First, we must agree, as a program, on what the steps of problem solving are. Second, we need to examine the possible range of responses provided by clients. We might use several raters in the pilot test to establish a protocol for scoring and, later, use the established procedures to train the people who collect the data.

Operationalization is a critical aspect of all types of evaluations and should not be taken lightly. Where possible, we need to look for means and methods to corroborate our data-generated results and strengthen the credibility of our results. Without at least the minimal pretesting of a measurement instrument, we cannot be confident about its ability to provide accurate data.

Step 3: Designing a Monitoring System

There are many procedural matters that must be thought through in carrying out a program outcome evaluation. The evaluation is more likely to go smoothly when these matters are considered in advance. Practical steps are dictated by the need to minimize cost and maximize the number of clients included in the evaluation.

Time and resources are important considerations for developing an outcome evaluation design. As we saw in Chapter 2, the monitoring approach to evaluation

Outcome evaluation is another important feature of any comprehensive evaluation plan. It assesses the short-term and long-term results of a project and seeks to measure the changes brought about by the project. Outcome evaluation questions ask: What are the critical outcomes you are trying to achieve? What impact is the project having on its clients, its staff, its umbrella organization, and its community? What unexpected impact has the project had?

Because projects often produce outcomes that were not listed as goals in the original proposal, and because efforts at prevention, particularly in complex, comprehensive, community-based initiatives, can be especially difficult to measure, it is important to remain flexible when conducting an outcome evaluation. Quality evaluations examine outcomes at multiple levels of the project. These evaluations focus not only on the ultimate outcomes expected but also attempt to discover unanticipated or important interim outcomes.

Potential Uses of Outcome Evaluations

Outcome evaluation can serve an important role during each phase of a project's development. Early on, you might focus outcome evaluation on:

- Determining what outcomes you expect or hope for from the project.
- Thinking through how individual participant/client outcomes connect to specific program or system-level outcomes.

These types of early evaluation activities increase the likelihood that implementation activities are linked to the outcomes you are trying to achieve, and help staff and stakeholders stay focused on what changes you are really attempting to make in participants' lives. In later phases of project maturity, an effective outcome evaluation process is critical to:

- Demonstrating the effectiveness of your project and making a case for its continued funding or for expansion/replication.
- Helping to answer questions about what works, for whom, and in what circumstances, and how to improve program delivery and services.

- Determining which implementation activities and contextual factors are supporting or hindering outcomes and overall program effectiveness.

We provide a range of information about outcome evaluation, along with some of the latest thinking about evaluating project outcomes, particularly for more complex, comprehensive, community-wide initiatives.

Types of Outcomes

Each project is unique and is aimed at achieving a range of different outcomes. The following provides a framework for thinking about the different levels of outcome when developing your outcome evaluation plan.

Individual, Client-Focused Outcomes

When people think about outcomes, they usually think about program goals. The problem is that, often, program goals are stated in terms of service delivery or system goals (e.g., reduce the number of women on welfare) rather than as clear outcome statements about how clients' lives will improve as a result of the program. Yet when we think about the purposes of social and human services programs, we realize that the most important set of outcomes are individual client/participant outcomes. By this, we mean, "What difference will this program/initiative make in the lives of those served?" When you sit down with program staff to answer this question, it will become clear that "reducing the number of women on welfare" is not a client-focused outcome; it is a program or system-focused outcome.

There are multiple ways to reduce the number of women on welfare (the stated outcome), but not all are equally beneficial to clients. The program might focus on quick-fix job placement for women into low-skill, low-paying jobs. However, if what many clients need is a long-term skill-building and support program, this method of "reducing the number of women on welfare" might not be the most appropriate or most beneficial program for the clients served.

If we change the outcome statement to be client-focused, we see how it helps us focus on and measure what is truly important to improving the lives of women on welfare. For example, the primary individual-level outcome for this program might be "Clients will gain life and job skills adequate to succeed in their chosen field," or "Clients will gain life and job skills necessary to be self-reliant and economically independent." The type of outcomes you may be attempting to achieve at the individual client level might include changes in circumstances, status, quality of life or functioning, attitude or behavior, knowledge, and skills. Some programs may focus on maintenance or prevention as individual client outcomes.

Program and System-Level Outcomes

Our emphasis on client-focused outcomes does not mean that we do not care about program and system-level outcomes. You do need to think through what outcomes you are trying to achieve for the program and for the broader system (e.g., improved access to case management, expanded job placement alternatives, or strengthened interagency partnerships); however, these outcomes should be seen as strategies for achieving ultimate client/participant outcomes. Once you have determined individual client outcomes, then you can determine which specific program and system-level outcomes will most effectively lead to your stated client improvements. Program and system-level outcomes should connect to individual client outcomes, and staff at all levels of the organization should understand how they connect so that they do not lose sight of client-level outcomes and focus on program outcomes, which are easier to measure and control.

Example

An initiative aimed at improving health care systems by strengthening local control and decision making, and restructuring how services are financed and delivered, has as its core an individual, client-centered outcome: "improved health status for those living in the community served." However, it quickly became clear to staff and key stakeholders that the road to improved health status entailed critical changes in health care systems, processes, and decision making—system-level goals or outcomes.

Specifically, the initiative focuses on two overarching system-level outcomes to support and achieve the primary individual/client–centered outcome of improved health status. These system-level outcomes include: inclusive decision-making processes and increased efficiency of the health care system. To achieve these system-level outcomes, the program staff have worked to (1) establish an inclusive and accountable community decision-making process for fundamental health care system reform; (2) achieve community-wide coverage through expansion of affordable insurance coverage and enhanced access to needed health care services; and (3) develop a comprehensive, integrated delivery system elevating the roles of health promotion, disease prevention, and primary care, and integrating medical, health, and human services. These key objectives and the activities associated with achieving them are linked directly to the system-level goals of inclusive decision making and increased efficiency of the health care system.

However, program staff found that it was easy in the stress of day-to-day work pressures to lose sight of the fact that the activities they were involved in to achieve system-level outcomes were not ends in themselves but a critical means to achieving the key client-level outcome of *improved health status*. To address this issue, project leaders in one community developed an effective method to assist staff and stakeholders in keeping the connection between systems and client-centered outcomes at the forefront of their minds. His method entailed "listening" to the residents of the communities where they operated. Program staff interviewed nearly 10,000 residents to gather input on how to improve the health status of those living in that community. Staff then linked these evaluation results to the system-level outcomes and activities they were engaged in on a daily basis. In this way, they were able to articulate clear connections between what they were doing at the system level (improving decision-making processes and efficiency) and the ultimate goal of improving the health status of community residents.

Broader Family or Community Outcomes

It is also important to think more broadly about what an individual-level outcome really means. Many programs are aimed at impacting families, neighborhoods, and, in

(continued)

Box 7.3 (continued)

some cases, whole communities. Besides individual outcomes, you and your staff need to think through the family and community level outcomes you are trying to achieve—both interim and long term. For instance, family outcomes might include improving communication, increasing parent–child-school interactions, and keeping children safe from abuse. Community outcomes might include increasing civic engagement and participation, decreasing violence, shifting authority and responsibility from traditional institutions to community-based agencies and community resident groups, or encouraging more intensive collaboration among community agencies and institutions.

Impacts on Organizations

In addition to a project's external outcomes, there will also be internal effects—both individual and institutional—which are important to understand and document. Many times these organizational outcomes are linked to how effectively the program can achieve individual client outcomes. They are also important to understand to improve program management and organizational effectiveness. Questions to consider in determining these outcomes include:

- *Impact on personnel.* How are the lives and career directions of project staff affected by the project? What new directions, career options, enhanced perceptions, or improved skills have the staff acquired?
- *Impact on the institution/organization.* How is the home institution affected? Does the presence of a project create ripple effects in the organization, agency, school, or university housing it? Has the organization altered its mission or the direction of its activities or the clientele served as a result of funding? Are collaborations among institutions strengthened?

Developing and Implementing an Outcome Evaluation Process

As we described above, an important first step of any outcome evaluation process is to help program staff and key stakeholders think through the different levels of program outcomes, and understand the importance of starting with individual client/participant outcomes rather than program or systems goals.

Once program staff and stakeholders have an understanding of outcome evaluation and how it can be used, you and your evaluation team can address the following questions which will facilitate the development of an outcome evaluation process (Patton, 1997):

1. Who are you going to serve?
2. What outcomes are you trying to achieve for your target population?
3. How will you measure whether you've achieved these outcomes?
4. What data will you collect and how will you collect them?
5. How will you use the results?
6. What are your performance targets?

Who Are You Going to Serve?

Before you and your program staff can determine individual client-level outcomes, you need to specify your target population. Who are you going to serve? Who are your clients/participants? It is important to be as specific as possible here. You may determine that you are serving several subgroups within a particular target population. For instance, a program serving women in poverty may find they need to break this into two distinct subgroups with different needs—women in corrections and women on welfare.

If your program serves families, you may have an outcome statement for the family as a unit, along with separate outcomes for parents and children. Here again, you would need to list several subgroups of participants.

What Outcomes Are You Trying to Achieve?

Once you have determined who you are serving, you can begin to develop outcome statements. What specific changes do you expect in your clients' lives? Again, these changes might include changes in behavior, knowledge, skills, status, or level of functioning. The key is to develop clear statements that directly relate to changes in individual lives.

How Will You Measure Outcomes?

To determine how effective a program is, you will need to have some idea of how well its outcomes are being achieved. To do this, you will need ways to measure changes the program is supposed to effect. This is another place where program staff and stakeholders can lose sight of individual participant outcomes and begin to focus exclusively on the criteria or indicators for measuring these outcomes.

Outcomes and indicators are often confused as one and the same, but they are actually distinct concepts. Indicators are measurable approximations of the outcomes you are attempting to achieve. For example, self-esteem, in and of itself, is a difficult concept to measure. A score on the Coopersmith self-esteem test is an indicator of a person's self-esteem level. Yet it is important to remember that the individual client-level outcome is not to increase the participants' scores on the Coopersmith but rather to increase self-esteem. The Coopersmith test simply becomes one way to measure self-esteem.

This program might also have constructed teacher assessments of a child's self-esteem to be administered quarterly. Here, the indicator has changed from a standardized, norm-referenced test to a more open-ended, qualitative assessment of self-esteem; however, the outcome remains the same—increased self-esteem.

What Data Will You Collect and How Will You Collect Them?

The indicators you select for each outcome will depend on your evaluation team's philosophical perspective about what the most accurate measure of your stated outcomes is; what the resources available for data collection are (some indicators are time and labor intensive to administer and interpret, such as student portfolios versus standardized achievement tests); and how privacy issues apply, and how intrusive the data collection methods are. Your team should also consider the current state of the measurement field, reviewing the indicators, if any, that currently exist for the specific outcomes you are attempting to measure. To date, little work has been completed to establish clear, agreed-upon measures for the less concrete outcomes attempted by comprehensive, community-based initiatives (e.g., changes in community power structures; increased community participation, and leadership development and community building) (Connell, Kubisch, Schorr, & Weiss, 1995).

Another common problem is that all too often programs start with this step: by determining what can be measured. Program staff may then attempt to achieve only the outcomes that they know how to measure or they find relatively easy to measure. Because the field of measurement of human functioning will never be able to provide an accurate and reliable measure for every outcome (particularly more complex human feelings and states), and because program staff and stakeholders often are knowledgeable about only a subset of existing indicators, starting with measures is likely to limit the potential for the program by excluding critical outcomes. The Kellogg Foundation believes it is important to start with the overall goals and outcomes of the program, and then determine how to go about measuring these outcomes. From our perspective, *it is better to have meaningful outcomes that are difficult to measure than to have easily measurable outcomes that are not related to the core of a program that will make a difference in the lives of those served.*

How Will You Use Results?

Ultimately, you want to ensure that the findings from your outcome evaluation process are useful. We suggest that you and your evaluation team discuss how you will use the results of the evaluation process from the beginning. Before you have even finalized data collection strategies, think through how you will use different outcome data and what specific actions you might take, depending on the findings. This will increase the likelihood that you will focus on the critical outcomes, select the most accurate and meaningful indicators, collect the most appropriate data, and analyze and interpret the data in the most meaningful ways. In addition, it will increase the likelihood that you and your staff will act on what you find, because you understood from the beginning what you were collecting and why you were collecting it.

What Are Your Performance Targets?

Think of performance targets as benchmarks or progress indicators that specify the level of outcome attainment you expect or hope for (e.g., the percentage of participants enrolled in postsecondary education; how many grade-level increases in reading ability). Setting meaningful performance targets provides staff

(continued)

Box 7.3 (continued)

and stakeholders with benchmarks to document progress toward achieving program outcomes. These benchmarks help clarify and provide specificity about where you are headed and whether you are succeeding.

It is often best to set performance targets based on past performance. Therefore, you may want to wait until you have some baseline outcome data before determining performance targets. However, if you do not have the luxury of waiting to collect baseline data, you can set initial performance targets based on levels attained in comparable or related programs.

Measuring the Impacts of System Change and Comprehensive Community-Based Initiatives

As discussed previously, we need to think differently about evaluating the impacts of more complex system change and comprehensive community initiatives. In these initiatives, implementation is difficult and long, and requires a collaborative, evolutionary, flexible approach. We may not see ultimate outcomes for many years, and many of the desired outcomes are difficult to measure using traditional quantitative methodologies. And yet these initiatives hold great promise for really making a difference in our communities.

When evaluating these initiatives, then, we need to use innovative methods, such as participatory and theory-based evaluation, to learn as much as we can about how and why these programs work. By working together to develop the key interim outcomes, we will be able to document better the progress of these initiatives and to understand better how they lead to the desired long-term outcomes.

There are two categories of interim outcomes you should think about measuring. The first includes interim outcomes associated directly with your target population. For example, interim outcomes associated with the long-term outcome of getting off public assistance might include leaving abusive relationships or conquering a drug problem.

The second category of interim outcomes includes changes in the project's or community's capacity to achieve the long-term desired outcomes (Schorr & Kubisch, 1995). For a project designed to increase the number of students going to college, important interim outcomes might be the implementation of a new professional development program to educate guidance counselors and teachers about how to encourage and prepare students for college; or to increase student access to financial aid and scholarship information; or to expand the number and type of summer and afterschool academic enrichment opportunities for students.

Measuring Impacts Through the Use of a Program Logic Model

One effective method for charting progress toward interim and long-term outcomes is through the development and use of a program logic model. As we discussed earlier, a program logic model is a picture of how your program works—the theory and assumptions underlying the program. A program logic model links outcomes (both short-term and long-term) with program activities/processes and the theoretical assumptions/principles of the program. This model provides a roadmap of your program, highlighting how it is expected to work, what activities need to come before others, and how desired outcomes are achieved.

There are multiple benefits to the development and use of a program logic model. First, there are *program design benefits*. By using a program logic model as part of the evaluation process, staff will be able to stay focused better on outcomes; connect interim outcomes to long-term outcomes; link activities and processes to desired outcomes; and keep underlying program assumptions at the forefront of their minds. In short, the process of creating a program logic model will clarify your thinking about the program, how it was originally intended to work, and what adaptations may need to be made once the program is operational.

Second, the program logic model provides a powerful base from which to conduct *ongoing evaluation of the program*. It spells out how the program produces desired outcomes. In this way, you can decide more systematically which pieces of the program to study in determining whether your assumptions were correct. A program logic model helps focus the evaluation on measuring each set of events in the model to see what happens, what works, what doesn't work, and for whom. You and your evaluation team will be able to discover where the model breaks down or where it is failing to perform as originally conceptualized.

As we discussed, a logic model or theory-based evaluation is also an effective approach for evaluating complex initiatives with intangible outcomes (such as increased community participation) or long-term outcomes that will not be achieved for several years. A program logic model lays out the interim outcomes and the more measurable outcomes on the way to long-term and intangible outcomes. As a result, it provides an effective way to chart the progress of more complex initiatives and make improvements along the way based on new information.

Finally, there is value in the *process of developing a logic model*. The process is an iterative one that requires stakeholders to work together to clarify the underlying rationale for the program and the conditions under which success is most likely to be achieved. Gaps in activities, expected outcomes, and theoretical assumptions can be identified, resulting in changes being made based on consensus-building and a logical process rather than on personalities, politics, or ideology. The clarity of thinking that occurs from the process of building the model becomes an important part of the overall success of the program. The model itself provides a focal point for discussion. It can be used to explain the program to others and to create a sense of ownership among the stakeholders.

Types of Program Logic Models

Although logic models come in many shapes and sizes, three types of models seem to be the most useful.

One type is an *outcomes model*. This type displays the interrelationships of goals and objectives. The emphasis is on short-term objectives as a way to achieve long-term goals. An outcomes logic model might be appropriate for program initiatives aimed at achieving longer-term or intangible, hard-to-measure outcomes. By creating a logic model that makes the connections among short-term, intermediate, and long-term outcomes, staff will be able better to evaluate progress and program successes, and locate gaps and weaknesses in program operations. See Figure 6 in Box 3.2 for an example of this type.

Another type of logic model is an *activities model*. This type links the various activities together in a manner that indicates the process of program implementation. Certain activities need to be in place before other activities can occur. An activities logic model is appropriate for complex initiatives that involve many layers of activities and interinstitutional partnerships. In these cases, every stakeholder needs to have the big picture of how the activities and processes pull together into a cohesive whole to achieve desired outcomes. It also provides an effective means to document and benchmark progress as part of the evaluation process. Which activities have been completed? Where did the program face barriers? How successfully were activities completed? What additional activities and processes were discovered along the way that are critical to program success? An example of this type of program logic model can be seen in Figure 7 in Box 3.2.

The third type of logic model is the *theory model*. This model links theoretical constructs together to explain the underlying assumptions of the program. This model is also particularly appropriate for complex, multifaceted initiatives aimed at impacting multiple target populations (e.g., multiple members of a family, whole communities, or multiple institutions or community organizations within a community). At the same time, a theory logic model is also effective for a simpler program because of its ability to describe why the program is expected to work as it does. See Figure 5 in Box 3.2 for an example of a theory logic model.

Oftentimes, program staff will find that they will need to combine two or three of these program logic models.

Monitoring system

The evaluation design, protocols, and procedures that ensure systematic, complete, and accurate data collection; also includes a schedule for reporting and disseminating evaluation findings.

incorporates evaluation activities and tasks into ongoing client service delivery. Thus, our **monitoring system** must be careful not to overburden the workers such that direct client service delivery is compromised. To gather valid and reliable data, we must consider the type and amount of changes we expect from the social workers.

How we design our evaluation can impact when the social workers meet with their clients. It may also change the nature of worker–client interaction in a first meeting, as is the case when standardized measuring instruments are administered. Evaluation activity almost always affects the way social workers record client data. Because these evaluation activities directly impact a social worker's behavior, they have important implications for how clients are served and how evaluation data are collected.

Deciding the Number of Clients to Include (Unit of Analysis)

In general, we want to collect outcome data for as many clients as possible in an outcome evaluation. For programs with a few clients, such as a single group home program or a private social worker working independently, 100 percent coverage of clients served is more likely. For programs with many clients, however, such as child protection services or a major family service agency, we can use basic sampling techniques to develop a representative sample of all clients receiving services. The major issue affecting sample size is whether program resources exist to collect data from all clients in the program. If it is not feasible to do so—an independent private social worker cannot afford to include 30 minutes of testing for each client, or a family service agency does not want to give up valuable "client time" for evaluation activities—then sampling is an option.

The number of clients needed for an outcome evaluation is affected by the number of subgroups that may be included in the evaluation. Suppose for example, our family support program wants to compare the levels of problem-solving skills (Program Objective 2) for single-parent and double-parent families. Ideally, we want to have roughly equivalent groups so that we do not end up comparing, say, 120 single parents with 240 double parents. Clearly, the double-parent families are better represented in this comparison. Ideally, we should aim to have a minimum of 30 clients for each subgroup included in our analyses. The more subgroups we include (say we are also interested in the age of parents, whether substance abuse is a factor, or what services our family has used previously), the more clients we need.

When there are not enough resources to support data collection from all clients, the task can be lightened by randomly selecting clients for inclusion in the evaluation. As we will see in Chapter 10, random selection can occur so long as the program aims to have a reasonable number of clients at critical points within the data analysis, such as when the program's annual or semiannual report are due. The idea behind random sampling is that each client has an equal chance of being included in the evaluation. In theory, this is a simple notion. In practice, however, there are many obstacles to consider.

The first matter to consider is deciding on what exactly constitutes the "total client population" served by the program. In our family support program, for example, it may be that parents periodically phone the program for crisis support and speak to a social worker on the telephone for a brief period; or at times, an inappropriate referral is made and program time is used to reroute the client to a better matched service. Although these clients may receive some assistance from our family support program, it would be unreasonable and even unimaginable to try and collect data related to the program's objectives. Rather, our family support program has as its primary client group families who are referred and accepted to the program to participate in the 12-week intervention.

Because clients of our family support program are referred on an ongoing basis, it is possible for random selection to occur by including every second or third client referred or by flipping a coin ("heads" our family is included, "tails" they are not) each time a client comes to the program, with a predetermined maximum number. If we are particularly interested in how outcomes relate to specific client groups (e.g., single-parent and double-parent families), we can use a stratified sampling strategy. The critical aspect of random selection is that the decision to include clients is made without bias. That is, a program administrator does not select families because they appear to be cooperative, or social workers do not exclude families because they are concerned that the families might not respond positively toward the program.

The philosophy behind monitoring evaluation is that evaluation is part and parcel of good practice. Just as we allow clients the right to self-determinism—to say whether or not a particular intervention fits for them—we must also be willing to give clients the option to participate in any given evaluation activity. When clients decline to answer questions or fill out questionnaires, then we are faced with the problem of missing data. That is, we will have some unknowns in our final client sample. The less missing data we have, the more confident we will be that our evaluation results are reflective of all clients served within our program.

Another matter to decide in sampling is whether we want to collect data from the *same* clients throughout the entire evaluation (a cohort analysis) or whether we want to collect data from a *different* set of clients at program intake and exit (a cross-sectional analysis). A cohort analysis permits us to address questions of change over time for a single group of clients. We could then compare, for example, the percentage of clients who showed an improvement in their problem-solving skills, and the amount of change.

A **cross-sectional analysis** would give us a slightly different set of data. In this case, we could determine the percentage of improvement in the average score for a group of clients at intake (Time 1) and another group at termination (Time 2). In this situation, we could not determine how many clients' problem-solving skills got better or worse, however.

Cross-sectional research design

A survey research design in which data are collected to indicate characteristics of a sample or population at a particular moment in time.

The advantage of using the same clients throughout the entire evaluation is that it reduces the difficulties associated with comparing two different groups of clients. The drawback of including only one set of clients in the evaluation is that they may, in effect, receive special treatment as a result of their inclusion, which will bias the representativeness of the results to the entire program.

Deciding When Data Will Be Collected

When the data are collected directly relates to the question asked in an outcome evaluation. An outcome evaluation indicates *whether* the program is working, but it says nothing about *how* it is working (or failing to work). Nor is there any mention of efficiency—that is, the time and dollar cost of client success (see the next chapter). After all, if a program achieves what it is supposed to achieve by the attainment of its program objectives, why does it matter how it achieves it? If the program is to be replicated or improved, it *does* matter, and efficiency assessments (Chapter 8) and process analyses (Chapter 6) can answer such questions.

Questions related to outcome generally fall into four major categories, which have a direct link to the type of evaluation design used. First, the evaluator wants to know to what degree the program is achieving its objectives. Does participation in our family support program, for example, increase positive social support for parents (Program Objective 1 in Box 3.1), and by how much? This question requires that we collect data at (or near) the beginning of the program and at (or near) the end of the program to detect how much *change* has occurred. As discussed earlier, we need to make a decision as to whether data will be collected for all incoming clients. Unless, the data are in some way used to plan and implement a treatment intervention, data collection from all clients might be excessive, so a sampling strategy can be used.

Second, we want to know whether people who have been through our family support program have more positive social supports than similar people who have not been through the program. This question suggests that we collect data not only from clients in the program but also from clients who did not participate in the program. These could be clients who were turned away or perhaps are on a waiting list for program services. The aim of this question is to directly *compare* outcomes for clients receiving program services with those who do not.

Causality

A relationship of cause and effect. The effect will invariably occur when the cause is present.

Third, there is the question of **causality**. Is there any evidence that services provided by our family support program *caused* the increase in positive social supports? This question is more sophisticated than the first two and requires the use of explanatory research designs.

Fourth, we might be interested in assessing the *longevity* of changes made by clients. In this case, we want to collect data from clients not only at program exit but also at some predetermined points afterward. Many clients who have exited from human service programs return to their previous social environments, which were at least partially responsible for their problems in the first place. Often, clients' gains are not maintained; equally often, programs have no follow-up procedures to find out if they in fact have been maintained. Ideally, **follow-up data** are collected at intervals, such as 3, 6, or 12 months after clients exit a program. The time span should allow for enough time to pass in order to comfortably say that the program effects were not simply temporary.

The challenge of collecting client follow-up data is that the task is not always easy. Sometimes it is very difficult to locate clients after they leave a program. Programs working with economically disadvantaged clients may have an especially difficult time because clients may not have telephones. Clients who are transient, clients with mental illness, clients with criminal backgrounds, and clients who are homeless are hard to track. The difficulties associated with locating clients are very expensive and time-consuming. Because of the additional costs, every effort should be made to collect posttest data just before clients leave the program.

Outcome data imply that we are interested in how clients change in terms of relevant program objectives at the end of our services. This assumption requires that a clear program end does in fact exist. In some cases, services to clients with ongoing difficulties may extend beyond those of the typical program. Suppose, for a moment, that a family within our family support program receives a two-week extension of services because our family needs additional assistance for one reason or another.

When brief extensions are granted, the end of the program is also extended. If, however, longer term extensions are given such that the client essentially repeats the program, then the *true* program end technically is decided by the predefined program service time. The downside of looking at things this way is that the client may not show positive improvement at the predefined end of the program. This is unfortunate for our evaluation results, but it is true. Frankly, we are in a better position to learn how to improve client service delivery if we work from objective data.

A related problem with collecting follow-up data is that clients may be receiving services from other social service programs during the follow-up period. How will we know if treatment effects are maintained as a result of our work with clients, or if the other current social service is somehow helping clients to do well? There are no perfect solutions to such a problem, but we can simply ask clients what additional social services they are involved with, if any. These data can be used to compare clients who are receiving additional social services with those who are not.

So far, we have been discussing data collection from the vantage point of program-level evaluation. As we will see in Chapters 11 and 14, it is also possible to use aggregated case-level data to evaluate a program's outcomes. When case-level data are used, there are usually many more data collection points. Just how many there are will be determined by the worker and the client in designing an individual monitoring system for their unique practice objectives.

Follow-up data
Collecting client data (as measured by a program's objectives) at specific points after clients have exited the program (e.g., three months, six months, one year).

Deciding How Data Will Be Collected

We can collect outcome data from clients by telephone, mail, or in person. Clearly, in-person costs are higher than if we collect data during our last contact with clients before they exit the program or if we contact clients by telephone (provided that the clients have phones). Ideally, we want to collect data from all clients who are represented in our program's objectives. In our example, Program Objective 2 within our family support program example focuses on problem-solving skills of all family members.

This raises the question of whether we should collect data from the children as well as the parents. We must decide how feasible it is to use more than one data source. If time and resources limit us to one data source, then we must pick the one we think is most representative or one that will provide the most meaningful data in relation to the program objective.

Who is going to be responsible for collecting data is a critical question. When data are collected at intake, workers usually will gather the facts from clients as part of the assessment process. When social workers collect data at program exit, there is great risk of biasing results, which can discredit the outcome evaluation. Because social workers and clients come to know each other well, the helping relationship can influence how clients respond to measuring instruments. Furthermore, having social workers evaluate their own performance is not generally accepted as a way to provide accurate data. Another reason for not using social workers to collect outcome data is that the additional task is likely to overload them. As clients exit a program, new clients are admitted. It becomes unwieldy for a single social worker to juggle a new admission, a termination, a clinical follow-up, and an evaluation follow-up in addition to his or her ongoing caseload.

Quality data collection requires several explicit procedures that need to be laid out and strictly followed. Minimal training is needed for consistent data collection. It is rather inefficient to train all social workers within a single program to collect data (in addition to the disadvantages already stated). Thus, it is advisable to assign data collection tasks to a small number of workers who are properly trained in the data collection effort. These individuals do not necessarily have to have any background in evaluation procedures; they simply need to have good interviewing skills and be able to follow basic standardized instructions.

Step 4: Analyzing and Displaying Data

It is possible that, by the time clients have answered questions on a program intake form and completed any standardized measuring instruments used by a program, they may have produced 50 or more separate pieces of data. From marital status, to service history, to the level of a social problem—we must decide how each unit of data will be presented and what the possibilities for analyses are. With outcome data, our data analyses tasks focus on the output of the program; that is, what is the condition (or situation) for clients at the time they exit the program and beyond? We may use demographic data on our intake form to present outcome data, according to subgroups, that reveal interesting results.

Suppose, for example, that overall family progress on problem-solving skills (Program Objective 2) for our family support program was rather mediocre. But with further analyses, we are able to show that families with toddlers had great improvement compared with families with teens; in the latter, almost no improvement was observed. The additional information that can be gained from analyzing data in subgroups gives important detail for program decision makers. It also helps to pinpoint a program's strengths and weakness, rather than simply looking at a program's results as a whole.

Although social workers may have some interest in analyzing client data on a question by question basis, outcome data are most useful when data can be aggregated and summarized to provide an overview on client outcomes. We must, therefore, decide how to aggregate responses to individual questions. When a standardized measuring instrument is used, the procedures for scoring and summarizing data derived from it are usually provided with the instrument.

Suppose we used a simple standardized measuring instrument to measure problem-solving skills, where a score of zero is considered "very low problem-solving skill" and a score of 100 is considered "very high problem-solving skill." If we measured clients at program intake (pretest data) and program exit (posttest data), we might report the average score for all clients at intake (e.g., 40) and the average score at program exit (e.g., 80), thereby reporting an "average" increase in problem-solving skills of 40 points.

We can report additional information when normative data are available with standardized measuring instruments. For example, if our measuring instrument reported that when tested on a clinical population, the mean score was 50, and when tested on a nonclinical population, the mean score was 70, we could use these data to compare our client scores with these normative data. Normative data are particularly helpful for interpreting client data when measurement occurs only at program exit.

Because many stakeholders desire concrete and objective results, it is also worthwhile to consider reporting outcome data according to preset expectations. We may have worded Program Objective 2, for example, as follows: "Seventy-five percent of families will show improvement in their problem-solving skills." We should only measure outcomes in this way if we have a sound rationale for estimating success. Estimates may be derived from previous evaluation data, research studies, or general expectations of a given **population**. Estimates may focus on the amount of

Population

An entire set, or universe, of people, objects, or events of concern to a research study, from which a sample is drawn.

"average improvement" rather than the number of clients expected to show success. Including such estimates serves to educate stakeholders who might not be as well-informed about a client population or a social problem.

It is important that stakeholders understand that 100 percent success in deterring runaways, family violence, drug addiction, child prostitution, crime, and welfare fraud is an unrealistic expectation for any social service program. In some cases, we may not expect a better than 50/50 chance of seeing improvement for clients. If this is the case, then outcome results should be interpreted in this context.

In addition to comparing outcome data with normative scores and with preset expectations, we may also choose to present outcome data over time. It is possible, for example, to report client outcomes from one year to the next to show program trends. If outcome data from similar programs exist, it also is possible to compare the results of one program with another.

For the most part, analysis of outcome data is done by summarizing key outcome measures and reporting either the amount of change or the number of clients achieving a certain level of change. In either case, it is helpful to report these data using actual numbers and percentages. The numbers provide stakeholders with a realistic view of how many clients are included in each analysis, while percentages offer an easy way of comparing data across categories. We can also use basic graphing techniques and statistics to gain further insight into our data analysis (see Chapter 12).

Step 5: Developing a Feedback System

Outcome evaluation can produce useful and telling data about what is happening for clients after they receive program services. The results are most useful when they are routinely shared with key stakeholders. In most cases, the emphasis on outcome data is for the benefit of the stakeholders who are external to the program.

Funders and policy makers learn about program outcomes through annual reports or perhaps new proposals. Program outcomes may be disseminated more broadly as well. The local newspaper may be interested in doing a feature article on the services a program offers. In addition to providing anecdotes and general descriptions of a social problem, program administrators have the option of reporting outcome data, thereby increasing public awareness.

When it comes to program-level evaluation, developing a feedback system for internal stakeholders such as program administrators and social workers is absolutely essential. Making outcome data available to them on a regular basis helps to keep them focused on the program's goal. Discussing outcome data can also stimulate important questions such as Why are our clients doing so well (or so poorly)? Are our program outcomes realistic? Are there any aspects of client outcomes that are being ignored? When program personnel have an opportunity to respond to concrete data, discussions become more purposeful and focused.

Step 6: Disseminating and Communicating Results

Disseminating and communicating results need be taken seriously if we want to see our outcome evaluation used. As we have seen, the findings that emerge from an outcome evaluation give us objective data from which to make decisions about how clients make changes. Such results can affect program operations, funding, and even what we believe about our clients and the expectations we have of our programs. The likelihood of having evaluation results used is increased when results are presented in a straightforward manner.

It is useful to think about the obstacles that get in the way of putting evaluation results into practice. One obstacle occurs when we fail to remember the law of parsimony when presenting the final report. As mentioned in the last chapter, a report should be straightforward, clear, and concise. It should be designed for the intended audience (stakeholder group). Note, however, that a program might have several versions of the same evaluation report—one version for each type of stakeholder. A report may be presented to the program's funders, while a pamphlet on the same information (presented differently) may be available for clients.

Another obstacle to using the findings of an outcome evaluation is created when the results contradict strong predetermined beliefs. It is fair to say, for example, that most social workers believe that their efforts are helpful to clients. We design programs with the hope and promise of improving human lives and social conditions. Thus, when our outcomes show that no, or little, client change has occurred or that a client problem has worsened, it is easy to become defensive and to question the integrity of the evaluation methods.

Given that evaluation research methods are fraught with threats to **internal** and **external validity**, it is tempting to raise such concerns and then continue practicing as we always have. In other instances, the public may hold strong convictions about a particular social problem. An evaluation of a prison program, for example, may show that the program is unsuccessful in preventing prisoners from committing further crimes once they have been released. Yet the general public may have a strong opinion that people who commit crimes should be punished by being sent to prison. In such a case, the evaluation results will have little influence on program changes.

Whatever the form of reporting and disseminating our evaluation findings, confidentiality is of utmost importance. Confidentiality is most easily established when data are reported in aggregate forms. By summarizing data by groups, we

Internal validity
The extent to which it can be demonstrated that the intervention (the independent variable) in an evaluation is the only cause of change in the program's objective (the dependent variable); soundness of the experimental procedures and measuring instruments.

External validity
The extent to which the findings of an evaluation study can be generalized outside the evaluative situation.

Box 7.4 Published Examples of Outcome Evaluations

Substantive areas are in **bold.**

Auslander, W., Haire-Joshu, D., Houston, C., Williams, J. H., & Krebill, H. (2000). The short-term impact of a health promotion program for **low-income African American women**. *Research on Social Work Practice, 10,* 78–97.

Bacha, T., Pomeroy, E. C., Gilbert, D. (1999). A psychoeducational group intervention for **HIV-positive children**: A pilot study. *Health and Social Work, 24,* 303–306.

Bagley, C., & Young, L. (1998). Long-term evaluation of group counseling of **women with a history of child sexual abuse**: Focus on depression, self-esteem, suicidal behaviors, and social support. *Social Work with Groups, 21,* 63–73.

Barber, J., & Gilbertson, R. (1998). Evaluation of a self-help manual for the **female partners of heavy drinkers**. *Research on Social Work Practice, 8,* 141–151.

Barker, S. B., Knisely, J. S., & Dawson, K. (1999). The evaluation of a consultation service for delivery of **substance abuse services** in a hospital setting. *Journal of Addictive Diseases, 18,* 73–82.

Burry, C. L. (1999). Evaluation of a training program for **foster parents** of infants with prenatal substance effects. *Child Welfare, 78,* 197–214.

Collins, M. E., Mowbray, C. T., & Bybee, D. (1999). Measuring coping strategies in an educational intervention for **individuals with psychiatric disabilities**. *Health and Social Work, 24,* 279–290.

Comer, E., & Fraser, M. (1998). Evaluation of six **family-support programs**: Are they effective? *Families in Society, 79,* 134–148.

Conboy, A., Auerbach, C., Schnall, D., & LaPorte, H. (2000). **MSW student** satisfaction with using single-system design computer software to evaluate social work practice. *Research on Social Work Practice, 10,* 127–138.

Deacon, S. A., & Piercy, F. P. (2000). Qualitative evaluation of **family therapy programs**: A participatory approach. *Journal of Marital and Family Therapy, 26,* 39–45.

de Anda, D. (1999). Project Peace: The evaluation of a skill-based violence prevention program for **high school adolescents**. *Social Work in Education, 21,* 137–149.

Deschenes, E., & Greenwood, P. (1998). Alternative placements for **juvenile offenders**: Results from the evaluation of the Nokomis challenge program. *Journal of Research in Crime and Delinquency, 35,* 267–294.

Ford, C. A., & Okojie, F. A. (1999). A multi-dimensional approach to evaluating **family preservation programs**. *Family Preservation Journal, 4,* 31–62.

Harrison, R. S., Boyle, S. W., Farley, W. (1999). Evaluating the outcomes of family-based intervention for **troubled children**: A pretest-posttest study. *Research on Social Work Practice, 9,* 640–655.

Hughes, R. H., & Kirby, J. (2000). Strengthening evaluation strategies for **divorcing family support services**: Perspectives of parent educators, mediators, attorneys, and judges. *Family Relations, 49,* 53–61.

Jenson, J. M., Jacobson, M., Unrau, Y. A., & Robinson, R. L. (1996). Intervention for victims of **child sexual abuse**: An evaluation of the children's advocacy model. *Child and Adolescent Social Work Journal, 13,* 139–156.

Jinich, S., & Litrownik, A. (1999). Coping with **sexual abuse**: Development and evaluation of a videotape intervention for nonoffending parents. *Child Abuse and Neglect, 23,* 175–190.

Myers, L., & Rittner, B. (1999). Family functioning and satisfaction of **former residents of a non-therapeutic residential care facility**: An exploratory study. *Journal of Family Social Work, 3,* 54–68.

Nicholson, B. C., Brenner, V., & Fox, R. A. (1999). A community-based parenting program with **low-income mothers of young children**. *Families in Society, 80,* 247–253.

Prior, V., Lynch, M. A., & Glaser, D. (1999). Responding to **child sexual abuse**: an evaluation of social work by children and their careers. *Child and Family Social Work, 4,* 131–143.

Raschick, M., & Critchley, R. (1998). Guidelines for conducting site-based evaluations of intensive **family preservation programs**. *Child Welfare, 77,* 643–660.

Salzer, M. S., Rappaport, J., & Segre, L. (1999). Professional appraisal of professionally led and **self-help groups.** *American Journal of Orthopsychiatry, 69,* 530–540.

Shifflett, K, & Cummings, E. M. (1999). A program for educating parents about the effects **of divorce and conflict on children:** An initial evaluation. *Family Relations, 48,* 79–89.

Short, J. L. (1998). Evaluation of a substance abuse prevention and mental health promotion program for **children of divorce**. *Journal of Divorce and Remarriage, 28,* 139–155.

Smith, L., Riley, E., Beilenson., P., Vlahov, D., & Junge, B. (1998). A focus group evaluation of drop boxes for safe **syringe disposal**. *Journal of Drug Issues, 28,* 905–920.

Stone, G., McKenry, P., & Clark, K. (1999). Fathers' participation in a **divorce education program:** A qualitative evaluation. *Journal of Divorce and Remarriage, 30,* 99–113.

Welsh, W., Jenkins, P., & Harris, P. (1999). Reducing **minority** over-representation in juvenile justice: Results of community-based delinquency prevention in Harrisburg. *Journal of Research in Crime and Delinquency, 36,* 87–110.

avoid singling out any one client. Box 7.4 lists some social work program outcome studies where their findings have been communicated to the general public (a stakeholder group) via professional journal publications.

SUMMING UP AND LOOKING AHEAD

Outcome evaluations are practical endeavors. We want to know whether client changes have occurred as a result of our intervention efforts. Thus, our evaluation plan is designed to give us valid and reliable data that can be used for decision making. To arrive at the best plan to answer our questions, we must consider how much time and money are available, what research design is feasible, and what biases exist. Program outcome assessment is an evaluation that determines to what degree the program is meeting its overall program objectives. In our profession, this usually means the degree to which our interventions are effective.

We usually do outcome evaluations before, or during, we do benefits evaluations, the topic of the following chapter.

RECAP AND ONLINE MATERIALS

In this chapter you learned how to do social work outcome evaluations.

You should also recall the concept of outcome evaluations from your foundational research course. If not, go online to take a free crash course in how to use various outcome evaluation tools.

You can also find the following materials online to help you master the concepts you just learned:

- Chapter Outline
- Learning Objectives
- Key Terms and Concepts
- Flash Cards
- Practice Multiple-Choice Tests
- Essay Questions with Answers
- Links

www.oup.com/us/swevaluation

STUDY QUESTIONS

1. Discuss why outcome evaluations are necessary in our profession. Use a social work example throughout your discussion.

2. List and describe in detail how program outcome evaluations can be used in our profession. Use a social work example throughout your discussion.

3. List and describe in detail the six steps you would have to undertake to do a outcome evaluation. Use one common social work example throughout your discussion.

4. Take a look at Box 7.1. Do you think that there are other myths that could be added. And if so, why?

5. Go to the library or use Box 7.4 and find a social work journal article that presents the results of an outcome evaluation. Did the author(s) of the article use the concepts found within this chapter? If so, what were they?

6. Describe the steps you would take to conduct an outcome evaluation of the social work program you are in (BSW or MSW).

7. In reference to question 6 above, what would be your outcome indicators? Why did you choose them?

8. In reference to question 6 above, who are your stakeholders? How would you involve them in your outcome evaluation?

9. From your field placement setting, obtain an outcome evaluation that was recently done. What concepts in this chapter were contained in the evaluation? Which ones were not?

10. Fully describe the similarities and differences among needs assessments (Chapter 5), process evaluations (Chapter 6), and outcome evaluations (this chapter). Are they complementary to one another? If so, why? If not, why not?

REFERENCES, FURTHER READING, AND RESOURCES

Connell, P. J., Kubisch, A. C., Schorr, L. B., & Weiss, C. H. (1995). *New approaches to evaluating communities initiatives: Concepts, methods, and contexts.* Washington, DC: Aspen Institute.

Patton, M. Q. (1997). *Utilization-focused evaluation.* Newbury Park, CA: Sage.

Schorr, L. B., & Kubisch, A. C. (September, 1995). New approaches to evaluation. Paper presented at the Casey Foundation Annual Research/Evaluation Conference.

W. K. Kellogg Foundation. (1998). *Evaluation handbook.* Battle Creek, MI: Author.

On Using Research Designs In Outcome Evaluations

Grinnell, R. M., Jr., Unrau, Y. A., & Williams, M. (2005). Group-level designs. In R. M. Grinnell, Jr., & Y. A. Unrau (Eds.), *Social work research and evaluation: Quantitative and qualitative approaches* (7th ed., pp. 185–210). New York: Oxford University Press.

Williams, M., Grinnell, R. M., Jr., & Unrau, Y. A. (2005). Case-level designs. In R. M. Grinnell, Jr., & Y. A. Unrau (Eds.), *Social work research and evaluation: Quantitative and qualitative approaches* (7th ed., pp. 171–184). New York: Oxford University Press.

On Gathering Original Data for Outcome Evaluations

Gochros, H. L. (2005). Interviewing. In R. M. Grinnell, Jr., & Y. A. Unrau (Eds.), *Social work research and evaluation: Quantitative and qualitative approaches* (7th ed., pp. 245–269). New York: Oxford University Press.

McMurtry, S. L. (2005). Surveys. In R. M. Grinnell, Jr., & Y. A. Unrau (Eds.), *Social work research and evaluation: Quantitative and qualitative approaches* (7th ed., pp. 271–287). New York: Oxford University Press.

Rogers, G., & Bouey, E. (2005). Participant observation. In R. M. Grinnell, Jr., & Y. A. Unrau (Eds.), *Social work research and evaluation: Quantitative and qualitative approaches* (7th ed., pp. 231–244). New York: Oxford University Press.

On Selecting the Best Data Gathering Methods for Outcome Evaluations

Unrau, Y. A. (2005). Selecting a data collection method and data source. In R. M. Grinnell, Jr., & Y. A. Unrau (Eds.), *Social work research and evaluation: Quantitative and qualitative approaches* (7th ed., pp. 339–349). New York: Oxford University Press.

On Analyzing Quantitative Data for Outcome Evaluations

Weinbach, R. W., & Grinnell, R. M., Jr. (2007). *Statistics for social workers* (7th ed.). Boston: Allyn & Bacon.

Williams, M., Tutty, L., & Grinnell, R. M., Jr. (2005). Analyzing quantitative data. In R. M. Grinnell, Jr., & Y. A. Unrau (Eds.), *Social work research and evaluation: Quantitative and qualitative approaches* (7th ed., pp. 353–369). New York: Oxford University Press.

On Constructing Survey Instruments for Outcome Evaluations

Mindel, C. H. (2005). Designing measuring instruments. In R. M. Grinnell, Jr., & Y. A. Unrau (Eds.), *Social work research and evaluation: Quantitative and qualitative approaches* (7th ed., pp. 133–146). New York: Oxford University Press.

DOING AN EFFICIENCY EVALUATION

8

The previous three chapters examined three different types of evaluations (i.e., needs assessments, process evaluations, and outcome evaluations). This chapter describes the final type—evaluations to determine how efficient our programs are. The basic question addressed in an evaluation of efficiency is "What did it cost to produce the program's outcomes?" A program that obtains its results (outcomes) at a lower cost than another similar program that achieves comparable results can be said to be more efficient.

Although the concept of "efficiency" is relatively straightforward, the techniques required to conduct an efficiency evaluation can be quite complex, technical, and costly. For this reason, many evaluators often stop at the evaluation of a program's outcomes and ignore the question of its efficiency. Yet any program evaluation without consideration of the program's costs provides only an incomplete understanding of the program being evaluated.

The question of efficiency arises for a number of reasons. At a practical level, think of your own purchasing practices; if you are like most people, you like to obtain the goods and services you use at the lowest possible cost. By doing so, you can "stretch your dollar." It is no different in the social services field. By being efficient, we create savings, which in turn can then be used to meet other social needs via the establishment of other social service programs.

In addition, because resources available to our profession are always scarce, it is a responsible practice to ensure that those resources are used wisely and used in the most efficient manner as possible. Finally, our profession has been under scrutiny for a number of years. There is a widely held perception among politicians and the general public alike that our social service programs are not good stewards of resources and that there is much waste in the delivery of the services we offer. Evidence of efficiency can serve to counteract such claims and shore up support for what we do.

COST EFFECTIVENESS VERSUS COST BENEFIT

The evaluation of efficiency has two types of analyses: cost effectiveness analyses and cost-benefit analyses. To illustrate the distinction between the two types, we will use an example of our Aim High Program described in Box 8.1. This program seeks to prepare social assistance recipients for employment.

Generally speaking, the **cost-effectiveness analysis** seeks to examine the costs of a program in relation to its outcomes, expressed in terms of the program's objectives. A **cost-benefit analysis** also looks at the costs of a program. However, when looking at a program's outcomes, a cost-benefit analysis takes a further step by assigning a monetary value to the outcomes achieved, a process referred to as monetizing outcomes. In our example, a cost-benefit analysis would determine the exact dollar value it costs for one participant to find employment.

Both types of analyses provide information regarding efficiency. Cost effectiveness analyses are somewhat easier to conduct than cost-benefit analyses because there is no requirement to place a monetary value on the outcomes produced. This saves a difficult step in the evaluation process. Placing a dollar value on outcomes is often difficult, particularly when we are dealing with intangible outcomes. For example, what dollar value should we assign to our clients' increased levels of self-esteem or their increased happiness?

The decision about which type of analysis to conduct depends on the circumstances and on the type of information required. If our intent is to assess the efficiency of a single program or to compare two or more programs producing the same outcomes, a cost-effectiveness analysis will provide the required information. If, on the other hand, our desire is to compare two or more programs that produce different outcomes, a cost-benefit analysis will be appropriate as this procedure places a dollar value on outcomes, thereby making it possible to make the desired comparison.

When to Evaluate for Efficiency

Ideally, efficiency-focused evaluations should be conducted in the planning phases of a social service program—that is, before the program is actually implemented. This is referred to as a prospective approach to efficiency-focused evaluations. The

Cost-effectiveness analysis

An analytical procedure that assesses the costs of the program itself; the monetary benefits of the program's effects are not assessed.

Cost-benefit analysis

An analytical procedure that not only determines the costs of the program itself but also considers the monetary benefits of the program's effects.

The Aim High Program is a state-funded program for the purpose of helping people who receive social assistance find competitive employment. One motivating factor in funding this program is to reduce the state's financial expenditures on social assistance. The program serves 130 unemployed social assistance recipients per year.

The program is designed as a 10-week on-site workshop followed by an eight-week follow-up session. The principal components of the program are delivered during the 10-week session. Some of these components are (1) short courses dealing with work-related issues, (2) job finding skills, (3) management of personal concerns; (4) adult academic upgrading; (5) a supported job search process; and (6) three weeks of work experience. During the eight-week follow-up, staff members contact participants several times per week and support them with the job search process or in their employment (if they have found a position by that point).

Using the previous chapter as a guide, the program's outcomes were evaluated. Some of them were (1) changes in reading and mathematics skills, (2) changes in self-esteem, (3) changes in employment status, (4) changes in income earned, and (5) changes in the amount of social assistance received.

purpose of such an approach is to provide information about the advisability of launching the program as potential program sponsors are provided information about the probable efficiency of the program. Sponsors often have to choose among several proposed social service programs; prospective efficiency-focused evaluations can shed light on the costs of each program in relation to its outcomes. This allows sponsors to make more meaningful comparisons among the proposed alternatives and therefore to make better informed decisions about which program(s) to fund.

A limitation of conducting a prospective efficiency-focused evaluation before a program gets up and running is that its costs and outcomes have to be estimated. Estimates, or best guesses, are seldom as accurate as actual records. Records, can be obtained from a program that is already operating. To compensate, evaluators often create a range of estimates including low, medium, and high for both costs and outcomes. The estimates for costs may come from a number of sources, including the plans for the proposed program and the costs of similar programs. The estimates of outcomes can come from the literature and from previously evaluated comparable programs.

From these sources, information can be provided to decision makers about the likely efficiency of the proposed program under a number of conditions ranging from "low efficiency" to "high efficiency." In a self-esteem program, for example, it might be possible to say that for each person who makes a 20-point improvement in his or her self esteem (as measured by Hudson's Index of Self-Esteem) in the best case scenario the cost will be $600/participant, in the most likely scenario the cost will be $700/participant, and in the worst case scenario the cost will be $800/participant. The limitations of using estimates cannot be ignored,

Box 8.2 A Comparison of Cost-Benefit and Cost-Effectiveness Analyses According to the National Institute of Drug Abuse

Cost-Effectiveness Analysis

A cost-effectiveness analysis is the relationship between program costs and program effectiveness—that is, patient outcome. Costs are measured as dollars spent, whereas effectiveness or outcome is measured as changes in patients' behaviors, thoughts, feelings, or biology. For example, the cost effectiveness of an opiate treatment program might be measured as the cost of generating an opiate-free month for the average patient.

There is no single standard for "cost effective." Generally, the term is used loosely as a way of saying that something probably costs less, or is more effective, than something else. Cost-effectiveness indices can be compared for different programs, different treatment modalities (such as residential versus outpatient clinics), and different treatment techniques (such as drug-free with or without acupuncture or drug-free versus methadone maintenance).

The overall cost effectiveness of a program can be improved by first finding which parts of the program contribute most to effectiveness and then discovering which of those program components have the lowest cost. Although substance abuse treatment programs are complex, it may be possible to improve cost effectiveness by enhancing use of these more effective and less expensive components while decreasing use of less effective and more expensive components.

However, cost-effectiveness indicators vary somewhat over time and over patients because of many factors, not all of which are controlled by the program. It is easy to find an apparent difference in the cost effectiveness of different program components or different programs. It is harder to show that the difference is real—for example, that it occurs reliably over months and for most patients and therefore should be used in program management decisions.

Cost-Benefit Analysis

A cost-benefit analysis is the measurement of both costs and outcomes in monetary terms. Costs and benefits can be compared between programs or contrasted within a single program. Cost-benefit analysis can also discover whether program expenditures are less than, similar to, or greater than program benefits. The time it takes for program benefits to exceed program costs is also measured in some cost-benefit analyses. Cost-benefit findings can often stand alone. For example, consider the inherent value of finding that every $1 spent for a particular substance abuse treatment program results in average savings of $4.96 to the taxpayer.

Some drug treatment programs produce measurable monetary outcomes, like increased days of legitimate employment and decreased job absences. Increased employment can yield increased income, which yields increased tax revenues. In addition, drug treatment programs may reduce patients' use of food stamps, public health services, and other public assistance—a potentially huge cost savings.

These cost savings may not occur as soon as patients begin treatment. Social service costs may actually rise as patients are guided to social services they need for recovery. In a few months or years, however, social service costs

but such analyses, known as sensitivity analyses, do provide decision-makers with useful information during the planning stages of a program. More commonly, efficiency-focused evaluations are undertaken as a final step of an outcome evaluation. When this is done, an efficiency evaluation is referred to as a retrospective approach.

For programs that are already operating, a completed outcome evaluation is required before an efficiency-focused evaluation can be undertaken. The basic logic of efficiency-focused evaluations requires that only incremental outcomes be considered—in other words, outcomes that would not have occurred without the may decrease, whereas patient income and taxes paid by patients may increase. Other major benefits of substance abuse treatment programs are indirect or secondary, such as reduction in crime-related costs, including property losses, medical services required by victims, time taken off from work by victims, and costs of apprehending, trying, and incarcerating offenders. All of these income increments, tax payments, and cost savings can add up to a considerable total benefit that exceeds the cost of treatment several times over.

There are several ways to report the relationships between costs and benefits:

- The *net benefit* of a program can be shown by subtracting the costs of a program from its benefits. For example, if a substance abuse treatment program cost $100,000 per year but generated in the same year $500,000 in increased patient income, increased tax payments by patients, and reduced expenditures for social and criminal justice services, the net benefit of the program would be $500,000 minus $100,000, or $400,000, for that year.
- The *ratio* of benefits to costs is found by dividing total program benefits by total program costs. For example, dividing the $500,000 benefit of the program by its $100,000 costs yields a cost-benefit ratio of 5:1.
- Because neither net benefits nor cost-benefit ratios indicate the size of the cost (*initial investment*) required for treatment to yield the observed benefits, it is important to report this as well. We cannot assume that the same exact relationships between costs and benefits will exist at different levels of investment. Sometimes an increase in cost allows new, more productive procedures to be used for treatment, increasing benefits dramatically. For example, increasing a program budget to allow hiring of a community liaison, vocational counselor, or physician might dramatically increase patient outcome. Therefore, it often is best to report the initial investment, the net benefit, and the cost-benefit ratio.

- The *time to return on investment* (the time it takes for program benefits to equal program costs) is yet another indicator used in cost-benefit analysis. For programs, benefits and costs occur at the same time, or at least in the same year. For individual patients, however, the investment in treatment may pay off substantially only after several months or years. Costs usually occur up front, but program benefits may take time to reach the point where they exceed costs.
- The decreasing value of benefits attained in the distant future can be calculated as the *present value* of benefits. When most of the cost of treatment occurs in the first year of treatment but most benefits occur only several years after treatment, the value of those delayed benefits needs to be adjusted (decreased) to reflect the delay.

Analyses of cost, cost-effectiveness, and cost-benefit relationships can provide valuable insights into how a program operates and how its operations could be improved to serve more people better for less. Analyses of costs, cost effectiveness, and cost-benefit also show funders that program managers are aware of the importance of accountability—accountability for how funds are used and what they are supposed to achieve.

program. Thus, it is important that the outcomes considered in an efficiency-focused evaluation can be attributed to the program and only to the program. As we know, evaluations that can attribute outcomes to an intervention require some form of an experimental design. Because such designs are, in practice, difficult to carry out, evaluators of efficiency often find themselves in a position where they must make the assumption that the outcomes they are using in their analyses can be directly attributed to the program.

The information provided by retrospective efficiency evaluations is useful in a number of ways. First, program administrators and sponsors can obtain a more complete understanding of the program. They can begin to weigh the outcomes against the costs and determine whether the costs are justifiable and whether it is worth to continue with the program. Such considerations are often relevant within multi-program agencies where administrators can use the information from efficiency assessments to manage their programs. The efficiency of a program is also an important consideration where there are plans to expand or replicate the program. Finally, where scarcity of resources dictates reductions or cuts, an understanding of the efficiency of alternative program options can greatly assist in making those difficult decisions.

STEPS IN CONDUCTING A COST-BENEFIT EVALUATION

This section describes the basic steps involved in conducting a cost-benefit evaluation and illustrates the procedures of conducing one by using an example of a social service program called the Aim High Program (Box 8.1). For purposes of this description, we will assume that we are conducting a retrospective cost-benefit analysis: An analysis is conducted after the program has performed an outcome evaluation using the procedures presented in the last chapter.

Step 1: Deciding on an Accounting Perspective

The first step in conducting a cost-benefit analysis is to decide on an accounting perspective to be used. A cost-benefit analysis can be conducted from a number of accounting perspectives. We will discuss only two of the perspectives: the individual program's participants' perspective, and the funding source's perspective. The perspective adopted determines what specific costs and benefits are to be considered in the analysis.

The Individual Program's Participants' Perspective

A program's participants' perspective is the narrowest perspective and is limited to considering the costs incurred and benefits obtained by the program's participants. For example, a cost-benefit analysis can be conducted using a participants' perspective to study the value, in monetary terms, of a college education.

Using hypothetical figures, suppose that the total cost to a student to obtain a college degree is $45,000 per year, or $180,000 over four years. These costs might include tuition and expenses for books, housing, and income not earned while attending college, to name a few. Census data along with and state and federal income statistics show that the average lifetime earnings of college graduates are $1,000,000 higher than those of non-college graduates. Having these data, we can now evaluate the cost-benefit of a college education; a graduate gains, on average, $820,000 over a lifetime as a result of graduating from college ($1,000,000 − $180,000 = $820,000).

The Funding Source's Perspective

Notice, however, that not all costs and benefits are included into the above calculations that use the individual program's participants' perspective. For example, the actual cost to the state-supported educational system of having students attend a college is typically much higher than the tuition paid by students—probably two thirds higher (one third state funds and one third grant funds). The state government usually provides annual funding to public universities to help make up the two thirds difference, but this is not counted when a program's participants' perspective is adopted. This is because the state funding was not a cost to students—the program's participants. On the other hand, the state will gain in future years from the higher income earned by college graduates in the form of additional income taxes collected. These benefits are not considered, however, as they are not directly relevant from the participants' perspective.

When a funding source's perspective is adopted, the costs that are incurred by the funder in sponsoring a program and the benefits that accrue to the funder as a result of the program are the focus. For example, a school district may wish to determine if it is efficient to fund English as a Second Language (ESL) instruction for students who have recently arrived in the country. The costs of the program to the district budget would then be considered in relation to the benefits obtained. Such benefits might include a reduction in costs related to providing other resources and supports within schools, as students with increased English language skills can manage without special assistance.

Which perspective is adopted in a cost-benefit analysis depends on the sponsor of the evaluation and the questions to be answered.

Applying the Procedure

In the case of our Aim High Program, a funding source perspective was adopted, specifically, that of the state government which funded the program. This perspective was taken because it was the state's senior managers who commissioned the evaluation as they sought to determine the impact of our Aim High Program on the state's budget. At the time of the evaluation, the state was very interested in employment training programs and were looking to identify the most efficient ones in order to establish similar programs throughout the state. This in turn would save the state money.

Step 2: Specifying the Cost-Benefit Model

Once an accounting perspective is decided on, it is now possible to describe the general cost-benefit model to be used. This model specifies which *specific* costs and which *specific* benefits will be included in the model.

Looking at Costs

For program administrators, the cost of simply delivering the program is usually the largest cost to be considered. And, for the individuals attending the program, the most obvious cost for them will be their enrollment fees. These costs are considered direct costs. There are other "less visible" costs as well, known as hidden, indirect, and overhead costs. To understand fully the costs from the individuals' perspectives, we need to look at these less obvious costs. For example, some participants may need to take time off from work and forego income, and they may need to acquire computer equipment and instructional texts. These are all hidden or indirect costs, and they need to be considered in a cost-benefit analysis from the individual's perspective.

Looking at Benefits

The same considerations apply to benefits as to costs. The students enrolled in our program may immediately benefit through an increase in salary from their current employers; that is, if they are currently employed. But, they might also be able to obtain higher paying positions shortly after completing the program. Perhaps previous evaluations have shown that graduates typically benefit in this manner. This benefit has a monetary value and might be included in a cost-benefit analysis. The participants may also gain in confidence and in their enjoyment of life. These are very important and real benefits but may be difficult, if not impossible, to convert into dollar terms. The evaluator would have to decide whether to monetize these benefits or to exclude them and note them as benefits to which a monetary value cannot be attached.

Having enumerated the exact costs and benefits from a selected accounting perspective, the cost-benefit model to be used can be specified.

Applying the Procedure

The model used in conducting the cost-benefit analysis of our Aim High Program enumerates the main expenses incurred in funding and supporting the program from the state's perspective.

The main cost factor of our Aim High Program was the funding provided by the state to run our program on a day-to-day basis. However, there are other costs of running our program as well. These include the costs incurred by the state in managing and administering the contract for our program. These are the professional, clerical, and other costs of contract management (at the state level), and these costs also need to be added to the model. In a nutshell, it costs the state money to administer the dollars in gives out for social service programs.

To make matters worse, our Aim High Program presently relies on state-funded social workers to refer clients to the program and to provide case management services. If we think about it, the time and state-funded resources expended in referring and providing case management services to the approximately 130 participants who attend the program yearly can be considerable. In short, the social workers are also employees of the state and thus the value of their services must also be included in the costs of our Aim High Program. They do not work for our program for free just because they are "not officially" on the program's budget line. There is no such thing as a free lunch.

The benefits to be included in the model are, as is often the case, more difficult to specify than are the costs. In the case of our Aim High Program, there are a number of benefits to consider from the state's budget perspective. The most obvious is a reduction in social assistance payments for our program's participants as they are able to find competitive employment and therefore decrease their reliance on assistance from the state. In addition, as income earners, the participants will now pay federal and state income taxes. As well, they will have more purchasing power and therefore engage in a variety of economic activities that benefit small businesses and corporations. This will result in more profitability for these businesses and hence more corporate taxes paid to the state.

It is important to keep in mind that our Aim High Program does produce other outcomes but the ones included in the model are the ones that represent the main financial benefits accruing to the state's budget office as a result of the program. If we were using a program's participants' perspective, we might include benefits such as increased self-confidence due to finding employment, higher levels of self-esteem, and better qualities of lives. The items included in the cost-benefit model for our Aim High Program are presented in Table 8.1.

Table 8.1 Costs and Benefits for the Aim High Program From a State Perspective

Costs	Benefits
1. Program payments	1. Reduction in social assistance payments
2. Contract administration costs	2. Increased state tax payments by participants
3. Costs of client referrals and case management services	3. Increased corporate taxes collected

Step 3: Determining Costs

When considering costs, it is important to assign an accurate market value to each cost element. Occasionally, some goods and services are obtained through special arrangements and thus at a lower cost than would be normal. For example, a university professor may be interested in providing training, on a voluntary basis, to the participants in our program as part of a research project. The professor, therefore, offers services without reimbursement. Because this service is unlikely to be obtained again without cost, it is common to use the normal market value (rather than the actual cost) of the service in the cost-benefit analysis. This process is known as shadow pricing.

Direct Costs

Direct costs
Day-to-day costs of running a social service program.

The first and usually most important cost factor to be accounted for is the **direct cost** of actually running the program. This information can usually be obtained from budgets, financial statements, or from contracts between the funders and the program's administrators. When an agency delivers a single program, the total budget, or funding, can be considered to be the program cost. However, in an agency that has several programs where it delivers its programs side by side, the accounting for direct costs becomes much more complicated. For example, some staff members may work in more than one program, and thus only a portion of their salary can be attributed to the program of interest. In some instances, separating out the costs to be attributed to a particular program can be a difficult and a time-consuming task.

Indirect Costs

Indirect costs
Those costs that are incurred for common or joint objectives and therefore can not be identified readily and specifically with a particular program.

Next, **indirect costs** must be considered. By their very nature, indirect costs are difficult to pinpoint. Often only a portion of such costs can be directly attributed to a particular program under review. For example, in a large agency operating several programs, part of the senior administration's time, some clerical time, as well as a portion of building costs and utilities would constitute overhead and would need to be attributed (via proportions) to the program being evaluated. The task of the evaluator in such circumstances is to identify the portion of indirect expenses that should be attributable to the cost of the program that is under review.

Applying the Procedure

Identifying direct costs for our Aim High Program was relatively simple as the agency and program were the same and thus had only our Aim High Program under its auspices. The total contract payment from the state to the program could be considered the direct cost for this program. Specifically, these costs were set by contract at $375,100 per year of program operations.

As described above, separating out the indirect costs that may be attributed to any single program can be a difficult exercise. Indeed, unless accurate accounting records are kept, it may be impossible to do so. Such was the case in examining the indirect costs of our Aim High Program. As indicated in the cost-benefit model, contract administration costs and the costs of case management services are the indirect costs to be considered. However, the departments within the state's government responsible for these functions did not keep records that would allow the costs associated with our Aim High Program to be separated from the costs of other activities within the various state departments.

The only way to identify these costs, under the circumstances, was to estimate them. After discussions with managers and accountants in the two state departments, it was estimated that indirect costs totaled 10% of direct costs. This formula was then used to complete the cost estimates for the program: $375,100 plus 10% equals $412,610, the total cost of the program per year—from the state's perspective. Dividing the sum ($412,610) by the total number of clients served annually (130 participants) equaled $3174 per participant. In sum, and on a general level, our program spent, on average, $3,174 per participant per year.

Estimates are typically substituted when actual costs cannot be determined from the records, as is often the case for at least some of the cost factors. Although evaluators attempt to make well-founded estimates, this nevertheless becomes a limitation of the evaluation. In the following section, we will see how estimates are also used in determining benefits.

Step 4: Determining Benefits

As we know, social service programs produce a variety of outcomes. These may include outcomes that are already expressed in dollar terms, such as an increase in annual income or a decrease in expenditures on medicines. However, more typically, programs produce outcomes that are not expressed in monetary terms. For example, a program might increase the self-esteem of its clients. Another program might result in better communications between parents and their teenage children. Other outcomes might be expressed even more generally, such as increasing the overall happiness or improving the quality of life for individuals. It is a major challenge in cost-benefit analyses to monetize, or express in amounts of money, outcomes that are not inherently "financially oriented."

Suppose, for example, we are looking at the benefits of a smoking cessation program from the participants' point of view, or perspective. When participants stop smoking, the direct benefits can be easily quantified by calculating the amount of money saved on tobacco products. Indirect benefits would include savings to the individuals on future medical costs among others. These indirect benefits can also be calculated with data obtained from findings derived from previous research studies and population statistics. The numbers from such analyses could be included in a cost-benefit evaluation.

However, other good outcomes will also be produced. For example, participants' children may be less likely to become smokers. A participant may also live longer and enjoy a better quality of life. These gains may well be more important than the financial savings that can be identified. However, it would be very difficult to monetize these important benefits. What financial value can be attached to a child not starting to smoke, from not being physically abused, or from not taking drugs?

Some evaluators use complicated and, at times, imaginative methods in an attempt to place a value on happiness, enjoyment of life, and other warm and fuzzy benefits. However, the fact remains that there is no easy way to monetize such outcomes without making huge and sometimes contentious assumptions. Under the circumstances, the most reasonable and prudent approach for evaluators to take is to monetize only those outcomes that can be reasonably converted into financial terms. Other outcomes, even if important, can be noted as unquantifiable benefits. The limitation of this approach is that other important benefits are not accounted for in the cost-benefit analysis.

Applying the Procedure

In the case of our Aim High Program, a variety of outcomes were produced and subsequently evaluated. These included changes in the basic educational levels of participants, changes in the self-esteem of participants, competitive employment for participants, wages earned by participants, and a reduction in social assistance payments to the participants. Although all of these outcomes could potentially be included in a cost-benefit analysis, not all were relevant to the accounting perspective selected, that of the state's budget office. For example, although there is a meaningful value for increasing the participants' confidence levels via furthering their basic educational skills, this outcome (increasing confidence levels of participants) is not relevant to the state. Consequently, only outcomes relevant to the state were included in the analysis; these three outcomes are specified in the cost-benefit model included in Table 8.1.

With reference to a reduction in social assistance payments (the first item in the list of benefits in the model), an outcome evaluation done prior to the cost-benefit analysis showed that social assistance payments to participants were reduced, on average, $230 per month.

The other financial benefits included in the model were increased state tax payments by participants resulting from their increased earnings as well as increased corporate taxes collected by the state government as a result of the increased economic activity generated by the program's participants. These benefits, although financial in nature, are very difficult to specify. To account for these benefits, a detailed examination of the income tax returns for each participant would be necessary. This was not possible because of the confidentiality provisions surrounding tax returns, and thus it was necessary to resort to estimates.

Tax accountants and economists were consulted, and, based on their assessments and recommendations, the assumption was made that the additional tax benefits to the state, resulting from the increased earnings of our program's participants, amounted to 3% of their earned income. As data relating to earned income was available from the outcome evaluation that was previously done, it was possible to calculate the tax benefits to the state at $5 per month, per participant. Adding the $5 per month tax increase to the $230 per month in reduced social assistance payments now provides $235 per month per participant to the state's coffers. In the state's eyes, this works out to $2,820 of benefits per participant per year to be added to the state's bank account ($235 per month × 12 months = $2,820).

Step 5: Adjusting for Present Value

In many instances, the benefits of a social service program may continue for a number of years. When that is the case, it is necessary to adjust the value of benefits in future years. This is a practice known as discounting and is based on the premise that the value of a sum of money at the present time (today) is higher than the value of the same amount in the future. For example, if someone offered you a choice between receiving $1,000 today or receiving the same sum next year, you would be better off taking the money now—don't wait, take the money and run. By having the money in your pocket now you could invest it, and by next year have $1,000 plus the amount earned through your investment. This is known as an opportunity cost.

Suppose it costs a participant $500 to complete a smoking cessation program and this results in savings of $1,200 per year on tobacco products. This means that the person will only save $700 for the first year when the $500 enrollment fee is figured in $1,200 − $500 = $700). The initial $500 cost of attending the program is incurred only once, but the benefit stream for the participants continues for years. When we decide to compute the savings, we cannot simply add $700 for each future year to arrive at the total benefit because, as explained above, the value of the $700 dollars decreases as time marches on.

In cost-benefit analyses, the following formula is used to discount the value of benefits in future years:

$$\text{Present Value} = \frac{\text{Amount}}{(1 + r)^t}$$

where

r = the discount rate
t = the number of years into the future

Tables providing discounted amounts at various rates are available from many financial institutions and on the Internet.

Before applying the discounting formula, the discount rate needs to be determined. There are a variety of ways for determining the discount rate, each requiring a number of economic assumptions that are far beyond the scope of our book. For purposes of the evaluation of social service programs, however, a reasonable way to set the discount rate is to set it at the opportunity cost of a safe investment (e.g., certified deposits). Thus, if the money could be safely invested at 4%, the discount rate should be set at 0.04.

A second decision is to determine the number of years that the benefits will last. In some instances, the benefits may last for a set period of time. In other cases, such as those of smoking cessation or employment training programs, the benefits may continue without a fixed end. However, projecting benefits into the future is an imprecise proposition at best because it requires the assumption that the participants' statuses will not substantially change in the future.

In the absence of longer term follow-up data, such assumptions are necessarily speculative; the farther into the future projections are made, the more speculative they become. Nevertheless, evaluators must make some assumptions regarding the length of time that the benefit stream will continue. Usually, this determination is made after examining the literature regarding similar programs and having consultations with knowledgeable stakeholders and experts. An alternative approach is to conduct multiple analyses, each assuming a different duration for each level of benefit.

Applying the Procedure

In the case of our Aim High Program, our interest is on the benefits accrued to the state. As can be seen in Table 8.1, we have specified these to be reductions in social assistance payments and increased taxes (state and corporate). These benefits, as we have seen, result from the increased earning power of the program's participants, and we can expect that their increased earning power, and hence the benefits, will continue for a number of years. For purposes of the cost-benefit analysis, it was decided to look at the efficiency of our program at three time periods after the participants exited our program (i.e., 12, 24, 36 months), rather than speculating about how long their benefit stream will continue. The cost-benefit data at three future points in time should provide decisions makers with a good understanding of the efficiency of the program—from the state's perspective, that is.

When examining the benefits in future years, it is therefore necessary to apply the discounting procedure to account for the reduced value of the benefits in future years. The discount rate was set at 0.045 to reflect the opportunity costs prevailing at the time.

As we know from Step 4, an outcome evaluation determined that the benefits on a per-participant basis were $2,820 per year. Using the formula to discount the value of benefits obtained in future years, it can be calculated that the present value of

Table 8.2 Calculating the Present Value of $2820 for Three Future Time Periods

Time Periods	Yearly Benefits*	Total Benefits Over a Three-Year Period	Present Value of Total Benefits
12 months	2,699	2,699	2,699
24 months	2,582	2,699 + 2,582	5,281
36 months	2,471	2,699 + 2,582 + 2,471	7,752

*After discounting, using a rate of 0.045.

"per-participant benefits" after Year 1 is $2,699. After Year 2 the value is $2,582, and after Year 3 it is $2,471. These values are then used to calculate the present value of the total benefits per participant. After 12 months, the total benefits are $2,699; after 24 months, the total benefits are $5,281; and after 36 months, the total benefits amount to $7,752. Table 8.2 shows these calculations in detail.

Step 6: Completing the Cost-Benefit Analysis

With the information obtained in the previous steps, a cost-benefit analysis can now be completed. This step involves a lot of numeric data, so tables are an effective way of presenting them. The program costs, benefits, and net benefit (or cost) are usually presented at this step, both on a per-participant basis and on a program basis as a whole.

Sometimes a benefit-cost ratio is reported. This ratio can be readily computed by dividing the benefits by the costs (benefits/cost). A ratio of 1.0 indicates that the program's benefits equal its costs; this is sometimes known as the breakeven point. A ratio greater than 1.0 indicates that benefits outweigh the costs. A ratio below 1.0 indicates that costs are higher than benefits. Thus, the higher the benefit-cost-ratio, the greater the efficiency of the program.

Applying the Procedure

As was shown in Step 3, the average annual cost for each participant in our Aim High Program was $3,174. As was shown in Step 4, the annual benefit for each participant was $2,820 per year. As was shown in Step 5, the adjusted benefit value was $2,669 for the first year. Table 8.3 reports the costs, benefits, net benefits, and benefit-cost ratios of our program at three time intervals after the participants completed our program. Note that the benefits have been adjusted, as described in Step 5.

As can be seen in Table 8.3, after 12 months, on a per participant basis, the costs exceed benefits by $475. At the program level, with 130 participants served per year,

Cost effective

When a social service program is able to achieve its program objectives in relation to its costs.

Intense competition for limited substance abuse program funds, combined with increased scrutiny of program costs and outcomes have created a need for better understanding of how costs and outcomes are related in substance abuse treatment. Programs are increasingly called on to show that their treatment of substance-abusing patients is a good investment of public and private funds. Program costs must be justified relative to program outcomes (and vice versa).

There are several advantages to analyzing costs, cost effectiveness, and cost benefits. Concise but accurate reports of how much a service costs can help raise funds. Potential contributors may be impressed that you know both where the money is going and how much it takes to run different parts of the program. Having solid reports of the effectiveness and cost effectiveness of your program will assure donors that their contributions will have the maximum impact possible.

Critics will find it harder to dismiss funding requests as being too high when a careful and complete accounting of all resources used by the program shows their true value and the true cost of providing the services. Critics also will find it more difficult to dismiss your funding requests as wasted money when you can show what is achieved as well as what is done with the funds.

Some funding agencies require regular cost analyses to justify reimbursement for services provided. They may require that you verify your implementation of treatment procedures to account for your expenses. Many agencies set a ceiling on costs. A few agencies may even require that you demonstrate at least minimum levels of effectiveness for no more than a maximum allowable cost. These agencies and critics may be more impressed if you can show that your program not only understands the relationship between funds spent and effectiveness achieved but also attempts to measure the social and other monetary benefits of treatment.

Acknowledging that substance abuse treatment benefits society by reducing the burden of substance-abusing patients on the health care, social service, and criminal justice systems helps to ensure continued funding for your program. One of the most powerful ways to acknowledge this purpose is to measure your program's savings in health care and other services. If your program saves substantially more money than it consumes, it will be easier to defend as a form of social investment that may deserve more attention and additional funds.

Do not worry that analyzing the cost effectiveness and cost benefit of your substance abuse program will produce negative findings. Programs and researchers have conducted cost-related analyses since the 1970s. Some of their findings have been included in this book, along with some of the methods they used to attain them. Program evaluators generally have answered the question "Is treatment of substance abuse cost effective or cost beneficial?" with a qualified or resounding *yes*.

Table 8.3 Cost-Benefit Analysis of the Aim High Program

Months after Program Completion	Participant Level	Program Level (130 clients per year)	Benefit/Cost Ratio
12	Benefit $2,699 Cost $3,174 Net (cost) benefit $(475)	Benefit $350,870 Cost $412,620 Net (cost) benefit $(61,750)	0.85
24	Benefit $5,281 Cost $3,174 Net (cost) benefit $2,107	Benefit $686,530 Cost $412,620 Net (cost) benefit $273,910	1.66
36	Benefit $7,752 Cost $3,174 Net (cost) benefit $4,578	Benefit $1,007,760 Cost $412,620 Net (cost) benefit $595,140	2.44

the costs exceed benefits by $61,750 ($475 × 130 participants = $61,750). The benefit to cost ratio for the first year was 0.85.

At 24 months, the benefits exceed costs by $2,107 on an individual client basis and by $273,910 at the program level; the benefit cost ratio rose from 0.85 at 12 months to 1.66 after two years out of the program.

After 36 months, the benefits exceed costs by $4,578 on an individual client basis and by $595,140 when looking at the program level; the benefit cost ratio was 2.44 after three years out of our program. As is the case with most social service programs, the efficiency of a program depends, in part, on the selection of time at which its results are viewed. The further into the future the benefits are projected, the higher the benefit-cost ratio and the more efficient the program appears.

Using cost-benefit data we can be calculate our program's breakeven point—when the cost of our program is balanced by its benefits. Dividing the present value of benefits (after 12 months, $2,699) by 12, it can the calculated that the monthly value of these benefits during the first year is $225. With benefits accruing at the rate of $225 per month, the program cost of $3,174 is recovered in just over 14 months.

COST-EFFECTIVENESS ANALYSES

As has been discussed, there are differences between a cost-benefit and a cost-effectiveness analysis. This section highlights those differences and describes how a cost-effectiveness evaluation is conducted.

As we now know, efficiency analyses require an "accounting minded" approach and are focused on the financial and economic aspects of a social service program and its outcomes. As we know, a program may produce other outcomes that cannot be readily or reasonably expressed in financial terms. An effectiveness analysis, which does not try to establish a monetary value for a program's outcomes, provides only one way of examining efficiency. Simply put, a cost-effectiveness evaluation establishes the cost of achieving each unit of a program's outcome.

On the cost side, a cost-effectiveness analysis proceeds in much the same way as cost-benefit analysis. In identifying outcomes, cost-effectiveness analyses depend on prior outcome evaluations, which will have identified relevant program outcomes. The process then continues by selecting the outcomes to be analyzed and determining the number of units of each outcome that have been achieved. For each outcome, it is then possible to determine the cost of each unit achieved by dividing the total program cost by the total number of units of outcome achieved.

As has been seen, in cost-benefit analyses, it is necessary to select an accounting perspective and to consider only those costs and benefits that are relevant to the chosen perspective. This results in some outcomes being excluded from the analyses. In cost-effectiveness analyses, it is possible to mix perspectives and to report the costs of outcomes that are relevant to individual participants as well as to the funding source or some other entity, such as the program's stakeholders.

Applying the Procedure

Like all social service programs, our Aim High Program produced a variety of outcomes. These included an increase in basic academic skills of participants, an increase in self-esteem of participants, and competitive employment for participants. With these results in hand, it is possible to calculate their cost per unit achieved.

For example, the outcome evaluation found that approximately 30% of our program participants found employment. Taking the program level data reported in Table 8.3, we know the annual cost of the program is $412,620. At the program level, with 130 clients served per year, we can expect that 30% or 39 clients will find employment at a total program cost of $412,620. We can now calculate the cost for each participant to find a job by dividing the total program costs by the number of participants who found jobs. In the case of our Aim High Program, it costs $10,580 per participant to find a job ($412,620/39 = $10,580). If all of our participants found jobs, the cost per job found would be much lower, $3,174. Thus, it should be noted that the very best our program could do, on the efficiency side of things, would be to have all of our 130 participants find jobs at $3,174 per participant.

A Few Words About Efficiency-Focused Evaluations

As shown, evaluations of efficiency put a clear focus on the financial and economic aspects of programs. This is particularly true in the case of cost-benefit analyses. Advocates of efficiency-focused evaluations argue that, unless there is a good understanding of the financial efficiency of a program, any evaluation will necessarily be incomplete. They contend that efficiency-focused evaluations will put decision makers in a position where they can make better and more rational decisions. As a result, the scarce resources available to support social service programs will be used most efficiently. Such thinking is consistent with the growing trend in our society to make decisions based on economic criteria.

Although there is a certain validity to these claims, critics point out that efficiency-focused evaluations are not without their limitations and shortcomings. First, from a practical point of view, as should be now evident by reading this chapter, the evaluation of efficiency, particularly cost-benefit analyses, requires a technical approach with a high level of skill on the part of the evaluator. Few social service organizations employ staff members with these skills; therefore, they face the additional expense of having to hire outside consultants to undertake such work. Maintaining the kind of financial records and data that are required to analyze the costs and benefits of social service programs also adds to the costs of such evaluations. These costs will further increase when an agency operates several programs at the same time, shares social workers between and among programs, and uses common space such as a gym or playground—the list can be endless. Also adding to the mix is that some clients are enrolled in more than one program within the same agency at the same time. Sometimes they are also being seen by another program in a different agency as well.

From a technical perspective, there may be a reliance on estimates and assumptions throughout the process. First, cost data are often not available to complete detailed cost analyses, and thus estimates must be used. Next, it is not easy to place a dollar value on many outcomes of interest, and assumptions must be made in assigning dollar values to such benefits. Moreover, some benefits cannot be monetized at all and are therefore ignored in the calculations. Further, projecting benefits into the future is difficult and again requires assumptions on the part of the evaluators. The more that estimates and assumptions are used in completing an evaluation, the more the results must be treated with caution.

From a more philosophical perspective, critics point to the fact that the evaluation of efficiency is based on a concept of utilitarianism. This is an economic–philosophical view that holds that social service organizations should weigh the costs and benefits of a proposed course of action and proceed to establish a program only if its "benefits" to the clients it will serve will exceed the program's "costs." This perspective is clearly dominant within the for-profit sector where investments and products are judged by whether they will produce a profit. In the social services, however, it is not always desirable to make decisions based on utilitarian considerations. The ethics and values of our professions calls for action based on what is right, just, and enhances human dignity and well-being. Thus, we strongly believe it may be desirable to proceed with a social service program even if its benefits cannot be shown to exceed its costs.

For example, many individual and group counseling programs are concerned with assisting people to live more effective and fulfilling lives. Although the costs of

Box 8.4 Published Examples of Efficiency Benefit Evaluations

Substantive areas are in **bold**.

Beshai, N. N., (1991). Providing cost efficient detoxification services to **alcoholic patients**. *Public Health Reports, 105*, 475–481.

Claiborne, N. (2006). Efficiency of a care coordination model: A randomized study with **stroke patients**. *Research on Social Work Practice, 16*(1), 57–66.

Egger, G. M., Friedman, B., & Zimmer, J. G. (1990). Models of **intensive case management**. *Journal of Gerontological Social Work, 15*, 75–101.

Ell, K. (1996). Social work and **health care practice** and policy: A psychosocial research agenda. *Social Work, 41*, 583–592.

Engelhardt, J. B., Toseland, R. W., Gao, J., & Banks, S. (2006). Long-term effects of outpatient geriatric evaluation and management on **health care utilization**, cost, and survival. *Research on Social Work Practice, 16*(1), 20–27.

Essock, S. M., Frisman, L. K., & Kontos, N. J. (1998). Cost-effectiveness of assertive **community treatment teams**. *American Journal of Orthopsychiatry, 68*, 179–190.

Fahs, M. C., & Wade, K. (1996). An economic analysis of two models of hospital care for **AIDS patients**: Implications for hospital discharge planning. *Social Work in Health Care, 22*, 21–34.

Greene, V. L., Lovely, M. E., & Ondrich, J. I. (1993). The cost-effectiveness of community services in a **frail elderly population**. *The Gerontologist, 33*, 177–189.

Grinnell, R. M., Jr., & Hill, L. S. (1979). Do agency administrative changes affect the effectiveness and efficiency of **DHR employees**? *Journal of Sociology and Social Welfare, 6*, 503–508.

Grinnell, R. M., Jr., & Hill, L. S. (1979). The perceived effectiveness and efficiency of **DHR employees**. *Social Service Review, 53*, 116–122.

Holosko, M. J., Dobrowolsky, J. Feit, M. D. (1990). A proposed cost effectiveness method for use in policy formulation in **human service organizations**. *Journal of Health and Social Policy, 1*, 55–71.

Holtgrave, D. R, & Kelly, J. A. (1998). Cost-effectiveness of an **HIV/AIDS prevention intervention for gay men**. *AIDS, and Behavior, 1*, 173–180.

Hughes, W. C. (1999). Managed care meets community support: Ten reasons to include **direct support services** in every behavioral health plan. *Health and Social Work, 4*, 103–111.

Jackson, N., Olsen, L., & Schafer, C. (1986). Evaluating the treatment of **emotionally disturbed adolescents**. *Social Work, 31*, 182–185.

Keigher, S. M. (1997). What role for social work in the new **health care practice** paradigm? *Health and Social Work, 22*, 149–55.

Knapp, M. (1988). Searching for efficiency in long-term care: De-institutionalisation and privatisation. *British Journal of Social Work, 18*, 149–171.

Levy, R. L., & Bavendam, T. G. (1995). Promoting **women's urologic self-care**: Five single-case replications. *Research on Social Work Practice, 5*, 430–441.

Padgett, D. K., & Gulcur, L., & Tsemberis, S. (2006). Housing first services for people who are **homeless with co-occurring serious mental illness** and substance abuse. *Research on Social Work Practice, 16*(1), 74–83.

Pike, C. L., & Piercy, F. P. (1991). Cost effectiveness research in **family therapy**. *Journal of Marital and Family Therapy, 16*, 375–388.

Pinkerton, S. D., & Holtgrave, D. R. (1998). A method for evaluating the economic efficiency of **HIV behavioral risk reduction interventions**. *AIDS and Behavior, 2*, 189–201.

Prentky, R., & Burgess, A. W. (1990). Rehabilitation of **child molesters**: A cost-benefit analysis. *American Journal of Orthopsychiatry, 60*, 108–117.

Rizzo, V. M., & Rowe, J. M. (2006). Studies of the cost-effectiveness of social work services in **aging**: A review of the literature. *Research on Social Work Practice, 16*(1), 67–73.

Robertson, E., & Knapp, M. (1988). Promoting **intermediate treatment**: A problem of excess demand or excess supply? *British Journal of Social Work, 8*, 131–147.

Saleh, S. S., Vaughn, T., Levey, S., Fuortes, L., Uden-Holmen, T., & Hall, J. A. (2006). Cost-effectiveness of case management in **substance abuse treatment**, *Research on Social Work Practice, 16*(1), 38–47.

Schreiner, M., Tin Ng, G., & Sherraden, M. (2006). Cost-effectiveness in **individual development accounts**. *Research on Social Work Practice, 16*(1), 28–37.

Segal, E. A., & Gustavsson, N. S. (1990). The high cost of neglecting **children**: The need for a preventive policy agenda. *Child and Adolescent Social Work Journal, 7*, 475–485.

Shilling, R., Dornig, K., & Lungren, L. (2006). Treatment of **heroin dependence**: Effectiveness, costs, and benefits of methadone maintenance. *Research on Social Work Practice, 16*(1), 48–56.

Toseland, R. W., & Smith, T. L. (2006). The impact of caregiver **health education** program on health care costs. *Research on Social Work Practice, 16*(1), 9–19.

Winegar, N., Bistline, J. L., & Sheridan, S. (1992). Implementing a **group therapy program** in a managed-care setting: Combining cost effectiveness and quality care. *Families in Society, 73*, 56–58.

such programs can be established, it would be very difficult to place a dollar value on the program's outcomes. Should such programs therefore be abandoned? Alternatively, consider the case of two assisted living programs for the elderly. Program A has been shown to be more **cost efficient** than Program B. However, the residents in Program B feel much happier and more comfortable than the residents in Program A. A decision based entirely on financial efficiency would dictate that the decision maker chose Program A to fund as the desirable model. In cost-benefit calculations, little or no weight is given to outcomes such as the happiness or comfort of the residents.

Cost efficient

When a social service program is able to achieve its program objectives at less cost, compared to another program striving for the same objectives.

SUMMING UP AND LOOKING AHEAD

This chapter discussed two common types of efficiency-focused evaluations: cost-benefit evaluations and cost-effectiveness evaluations. There is little doubt that such evaluations have the potential to provide valuable information to decision makers and stakeholders. At the same time, it is important to understand and recognize the limitations inherent in efficiency-focused evaluations.

RECAP AND ONLINE MATERIALS

In this chapter, you learned how to do social work efficiency evaluations.

You should also recall the concept of efficiency evaluations from your foundational research course. If not, go online to take a free crash course in how to use various efficiency evaluation tools.

You can also find the following materials online to help you master the concepts you just learned:

- Chapter Outline
- Learning Objectives
- Key Terms and Concepts
- Flash Cards
- Practice Multiple-Choice Tests
- Essay Questions with Answers
- Links

www.oup.com/us/swevaluation

STUDY QUESTIONS

1. In your own words list and discuss thoroughly the similarities and differences between cost-effectiveness analyses and cost-benefit analyses.

2. With your discussion from question 1, how could your school's director use the results from these two forms evaluations to improve the social work program (BSW, or MSW) that you are now enrolled in? Discuss how your program could be made better via a cost-benefit analysis. Discuss how your program could be made better via a a cost-effectiveness analysis.

3. With your discussion from question 2, discuss how a cost-effectiveness analysis could be done on your social work program from your point of view. Then discuss it from your state's point of view.

4. With your discussion from question 3, what would you consider to be the costs and benefits of your program from your own point of view? What would be the costs and benefits of your program from your state's point of view?

5. List and describe thoroughly the direct and indirect costs for you from obtaining a social work degree.

6. What is shadow pricing? How is this concept relevant to you when you are at your field practicum?

7. How would you go about doing a cost-benefit analysis of the Ronald McDonald's House? What would you use as the outcome indicators, and why?

8. How would you go about doing a cost-effectiveness analysis of the Ronald McDonald's House? What would you use as the outcome indicators, and why?

9. Go on the Internet (or refer to Box 8.4) and find a social work journal article that presents the results of a *cost-benefit analysis*. Did the authors use the concepts contained within this chapter? If so, what were they and how were they used? If not, which ones were not used?

10. Go on the Internet (or refer to Box 8.4) and find a social work journal article that presents the results of a *cost-effectiveness analysis*. Did the authors use the concepts contained within this chapter? If so, what were they and how were they used? If not, which ones were not used?

REFERENCES, FURTHER READING, AND RESOURCES

Chen, H. T. (2006). *Practical program evaluation: Assessing and improving planning, implementation, and effectiveness.* Thousand Oaks, CA: Sage.

Claiborne, N. (2006). Efficiency of a care coordination model: A randomized study with stroke patients. *Research on Social Work Practice, 16*(1), 57–66.

Drummond, M., & McGuire, A. (2001). *Economic evaluation in health care: Merging theory with practice.* New York: Oxford University Press.

Drummond, M., O'Brien, B., Stoddart, G., & Torrance, G. (1997). *Methods for the economic evaluation of health care programs* (2nd ed.). New York: Oxford University Press.

Engelhardt, J. B., Toseland, R. W., Gao, J., & Banks, S. (2006). Long-term effects of outpatient geriatric evaluation and management on health care utilization, cost, and survival. *Research on Social Work Practice, 16*(1), 20–27.

Gold, M., Siegel, J., Russell, L., & Weinstein, M. (1996). *Cost-effectiveness in health and medicine.* Oxford, United Kingdom: Oxford University Press.

Holosko, M., Dobrowolsky, J., & Feit, M. (1989). Using cost-effectiveness analysis in policy formulation in human service organizations. *Journal of Health and Social Policy, 1*(1), 43–60.

Holosko, M., Dobrowolsky, J., & Feit, M. (1990). A proposed cost-effectiveness method for use in policy formulation in human service organizations. *Journal of Health and Social Policy, 1*(3), 55–77.

Juvenile Justice Evaluation Center. (2002). *Cost-benefit analysis for juvenile justice programs* (Program Evaluation Briefing Series No. 4). Washington, DC: Justice Research & Statistics Association.

Kassirer, J. (2005). *On the take: How medicine's complicity with big business can endanger our health.* New York: Oxford University Press.

Kassirer, J., & Angell, M. (1994). The *Journal's* policy on cost-effectiveness analyses. *The New England Journal of Medicine, 331,* 669–670.

Kee, J.E. (1994). Benefit-cost analysis in program evaluation. In J. Wholey, H. P. Hatry, & K. E. Newcomer (Eds.), *The handbook of practical program evaluation.* San Francisco: Jossey-Bass.

Levin, H. M., & McEwan, P. J. (2000). *Cost-effectiveness analysis: Methods and applications* (2nd ed.). Thousand Oaks, CA: Sage.

Mohr, L. B. (1995). *Impact analysis for program evaluation* (2nd ed.). Thousand Oaks, CA: Sage.

Nas, T. F. (1996*). Cost-benefit analysis: Theory and application.* Thousand Oaks, CA: Sage.

Neumann, P. (2005). *Using cost-effectiveness analysis to improve health care.* New York: Oxford University Press.

Padgett, D. K., & Gulcur, L., & Tsemberis, S. (2006). Housing first services for people who are homeless with co-occurring serious mental illness and substance abuse. *Research on Social Work Practice, 16*(1), 74–83.

Rizzo, V., & Fortune, A. E. (2006). Cost outcomes and social work practice. *Research on Social Work Practice 16,* 5–8.

Rizzo, V., & Rowe, J. (2003). *Studies of the efficacy and cost-effectiveness of social work services in aging: A report commissioned by the National Leadership Coalition.* New York: Academy of Medicine.

Rizzo, V. M., & Rowe, J. M. (2006). Studies of the cost-effectiveness of social work services in aging: A review of the literature. *Research on Social Work Practice, 16*(1), 67–73.

Saleh, S. S., Vaughn, T., Levey, S., Fuortes, L., Uden-Holmen, T., & Hall, J. A. (2006). Cost-effectiveness of case management in substance abuse treatment, *Research on Social Work Practice, 16*(1), 38–47.

Schreiner, M., Tin Ng, G., & Sherraden, M. (2006). Cost-effectiveness in individual development accounts. *Research on Social Work Practice, 16*(1), 28–37.

Shilling, R., Dornig, K., & Lungren, L. (2006). Treatment of heroin dependence: Effectiveness, costs, and benefits of methadone maintenance. *Research on Social Work Practice, 16*(1), 48–56.

Thompson, M. (1980). *Benefit-cost analysis for program evaluation.* Beverly Hills, CA: Sage.

Toseland, R. W., & Smith, T. L. (2006). The impact of caregiver health education program on health care costs. *Research on Social Work Practice, 16*(1), 9–19.

U.S. Department of Health and Human Services Public Health Services, Agency for Health Care Research and Quality. (2001). *Focus on cost-effectiveness analysis at the Agency for Healthcare Quality and Research fact sheet.* Rockville, MD: Author.

Weinstein, M., Siegel, J., Gold, M., Kamlet, M., & Russell, L. (for the U.S. Panel on Cost-Effectiveness in Health and Medicine). (1996). Recommendations of the Panel on Cost-Effectiveness in Health and Medicine. *Journal of the American Medical Association, 276,* 1253–1258.

Yates, B. T. (1994). Toward the incorporation of costs, cost-effectiveness analysis, and cost-benefit analysis into clinical research. *Journal of Consulting and Clinical Psychology, 62,* 729–736.

Yates, B. T. (1995). Cost-effectiveness analysis, cost-benefit analysis, and beyond: Evolving models for the scientist-manager-practitioner. *Clinical Psychology: Science and Practice, 2,* 385–398.

Yates, B. T. (1996). *Analyzing costs, procedures, processes, and outcomes in human services: An introduction.* Thousand Oaks, CA: Sage.

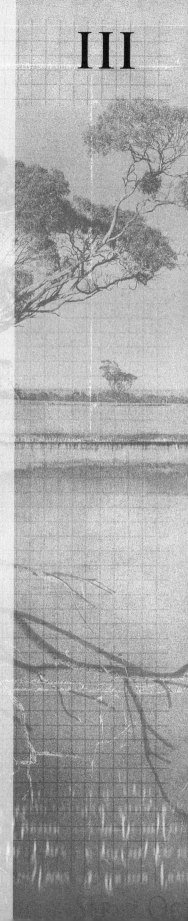

III

GATHERING DATA AND MAKING DECISIONS

Now that we know the four basic types of program evaluations as described in Part II, this part contains chapters that provide the skills that are needed to actually do them. Chapter 3, for example, only introduced the concepts of practice and program objectives and how important they are for doing any kind of evaluation (practice or program). Chapter 9 discusses how to measure them via nonstandardized and standardized measures. It presents creative ways to measure practice and program objectives when standardized ones cannot be used or found.

Chapter 10 presents how to obtain existing and new data for practice and program objectives using various data sources and data collection methods. It stresses the use of more than one source and method for collecting data on any given objective. Sampling is also included, with a brief presentation of nonprobability and probability sampling procedures. It also presents the need for fitting the evaluation's data-gathering enterprise into the program's day-to-day operations.

Chapter 11 describes how to develop, maintain, and evaluate a data information system within a program. It stresses data collection at the case level and the program level and presents a framework for how case-level data can be used at the program level.

Chapter 12 discusses the basic ways that quantitative data derived from a program evaluation can be displayed in graphic forms via the use of bar charts, pie charts, line graphs, illustrations, and photographs.

Chapter 13 presents how to collect, analyze, and display qualitative program evaluation data. It provides a step by step approach to analyzing narrative program evaluation data. The chapter also contains pointers on what pitfalls to avoid when analyzing qualitative data.

The final chapter of Part III, Chapter 14, discusses how to make decisions from the data that have been collected (Chapter 10), measured (Chapter 9), and analyzed (Chapters 12 and 13). It stresses decision making at the case and program levels.

MEASURING PRACTICE AND PROGRAM OBJECTIVES

A **concept** such as depression can be defined in words, and, if the words are sufficiently well chosen, the reader will have a clear idea of what depression is. When we apply the definition to a particular client, however, words may be not enough to guide us. The client may seem depressed according to the definition, but many questions may still remain. Is the client more or less depressed than the average person? If more depressed, how much more? Is the depression growing or declining? For how long has the client been depressed? Is the depression continuous or episodic? If episodic, what length of time usually elapses between depressive episodes? Is this length of time increasing or diminishing? How many episodes occur in a week? To what degree is the client depressed? Answers to questions such as these will enable you to obtain greater insight into your client's depression—an insight essential for planning and evaluating a treatment intervention.

WHY MEASUREMENT IS NECESSARY

The word **measurement** is often used in two different senses. In the first sense, a measurement is the result of a measuring process:

- The *number of times* Bobby hits his brother in a day (a possible *frequency* practice objective).

Concept

An understanding, an idea, or a mental image; a way of viewing and categorizing objects, processes, relations, and events.

Measurement

The assignment of labels or numerals to the properties or attributes of observations, events, or objects according to specific rules.

247

- The *length of time* for which Jenny cries (a possible *duration* practice objective).
- The *intensity* of Ms. Smith's depression (a possible *magnitude* practice objective).

In the second sense, measurement refers to the measuring process itself; that is, it encompasses the event or attribute being measured, the person who does the measuring, the method employed, the measuring instrument used, and often also the result. Throughout our book, *measurement* will be taken to refer to the entire process, excluding only the results. The results of any measurement process will be referred to as **data**. In other words, measurement is undertaken to obtain data—objective and precise data, that is.

In any profession, from the social services to plumbing, an instrument is a tool designed to help the user perform a task. A tool need not be a physical object; it can just as easily be a perception, an idea, a new synthesis of known facts, or a new analysis of a known whole. As we now know, an evaluation is an appraisal: an estimate of how effectively and efficiently objectives are being met in a practitioner's individual practice or in a social service program. In other words, an evaluation can compare the change that has actually taken place against the predicted, desired change.

Thus, an evaluation requires knowledge of both the initial condition and the present condition of the objective undergoing the proposed change. Therefore, it is necessary to have at least two *measurements,* one at the beginning of the change process and one at the end. In addition, it is always useful to take measurements of the objectives during the change process as well. Measurement, then, is not only necessary in the quality improvement process—it is the conceptual foundation without which the evaluative structure cannot exist.

A definition, no matter how complete, is useful only if it means the same thing in the hands of different people. For example, we could define a distance in terms of the number of days a person takes to walk it; or the number of strides needed to cross it, or the number of felled oak trees that would span it end to end. But since people, strides, and oak trees vary, none of these definitions is very exact. To be useful to a modern traveler, a distance must be given in miles or some other precisely defined unit.

Similarly, shared understanding and precision are very important in the social services. A worker who is assessing a woman's level of functioning needs to know that the results of the assessment are not being affected by her feelings toward the woman, her knowledge of the woman's situation, or any other biasing factor; that any other worker who assessed the same woman under the same conditions would come up with the same result.

Further, you will need to know that the results of the assessment will be understood by other professionals, that the results are rendered in words or symbols that are not open to misinterpretation. If the assessment is to provide the basis for decisions about the woman's future, via your chosen treatment intervention, objectivity and precision on your part are even more important.

Data

Isolated facts, presented in numerical or descriptive form, on which client or program decisions are based; not to be confused with information.

Objectivity

Some social workers believe that they are entirely **objective;** that is, they will not judge clients by skin color, ethnic origin, religious persuasion, sexual orientation, social class, income level, marital status, education, age, gender, verbal skill, or personal attractiveness. They may believe they are not influenced by other people's opinions about a client—statements that the client has severe emotional problems or a borderline personality will be disregarded until evidence is gathered. No judgments will be made on the basis of the worker's personal likes and dislikes, and stereotyping will be avoided at all costs.

Social workers who sincerely believe that their judgment will never be influenced by any of the above factors are deluding themselves. Everyone is prejudiced to some degree in some area or another; everyone has likes and dislikes, moral positions, and personal standards; everyone is capable of irrational feelings of aversion, sympathy, or outrage. Workers who deny this run the risk of showing **bias** without realizing it, and a worker's unconscious bias can have devastating effects on the life of a client.

A client may unwittingly fuel the bias by sensing what the practitioner expects and answering questions in a way that supports the worker's preconceptions. In extreme cases, clients can even become what they are expected to become, fulfilling the biased prophecy. The art of good judgment, then, lies in accepting the possibility of personal bias and trying to minimize its effects. What is needed is an unprejudiced method of assessment and an unbiased standard against which the client's knowledge, feelings, or behaviors can be gauged. In other words, we require a measurement method from which an impartial measure can be derived.

Precision

The other ingredient of the quality improvement process is precision, whose opposite is vagueness. A vague statement is one that uses general or indefinite terms; in other words, it leaves so many details to be filled in that it means different things to different people. There are four major sources of vagueness.

The first source of vagueness is terms such as *often, frequently, many, some, usually,* and *rarely,* which attempt to assign degrees to a client's feelings or behaviors without specifying a precise unit of measurement. A statement such as "John misses many appointments with his worker" is fuzzy; it tells us only that John's reliability *may* leave much to be desired. The statement "John missed 2 out of 10 appointments with his worker" is far more precise and does not impute evil tendencies to John.

The second source of vagueness is statements that, although they are intended to say something about a particular client, might apply to anyone; for example, "John often feels insecure, having experienced some rejection by his peers." Who has not

Objectivity

A research stance in which a study is carried out and its data are examined and interpreted without distortion by personal feelings or biases.

Bias

Not neutral; an inclination to some form of prejudice or preconceived position.

Measuring instrument
Any instrument used to measure a variable.

Rating scale
A type of measuring instrument in which responses are rated on a continuum or in an ordered set of categories, with numerical values assigned to each point or category.

Practice objective
A statement of expected change identifying an intended therapeutic result tailored to the unique circumstances and needs of each client; logically linked to a program objective. Practice objectives, like program objectives, can be grouped into affects, knowledge, and behaviors.

Program objective
A statement that clearly and exactly specifies the expected change, or intended result, for individuals receiving program services. Qualities of well-chosen objectives are meaningfulness, specificity, measurability, and directionality. Program objectives, like practice objectives, can be grouped into affects, knowledge, and behaviors. Not to be confused with program goal.

experienced peer rejection? Nevertheless, the statement will be interpreted as identifying a quality specific to John. Our profession abounds with statements like this, which are as damaging to the client as they are meaningless.

A third source of vagueness is professional jargon, the meaning of which will rarely be clear to a client. Often professionals themselves do not agree on the meaning of such phrases as "expectations–role definition" or "reality pressures." In the worst case, they do not even know what they mean by their own jargon; they use it merely to sound impressive. Jargon is useful when it conveys precise statements to colleagues; when misused, it can confuse workers and alienate clients.

The last source of vagueness is tautology: a meaningless repetition disguised as a definition; for example, "a delinquent is a person who engages in delinquent behaviors," "John is agoraphobic because he is afraid of open spaces," "Betty is ambivalent because she cannot make up her mind," "Marie hits her brother because she is aggressive," "John rocks back and forth because he is autistic." Obviously, tautological statements tell us nothing and are to be avoided.

In summary, we need to attain objectivity and precision and avoid bias and vagueness. Both objectivity and precision are vital in the quality improvement process and are readily attainable through measurement.

TYPES OF MEASURING INSTRUMENTS

There are many types of **measuring instruments,** and Chapter 9 on this book's Web page provides numerous links that you can use to find them. We will present only three types to give you a flavor of what they can look like: (1) rating scales, (2) summated scales, and (3) goal attainment scaling.

Rating Scales

Rating scales use judgments by oneself or others to assign an individual (or program) a single score in relation to the **practice or program objective** being measured. What the various types of rating scales have in common is that they all rate clients on various traits or characteristics by locating them at some point on a continuum or in an ordered set of response categories, where numerical values are assigned to each category. Rating scales may be completed by the person being evaluated (self-rating) or by some significant other, such as a parent, supervisor, spouse, or practitioner. Sometimes a client and a significant other are asked to complete the same rating scale to provide the worker with two different views.

There are many different types of rating scales that are useful for evaluative purposes. We will only present two of them: (1) graphic rating scales and (2) self-anchored rating scales.

Graphic Rating Scales

Graphic rating scales are structured with a practice or program objective described on a continuum from one extreme to the other, such as "low to high" or "most to least." The points of the continuum are ordered in equal intervals and are assigned numbers. Some or most points have descriptions to help people locate their positions on the scale. Below is one such scale, a "feeling thermometer" that asks children to rate their level of anxiety from "very anxious" to "very calm." The practice objective in this situation might be "to decrease Bob's anxiety at home."

Graphic rating scale
A rating scale that describes an attribute on a continuum from one extreme to the other, with points of the continuum ordered in equal intervals and then assigned values.

Check below how anxious you are at home:

_____ 100 Very anxious
_____ 90
_____ 80
_____ 70
_____ 60
_____ 50 Neither anxious nor calm
_____ 40
_____ 30
_____ 20
_____ 10
_____ 0 Very calm

The major advantage of graphic rating scales is that they are easy to use, though one must take care to develop appropriate descriptive statements. For example, end statements so extreme that it is unlikely anyone would choose them, such as "extremely hot" or "extremely cold," should not be used.

Self-Anchored Rating Scales

Self-anchored rating scales are similar to graphic rating scales in that clients are asked to rate themselves on a continuum, usually a 7-point or 9-point scale from low to high. They differ in that *clients* define the specific referents, or *anchors,* for three points on the continuum on a self-anchored scale. An anchor point is the point on a scale where a concrete descriptor is given to define the condition represented by that point. This type of scale is often used to measure such attributes as intensity of feeling or pain. A self-anchored scale is an excellent source of data because it is essentially developed by the person most familiar with the subtleties of the problem—the client.

For example, one of your clients, Jim, has difficulty being honest in group sessions; he could complete a question that is intended to measure his own perceptions of his honesty (the three anchor points are put in by the client). In the example below, he writes in the three anchor points (i.e., can never be honest, can sometimes

Self-anchored rating scales
A rating scale in which research participants rate themselves on a continuum of values, according to their own referents for each point.

be honest, and can always be completely honest). Jim's practice objective in this case could be to increase his honesty within the group.

Indicate the extent to which you feel you can be honest in the group.

1	2	3	4	5	6	7	8	9
I can never be honest				I can sometimes be honest			I can always be completely honest	

Suppose that another one of your clients, Betty, is feeling trapped in her marriage and in her role as a homemaker. She might develop a 9-point scale such as the one shown below, ranging from "I feel completely trapped," to "I feel I have some options," to "I do not feel trapped at all." If she is not able to analyze her feelings well enough to identify three distinct emotional levels between 5 and 9 or 1 and 5, she may prefer to use a 5-point scale instead. She should certainly be told that the intervals are equal; the distance between 8 and 9 is the same as the distance between 7 and 8, and so forth.

1	2	3	4	5	6	7	8	9
I do not feel trapped at all.				I feel I have some options.			I feel completely trapped.	

If the problem is not the extent to which Betty feels trapped but the intensity of the trapped feelings, she might consider what sort of emotions she experiences when she feels most and least trapped. If being most trapped involves desperate or suicidal feelings, these feelings will define the high end of the scale.

From this example, we can deduce the two major advantages of self-anchored scales. First, they are specific to the client in a way that a scale developed by someone else cannot be. They measure emotions known only to the client and may therefore yield the most complete and accurate portrayal of the situation. Second, they can measure the intensity of a feeling or attitude. Clients who suffer from feelings of anxiety or guilt or from physical ailments such as migraine headaches are often primarily concerned with intensity, and they may be more willing to fill out an instrument that reflects this concern.

There are also disadvantages to an instrument that is completed by the client. One major drawback is that clients may consciously or unconsciously distort their responses so as to appear more worthy or more deserving in the eyes of the worker. Analyzing an emotion thoroughly enough to rate it on a scale may result in changes to the emotion. This problem is known as "reactivity."

Self-anchored scales, then, are of particular value when the quality being measured is an emotion or thought pattern known only to the client, or when intensity is the primary concern. These scales can be used alone or in conjunction with other types of measuring instruments. They can also be used to supply data peripheral to the central problem: For example, a client whose practice objective is weight loss might use a self-anchored scale to measure changes in self-esteem associated with the weight loss.

Summated Scales

Where rating scales obtain data from one question, or item, about the practice or program objective, **summated scales** present multiple questions, or items, to which the client is asked to respond. Thus, summated scales combine responses to all of the questions on an instrument to form a single, overall score for the objective being measured. The responses are then totaled to obtain a single composite score indicating the individual's position on the objective of interest.

Summated scales are widely used to assess individual or family problems, to perform needs assessments, and to assist other types of case-level and program-level evaluation efforts. The scale poses a number of questions and asks clients to indicate the degree of their agreement or disagreement with each. Response categories may include such statements as "strongly agree," "agree," "neutral," "disagree," and "strongly disagree."

It is our opinion that summated scales provide more objectivity and precision in the variable that they are measuring than the two types of rating scales mentioned above. Figure 9.1 presents an excellent example of a standardized summative scale and Box 9.1 shows how it can be scored. It measures one variable: client satisfaction with services. Figure 9.2 is another example of a standardized summative scale that measures client satisfaction with services, only this one has three related subscales in it, all combined in one measuring instrument.

A unidimensional summative measuring instrument (e.g., Figure 9.1) only measures one variable. On the other hand, a multidimensional one measures a number

The questions below are designed to measure the way you feel about the services you have received. This is not a test, so there are no right or wrong answers. Answer each item as carefully and as accurately as you can by circling the appropriate number on the right.	None of the time	Very rarely	A little of the time	Some of the time	A good deal of the time	Most of the time	All of the time
1. People here really seem to care about me.	1	2	3	4	5	6	7
2. I would come back here if I need help again.	1	2	3	4	5	6	7
3. I would recommend this place to people I care about.	1	2	3	4	5	6	7
4. People here really know what they are doing.	1	2	3	4	5	6	7
5. I get the kind of help here that I really need.	1	2	3	4	5	6	7
6. People here accept me for who I am.	1	2	3	4	5	6	7
7. People here seem to understand how I feel.	1	2	3	4	5	6	7
8. I feel I can really talk to people here.	1	2	3	4	5	6	7
9. The help I get here is better that I expected.	1	2	3	4	5	6	7

Figure 9.1 Client Satisfaction Inventory (CSI-SF).

Box 9.1 Scoring Instructions for the Short-Form
Client Satisfaction Inventory (CSI-SF)

Step 1: Add up the value of the valid responses. This
value is called SUM. Use a value of "0" for items
marked "x" or items left blank. Write the sum of
the valid items at the right.   SUM_____

Step 2: Determine the number of valid responses.
This value is called N. Items left blank or marked
"x" are not added to N. Also, do not score any
form in which fewer than seven items were
answered. N_____

Step 3: Subtract N from SUM.   SUM – N_____

Step 4: Multiple (SUM – N) by 100.   (SUM – N) (100)_____

Step 5: Divide the value obtained in Step 4 by (N) (6).

Example: Sum = 51, N = 8.
Therefore: Score = (51 – 8) (100)/(8 * 6) = 89.6   SCORE_____

---

of highly related subvariables at the same time (e.g., Figure 9.2). In short, a multidimensional instrument is nothing more than a number of unidimensional instruments stuck together. For example, Figure 9.2 is a multidimensional summative measuring instrument that contains three unidimensional ones:

1. Relevance of received social services (items 1–11).
2. The extent to which the services reduced the problem (items 12–21).
3. The extent to which services enhanced the client's self-esteem and contributed to a sense of power and integrity (items 22–34).

Goal Attainment Scaling (GAS)

Goal attainment scale (GAS)

A modified measurement scale used to evaluate case or program outcomes.

A **goal attainment scale** (GAS) is an excellent device for measuring practice objectives. However, we do not recommend that they be used in evaluating a program's objective because they are not standardized. As we know by now, we ultimately try to achieve program objectives with our clients. We do this by creating practice objectives which, if resolved, will accomplish one of the program's objectives. The underlying program objective, however, is not the direct focus of a worker's atten-

Using the scale from one to five described below, please indicate on the line to the left of each item the number that comes closest to how you feel.

1 Strongly agree
2 Agree
3 Undecided
4 Disagree
5 Strongly disagree

_____ 1 The social worker took my problems very seriously.
_____ 2 If I had been the social worker, I would have dealt with my problems in just the same way.
_____ 3 The worker I had could never understand anyone like me.
_____ 4 Overall the agency has been very helpful to me.
_____ 5 If friends of mine had similar problems I would tell them to go to the agency.
_____ 6 The social worker asks a lot of embarrassing questions.
_____ 7 I can always count on the worker to help if I'm in trouble.
_____ 8 The agency will help me as much as it can.
_____ 9 I don't think the agency has the power to really help me.
_____10 The social worker tries hard but usually isn't too helpful.
_____11 The problem the agency tried to help me with is one of the most important in my life.
_____12 Things have gotten better since I've been going to the agency.
_____13 Since I've been using the agency my life is more messed up than ever.
_____14 The agency is always available when I need it.
_____15 I got from the agency exactly what I wanted.
_____16 The social worker loves to talk but won't really do anything for me.
_____17 Sometimes I just tell the social worker what I think she wants to hear.
_____18 The social worker is usually in a hurry when I see her.
_____19 No one should have any trouble getting some help from this agency.
_____20 The worker sometimes says things I don't understand.
_____21 The social worker is always explaining things carefully.
_____22 I never looked forward to my visits to the agency.
_____23 I hope I'll never have to go back to the agency for help.
_____24 Every time I talk to my worker I feel relieved.
_____25 I can tell the social worker the truth without worrying.
_____26 I usually feel nervous when I talk to my worker.
_____27 The social worker is always looking for lies in what I tell her.
_____28 It takes a lot of courage to go to the agency.
_____29 When I enter the agency I feel very small and insignificant.
_____30 The agency is very demanding.
_____31 The social worker will sometimes lie to me.
_____32 Generally the social worker is an honest person.
_____33 I have the feeling that the worker talks to other people about me.
_____34 I always feel well treated when I leave the agency.

Figure 9.2 Reid-Gundlach Social Service Satisfaction Scale.

tion. Instead, workers create and focus their attention on their clients' practice objectives that are directly linked to the program's objectives. A useful medical analogy is to think of a disease as a program objective and the symptoms of the disease as practice objectives.

Creating Practice Objectives From Program Objectives

By way of example, suppose that a residential home for delinquent children accepts a boy, Ron, who is experiencing trouble at school as well as with the police. Ron's teacher reports that he is two grade levels behind on every subject, he has violent temper outbursts in the classroom, and he acts as a negative leader to other students. The worker sets three practice objectives for Ron: first, that he should perform academically at his own grade level; second, that he should express anger in appropriate ways; third, that he should display positive leadership behaviors. In using the medical analogy above, delinquency is the disease, and Ron's poor grades, inappropriate anger expression, and few leadership skills are symptoms of the disease—the practice objectives. It should be noted that Ron could have exhibited other delinquent behaviors (e.g., skipping school, criminal behavior, or joining a street gang).

Weighting Practice Objectives. Each of the three practice objectives for Ron presented in Table 9.1 is assigned a weight between 1 and 10, based on the worker's perception of its clinical importance. The first practice objective receives a weighting of 7, the second of 3, and the third of 9. These practice objectives, with their weights, are shown at the top of Ron's goal attainment scale (Alter & Evens, 1990).

Next, each practice objective is operationalized; that is, a precise meaning is assigned to such phrases as "displays positive leadership" and "expresses anger in appropriate ways" so that the objective is measurable. Each objective is then rated on a 5-point scale ranging from -2 to $+2$ (see left column of Table 9.1), where:

- $-2 =$ Much less than expected level of outcome
- $-1 =$ Somewhat less than expected level of outcome
- $0 =$ Expected level of outcome
- $+1 =$ Somewhat more than expected level of outcome
- $+2 =$ Much more than expected level of outcome

As can be seen from Table 9.1, each point on the scale is anchored; that is, each of the five possible outcomes is operationalized in fairly precise terms. For example, the first practice objective, "Much more than expected level of outcome," is defined as an increase from Ron's present grade level to a gain of one year. Similarly, the second practice objective, "Somewhat more than expected level of outcome," is defined in terms of a decrease in number of tantrums, specifically, their becoming "rare."

Table 9.1 Ron's Goal Attainment Scale

Levels of Predicted Attainment	Scale 1 Ron Achieves Appropriate Grade (Weight=7)	Scale 2 Ron Expresses Anger Appropriately (Weight=3)	Scale 3 Ron Displays Positive Leadership (Weight=9)
Much less than expected level of outcome (−2)	Falls behind current grade level	Acts out in more destructive ways	Uses others all the time to achieve negative goals
Somewhat less than expected level of outcome (−1)	Stays at current grade level	Stays the same	Sometimes uses others to achieve negative goals
Expected level of outcome (0)	Gains three months	Shows some signs expresses anger in acceptable ways	Sometime functions as a positive leader
Somewhat more than expected level of outcome (+1)	Gains six months	Rarely has tantrums	Has become a strong but inconsistent leader
Much more than expected level of outcome (+2)	Gains a year	Always expresses anger in acceptable ways	Never functions as a negative leader

The Generation of Data. Once the scale has been established, a baseline score is obtained. A baseline measure is a measure of the client's state *before* any intervention. Without this measure, it is impossible to know whether change has occurred, so a baseline measurement is always critically important to any series of repeated measurements. Ron's baseline score is determined by rating him on the scale very soon after he enters the home, when nothing in his behavior will have yet changed. The worker assigns him a score of −1 on the first practice objective, −1 on the second, and −2 on the third. Because the objectives are weighted, the goal attainment score is determined by multiplying each rating by the assigned weight and summing the results. Ron's baseline goal attainment score would then be calculated as follows:

First Practice Objective

Weight = 7
Rating = − 1
Score = 7 (−1) = −7

Second Practice Objective

Weight $= 3$
Rating $= -1$
Score $= 3(-1) = -3$

Third Practice Objective

Weight $= 9$
Rating $= -2$
Score $= 9(-2) = -18$

Total Goal Attainment Score $= (-7) + (-3) + (-18) = -28$

As the ratings reflect the opinion of the rater, it is always preferable to have two or more people simultaneously rate the client. Let us say that Ron's teacher gives him the same rating as his worker on the first two practice objectives, but on the third she gives him a -1 instead of a -2. Ron's score on the third practice objective is then $9(-1) = -9$ according to his teacher, bringing his total score to -19 from the teacher's point of view. Ron's baseline goal attainment score is then calculated as the average of the two scores, that is, $[(-28) + (-19)]/2 = -23.5$.

If the scores assigned by the two raters differ greatly, this is a sign that the anchor points on the scale have not been defined with sufficient precision. They will then have to be redefined and the ratings redone. The calculation of a baseline score therefore provides an initial score against which change can be measured. Once a baseline score is established, the intervention is implemented, and the client is repeatedly rated at whatever intervals seem appropriate. If the scale becomes outdated in light of the client's achievements, a new scale can be constructed for one or more practice objectives.

Measurement by the Numbers

Box 9.2 presents two actual examples of how two social service programs' initial outcomes, intermediate outcomes, and long-term outcomes (program objectives) can be easily measured with only simple numbers and percentages. The two programs in Box 9.2, emergency shelters and transitional shelters, do not use any "measuring instruments" per se, but rather simply measure their respective program outcomes via numbers. In short, they do not use rating scales, summated scales, or GASs of any kind. Sometimes simple numbers are all that is needed to measure client and program outcomes. (Also see Box 7.2 for more examples of how objectives can be measured with just numbers.)

Emergency Shelters

Initial Outcome: Clients receive emergency food and shelter.

Indicator 1: Total number of different clients who received shelter.

> This is an unduplicated count of all the individuals who received shelter at your location during the fiscal year. In the case of families, count each member of the family separately.

Indicator 2: Average number of bed-nights used per client.

> Count the total number of bed-nights for the fiscal year and divide by the total number of different clients who received shelter during that fiscal year (i.e., the value for Indicator 1 above).

Intermediate Outcome: Clients begin to access needed services.

Indicator 3: Number and percent of clients who agree to a recovery/treatment/ service plan by the end of their 30th day of shelter at that site.

> In this indicator, "clients" refers to adult clients whose 30th day of shelter at your site occurs during the current fiscal year. These days do not have to be consecutive or all in the same fiscal year.
>
> If the client's first 30 days of shelter spans two fiscal years, that client should be included in the first fiscal year calculation (both numerator and denominator for the percentage) only if s/he agreed to a recovery/treatment/service plan during that fiscal year. Otherwise such clients should be included in the computation of this indicator for the next fiscal year.

Indicator 4: Number and percent of clients who, as a result of their service plan, connected with supportive services within 30 days of the start of case management.

> In this indicator, "clients" refers to adult clients.
>
> If a client's 30 days following the start of case management spans two fiscal years, that client should be included in the first fiscal year calculation (both numerator and denominator for the percent) only if the client connected with supportive services that fiscal year. Otherwise such clients should be included in the computation of this indicator for the next fiscal year.
>
> Supportive services include any of the following:
>
> - Alcohol or drug abuse services
> - Mental health services
> - HIV/AIDS-related services
> - Other health care services
> - Education
> - Child care services
> - Legal services
> - Housing placement services
> - Employment assistance services

(continued)

Box 9.2 (continued)

Long-Term Outcome: Clients move to more stable housing.

Indicator 5: Number and percent of clients who move to a transitional shelter, long-term housing, a rehabilitative setting, or the home of a friend or family member.

In this indicator, "clients" refers to all clients, not just adults. Consequently, the denominator for the percent calculation will be the number of different clients who received shelter at your location during the fiscal year.

Transitional Shelters

Initial Outcome: A client develops a treatment/ recovery/service plan and implements it.

Indicator 6: Number and percent of clients who have met with counselor/case manager and developed a plan within 30 days of entering program.

In this indicator, "clients" refers to adult clients only.

If the 30 days following admission to the program spans two fiscal years, that client should be included in the first fiscal year calculation (both numerator and denominator for the percent) only if s/he has developed a treatment/recovery/service plan during that fiscal year. Otherwise such clients should be included in the computation of this indicator for the next fiscal year.

Indicator 7: Number and percent of clients who within 30 days of agreeing to a treatment/recovery/service plan are involved in recuperative daytime activities related to that plan.

In this indicator, "clients" refers to adult clients only.

If the 30 days following the development of a treatment/recovery/service plan spans two fiscal years, that client should be included in the first fiscal year calculation (both numerator and denominator for the percent) only if s/he has become involved in recuperative daytime activities during that fiscal year. Otherwise such clients should be included in the computation of this indicator for the next fiscal year. Recuperative daytime activities include any of the following:

- Mental health or substance abuse programs
- Psychiatric rehabilitation programs
- Job-skills training
- Education or vocational education programs
- Employment
- Day programs

Intermediate Outcome: Clients diagnosed with substance abuse and/or mental health problems receive treatment.

Indicator 8: Number and percent of the clients diagnosed with substance abuse and/or mental health problems who are receiving professional treatment within 90 days of entering the program.

In this indicator, "clients" refers to adult clients only.

If the 90 days following the admission to the program spans two fiscal years, that client should be included in the first fiscal year calculation (both numerator and denominator for the percent) only if s/he begins receiving professional treatment during that fiscal year. Otherwise such clients should be included in the computation of this indicator for the next fiscal year.

Long-Term Outcome 1: Client's income increases.

Indicator 9: Number and percent of clients whose income is greater upon discharge from the program than when they entered.

In this indicator, "clients" refers to adult clients only.

The denominator of the percent calculation is the number of adult clients discharged from the program during the fiscal year.

Long-Term Outcome 2: Client moves to permanent housing.

Indicator 10a: Number and percent of *adult* clients who moved to permanent housing.

Indicator 10b: Number and percent of *child* clients who moved to permanent housing.

This indicator measures the outcome separately for adults and children. Consequently, the denominator for the percent calculation for *Indicator 10a* will be the number of different adult clients who received shelter at your location during the fiscal year, and the denominator for the percent calculation for *Indicator 10b* will be the number of different child clients who received shelter at your location during the fiscal year.

For purposes of this indicator, permanent housing is one of the following:

- Rental house or apartment
- Public housing
- Section 8 housing
- Shelter Plus Care housing
- Homeownership
- Moving in with family or friends

In measuring this indicator a foster home for a child is not considered permanent housing.

Long-Term Outcome 3: Client remains in permanent housing.

Indicator 11a: Number and percent of adult clients who do not reenter the Montgomery County homeless system within one year of obtaining permanent housing.

Indicator 11b: Number and percent of child clients who do not reenter the Montgomery County homeless system within one year of obtaining permanent housing.

(continued)

Box 9.2 (continued)

This indicator measures the outcome separately for adults and children. The numerators for the percent calculations are the number of clients who had obtained permanent housing during the previous year and as of one year later had not reentered the Montgomery County homeless system. The denominator for the percent calculation for *Indicator 11a* is the number of adult clients previously sheltered at your site who moved to permanent housing during the prior fiscal year. The denominator for the percent calculation for *Indicator 11b* is the number of child clients previously sheltered at your site who moved to permanent housing during the previous fiscal year.

STANDARDIZED MEASURING INSTRUMENTS

Standardized measuring instrument

A professionally developed measuring instrument that provides for uniform administration and scoring and generates normative data against which later results can be evaluated.

A **standardized measuring instrument** is one that has been constructed by researchers to measure a particular knowledge level, attitude or feeling, or behavior of clients. It is a paper-and-pencil instrument and may take many forms. Two factors differentiate a standardized measuring instrument from any other instrument: the effort made to attain uniformity in the instrument's application, scoring, and interpretation, and the amount of work that has been devoted to ensuring that the instrument is valid and reliable.

Every instrument, whether standardized or not, is designed to measure some specific quality; if it is valid, it will measure only that quality. The information sheet that usually accompanies a standardized instrument will state the instrument's purpose: to measure anxiety about academic achievement, say, or to measure three aspects of assertiveness. In addition, the sheet will usually describe how the questions (items) on the instrument relate to that purpose and will say something about the clinical implications of the quality being measured.

The information sheet may also indicate what the instrument does not measure. A description of an instrument to measure aggression, for example, may specifically state that it does not measure hostility. This statement of purpose and the accompanying description improve chances that the instrument will be used as it was intended, to measure what it was designed to measure. In other words, it is more likely that the application of the instrument will be uniform.

The information sheet may also discuss the research studies done to ensure the instrument's validity, often including the instrument's ability to discriminate between clinical and nonclinical populations. It may mention other instruments or criteria with which the instrument was compared so that users will better understand what validity means in this particular instance. Information about reliability will usually be given via descriptions of the research studies undertaken to ensure reliability and their results. Again, this information will help the worker who uses the instrument to know what kind of reliability can be expected.

Information will also be given about the characteristics of people on whom the instrument was tested. For example, an instrument to measure loneliness may be accompanied by the information that it was tested on a sample of 399 undergraduate students (171 males, 228 females) from three university campuses. An instrument to measure self-esteem may have been tested on a sample of 240 eighth graders—110 African American and 130 Caucasian. In each case, scores will be given for the tested group and subgroups so that the user can see what the norms are for people with particular demographic characteristics. A **norm** is an established score for a particular group against which the score of a client can be measured.

Let us say, for example, that the mean score of African American eighth graders on the self-esteem instrument was 40, with a small range in scores about the mean given in terms of a standard deviation. In comparison, the mean score for Caucasian eighth graders was 60. A practitioner who read this information on the sheet accompanying the instrument would know that an African American client's score should be compared with the African American average score of 40, and a Caucasian client's score should be compared with the Caucasian average of 60. Without this information, the worker might think that an African American client who scored 42 was suffering from low self-esteem—although, in such a case 42 is really close to the average self-esteem score for African American eighth graders.

The concept of norms has an important place in our profession, particularly in the administering of measuring instruments. What is "normal" for an African American child from a poor, urban neighborhood is not necessarily "normal" for a Caucasian child from a prosperous rural neighborhood; what is "normal" for one ethnic group may not be "normal" for another; what is "normal" for an adolescent female may not be "normal" for an adolescent male. It is very important that a client's score be compared with the average score of people with similar demographic characteristics. If this information is not available, as it sometimes is not, the social worker should bear in mind that an "unusual" score may not be at all unusual; that is, it may be normal for the type of client being measured. Conversely, a normal-looking score may turn out to be unusual when the demographic characteristics of the client are taken into account.

The documentation sheet should also explain how to score the instrument and how to interpret the score. Scoring may be simple or relatively complex; it may involve summing specific items, reversing entered scores, or following a preset template. Often, it may also be accomplished on a computer. Some instruments may yield one global score while others may provide several scores, each representing a dimension such as self-esteem or assertiveness. Interpretation of the scores also varies depending on the instrument. When interpreting scores, it is particularly important to be aware that some scores represent the magnitude of problems while others indicate the magnitude of positive attributes such as skills or knowledge.

Norm

In measurement, an average or set group standard of achievement that can be used to interpret individual scores; normative data describing statistical properties of a measuring instrument, such as mean and standard deviation.

Depending on what is measured, increasing scores may indicate improvement or deterioration; the same is true for decreasing scores.

A standardized measuring instrument, then, should be accompanied by at least six kinds of information:

1. The purpose of the instrument
2. A description of the instrument
3. The instrument's validity
4. The instrument's reliability
5. Norms
6. Scoring and interpretation procedures

McDowell and Newell (1996) provide a list of 17 questions that need to be answered when it comes to evaluating the generalizability of standardized instruments across populations:

1. What is the name of the measurement tool?
2. What is/are the name(s) of the measurement tool developer(s)?
3. In which population(s) and age group(s) was the tool developed (e.g., Caucasians, men, college students)?
4. To which population(s) has the tool been applied since its original publication?
5. Has the tool been tested in the population(s) of interest?
6. Has the tool been tested in older populations? If so, in which age cohort(s) was it tested?
7. Is the tool a general measure or a disease-specific measure?
8. What is the reading level of the measurement tool?
9. What are barriers to using the measurement tool?
10. What are the reliability coefficients of the tool components or the overall reliability of the tool, by population?
11. In what ways has the tool been validated?
12. Is the tool self-administered or professionally administered?
13. What is the average length of time for completing the tool?
14. What is the conceptual approach to the topic area (such as psychological well-being)?
15. Is this conceptual approach relevant to/appropriate for the population of interest?
16. Is the original purpose of the tool appropriate for use in the proposed study?
17. What are the published citations of the measurement tool?

The amount and quality of information provided may be taken as an indicator of whether an instrument is standardized, and, if it is, to what degree. There are

Box 9.3 A Catalog of Family Process Measures

Developmental research has confirmed the importance of family processes and of the home environment in child and youth development and learning. How do intervention programs measure changes in family processes? To address this question, the Family Involvement Network of Educators (FINE) at Harvard Family Research Project reviewed rigorously evaluated intervention and prevention programs that sought to change children's cognitive and socioemotional development by supporting both children and parents. Using the database of effective interventions developed by the Substance Abuse and Mental Health Service Administration of the U.S. Department of Health and Human Services, 13 programs were identified that measured family processes along four dimensions: (1) family context, (2) parent–child relationships, (3) parenting practices, and (4) parent involvement in children's learning in the home and school.

- *Family context* refers to attempts on the part of the program to address issues of family functioning and the family environment, including stress, isolation, family cohesion, and problems related to child and substance abuse.
- *Parent–child relationships* relate to efforts to affect parent–child bonding, including increasing parent–child communication, positive interactions, and attachment.
- The *parenting practices* dimension examines programs' impact on parenting strategies as regards effective and positive discipline practices, appropriate parental expectations, and monitoring.
- *Parent involvement in the home and in the school* refers to a program's intent both to increase parents' skills, beliefs, and attitudes in supporting children in homework and literacy activities, and to bolster family and school relationships and parent–teacher communication. Table 1 is a breakdown of the various measures programs use to evaluate family processes.

Table 1 Measures Used to Evaluate Family Processes

Family Processes	Measures of Family Processes	Measure Description
Family Context	Family Environment Scale (FES; Moos & Moos, 1984)	Respondents (parents or adolescents) describe their family interactions in terms of cohesiveness, expressiveness, conflict, independence, organization, and control.
	Structural Family Systems Rating (SFSR; Szapocznik et al., 1991)	Trained observers rate family interactions for closeness, distance, and boundaries between family members, based on audiotaped recordings of three standardized tasks (e.g., deciding on a menu for a meal).
	Internal Control, Power of Others, Chance Scales (IPC; Levenson, 1981)	Parents report their sense of internal control over their lives.
	Social Network Questionnaire (SNQ; Antonucci, 1986)	Parents report about their social and frequency of contact networks, including size and who is relied upon.
	Parenting Stress Index (PSI; Abidin, 1995)	Parents report their sources of stress (depression, isolation, and health).
	Family Relationship Scale (FRS; Tolan, Gorman-Smith, Huesmann, & Zelli, 1997)	Parents report about family cohesion, beliefs about the family, and structure (organization).

(continued)

Box 9.3 (continued)

Table 1 (continued)

	Developmental History & Life Changes (Miller-John son & Maumary-Gremaud, 1995)	Parents respond to open-ended questions and describe how they would respond to a series of six standardized vignettes.
	Family Adaptability and Cohesion Evaluation Scales (FACES III; Olson, Portner, & Lavee, 1985)	Families report about family adaptability and cohesion.
Parent–Child Relationships	Parent–Child Interaction Task (PCIT; Forehand & McMahon, 1981)	Parents engage in four tasks with their child, including free play, a parent control situation, a task using LEGO plastic construction toys, and cleanup.
	Parent–Child Affective Quality (Spoth, Redmond, & Shin, 1998)	Parents report about positive and negative affect in the parent–child relationship. Trained observers rate warmth and relationship quality of the parent–child interaction in a videotaped family interaction task (e.g., discuss questions on cards related to family life).
	Dyadic Parent–Child Interactive Coding System Revised (DPICS-R; Webster-Stratton, 1985)	Trained observer rates mother interacting with her child for 30 minutes in the home environment.
Parenting Practices	Self-Perceptions of the Parental Role scale (SPPR; MacPhee, Benson, & Bullock, 1986)	Parents report their self-perceived competence in the parental role and their satisfaction with the role.
	Alabama Parenting Questionnaire (APQ; Shelton, Frick, & Wooten, 1996)	Parents report their involvement, positive parenting, monitoring and supervision, and inconsistent discipline and punishment practices.
	Parenting Practices Questionnaire (PPQ; Gorman-Smith, Tolan, Zelli, & Huesmann, 1996)	Parents report their discipline and monitoring techniques.
	Parenting Practices Scale (PPS; Strayhorn & Weidman, 1988)	Parents report about their discipline and warmth.
	Ratings of Parent Change (Conduct Problems Prevention Research Group, 1999)	Parents describe the extent of change in their own parenting practices and social cognitions over the past year.
Parent Involvement in the Home and in the School	Parent as a Teacher Inventory (PAAT; Strom, 1984)	Parents report their feelings about their child's need for creativity and play, about their own role as teacher of their child, and about their level of patience with their child.

Table 1 (continued)

Parent–Teacher Involvement Questionnaire (Conduct Problems Prevention Research Group, 1999)	Teachers and parents respond to questions about parent–teacher contact and relationships, parent involvement in school, parent involvement at home, and parent endorsement of the school.
Parent–Teacher Involvement Questionnaire (INVOLVE-P/T; Reid, Webster-Stratton & Beauchaine, 2001)	Parents report the amount and quality of their involvement with their children's education and activities at home and at school. Teachers rate parents' involvement in their child's education and their frequency of contact with teachers and school personnel.

The following is a list of questions regarding resources available in the Calgary area. Please write down as many resources as you know about in responding to each question.

1. Where would you go for help in caring for your children?
2. Where would you go for financial assistance?
3. Where would you go for help with parenting?
4. Where would you go for medical assistance or information?
5. Where would you go for information on improving your education?
6. Whom would you call to help at home?
7. Where would you go for help in finding a job?
8. Where would you go to get help in finding a place to stay?
9. Who would you call if you had an immediate crisis?
10. Where would you go for assistance for food or clothing?
11. Where would you go for legal assistance?
12. Where would you go for counseling?

Figure 9.3 Questionnaire on support systems in Calgary.

thousands of standardized measuring instruments available on the market today. This book's Web site provides links to these instruments. Box 9.3 displays the various standardized measuring instruments (and a brief description of how the instruments are completed) that can be used to measure changes in four dimensions of family processes: family context, parent–child relationships, parenting practices, and parent involvement in the home and in the school.

Box 9.4 Program Structure of a Social Service Program to Help High School Teenagers Who Are Pregnant

— **Program Goal:** To provide social services to pregnant teenagers in high school who have elected to keep their babies in an effort to help these students become adequate mothers when they graduate from high school.

  • **Program Objective:** To increase the self-sufficiency of pregnant adolescents after they have their babies.

      • **Measurement of Program Objective:** Self-Sufficiency Inventory.

          • **Practice Objective (A):** To increase parenting skills.

              • **Measurement of Practice Objective (A):** Adult-Adolescent Parenting Inventory.

                  – **Practice Activities (A):** Teach specific child-rearing skills, role-model/role-play effective parenting skills, teach effective child/adult communication skills, teach and model alternative discipline measures, teach age-appropriate response of children, and establish family structure (e.g., meal times, bath times, and bed times).

          • **Practice Objective (B):** To increase the number of support systems with which client is knowledgeable.

              • **Measurement of Practice Objective (B):** Instrument specially constructed for the particular city. To show how simple measuring instruments can be, Figure 9.3 presents one that was used with this practice objective. Figure 9.4 presents the correct answers.

                  – **Practice Activities (B):** Review the city's information resource book with the client, provide information sheet on key resources relevant to the client, provide brochures on various agencies, escort client to needed resources (e.g., career resource center, health clinic), and go through specific and appropriate sections of the Yellow Pages with the client.

Is the Measurement Useful?

An important characteristic of any measuring instrument is its utility. Does it fit within the program's structure and logic model? For example, Box 9.4 presents a goal and only one of eight program objectives for a social service program that helps pregnant teenagers in high school. Also included is the measurement of the program

1. Alberta Social Services, Community Daycare/Day Home, City of Calgary Social Services, Children's Cottage
2. Alberta Social Services, church, Alberta Consumer Corporate Affairs, Alberta Student Finance Board
3. Calgary Health Services, family doctor, Parent Support Association, Calgary Association of Parents, Parent Aid, City of Calgary Social Services, Children's Hospital
4. Family doctor, hospitals, Calgary Birth Control Association, Calgary Health Services, Birthrite
5. Alberta Vocational College, Viscount Bennet School, SAIT, Mount Royal College, Canada Manpower, Alberta Social Services, Women's Career Center, Louise Dean School, University of Calgary
6. Homemaker Services (FSB), Landlord & Tenant Board, Calgary Housing Authority, Relief Society (Mormon Church), Alberta Social Services, City of Calgary Social Services
7. Alberta Social Services, Canada Manpower, Career Center, Volunteer Center, Hire-A-Student, newspapers, 12 Avenue, job boards
8. Alberta Social Services, YWCA Single Mother Program, Renfrew Recovery, Women's Emergency Shelter, Park Wood House, Discovery House, church, Avenue 15, Single Men's Hostel, JIMY Program, Alpha House, Sheriff King, McMan Youth Services, Birthrite
9. Emergency Social Services, Distress Center, Sexual Assault Center, Suicide Line (CMH), Children's Cottage, Wood's Stabilization Program, Alberta Children's Hospital, church, police/fire department
10. Interfaith Food Bank, Milk Fund, Salvation Army, church, Emergency Social Services, Alberta Social Services
11. Legal Aid, Legal Guidance, University of Calgary Legal Line, Women's Resource Center, Women's Shelter, Dial-A-Law
12. Family Service Bureau, church, Alberta Mental Health, Pastoral Institute, Sexual Assault Center, Children's Cottage, Alberta Social Services, City of Calgary Social Services, Catholic Family Services, Parents Anonymous, Distress Center

Note: Clients may respond to the questionnaire with answers not listed above but which may be entirely appropriate to their own unique situations and thus be evaluated as correct.

Figure 9.4 Answers to questionnaire on support systems in Calgary (see Figure 9.3).

objective. In addition, two practice objectives (*A* and *B*) are outlined and their corresponding measurements are given.

Practice activities that are believed to achieve the two program objectives are also delineated. Notice the consistency among the concepts of the program's goal, the stated program's objective, the two practice objectives related to the program's objective, the various activities, and the two measurements.

SUMMING UP AND LOOKING AHEAD

This chapter discussed the need to measure our practice and program objectives via the use of measuring instruments. We provided a few examples of how practice and program objectives can be measured in addition to considering the features required of a good one. The next chapter builds upon this one in that it presents the various data sources (e.g., clients, practitioners, supervisors, and significant others) and data collection methods (e.g., surveys, interviews, and observations) that can be used to measure practice and programs objectives. So far we have only discussed how we can measure practice and program objectives. We now need to know specifically who we will be measuring (data sources) and how will we be measuring them (data collection method)—the topic of the next chapter.

RECAP AND ONLINE MATERIALS

In this chapter, you learned how to measure social work program and practice objectives.

You should also recall the concept of measurement from your foundational research course. If not, go online to take a free crash course in measurement.

You can also find the following materials online to help you master the concepts you just learned:

- Chapter Outline
- Learning Objectives
- Key Terms and Concepts
- Flash Cards
- Practice Multiple-Choice Tests
- Essay Questions with Answers
- Links

www.oup.com/us/swevaluation

STUDY QUESTIONS

1. How can demographic information used in developing a standardized measurement instrument influence the interpretation of scores obtained by a single client? When measuring practice or program objectives, why is it important to choose the instrument that will measure the objective and not anything else?
2. In groups of four, have each member list his or her biases or beliefs about the use of measuring instruments in the human services. As a group, discuss the nature

of each individual bias and determine how such biases affect client service delivery.

3. In groups of four, develop a hypothetical practice objective for a client who has difficulty in managing anger. Assign one type of measuring instrument to each member of the group, and have each individual develop a scale to measure the stated practice objective. Discuss the advantages and disadvantages of each type of scale, and select the best one. Present your decision to the class.

4. Your colleagues wonder why measurement of the practice objectives they have established for their clients is necessary. How do you respond?

5. Why are objective methods of assessment so important in the human services? Why are objective definitions of program and practice objectives important in the human services?

6. What are standardized measuring instruments? What types of information should accompany them?

7. You are a worker at a local immigrant society. You have all Asian American clients undergo a standardized instrument measuring self-esteem. They all perform poorly on the instrument. Would you immediately specify increased self-esteem as a practice or program objective with your clients? Why or why not?

8. Specify a practice objective that can be described on a continuum from one extreme to another. Develop a graphic rating scale for this objective. Develop a summated rating scale to measure the practice objective you specified.

9. Suppose you are a member of a self-help group designed to enhance your ability to interact with others and overcome your shyness. Define your practice objective and develop a 9-point self-anchored rating scale to measure this objective. Why would it be important for your group leader to cross-validate the data gathered from your scale with other sources? What are other possible sources of data?

10. Under what circumstances would a worker measure a practice objective with a summated scale? Why? Explain in detail. As a practitioner you will want to choose good measuring instruments when measuring a particular objective. How will you be able to distinguish good instruments from poor ones?

REFERENCES, FURTHER READING, AND RESOURCES

Abidin, R. R. (1995). *Parenting Stress Index professional manual* (3rd ed.). Odessa, FL: Psychological Assessment Resources.

Alter, C., & Evens, W. (1990). *Evaluating your practice: A guide to self-assessment.* New York: Springer.

Antonucci, T. C. (1986). Social support networks: A hierarchical mapping technique. *Generations, 10,* 10–12.

Conduct Problems Prevention Research Group. (1999). Initial impact of the Fast Track prevention trial for conduct problems: The high risk sample. *Journal of Consulting and Clinical Psychology, 67*(5), 631–647.

Forehand, R., & McMahon, R. J. (1981). *Helping the noncompliant child: A clinician's guide to parent training.* New York: Guilford Press.

Gorman-Smith, D., Tolan, P. H., Zelli, A., & Huesmann, L. R. (1996). The relation of family functioning to violence among inner-city minority youths. *Journal of Family Psychology, 10,* 115–129.

Levenson, H. (1981). Differentiating among internality, powerful others, and chance. In H. M. Lefcourt (Ed.), *Research with the locus of control construct: Vol. 1. Assessment methods* (pp. 15–62). Orlando, FL: Academic Press.

MacPhee, D., Benson, J. B., & Bullock, D. (1986, April). *Influences on maternal self-perceptions.* Poster session presented at the biennial International Conference on Infant Studies, Los Angeles.

Miller-Johnson, S., & Maumary-Gremaud, A. (1995). *Developmental history and life changes* (Fast Track Project Technical Report). Durham, NC: Duke University.

Moos, R. H., & Moos, B. S. (1984). *Family Environment Scale test and manual.* Palo Alto, CA: Consulting Psychologists Press.

Olson, D. H., Portner, J., & Lavee, Y. (1985). *FACES III.* St. Paul: Department of Family Science, University of Minnesota.

Reid, M. J., Webster-Stratton, C., & Beauchaine, T. P. (2001). Parent training in Head Start: A comparison of program response among African American, Asian American, Caucasian, and Hispanic mothers. *Prevention Science, 2*(4), 209–227.

Shelton, K. K., Frick, P. J., & Wooten, J. (1996). Assessment of parenting practices in families of elementary school-age children. *Journal of Clinical Child Psychology, 25,* 317–329.

Spoth, R., Redmond, C., & Shin, C. (1998). Direct and indirect latent variable parenting outcomes of two universal family-focused preventive interventions: Extending a public health-oriented research base. *Journal of Consulting and Clinical Psychology, 66*(2), 385–399.

Strayhorn, J. M., & Weidman, C. S. (1988). A parent practices scale and its relation to parent and child mental health. *Journal of the American Academy of Child and Adolescent Psychiatry, 27,* 613–618.

Strom, R. D. (1984). *Parent as a teacher inventory manual.* Bensenville, IL: Scholastic Testing.

Szapocznik, J., Rio, A. T., Hervis, O. E., Mitrani, V. B., Kurtines, W. M., & Faraci, A. M. (1991). Assessing change in family functioning as a result of treatment: The Structural Family Systems Rating Scale (SFSR). *Journal of Marital and Family Therapy, 17,* 295–310.

Tolan, P. H., Gorman-Smith, D., Huesmann, L. R., & Zelli, A. (1997). Assessment of family relationship characteristics: A measure to explain risk for antisocial behavior and depression among urban youth. *Psychological Assessment, 9,* 212–223.

Webster-Stratton, C. (1985). *Dyadic Parent-Child Interactive Coding System Revised (DPICS-R): Manual.* Unpublished manuscript, University of Washington at Seattle.

On Measuring Your Practice and Program Objectives

Bloom, M., Fischer, J., & Orme, J. (2006). *Evaluating practice: Guidelines for the accountable professional* (5th ed.). Boston: Allyn & Bacon.

Bostwick, G., & Kyte, N. S. (2005). Measurement. In R. M. Grinnell, Jr., & Y. A. Unrau (Eds.), *Social work research and evaluation: Quantitative and qualitative approaches* (7th ed., pp. 98–111). New York: Oxford University Press.

Corcoran, K. J., & Fischer, J. (2007). *Measures for clinical practice*: Vol. 1. Couples, families, and children (4th ed.). New York: Oxford University Press.

Corcoran, K. J., & Fischer, J. (2007). *Measures for clinical practice*: Volume 2. Adults (4th ed.). New York: Oxford University Press.

Jordan, C., Franklin, C., & Corcoran, K. (2005). Measuring instruments. In R. M. Grinnell, Jr., & Y. A. Unrau (Eds.), *Social work research and evaluation: Quantitative and qualitative approaches* (7th ed., pp. 114–131). New York: Oxford University Press.

McDowell, I., & Newell, C. (1996). *Measuring health*. New York: Oxford University Press.

Mindel, C. H. (2005). Designing measuring Instruments. In R. M. Grinnell, Jr., & Y. A. Unrau (Eds.), *Social work research and evaluation: Quantitative and qualitative approaches* (7th ed., pp. 134–146). New York: Oxford University Press.

Data Sources, Sampling, and Data Collection Methods

10

This chapter presents the basic tools for the evaluation enterprise. These tools are borrowed from quantitative and qualitative research methods that are common in social work research. As is the case in any line of work, evaluators who master the proficient use of their tools produce better quality products than those who do not. The evaluation toolbox is filled with strategies to create, maintain, and repair evaluation plans. This chapter covers the tools that assist us in determining where our evaluation data will come from and how to obtain these data.

Using the image of an evaluation toolbox helps us to understand that there is little use in rummaging through our tools without having a project or purpose in mind. It is fruitless, for example, to debate strategies for measuring client outcomes when program objectives have not yet been formulated. It is also unproductive to deliberate who ought to supply evaluation data in the absence of clearly articulated evaluation questions. When program structure and logic models are ambiguous and/or reasons for conducting an evaluation are vague, there is not much in the evaluation toolbox that will help us produce a meaningful evaluation.

In this chapter we present well-known strategies to select data sources and methods to collect data that will address our evaluation questions. These two tool sets are more commonly known as sampling and data collection. Thus, our discussion ought to bring back fond memories of basic research principles and concepts learned in previous research courses.

DATA SOURCES

Data sources
People or records that are the suppliers of data.

Data sources furnish either new or existing data that are used in an evaluation. *New data sources* are **original data** obtained specifically for the purpose of answering evaluation questions. Who provides the data? There could be any number of individuals who represent our stakeholder groups (Chapter 1). For example, federal and state personnel such as politicians, government officials, and staff from professional organizations can be data sources. Among program workers there are therapists, caseworkers, and case aides as well as many collateral professionals such as teachers, psychologists, and workers from other programs to supply data. Clients, as a stakeholder group, are a common data source. A client can refer to an individual, a family, a group, a community, or an organization, depending on how a program defines it. Table 10.1 provides a simple display of six program outcomes (left column), the measurement of each outcome (middle column), and the respective data source (right column).

Original data
Data that have never been collected before.

Existing data sources are previously recorded documents or artifacts that contain data relevant to current evaluation questions. Generally speaking, existing data were originally collected for some purpose other than our current evaluation. Most likely, stakeholders supplied the data some time ago, but data can be found in documents or databases in one of three areas:

Existing data
Data that exist now in some form or another.

- *Client data and information,* such as client records, social histories, genograms, service plans, case notes, clinical assessments, or progress reports
- *Program data and information,* such as program logic models, previous evaluation reports, program contracts or funding applications, meeting minutes, employee time and activity logs, employee resumes, quality assurance records, or accounting records
- *Public data and information,* such as census data, government documents, or published literature

How do we decide whether to use new or existing data sources? It depends on the specific focus of our evaluation. In particular, the final questions developed for an evaluation guide us to who or what is our best data source for our inquiry. For example, a needs assessment aimed at increasing understanding about the adolescents involved in crime in their community may phrase its evaluation questions to emphasize different data sources:

- Do adolescents who commit crimes see themselves as having a future in their community?
- To what degree do parents feel responsible for their children's criminal behavior in the community?
- What are the legal consequences for adolescents who commit crimes in the community?

Table 10.1 Linking Outcomes to Outcome Indicators to Data Sources

Example: Foster Home Services

Mission/Objective: Ensure the physical and emotional well-being (safety) and normal development of children by placing them into stable, safe, high-quality foster homes.

Outcome	Outcome Indicator	Data Source
Child safety		
Physical well-being	Number and percentage of children with serious health problems at follow-up.	Agency records; trained observer ratings
Repeated abuse and neglect	Number and percentage of children identified as either abused or neglected by time of follow-up.	Agency records; trained observer ratings; client survey
Safety concerns	Number and percentage of children removed from foster home by time of follow-up for other than permanent placement.	Agency records; trained observer ratings
Child development		
Physical development	Number and percentage of children who met normal growth curves and height/ weight expectations at time of follow-up.	Agency records; trained observer ratings
Social development	Number and percentage of children who displayed "age-appropriate" social skills at time of follow-up.	Trained observer ratings; client survey
Educational development	Number and percentage of school-age children who were progressing satisfactorily in school at time of follow-up.	Agency records; client survey

Clearly, the first question targets adolescents as an essential data source, but the latter questions give priority to parents of adolescents and legal professionals or documents, respectively. Each question, of course, can be answered by any number of data sources. No doubt, parents have opinions about their children's futures, and, certainly, the legal community has a perspective on adolescent crime. Each data source, however, can only speculate about questions that ask what others are thinking or feeling.

The *best* data sources are those that provide firsthand or direct knowledge regarding the experience that is the subject of evaluation. Adolescents, for example, have firsthand data relating to their perceptions about their futures. In contrast, data sources that have indirect knowledge about an experience can provide only secondhand data. Adolescents, for example, can offer secondhand data about their parents' feelings either through speculation or by sharing observations about their parents' behaviors.

Given that firsthand data sources are not always available or easily accessible for evaluation purposes, we often look to secondhand data to inform us. Client records, for example, are filled with data that describe client problems and strengths as well as their patterns of change. Practitioners and not the clients themselves, however, typically provide these data. As such, evaluation findings that are based solely on client records as a data source are weaker than those that use firsthand data sources or multiple data sources.

This discussion of firsthand and secondhand data sources raises questions as to which can provide the most accurate and truthful data. Who is in a better position to say which interventions most effectively help clients? Is it the clients themselves,

Table 10.2 Refining the Initial Evaluation Questions When Different Data Collection Strategies Are Considered

Evaluation Questions	Key Data Collection Strategies
Sample 1	
How many people were affected by the project after 2 years?	Usually administrative data available in the project (such as project enrollment; case files; or attendance logs for meetings, seminars, or workshops) will provide the information needed to answer this question.
How much change occurred in the participants after 2 years in the project?	The evaluator will need to identify the nature of changes reported by participants or by external observers and measure them (usually *before* the project starts and *after* a determined time period) using surveys, tests, interviews, focus groups, observations, etc.
Sample 2	
What changes could be observed in the participants after 3 years in the project?	A descriptive study that might include surveys, observations, tests, focus groups, and/or interviews aiming to document the changes over time in the targeted audience will probably suffice to answer this evaluation question.
How much of the observed changes can be attributed to the project?	Answering this question requires the development of strategies to assess casual links between the program and the observed changes that may include logical elimination of competing explanations and quasi-experimental study of a control group.

the practitioners who work with them, or the funders who shell out the money to pay for services? Do practitioners' case notes truly reflect their perceptions about their cases? Or is it necessary to interview them firsthand? These types of questions have no easy answers. As a result, it is desirable to include a variety of data sources in any evaluation so that multiple perspectives are considered.

Our bias is to give priority to data sources who have directly experienced the social need, the program process, or the program outcome that is being evaluated. As mentioned earlier, firsthand data sources generally convey their experiences with more candor and accuracy than anyone who has had only indirect involvement. A pregnant teenager, for example, can more aptly speak to her fears of motherhood than anyone else, including her own mother. Likewise, a worker can more succinctly describe the details of an interaction with a client than can a supervisor or a professional colleague. Generally speaking, the farther removed a data source is from the experience or event in question, the greater the possibility for misrepresentation of the actual experience, or the more vague the data will be.

As the W. K. Kellogg Foundation points out in its *Evaluation Toolkit* (2006), "as the evaluation design progresses and the actual data collection plans are developed, the evaluation questions become clearer. You will undoubtedly discover that subtle differences in how a question is worded lead to different ways of thinking about collecting data, which will cause you to continually clarify your thinking." Table 10.2 illustrates this point.

SAMPLING

After selecting data sources for an evaluation, our next step is to develop a comprehensive list of every single person, document, or artifact that could possibly provide the data for our evaluation. This list is called a *sampling frame* and identifies all units (i.e., people, objects, or events) of a population from which a **sample** is drawn. A needs assessment, for example, may target *people*—every community member, regardless of what stakeholder group they represent. A process evaluation, on the other hand, may target *objects*—all client records opened in the last fiscal year. Or an outcome evaluation may target *events*—every client discharge after a minimum of two weeks of program services. Of course, each evaluation type can sample people, objects, or events, depending on its focus.

If our sampling frame includes only a small number of units, then it is feasible to include each one as a data source. A social service program employing 12 practitioners can easily collect data from all of its workers. On the other hand, the 12 practitioners, each with caseloads of 40, together serve 480 clients at one time, which amounts to oodles of data collection activity—perhaps more than the program can manage. Having more data source units than we can handle is a problem that our sampling tools can help fix.

Sample

A subset of a population of individuals, objects, or events chosen to participate in or to be considered in an evaluation; a group chosen by unbiased sample selection from which inferences about the entire population of people, objects, or events can be drawn.

After a sampling frame is defined, we then want to develop a plan that tells us how many units to pick and which specific units to choose. Do we want every member of a community to provide data or only a select number? Do we review every client record opened in the last fiscal year, or just a portion of them? A sampling plan gives us explicit criteria so that there is no question as to which units will provide data for our evaluation and which units will not.

There are two sampling approaches to consider for any evaluation: probability and nonprobability sampling. A **probability sampling** approach is one that ensures that each unit in a sampling frame has an equal chance of being picked for an evaluation. Units are selected randomly and without bias. Those that are chosen will provide data for the evaluation, and units that are not picked will not. Four common probability sampling strategies are summarized in Box 10.1.

Probability sampling
Sampling procedures in which every member of a designated population has a known chance of being selected for a sample.

Probability Sampling

The major benefit of probability sampling approaches is that they produce samples that are considered to be representative of the larger sampling frame from which they were drawn. As such, data collected from the sample can be generalized or applied to the sampling frame as a whole. Suppose that we randomly pick 100 out of a possible 821 members of the community that is the focus of a needs assessment evaluation. If the 100 people in our sample were picked using probability sampling approaches, then we can be confident that the data they provide will give the same information as if we had collected data from all 821 members. Probability sampling, therefore, saves time and money by using a randomly selected subset to provide information about a larger group.

Nonprobability Sampling

Nonprobability sampling
Sampling procedures in which all of the persons, events, or objects in the sampling frame have an unknown, and usually unequal, chance of being included in a sample.

In contrast, **nonprobability sampling** methods do not give each unit in a sampling frame an equal chance of being picked for an evaluation study. In other words, individual people, objects, or events do not have an equal opportunity to supply data to an evaluation. Four types of nonprobability sampling strategies are summarized in Box 10.2.

Nonprobability sampling methods are used in situations where it is desirable to limit or pick our data sources based on some unique characteristic. It may be that we want to collect data only from clients who drop out of treatment before completion. Or we may want only data related to cross-cultural worker–client interactions. When it is possible to decisively identify conditions or characteristics that define a subset of data sources, it is not necessary to sample beyond it. In other words, it is not necessary to sample from all units when the data of interest are possessed by only a select few.

Box 10.1 Types of Probability Sampling Strategies

Simple Random Sampling

Select each unit included in the sample using a chance procedure (e.g., rolling dice, picking random numbers, or flipping a coin).

Systematic Random Sampling

1. Determine the total number of units in a population (e.g., $N = 400$ client sessions).
2. Determine the desired sample size for the evaluation (e.g., $N = 100$ client sessions).
3. Calculate the interval to select units; that is, divide the total number of units by the desired sample size (e.g., 400/100 = 4, so every fourth session will be selected).
4. Randomly select the starting point using a chance procedure (e.g., rolling dice) to pick a number between 1 and 4 (e.g., 3).
5. Begin with session 3, and pick every fourth one thereafter (e.g., 003, 007, 011, up to session 399).

Stratified Random Sampling

1. Identify the variables or strata relevant to the evaluation (e.g., African American, Caucasian, and Latino community members).
2. Determine the percentage of each variable category in the population (e.g., African American, 28%; Caucasian, 60%; and Latino, 12%).
3. Determine the total sample size (e.g., $N = 100$).
4. Calculate the strata totals (e.g., 28% of 100 = 28 African American, 60% of 100 = 60 Caucasian, and 12% of 100 = 12 Latino).
5. Use simple random sampling procedures to select units for each strata until all totals are filled.

Cluster Sampling

1. Determine the sample size (e.g., $N = 250$).
2. Determine the percentage of each variable category in the population (e.g., African American, 28%; Caucasian, 60%; and Latino, 12%).
3. Use simple random sampling to select a portion of clusters (e.g., 40 residential blocks).
4. Calculate the number of units within the selected clusters (e.g., 10 homes per block = 400 units).
5. Use random sampling procedures to select 250 homes from 400.

Box 10.2 Types of Nonprobability Sampling Strategies

Convenience or Availability Sampling

Include the nearest or most available units.

Purposive Sampling

Include units known or judged to be good data sources based on some theoretical criteria.

Quota Sampling

1. Identify variables relevant to the evaluation (e.g., gender and age).
2. Combine the variables into discrete categories (e.g., younger female, younger male, older female, and older male).
3. Determine the percentage of each category in the population (e.g., 35% younger female, 25% younger male, 30% older female, and 10% older male).
4. Determine the total sample size (e.g., $N = 200$).
5. Calculate quotas (e.g., 35% of 200 = 70 younger females, 25% of 200 = 50 younger males, 30% of 200 = 60 older females, and 10% of 200 = 20 older males).
6. Select the first available data sources possessing the required characteristics until each quota is filled.

Snowball Sampling

1. Locate a small number of data sources in the population of interest.
2. At the same time that data are collected from these sources, ask them to identify others in the population.
3. Contact the newly identified data sources, obtain their data, and request additional data sources from them.
4. Continue until the desired sample size is obtained.

Purposive sampling

A nonprobability sampling procedure in which individuals with particular characteristics are purposely selected for inclusion in the sample; also known as judgmental or theoretical sampling.

Nonprobability sampling strategies aim to produce quality firsthand data from sources that share something in common. They are often used when an evaluation question seeks a fuller understanding of the dynamics of a particular experience or condition rather than to generalize the characteristics of a sample to the larger sampling frame from which it was drawn. This latter aim is achieved by using probability sampling methods.

When is it necessary to use sampling strategies in an evaluation plan? Sampling strategies or tools can effectively address the following problems that are commonplace in all types of evaluations:

- The sampling frame is so large that data cannot realistically be collected from every unit (e.g., needs assessment of a community of 10,000 people, or a process evaluation of daily worker–client interactions in an institutional setting).

- Previous efforts to include all units in a sampling frame have failed (e.g., client response rate to satisfaction surveys is low, or client records are voluminous and not systematically organized).
- Only data sources with unique characteristics are desired (e.g., practitioners who balance their workload well, clients who successfully complete treatment, or client reports that influence courtroom decisions).
- Program resources are limited and can support data collection from only a portion of the sampling frame (e.g., program costs for evaluation are limited, or the program only employs one or two practitioners who are responsible for data collection).
- Multiple data sources are desired (e.g., data are collected from clients, workers, and/or records).

DATA COLLECTION METHODS

Data sources supply data, but **data collection methods** are concerned with the manner in which data are obtained. Data collection methods consist of detailed plans of procedures that aim to gather data for a specific purpose—that is, to answer our evaluation questions. No matter what data collection method is used, we want to develop protocols that will yield credible data. That is, we want our data to be judged as accurate and trustworthy by any reviewer.

Data collection methods
The various ways in which data can be collected, such as surveys (i.e., telephone, mail), participant observations, interviews, secondary analyses, and document reviews.

It should be clear by now that how an evaluation question is stated guides the selection of the data collection method(s). As discussed earlier, we do not want to subscribe to a data collection method before we know our evaluation questions. To do so risks collecting a flurry of data that in the end are worthless. Put simply, the combination of data sources and data collection methods chosen can influence the nature and type of data collected. Having well-thought-out and meaningful evaluation questions before we reach for our data collection tools helps to steer us clear of the disaster that can come when evaluation plans drift apart from an evaluation's purpose. There are many ways to collect data, as displayed in Table 10.3. Like all things in life, each data collection method also has its advantages and disadvantages when it comes to colleting data.

How we go about collecting data to answer evaluation questions depends on many practical considerations—such as how much time, money, and political support is available at the time of the study. Political factors affecting an evaluation study are discussed in Chapter 15. For now, it is enough to say that, given the resource limitations affecting most programs and the importance of a program's developmental history, it is worthwhile to explore existing data before making data collection plans.

In the vast majority of evaluations, existing data are not adequate to answer current evaluation questions, and new data must be collected. For comprehensive coverage, an evaluation ought to use multiple data sources and data collection methods—as many as are feasible for a given program.

Table 10.3 Common Data Collection Methods Used to Evaluate Social Service Programs

Data Collection Method	Description	Advantages	Disadvantages
Questionnaire (General)	A paper and pencil method for obtaining responses to statements or questions by using a form on which participants provide opinions or factual information.	• Relatively inexpensive, quick way to collect large amounts of data from large samples in short amount of time • Convenient for respondents to complete • Anonymity can result in more honest responses • Questionnaires are available • Well suited for answering questions related to "What?" "Where?" and "How many?"	• Limited ability to know if one is actually measuring what one intends to measure • Limited ability to discover measurement errors • Question length and breadth are limited • No opportunity to probe or provide clarification • Relies on participants' ability to recall behavior, events • Limited capability to measure different kinds of outcomes • Must rely on self-report • Not well suited to answering questions related to "How?" and "Why?" • Difficult with low-literacy groups
One-to-One Interview—General	An interaction between two people in which information is gathered relative to respondent's knowledge, thoughts, and feelings about different topics.	• Allows greater depth than a questionnaire • Data is deeper, richer, has more context • Interviewer can establish rapport with respondent • Interviewer can clarify questions • Good method for working with low-literacy respondents • Higher response and completion rates • Allows for observation of non-verbal gestures	• Requires a lot of time and personnel • Requires highly trained, skilled interviewers • Limited number of people can be included • Is open to interviewer's bias • Prone to respondents giving answers they believe are "expected" (social desirability) • No anonymity • Potential invasiveness with personal questions

Method	Description	Advantages	Disadvantages
One-to-One Interview—Unstructured	Totally free response pattern; allows respondent to express ideas in own way and time.	• Can elicit personal information • Can gather relevant unanticipated data • Interviewer can probe for more information	• Requires great skill on part of interviewer • More prone to bias in response interpretation • Data are time-consuming to analyze
One-to-One Interview—Semistructured	Limited free response, built around a set of basic questions from which interviewer may branch off.	• Combines efficiency of structured interview with ability to probe and investigate interesting responses	• Cannot do true exploratory research • Predetermined questions limit ability to probe further
One-to-One Interview—Structured	Predetermined questions, often with structured responses.	• Easy to administer • Does not require as much training of interviewer	• Less ability to probe for additional information • Unable to clarify ambiguous responses
Focus Group	Interviews with groups of people (anywhere from four to 12) selected because they share certain characteristics relevant to the questions of study. Interviewer encourages discussion and expression of differing opinions and viewpoints.	• Studies participants in natural, real-life atmosphere • Allows for exploration of unanticipated issues as they are discussed • Can increase sample size in qualitative evaluation • Can save time and money • Can stimulate new ideas among participants • Can gain additional information from observation of group process • Can promote greater spontaneity and candor	• Interviewer has less control than in a one-to-one interview • Data is sometimes difficult to analyze • Must consider context of comments • Requires highly trained observer-moderators • Cannot isolate one individual's train of thought throughout

continued

Table 10.3 (continued)

Method	Description	Advantages	Disadvantages
Phone Interview	One-to-one conversation over the phone.	• Potentially lower cost • Anonymity may promote greater candor	• Not everyone has a phone • Unlisted numbers may present sampling bias • No opportunity to observe non-verbal gestures
Participant Observation—General	Measures behaviors, interactions, processes by directly watching participants.	• Spontaneous quality of data that can be gathered • Can code behaviors in a natural setting such as a lunchroom or a hallway • Can provide a check against distorted perceptions of participants • Works well with a homogeneous group • Good technique in combination with other methods • Well suited for study of body language (kinesics) and study of people's use of personal space and its relationship to culture (proxemics)	• Quantification and summary of data is difficult • Recording of behaviors and events may have to be made for memory • Difficult to maintain objectives • Very time-consuming and expensive • Requires a highly trained observer
Participant Observation—Participant as Observer	Evaluator's role as observer known to the group being studied and is secondary to his or her role as participant.	• Evaluator retains benefits of participant without ethical issues at stake	• Difficult to maintain two distinct roles • Other participants may resent observer role • Observer's presence can change nature of interactions being observed

Method	Description	Strengths	Weaknesses
Participant Observation—Observer as Participant	Evaluator's observer role known and his or her primary role is to assess the program.	• Evaluator can be more focused on observation role while still maintaining connection to other participants	• Evaluator is clearly an outsider • Observer's presence can change nature of the interactions being observed
Participant Observation—Complete Observer	Evaluator with no formal role as participant; is a silent observer; may also be hidden from the group or in a completely public setting where his or her presence is unnoticed and unobtrusive.	• More objective observations possible • Evaluator is not distracted by participant role • Evaluator's observations do not interfere in any way with the group's process if his or her presence is hidden	• If evaluator's presence is known, it can inhibit or change interactions of participants • If evaluator's presence is hidden, it raises ethical questions
Document Analysis	Unobtrusive measure using analysis of diaries, logs, letters, and formal policy statements to learn about the values and beliefs of participants in a setting or group. Can also include class reviews, letters to teachers, letters from parents, and letters from former students to learn about the processes involved in a program and what may be having an impact.	• Diaries reduce problems of memory relating to when, where, with whom • Provides access to thoughts and feelings that may not otherwise be accessible • Can be less threatening to participants • Evaluator can collect and analyze data on own schedule • Relatively inexpensive	• Quality of data varies between subjects • Diaries may cause change in subjects' behaviors • Not well suited for low-literacy groups • Can be very selective data • No opportunities for clarification of data

continued

Table 10.3 (continued)

Archival Data	Analysis of archival data from a society, community, or organization. Can include birth rates, census data, purchase data, and number of visits to hospitals.	• More accurate than self-report	• Not all data is available or fully reported • Difficult to match data geographically or individually
Historical Data	Analysis of historical data is a method of discovering, from records and personal accounts, what happened in the past. It is especially useful for establishing a baseline or background of a program or of participants prior to measuring outcomes.	• Baseline data can help with interpretation of outcome findings • Can help answer questions about why a program is or is not successful in meeting its goals • Provides a picture of the broader context within which a program is operating	• Can be difficult to obtain data • Relies on data that may be incomplete, missing, or inaccurate • May rely on participant's selective memory of events and behaviors • Difficult to verify accuracy

There are various data collection methods available, and each one can be used with a variety of data sources, which are defined by who (or what) supplies the data. As discussed previously, data collection methods are concerned with either existing or new data.

Obtaining Existing Data

Given that existing data are previously recorded, they can be used to address questions that have an historical slant. Existing data can be used to profile recent and past characteristics or patterns that describe communities, clients, workers, or program services. For example, we may be interested in knowing the past demographic characteristics of a community, or a synopsis of worker qualifications for recent employees, or the general service trends of a program since its beginning.

When existing data are used, the method of data collection is primarily concerned with detailing the steps taken to assemble relevant materials. In other words, what are the rules for including or excluding existing data? The challenge of gathering existing data is in recovering old documents or artifacts that may not be easily accessible. It may be, for example, that program start-up events were recorded but they are in the possession of a former employee, or that client records are sealed by court orders. It may also be that there are no existing data because none was ever recorded. Existing data can be found in (1) documents and reports, and (2) data sets.

Documents and Reports

Reviewing existing documents is a process whereby we examine data that have been previously analyzed and summarized. In other words, someone has already studied the raw, or original, data and presented his or her interpretations or conclusions. Examples of such materials include published research studies, government documents, news releases, social service agency directories, agency annual reports, client reports, and worker performance reviews.

The data available in existing documents and reports are typically presented in either narrative or statistical form. *Existing narrative data* are presented as words or symbols that offer insight into the topic being addressed. Reading the last 10 annual reports for a program, for example, can shed light on the program's evolution. Examining training materials for workers can reveal strengths and weaknesses of program services. Reviewing client files can provide strong clues about underlying practice principles that drive client service delivery.

Existing statistical data involve numbers and figures that have been calculated from original raw data. These data provide us with information about specific client or program features in a summarized form. The most recent program annual report, for example, may state that client racial makeup is 35 percent African American,

Existing statistical data
Data that involve numbers and figures that have been calculated from original raw data.

40 percent Caucasian, 15 percent Hispanic or Latino, and 10 percent other. Or it may report that program clients, on average, received 10 more service hours compared with clients from the previous year. These reports rarely include the raw data used to formulate such summary statements, but they are informative.

By looking at what others have already done, we can save valuable time and frustration—learning from mistakes made by others and avoiding unnecessarily reinventing the wheel. Data and information gleaned from existing published reports and articles provide us with a picture of how much attention our evaluation questions have previously received, if any. Additionally, we can find out if other similar evaluations or studies have taken place. If so, what did they find? What measurement instruments were used, either successfully or unsuccessfully? In short, existing reports provide a starting point from which to begin and refine current evaluation plans.

Data Sets

Data set

A collection of related data items, such as the answers given by respondents to all the questions in a survey.

Data sets, also called databases, store existing raw or original data and organize them such that all data elements can be connected to the source that provided them. For example, a typical client database for a program stores demographic data (e.g., age, race, and gender) for each client. Because data in existing data sets were collected for purposes other than answering our evaluation questions, they are called secondary data.

Before we get ahead of ourselves, it is important to note that data sets or databases can be manual or automated. Most social service programs use *manual* data sets, which amount to no more than a collection of papers and forms filed in a folder and then stored in a filing cabinet. In contrast, *automated* data sets store data electronically in computers. The format or setup of an automated database can mirror its manual predecessors, but because of the power of computers, it is far more sophisticated and efficient.

Even though many social service programs are beginning to automate, old data sets will likely remain in manual form until the day comes when an ambitious evaluator determines that the old data are needed to inform current evaluation questions. Whether manual or automated, databases can accommodate secondary data in both narrative and statistical form. Two common data sets that evaluators can tap into are census and client and/or program data sets.

Census data

Data from the survey of an entire population in contrast to a survey of a sample.

Census Data. **Census data** are periodic summaries of selected demographic characteristics, or variables, that describe a population. Census takers obtain data about variables such as age, gender, marital status, and race. To obtain data in specific topic areas, census takers sometimes obtain data for such variables as income level, education level, employment status, and presence of disabilities. Census data are extremely useful for evaluations in that they aim to compare a program sample with the larger population. For example, is the racial or gender makeup of a program's clientele similar to that of the community at large?

Census data also are useful for providing a general picture of a specific population at a certain point in time. The more data obtained during a census taking, the more detailed the description of the population. The disadvantage of census data is that they can become outdated quickly. Census surveys occur every 10 years and take considerable time to compile, analyze, and distribute. In addition, they give only a general picture of a population. The census, for example, provides data only on the average age of residents in a community or the percentage of childless couples living in a certain area. Although these data are useful for developing an average community profile, they do not provide us with a clear idea of individual differences or how the members of the community describe themselves.

Client and Program Data. More and more social service programs rely on client and program data to produce reports that describe the services they provide. They most likely use data taken from client and program records. **Client data** sets consist of data elements that are collected as part of normal paperwork protocols. Intake forms, assessments, progress reports, and critical incident reports all produce a wealth of client data that range from client demographics to rates of treatment progress.

Client data
Collected as part of the normal paperwork protocols within a program such as intake forms, progress reports, and critical incident reports.

Program data sets encompass various administrative forms that are part and parcel of program operations. They include such things as time sheets, employee resumes and performance evaluations, audit sheets, accreditation documents, training and supervision schedules, and minutes of meetings. Program data sets also yield rich data, including variables such as number of clients served, worker demographics and qualifications, type of service provided, amount of supervision and training, and client outcomes.

There are two problems associated with client and program data sets. First, the data are often incomplete or inconsistently recorded. Because data collection occurred previously, it is usually not possible to fill in missing data or correct errors. Second, the data apply to a specific point in time. If program conditions are known to change rapidly, then past data may no longer be relevant to present evaluation questions. For example, social service programs that rely on workers to collect client and program data and that suffer from high staff turnover rates are faced with the problem that data collected by past workers may not be pertinent to present situations.

Program data
Collected via the forms used in the day-to-day administration of the program, such as timesheets, employee resumes, performance evaluations, audit sheets, and accreditation documents.

Obtaining New Data

Existing data provide us with general impressions and insights about a program, but rarely can they address all questions of a current evaluation. As such, the activities of an evaluation almost always involve the process of collecting new or original data.

Four basic strategies for collecting new data are: (1) face-to-face individual interviews, (2) surveys, (3) group interviews, and (4) observation.

Face-to-Face Individual Interviews

Individual interviews with data sources can produce new, or original, data about social needs, program processes, or program outcomes. **Interviewing** is a data collection method that requires us to identify, approach, and interview specific people who are considered knowledgeable about our questions. Interviewees are sometimes referred to as key informants and can include various people: professionals, public officials, agency directors, program clients, and select citizens, minorities, to name a few.

Interviews can be formal, and they can use a structured interview schedule such as the one presented for a needs assessment in Box 5.1 in Chapter 5. Overall, face-to-face interviews with individuals are generally used to ask questions that permit open-ended responses. To obtain more detailed data, we simply develop additional questions to provide more structure and help probe for answers with more depth. Question 4 in Box 5.1, for example, could be expanded so that key informants are asked to consider past or present services, or gaps in services. Structured interview schedules are used when we have some prior knowledge of the topic being investigated and we want to guide data sources to provide us with particular kinds of information. On the other hand, when very little is known about our problem area, we can use informal unstructured interviews to permit more of a free-flowing discussion. Informal interviews involve more dialogue, which produces not only rich and detailed data but also more questions.

Suppose, for example, we want to learn more from a group of community residents who stay away from using our social service program (needs assessment). We might begin each interview by asking a general question: What keeps you from using our social service program? Depending on the responses given, subsequent questions may focus on better understanding the needs of our interviewees, or on changing existing services to become more accessible. Both structured and unstructured interviews rely on interviewer–interviewee interaction to produce meaningful data.

Surveys

The main goal of **surveys** is to gather opinions from numerous people to describe them as a group. Such data can be collected using in-person or telephone interviews, or via mailed surveys. Surveys differ from the structured and unstructured interview schedules used in face-to-face data collection. Specifically, survey questions are more narrow and yield shorter responses. Additionally, they do not rely on interviewer skills to generate a response.

Creating survey questions that yield valid and reliable responses is a prickly problem because it is a task that appears simple but is not. Consider the likely reac-

Box 10.3 Basic Tasks in Implementing a Regular Client Survey Process

1. Identify the specific information needed.
2. Develop the questionnaire, with help from an expert if possible. Each question included should provide information related to one or more of the outcome indicators.
3. Decide when to administer the questionnaire. For example, if a program seeks to help clients sustain an improved condition, then each client might be surveyed 6 or 12 months after completing the service. In other programs, clients could provide outcome information at the time the services are completed. Institutionalized clients might be surveyed periodically, for example, at one-year intervals.
4. Determine how the questionnaire will be administered. Common options include:

    - Mail, if addresses are available and most clients are literate (a low-cost method);
    - Telephone interview, if clients have telephones (a more time-consuming and expensive method);
    - In-person interviews, which will likely be too costly unless the questionnaire can be administered at the program's offices; or
    - A combination of these methods.

    Consider low-cost incentives (free meals, movie tickets, or a chance to win a TV or other items) to improve the response rate.

5. Assign staff to track which clients should be surveyed and when, and to oversee the survey administration and ensure completion, including arranging for second or third mailings or telephone calls to nonrespondents.
6. Enter and tabulate survey information, preferably using a computer to prepare reports.
7. Provide and disseminate easily understood reports to staff and interested outsiders at regular intervals. Usually, it is not appropriate to report on the responses of individual clients (and some programs may provide clients with a guarantee of confidentiality).
8. Encourage use of the survey information to identify program weaknesses and improvement needs.

tions of students if a teacher were to include a vague or confusing question on a class test. Generally speaking, people do not like or do not respond to questions that do not make sense or are presented ambiguously.

Whether surveys are conducted in-person, by telephone, or by mail depends on several factors. Whatever is the given method of collecting data, all types of surveys contain basic tasks in their implementation. Box 10.3 presents various tasks that must be followed when sending a survey to clients, such as a mailed satisfaction with services questionnaire.

Given that one of the major disadvantages of mail surveys is a low response rate, we present the following strategies for increasing the number of respondents.

- Include a cover letter stating the purpose of the evaluation with each mailed survey. The letter confirms that all responses are confidential and is most effective when signed by a high-ranking official (e.g., program executive director, minister, school principal, or politician).
- Use extremely clear and simple instructions.
- Include a stamped, self-addressed return envelope with the survey.
- Include free incentives to potential respondents (e.g., movie passes, fast-food coupons, or a pencil with the agency logo).
- Send a follow-up letter to all respondents as a prompt to complete the survey.
- Offer respondents the opportunity to request the results of the evaluation.

Group Interviews

Conducting group interviews is a data collection method that allows us to gather the perspectives of several individuals at one time. They are more complex than individual interviews because they involve interaction between and among data sources. Three strategies for group interviews—presented from the least to most structured—are open forums, focus groups, and nominal groups. The procedures for carrying out each type of group interview are summarized in Box 10.4.

Open Forums. Open forums have the least structure of the three group interview strategies. They are generally used to address general evaluation questions. Holding an open forum involves inviting stakeholders to discuss matters of interest to our evaluation. Open forums include such things as town hall meetings or phone-in radio talk shows. They simply provide a place and an opportunity for people to assemble and air their thoughts and opinions about a specific topic.

Open forums are generally most useful for gaining reactions or responses to a specific event or problem. An executive director, for example, might hold an open forum for all program stakeholders to announce plans to conduct a program evaluation. The forum would provide stakeholders the opportunity to respond to the idea as well as give input. The advantage of public forums is that they offer widespread involvement. Their main disadvantage is that they tend to draw a deliberate and select group of people who have strong opinions (one way or another) that are not necessarily shared by all.

Focus group interview
A group of people brought together to talk about their lives and experiences in free-flowing, open-ended discussions that usually focus on a single topic.

Focus Groups. **Focus groups** aim to gather data for the purposes of exploring or testing ideas. They consist of individuals who are reasonably familiar with the topic slated for discussion but not necessarily familiar with each other. Focus groups involve an interactive discussion that is designed to gather perceptions about a predefined topic of interest from a group of select people in an accepting and nonthreatening setting.

Conducting focus groups requires the skills of a group facilitator who sets the ground rules for the group and helps to guide discussion. The facilitator, as a group

Box 10.4 Group Interviewing Strategies and Procedures

Open Forums

- Identify the event or problem to be addressed.
- Allow individuals to spontaneously share responses and reactions.
- Record responses as given, without editing or discussion.

Focus Groups

- Develop open-ended questions.
- Provide an orientation or introduction to the topic of focus.
- Allow time for participants to read or review material if necessary (maximum 30 minutes).
- Determine how data are going to be recorded (e.g., audiotape, videotape, observation, or note-taking).
- Have the facilitator begin with open-ended questions and facilitate the discussion.
- The four major facilitation tasks are

    1. Prevent one person or a small group from dominating the discussion.
    2. Encourage the quiet ones to participate.
    3. Obtain responses from the entire group to ensure the fullest possible coverage.
    4. Maintain a balance between the roles of moderator (managing group dynamics) and interviewer.

- When the responses have been exhausted, move to the next question.
- Analyze data from the group.

Nominal/Delphi Method

- Develop open-ended questions.
- Provide six to nine people with a comfortable seating arrangement, preferably a circle.
- Procedures are to give overview of the group task, give each member a sheet with questions on it (and room to record answers), instruct members NOT to talk to each other, allow time for individuals to record responses privately.
- Use round-robin approach to list all answers from step 3. No discussion.
- Discussion focuses on clarifying what responses mean to ensure that everyone has a common understanding of each response.
- Individually rank top 5 responses.
- Round-robin to list rankings.
- Brief discussion for clarification if necessary.

leader, provides guidelines for the group process and aids the dialogue for group members. Questions prepared in advance help to set the parameters for discussion. Indeed, the questions presented earlier in Box 5.1 could be used to guide a focus group for a needs assessment.

The main task of focus group facilitators is to balance group discussion such that group members stay centered on the questions being asked but also stimulate one another to produce more in-depth and comprehensive data. The results of a focus group may show similar and divergent perceptions of participants.

Nominal Groups. The **nominal group technique** is a useful data gathering tool for evaluation because it provides for an easy way to collect data from individuals in a group situation. The composition of a nominal group is similar to that of a focus group in that it includes individuals who can answer a particular question of interest but may or may not know each other. A nominal group, however, is far more structured than a focus group, and group interaction is limited. The nominal group process involves members working in the presence of others but with little interaction. Refer again to Box 10.4 for a summary of the steps for conducting a nominal group.

The most obvious advantage of a nominal group is collecting data from numerous sources in an efficient manner. The nominal group process typically takes two to four hours, depending on the size of the group and the number of questions asked. Because of the game-like nature of the technique, participants can find the experience fun. When a cross section of group participants is recruited, the process can yield a comprehensive response to evaluation questions.

Observation

Observation as a data collection method is different from interviewing and surveying in that the data source watches a person, event, or object of interest and then records what was seen. A major tenet of observation as a data collection method is that it produces objective data based on observable facts. Two types are structured observation and participant observation.

Structured Observation. **Structured observations** occur under controlled conditions and aim to collect precise, valid, and reliable data about complex interactions. An impartial **observer** is trained to fix his or her eyes on particular persons or events and to look for specifics. The observation can take place in natural or artificial settings, but the conditions and timing of the observation are always predetermined. The data recorded reflect the trained observers' perceptions of what they see; and the observers are not directly involved with the people or the event being observed.

For example, a program may want to set up observations of parent–adolescent dyads to better understand how families learn to problem-solve together. The dimensions of problem solving are predefined such that the observer knows precisely what to look for. It may be that the observer watches for each time the parent or child verbally expresses frustration with the other as they work through a problem. Another dimension of problem solving to watch for may be the degree of confidence parents convey to their children at the beginning, middle, and end of the problem-

Nominal group technique
A group of people brought together to share their knowledge about a specific social problem; a structured group interview. The process is structured using a round-robin approach and permits individuals to share their ideas within a group but with little interaction between group members.

Structured observation
A data collection method in which people are observed in their natural environments using specified methods and measurement procedures.

Observer
One of four roles on a continuum of participation in participant observation research. The level of involvement of the observer participant is lower than of the complete participant and higher than of the participant observer.

> **Box 10.5** Basic Tasks in Implementing Regular Trained Observer Measurements
>
> - Identify what specific data are wanted.
> - Develop the trained observer rating guide. Test the guide with a number of raters to make sure the rated items and rating categories are clear.
> - Decide when the ratings will be made and how frequently they will be reported during the year.
> - Select and train the observers.
> - Assign staff to oversee the process, including (a) making sure the ratings are done on schedule, (b) periodically checking the ratings to make sure that each trained observer is still providing accurate ratings. and (c) providing retraining when necessary and training for new observers.
> - Arrange for the ratings to be entered and tabulated, preferably electronically and using a computer to tabulate that information and prepare reports. (In recent years, many organizations have begun using handheld computers to record the ratings. The use of such computers can greatly reduce data entry, tabulation, and reporting time.)
> - Provide and disseminate regular reports on the findings to staff and interested outside organizations. The reports should be clear and understandable.
> - Encourage use of the rating information to identify program weaknesses and improvement needs.

solving exercise. To obtain objective data, the observer cannot be directly or indirectly involved with the case being observed. In other words, workers and their supervisors are not eligible to observe families who are in their caseload.

Another evaluation effort may seek to describe exemplary cross-cultural supervision practices. In this scenario, the observer follows a protocol to tease out supervisory behaviors that demonstrate cultural competence. Once again, the rules for observation and recording data are set out ahead of time, and the observer adheres to these fixed guidelines. In this case, the observer records only observations related to cultural competence and not general competence, for example.

Because structured observations rely on observer interpretation, it is useful to capture the observation episode on videotape to allow for multiple viewing and multiple viewers. Also, training observers to a level of unmistakable clarity about what to watch for and what to document is essential, as presented in Box 10.5. The more precise the protocols for structured observation, the more consistent the data.

Participant Observation. **Participant observation** differs from structured observation on two main features: The observer is not impartial, and the rules for observation are far more flexible. As participant to the event under scrutiny, the observer has a vested interest in what is taking place. An executive director could be a participant observer in a sobriety support group offered by her program, for example,

Participant observation
An obtrusive data collection method in which the researcher, or the observer, participates in the life of those being observed. Both an obtrusive data collection method and a research approach, this method is characterized by the researcher undertaking roles that involve establishing and maintaining ongoing relationships with research participants who are often in the field settings, and observing and participating with the research participants over time.

Participant observer
The participant observer is one of four roles on a continuum of participation in participant observation research. The level of involvement of the participant observer is higher than of the complete observer and lower than of the observer participant.

Complete observer

A term describing one of four possible research roles on a continuum of participant observation research. The complete observer acts simply as an observer and does not participate in the events at hand.

Complete participant

The complete participant is at the far end of the continuum from the complete observer in participant observation research. This research role is characterized by total involvement.

given that she has influence in how the group is run and has a stake in the group's success.

The challenge for **participant observers** is to balance their dual roles so that data are based on fact and not personal impressions. The benefit of participant observation is that members of group are in a better position to pick up subtle or cultural nuances that may be obscure to an impartial viewer. Consider the scenario of the parent–adolescent dyad working toward improving their problem-solving skills. Choosing to use a participant observer such as the assigned worker or another family member may well influence data collection. Specifically, an observer who is personally known to the parent and adolescent can better detect verbal expressions of frustration or parent behaviors displaying confidence than can a stranger.

Unlike structured observers, participant observers interact with the people they are watching. In other words, the participant observer is free to have a dialogue with his or her research participants to verify observations and to check out interpretations. Participant observer interviews are unique in their tone and how they are carried out.

FITTING DATA COLLECTION TO THE PROGRAM

Program workers conduct most data collection for program evaluations. As a result, it is necessary to choose data collection instruments that fit well within the normal range of paperwork duties for workers. Feasible data collection methods possess three qualities: (1) they are easy to use, (2) they fit within the flow of program operations, and (3) they are designed with user input.

Ease of Use

Data collection methods should help workers to do their jobs better, not tie up their time with extensive paperwork. Data collection tools that are easy to use also minimize the amount of writing that workers are expected to do and the amount of time it takes to complete them. Data collection instruments that are easy to use develop through a process of trial and error. Often other programs have already created such instruments. Box 6.1 contains an example of an instrument that collects client–practitioner data in an easy-to-use format.

When data collection instruments have not yet been created, program staff are faced with developing their own. Suppose, for example, that we asked workers employed at a youth drug and alcohol counseling program to record their daily intervention activities with clients by listing them out on a piece of paper. After reviewing their written annotations, we note that the following activities were recorded: gave positive feedback, rewarded youth for reduced alcohol consumption, discussed positive aspects of the youth's life, cheered youth on, and celebrated youth's new job. These descriptors all serve a common function—praise. Thus, for this group of workers, we might create a single checklist item called "praise."

Clearly, the checklist approach loses important detail that was captured by workers in their handwritten notes, but a frequency of checklist items does give a picture as to what type of activities are being used by workers. The point here is that it is much easier for workers to check off items on a list than it is to record details of every interaction with a client.

Appropriateness to the Flow of Program Operations

Data collection instruments should be designed to fit within the context of the social service program, facilitate the program's day-to-day operations, and provide data that will ultimately be helpful in improving program operations and client service delivery. Data that are routinely collected from clients ought to have both case-level and program-level utility. For instance, if client intake forms have workers identify client referral problems, then these data ought to have utility for client assessment and intervention as well as value for describing typical referral problems of program clientele. Data that are not used (i.e., not summarized or reviewed) should not be collected in the first place.

Ideal data collection instruments serve multiple program functions. First, they offer a record of case-level intervention that can be used to review individual client progress. Second, components of the data collection instruments can be aggregated to produce a program summary. Third, the instruments can be used as a principal component of supervisory meetings. Finally, they can also inform case review discussion as they can convey the major client problems, treatment interventions, and worker activities in a concise manner. Overall, data collection instruments that are well integrated with program operations function to capture resourcefulness and innovativeness among workers; they do not thwart creativity by burying workers in unreasonable paperwork expectations.

Design With User Input

It should be clear by now that the major users of data collection instruments are line-level workers. Social workers often are responsible for gathering the necessary data from clients and others. Therefore, their involvement in the development and testing of the data collection instruments is critical. Workers can provide valuable input in many areas. They can provide suggestions for formatting, procedures, and use. Social workers who see the relevance of recording data will likely record more accurate data than workers who do not. Regardless of what data collection methods and instruments are used, training is inevitable if data collection is to produce consistent data.

Developing a Data Collection Monitoring System

The monitoring system for data collection is closely linked to administration and supervision practices within a program. This is because program data are integral to delivering client services. Data about a program's background, client profile, and staff characteristics can, more or less, be collected at one time period. These data can be summarized and stored for easy access. Program changes such as staff turnover, hours of operation, or caseload size can be duly noted as they occur.

In contrast, data that are routinely collected ought to be monitored and checked for reliability and validity. Time and resources are a consideration for developing a monitoring system. When paperwork becomes excessively backlogged, it may be that there is simply too much data to collect, data collection instruments are cumbersome to use, or staff are not invested in the evaluation process.

Quality data collection requires several explicit procedures that need to be laid out and strictly followed. Minimal training is needed for consistent data collection. It is rather inefficient to train all social workers within a single program to collect data. Alternatively, it is advisable to assign data collection tasks to a small number of workers who are properly trained in the data collection effort. These individuals do not necessarily have to have any background in evaluation procedures; they simply need to have good interviewing skills and be able to following basic standardized instructions.

A monitoring system also functions as a feedback loop for data collected; that is, data collected are routinely shared with key stakeholders. Funders and policy makers receive feedback from annual reports or, perhaps, new proposals. Program data may also be disseminated more broadly, such as in an article in the local newspaper.

Developing a feedback system for internal stakeholders such as program administrators and workers is absolutely essential. Making data available on a regular basis helps to keep staff focused on the program's goal and objectives and allows them make incremental changes as needed. Discussing data can also stimulate important questions, such as, What activities best explain client progress? Or regress? Are program services realistic? Are any client groups being ignored? When program personnel have an opportunity to respond to data they have collected, program development becomes much more purposeful and focused.

SUMMING UP AND LOOKING AHEAD

This chapter covered some of the basic tools of evaluation—sampling and data collection. These tools are used only after programs have developed their logic models and articulated their evaluation questions. Evaluators can choose from numerous sampling and data collection methods. The pros and cons of each must be assessed in light of the unique context for each program. Ultimately, programs should strive to collect data from firsthand sources. Additionally, data collection methods ought to be easy for workers to use, fit within the flow of a program, and be designed with user input.

RECAP AND ONLINE MATERIALS

In this chapter, you learned how to identify potential data sources and data collection methods in addition to how to obtain samples of them.

You should also recall the concept of sampling from your foundational research course. If not, go online to take a free crash course in sampling.

You can also find the following materials online to help you master the concepts you just learned:

- Chapter Outline
- Learning Objectives
- Key Terms and Concepts
- Flash Cards
- Practice Multiple-Choice Tests
- Essay Questions with Answers
- Links

www.oup.com/us/swevaluation

STUDY QUESTIONS

1. Imagine that you are asked to design an evaluation of your social work education program. List all data sources that you might include to inform the evaluation. What are the strengths and weaknesses of each? Identify the top three sources that you would recommend for use in the evaluation.
2. A social service program aims to collect satisfaction data from every client (over 200 per year) at termination of services using a mailed satisfaction questionnaire. Unfortunately, only 20 percent of clients ever return the questionnaire. How can random sampling be used to assist with this problem of low response

rate? Given what you know about sampling, devise a strategy that might increase the program's response rate.

3. What are the advantages and disadvantages of using new data (and existing data) in an evaluation?

4. You are asked to develop an evaluation plan to address the following question: How do clients experience the intake process in a social service program? What data collection method would provide the "best" data for this evaluation? Explain your choice.

5. Surveys are one of the most common data collection methods used in program evaluation, but response rates are typically poor. Discuss strategies that an evaluator could use to increase the number of surveys that get returned.

6. What are the three different types of group interviews? Describe a program evaluation situation that would be ideal for use for each type.

7. Observation, as a data collection method, relies on the observer to interpret what he or she sees. What steps can observers take to minimize bias in their observations?

8. Discuss why it is important for data collection procedures to fit within the normal range of paperwork duties for workers in a social service program. What problems are likely to occur if evaluation data result in an excessive amount of paperwork?

9. What are three qualities of data collection methods that are considered *feasible?* Give an example of each.

10. Discuss why a data collection monitoring system is important to an evaluation.

REFERENCES, FURTHER READING, AND RESOURCES

On Obtaining Samples

Gabor, P. A., & Ing, C. (2001). Sampling. In R. M. Grinnell, Jr. (Ed.), *Social work research and evaluation: Quantitative and qualitative approaches* (6th ed., pp. 207–223). Itasca, IL: F. E. Peacock.

On Gathering New Data for Evaluations

Gochros, H. L. (2005). Interviewing. In R. M. Grinnell, Jr., & Y. A. Unrau (Eds.), *Social work research and evaluation: Quantitative and qualitative approaches* (7th ed., pp. 245–269). New York: Oxford University Press.

McMurtry, S. L. (2005). Surveys. In R. M. Grinnell, Jr., & Y. A. Unrau (Eds.), *Social work research and evaluation: Quantitative and qualitative approaches* (7th ed., pp. 271–287). New York: Oxford University Press.

Rogers, G., & Bouey, E. (2005). Participant observation. In R. M. Grinnell, Jr., & Y. A. Unrau (Eds.), *Social work research and evaluation: Quantitative and qualitative approaches* (7th ed., pp. 231–244). New York: Oxford University Press.

On Gathering Existing Data for Evaluations

Krysik, J. L. (2005). Secondary analysis. In R. M. Grinnell, Jr., & Y. A. Unrau (Eds.), *Social work research and evaluation: Quantitative and qualitative approaches* (7th ed., pp. 291–301). New York: Oxford University Press.

LeCroy, C. W., & Solomon, G. (2001). Content analysis. In R. M. Grinnell, Jr. (Ed.), *Social work research and evaluation: Quantitative and qualitative approaches* (6th ed., pp. 367–381). Itasca, IL: F. E. Peacock.

Sieppert, J., McMurtry, S. L., & McClelland, R. (2005). Utilizing existing statistics. In R. M. Grinnell, Jr., & Y. A. Unrau (Eds.), *Social work research and evaluation: Quantitative and qualitative approaches* (7th ed., pp. 315–328). New York: Oxford University Press.

On Constructing Survey Instruments for Evaluations

Mindel, C. H. (2005). Designing measuring instruments. In R. M. Grinnell, Jr., & Y. A. Unrau (Eds.), *Social work research and evaluation: Quantitative and qualitative approaches* (7th ed., pp. 133–146). New York: Oxford University Press.

On Selecting the Best Data Gathering Method

Unrau, Y. A. (2005). Selecting a data collection method and data source. In R. M. Grinnell, Jr., & Y. A. Unrau (Eds.), *Social work research and evaluation: Quantitative and qualitative approaches* (7th ed., pp. 339–349). New York: Oxford University Press.

W. K. Kellogg Foundation. (2006). *Evaluation toolkit.* Retrieved January 2, 2006, from W. K. Kellogg Foundation Web site: http://www.wkkf.org/default.aspx?tabid=75&CID=281&NID=61

Developing a Data Information System

Data
Isolated facts, presented in numerical or descriptive form, on which client or program decisions are based

Data information system
On a general level, the systematic collection and storage of data that are subsequently analyzed and reported.

Project approach to quality improvement
Evaluations whose purpose is to assess a completed or finished program (or project); complements the monitoring approach.

Monitoring approach to quality improvement
An evaluation that aims to provide ongoing feedback so that a program (or project) can be improved while it is still underway; contributes to the continuous development and improvement of a human service program. This approach complements the project approach.

As we know, **data** collection is not an indiscriminate activity. In short, it is not undertaken in the hope that the data collected will somehow be useful to someone in some place at some time. Data collection procedures must reflect a careful analysis of information needs at all levels within the social service program and should provide for the collection of useful data in the least disruptive, most economical and efficient manner possible.

The data collected for evaluations of all kinds can be loosely characterized as a **data information system.** Within this system, specific data are collected, analyzed, and reported. Of course, systems of any kind may function well or not so well. Some evaluations are inadequately planned, resulting in a lack of coherence in data collection, analyses, and reporting. On the other hand, others are well planned and function well in that they collect the right data in a form that can be readily analyzed and subsequently reported to the stakeholders.

The concept of a data information system applies whether the evaluation process involves a **project approach** or a **monitoring approach to quality improvement.** In a project type of situation, the information system will usually be active for a shorter period of time—the duration of the project. As well, project evaluations tend to be concerned with fewer variables, usually program outcomes, resulting in smaller information systems. Conversely, in a monitoring situation, the evaluation system will be active on an open-ended basis; it will also usually be concerned with a larger number of variables, resulting in a larger information system. In particular, monitoring types of evaluations are more likely to include a larger number of process issues than are project evaluations.

Whether an information system is created for a monitoring or a project evaluation, it should be designed in a way that data collected at any stage are demonstrably relevant to the decisions to be made. Data collected by front-line workers, for example, should bear upon, in the first instance, the decisions they are required to make. In other words, the data collected by workers must guide clinical decision making. At the same time, these data must be capable of being aggregated in a manner that is relevant to administrators and other stakeholders interested in outcomes. Essentially, an effective information system should:

- Recognize that different data needs exist among different stakeholders
- Be capable of delivering needed information to all levels of stakeholders in a timely manner and in a format usable at that level

Because we have emphasized the benefits of a monitoring approach to quality improvement throughout this book, this chapter provides illustrations and examples from monitoring situations. However, the discussion and illustrations do apply to project-type evaluations as well.

STAFF MEMBERS' ROLES IN DEVELOPING A DATA INFORMATION SYSTEM

Designing, developing, and maintaining an effective information system is not only a technical matter; social service issues also need consideration. Staff members, as human beings, may have reactions that range from skepticism to resistance when faced with the introduction of an information system. These reactions are related not only to the personality and experience of the individual but also to the collective experience of the workgroup and of the organization. Where recent experience includes reorganization, restructuring, and questionable use of previous evaluation results, staff members will understandably react with suspicion, if not outright hostility (Gabor & Sieppert, 1999).

Establishing and maintaining an information system requires the cooperation of all program staff, from line-level workers through senior administrators. Inevitably, much of the burden of data collection falls on the line-level workers. Involving them in the planning and design of the information system helps to ensure that information needs at the direct-service level will be met and that data can be collected without undue disruption to service provision. Moreover, the involvement of line-level workers helps to secure their cooperation and commitment to the evaluation process.

Administrators must contribute by committing the necessary resources for the implementation of the system, including providing training and support. The design and implementation of an information system is expensive. Computer hardware and software may have to be purchased, and consultation fees and training costs probably will be incurred. Providing adequate training and support to professional and staff is a vital consideration. Training is particularly necessary if the new system introduces computerization. Often, administrators will not hesitate to spend tens of thousands of dollars on equipment but will skimp on training the personnel who are to use it. This is shortsighted; as a general rule, administrators should expect to spend at least one dollar for training for every dollar spent on equipment.

It is very important that an evaluation be carried out within an organizational culture that acknowledges that social service programs inevitably fall short of perfection. The purpose of an evaluation is not to assign blame; it is to provide better services by identifying strengths and limitations so that the former can be reinforced and the latter corrected. An attitude of continuous learning and developing is the essence of the learning organization; the information system generates feedback that facilitates the process. When the objective is improvement and development, and workers can see the contribution of an effective information system to that objective, they are more likely to cooperate and contribute to the effective functioning of that information system.

Establishing an Organizational Plan

As previously discussed, effective information systems are the result of careful planning and design as well as negotiation and compromise. Early involvement in the planning of the system by front-line workers, administrators, and other relevant stakeholders is important. Any data collection plan must take into account at least three sets of needs:

1. Data collection must meet case-level decision-making needs, serving decisions to be made immediately as well as those made throughout the client's progress within the program. Certain data, for example, are required at client intake to decide whether to accept the referral. Once accepted, the client may go through a formal assessment procedure, at which point further data likely will be collected. Other stages of service provision will require yet more data. The case-level information system should be designed to take advantage of and build on existing data collection.
2. The system design must accommodate the program-level decision-making responsibilities of the administrators and other stakeholders. To avoid the creation of parallel evaluation systems at the case and program levels, the latter should be designed to make as much use of data collected for case-level evaluation as is possible. This often entails the aggregation of case-level data.
3. Technical requirements of the system must also be considered. The system will require certain types of data, formats, data collection procedures, and analytic capabilities.

CASE-LEVEL DATA COLLECTION

Client flowchart

Used to graphically display how a client goes through the program.

Perhaps the best way to decide what data are needed at the case level is to follow a client through the program by way of a client case-flow analysis. Figure 11.1 presents an example of a **client flowchart** illustrating the sequence of events in a child protection program. (See Figure 6.4 for an additional example.)

The beginning of the process is the referral. Suspected neglect or abuse may be reported by a variety of people, including relatives, teachers, neighbors, and health care workers. All referrals are immediately directed to the screening unit. Because every allegation of child abuse must be looked into, at this point the two most relevant pieces of data are the age and place of residence of the alleged victim. Within a short period, a screening worker normally contacts the referring source as well as the

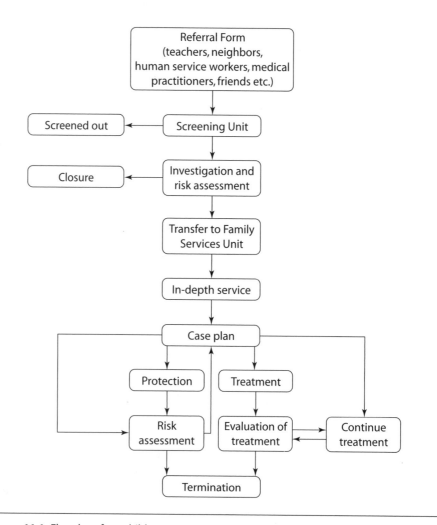

Figure 11.1 Flowchart for a child protection program.

family to verify the complaint and to obtain further details. Based on this information, the worker decides whether a full investigation is warranted. If so, an investigating worker will likely interview the alleged victim and will probably also interview relevant others.

As with every activity, each interview has a specific purpose. The purpose of interviewing the alleged victim is fourfold:

1. To verify that the alleged abuse has in fact occurred
2. To ensure the immediate safety of the child
3. To determine whether treatment is needed
4. To determine what treatment would be best to inform the child and others connected to the case about what will happen next

The investigating worker will conduct this interview on the basis of data collected by the screening worker and will need data in the following general areas:

- Specific circumstances of the alleged abuse
- Specific circumstances in which it was disclosed
- Data about the child
- Data about the family

The screening form thus must be designed to incorporate these different data needs. From a case-level perspective, then, the data collected at screening serves two broad purposes:

1. To make a decision about whether further investigation is warranted
2. To provide the investigating worker with initial information data

Because a monitoring system is intended to provide needed and timely data to staff members, and because front-line workers themselves will be in the best position to know what data they need to help them in their decision making, front-line workers should be involved in designing forms.

When the investigation is complete, the data are used to assess the degree of continuing risk to the child. On this basis, the worker determines whether further services are required. Continuing cases are transferred from the screening unit to the family services unit, where a worker is assigned to the family to coordinate protection and treatment functions. The family services unit worker then conducts a full assessment based on the data provided by the investigating worker in the screening unit as well as any additional data collected. The purpose of assessment is to develop an in-depth understanding of the situation and of child and family needs so that an appropriate intervention plan can be established. In other words, data collected during assessment are used in making decisions about the client's case plan.

As Figure 11.1 indicates, the case plan formulated may have both a protection component and a treatment component. Practice objectives are established in relation to both of these components, and data collected during service provision are used to assess the degree to which interventions are achieving practice objectives. Case-level data will also be needed subsequently, in aggregated form, for program evaluation purposes. Thus, when determining what data are to be collected for **case-level evaluation,** it is important to take into consideration program evaluation needs..

Termination criteria for protection and treatment often differ. Protection workers are likely to focus on the continuing safety of the child whereas treatment workers may focus on family functioning. The family may therefore still be undergoing treatment when protection services have been discontinued. Ultimately, when the decision to terminate all services is made, the case can be closed.

As is evident, data collection is not a matter of randomly assembling whatever data come to hand. The data collected in each phase should be fully and firmly linked to the objectives of the particular phase, the decisions to be made during the phase, and the data needs of subsequent phases. Insufficient data lead to poor decision making; overly profuse and irrelevant data result in a lack of clarity and unnecessary costs.

To ensure that there is adequate congruence between the data collected and the decisions to be made, a data collection analysis can be undertaken. This analysis lists, in chronological order:

1. The decisions to be made
2. The data needed to make each decision
3. The actual data collected

If there is a discrepancy between what is needed and what is being collected, data collection protocols need to be revised.

PROGRAM-LEVEL DATA COLLECTION

Data collection at any program stage must be designed to fulfill the data needs of both line-level workers and administrators alike. From the perspective of a multi-program agency, for example, it is often useful to identify the main data collection events for each program. Typically, a program collects data at intake, at every contact with a client, and at termination. Other data collection events may be planned, depending on circumstances and needs.

A specific plan for identifying the key data collection events for a family service agency, for example, across five of its programs is presented in Figure 11.2. As you can see, the agency has five programs. It has: an Information Program, an Education Program, a Parent Support Program, a Counseling Program, and a Mediation Program. Each cell marked with an "X" represents a major data collection event for which a corresponding data collection instrument (or form) can be designed. In the case of this agency, the four major data collection events are at client intake, assessment, client contacts (intervention period), and termination.

	Programs				
Forms	Information	Education	Parent Support	Counseling	Mediation
• Intake	X	X	X	X	X
• Assessment				X	X
• Contact Notes			X	X	X
• Termination			X	X	X
• Self-Report Satisfaction					
Nonstandardized		X		X	X
Standardized	X	X	X	X	X

Figure 11.2 Example of a data collection plan.

In addition, two kinds of client outcome data relating to **client satisfaction** are also included in Figure 11.2: (1) nonstandardized self-report data, and (2) standardized self report data, The nonstandardized data could be collected via Figure 11.8, for example, and the standardized data could be collected via Figures 9.1 and/or 9.2. Once the information needs are identified, data collection forms can be designed for each of these purposes.

To illustrate this point, consider the counseling program operated by the agency. The service is funded by the Department of Social Services (DSS) to provide counseling services to DSS clients with psychosocial problems who need more help than the brief instrumentally oriented counseling of the DSS can provide. Figure 11.3 shows part of an intake form that new clients might complete in the center's office while they are waiting for a first interview.

Client satisfaction

A program variable that measures the degree to which clients are content with various aspects of the program services that they received.

Data Collection at Intake

The intake form is usually the first document in the client's file. Of course, different programs need different or additional data. A job-training program, for example, will likely ask about jobs previously held, previous income, reason for present unemployment, and participation in other job-training programs.

An individual intake form provides data for a case record, but it is not very useful for program evaluation purposes unless the data are aggregated with other intake forms. Figure 11.4 provides four simple tabular reports on the counseling service compiled by aggregating the data from 200 individual client intake forms for the month of January 2008. These reports are examples of information related to client characteristics.

Figure 11.4 shows at a glance that 200 new clients were accepted into the program during the month of January, 63 percent of whom were referred by DSS. The

```
Name: _____

Current Address: _____

Telephone Number: _____

• TYPES OF SERVICE SOUGHT (circle one number below):
   1. Individual counseling
   2. Couple counseling
   3. Family counseling
   9. Other (please specify _____ )

• SEX (circle one number below):
   1. Male
   2. Female

• BIRTH DATE _____

• REFERRAL SOURCE (circle one number below):
   1. Self
   2. Friends, family
   3. Physician
   4. Clergy
   5. Department of Social Services
   6. Other agency
   9. Other (please specify _____ )

• REASONS FOR SEEKING SERVICES (circle one number below):
   1. Marital problems
   2. Family problems
   3. Problems at school
   4. Problems at work
   5. Parent–child problems
   6. Health problems
   7. Substance abuse
   8. Personal adjustment problems
   9. Other (please specify _____ )
```

Figure 11.3 Example of a client intake form.

program is thus able to document the degree to which it is achieving one of its maintenance objectives: providing services to clients referred by DSS. Equally important, if referrals from DSS fall short of objectives, staff members will be able to spot this trend immediately and take steps to better meet the program's mandate, or perhaps to negotiate an adjustment of this mandate if new circumstances have arisen. The point of importance is that monitoring provides ongoing feedback that helps to ensure continuing achievement of a program's mandate—to see clients referred by DSS.

Contrast this with the situation of a program that undertakes occasional evaluations. By the time data indicating a problem with DSS referrals are analyzed

Sex of Client		
Sex	Number	Percent
Male	90	45
Female	110	55
Total	200	100

Age of Clients		
Age Range	Number	Percent
10–19	30	15
20–29	78	39
30–39	42	21
40–49	28	14
50–59	12	6
60+	10	5
Total	200	100

Referral Sources of Clients		
Sources	Number	Percent
Self	8	4
Friends, family	12	6
Physicians	8	4
Clergy	10	5
DSS	126	63
Other agencies	28	14
Other	8	4
Total	200	100

Reasons Clients Requesting Services		
Presenting Problems	Number	Percent
Marital problems	18	9
Family problems	40	20
Problems at school	28	14
Problems at work	12	6
Parent–child problems	30	15
Health problems	20	10
Substance abuse	22	11

Figure 11.4 Excerpts from a monthly intake report for January 2008 (from Figure 11.3).

and reported, the problem will have existed for a period of time and is likely to have serious consequences. In all likelihood, the program's reputation among the DSS workers will have suffered. The DSS may even have concluded that, because this program is not providing adequate service, alternative services should be contracted.

The report also provides other useful data. Tables reporting the frequency distribution of the sex and age of new clients provide the data required to ensure that the program is attracting the type of clients for whom it was established. Assume that another one of the program's maintenance objectives is to attract 100 adolescents and young adults each month. Figure 11.4 indicates that 54 percent of new clients are 29 years of age or under. These kind of data indicate that the program is on the right track.

On the other hand, if an objective had been to provide services to a large number of senior citizens, data revealing that only 5 percent of new clients are 60 years of age or over would be cause for concern (see Figure 11.4). A program is unlikely to undertake extensive changes on the basis of data for one month, but if several consecutive monthly reports were to indicate that older people constitute only a small percentage of new clients, staff may well conclude that a problem exists and needs to be addressed.

Data Collection at Client Contact

The course of service provision can be followed by completing, after each session, a client contact form, such as the one illustrated in Figure 11.5. The form is designed to provide workers with the information they need to maintain a record of services provided and also to provide data to the information system for evaluation purposes. The form is designed for easy completion, using primarily a check-box format for entering the data. At the end of the form, there is a space for the workers' anecdotal notes, which may be made in the manner preferred by each worker. All but the anecdotal information is designed to be ultimately transferred into the information system. After identifying data for the client and worker are entered, the type of service and service location are specified.

As discussed, these are the types of data that make it possible for service statistics to be compiled and reported on a regular basis. In this case, counseling is the service provided. Because the data are captured at this point, it will later be possible to track the number of counseling sessions provided to the client. The record also makes it possible to track the total number of counseling sessions provided within the program and the agency. Similarly, noting the service location or whether the service was provided by telephone will make it possible to generate a description of services provided by location.

Quality standards were also identified as one possible focus of evaluation. The present client contact form records data about whether the service was provided to an individual or a larger unit within the family and also whether community resource suggestions were made. These data can later be compiled to provide a profile of the client system to which services are provided and the number of community resources suggested in this case. Because the agency had set objectives regarding

- Date: January 15, 2008

- Worker: Mary Carnes

- Client Name: Jane Harrison

- ID Number: 144277

- Type of Service
  - ___ Family support
  - ___ Mediation
  - X Counseling
  - ___ Interactive play
  - ___ Other: _____

- Service Location
  - ___ Phone
  - ___ Center
  - X School
  - ___ Other

- Type of Contact
  - ___ Individual: parent
  - ___ Individual: child
  - ___ Family
  - ___ Couple
  - X Parent–child dyad
  - ___ Collateral: _____

- Community Resources Suggested
  1. None
  2. _____
  3. _____

- Length of session, in minutes: 40

- Length of travel, in minutes: 25

- Measures

Objective	Measure	Score
Self-esteem	Index of Self-Esteem	39

- Notes

Figure 11.5 Excerpts from a client contact form.

these standards, capturing the data on the client contact form tracks the extent to which these standards have been met.

On this contact form, provision is also made for recording the length of the session and the length of preparation, including travel time and paperwork. These data reflect administrative needs. Management wanted to track the costs associated with moving services out of the center and decided that, for a period of time, data should be collected that would provide information about such costs. By tracking time spent in travel and preparation, the additional costs related to moving services out of the center can be easily determined.

Finally, the client contact form records the results of any measurements that were completed during service provision. In this case, a practice objective was self-esteem improvement, and Hudson's Index of Self-Esteem was used as the measure.

Client's Name: _____   Date (M-D-Y) ____ ____ ____

Client Identification Number: _____

   CLOSURE DECISION WAS:

   1. Mutual
   2. Client's
   3. Worker's
   9. Other (specify _____)

   REASON FOR CLOSURE:

   1. Service no longer needed
   2. Further service declined
   3. Client stopped coming
   4. Client moved
   5. Referred elsewhere
   9. Other (specify _____)

   PRACTICE OBJECTIVES:

Objective	Score	Measuring Instrument
1.		
2.		
3.		
4.		

   IS FOLLOW-UP REQUIRED?

   1. Yes (if so, why _____)
   2. No (if so, why not _____)

Figure 11.6 Example of a client termination form.

The current week's score on the instrument, 39, is recorded for this practice objective. There is a provision for recording other scores, as well. These data can be used to follow changes in practice objectives during the course of the intervention, can be aggregated into monthly summaries (as shown at the bottom-half of Figure 11.7), and, ultimately, can be employed in a pretest–posttest group evaluation design.

Data Collection at Termination

When the case is closed, a termination form is completed. On this form, data regarding the nature of termination as well as the final level of outcomes can be recorded. Moreover, the need for any follow-up can also be noted. An example of a client termination form is provided in Figure 11.6. Data from client terminations can also be aggregated and summarized.

Figure 11.7 provides excerpts from a summary report of cases closed in the counseling unit during one recent month. These data are the result of aggregating data from clients' intake and termination forms. Aggregating data in this manner

Cases Terminated		
Method of Termination	Number	Percent
Mutual consent	25	50
Client's decision	18	36
Worker's decision	7	14
Total	50	100

Average of Clients' Practice Objectives			
Practice Objectives	Beginning	End	n
Self-esteem	61	42	12
Peer relations	57	37	4
Depression	42	27	4
Marital satisfaction	51	48	6
Clinical stress	47	41	9
Alcohol involvement	40	31	4
Partner abuse	52	42	1
Sexual satisfaction	66	60	5
Anxiety	52	41	5
Total			50

Note: All practice objectives are measured with Hudson's Scales as reported in Nurius and Hudson, 1993. High scores = higher levels of problem.

Figure 11.7 Excerpts from a monthly summary report of closed cases.

provides information that is very useful in understanding program functioning. We can readily see, for example, that over a third (36 percent) of the clients who terminated did so unilaterally.

Depending on the program's norms, expectations, and past experiences, these data may be considered problematic. If the data are further analyzed to learn more about the termination process, program staff can determine whether unilateral termination is characteristic of any particular client group, such as males, older clients, or clients with specific practice objectives. Such data are invaluable in diagnosing the problem and deciding on program adjustments and modifications. Data from subsequent reports will then shed light on the success of the measures adopted.

Data pertaining to specific client's practice objectives are also useful. Comparing the average practice objective score at the beginning with the average score at termination for a group of clients provides data about net change achieved with respect to each practice objective. Doing so takes the form, in research terms, of a one-group, pretest–posttest design. Such designs make it possible to describe change but allow only limited inferences about the cause of that change.

Of course, data in themselves do not tell the whole story. They are very useful indicators, but their full interpretation requires careful attention to contextual variables and issues. For instance, it is possible that the relatively modest results achieved with clients experiencing marital and family problems is attributable to factors other than the way in which the program is designed and delivered. It may be that two of the more experienced workers have been on leave for the past several months.

Perhaps one of these positions was covered by temporarily reassigning a less experienced worker while the other position was left vacant. Thus, during the preceding several months, fewer marital counseling and family therapy hours may have been delivered, by less experienced staff. This could obviously have affected client outcomes. In general, interpreting the data resulting from evaluation requires consideration of contextual variables and cannot be done purely on the basis of quantitative results.

Data Collection to Obtain Feedback

Satisfaction with a social service program often becomes a focus for evaluation. Thus, staff members depicted in the illustrations above have determined that it would be useful to obtain feedback from program participants regarding various aspects of their satisfaction. Consequently, a satisfaction survey was developed, which clients are asked to complete at the time of service closure. An example of a very simple nonstandardized client satisfaction survey instrument is provided in Figure 11.8. Also see Figures 9.1 and 9.2 for standardized instruments for assessing clients' satisfaction with the services they have received.

Again, such data are most useful when aggregated across clients. An excerpt

Please provide us with feedback on our services by completing the following brief questionnaire. For each question, circle one response.

- The services received were helpful:

  Strongly Disagree   Disagree   Agree   Strongly Agree

- Staff members were supportive:

  Strongly Disagree   Disagree   Agree   Strongly Agree

- I am better off as a result of these services:

  Strongly Disagree   Disagree   Agree   Strongly Agree

- I would recommend these services to others:

  Strongly Disagree   Disagree   Agree   Strongly Agree

- My overall satisfaction with these services is:

  Low   Moderate   High   Very High

- Comments or suggestions:

Figure 11.8 Example of a nonstandardized client satisfaction survey.

from such an analysis is provided in Figure 11.9. As may be seen, a large majority of clients consider the services helpful and the staff members supportive, and think themselves better off as a result of services. As well, two thirds would recommend the services to others, and about 68 percent indicate a high or very high level of overall satisfaction with the program.

Staff members may react to summaries such as those shown in Figures 11.7 and 11.9 in a number of ways. They may resent that their work is being scrutinized, particularly if the monthly summary has been newly instituted. Where the results suggest that there is room for improvement (which is often the case), they may be uncertain of their own competence and, perhaps, feel that they are being judged. Alternatively, or perhaps in addition, they may be alerted to the fact that they need to modify their approaches to improve results.

Which of these feelings predominates depends to some extent on the way the information system was introduced to the practitioners. Workers who were consulted about the system's development, informed about its advantages, and involved in its design and implementation are more likely to regard the monthly summaries as useful feedback. Staff who were neither consulted nor involved are likely to regard them with apprehension and resentment.

Equally important in shaping attitudes to monitoring is how the agency's management uses, or abuses, the data generated. If the data are used in a judgmental, critical manner, staff are likely to remain skeptical and defensive about the monitoring

The services I received were helpful.

	Number	Percent
Strongly Disagree	22	11
Disagree	36	18
Agree	94	47
Strongly Agree	48	24
Total	200	100

Staff members were supportive.

	Number	Percent
Strongly Disagree	18	9
Disagree	38	19
Agree	88	44
Strongly Agree	56	28
Total	200	100

I am better off as a result of these services.

	Number	Percent
Strongly Disagree	30	15
Disagree	46	23
Agree	98	49
Strongly Agree	26	13
Total	200	100

I would recommend these services to others.

	Number	Percent
Strongly Disagree	40	20
Disagree	30	15
Agree	74	37
Strongly Agree	56	28
Total	200	100

My overall satisfaction with these services is . . .

	Number	Percent
Low	24	12
Moderate	40	20
High	90	45
Very High	46	23
Total	200	100

Figure 11.9 Program level report of results from a client satisfaction survey (from data collected via the form in Figure 11.8).

process. Where the data are regarded as useful feedback and are used in a genuine, cooperative effort to upgrade and further develop services, workers will likely welcome such reports as tools that can help them—and the program—improve.

These considerations suggest that administrators should view evaluation data as a means of assisting them in identifying areas for improvement and in identifying factors in problems and difficulties. Obviously, this approach is far more likely to evoke a positive response than one in which undesirable results signal the beginning of a search to assign blame.

Administrators' responsibilities do not, however, end here. To foster a truly positive environment for evaluation, administrators should not only be concerned with pinpointing potential trouble spots but should also be committed to supporting workers' efforts to improve program effectiveness. These are key roles for an administrator of any social service organization.

DATA MANAGEMENT

Effective evaluation systems are powered by information gleaned from the data. As programs become more complex, and as evaluation becomes an increasingly important function, organizations require increasingly sophisticated data management capabilities. Data management includes collection and recording; aggregation, integration, and analyses; and reporting. These functions may be carried out manually, through the use of computers, or through a combination of manual and computer-based methods.

Manual Data Management

Not long ago, most data management functions were undertaken manually. Data collection forms were designed, completed in longhand or by typewriter, and filed, usually in case files. The need to produce specific data—for example, looking at the referral sources of all new cases in the last six months—usually entailed a manual search of all new case files as well as manual aggregation and analyses of the data. Although such a system could unearth the required data, the process was cumbersome and labor-intensive.

As organizations found that they were called upon to generate certain types of data on a regular basis, they developed methods for manually copying specific data (e.g., referral sources, age and sex of client, and presenting problem) from client records onto composite forms or spreadsheets. In this way, manually searching files for the required data could be avoided. However, the composite forms or spreadsheets were still analyzed manually. Although these procedures were an improvement, such a system was limited not only because manual analyses were time-consuming but also because they could provide only the data that had been identified for aggregation. A need for data other than that which had been included on the spreadsheet still entailed a manual search of all relevant files.

Obviously, manual methods are labor-intensive and costly. They are also limited in their flexibility and in their capacity to quickly deliver needed data. It is not surprising that, with the ready availability of powerful desktop computers, social service organizations have increasingly turned to computer-based data management systems.

Computer-Assisted Data Management

Computers can be used in both case-level and program-level evaluations. Because computers increase the capacity for data management and make the process more efficient, their use in recent years has dramatically increased.

Even so, at this time, few social service organizations rely entirely on computers for data management. Usually, data management systems are a combination of manual and computer-based methods. Manual functions, however, are decreasing, and, correspondingly, computer-based functions are increasing. The trend is clear: Computers are becoming increasingly important in evaluation. Typically, data are collected manually through the completion of forms and measuring instruments. At this point, the data are often entered into the computer, which maintains and manages the data and carries out the required aggregation and analyses.

The computer can easily assist, for example, with the aggregation and analysis of case-level monitoring data. Figure 11.7 illustrated this process, using the example of an agency where workers routinely use standardized measuring instruments to track changes in clients' practice objectives. As may be seen, the computer has selected all clients who had practice objectives related to self-esteem during a specified period of time and calculated the average initial (Beginning) and final (End) self-esteem scores for those clients. There were 12 clients in the group, and the average score for the group dropped from 61 at the beginning of service to 42 at termination, a considerable decline in problems with self-esteem. In this instance, the data management capabilities of the computer readily allowed a one-group pretest–posttest evaluation design to be carried out.

Data analyses

The process of turning data into information; the process of reviewing, summarizing, and organizing isolated facts (data) such that they formulate a meaningful response to a research question.

Further analyses can be conducted on these results to determine if the decline is statistically significant. A variety of computer programs can rapidly carry out such **data analyses.** This represents a major advantage over manual data analyses, as most statistical computations tend to be complex, cumbersome, and time-consuming. With today's statistical software packages, the required computations can be easily and accurately accomplished; indeed, more sophisticated procedures, prohibitively time-consuming when done by hand, also become possible.

Similarly, the computer analysis can readily provide data on other points of focus: service data, client characteristics, quality indicators, and client satisfaction. As in the case of the outcome data discussed previously, computers can refine analyses not only to provide data about the entire group but to answer more specific questions. A computer can easily select clients who received services in conjunction with other family members (a quality indicator) and compare their outcomes with those who received individual services. Similarly, data pertaining to two or more operating periods can be compared. These are just two examples of powerful analyses that become possible through computers; the result is information that allows a deeper understanding of programs and services.

There is a potential danger in the ready availability of such analytical power; people who have little knowledge or understanding of data analyses or statistics can easily carry out inappropriate procedures that may serve to mislead rather than inform. Nevertheless, when used knowledgeably, such statistical power makes more incisive analyses possible.

Another group of software programs known as *relational databases* are also increasingly being used in data management. As the name suggests, these programs enable the linking of disparate data in a way that makes it possible to look at and understand data in different ways. Through linking the data contained on client contact forms with information on intake and termination forms, for example, it may be possible to analyze the relationship between initial presenting problems, the course of service provision, and client outcomes. Virtually unlimited flexibility in analyzing data is provided by such programs, which leads to an increasingly more sophisticated understanding of programs, services, and their specific elements. Gabor and Sieppert (1999) provide a detailed example of one such system.

Reporting

Regular reports provide continuous feedback, which is the essence of monitoring. Essentially, reports provide the same data, updated for new cases, on a regular basis. Examples of such reports are provided in Figures 11.4, 11.7, and 11.9.

As with other data management, computers are particularly useful in generating such reports. Software packages used to conduct statistical analyses or to maintain relational databases usually have provisions for repeating the same analyses. Basically, once a data analysis is specified, it can be run over and over again using updated data and producing updated reports. Moreover, formats for reports containing tables, graphs, and charts as well as headings and labels can also be specified in advance. Using computers, there is little limit to the number of reports that can be generated, making it possible to provide timely information, tailored to the needs of staff members at all organizational levels. This, in turn, makes possible an ongoing, organization-wide quality improvement process.

A Look to the Future

It is probably safe to predict that over the next few years computers will play an increasingly important role in data management. With the ready availability of more powerful computer hardware and software programs, it is likely that many organizations will attempt to automate as much of their data management processes as is possible.

One prominent area for automation is the data entry process. Laptop computers make direct data entry feasible. Workers and clients will increasingly use electronic versions of forms, instruments, and questionnaires, entering data directly into laptop computers. Although it may be hard to picture workers and clients in the social services engaging in such activities, they are common practice in the business world. It is only a matter of time until most people will have sufficient familiarity with computers to feel comfortable in interacting with and entering data into them. Already, many people are doing so through automatic tellers, voice mail, and electronic travel reservations.

Data entered directly into laptop computers will be electronically transferred into the organization's data management system, eliminating the need for completing paper copies and manually entering data into the system. This development will not only make data management more accurate and efficient but will also make possible the creation of larger, more powerful systems.

Such developments are probably inevitable. Though some might regard them with suspicion, computer-based information systems can be powerful tools in the service of quality improvement efforts. Ultimately, the technology represented by computerization is, in itself, neither good nor bad. Like any technology, it can be used well but it can also be misused. Clearly, evaluators and social service professionals alike will need to keep a close eye on such developments and ensure that computer use is congruent with professional values and ethics.

Summing Up and Looking Ahead

This chapter stressed that the development of an information system in an existing social service program requires the full cooperation of both line-level workers and administrators. Front-line workers have an important role to play in the design and development of the system. Administrators must be prepared to provide training, support, and resources in addition to demonstrating that the monitoring system is intended to improve the program, not to assign blame.

The following chapter builds upon this one in that it presents how to use graphics when reporting data from a program evaluation.

RECAP AND ONLINE MATERIALS

In this chapter, you learned how to identify and use data that can be used in social work data information systems.

You should also recall the concept of using computers to sort and manage data from your foundational research course. If not, go online to take a free crash course in computers.

You can also find the following materials online to help you master the concepts you just learned:

- Chapter Outline
- Learning Objectives
- Key Terms and Concepts
- Flash Cards
- Practice Multiple-Choice Tests
- Essay Questions with Answers
- Links

www.oup.com/us/swevaluation

STUDY QUESTIONS

1. Data information systems contain data that ultimately will answer questions raised by various stakeholder groups. Identify five generic questions that might be asked of a social service program. Given your questions, what data (or variables) must be included in a program's data information system?

2. Imagine that you are the evaluator hired to set up a data information system for your social work education program (bachelor's or master's degree level). Name the different stakeholder groups that you would consult. Identify key data (or variables) that each stakeholder group would likely insist on including in the system. (*Hint: Think of likely questions that would be of interest for each stakeholder group.*)

3. Review the list of stakeholder groups that you identified in the previous question. Rank the groups in order, starting with the group that you believe should have the most say-so with respect to what data ought to be included in the data information system. What rationale can you offer for your rankings? Do other students in your class agree or disagree with your rankings and rationales?

4. This chapter stresses that program-level and case-level data information systems ought to parallel each other in any given program. How do parallel systems benefit program administrators, program workers, and clients? What problems are likely to occur for each of these stakeholder groups when program and case-level data information systems are unrelated?

5. Look at the flowchart presented in Figure 11.1. Identify a case-level question at each step in the chart that would assist you in monitoring an individual client's progress. Identify a program-level question at each step in the chart that would assist you in monitoring overall client progress (i.e., all clients).

6. Intake forms are common to most social service programs. Identify generic data (or variables) that would likely appear on such a form. What case-level decisions could you make with these data, if any? What program-level decisions could you make with these data, if any?

7. A social worker exclaims, "There is no point in collecting data from clients at termination because the feedback will not be used to benefit their individual cases." Explain why you agree or disagree with this statement. Compare your answer with those of other students in your class.

8. Look at the excerpt from a summary report presented in Figure 11.7. What questions does the information presented in the figure raise for you? Is it possible to make recommendations for program development based on the numbers presented? Why or why not? Discuss your answers with other students in your class.

9. Compare Figure 11.8 with Figures 9.1 and 9.2. Which client satisfaction survey would you use? Why?

10. Discuss the reasons why it is better to use standardized measures within a data information system than nonstandardized ones. You may need to reread Chapter 9 and look into the references at the end of this chapter before answering this question.

REFERENCES, FURTHER READING, AND RESOURCES

Ames, N. (1999). Social work recording: A new look at an old issue. *Journal of Social Work Education, 35*(2), 227–237.

Auslander, G. K., & Cohen, M. E. (1992). Issues in the development of social work information systems: The case of hospital social work departments. *Administration in Social Work, 16,* 73–88.

Aydin, C. E., & Rice, R. E. (1991). SOS, social worlds, individual differences, and implementation predicting attitudes toward a medical information system. *Information and Management, 20,* 119–136.

Barrett, S. (1999). Information systems: An exploration of the factors influencing effective use. *Journal of Research on Computing in Education, 32*(1), 4–17.

Benbenishty, R. (1989). The design of computerized clinical information systems to monitor interventions on the agency level. *Computers in Human Service Organizations, 5,* 69–78.

Benbenishty, R., & Treistman, R. (1998). The development and evaluation of a hybrid decision support system for clinical decision making: The case of discharge from the military. *Social Work Research, 22,* 195–204.

Caputo, R. (1988). *Management and information systems in human services implications for the distribution of authority and decision making.* New York: Haworth Press.

Carrilio, T., Cohen, R., & Goldman, A. (1980). The team method of delivering services to the elderly: An interim report. *Journal of Jewish Communal Service, 52*(1), 56–62.

Carrilio, T., Kasser, J., & Moretto, A. H. (1985). Management information systems: Who is in charge? *Social Casework: The Journal of Contemporary Social Work. 42,* 417–423.

Clapp, J. D., Burke, A. C., & Stanger, L. (1998). The institutional environment, strategic response and program adaptation: A case study. *Journal of Applied Social Sciences, 22*(1), 87–95.

Collins, M. E., Epstein, I., Barbarin, O., & Savas, S. A. (1996). Re-designing a clinical information system: A description of the process in a human service agency. *Computers in Human Services, 13,* 19–36.

Compeau, D. R., & Higgins, C. A. (1995). Computer self-efficacy; development of a measure and initial test. *MIS Quarterly, 19,* 189–211.

Damodaran, L. (1996). User involvement in the systems design process—a practical guide for users. *Behavior & Information Technology, 15,* 363–377.

Dodd, J. L., & Carr, H. C. (1994). Systems development led by end-users: An assessment of end-users involvement in information systems development. *Journal of Systems Management,* 45, 34–40.

Doll, W. J., & Torkzadeh, G. (1988). The measurement of end-user computing satisfaction. *MIS Quarterly, 12,* 259–274.

Dorsey, D. (2002) Information technology. In J. Hedge, & E. Pulkalos (Eds.), *Implementing organizational interventions* (pp. 110–132). San Francisco: Jossey-Bass.

Fancett, S., & Hughes, M. (1996). The development of a client record system within a non-governmental child care organization. *Computers in Human Services, 13,* 63–72.

Fitzgerald, B., & Murphy, C. (1994). Introducing executive information systems into organizations: Separating fact from fallacy. *Journal of Information Technology, 9,* 288–296.

Gabor, P. A., & Grinnell, R. M., Jr. (1994). *Evaluation and quality improvement in the human services.* Boston: Allyn & Bacon.

Gabor, P. A., & Sieppert, J. (1999). Developing a computer supported evaluation system in a human service organization. *New Technology in the Human Services, 12,* 107–119.

Gabor, P. A., Unrau, Y. A. (1998). *Evaluation for social workers: A quality improvement approach for the human services* (2nd ed.). Boston: Allyn & Bacon.

Grasso, A. J., & Epstein, I. (Eds.). (1993). Information systems in child, youth, and family agencies: Planning, implementation, and service enhancement. Binghamton, NY: Haworth Press. (Original work published as *Child and Youth Services, 16*(1).)

Harachi, T. W., Abbott, R. D., Catalano, R. F., Haggerty, K. P. & Fleming, C. B. (1999). Opening the black box: Using process evaluation measures to assess implementation and theory building. *American Journal of Community Psychology, 27*(5), 711–731.

Hasenfeld, Y., & Patti, R. (1992). The utilization of research in administrative practice. In A. Grasso, & I. Epstein (Eds.), *Research utilization in the social services* (pp. 221–239). New York: Haworth Press.

Herie, M., & Martin, G. (2002). Knowledge diffusion in social work: A new approach to bridging the gap. *Social Work, 47*(1), 85–95.

Hernandez, M. (2000) Using logic models and program theory to build outcome accountability. *Education and Treatment of Children, 23*(1), 24–40.

Hodges, S., & Hernandez, M. (1999). How organizational culture influences outcome information utilization. *Evaluation and Program Planning, 22,* 183–197.

Hornby, P., Clegg, C. W., Robson, J. I., Maclaren, C. R., Richardson, C. S., & O'Brien, P. (1992). Human and organizational issues in information systems development. *Behavior and Information Technology, 11,* 160–174.

Horsch, K. (1996). Results-based accountability systems: Opportunities and challenges. *Evaluation Exchange, 2,* 2–3.

Howell, J. M., & Higgins, C. A. (1990). Champions of change: Identifying, understanding, and supporting champions of technological innovations. *Organizational Dynamics, 19,* 40–55.

Igbaria, M. (1994). An examination of the factors contributing to technology acceptance. Accounting. *Management and Information Technologies, 4,* 205–224.

Igbaria, M., Iivari, J., & Maragahh, H. (1995). Why do individuals use computer technology? A Finnish case study. *Information and Management, 29,* 227–238.

Iivari, J., & Igbaria, M. (1997). Determinants of user participation: A Finnish survey. *Behavior and Information Technology, 16,* 111–121.

Kagle, J. D. (1993). Record keeping: directions for the 1990s. *Social Work, 38*(2), 190–196.

Kettner, P., Moroney, R., & Martin, L. (in press). *Designing and managing programs: An effectiveness based approach* (3rd ed.). Thousand Oaks, CA: Sage.

Leff, H. S., & Mulkern, V. (2002). Lessons learned about science and participation from multisite evaluations. In J. M. Herrell, & R. B. Straw (Eds.), *Conducting multiple site evaluations in real-world settings: New directions for evaluation.* (pp. 89–100). San Francisco: Jossey-Bass.

Leonard-Barton, D., & Sinha, D. K. (1993). Developer-user interaction and user satisfaction in internal technology transfer. *Academy of Management Journal, 36,* 1125–1139.

Martin, L. (2000). Performance contracting in the human services: An analysis of selected state practices. *Administration in Social Work, 24*(2), 29–44.

Monnikendam, M. (1999). Computer systems that work: A review of variables associated with system use. *Journal of Social Service Research, 26,* 71–94.

Monnikendam, M. (2000). Participative system implementation for creating user oriented computer systems in human services. *Administration in Social Work, 24,* 57–74.

Monnikendam, M., & Morris, A. (1989). Developing an integrated computerized case management system for the Israeli defense forces: An evolutionary approach. *Computers in Human Services, 5,* 133–149.

Moser, K., & Ramirez, R. G. (1995). Should end-users be considered last? *Journal of Systems Management, 46,* 48–53.

Mutschler, E. (1992). Computers in agency settings. In A. Grasso, & I. Epstein, (Eds.), *Research utilization in the social services* (pp. 325–344). New York: Haworth Press.

Mutschler, E., & Hasenfeld, Y. (1986). Integrated information systems for social work practice. *Social Work, 42,* 345–349.

Nugent, W. R., Sieppert, J. D., & Hudson, W. W. (2001). *Practice evaluation for the 21st century.* Belmont, CA: Brooks/Cole.

Nurius, P., & Hudson, W. (1989). Workers, clients, and computers. *Computers in Human Services, 4,* 71–81.

Nurius, P. S., & Hudson, W. (1993). *Human services: Practice, evaluation, and computers.* Belmont, CA: Brooks/Cole.

Ogborne, A. C., Braun, K., & Rush, B. R. (1998). Developing an integrated information system for specialized addiction treatment agencies. *Journal of Behavioral Health Services and Research, 25*(1), 100–107.

Oyserman, D., & Benbenishty, R. (1997). Developing and implementing the integrated information system for foster care and adoption. *Computers in Human Services, 14,* 1–20.

Pare, G., & Elam, J. J. (1995). Discretionary use of personal computers by knowledge workers: Testing of a social psychology theoretical model. *Behavior and Information Technology, 14,* 215–228.

Poertner, J. (2000). Managing for service outcomes. In R. Patti (Ed.), *The handbook of social welfare management* (pp. 267–281). Thousand Oaks, CA: Sage.

Poertner, J., & Rapp, C. A. (1987). Designing social work management information systems: The case for performance guidance systems. *Administration in Social Work, 11,* 177–190.

Poole, D. L., Nelson, J., Carnahan, S., Chepenik, N. G., Tubiak, C. (2000). Evaluating performance measurement systems in nonprofit agencies: The Program Accountability Quality Scale (PAQS). *American Journal of Evaluation, 21*(1), 15–26.

Proctor, E. K. (2002). Quality of care and social work research. *Social Work Research, 26*(4), 195–197.

Raider, M., & Moxley, D. (1990). A computer-integrated approach to program evaluation: A practical application within residential services. *Computers in Human Services, 12,* 133–148.

Rapp, C., & Poertner, J. (1992). *Social administration: A client-centered approach.* New York: Longman.

Rossi, P. H., Freman, H. E., & Lipsey, M. W. (1999). *Evaluation: A systematic approach* (6th ed.). Thousand Oaks, CA: Sage.

Savaya, R., & Spiro, S. (1997). Reactions of practitioners to the introduction of a standard instrument to monitor clinical outcomes. *Journal of Social Service Research, 22,* 39–55.

Savaya, R., & Waysman, R. (1996). Factors implicated in the integration of clinical information systems into human service agencies: A concept mapping. *New Technology in the Human Services*, 9, 15–22.

Scheirer, M. A. (2000). Getting more "bang" for your performance measures buck. *American Journal of Evaluation, 21*(2), 139–149.

Schoech, D. (1995). Information systems. In R. Edwards (Ed.), *Encyclopedia of social work* (19th ed., pp. 1470–1479). Washington, DC: NASW Press.

Schoech, D. (1999). *Human services technology: Understanding, designing, and implementing computer and internet applications in the social services.* New York: Haworth Press.

Schoech, D., Fitch, D., MacFadden, R., & Schkade, L. (2001). From data to intelligence: Introducing the intelligent organization. *Administration in Social Work, 26*(1), 1–21.

Schoech, D., Schkade, L. L., & Mayers, R. S. (1981). Strategies for information system development. *Administration in Social Work, 5,* 11–26.

Schorr, L. (1997). *Common purpose.* New York: Anchor Books/Doubleday.

Spiro, S. E., Savaya, R., Waysman, M., & Golan, M. (1998, October 7–9). *A formative evaluation of the development of a clinical information system for a network of juvenile institutions.* Paper presented at the Australian Evaluation Society international conference, Melbourne, Victoria, Australia.

Straw, R. B., & Herrell, J. M. (2002). A framework for understanding and improving multisite evaluations. In J. M. Herrell, & R. B. Straw (Eds.), *New directions for evaluation* (pp. 5–15). San Francisco: Jossey-Bass.

Swanson, E. B. (1974). Management information systems: Appreciation and involvement. *Management Science,* 21, 178–188.

Tichy, N. (1983). *Managing strategic change.* New York: Wiley.

Yin, R. K. (1994). *Case study research: Design and methods* (2nd ed.). Thousand Oaks, CA: Sage.

On Measuring Your Practice and Program Objectives

Bloom, M., Fischer, J., & Orme, J. (2006). *Evaluating practice: Guidelines for the accountable professional* (5th ed.). Boston: Allyn & Bacon.

Bostwick, G., & Kyte, N. S. (2005). Measurement. In R. M. Grinnell, Jr., & Y. A. Unrau (Eds.), *Social work research and evaluation: Quantitative and qualitative approaches* (7th ed., pp. 98–111). New York: Oxford University Press.

Corcoran, K. J., & Fischer, J. (2007). *Measures for clinical practice: Vol. 1. Couples, families, and children.* (4th ed.) New York: Oxford University Press.

Corcoran, K. J., & Fischer, J. (2007). *Measures for clinical practice: Vol. 2: Adults.* (4th ed.) New York: Oxford University Press.

Jordan, C., Franklin, C., & Corcoran, K. (2005). Measuring instruments. In R. M. Grinnell, Jr., & Y.

A. Unrau (Eds.), *Social work research and evaluation: Quantitative and qualitative approaches* (7th ed., pp. 114–131). New York: Oxford University Press.

McDowell, I., & Newell, C. (1996). *Measuring health.* New York: Oxford University Press.

Mindel, C. H. (2005). Designing measuring Instruments. In R. M. Grinnell, Jr., & Y. A. Unrau (Eds.), *Social work research and evaluation: Quantitative and qualitative approaches* (7th ed., pp. 134–146). New York: Oxford University Press.

Nugent, W. R., Sieppert, J. D., & Hudson, W. W. (2001). *Practice evaluation for the 21st century.* Belmont, CA: Brooks/Cole.

Unrau, Y. A., Gabor, P. A., & Grinnell, R. M., Jr. (2001). *Evaluation in the human services* (3rd ed.). Belmont, CA: Wadsworth.

12

USING GRAPHICS TO REPORT EVALUATION DATA

Ed Minter and Mary Michaud

People "consume" **information** in different ways and presenting information graphically can help clarify evaluation results. One of the best ways to clarify evaluation results is through simple **graphics**—bar charts, pie charts, illustrations, and photographs. They can simplify complex information, emphasize key points, and create a picture of the data. Graphics can also tell a story, showing proportions, comparisons, trends, geographic and technical data and, in the case of photographs, putting a "human face" on a project.

This chapter provides a brief overview of how to choose among common types of graphics and ensure that they accurately represent the data derived from a program evaluation. Why use graphics to present evaluation results? Before choosing a graphic to illustrate evaluation results, ask the following questions:

- What is the purpose of this report?
- Who will use the information?
- What are the key messages for this audience?

Think about the types of graphics readers are used to seeing. For example, are members of the general public ready for a complex line graph showing trends or will a simpler graphic do a better job of helping them understand the main points? Using graphics may not always be the best approach. Ask yourself whether readers will take time to decipher complex pie charts with multiple categories or whether a simple

Information
The interpretation given to data that have been collected, collated, and analyzed. Information is used to help in the decision-making process and should not to be confused with data.

Information anxiety
A feeling attributable to a lack of understanding of information, being overwhelmed by the amount of information to be accessed and understood, or not knowing if certain information exists.

Graphics
Visual elements that supplement type to make printed messages clearer or more interesting.

Table 12.1 When to Use Common Graphics

Type	When to Use	Tradeoffs	Tips
Bar Chart	Versatile and good for comparisons. Relatively easy to construct.	Units on y axis (vertical axis) can sometimes be too small to show meaningful differences.	• Label the horizontal (x) and vertical (y) axes. • Use as few bars or lines as possible (maximum 6 bars or 3 lines).
Line Graph	Useful for showing trends and differences between groups.	Too many data lines can confuse.	• Emphasize one aspect of the data by changing a bar's color or texture. • Clarify values by adding value labels at the top of the bar. • Label lines on line graphs, and, if possible, use different colors. • Use gridlines, horizontal lines across the chart, beginning at each interval on the vertical axis.
Pie Chart	Shows proportions (percentages) of a whole.	Too many categories can mislead. Not ideal for showing trends.	• Use six or fewer slices. • Use contrasting colors, shades of gray, or simple patterns to increase readability. • Label the slices. • Emphasize a certain piece of data by moving its slice out from the circle.
Illustration (Examples: Diagrams, maps, drawings)	Conveys lots of information in a small space. Shows technical and geographic data.	May take up a lot of space. Complex illustrations may not photocopy well.	• Position the title above the illustration. • Keep illustrations simple. If the illustration needs a lot of explanation, it is probably too complicated for an illustration. • Provide ample white space around and within the illustration
Photograph	Adds a "human face" to data. Captures before-and-after pictures of a program or intervention.	May be costly. Sometimes difficult to take high-quality photos. Can take up a lot of space in a report. May not photocopy well.	• Get written permission to take the picture as well as permission to use the photo in a publication. • Figure out ahead of time what you want to photograph and how pictures will be used. • Use several photographers to capture multiple perspectives.

table will do the trick. After glancing over Table 12.1, you need to remember three rules for presenting data using graphics:

1. Keep it simple.
2. Choose a graphic that communicates the most important message.
3. Don't assume people will read text that accompanies a graphic.

This chapter does not provide exhaustive rules on how to present data graphically. It does, however, offer guidelines on how to choose the most appropriate graphic to communicate data to different audiences.

CHARACTERISTICS OF AN EFFECTIVE GRAPHIC

Graphics that use data will benefit from several key elements, illustrated in the simple bar chart as presented in Figure 12.1. In this example, the title clearly states the units of analysis (Williams County and Wisconsin worksites), the statistic used to describe the data (percentage), and the dates data were collected (2001). The note draws attention to information sources.

Audiences who do not regularly consume technical information may find that these details clutter the graphic. However, be prepared to answer questions about sampling and analysis methods, and include a description of the methods in written reports.

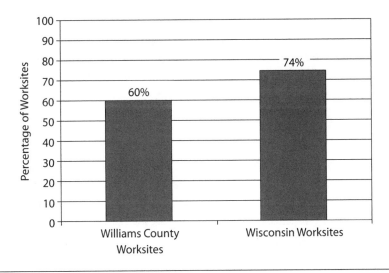

Figure 12.1 Percentage of Williams County and Wisconsin worksites that ban smoking indoors. (Note: Worksites for both surveys are defined as those with more than five employees. (*Source:* University of Wisconsin Monitoring and Evaluation Program. *Results of 2001 Wisconsin Worksite Smoking Policy Survey.* March 2002. Williams County Tobacco-Free Coalition.)

BAR CHARTS

Bar chart
A chart used to graphically summarize and display the differences between groups of data.

Bar charts show comparisons and are relatively easy to construct. Take a moment to study the bar chart depicted in Figure 12.1. What does it show you? What do you conclude? What questions does the chart prompt? Depending on the audience, this bar chart may require more information about methods used, such as the sampling process that was used to collect the data. Notice that the note says worksites are defined the same way in these two studies, making their findings comparable. However, if this was a chart on smoking prevalence among youth, the findings would not be comparable. That's because the Williams County survey defines youth as between 11 and 18, while the statewide survey defines youth as younger than 21. A few simple steps make the chart less cluttered:

- Value labels (percentages listed above the bars) add precision.
- The title uses precise language. "Worksites that ban smoking indoors" is less ambiguous than "worksites that have smoking policies."
- Gridlines add depth and dimension, helping readers see the difference between each bar of data.
- Although the *y*-axis data label may seem redundant, it ensures that readers know what the values mean.

PIE CHARTS

Pie chart
A circle graph used for comparing the parts of a whole with the whole. The area of the circle represents the whole, and the areas of the sectors of the circle represent the parts.

Pie charts show proportions of a whole. The pie chart depicted in Figure 12.2 gives a breakdown of restaurant smoking policies in Ozaukee County. With only the information in the graphic, readers may wonder whether this survey represents all restaurants in the county, only restaurants that responded to the survey, or restaurants that include bars. To avoid confusion, supplement the graphic with information about sampling methods, response rates, and limitations of results.

LINE GRAPHS

Line graphs
Graph that uses connected data points to plot the relationship between two or more variables.

Line graphs such as the one shown in Figure 12.3 show trends over time. They also show the ways groups differ over time. For example, lines on the graph may show that behavior patterns between two or more groups converge, diverge, or stay the same. Figure 12.3 is a line graph that shows that, between September 2001 and November 2002, teen involvement in the Williamsburg Fight Against Corporate Tobacco (FACT) group increased. Not surprisingly, the graph tells us that fewer teens were involved over the summer and that membership increased significantly when the school year began. Testimonials from teens involved in the program from the beginning might help tell the story of what they gained from their participation. Combining quantitative and qualitative data can tell a powerful story about community change and the forces behind it.

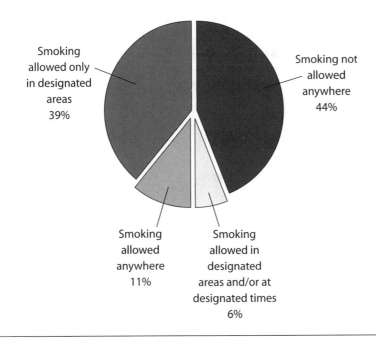

Figure 12.2 Smoking policies in Ozaukee County restaurants, 2001 (57 restaurants surveyed). (*Source*: Ozaukee Tobacco-Free Coalition. *2001 Ozaukee County Restaurant Survey.*)

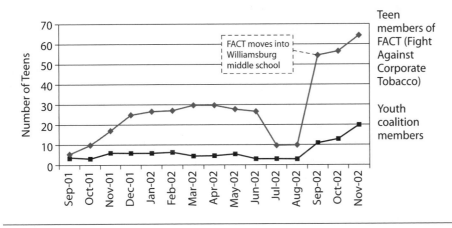

Figure 12.3 Youth involvement in Williams County Tobacco-Free Coalition, 2001–2002. (*Source*: Williams County Tobacco-Free Coalition, 2002.)

ILLUSTRATIONS

Illustrations can convey a lot of information in a small space. They can also convey technical information and geographic references. The illustration in Figure 12.4 was created using the "Drawing" toolbar in Microsoft Word. It shows a map of tobacco retailers and advertisements within a mile of a high school and a middle school. For

Illustrations
Line art, photos, and other graphic images used in printed material.

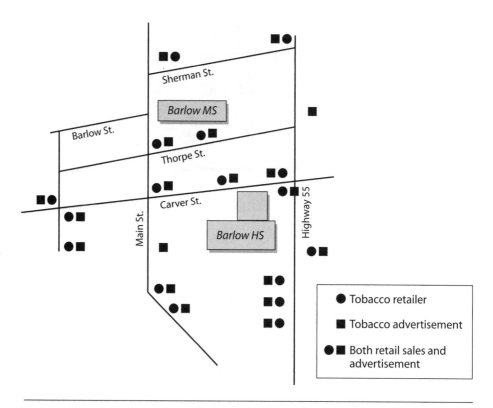

Figure 12.4 Tobacco retailers and advertisements within one mile of Barlow High School and Middle School. (*Source:* Williamsburg FACT group, Community Ad Watch, 2001.)

parents and administrators, this illustration tells a compelling story about the presence of the tobacco industry in their children's daily environment. Text or oral explanations accompanying this illustration might explain how "Ad Watch" was conducted and how "tobacco retailer" and "tobacco advertisement" were defined. Another map a year or two later might show a decrease in the number of locations that advertise tobacco by crossing out the squares on the illustration.

Photographs

Photographs Images on paper.

Photographs often convey information better than text. They can show what happens before and after a program intervention, such as the number of tobacco ads in front of a store before and after an Ad Watch campaign. The example in Figure 12.5 combines text with a picture showing how and where tobacco products are placed in retail spaces. Text without a photograph would not convey such a powerful message. Use photography to

- Capture before and after information.
- Help the audience understand participants' experiences.

Figure 12.5 Example of a picture used in a program evaluation. (*Source:* Omaha Tobacco-Free Coalition, Operation Storefront, 2000.)

- Show unexpected or secondary effects of a program.
- Document how a program was implemented.
- Compare, count, measure, qualify, or track changes in the environment (such as signage in a school district or advertising in a community).

CHECKLIST

The following questions will help ensure your graphic conveys an accurate message appropriate for your intended audience.

Question 1: **Before you start the graphic, ask:**

- What audience are you trying to reach?
- What type of graphic is the audience used to seeing?
- What is the purpose of the graphic? What is the main message you want to convey?
- Is the type of graphic the most appropriate one to use for this message?
- Will more than one graphic deliver the message more effectively?
- Will text or oral explanation clarify the message, or is the graphic clear enough to stand on its own?

Question 2: After you create the graphic, ask:

- Is the graphic easy to understand?
- Is the graphic presentation easy to interpret for someone not familiar with the material?
- Does the graphic accurately reflect the data?
- Is the graphic close to the relevant text?

Summing Up and Looking Ahead

This chapter presented a very brief overview of how program evaluation results that are quantitative in nature can be displayed in the form of graphics. The following chapter presents how qualitative data derived from a program evaluation can be collected, analyzed, summarized, and displayed.

Recap and Online Materials

In this chapter, you learned how to display quantitative data in graphic form.

You should also recall the concept of quantitative data analysis from your foundational research course. If not, go online to take a free crash course in quantitative data analysis.

You can also find the following materials online to help you master the concepts you just learned:

- Chapter Outline
- Learning Objectives
- Key Terms and Concepts
- Flash Cards
- Practice Multiple-Choice Tests
- Essay Questions with Answers
- Links

www.oup.com/us/swevaluation

Study Questions

1. What three questions must you ask yourself before you display data from a program evaluation study in graphics form? Provide a social work example throughout your discussion.
2. Discuss how you can use bar charts when displaying data from a program evaluation study. When are they most useful? When are they least useful? Go to the

published social work literature and find an evaluation study that presented some, if not all, of its findings in the form of bar charts. How would you have displayed the data differently? Why?

3. Discuss how you can use pie charts when displaying data from a program evaluation study. When are they most useful? When are they least useful? Go to the published social work literature and find an evaluation study that presented some, if not all, of its findings in the form of pie charts. How would you have displayed the data differently? Why?

4. Discuss how you can use line graphs when displaying data from a program evaluation study. When are they most useful? When are they least useful? Go to the published social work literature and find an evaluation study that presented some, if not all, of its findings in the form of line graphs. How would you have displayed the data differently? Why?

5. Discuss how you can use illustrations when displaying data from a program evaluation study. When are they most useful? When are they least useful? Go to the published social work literature and find an evaluation study that presented some, if not all, of its findings in the form of illustrations. How would you have displayed the data differently? Why?

6. Discuss how you can use photographs when displaying data from a program evaluation study. When are they most useful? When are they least useful? Go to the published social work literature and find an evaluation study that presented some, if not all, of its findings in the form of photographs. How would you have displayed the data differently? Why?

REFERENCES, FURTHER READING, AND RESOURCES

Baron, M. E. (1969). A note on the historical development of logic diagrams: Leibniz, Euler, and Venn. *Mathematical Gazette, 52,* 113–125.

Brinton, W. C. (1980). *Graphic methods for presenting facts.* New York: Arno Press. (Original work published 1914)

Chin, M. (2002, July). *Caledonia/Mt. Pleasant/North Bay restaurant survey findings.* Unpublished manuscript.

Cleveland, W. S., & McGill, R. (1984). Graphical perception: Theory, experimentation, and application to the development of graphical methods. *Journal of the American Statistical Association, 79,* 531–540.

Croxton, F. E. (1927). Further studies in the graphic use of circles and bar II: Some additional data. *Journal of the American Statistical Association, 22,* 36–39.

Croxton, F. E., & Stein, H. (1932). Graphic comparisons by bars, squares, circles, and cubes. *Journal of the American Statistical Association, 27,* 54–60.

Croxton, F. E., & Stryker, R. E. (1927). Bar charts versus circle diagrams. *Journal of the American Statistical Association, 22,* 473–482.

Culbertson, H. M., & Powers, R. D. (1959). A study of graph comprehension difficulties. *AV Communication Review, 7,* 97–110.

Donnant, D. F. (1805). *Statistical account of the United States of America.* (William Playfair, Trans.) London: Greenland and Norris.

Eells, W. C. (1926). The relative merits of circles and bars for representing component parts. *Journal of the American Statistical Association, 21,* 119–132.

Funkhouser, H. G. (1937). Historical development of the graphical representation of statistical data. *Osiris, 3,* 269–404.

Hollands, J. G., & Dyre, B. P. (2000). Bias in proportion judgments: The cyclical power model. *Psychological Review,* 107, 500–524.

Hollands, J. G., & Spence, I. (1992). Judgments of change and proportion in graphical perception. *Human Factors, 34,* 313–334.

Hollands, J. G., & Spence, I. (1998). Judging proportion with graphs: The summation model. *Applied Cognitive Psychology, 12,* 173–190.

Jan-Aage, H., Jorner, U., Persson, R., Wallgren, A., & Wallgren, B. (1996). Chapters 1, 11, and 14. In *Graphing statistics & data: Creating better charts.* Thousand Oak, CA: Sage.

Marten, S. (2001, November). *Tobacco Free Coalition 2001 smoke free restaurant survey.* Paper presented at the Ozaukee County Tobacco Free Coalition Meeting. Grafton, WI.

Piontek, M. E., Preskill, H. S., & Torres, R. T. (1996). Chapters 4 and 5. In *Evaluating strategies for communicating & reporting: Enhancing learning in organizations.* Thousand Oak, CA: Sage.

Spence, I. (2005). No humble pie: The origins and usage of a statistical chart. *Journal of Educational and Behavioral Statistics, 30*(4), 353–368.

Spence, I., & Lewandowsky, S. (1991). Displaying proportions and percentages. *Applied Cognitive Psychology, 5,* 61–77.

Spence, I., & Wainer, H. (1997). William Playfair: A daring worthless fellow. *Chance, 10,* 31–34.

Tufte, E. R. (1983). *The visual display of quantitative information.* Cheshire, CT: Graphics Press.

ANALYZING QUALITATIVE DATA

13

Ellen Taylor-Powell and Marcus Renner

Qualitative data consist of raw words and observations, not numbers. These words and observations have to be analyzed and interpreted. This requires creativity, discipline, and a systematic approach. There is no single or best way to go about this, and your process will depend on: (1) the questions you want to answer, (2) the needs of those who will use the information, and (3) your resources.

This chapter briefly outlines a basic approach for analyzing and interpreting narrative data that you can adapt to your own evaluations that include a qualitative component such as an open-ended question on a client satisfaction questionnaire. (For descriptions of other types of qualitative data analysis see Ratcliff, 2002.)

NARRATIVE DATA

As we know by now, text or narrative data can come in many forms and from a variety of sources. You might have brief responses to **open-ended questions** on a survey, the complete transcript from an interview or focus group, notes from a log or diary, field notes, or the text of a published report. Your **narrative data** may come from

---

Qualitative data
Data that measure a quality or kind; when referring to variables, qualitative is another term for categorical or nominal variable values; when speaking of kinds of research, qualitative refers to studies of subjects that are hard to quantify; interpretive research produces descriptive data based on spoken or written words and observable behaviors.

Narrative data
Words that describe a story or an idea.

Open-ended questions
Unstructured questions in which the response categories are not specified or detailed.

many people, a few individuals, or a single case. Any of the following may produce narrative data that require analysis.

Member checking
A process of obtaining feedback and comments from research participants on interpretations and conclusions made from the qualitative data they provided; asking research participants to confirm or refute the conclusions made.

- Open-ended questions and written comments on questionnaires may generate single words, brief phrases, or full paragraphs of text.
- Testimonials may give reactions to a social service program in a few words or lengthy comments, either in person or in written correspondence.
- Individual interviews can produce data in the form of notes, a summary of an individual interview, or word-for-word transcripts.
- Discussion group, or focus group interviews, often involve full transcripts and notes from a moderator or observer.
- Logs, journals, and diaries can provide structured entries or free-flowing text that you or others have produced.
- Observations might be recorded in your field notes or descriptive accounts as a result of watching and listening.
- Documents, reports, news articles, and any published written material may serve as evaluation data.
- Stories may provide data from personal accounts of experiences and results of programs in people's own words.
- **Case studies** typically include several of the above.

THE ANALYSIS PROCESS

Once you have these data, what do you do? The following steps describe the basic elements of narrative data analysis and interpretation. This process is fluid, so moving back and forth between steps is likely.

Case study
Using research approaches to investigate a research question or hypothesis relating to a specific case; used to develop theory and test hypotheses; an in-depth form of research in which data are gathered and analyzed about an individual unit of analysis, person, city, event, or society. Case studies allow more intensive analysis of specific details; the disadvantage is that it is hard to use the results to generalize to other cases.

Step 1: Get to Know Your Data

A good qualitative analysis depends on a good understanding of the data. For a qualitative analysis, this means you will have to read and re-read the text. If you have tape recordings, you will have to listen to them several times. Write down any impressions you have as you go through the data. These impressions will more than likely be useful later.

Also, just because you have narrative data does not mean you have quality data. Sometimes narrative data does not add any meaning or additional value to your evaluation. Or they may have been collected in a biased manner. Before beginning any narrative analysis, consider the quality of the data and proceed accordingly. Eventually, down the "analysis road," you will need to explain the limitations and the level of analysis you deem appropriate given your data.

Step 2: Focus the Analysis

You will first need to review the purpose of your evaluation and what you want to find out. Identify a few key questions that you want your analysis to answer. Write these down. These questions will help you to decide on how to begin and will more than likely change as you work with your data. How you focus your analysis depends on the purpose of your evaluation and how you will use the results. There are two common approaches you can use to focus your narrative analysis: (1) focus by questions or topic, time period, or event, or (2) focus by case, individual, or group.

Focus by Question or Topic, Time Period, or Event

In this approach, you will need to focus your analysis to look at how all individuals or groups responded to each question or topic, or for a given time period or event. This is often done with open-ended questions. You will need to organize the data by question and look across all respondents' answers to identify consistencies and differences. You will also need to put all the respondents' responses for each question together. You can apply the same approach to particular topics, or a time period or an event of interest. Later, you may explore the connections and relationships between questions (topics, time periods, or events).

Focus by Case, Individual, or Group

You may want an overall picture of (1) one case such as one family or one agency, (2) one individual such as a first-time or teen participant in a program, or (3) one group such as all first-time participants in a program or all teens ages 13 to 18.

Rather than grouping the respondents' answers by question or topic, you may want to organize your data set (from or about the case, individual, or group) and analyze it as a whole. Or you may want to combine these approaches and analyze the data both by question and by case, individual, or group.

Step 3: Categorize Information

Some people refer to categorizing information as coding the data or indexing the data. However, categorizing does not involve assigning numerical codes as you would in a quantitative analysis where you label exclusive variables with preset codes or values. To bring meaning to the words, you will need to (1) identify **themes** or patterns—ideas, concepts, behaviors, interactions, incidents, terminology, or phrases used within the data set, and (2) organize the data into coherent categories that summarize and bring meaning to the text.

This can be fairly labor-intensive depending on the amount of data you have.

Theme

In a qualitative data analysis, a concept or idea that describes a single category or a grouping of categories; an abstract interpretation of qualitative data.

Table 13.1 Sorting Responses to Questions

Questions	Categories Responses to the question were sorted into:
1. What makes a quality educational program?	Staff (Stf), relevance (Rel), participation (Part), timeliness (Time), content (Con)
2. What is the benefit of a youth mentoring program?	Benefits to youth (Y), benefits to mentor (M), benefits to family (Fam), benefits to community (Comm)
3. What do you need to continue your learning about evaluation?	Practice (P), additional training (Trg), time (T), resources (R), feedback (Fdbk), mentor (M), uncertain (U)

Possible code abbreviations are designated in parentheses.

But this is the crux of a qualitative analysis. It involves reading and re-reading the text and identifying coherent categories. You may want to assign abbreviated codes of a few letters, words, or symbols and place them next to the themes and ideas you find. This will help you to organize your data into categories. You must provide a descriptive label (name) for each category you create. Be clear about what you included in the category and what you excluded.

As you categorize the data, you might identify other themes that will serve as subcategories. Continue to categorize your data until you have identified and labeled all relevant themes. The right side of Table 13.1 shows the categories that were identified to sort the responses to the three questions on the left side, for example.

There are two basic ways to categorize narrative data: (1) using preset categories or (2) using emergent categories.

Preset Categories

You can start with a list of preconceived themes, or categories, in advance and then search the data for these topics within your data set. For example, you might start with concepts that you really want to know about. Or you might start with topics derived from the professional research literature. These themes provide direction for what you look for in the data.

Emergent Categories

Rather than using preconceived themes, or categories, you can read through the text and let the themes emerge from the data. These reoccurring themes then become your categories. They may be ideas or concepts that you had not thought about before. In short, categories are defined as a result of working with the data.

Sometimes, you may combine these two approaches, starting with some preset categories and adding others as they become apparent. Your initial list of categories may change as you work with the data. This is an interactive process. More often

Table 13.2 Responses to a Question Broken Down
Into Categories

Question	Categories
What is the benefit of a youth mentoring program?	Benefits to youth (Y)
	School performance (Y-SP)
	Friendship (Y-Friends)
	Self-concept (Y-SC)
	Role modeling (Y-RM)
	Benefits to mentor (M)
	Benefits to family (Fam)
	Benefits to community (Comm)

than not, you may have to adjust the definition of your categories, or identify new categories to accommodate data that do not fit into the existing labels.

Main categories can also be broken into subcategories. If this is the case, you will need to re-sort your data into these smaller and hence more defined subcategories. This allows for greater discrimination and differentiation among the data. For example, in a question about the benefits of a youth mentoring program, data within the category "benefits to youth" were broken down into four subcategories as presented in Table 13.2.

You will need to continue to build categories until no new themes or subcategories are identified from your data set. You can add as many categories as you need in order to reflect the nuances within the data and to interpret the data clearly. You will want to try to create mutually exclusive and exhaustive categories, but sometimes sections of data will fit into two or more categories. Thus, you may need to create a way to cross-index. Reading and re-reading the text helps ensure that the data are correctly categorized.

Figure 13.1 displays the labeling of one open-ended question on an end-of-session questionnaire. In this example, all 21 responses were numbered and given a label to capture the idea(s) in each comment. Later, they can be sorted and organized into their categories in an effort to identify patterns and bring meaning to the responses for Question 5.

Step 4: Identify Patterns and Connections Within and Between Categories

As you organize the data into categories and subcategories—either by question or by case—you will begin to see patterns and connections both within and between the categories. Assessing the relative importance of different themes or highlighting subtle

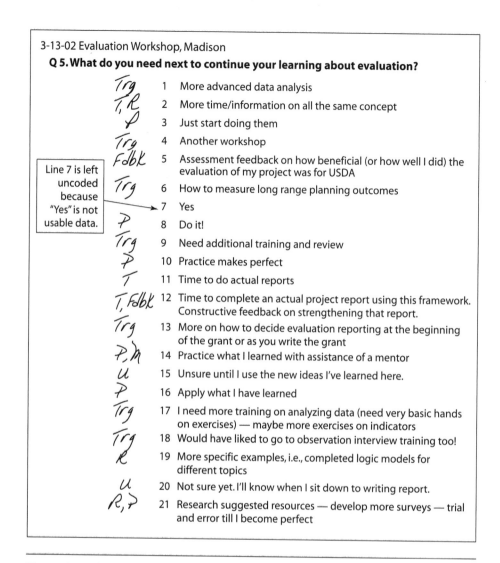

Figure 13.1 Labeling data from an end-of-session questionnaire.

variations may be important to your particular analysis. The following are some ways to do this.

Within Category Description

You may be interested in summarizing the information pertaining to one theme, or capturing the similarities or differences in people's responses within a category. To do this, you need to assemble all the data pertaining to the particular theme (category). What are the key ideas being expressed within the category? What are the similarities and differences in the way people responded, including the subtle variations? It is helpful to write a summary for each category that describes these points.

Larger Categories

You may wish to create larger super categories that combine several categories. You can work up from more specific categories to larger ideas and concepts. Then you can see how the parts relate to the whole.

Relative Importance

To show which categories appear more important, you may wish to count the number of times a particular theme comes up or the number of unique respondents who refer to certain themes. These counts provide a very rough estimate of relative importance. They are not suited to statistical analyses, but they can reveal general patterns within the data.

Relationships

You also may discover that two or more themes occur together consistently in the data; that is, whenever you find one, you find the other. For example, youth with divorced parents may consistently list friendship as the primary benefit of a mentoring program. You may decide that some of these connections suggest a cause and effect relationship or create a sequence through time. For example, respondents may link improved school performance to a good mentor relationship. From this, you might argue that good mentoring causes improved school performance.

Such connections are important to look for, because they can help explain why something occurs. But be careful about simple cause and effect interpretations. Seldom is human behavior or narrative data so simple. Ask yourself: How do things relate? What data support this interpretation? What other factors may be contributing to this relationship? You may wish to develop a table or matrix to illustrate relationships across two or more categories. You need to look for examples of responses or events that run counter to the prevailing themes. What do these countervailing responses suggest? Are they important to the interpretation and understanding of the data? Often, you learn a great deal from looking at and trying to understand items that do not fit into your categorization scheme.

Step 5: Interpretation—Bringing It All Together

Use your themes and connections to explain your findings. It is often easy to get sidetracked by the details and the rich descriptions within the data. But what does it all mean? What is really important within the data?

This is what we call interpreting your data—attaching meaning and significance to your analysis. A good place to start is to develop a list of key points or important findings you discovered as a result of categorizing and sorting your data. Stand back and think about what you have learned. What are the major lessons? What new things did you learn? What findings have application to other settings, programs, and future evaluation studies? What will those who use the results of the evaluation be most interested in knowing? Too often, we list an evaluation's findings without synthesizing them and tapping their meanings.

You will need to develop an outline for presenting your results to other people or for writing a final report. The length and format of your report will depend on your audience. It is often helpful to include quotes or descriptive examples to illustrate your points and bring the data to life. A visual display might help communicate the findings.

Sometimes a diagram with boxes and arrows can help show how all the pieces fit together, such as the program and logic models presented in Boxes 2.3 and 3.2. Creating such a model may reveal gaps in your investigation and connections that remain unclear. These may be areas where you can suggest further study.

"NUTS AND BOLTS" OF NARRATIVE ANALYSIS

Moving from a mass of words to a final report requires a method for organizing and keeping track of the text. This is largely a process of cutting and sorting. You can work by hand, with a hardcopy (print copy) or directly on the computer. Exactly how you manage the data depends on your personal preferences and the amount and type of qualitative data you have.

Data Management Tips

Check Your Data

Often, there are data from multiple respondents, multiple surveys, or documents. Make sure you have everything together. Decide whether your data are of sufficient quality to analyze, and what level of investment is warranted.

Add ID Numbers

Add an identification (ID) number to each questionnaire, respondent, group, or site.

Prepare Data for Analysis

You may need to transcribe taped interviews. How complete to make your transcription depends on your purpose and resources. Sometimes, you may make a summary of what people have said and analyze that. Or certain parts of an interview may be particularly useful and important and just those sections may be transcribed. Other times, you will want to have every word of the entire interview transcribed. Transcription is time-consuming, so be sure both data quality and your use of the data are worth the investment.

With small amounts of narrative data, you may work directly from the original hardcopy. However, text is usually typed into a computer software program such as Microsoft Word, Word Perfect, or Excel. You may decide to use a relational database management program such as ACCESS or a special qualitative data analysis software program such as, AskSam, Atlis/ti, Ethno 2, Ethnograph v.5.08, HyperRESEARCH v.2.06, N6 (formally NUD*IST), NVIVO, PolyAnalyst v.4.6, VisualText v.1.7, or XSIGHT, to name just a few on the market today.

Your decision on which one to use will depend on the size of your narrative data set, the resources available, your preferences, and the level of analysis needed or warranted. You will need to decide whether you will enter all responses question by question, or whether you want to keep all text concerning one case, individual, group, or site together (see Step 2). Save the file. If you type the data into a word processing program, it is helpful to leave a wide margin on the left so you have space to write labels for text and any notes you want to keep. Number each line to help with cutting and sorting later.

Make Copies

Make a copy of all your data (hardcopy and electronic files). This gives you one copy to work from and another for safekeeping.

Identify the Source of All Data

As you work with the data, you will need to keep track of the source of the information or the context of the quotes and remarks. Such information may be critical to the analysis. Make sure you have a way to identify the source of all the data, such as by individual, site, and date.

Think about what information to keep with the data. For example, you might use identifiers to designate the respondent, group, site, county, date, or other sources information. Or you may wish to sort by variables such as age, gender, or position. Will you want to compare and contrast by demographic variables, sites, and dates? These identifiers stay with the data as you cut and sort them, either by hand or by the computer. If you are working with hardcopies, you might use different colors of paper to color code responses from different people or groups (e.g., Krueger, 1998).

Mark Key Themes

Read through the all narrative text very carefully and look for key themes. Use abbreviations or symbols (codes) to tag key themes—ideas, concepts, beliefs, incidents, terminology, or behaviors. Or you might give each theme a different color. Keep notes of emerging ideas or patterns and how you are interpreting the data. You can write or type these in the margins or in a specified column. It is important to keep a separate notebook that records your thoughts and observations about the data as you look for themes (Figure 13.2).

Define Categories

Organize or combine related themes into categories. Name (label) these categories by using your own descriptive phrases or choose words and key phrases from the text. Be clear about what each category stands for. Would someone unfamiliar with the data understand the label you have chosen for your categories? Write a short description or definition for each category and provide examples or quotes from the

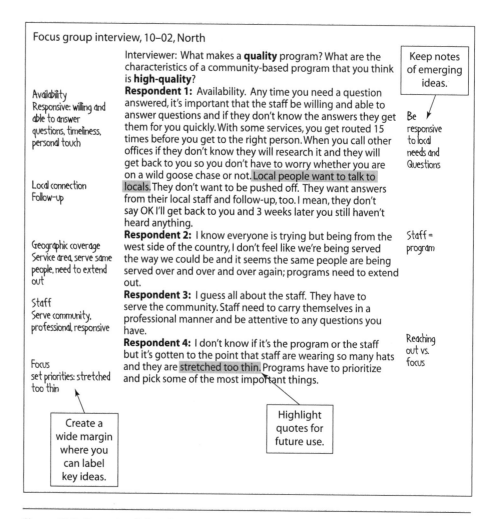

Figure 13.2 Example of identifying themes and labeling data.

text that illustrates the category's meaning. You may also describe what each category does not include to clarify what is does include.

Cut and Sort

Defining the categories within the data and appropriately labeling them involves some form of cutting and sorting. This is a process of selecting sections of data and putting them together in their respective categories.

Hardcopy. A simple method is to cut text out of the printed page and sort all of it into different piles. Each pile represents a category and has a name. As you work with the data, you may make new piles, combine piles, or divide piles into subcategories. Remember to keep the identifier (source of data) with the data so that you know where the text originally came from. Also, remember that you should be working with a copy of your narrative data, not with the original material.

Electronic Copy. It is relatively simple and fast to move text around in a word processing program using the Windows platform. You can cut and paste text into different windows, each representing a single category. If you type the category label directly into the computer file, you can use the search function to gather chunks of text together to copy and paste. Or you can separate the text into paragraphs, code the beginning of each paragraph, and then sort the paragraphs. You may prefer to use Excel. If the data are in Microsoft Word, you can easily transfer them to Excel. Set up an Excel file that includes columns for the ID number, identifiers, categories (themes), codes, and text (Figure 13.3).

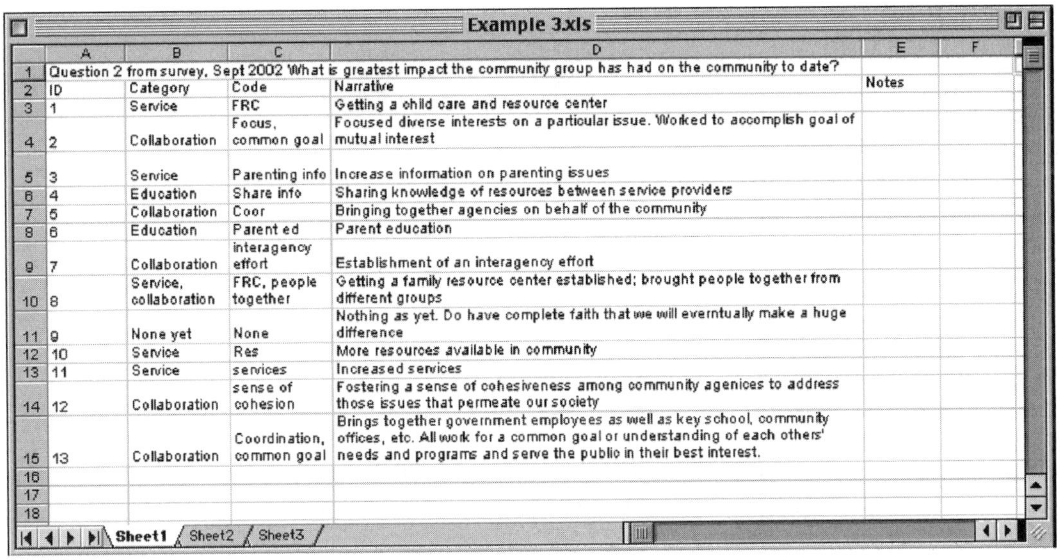

	A	B	C	D	E	F
1	Question 2 from survey, Sept 2002 What is greatest impact the community group has had on the community to date?					
2	ID	Category	Code	Narrative	Notes	
3	1	Service	FRC	Getting a child care and resource center		
4	2	Collaboration	Focus, common goal	Focused diverse interests on a particular issue. Worked to accomplish goal of mutual interest		
5	3	Service	Parenting info	Increase information on parenting issues		
6	4	Education	Share info	Sharing knowledge of resources between service providers		
7	5	Collaboration	Coor	Bringing together agencies on behalf of the community		
8	6	Education	Parent ed	Parent education		
9	7	Collaboration	interagency effort	Establishment of an interagency effort		
10	8	Service, collaboration	FRC, people together	Getting a family resource center established; brought people together from different groups		
11	9	None yet	None	Nothing as yet. Do have complete faith that we will everntually make a huge difference		
12	10	Service	Res	More resources available in community		
13	11	Service	services	Increased services		
14	12	Collaboration	sense of cohesion	Fostering a sense of cohesiveness among community agenices to address those issues that permeate our society		
15	13	Collaboration	Coordination, common goal	Brings together government employees as well as key school, community offices, etc. All work for a common goal or understanding of each others' needs and programs and serve the public in their best interest.		
16						
17						
18						

Figure 13.3 Screen image of an Excel spreadsheet.

Be sure to keep identifiers attached to all sections of your data. Keep enough text together so that you can make sense of the words in their context. As you cut and move data, text can easily become fragmented and lose its contextual meaning. Be sure to include enough surrounding text so that the meaning is not open to misinterpretation. When data do not seem to fit, place those in a separate file for possible use later.

Make Connections

Once you have sorted the data, you now need to think about how the categories fit together and relate to one another. What seems more important or less important? Are there exceptions or critical cases that do not seem to fit? You will need to consider **alternative explanations** and explore paradoxes, conflicting themes, and evidence that seems to challenge or contradict your interpretations.

To trace connections, you can spread note cards across a table, use sticky notes on walls, or draw diagrams on newsprint showing the categories and relationships. Another approach is to create a two-dimensional or three-dimensional matrix. List the categories along each axis, and fill the cells with corresponding evidence or data (for further explanation, see Patton, 1990). You can use simple hand tabulations or a computer program to (1) search and count the frequency a particular topic occurs or how often one theme occurs with another, and (2) keep track of how many respondents touch on different themes. Such counts may be illuminating and indicate relative importance. But treat them with caution, particularly when responses are not solicited the same way from all respondents or not all respondents provide a response.

ENHANCING THE PROCESS

As with any data analysis process, bias can influence your results. Consider the following ways to increase the credibility of your data analysis and hence your evaluation findings.

Use Several Sources of Data

As we know from Chapter 10, using different **data sources** can help you check your findings. For example, you might combine one-on-one interviews with information from focus groups and an analysis of written material on the topic. If the data from these different sources point to the same conclusions or converge, you will have more confidence in your results.

Alternative explanation

A hypothesis that is a plausible alternative to the research hypothesis and might explain the results as well or better; a hypothesis involving extraneous or intervening variables other than the independent variable in the research hypothesis; also referred to as an alternative hypothesis.

Data source

The provider of the data, whether it be primary (the original source) or secondary (an intermediary between the research participant and the researcher analyzing the data).

PART III Gathering Data and Making Decisions

Track Your Choices

As we have said before, your results will be more credible if others understand how you came to your conclusions. Thus, keep a **journal** or notebook of how you came to your decisions during the analysis process to help others follow your reasoning. Document your reasons for the focus you took, the category labels you created, the revisions to the categories you made, and any observations you noted concerning the data as you worked with the text.

People tend to see and read only what supports their interest or point of view. Everyone sees data through their own lens and filters, so it is important to recognize and pay attention to this. Your analysis process should be documented so that another person can see the decisions that you made, how you did the analysis, and how you arrived at the interpretations from your analysis.

Involve Others

Getting feedback and input from others can help you with your analysis and interpretation. You can involve others in the entire analysis process or in any one of the steps. For example, several people or one other person might review the data independently to identify themes and categories. Then you can compare categories and resolve any discrepancies in meaning.

You can also work with others in picking out important lessons once the cutting and sorting has been done. Or you can involve others in the entire analysis process, reviewing and discussing the data and their meaning, arriving at major conclusions, and presenting the results. Involving others may take more time, but often this results in a better analysis and greater ownership of the results.

PITFALLS TO AVOID

Finally, keep in mind the following cautions: (1) avoid **generalizing,** (2) choose quotes carefully, and (3) address limitations and alternative explanations.

Avoid Generalizing

The goal of the qualitative research approach is not to generalize across a population. Rather, it seeks to provide an understanding from the respondent's perspective. It tries to answer the questions "What is unique about this individual, group, situation, or issue? Why?" Even when you include an open-ended question on a mailed survey, for example, you are seeking insight and differences, the individual's own

Journal
A written record of the process of an interpretive research study. Journal entries are made on an ongoing basis throughout the study and include study procedures as well as the researcher's reactions to emerging issues and concerns during the data analysis process.

Generalizing results
Extending or applying the findings of a research study to individuals or situations not directly involved in the original research study; the ability to extend or apply the findings of a research study to subjects or situations that were not directly investigated.

perspective and meaning. Thus, the focus is always on the individual's own unique response. Narrative data provide clarification, understanding, and explanation, not generalizations.

Choose Quotes Carefully

Using quotes can lend valuable support to data interpretation, but they should never be used selectively to only support the argument or illustrate success. This can lead to using people's words out of context or editing quotes to exemplify a point. When putting together your final report, think about the purpose for including quotes. Do you want to show the differences in people's comments, give examples of a typical response relative to a certain topic, or highlight your success? In any event, specify why you chose the quotes. Include enough of the text to allow the reader to decide what the respondent is trying to convey.

Confidentiality and anonymity are also concerns when using direct quotes. Even if you do not give the person's identity, others may be able to tell who made the remark. You always need to consider the consequences of including certain quotes. Are they important to your analysis and interpretation? Do they provide a balanced viewpoint? You will need to obtain people's permission to use their words. Check with others about the usefulness and value of the quotes you select to include.

Address Limitations and Alternative Explanations

Every evaluation study has limitations. Presenting the problems or limitations you had while collecting and analyzing your data will help others better understand how you arrived at your conclusions. Similarly, it is important for you to address possible alternative explanations. What else might explain the results? Show how the evidence, via your analysis, supports your interpretation.

SUMMING UP AND LOOKING AHEAD

This chapter presented a very brief discussion of how to analyze qualitative data. Working with qualitative data is a rich and enlightening experience. The more you practice, the easier and more rewarding it becomes. As both a science and an art, it involves critical, analytical thinking and creative, innovative perspectives (Patton, 1990). The following chapter discusses how to make decisions from data generated via a program evaluation.

Box 13.1 Looking at It All Together

One thing is for certain—all of the formative and summative data that you collect can quickly add up, even for a small program. What does it all tell you? How can you use it to judge your programs? How can you present it to your board, your funders, the community, and others who might have a stake in your efforts?

Looking for Themes

As part of the documentation and *formative evaluation,* you will have accumulated some important information that can help you make sense of things. Reviewing the data periodically as it accumulates has several advantages: It helps you to begin to identify themes; it makes the analysis process less intimidating than if you wait until all of the data have been collected; and most importantly, it enables you to use the results to improve your program.

Your first step in *data analysis* will be to look for recurring themes. As you review data from documents, observations, interviews, and surveys, some ideas will occur more often than others. Learning to recognize these patterns and their relevancy as they emerge in each of these formats is crucial to your evaluation. These key themes are what you must capture in your evaluation report.

What is the most important thing to remember when interpreting and reporting your data? The *intermediate indicators* and *final program outcomes* that you defined at the beginning of your program! Framing your thinking and your results in those terms can help you to understand and present your data clearly.

Be Flexible

In your review of formative data, you may discover key issues other than the ones you originally thought to examine when you designed your evaluation. It is important to be flexible enough to explore these unexpected issues, within the limits of your resources.

Be sure to note new ideas, different patterns or themes, and questions that need further investigation. Interview or observation guides and surveys can be adjusted over time in response to what you learn through the review and interpretation of your formative data. Here is an example of how you must be flexible when collecting data.

During the summer camps for middle school students and their mentors, *Youth Action Today!* found that parental support and involvement was particularly strong this year. Unlike previous years, program staff actually had the luxury of selecting volunteers from a pool of over 20 parents who had agreed to help. The staff originally planned to survey all parents as part of their evaluation. However, when they noticed the increase in parental support this year, they changed their evaluation plan to include interviews. The staff decided to conduct interviews with a *sample* of parents to get more in-depth information on what prompted their involvement in the program this year.

Putting It Together

Once you have taken the trouble to collect data from a variety of sources (students, staff, parents, or others), it is important to look at all of these perspectives together to get a full picture of your program. The various pieces of the evaluation (formative and summative) and each *data collection* activity (*document review, observations, interviews,* and *surveys*) all add up to tell you about the quality and success of your program. Looking at all of this evidence together and considering it in terms of your *objectives* will enable you to say with some accuracy whether your program achieved what you intended.

The amount of time that you can devote to this process will depend on the level of resources available to your community based organization (CBO). For example, a small CBO may just do a quick review of interview notes to get the main points; a CBO with extensive resources and staff might do a more in-depth analysis—summarizing each interview in writing, developing charts that compare the responses of different groups of people, and writing up common themes that emerge from the interviews.

Working With What You've Got . . . Again

In some cases, interpreting the data you collect may require some additional expertise. For example, science

(continued)

Box 13.1 (continued)

or mathematics content may play a central role in some program activities, so having knowledge in these areas may help with the analysis of student misconceptions about certain topics.

In a case like this, you might want to discuss your observations or share observation notes with someone who has this expertise and can help shed light on your descriptions of student questions or discussions. (Better yet, have such persons do the observations.) In a larger CBO, there may be individuals on staff who can help. If you do not have this expertise on staff, you might look to your board members or volunteers who may bring these skills to your organization.

Telling the Story: How to Report Your Evaluation Results

Interpreting your evaluation data for in-house use can be done informally, but making it available and useful to others requires a more polished product. Formal evaluation reports can provide information to your board members, the community, and your funders about the program's progress and success. Portions of these reports can also be a valuable public relations tool. When distributed to newspapers or other media, this information can increase community awareness and support for your organization's programs. Here are several things you will want to include in your evaluation report:

- The objectives of your program and your targeted audience.
- What data you collected for your evaluation and how they were collected.
- The evaluation results in terms of program *goals* and *objectives*.
- The plan for using the evaluation to improve the program.

In addition to these pieces, you will want to include a description of the context in which your program occurs. This might consist of a brief summary of *needs assessment* data, the demographic and socioeconomic characteristics of the community and your program participants, and documentation of the level of impact (such as the number of young people served compared with the number of youth in the community). Your report should also highlight tactics you used to attract your targeted audience as well as other strategies to ensure that your program was well implemented. Here are some tips to help you tell your program's story:

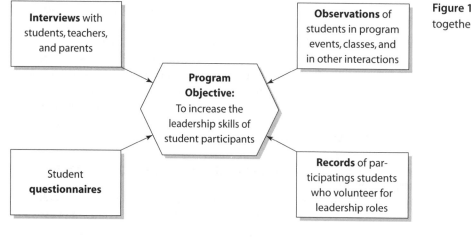

Figure 1 Looking at it all together.

Interviews with students, teachers, and parents

Observations of students in program events, classes, and in other interactions

Program Objective: To increase the leadership skills of student participants

Student **questionnaires**

Records of participatings students who volunteer for leadership roles

- *Know your audience.* A report for a funder will look different from an in-house summary.
- *Leave the jargon at home.* Be straightforward and clearly state your major findings.
- *Blend the presentation of quantitative and qualitative data.* Quotes from relevant persons interspersed with tables and graphs illustrating quantitative data (numbers or percents) make the report more readable and strengthen your summary of the data.
- *Be honest.* Your report will be considerably more credible if you note both the strengths and weaknesses of your program.

Presenting your data simply and concisely can help your audience get a clear and accurate picture of your program. For example, it is unlikely that you would include long excerpts from interviews in your report (although these might be included in an appendix). Instead, pick a few powerful, short quotes that really make your point and sprinkle them throughout your summary or analysis of other data.

Another strategy is to include a brief description of a particularly effective program activity. Blending your qualitative data, such as quotes from interviews or descriptions from observations, with your quantitative data from surveys is a useful way to report your evaluation results. Simple charts, tables, and graphs that show how many students participated or what percent demonstrated changes after the program can help illustrate the impact of your program (see Chapter 12).

RECAP AND ONLINE MATERIALS

In this chapter, you learned how to analyze qualitative data.

You should also recall the concept of qualitative data analysis from your foundational research course. If not, go online to take a free crash course in qualitative data analysis.

You can also find the following materials online to help you master the concepts you just learned:

- Chapter Outline
- Learning Objectives
- Key Terms and Concepts
- Flash Cards
- Practice Multiple-Choice Tests
- Essay Questions with Answers
- Links

www.oup.com/us/swevaluation

STUDY QUESTIONS

1. In your own words, discuss the commonalities and differences between analyzing and displaying quantitative data (discussed in the previous chapter) and qualitative data.
2. Discuss how quantitative data and qualitative data differ. Discuss how the two types of data can be collected in one evaluation study.

3. Discuss when it is more appropriate to gather quantitative data for a program evaluation study than qualitative data. Use a common social work example throughout your discussion.

4. List and describe in detail the steps you would need to go through to gather and analyze qualitative data derived from a program evaluation study. Use one common social work example throughout your discussion.

5. List and discuss the major process you could use to enhance the qualitative data analysis process. Use one common social work example throughout your discussion.

6. List and discuss the major pitfalls you need to avoid when analyzing qualitative data that were derived from a program evaluation study. Use one common social work example throughout your discussion.

7. Through the Internet, locate a social work evaluation study that reported qualitative data of some kind. Discuss how the author(s) used the concepts of this chapter to analyze the data presented. Would you have done it differently? Why or why not?

8. Discuss how you would go about doing a program evaluation study that would collect quantitative data (discussed in the previous chapter) and qualitative data (this chapter) at the same time.

9. Using your answer to Question 8, show how you would display the quantitative data and qualitative data that you collected and analyzed.

10. Discuss the steps you would need to go through when you identify the patterns and connections within and between categories with a qualitative data set. Use one common social work example throughout your discussion.

References, Further Reading, and Resources

Barone, T. (2001). Science, art, and the predispositions of educational researchers. *Educational Researcher, 30*(7), 24–28.

Barone, T., & Eisner, E. (1997). Arts-based educational research. In R. M. Jaegar (Ed.), *Complementary methods for research in education* (2nd ed., pp. 75–116). Washington, DC: American Educational Research Association.

Berk, R. A., & Rossi, P. H. (1999). *Thinking about program evaluation* (2nd ed.). Thousand Oaks, CA: Sage.

Bruner, J. (1986). *Actual minds, possible worlds.* Cambridge, MA: Harvard University Press.

CDC EZ-Text. (2000, August 14). Retrieved January 2, 2006, from Behavioral Intervention Research Branch, Divisions of HIV/AIDS Prevention, National Center for HIV, STD, and TB Prevention, Centers for Disease Control & Prevention Web site: Web site: http://www.cdc.gov/hiv/software/ez-text.htm

Clandinin, D. J., & Connelly, M. (2000). *Narrative inquiry: Experience and story in qualitative research.* San Francisco, CA: Jossey-Bass.

Coffey, A., & Atkinson, P. (1996). *Making sense of qualitative data.* Thousand Oaks, CA: Sage.

Datta, L. E. (1994). Paradigm wars: A basis for peaceful coexistence and beyond. *New Directions for Program Evaluation, 61,* 53–71.

Denzin, N. K. (1989). *Interpretive interactionism.* Newbury Park, CA: Sage.

Denzin, N. K., & Lincoln, Y. S. (Eds.). (2000). *Handbook of qualitative research* (2nd ed.). Thousand Oaks, CA: Sage.

Fetterman, D. M., (1996). Empowerment evaluation: An introduction to theory and practice. In D. M. Fetterman, S. Kaftarian, & A. Wandersman (Eds.), *Empowerment evaluation: Knowledge and tools for self-assessment and accountability.* Thousand Oaks, CA: Sage.

Greene, J. C., & Abma, T. A. (Eds.). (2001). *Responsive evaluation. New directions for evaluation* (Vol. 92). San Francisco, CA: Jossey-Bass.

Guba, E. G., & Lincoln, Y. S. (1989). *Fourth generation evaluation.* Thousand Oaks, CA: Sage.

Karlsson, O. (2001). Critical dialogue: Its value and meaning. *Evaluation, 7,* 211–227.

Krueger, R. A. (1988). *Focus groups: A practical guide for applied research.* Thousand Oaks, CA: Sage.

Krueger, R. A. (1998). *Analyzing and reporting focus group results.* Thousand Oaks, CA: Sage.

Kuhn, T. S. (1962). *The structure of scientific revolutions.* Chicago: University of Chicago Press.

Kushner, S. (2000). *Personalizing evaluation.* London: Sage.

Kvale, S. (1996). *InterViews.* Thousand Oaks, CA: Sage.

Lincoln, Y., Thorp, L., & Russon, C. (2002). *The storied nature of agriculture and evaluation: A conversation.* Paper presented at the annual meeting of the American Evaluation Association, Arlington, VA.

MacNeil, C. (2002). *The politics of narrative: Realizing, re-presenting, and re-authoring=re-form.* Paper presented at the annual meeting of the American Evaluation Association, Arlington, VA.

Maxwell, J. A. (2002). Understanding and validity in qualitative research. In A. M. Huberman, & M. B. Miles (Eds.), *The qualitative researcher's companion* (pp. 37–64). Thousand Oaks, CA: Sage.

Mayer, R. A. (2001). Resisting the assault on science: The case for evidence-based reasoning in educational research. *Educational Researcher, 30*(7), 29–30.

McCollum, E., & Callahan, J. (2002). *Understanding changes in sense of self in a leadership development program: The narrative assessment interview.* Paper presented at the annual meeting of the American Evaluation Association, Arlington, VA.

Miles, M. B., & Huberman, A. M. (1994). *Qualitative data analysis: An expanded sourcebook* (2nd ed.). Thousand Oaks, CA: Sage.

Mohr, L. B. (1999). The qualitative method of impact analysis. *American Journal of Evaluation, 20*(1), 69–84.

Murphy, E., Dingwall, R., Greatbatch, D., Parker, S., & Watson, P. (1998). Qualitative research methods in health technology assessment: A review of literature. *Health Technology Assessment, 2*(16), 1–274.

Patton, M. Q. (1990). *Qualitative evaluation and research methods* (2nd ed.). Thousand Oaks, CA: Sage.

Patton, M. Q. (1997). *Utilization-focused evaluation* (3rd ed.). Thousand Oaks, CA: Sage.

Patton, M. Q. (2003). *Qualitative evaluation checklist.* Retrieved January 2, 2006, from http://www.wmich.edu/evalctr/checklists/qec.pdf

Polkinghorne, D. (1997). Reporting qualitative research as practice. In W. G. Tierney & Y. S. Lincoln (Eds.), *Representation and the text: Re-framing the narrative voice* (pp. 3–21). Albany, NY: SUNY Press.

Ratcliff, D. (2002). *Qualitative research, Part five: Data analysis.* Retrieved February 20, 2006, from http://don.ratcliffs.net/qual/5.htm

Reichardt, C. S., & Rallis, S. F. (1994). Qualitative and quantitative inquiries are not incompatible: A call for a new partnership. *New Directions for Program Evaluation, 61,* 85–91.

Rose, D. S., & Davidson, E. J. (2003). Overview of program evaluation. In J. E. Edwards, J. C. Scott,

& N. S. Raju (Eds.), *The human resources program evaluation handbook* (pp. 3–26). Thousand Oaks, CA: Sage.

Santos, J., Reynaldo A., Mitchell, D., & Pope, P. (1999, August). Are open-ended questions tying you in knots? *Journal of Extension, 37*(4). Retrieved February 20, 2006, from http://www.joe .org/joe/1999august/iw2.html

Scriven, M. (1993). *Hard-won lessons in program evaluation.* San Francisco, CA: Jossey-Bass.

Stake, R. (1987). Program evaluation, particularly responsive evaluation [keynote address at the conference "New Trends in Evaluation," Institute of Education, University of Goteborg, Sweden, 1973]. In G. F. Madaus, M. Scriven, & D. Stufflebeam (Eds.), *Evaluation models: Viewpoints on educational and human services evaluation.* Boston: Kluwer-Nijhoff.

Stake, R. (1995). *The art of case study research.* Thousand Oaks, CA: Sage.

Tutty, L. M., Rothery, M., & Grinnell, R. M. (Eds.). (1996) *Qualitative research for social workers: Phases, steps, and tasks.* Boston: Allyn & Bacon.

Van Maanen, J. (1988). *Tales of the field: On writing ethnography.* Chicago: University of Chicago Press.

Making Decisions With Data 14

I deally, all professional decisions should be arrived at via a rational process based on the collection, synthesis, and analysis of relevant, objective, and subjective **data.** Objective data are obtained by an explicit measurement process that, when carefully followed, reduces bias and increases the data's objectivity. Subjective data, on the other hand, are obtained from impressions and judgments which, by their very nature, incorporate the values, preferences, and experiences of the individuals who make them.

It is our position that objective data *when combined with* subjective data offer the best basis for decision making. The best practice and program relevant decisions are made when we understand the advantages and limitations of both objective and subjective data and are able to combine the two as appropriate to the circumstances.

OBJECTIVE DATA

The main advantage of using objective data when making decisions is in the data's precision and objectivity. At the **program** level, for example, an **agency** may receive funding to provide an employment skills training program for minority groups such as our Aim High Program described in Chapter 8. If appropriate data are kept, it is easy to ascertain to what degree the eligibility requirement is being met, and it may be possible to state, for example, that 85 percent of service recipients are in fact from minority groups.

Data
Isolated facts, presented in numerical or descriptive form, on which client or program decisions are based; not to be confused with information.

Program
An organization that exists to fulfill some social purpose; must be logically linked to the agency's goal.

Agency
A social service organization that exists to fulfill a broad social purpose; it functions as one entity, is governed by a single directing body, and has policies and procedures that are common to all of its parts.

Without objective data, the subjective impressions of community members, staff members, funders, and program participants would be the sources of the data. Individuals may use descriptors such as "most," "many," or "a large number" to describe the proportion of minority people served by the employment skills training program. Obviously, such subjective judgments are far less precise than objective data and they are also subject to biases.

Objective data, however, are not without their own limitations. Among these are

- Some variables are difficult to measure objectively.
- Data may be uncertain or ambiguous, allowing conflicting interpretations.
- Objective data may not take all pertinent contextual factors into account.

Although considerable progress has been made in recent years in the development of **standardized measuring instruments,** not all variables of conceivable interest to social workers are convenient and feasible to measure. Thus, objective data may not be available to guide certain practice and program decisions. In the same vein, even if a variable can be measured, data collection plans may not call for its measurement—or the measurement may have been omitted for any of a variety of reasons that arise in day-to-day professional activity. Consequently, objective data are not always available to guide practice and program decision making.

Where objective data are available, their meaning and implications may not always be clear. At the **case** level, a series of standardized measures intended to assess a 10-year-old's self-esteem may yield no discernable pattern. It would thus be difficult, on the basis of such objective data alone, to make decisions about further interventions and services. At the program level, objective data may indicate that, over a three-month period, people participating in a weight-loss program lose an average of five pounds per person. Although the results seem favorable, the average weight loss is not very great, making it unclear whether the program should be continued as is, or whether modifications should be considered.

Finally, objective data seldom provide contextual information—although the context relating to them is important in their interpretation. In the example of our weight-loss program, the average five-pound loss would probably be considered inadequate if the clientele were known to be a group of people who, for medical reasons, needed to lose an average of sixty pounds each. On the other hand, if the clientele were known to be a group of skiers preparing for the ski season, the program could be considered quite successful.

Subjective Data

Although it might seem desirable to base all decisions on logically analyzed objective data, such information on all factors affecting a given practice or program decision is seldom available. Consequently, objective data are often supplemented by

Standardized measuring instrument

A professionally developed measuring instrument that provides for uniform administration and scoring and generates normative data against which later results can be evaluated.

Case

The basic unit of social work practice, whether it be an individual, a couple, a family, an agency, a community, a county, a state, or a country.

more subjective types of data, such as the workers' impressions, judgments, experiences, and intuition.

As human beings, we assimilate subjective data continuously as we move through our daily life; competent social work professionals do the same, noting the client's stance, gait, gestures, voice, eye movements, and set of mouth, for example. At the program level, an administrator may have a sense of awareness of staff morale, history and stage of development of the organization, external expectations, and the ability of the organization to absorb change. Seldom are any of these subjective data actually measured, but all of them are assimilated. Some subjective data are consciously noted; some filter through subconsciously and emerge later as an impression, opinion, or intuition. Clearly, such subjective data may considerably influence case and program decision making.

At the case level, for example, perceptions, judgments, and intuition—often called clinical impressions—may become factors in decision making. A worker may conclude, based on body language, eye contact, and voice, that a client's self-esteem is improving. Further case-level decisions may then be based on these subjective impressions.

At the program level, objective data may suggest the need to modify the program in the face of inadequate results. The administrator, however, may put off making any modifications on the basis of a subjective judgment that, because several other program changes had recently been implemented, the team's ability to absorb any more changes is limited. To the extent that subjective data are accurate, such a decision is entirely appropriate.

The main limitation of subjective data, however, is that impressions and intuition often spring to the mind preformed, and the process by which they were formed cannot be objectively examined. By their nature, subjective data are susceptible to distortion through the personal experience, bias, and preferences of the individual. These may work deceptively, leaving workers unaware that the subjective data upon which they are relying actually distort the picture.

In reality, case-level and program-level decision making uses a blend of objective and subjective data. Together, the two forms of data have the potential to provide the most complete information upon which to base decisions. Ultimately, the practitioner will have to use judgment in reconciling all relevant sources of data to arrive at an understanding of the situation. In building an accurate picture, it is important not only to consider all sources of data but also to be aware of the strengths and limitations of each of these sources. Quality case and program decisions are usually the result of explicitly sifting through the various sources of data and choosing those sources in which it is reasonable to have the most confidence under the circumstances.

Having considered decision making in general, we now turn to an examination of the specifics of the process at the case and program levels.

If high-quality case-level decisions are to be reached, the social worker should know what types of decisions are best supported by objective data and what types will likely require the use of subjective data.

A helping relationship with a client is a process that passes through a number of phases and follows logically from one to the next. There are essentially four phases: (1) the engagement and problem-definition phase, (2) the practice objective setting phase, (3) the intervention phase, and (4) the termination and follow-up phase. In practice, these phases are not likely to follow a clear sequence. Engagement, for example, occurs most prominently at the beginning of the professional relationship, but it continues in some form throughout the entire helping process. Problem definition is logically the first consideration after engagement, but if it becomes evident during intervention that the client's problem is not clearly understood, the problem-definition and objective-setting phases will have to be readdressed. Nevertheless, discernible phases do exist. The following describes how case-level decisions can be made in each phase.

The Engagement and Problem-Definition Phase

Suppose a married couple, Mr. and Ms. Wright, come to a family service agency to work on their marriage problems and have been assigned to a worker named Maria. From Ms. Wright's initial statement, the problem is that her partner does not pay enough attention to her. In Maria's judgment, Ms. Wright's perception is a symptom of yet another problem that has not been defined. The client's perception, however, is a good starting point, and Maria attempts to objectify Ms. Wright's statement: In what ways, precisely, does her partner not pay enough attention to her? Ms. Wright obligingly provides data: Her partner has not gone anywhere with her for the past three months, but he regularly spends three nights a week playing basketball, two nights with friends, and one night at his mother's.

Mr. Wright, protestingly brought into the session, declares that he spends most nights at home and the real problem is that his partner constantly argues. Further inquiry leads Maria to believe that Mr. Wright spends more nights away from home than he reports but fewer than his partner says; Ms. Wright, feeling herself ignored, most likely is argumentative; and the underlying problems are actually poor communication and unrealistic expectations on the part of both.

A host of other problems surfaced subtly during the interview and cannot be addressed until the communications problem is solved; communication, therefore, should be the initial target of the intervention—the first practice objective.

A second practice objective could be to reduce the Wrights' unrealistic expectations of each other. Let us consider that the Wrights have these two practice objectives that are specifically geared toward the **program objective,** "to increase their marital satisfaction." Maria believes that the attainment of the two practice objectives will increase the Wrights' marital satisfaction—the main purpose for which they are seeking services. Remember, the Wrights want a happier marriage (that is why they sought out services); they did not seek out help with their dysfunctional communication patterns and unrealistic expectations of one another. Thus, to increase their marital satisfaction becomes the program objective, and communications and expectations become the two practice objectives.

So far, Maria's conclusions have been based on her own impressions of the conflicting data presented by the Wrights. Unless the problem is straightforward and concrete, the engagement and problem-definition phase often depends more on the worker's subjective judgment, experience, and intuition than it does on objective data. Even when standardized measuring instruments are used to help clients identify and prioritize their problems, the choice of the problem to be first addressed will largely be guided by the worker's subjective intuition and judgment. Once intuition has indicated what the problem might be, however, the magnitude of the problem can often be measured with more objectivity through the use of standardized measuring instruments.

In the Wrights' case, Maria has tentatively decided to formulate a practice objective of increasing the Wrights' communication skills. To confirm that communication skills are problematic, she asks Mr. and Ms. Wright to independently complete a 25-item standardized measuring instrument designed to measure marital communications skills. The instrument contains such items as "How often do you and your spouse talk over pleasant things that happen during the day?" with possible responses of "very frequently," "frequently," "occasionally," "seldom," and "never." This instrument has a range of 0 to 100, with higher scores showing better communication skills. It has a clinical cutting score of 60, indicating effective communications above that level, and it has been tested on people of the same socioeconomic group as the Wrights and may be assumed to yield valid and reliable data.

The introduction of the measuring instrument at this stage serves two basic purposes. First, the scores will show whether communication is indeed a problem and to what degree it is a problem for each partner. Second, the scores will provide a **baseline** measurement that can be used as the first point on a graph in whatever case-level design Maria selects.

The Practice Objective Setting Phase

In the Wrights' case, the program objective is to increase their marital satisfaction. Thus, a related practice objective (one of many possible) is to increase the couple's communication skills to a minimum score of 60, the clinical cutting score on the standardized measuring instrument. The practice objective setting phase in this example

Program objective
A statement that clearly and exactly specifies the expected change, or intended result, for individuals receiving program services. Qualities of well-chosen objectives are meaningfulness, specificity, measurability, and directionality. Program objectives, like practice objectives can be grouped into affects, knowledge, and behaviors. Not to be confused with program goal.

A phase
In case-level evaluation designs, a phase (A Phase) in which the baseline measurement of the target problem is established before the intervention (B Phase) is implemented.

Baseline
A period of time, usually three or four data collection periods, in which the level of the client's target problem is measured while no intervention is carried out; designated as the A Phase in single-system designs (case-level designs).

thus relies heavily on objective data: It is framed in terms of a change from very in-effective communication (score of 0) to very effective communication (score of 100).

The same process applies in cases where the standardized measuring instrument selected is less formal and precise. Maria, for example, may ask each partner to complete a self-anchored rating scale indicating his and her level of satisfaction with the degree of communication achieved. The scoring range on this instrument could be from 1 to 6, with higher scores indicating greater levels of satisfaction and lower scores indicating lesser levels of satisfaction. If Mr. Wright begins by rating his satisfaction level at 3 and Ms. Wright indicates hers at 2, the practice objective chosen may be to achieve a minimum rating of 4 for each partner. Here again, practice objective setting is based on objective data collected at the beginning of Maria's intervention.

The Intervention Phase

The selection of the intervention strategy itself will be based on objective and subjective data only to a limited degree. Perhaps Maria has seen previous clients with similar practice objectives and also has objective evidence, via the professional literature, that a specific treatment intervention is appropriate to use in this specific situation. But even though the intervention is chosen on the basis of data accumulated from previous research studies and past experience, each intervention is tailored to meet the needs of the particular client system, and decisions about strategy, timing, and its implementation are largely based on subjective data—the worker's experience, clinical judgment, and intuition.

Objective data may play only one part in the selection of an intervention strategy, but once the strategy is selected, its success is best measured on the basis of consistently collected objective data. Ideally, objective data are collected using a number of different standardized measures. In the Wrights' case, for example, the scores from repeated administrations of the standardized instrument that measures the degree of communication will comprise one set of objective data for one particular practice objective.

Frequency counts of specifically selected behaviors may comprise another set: for example, a count of the number of conversations daily lasting at least five minutes, or the number of "I" statements made daily by each partner. The self-anchored rating scale, described in the previous section, could be a third source of data. These sets of data together provide considerable information about whether, and to what degree, progress is being made.

Maria is also likely to come to a more global opinion about how the couple are doing in regard to their communication patterns. This opinion will be based on a variety of observations and impressions formed as she works with the couple. The process by which such an opinion is formed is intuitive and—depending on the worker's skill, experiences, and the circumstances—may be quite accurate. The method by which it is arrived at, however, is idiosyncratic and is, therefore, of unknown validity and reliability. For this reason, relying on clinical impressions exclusively is inadvisable.

On the other hand, objective measures may have their own problems of validity and reliability. The best course is a middle one: Determination of a client's progress should be based on a combination of objective data *and* subjective data. Where objective and subjective data point in the same direction, Maria can proceed with considerable confidence that she has a clear and accurate picture of her clients' progress. Where objective and subjective data diverge, Maria should first attempt to determine the reasons for the difference and ensure that she has a good understanding of her clients' problems and needs. When Maria is satisfied that she has an accurate grasp of her client system's progress, she is ready to proceed to decisions about the most appropriate treatment intervention to use.

These decisions are guided by changes in the practice objective. Three patterns of change are possible: (1) deterioration, or no change; (2) insufficient, or slow change; and (3) satisfactory change.

Deterioration, or No Change

Suppose that Ms. Wright scored a 40 on the first administration of the standardized measuring instrument that measures the degree, or level, of communication patterns. Then she scores a 41 on the second, a 43 on the third, and a 42 on the fourth (Figure 14.1). Mr. Wright scores 50, 51, 53, and 52, respectively. How would Maria analyze and interpret such data?

First, Maria will want to consider what the other available sources of data indicate. Let us assume that, on the self-anchored communication satisfaction scale, Ms. Wright still rates her satisfaction at 2 and that, during the sessions, she avoids eye contact with Mr. Wright and tries to monopolize the worker's attention with references to "he" and "him." In this situation, the data all seem to point to the same conclusion: There has been virtually no change or progress. Under such circumstances, it is reasonable to place considerable reliance on the data contained in Figure 14.1.

As Figure 14.1 also indicates, the slope of the line connecting the measurement points is virtually flat—that is, it is stable, indicating neither improvement nor deterioration. Moreover, the level of the problem is well below the desired minimum score of 60. Such data would normally lead Maria to conclude that a change in the intervention is warranted—resulting in a *BC* design.

Here, qualitative considerations may also enter the case-level decision-making process. Maria, for example, may be aware of disruptions in the lives of Mr. and Ms. Wright. Perhaps Mr. Wright received a lay-off notice from his job during the second week of the intervention. Maria may now need to consider whether the effects of the intervention might not have been counteracted by these adverse circumstances. Ultimately, she will need to decide whether to continue the intervention in the hope

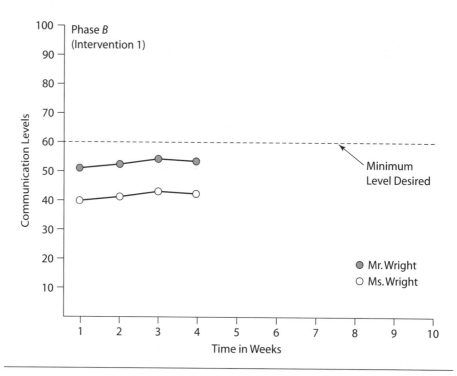

Figure 14.1 *B* design: The Wrights' communication levels over time, indicating no change.

that, once the couple have dealt with the shock of the impending lay-off, the intervention will begin to have the desired effect.

It is also possible that the intervention is known to have a delayed impact. This characteristic could have been determined from the professional literature or from Maria's previous experience with using the intervention. Under such circumstances it may, again, be reasonable to maintain the intervention for some time longer and see whether movement toward the practice objective begins.

How long it is sensible to continue an intervention in the absence of documented progress is a matter best left to Maria's and the couple's judgment. As long as there is reason to believe that an intervention may yet have the desired impact, it is justified to pursue that intervention. If there is no evidence of change for the better, however, the intervention will need to be changed. Note that data will provide objective evidence supporting the need for a change in the intervention, but they will not indicate what future intervention strategies might be used instead. Formulation of a new intervention strategy will again call upon Maria's and her clients' judgment.

Insufficient, or Slow Change

Insufficient or slow change is a familiar scenario in the social services. A gradual but definite improvement in the communication scores may be noted, indicating that Mr. and Ms. Wright are slowly learning to communicate. Their relationship continues to deteriorate, however, because their communication scores are still below 60—the minimum level of good communication; progress needs to be more rapid if the marriage is to be saved.

In general, many clients improve only slowly, or improve in spurts with regressions in between. The data will reflect what is occurring—what the problem level is, and at what rate and in what direction it is changing. No data, however, can tell a worker whether the measured rate of change is acceptable in the particular client's circumstances. This is an area in which subjective clinical judgment again comes into play.

The worker may decide that the rate of change is insufficient, but just marginally so; that is, the intervention is successful on the whole and ought to be continued, but at a greater frequency or intensity. Perhaps the number of treatment sessions can be increased, or more time can be scheduled for each session, or more intensive work can be planned. In other words, a B design will now become a B_1B_2 design (Figure 14.2). Or, if baseline data have been collected, an AB design will become an AB_1B_2 design. If, on the other hand, the worker thinks that intensifying the intervention is unlikely to yield significantly improved results, a different intervention entirely may be adopted. In this case, the B design will become a BC design (Figure 14.3), or the AB design will become an ABC design.

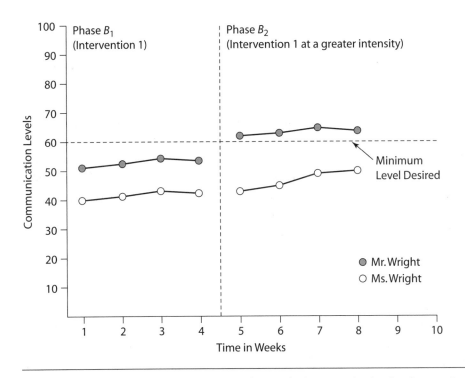

Figure 14.2 B_1B_2 changing intensity design: The Wrights' communication levels over time, indicating insufficient change at B_1 followed by a more intensive B_2.

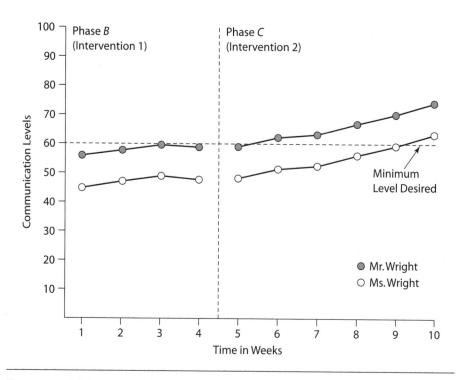

Figure 14.3 *BC* design: The Wrights' communication levels over time, indicating insufficient change at the *B* intervention followed by a *C* intervention.

Sometimes improvement occurs at an acceptable rate for a period and then the client reaches a plateau, below the desired minimal level; no further change seems to be occurring. The data will show the initial improvement and the plateau (Figure 14.4), but they will not show whether the plateau is temporary, whether it is akin to a resting period, or whether the level already achieved is as far as the improvement will go. Again, this is a matter for clinical judgment. The worker and client system may decide to continue with the intervention for a time to see if improvement begins again. The exact length of time during which perseverance is justified is a judgment call. If the client system remains stuck at the level reached beyond that time, the worker and client system will have to decide whether to apply the intervention more intensively, try a new intervention, or be content with what has been achieved.

Satisfactory Change

Frequently objective data will show an improvement. At times the improvement will be steady and sustained, and at other times an overall trend of improvement will be punctuated with periods of plateau or even regression. This latter scenario is illustrated in Figure 14.5. Essentially, continuation of the treatment intervention is justified by continuing client progress, although Maria may wish at times to make minor modifications in the intervention.

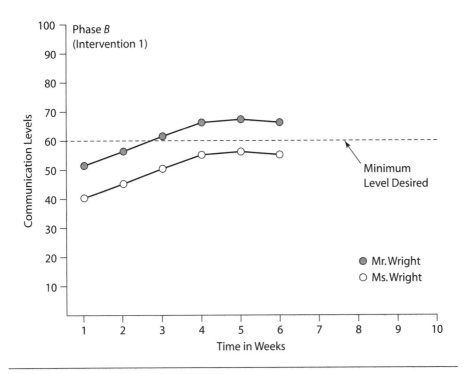

Figure 14.4 *B* design: The Wrights' communication levels over time, indicating an initial improvement leveling off to a plateau.

It is important to keep in mind that not all case-level designs permit the worker to conclude that the intervention has caused the change for the better. With many designs that are likely to be used in the monitoring of social work interventions, it is possible to conclude only that the client's practice objective has changed for the better. This is the situation in the *B* design shown in Figure 14.4 where Mr. Wright has obtained communication scores over 60 but Ms. Wright has yet to reach the minimum acceptable level of 60. From a service perspective, however, evidence that Mr. and Ms. Wright are improving is sufficient justification for continuing the intervention; it is not necessary to prove that the intervention is causing the change.

When the data show that a client has reached the program or practice objective, the worker will, if possible, initiate a maintenance phase, perhaps gradually reducing the frequency of contact with a view to service termination but also trying to ensure that the gains achieved are not lost. If other practice objectives need to be resolved, the maintenance phase for one objective may coincide with the baseline or intervention phase for another. It is quite possible to engage in a number of case-level designs at the same time with the same client; because client practice objectives are usually interrelated, data obtained in one area will often be relevant to another.

The maintenance phase is important, ensuring that the practice objective really has been satisfactorily resolved. Assume that data show a steady improvement, culminating at a point above the target range (as in Figure 14.3). One measurement below

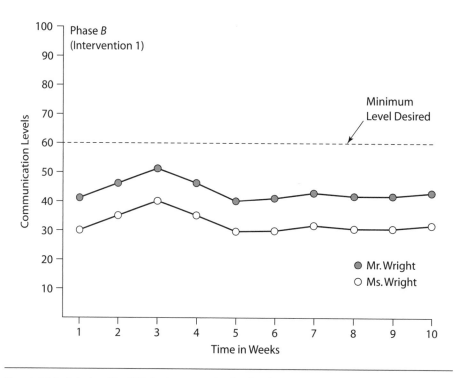

Figure 14.5 *B* design: The Wrights' communication levels over time, indicating some improvement with periods of plateaus and regressions.

the minimum desired level means only that the practice objective was not at a clinically significant level when that measurement was made. Subsequent measurements may show that a significant problem still exists. A number of measurements are required before Maria can be confident that the practice objective has stabilized at the desired level. Similarly, where the trend to improvement included plateaus and regressions, measurements must continue beyond the achievement of the practice objective to ensure that the objective has indeed stabilized in the desired level and direction.

The Termination and Follow-Up Phase

Once it is decided that the program objective (not the practice objective) has been accomplished, the next step is termination and follow-up. The termination decision is straightforward, in theory: When the data show that the program objective has been achieved via the attainment of practice objectives, and the objective level is stable, services can be terminated. In reality, however, other factors need to be taken into account, such as the number and type of support systems available in the client's social environment and the nature and magnitude of possible stressor events in the client's life. We must carefully weigh all these factors, including information yielded by objective and subjective data, in making a decision to end services.

Ideally, the follow-up phase will be a routine part of the program's operations. Many social work programs, however, do not engage in any kind of follow-up activities, and others conduct follow-ups in a sporadic or informal way. If the program does conduct routine follow-up, decisions will already have been made concerning how often and in what manner the client should be contacted after the termination of services. If no standardized follow-up procedures are in place, we will have to decide whether follow-up is necessary and, if so, what form it should take.

Data can help decide whether a follow-up is necessary. If data reveal that a client has not reached a program objective, or has reached it only marginally, a follow-up is essential. If data show a pattern of improvement followed by regression, a follow-up is also indicated to ensure that regression will not occur again.

The follow-up procedures that measure program objectives may be conducted in a number of ways. Frequently used approaches include contacting former clients by letter or telephone at increasingly longer intervals after the cessation of services. A less frequently used approach is to continue to measure the program objectives that were taken during the intervention period. As services to the Wrights are terminated, Maria could arrange to have them each complete, at monthly intervals, the Marital Satisfaction Scale (the measure of the program objective). Maria could mail the scale to the Wrights, who, because they have already completed it during the course of the intervention, should have no problem doing so during follow-up. The inclusion of a stamped, self-addressed envelope can further encourage them to complete this task. In this manner, Maria can determine objectively whether marital satisfaction gains made during treatment are maintained over time.

At a minimum, collecting program-level data (not case-level data) during follow-up results in a *BF* design, as illustrated in Figures 14.6 and 14.7. If an initial baseline phase had been used, the result would be an ABF design. Where follow-up data indicate that client gains are being maintained, a situation illustrated in Figure 14.6, termination procedures can be completed. Where follow-up data reveal a deterioration after termination, as illustrated in Figure 14.7, Maria is at least in a position to know that her clients are not doing well. Under such circumstances, complete termination is not warranted. Instead, Maria should consider whether to resume active intervention, provide additional support in the clients' social environment, or offer some other service. The follow-up data will not help Maria to decide what she should do next, but they will alert her to the need to do something.

It should be noted that Figures 14.6 and 14.7 provide data for marital satisfaction scores and do not represent the couple's communication scores, as in Figures 14.1 through 14.5. This is because follow-up data are concerned only with program objectives (in this case, marital satisfaction), not practice objectives (in this case, communication and expectations of one another).

One other point needs to be clarified. All standardized measuring instruments do not measure their variables in the same way when it comes to what their high and

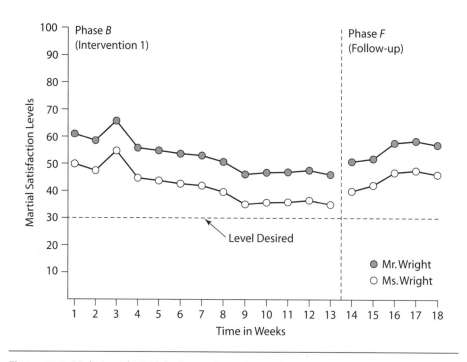

Figure 14.6 *BF* design: The Wrights' marital satisfaction levels during treatment (*B*) and after termination (*F*), indicating maintained improvement after termination.

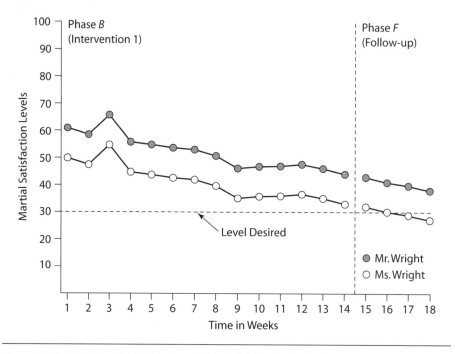

Figure 14.7 *BF* design: The Wrights' marital satisfaction levels during treatment (*B*) and after termination (*F*), indicating a deterioration after termination.

low scores mean. For example, high scores on some instruments indicate there is more of a "problem" being measured than lower scores on the same instrument. For example, see Figures 14.6 and 14.7, where higher the score, the worse their marital satisfaction. Thus, we try to get our clients' scores *below* the clinical cutting score of 30, where the lower the score, the better.

Some instruments are scored exactly the opposite, where higher scores indicate the "problem" is less present than lower scores. For example, see Figures 14.1 through 14.5, where the higher the score, the better the communication. We try to get our clients' scores *above* the clinical cutting score of 60, where the higher the score, the better. All of this can be very confusing to novice and expert alike. It is always necessary to know exactly how each standardized measuring instrument is scored and what the scores mean.

PROGRAM-LEVEL DECISION MAKING

The primary purpose of the monitoring approach at the program level is to obtain feedback on the program in an ongoing manner so that the services provided can be continually developed and improved.

In the first instance, the program may be assessed with regard to the achievement of process objectives. Process objectives are analogous to facilitative practice objectives; their achievement makes it more likely that program objectives will also be achieved. In a sense, they speak to the effectiveness and efficiency of the service operation. Process objectives, for example, might address the type of clientele to be served, indicating that a minimum of 75 percent should come from minority backgrounds.

Or these objectives could speak to the length of waiting lists, specifying that no one should have to wait longer than two weeks before the commencement of services. Other process objectives could deal with the number of continuing education hours provided to staff members, premature termination of cases, service hours provided, and similar other matters.

The actual program objectives may be assessed in various ways. Success rates may vary with problem type. A particular social service program, for example, may achieve good success with children who have family-related problems but less success with children whose problems are primarily drug related. Or perhaps desirable results are achieved with one type of client but not another: A drug rehabilitation program may be more successful with adults than it is with adolescents. Or, again, a particular program within an agency may achieve its program objectives better than another program within the same agency. A child welfare agency, for example, may successfully operate an adolescent treatment foster-care program but have less success with its adolescent group-care program. If several residential programs are operated, one may achieve its program objectives to a higher degree than another.

Finally, the agency must be considered as a whole. How successful is it when all of its programs are assessed together? What might be done on a general organizational level to improve the agency's effectiveness and efficiency?

A picture of results can be readily achieved through the collection and analysis of objective and subjective data. The kinds of data collected and analyses performed will depend on the program being considered. This section begins with a few words about process evaluation and then deals in detail with outcome evaluation.

Process

Usually, data can be readily gathered on matters of interest in a process evaluation as discussed in Chapter 6. Collecting data, for example, on the demographic characteristics of clients, the length of time spent on waiting lists, the types of services provided, and the total number of hours of each is a relatively straightforward matter. In the monitoring approach, these and similar data are collected continuously and analyzed on a regular basis. Reports available to staff members make clear to what degree process objectives are being met. Process objectives usually pertain to good and desirable practices that are thought to lead to desired results.

Outcome

Outcomes can be classified into three nonmutually exclusive areas: (1) problems and cases, (2) program, and (3) agency.

Problems and Cases

As we know, many social service agencies offer services to people with a variety of needs: pregnant teens, disabled seniors, preadolescents with self-esteem problems, couples seeking help with their marriages, and people who are trying to stop smoking. The agency will be interested in knowing, and is usually required by funders to document, to what degree its programs are helping people with particular types of social problems.

The results achieved by any one client, satisfactory or not, do not say much about the general effectiveness of the program as a whole. Program effectiveness is determined only by examining data from groups of clients, often using simple aggregation methods.

Assume, for example, that during a six-month period of a smoking cessation program, the program served 80 clients, 40 male and 40 female. Using the case-level monitoring techniques previously described, data will be available showing the number of cigarettes smoked by each client at the beginning and at the end of the intervention.

Table 14.1 Average Number of Cigarettes Smoked at the Beginning and End of the Smoking Cessation Program (*N* = 80)

Beginning	−	After	=	Difference
34		11		23

Aggregating the individual client results indicates that the average number of cigarettes smoked daily at the beginning of the intervention was 34, and the average number smoked at the end of the program was 11. Thus, the clients smoked, on average, 23 fewer cigarettes after they completed the stop-smoking program. These aggregated data, after analysis, provide a method of assessing the outcome of the program. The aggregated data and the results of the analysis for all 80 clients are presented in Table 14.1.

The analysis presented in Table 14.1 is a simple one—the calculation of the difference between the beginning and ending average number of cigarettes smoked. The analysis could be extended to determine whether this difference might have come about by chance alone. This is what is meant by the term "statistical significance." Detailed treatment of statistical procedures is beyond the scope of this text but is readily available in any introductory statistics book such as the Weinbach and Grinnell text (2007).

To return to our example, the decline in smoking can be documented as a net change of 23 cigarettes, on average, per client. Although the data available in this situation permit documentation of the program's objective, or outcome, it is not possible to attribute this change to the intervention. The particular evaluation design used was the one-group pretest–posttest design, and as we know, it does not support inferences about causality. Nevertheless, this type of design enables staff members to document the overall results of their services.

Further analyses of these data may provide additional and more specific information. Suppose, for example, that program staff had the impression that they were achieving better results with female smokers than with male smokers. Examining the results of males and females as separate groups would permit a comparison of the average number of cigarettes each group smoked at the end of the program. The data for this analysis are presented in Table 14.2. Note that the average number of cigarettes smoked at the beginning of the program was exactly the same for the males and females, 34. Thus, it could be concluded that there were no meaningful differences between the males and females in reference to the average number of cigarettes they smoked *at the start* of the intervention.

As Table 14.2 shows, at the end of the program males smoked an average of 18 cigarettes daily and females an average of 4 cigarettes. On average, then, females smoked 14 fewer cigarettes per day than did males. Essentially, this analysis confirms workers' suspicion that they were obtaining better results with female smokers than with male smokers.

Table 14.2 Average Number of Cigarettes Smoked at the Beginning and End of the Smoking Cessation Program by Sex ($N = 80$)

Sex	Beginning	−	After	=	Difference	n
Males	34		18		16	40
Females	34		4		30	40
Totals	34		11		23	80

The information obtained via the simple analysis presented above provides documentation of outcomes, a vitally important element in this age of accountability and increased competition for available funding. There is, however, a further advantage to compiling and analyzing evaluation data. By conducting regular analyses, social work administrators and workers can obtain important feedback about program strengths and weaknesses. These data can be used to further develop services. The data discussed above, for example, may cause the services to be modified in ways that would improve effectiveness with male clients while maintaining effectiveness with female clients. This would not only improve services to the male client group but would also boost overall program outcomes.

Program

As we know from Chapter 3, a program is a distinct unit, large or small, that operates within an agency. An agency, for example, may comprise a number of treatment programs, or a child welfare agency may operate a treatment foster-care program and a residential child abuse treatment program as part of its operations. The residential program itself may comprise a number of separate homes for children of different ages or different problem types.

These programs should be evaluated if the agency as a whole is to demonstrate accountability and provide the best possible service to its clientele. A thorough evaluation will include attention to needs, process, and outcomes as well as efficiency. Because the greatest interest is often in outcome, however, this section focuses on outcome evaluation (see Chapter 7), where the question is, "To what degree has a program succeeded in reaching its program objectives?"

If this question is to be answered satisfactorily, the program's objectives must be defined in a way that allows them to be measured (see Chapter 9). Let us assume that one of the objectives of the residential child abuse treatment program is to enable its residents to return to their homes. The degree of achievement of this program objective can be determined through simple math: What percentage of the residents returned home within the last year?

If the agency includes several programs of the same type, in different locations, lessons learned from one can be applied to another. In addition, similar programs will likely have the same program objectives and the same ways of measuring them so that results can be aggregated to provide a measure of effectiveness for the entire agency. If the programs are dissimilar—for example, a treatment foster-care program and a victim-assistance program—aggregation will not be possible, but separate assessment of program outcomes will nevertheless contribute to the evaluation of the agency as a whole.

Agency

An outcome evaluation, whether in respect to an agency, a program, or a case, always focuses on the achievement of objectives. How well has the agency fulfilled its mandate? To what degree has it succeeded in meeting its goal, as revealed by the measurement of its program objectives? Again, success in goal achievement cannot be determined unless the agency's programs have well-defined, measurable program objectives that reflect the agency's mandate.

As seen in Chapter 3, agencies operate on the basis of **mission statements,** which often consist of vaguely phrased, expansive statements of intent. The mission of a sexual abuse treatment agency, for example, may be to ameliorate the pain caused by sexually abusive situations and to prevent sexual abuse in the future. Although there is no doubt that this is a laudable mission, the concepts of pain amelioration and abuse prevention cannot be measured until they have been more precisely defined.

This agency's mandate may be to serve persons who have been sexually abused and their families living within a certain geographical area. If the agency has an overall goal, "to reduce the trauma resulting from sexual abuse in the community," for example, the mandate is reflected and measurement is implied in the word "reduce." The concept of trauma still needs to be operationalized, but this can be accomplished through the specific, individual practice objectives of the clients whose trauma is to be reduced: The primary trauma for a male survivor may be fear that he is homosexual, whereas the trauma for a nonoffending mother may be guilt that she failed to protect her child.

If logical links are established between the agency's goal, the goals of the programs within the agency, and the individual practice objectives of clients served by the program, it will be possible to use the results of one to evaluate the other. Practice objective achievement at the case level will contribute to the success of the program, which will in turn contribute to the achievement of the agency's overall goal.

Mission statement

A unique written philosophical perspective of what an agency is all about; states a common vision for the organization by providing a point of reference for all major planning decisions.

USING OUTCOME MONITORING DATA IN PROGRAM-LEVEL DECISION MAKING

Just as a program outcome for any client may be acceptable, mixed, or inadequate, evaluation results can also be acceptable, mixed, or inadequate, reflecting the degree to which its program objectives have been achieved.

Acceptable Results

Before a result can be declared "acceptable," it is necessary to define clearly what counts as an acceptable result for a specific program objective. Let us return to the example of the residential program, where one of the program's objectives included enabling residents to return home: If 90 percent of residents succeed in making this move within six months of entry into the program, has the program's objective been achieved to an acceptable degree? What if 80 percent of residents return home within six months and a further 10 percent return home within a year? Or suppose that 100 percent return home within six months but half of the adolescents are eventually readmitted to the program.

Evidently, an acceptable result is largely a matter of definition. The program administrators and funders must decide what degree of objective achievement can reasonably be expected given the nature of the problems, the resources available, and the results of similar programs. Are the results for the smoking cessation program, for example, shown in Tables 14.1 and 14.2, indicative of success? If the program comprises a number of subprograms, the same considerations apply with regard to each. Defining criteria for success should be done in advance of obtaining results, to avoid politicizing the results and to make it possible to set relevant program objectives.

Once the standards for an acceptable level of achievement have been set, evaluation becomes a matter of comparing actual outcomes against these standards. Where standards are met, program personnel can, with some degree of confidence, continue to employ existing procedures and practices. If a monitoring approach to evaluation is used and outcomes are analyzed on a regular basis, workers will be able to see not only whether program objectives are being achieved to an acceptable degree but also whether the level of achievement is rising or falling. Any persistent trend toward improvement or decline is worth investigating so that more effective interventions and processes can be reinforced and potential problems can be detected and resolved.

Mixed Results

Occasionally, the results of an outcome evaluation will show that the program is achieving its objectives only partially. A program may be successful in helping one group of clients, for example, but less successful with another. This was the situation in the smoking cessation program mentioned previously: Female clients were being helped considerably, but male clients were obtaining much less impressive results (see Table 14.2). Similarly, an evaluation may reveal seasonal variations in outcomes: At certain times of the year a program may achieve its program objectives to an acceptable degree, but not at other times. Clients in farming communities, for instance, may be able to participate in the program in the winter more easily than during the growing season, when they are busy with the tasks of farming. This factor alone may result in reduced achievement at both the case and program levels. It is also possible that one program within an agency is achieving its objectives to a greater degree than another similar program.

In such situations, staff members will undoubtedly wish to adjust practices and procedures so that the underperforming components can be upgraded. In making any adjustments, however, care must be taken not to jeopardize those parts of the operation that are obtaining good outcomes. In the case of the smoking cessation program, for example, the workers may be tempted to tailor several sessions more to the needs of male clients. Although this may indeed improve the program's performance with male clients, the improvement may come at the expense of effectiveness with females.

A preferable strategy might be to form separate groups for males and females during some parts of the program, leaving the program unchanged for female clients but developing new sessions for male clients to better meet their needs. Of course, it is impossible to predict in advance whether changes will yield the desired results, but ongoing monitoring will provide feedback about their efficacy.

Inadequate Results

One of the strengths of a program-level monitoring system is that it takes into account the entire program process, from intake to follow-up. A low level of program objective achievement is not necessarily attributable to the interventions used by the workers with their clients. It is possible that the problem lies in inappropriate eligibility criteria, unsatisfactory assessment techniques, inadequate staff training, or a host of other factors, including unforeseen systematic barriers to clients' involvement in the program.

If an outcome evaluation shows that results are unsatisfactory, further program development is called for. To diagnose the problem or problems, the program administrator and workers will want to examine data concerning all the stages that lead up to intervention as well as the intervention process itself. Once they have ideas about the reasons for suboptimal performance, usually obtained by process evaluations (see Chapter 6), they are in a position to begin instituting changes to the program's procedures and practices—and monitoring the results of those changes.

SUMMING UP AND LOOKING AHEAD

One of the most important reasons for monitoring is to obtain timely data on which further decisions about intervention plans or program development can be based. At the case level, the worker will continually monitor changes in the client problem; at the program level, data relating to needs, processes, and outcomes can help staff make informed decisions about program modifications and changes.

This chapter is the last chapter in Part III of our book. This chapter, along with the five preceding ones, discussed how you can collect and analyze quantitative and qualitative data from various data sources and use these data in management information systems where you then can make decisions from them.

The next part, Part IV, presents the contexts of the evaluation enterprise by concentrating on ethical (Chapter 15) and culturally appropriate (Chapter 16) evaluation practices along with a final chapter on writing grant proposals (Chapter 17).

RECAP AND ONLINE MATERIALS

In this chapter, you learned how to make decisions with data.

You should also recall the concept of single-subject designs from your foundational research course. If not, go online to take a free crash course in single-subject designs.

You can also find the following materials online to help you master the concepts you just learned:

- Chapter Outline
- Learning Objectives
- Key Terms and Concepts
- Flash Cards
- Practice Multiple-Choice Tests
- Essay Questions with Answers
- Links

www.oup.com/us/swevaluation

STUDY QUESTIONS

1. Explain the difference between empirical and subjective data. In your own words, briefly outline the limitations of empirical data. Compare your list with those identified in this chapter. In your own words, briefly outline the limitations of subjective data. Compare your list with those identified in this chapter. What is meant by the phrase "garbage in, garbage out" in monitoring evaluations? What suggestions can you offer for workers to avoid the "garbage in, garbage out" scenario?

2. Suppose a worker intuitively feels that her client is at risk for experiencing more serious episodes of loneliness. What suggestions can you offer to assist the worker in obtaining empirical data to support her subjective conclusion? What is meant by the "clinical significance" of data? How does the clinical significance of data affect decision making for social service workers? What options for program

development might an administrator have when program results prove to be inadequate? What ethical considerations must be addressed?

3. In groups of four, agree on a social service problem and the criteria for client termination. Identify four different methods of measuring the problem that will assist you in deciding whether or not the client is ready for termination. To what degree will the information obtained from each of these methods be consistent? Will the decision to terminate client services tend to rely more on empirical or subjective data? Present your findings to the class.

4. In groups of five, develop a hypothetical social service program, complete with a mission statement, a goal, objectives, activities, and measurements of the program objectives. Choose an exploratory design to monitor and appraise case-level client outcomes, and identify the type of data to be collected for various practice objectives. Suppose the data obtained indicate mixed results. What adjustments would you make to the interventions to increase client success? Review your list of adjustments and prioritize them according to order of implementation. Present your discussion to the class.

5. Social service decision making is based upon two different types of data. What are they? As you briefly describe each type, explain how they guide the decision-making process. What are the advantages of using empirical data in decision making? Justify your response. Be specific and clear. Use a social service example throughout your discussion. What are the limitations of using empirical data in decision making? Justify your response. Be specific and clear. Use a social service example throughout your discussion. Under what conditions do workers use subjective data in decision making? When is the use of subjective data useful to the decision-making process? Justify your response. Be specific and clear. Use a social service example throughout your discussion. Identify and discuss the major drawback to using subjective data in decision making. Justify your response. Be specific and clear. Use a social service example throughout your discussion.

6. How do practitioners make decisions at the case level? How are the highest quality decisions reached? Justify your response. Be specific and clear. Use a social service example throughout your discussion.

7. You are currently working with a client named Jennifer who wants to lose weight. You also see her mother, Irene, who is having problems with her boss at work. What types of decisions do you make with each of these clients in the engagement and problem definition phase of intervention? On what types of data are these decisions based? Justify your response. Be specific and clear. Define a practice objective for Irene. To what degree does this phase rely on empirical data? Justify your response. Be specific and clear. In what ways are your intervention strategies with clients like Jennifer and Irene based on empirical data? Justify your response. Be specific and clear. How would your success with Irene be measured on the basis of consistently collected data? On what basis should you determine Irene's progress? Justify your response. Be specific and clear. You

realize your intervention decisions regarding Irene are based of her progress and your interpretation of her progress. How would you interpret a deterioration or no change in Irene as she works toward her practice objective? How would you interpret an insufficient or slow change in Irene's progress? Justify your response. Be specific and clear. What kind of data would you take into account when deciding when Irene's case should be terminated? How can data aid your decision about whether to follow up with Irene? Justify your response. Be specific and clear.

8. What is the purpose of using a monitoring approach to quality improvement at the program level? How can program progress be assessed? Justify your response. Be specific and clear. What kinds of data must be collected and analyzed when measuring the outcomes of a particular program? How is an evaluation of program outcomes conducted? Justify your response. Be specific and clear. Use a social service example throughout your discussion.

9. Suppose a program-level evaluation indicated *acceptable* results. How would such a result affect staff and administrative behavior? Justify your response. Be specific and clear. Use a social service example throughout your discussion. Suppose a program-level evaluation indicated *mixed* results. How would such a result affect staff and administrative behavior? Justify your response. Be specific and clear. Use a social service example throughout your discussion. Suppose a program-level evaluation indicated *inadequate* results. How would such a result affect staff and administrative behavior? Justify your response. Be specific and clear. Use a social work example throughout your discussion.

10. In your own words, discuss in depth why program objectives are measured at follow-up and not practice objectives. What is the rationale behind this? What are the limitations of follow-up data if practice objectives are not being measured? Under what circumstances would the measurement of practice objectives be justified for follow-up data? Justify your answer. Use one common social service example throughout your discussion.

REFERENCES, FURTHER READING, AND RESOURCES

On Social Work Decision Making

Alter, C., & Murty, S. (1997). Logic modeling: A tool for teaching practice evaluation. *Journal of Social Work Education, 33*(1), 103–117.

Au, C. (1994). The status of theory and knowledge development in social welfare administration. *Administration in Social Work, 18*(3), 27–57.

Austin, D. M. (2002). *Human services management: Organizational leadership in social work practice.* New York: Columbia University Press.

Bridges, E. M. (1992). *Problem-based learning for administrators.* Eugene, OR: ERIC Clearinghouse on Educational Management.

Brody, R. (2000). *Effectively managing human service organizations* (2nd ed.). Thousand Oaks, CA: Sage.

Edwards, R., Yankey, J. A., & Altpeter, M. A. (Eds.). (1998). *Skills for effective management of nonprofit organizations.* Washington, DC: NASW Press.

Fleming, N. D. (2001). *Teaching and learning styles: VARK strategies.* Christchurch, NZ: Author.

Ginsberg, L., & Keys, P. (Eds.). (1995). *New management in human services* (2nd ed.). Washington, DC: NASW Press.

Kettner, P. (2002). *Achieving excellence in the management of human service organizations.* Boston: Allyn & Bacon.

Lewis, J., Lewis, M., Packard, T., & Soufflee, F. (2001). *Management of human service programs* (3rd ed.). Belmont, CA: Brooks/Cole.

Lohmann, R. A., & Lohmann, N. (2002). *Social administration.* New York: Columbia University Press.

Mayers, R. S., Souflee, F., & Schoech, D. J. (1994). *Dilemmas in human services management: Illustrative case studies.* New York: Springer.

Menefee, D. T. (2000). What managers do and why they do it. In R. Patti (Ed.), *The handbook of social welfare management* (pp. 247–266). Thousand Oaks, CA: Sage.

Menefee, D. T., & Thompson, J. J. (1994). Identifying and comparing competencies for social work management: A practice-driven approach. *Administration in Social Work, 18*(3), 1–25.

Patti, R. (Ed.). (2000). *The handbook of social welfare management.* Thousand Oaks, CA: Sage.

Rapp, C., & Poertner, J. (1992). *Social administration: A client-centered approach.* New York: Longman.

Skidmore, R. A. (1995). *Social work administration: Dynamic management and human relationships* (3rd ed.). Boston: Allyn & Bacon.

Unrau, Y. A., Gabor, P. A., & Grinnell, R. M., Jr. (2001). *Evaluation in the human services* (3rd ed.). Belmont, CA: Wadsworth.

Weinbach, R. W. (1998). *The social worker as manager: A practical guide to success* (3rd ed.). Boston: Allyn & Bacon.

Whetten, D. A., & Cameron, K. M. (2002). *Developing management skills* (5th ed.). Upper Saddle River, NJ: Prentice Hall.

On Measuring Your Practice and Program Objectives

Bloom, M., Fischer, J., & Orme, J. (2006). *Evaluating practice: Guidelines for the accountable professional* (5th ed.). Boston: Allyn & Bacon.

Bostwick, G., & Kyte, N. S. (2005). Measurement. In R. M. Grinnell, Jr., & Y. A. Unrau (Eds.), *Social work research and evaluation: Quantitative and qualitative approaches* (7th ed., pp. 98–111). New York: Oxford University Press.

Corcoran, K. J., & Fischer, J. (2007). *Measures for clinical practice: Vol. 1. Couples, families, and children* (4th ed.). New York: Oxford University Press.

Corcoran, K. J., & Fischer, J. (2007). *Measures for clinical practice: Volume 2. Adults* (4th ed.). New York: Oxford University Press.

Nugent, W. R., Sieppert, J. D., & Hudson, W. W. (2001). *Practice evaluation for the 21st century.* Belmont, CA: Brooks/Cole.

Jordan, C., Franklin, C., & Corcoran, K. (2005). Measuring instruments. In R. M. Grinnell, Jr., & Y. A. Unrau (Eds.), *Social work research and evaluation: Quantitative and qualitative approaches* (7th ed., pp. 114–131). New York: Oxford University Press.

McDowell, I., & Newell, C. (1996). *Measuring health.* New York: Oxford University Press.

Mindel, C. H. (2005). Designing measuring Instruments. In R. M. Grinnell, Jr., & Y. A. Unrau (Eds.), *Social work research and evaluation: Quantitative and qualitative approaches* (7th ed., pp. 134–146). New York: Oxford University Press.

On Analyzing Group-Level Data

Grinnell, R. M., Jr., Unrau, Y. A., & Williams, M. (2005). Group-level designs. In R. M. Grinnell, Jr., & Y. A. Unrau (Eds.), *Social work research and evaluation: Quantitative and qualitative approaches* (7th ed., pp. 185–210). New York: Oxford University Press.

Weinbach, R. W., & Grinnell, R. M., Jr. (2007). *Statistics for social workers* (7th ed.). Boston: Allyn & Bacon.

Williams, M., Tutty, L., & Grinnell, R. M., Jr. (2005). Analyzing quantitative data. In R. M. Grinnell, Jr., & Y. A. Unrau (Eds.), *Social work research and evaluation: Quantitative and qualitative approaches* (7th ed., pp. 353–369). New York: Oxford University Press.

On Analyzing Case-Level Data

Bloom, M., Fischer, J., & Orme, J. (2006). *Evaluating practice: Guidelines for the accountable professional* (5th ed.). Boston: Allyn & Bacon.

Corcoran, K. J., & Fischer, J. (2007). *Measures for clinical practice: Vol. 1. Couples, families, and children* (4th ed.). New York: Oxford University Press.

Corcoran, K. J., & Fischer, J. (2007). *Measures for clinical practice: Volume 2. Adults* (4th ed.). New York: Oxford University Press.

Gabor, P. A., & Grinnell, R. M., Jr. (1994). *Evaluation and quality improvement in the human services.* Boston: Allyn & Bacon.

Gabor, P. A., Unrau, Y. A. (1998). *Evaluation for social workers: A quality improvement approach for the human services* (2nd ed.). Boston: Allyn & Bacon.

Williams, M., Grinnell, R. M., Jr., & Unrau, Y. A. (2005). Case-level designs. In R. M. Grinnell, Jr., & Y. A. Unrau (Eds.), *Social work research and evaluation: Quantitative and qualitative approaches* (7th ed., pp. 171–184). New York: Oxford University Press.

IV

KNOWING THE CONTEXTS OF EVALUATIONS

All evaluations are influenced, to some degree, by politics. Chapter 15 discusses how these political influences affect the evaluation process and highlights the appropriate and inappropriate uses of evaluations. It also discusses how the four professional standards for evaluations influence our evaluative efforts. The chapter highlights the informed consent process and the role that institutional review boards play on submitting an evaluation proposal.

Chapter 16 describes how evaluations in the social services must be culturally appropriate. It discusses various cultural frameworks and presents mechanisms that we can use to be sure our evaluations are not only culturally appropriate but also produce findings and implications that are useful to marginalized populations.

The final chapter, Chapter 17, briefly describes how to write grants to obtain funding for a program. It assumes that the 16 previous chapters have been read as it incorporates most of their content in describing how to ask for funds to create a new social service program. Thus, it assumes that readers are familiar with the terms that were introduced in the previous chapters.

EVALUATION POLITICS, ETHICS, AND STANDARDS

15

A s you know by now, our book is intended to provide an approach to planning, implementing, reporting, and using evaluations. The actual implementation of an evaluation, however, occurs in the real world and thus is subject to the multiple influences and pressures that exist there. In this chapter, professional and ethical guidelines for evaluations are discussed and presented as a way of ensuring that evaluations are properly and competently conducted and appropriately used.

POLITICS OF EVALUATION

The real-world pressures that affect and sometimes buffer evaluation work exist because evaluations are often perceived to have serious consequences affecting people's interests. Consequently, people, factions, or groups sometimes seek to advance their interests by influencing the evaluation process. **Politics** may be at work within a program or outside of a program; these can result in very strong pressure on the evaluation process. Further, because politics often lead to personal contention, the actual conduct of the evaluation may become difficult.

Politically charged situations may emerge within a social service program, in which case individuals internal to the program are primarily involved. Administrators and staff are key players when it comes to internal politics. Program politics become

Politics

Individual actions and policies that govern human behavior, which, in turn, influence program decisions. Politically charged situations usually have an element of self-interest.

apparent in situations where staff interests are involved; the evaluation may lead to changes in philosophy, organization, or approach to service provision. An evaluation must be prudent in dealing with internal politics because the cooperation of administrators and staff needs to be maintained to facilitate the evaluation process. At other times, individuals who are *outside* of the program may wish to influence decisions about the future development or the allocation of resources. When individuals outside the program attempt to influence the evaluation, external politics are at work.

Further contention may develop when a program's staff members and external stakeholder groups hold different views about what events should take place and what decisions ought to be made. The nature of the decisions to be made, the invested interests of the respective parties, and the magnitude of potential change can all serve to raise the perceived consequences of the evaluation and the intensity of the political climate.

Appropriate and Inappropriate Uses of Evaluation

Any human endeavor, including evaluation, can be appropriately or inappropriately used; when stakes are high, the probability of misuse increases. A good evaluation results in the production of fair, balanced, and accurate data about the program; appropriate use of these data is in the decision-making process as presented in the last chapter. At its best, this should be an open, transparent process with decisions evolving from evaluation results. However, in politicized situations, there is little intention to use evaluation results in an open decision-making process; the intent is to use the evaluation process to further some other purpose. Inevitably, a misuse of an evaluation's findings occurs.

Misuses of Evaluation

Evaluations can be misused in various ways. Some of the more common misuses include: (1) justifying decisions already made, (2) inappropriate use of public relations, (3) used for performance appraisals, and (4) fulfilling funding requirements.

Justifying Decisions Already Made

Perhaps the most frequent misuse of an evaluation is to justify decisions that were already made in advance of the evaluation. At the case level, for example, a worker may have decided, if only at the subconscious level, that a youngster in treatment foster care should be referred to a group-care program. The worker may then select a standardized measuring instrument (see Chapter 9) that is likely to show that the youngster's functioning is highly problematic, and then use these data to justify the previously taken decision.

At the program level, an administrator may already have decided that a certain program within the agency should be reduced in size. The administrator may then commission an evaluation in the hope that the results will show the program to be ineffective. Inevitably, any evaluation will uncover some shortcomings and limitations; the administrator can then use these to justify the decision to reduce the size of the program. Similarly, **outside funders** who have already decided to curtail or cancel funding for a program may first commission an evaluation in the hope that the results will justify the preexisting decision.

Inappropriate Use of Public Relations

A second misuse of an evaluation is to distract attention from negative events, as a **public relations** tool. From time to time within the social services, problems and incidents occur that bring unwelcome publicity. A worker in a group home, for example, may be indicted for sexual abuse of residents, or a preschooler may be returned from a treatment foster home to her birth home and be subsequently physically abused by her biological parents. These types of incidents inevitably attract intense media scrutiny and public interest.

Some administrators may immediately respond to such incidents by commissioning an evaluation and then declining any comment. An administrator might announce, "I have today engaged Professor Rodriguez from the university to undertake a comprehensive evaluation of this program; until the evaluation results are available, I do not want to say anything further that might prejudge the findings." An evaluation may be an appropriate response in such a situation. However, its findings must be used to help decide on changes that need to be made to increase the likelihood that a similar problem will never again occur. When an evaluation is commissioned merely to distract attention, to avoid having to comment, much of the time, effort, and resources invested will be wasted as there is unlikely to be any genuine interest in the evaluation's results. An evaluation in such a situation is mere window dressing—a diversion.

Used for Performance Appraisals

The third serious misuse of an evaluation occurs when it is used for purposes of **performance appraisal**. For example, data can be aggregated inappropriately across a worker's caseload, and the resulting "cumulative data" are then used for a performance appraisal. At the program level, the contents of an evaluation report, which focuses on an operating unit, may be used to evaluate the performance of a supervisor or administrator. Although administrators do have some responsibility for the performance of their unit, program, or department, other factors—beyond the control of the administrator—may also be involved; the point is that a program evaluation is

Outside funder
The sponsoring body who provides funding for the creation of a social service program.

Public relations
The business of generating goodwill toward an individual, cause, or social service agency.

Performance appraisals
An evaluation of a social worker's efficiency and/or effectiveness.

not meant to link program performance and outcomes to individual social workers and their performances.

When an evaluation is used for purposes of a performance appraisal, the findings are likely to be used for political goals—to promote or undermine an individual. Such misuse of an evaluation is destructive, as administrators and workers alike will undoubtedly become defensive and concentrate their efforts on ensuring that evaluation data show them in the best possible light. These efforts detract from the delivery of effective services and will also likely result in less reliable and valid data. Performance appraisals and program evaluations are two distinct processes, with different purposes. Both are compromised if they are not kept separate.

Fulfilling Funding Requirements

Nowadays, funders are commonly requiring an evaluation of some kind as a condition of a program's funding, particularly in the case of new projects. Staff members who are trying to set up a new program or maintain an old one, for example, may see the evaluation requirement as a ritual without any direct relevance to them. They may thus incorporate an evaluation component into the funding proposal or graft evaluation activities onto an existing program, obediently jumping through hoops to satisfy funders that they are in compliance with evaluation requirements.

Often, these evaluation plans are not even implemented because they were designed for "show" only. At other times, the evaluation activities are undertaken but without any intention of making use of the results. It is, of course, a serious misuse (not to mention a waste of time, effort, and resources) to undertake an evaluation only to obtain program funds, without any thought of using the data that were derived from the evaluation in any meaningful way.

Proper Uses of Evaluation

Having described a variety of possible misuses, it is appropriate to conclude this section of the discussion by reviewing two appropriate uses of evaluations. As discussed previously, evaluations are most properly used to guide an open and transparent decision-making process, where evaluation findings will be weighed and considered.

Internal Decision Making

The primary internal use of evaluation data is feedback; evaluation findings provide data about the degree to which a program's objectives are being met. When these data are available in a timely fashion, administrators and workers alike can continually monitor the impacts of their decisions, and, where required, make adjustments to activities and program operations.

Decision making
The cognitive process of reaching a decision.

At the case level, for example, evaluation data can provide an objective basis for making clinical decisions. As has been described in Chapters 9 and 14, selected practice objectives are measured repeatedly while the client is receiving services. These data are then used as feedback on client progress and become an important consideration in decisions to maintain, modify, or change treatment interventions.

At the program level, staff members' interest is in a broader picture of how the program functions. The monitoring approach to evaluation allows a program to gather data continuously about its various components, practices, and procedures. The principal internal use for such data is developmental. The process is essentially as follows: Data are collected continuously and analyzed periodically to provide ongoing feedback about the functioning of various aspects of the program. Where the program is not performing as desired, there is an opportunity to make changes in structures, procedures, and practices. Subsequent data will then provide information about the impact of these changes. Through this process, administrators and staff can continuously fine-tune and improve the program.

Because the purpose of the evaluation is development, not judgment, people are more likely to take risks, innovate, and experiment. In such an environment, growth and development are more likely to occur. When staff members and teams feel encouraged to grow and learn, the program itself grows and learns.

External Decision Making

External uses of evaluation data usually involve funders, policymakers, other stakeholder groups, and researchers. Appropriate uses include the demonstration of accountability, decision making about program and policy, and knowledge building.

Social service programs are, in a general sense, accountable to their clients, to their communities, and to professional peers. In a more specific way, they are also accountable to their funders. Accountability generally requires evidence that goals are consistent with community needs, that contracted services are actually provided as planned, and that these services are being provided effectively and efficiently. These are among the most common uses of evaluation data: to account for program activities and program results.

At the policy level, it is sometimes necessary to make decisions among various ways of meeting particular social needs. Or policymakers may decide to encourage the development of programs that are organized along certain intervention models. For example, in many jurisdictions, the development of treatment foster homes has been encouraged in recent years, while group-care facilities for young people are supported much more reluctantly. At other times, funders must make decisions regarding future funding for a specific program. In all three situations, evaluation will provide data that can help guide decisions.

Knowledge building is another way in which an evaluation's results may be used. Each completed evaluation study has the potential of adding to our profession's knowledge base. Indeed, at times, evaluations are undertaken specifically for the purpose of acquiring knowledge. Because evaluations are conducted in field settings, they are particularly useful for testing the effectiveness of interventions and treatment models that actually occur in these settings.

Evaluations for external purposes are usually initiated by people outside the program, typically funding bodies such as governments or foundations. They are often also externally conducted by evaluation specialists on a project by project basis. When evaluations are externally initiated and externally conducted, there is a higher potential for problems in the evaluation process and for the misuse of the findings. This is because an external evaluator may impose an evaluation framework that does not fit well with a program's operations or is not consistent with staff members' or administrators' expectations.

An effective safeguard is provided when administrators and staff are involved in decisions relating to the planning and execution of the evaluation. An alternative to the externally conducted project evaluation is available to programs that establish internal evaluation systems. When internal systems are developed with **stakeholders** participating, the data collected through them often satisfy many of the data needs of the external stakeholders.

Stakeholders

A person or group of people having a direct or indirect interest in the results of an evaluation.

POLITICAL INFLUENCES ON THE EVALUATION PROCESS

We have seen how internal and external politics can lead to inappropriate reasons for conducting case-level and program-level evaluations. Moreover, we should also be aware that political influences may have an impact once the evaluation is underway. Individuals may attempt to influence the evaluation process itself, in an attempt to obtain results that support their views and positions.

Manipulating the Evaluation Process

Stakeholders usually have legitimate interests in relation to a social service program and, quite appropriately, may attempt to further these interests. For example, some staff members may believe strongly that a new intervention approach would work better than the existing one. They may then try to convince and influence others that the new intervention approach should be adopted. Or an administrator may believe that a certain approach to intake will produce better results.

Attempting to influence program development so that the new approach or intake method is adopted is quite natural and entirely appropriate. In the normal course of an evaluation, data may emerge that would, in fact, confirm the superiority of the intervention approach or the benefits of the new intake process.

However, people sometimes move beyond the legitimate use of influence and attempt to manipulate the evaluation process itself. Thus, staff members may selectively provide data that tend to show the benefits of their preferred approach or the shortcomings of the existing approach, hoping to influence the outcome of the evaluation. Or an administrator may offer to an evaluator a comparison situation between two units, one using the old intake approach and one using the new intake approach. However, the administrator might also know that the unit using the old intake approach has encountered large staff turnover recently and currently faces other difficulties as well. If the evaluator collected data from the two proposed units, the resulting comparison might well reflect the functioning of the units rather than the effectiveness of the intake processes.

Any number of other examples could be cited, ranging from relatively mild examples of attempting to exert undue influence to very flagrant attempts at manipulating the process.

Misdirecting the Evaluation Process

We know that social service programs (including interventions) do not exist in a single static state. They exist in many states or are multifaceted, and the particular state revealed by an evaluation depends on the purpose and focus of the evaluation and the methodology employed. Individuals and groups may attempt to further their interests by misdirecting the evaluation process, in the hope that the state of the program revealed in the evaluation will serve to promote their agenda. Misdirecting the process may be accomplished through (1) program objectives, (2) the evaluation sample, (3) data collection methods, and (4) interpretation of findings.

Evaluators have considerable latitude in establishing the methodology and process concerning these matters. However, these methodological and process choices are subject to political pressures from individuals and groups who hope to influence the findings. It is, therefore, particularly important that evaluators avoid becoming unwitting pawns in a manipulative political process; they need to be keenly aware of the implications of each choice they make. Let us now consider these four key decision-making points in evaluations and take a closer look at the role that politics may play within each.

Program Objectives

Unfortunately, many social service programs do not have clearly stated and measurable program objectives. How can a program be evaluated if its objectives are not explicitly stated? What is to be evaluated in such a situation? If specific objectives are lacking, they will need to be developed early in the evaluation process. The task of defining a program's objectives may heighten political contention because, in reality, a program's objectives define the criteria on which the program will be evaluated (see Chapter 3).

Administrators and workers, understandably, will wish to be evaluated against criteria that they feel reflect their program's philosophy, practices, and focus. They would also like to see the objectives set in a manner that takes into account the constraints imposed by mandate, resources, and context. In addition, they will wish to emphasize objectives that they believe they are meeting or exceeding. On the other hand, stakeholders from the outside may wish to set objectives around matters that are important to them. Funders, for example, may wish to define outcome objectives; other agencies may identify partnership-related objectives; service recipients may emphasize access.

Of course, the program will inevitably fare better on some objectives than on others; thus, if any of these stakeholder groups have political goals or are trying to advance a hidden agenda, they may be furthered depending on the selection of the objectives that will frame the evaluation.

The evaluator thus has a responsibility to ensure that the program is evaluated against existing program objectives, if there are any. If there are none, objectives need to be identified, and the evaluator must ensure that the objectives are fair and reasonable and include a balance of perspectives from all relevant stakeholder groups.

Sample Selection

Sample

A subset of a population of individuals, objects, or events chosen to participate in or to be considered in a study; a group chosen by unbiased sample selection from which inferences about the entire population of people, objects, or events can be drawn.

As we know from Chapter 10, whom we decide to include in an evaluation **sample** influences the data that are collected and, ultimately, the findings that are derived from the evaluative effort. Because all social service programs have a number of stakeholder groups, it is possible to gather evaluation data from many different sources. In a family support program (e.g., Box 3.1), for example, we could sample the program's workers (Data Source 1), other helping professionals involved with the clients (Data Source 2), the clients themselves (Data Source 3), or even the general public (Data Source 4) to obtain relevant data.

Further, after the sources are decided on, questions often arise about the criteria for sample inclusion. Suppose it was agreed in a family support program that the families would be the main data source. Evaluation results may be influenced considerably by how a "family" is defined. Are data collected from parents only, or are children included as well? Sometimes data are collected from *available* family members. Data for one family can be collected from the mother, while data for another family can be collected from both parents, the children, and a live-in grandparent. Clearly, decisions regarding these matters will influence results.

Another consideration in sampling is whether all clients who started in the program are to be included in the sample. If, for example, clients complete a self-administered satisfaction survey at termination (e.g., Figures 9.1 and 9.2), those who have dropped out of the program early and who are presumably less satisfied will not be included. Thus, the results will likely reflect more satisfaction with the program than is actually the case.

Or if a focus group is to be conducted, who will participate? Often, such groups are composed on the basis of recommendations of staff members, who tend to suggest their "best" clients, those who are articulate, cooperative, have made the most improvement, and generally hold the most favorable attitudes toward the program. Obviously, such a sample would not likely result in data that are representative of all clients.

Again, it is the evaluator's responsibility to consider the implications of how the sample is selected and to ensure that the sampling method is reasonable under the circumstances.

Data Collection Methods

The **data collection methods** may also influence results. For example, in an evaluation of the stability of client gains made during a program, a follow-up of closed cases may be undertaken and telephone interviews conducted to collect data. Clearly, clients without telephones or those who have moved and not left forwarding information will be excluded. It is, however, likely that these clients may be different from those who are included; they are probably not doing as well as clients who have a stable residence and can be contacted through telephone calls. Thus, follow-up data collected by this method may tend to overstate the level of functioning of former clients.

The timing of data collection can also have a considerable effect on an evaluation's results. At both the case and program levels, different conclusions may be drawn about client success if progress is measured at the time of termination of services rather than at some time after termination. In the case of adolescents discharged from a group-care program, for example, deterioration often takes place subsequent to termination because less structure and fewer supports are available in the community.

Outcome measures taken at the time of termination (as well as at follow-up) are both legitimate reflections of a program's objectives, but they represent unique perspectives and may show different results. Clients, for example, may show considerable gains at posttest immediately after exiting the program, but may show only marginal gains at follow-up three months later.

Who collects the data is another important decision. As discussed in previous chapters, many programs use front-line workers to collect data in an effort to keep data collection costs at a minimum. If the data are collected by their workers, service recipients may not feel free to express their true opinions, particularly if their opinions are somewhat critical. Alternatively, if workers are asked to rate their own clients' functioning, they may overstate the case, in a conscious or subconscious effort to reflect their own efforts in the best possible light.

Data collection methods
The various ways in which data can be collected, such as surveys (i.e., telephone, mail), participant observations, interviews, secondary analyses, document reviews, and the like.

Because data collection has implications for the results, evaluators have a responsibility to ensure that the methods used are appropriate, will provide for the integrity of the resulting data, and are without biasing effects (see Table 10.3).

Interpretation of Findings

In this book, evaluation is described as a way of monitoring interventions, program processes, and outcomes to provide feedback that can support a process of continuous improvement and development. The degree to which a program achieves its objectives is a measure of success, but it is essentially a matter of opinion what level of achievement actually constitutes *success*. Suppose for a moment that 60 percent of the graduates of a job-training program find employment in our Aim High Program discussed in Chapter 8. This figure may be interpreted as indicating success, in that *fully* 60 percent of graduates are employed; or it may be taken to indicate failure, in that *only* 60 percent of graduates find work.

Moreover, such data as the percentage of former clients who find employment represent only a part of the evaluative picture. Relevant contextual factors should also be considered; these could include the rate of unemployment in the community, the income earned by former participants, and the level of job satisfaction experienced by them. The way in which evaluation findings are interpreted is a process known as **valuation**.

Valuation

The way evaluation findings are interpreted.

Because criteria for a program's success are seldom predefined, evaluators often play an influential part in the valuation process; depending on the judgment of an evaluator, the same result may be classified as either a success or a failure. It goes without saying that evaluators must ensure that the valuation process is fair and reasonable.

PROFESSIONAL STANDARDS FOR EVALUATION

To safeguard against the misdirection of the evaluation process or the misuse of the results, evaluators turn to professional standards for guidelines regarding the conceptualization and implementation of their work. There are various standards that exist as well; this section provides a description of one widely accepted set of standards for evaluation.

The oldest professional standards for program evaluation are those issued by the Joint Committee on Standards of Educational Evaluation (1994). The Committee was formed in 1975 and now includes a large number of organizations concerned with maintaining high professional standards in evaluation practice. As displayed in Box 15.1, the Committee has identified four overlapping criteria against which evaluation practice should be judged: (1) utility, (2) feasibility, (3) propriety, and (4) accuracy. Although the Committee standards were written specifically as guidelines for program-level evaluation, many of the standards are relevant and can be applied to case-level evaluation as well.

Box 15.1 Summary of Program Evaluation Standards

Utility Standards

The utility standards are intended to ensure that an evaluation will serve the information needs of intended users.

- *Stakeholder Identification:* Persons involved in or affected by the evaluation should be identified so that their needs can be addressed.
- *Evaluator Credibility:* The persons conducting the evaluation should be both trustworthy and competent to perform the evaluation so that the evaluation findings achieve maximum credibility and acceptance.
- *Information Scope and Selection:* Information collected should be broadly selected to address pertinent questions about the program and be responsive to the needs and interests of clients and other specified stakeholders.
- *Values Identification:* The perspectives, procedures, and rationale used to interpret the findings should be carefully described so that the bases for value judgments are clear.
- *Report Clarity:* Evaluation reports should clearly describe the program being evaluated, including its context and the purposes, procedures, and findings of the evaluation so that essential information is provided and easily understood.
- *Report Timeliness and Dissemination:* Significant interim findings and evaluation reports should be disseminated to intended users so that they can be used in a timely fashion.
- *Evaluation Impact:* Evaluations should be planned, conducted, and reported in ways that encourage follow-through by stakeholders so that the likelihood that the evaluation will be used is increased.

Feasibility Standards

The feasibility standards are intended to ensure that an evaluation will be realistic, prudent, diplomatic, and frugal.

- *Practical Procedures:* The evaluation procedures should be practical, to keep disruption to a minimum while needed information is obtained.
- *Political Viability:* The evaluation should be planned and conducted with anticipation of the different positions of various interest groups so that their cooperation may be obtained and so that possible attempts by any of these groups to curtail evaluation operations or to bias or misapply the results can be averted or counteracted.
- *Cost Effectiveness:* The evaluation should be efficient and produce information of sufficient value so that the resources expended can be justified.

Propriety Standards

The propriety standards are intended to ensure that an evaluation will be conducted legally, ethically, and with due regard for the welfare of those involved in the evaluation as well as those affected by its results.

- *Service Orientation:* Evaluations should be designed to assist organizations to address and effectively serve the needs of the full range of targeted participants.
- *Formal Agreements:* Obligations of the formal parties to an evaluation (what is to be done, how, by whom, when) should be agreed to in writing so that these parties are obligated to adhere to all conditions of the agreement or formally to renegotiate it.
- *Rights of Human Subjects:* Evaluations should be designed and conducted to respect and protect the rights and welfare of human subjects.
- *Human Interactions:* Evaluators should respect human dignity and worth in their interactions with other persons associated with an evaluation so that participants are not threatened or harmed.
- *Complete and Fair Assessment:* The evaluation should be complete and fair in its examination and recording of strengths and weaknesses of the program being evaluated so that strengths can be built upon and problem areas addressed.
- *Disclosure of Findings:* The formal parties to an evaluation should ensure that the full set of evaluation findings along with pertinent limitations are made accessible to the persons affected by the evaluation and any others with expressed legal rights to receive the results.
- *Conflict of Interest:* Conflict of interest should be dealt with openly and honestly so that it does not compromise the evaluation processes and results.

(continued)

Box 15.1 (continued)

- *Fiscal Responsibility:* The evaluator's allocation and expenditure of resources should reflect sound accountability procedures and otherwise be prudent and ethically responsible so that expenditures are accounted for and appropriate.

Accuracy Standards

The accuracy standards are intended to ensure that an evaluation will reveal and convey technically adequate information about the features that determine worth or merit of the program being evaluated.

- *Program Documentation:* The program being evaluated should be described and documented clearly and accurately so that the program is clearly identified.
- *Context Analysis:* The context in which the program exists should be examined in enough detail so that its likely influences on the program can be identified.
- *Described Purposes and Procedures:* The purposes and procedures of the evaluation should be monitored and described in enough detail so that they can be identified and assessed.
- *Defensible Information Sources:* The sources of information used in a program evaluation should be described in enough detail so that the adequacy of the information can be assessed.
- *Valid Information:* The information-gathering procedures should be chosen or developed and then implemented so that they will assure that the interpretation arrived at is valid for the intended use.

- *Reliable Information:* The information-gathering procedures should be chosen or developed and then implemented so that they will assure that the information obtained is sufficiently reliable for the intended use.
- *Systematic Information:* The information collected, processed, and reported in an evaluation should be systematically reviewed, and any errors found should be corrected.
- *Analysis of Quantitative Information:* Quantitative information in an evaluation should be appropriately and systematically analyzed so that evaluation questions are effectively answered.
- *Analysis of Qualitative Information:* Qualitative information in an evaluation should be appropriately and systematically analyzed so that evaluation questions are effectively answered.
- *Justified Conclusions:* The conclusions reached in an evaluation should be explicitly justified so that stakeholders can assess them.
- *Impartial Reporting:* Reporting procedures should guard against distortion caused by personal feelings and biases of any party to the evaluation so that evaluation reports fairly reflect the evaluation findings.
- *Metaevaluation:* The evaluation itself should be formatively and summatively evaluated against these and other pertinent standards so that its conduct is appropriately guided and, on completion, stakeholders can closely examine its strengths and weaknesses.

Utility

Utility

An evaluation standard that says an evaluation must provide useful data to one or more of the program's stakeholder groups.

The **utility** criteria are intended to ensure that evaluations will provide useful data to one or more of the program's stakeholder groups. In other words, evaluators are required to establish links between an evaluation's findings and the decisions to be derived from them. Data obtained from an evaluation must be relevant to decision makers and reported in a manner that decision makers can understand.

At the case level, the participant and the front-line worker are, in most cases, joint decision makers. Because workers usually carry out case-level evaluations, they will be able to decide on the type of data to be gathered, the method of analyses, and the way in which evaluation findings will impact case-level decision making.

At the program level, evaluation findings are usually documented in a written report. In a monitoring situation, the report may be one of a regular series, without formal recommendations; in a project evaluation, there is likely to be a formal report, often ending with a series of recommendations. In either case, to ensure that an evaluation has utility, the evaluator is responsible for determining in advance, with as much clarity as possible, the decisions that are to be based on the evaluation's findings.

The evaluator is then responsible for reporting results in a manner that can inform the decisions to be taken. It is obviously important that the report be tailored to the decision makers, who usually do not have an extensive background in evaluation, research methods, or statistics. Thus, statistical results, for example, should be provided so they are comprehensible to the users. When drafting recommendations, it is important that evaluators keep in mind the social, political, economic, and professional contexts within which recommendations will be implemented. The challenge is to provide recommendations that can result in meaningful and feasible improvement within existing constraints.

Feasibility

Feasibility standards attempt to ensure that evaluations shall be conducted only when feasible, practical, and economically viable. These standards speak to minimizing disruption within the organization where the evaluation is conducted; evaluators need to consider the impact of evaluation activities such as data collection and ensure that they do not impose an unreasonable burden on staff and on the organization itself.

As well, these standards address the issue of "political viability," suggesting that evaluators should anticipate political influence and possible attempts to misdirect the process or to misapply the results. These matters have already been discussed in detail in previous sections of this chapter. The standards require that the evaluators be aware of these possibilities and ensure that the integrity of the evaluation process is maintained throughout.

Feasibility
An evaluation standard that says an evaluation can only be done when it is feasible, practical, and economically viable.

Propriety

Propriety standards provide the framework for the legal and ethical conduct of evaluations and describe the responsibilities of evaluators to ensure due regard for the welfare of those involved in the evaluation as well as of those affected by the evaluation.

These standards emphasize the obligation of those undertaking evaluations to act within the law, to respect those involved in the evaluation, and to protect the rights and well-being of all human subjects. These standards are similar to, but not as detailed as, the normal ethical standards that apply to the protection of human subjects in any research project.

Propriety
An evaluation standard that says all evaluations must be done in a legal and ethical manner.

Universities generally maintain institutional review boards or their equivalent, which are concerned with ensuring that research methods are implemented in an ethical manner and that human subjects are protected from harm or undue risk. Most professions also address research procedures in their ethical codes. An evaluation project usually entails the implementation of research procedures; consequently, applicable professional and institutional ethical standards for conducting research should be met. Box 15.2 displays an actual example of the procedures that were gone over with adolescents who were in foster care to obtain their permission to participate in an outcome evaluation study. The procedures were not only given to the adolescents to read (Box 15.2), but the procedures were also read to them by their social worker before they read and signed an assent form (Box 15.3). Notice the great deal of caution that is used when an evaluation is done with children and adolescents.

Finally, the propriety standards address completeness and fairness. These standards seek to ensure that a complete, fair, and balanced assessment of the program being evaluated results from the process. As we have seen in Chapter 4, evaluation is only a representation. This means that there are multiple possible pictures of a program, each representing a different perspective. Evaluators are responsible for creating a fair and balanced representation that can take into account all reasonable perspectives. Often this means that no single picture will emerge as the result of an evaluation and that evaluators will need to explain how the several perspectives fit together and how they relate to the overall social, economic, political, and professional context in which the program operates.

Accuracy

Accuracy
An evaluation standard that says all evaluations must be accurate and provide their methodological shortcomings.

The final set of standards address **accuracy**. This has to do with the technical adequacy of the evaluation process and involves such matters as validity and reliability, measurement instruments, samples, comparisons, and research designs. These standards make clear the evaluator's responsibility for maintaining high technical standards in all aspect of the process. The evaluator is also responsible for describing any methodological shortcomings and the limits within which findings can be considered to be accurate.

PRINCIPLES OF EVALUATION PRACTICE

The discussion in this chapter has addressed a variety of matters ranging from technical approaches to evaluation to appropriate uses of the resulting products. We conclude by providing some guidelines for effective evaluation practice. These guidelines result in high-quality, principled practices that can ensure that political influences are kept to a minimum and the integrity of the evaluation process is maintained.

Chatham-Kent Children's Services (CKCS) Help-Seeking Project for Adolescents in Out-of-Home Placement

You are invited to participate in **Chatham-Kent Children's Services (CKCS) Help-Seeking Project for Adolescents in Out-of-Home Placement**. The project is being funded by The Provincial Centre of Excellence for Child and Youth Mental Health at CHEO. The primary person in charge of the project is Mike Stephens, Chief Executive Officer of CKCS.

What Is This Handout?

This handout lets you know about the project and will help you decide if you want to participate. You are free to choose whether or not you will take part. Before you decide, however, you need to know the risks and benefits of your participation and what will be expected of you if you decide to participate.

Please take time to read this handout. A staff member will also explain the project to you and answer any questions you might have. There are no negative consequences for not participating in the project or quitting it later on if you decide to begin participating. You can drop out at any time without any penalties to you. The services you receive from CKCS will not be affected by your decision to participate in this project.

If you agree to take part, then you will be asked to sign a separate assent form. The assent form is a shorter version of this handout and contains important information about the project. When you sign the assent form, you give your "consent," which means that you give your "OK" to be a participant in the project. You should read this handout and the consent form carefully and be sure to ask any questions before signing the consent form.

What Is the CKCS Help-Seeking Project for Adolescents in Out-of-Home Placement?

The main purpose of the project is to test whether a workshop and additional support given to youth living in out-of-home placement at CKCS will make youth more skilled at asking for help when personal or emotional problems arise.

We don't yet know if our help-seeking intervention works. So we have designed a project that will involve over 100 youth age 12 years and older who are living in out-of-home placement at CKCS. Half of the youth who participate in the project will attend a special workshop and the other half will not. The special workshop will give you information and ideas about how to seek help when personal or emotional problems arise. We will then compare the help-seeking skills of youth who received the intervention with those who did not in order to learn whether the workshop helped in the way it was supposed to.

You will be assigned to either a group of youth who receive the help-seeking intervention, *or* to a group of youth who do not receive it. That is, you may or may not receive the help-seeking intervention even though you agree to participate in the project. But if we learn that the intervention is helpful in the way we expected, then all youth that did not get to go to the workshop will be offered a chance to participate in it at a later date if they are still living in the care of CKCS.

What Will Be Asked of You If You Choose to Become a Participant in Our Project?

If you agree to participate in the project you will be assigned to one of two groups.

In total about 120 youth will participate in the project. All of them will be invited to complete a set of questionnaires at four different points in time: this week, 5 weeks from now, 10 weeks from now, and 20 weeks from now (see the picture). Next, we describe what you can expect to happen if you decide to participate in the project.

- You will be contacted twice by telephone to answer a questionnaire. Some time during this week and then again 20 weeks from now, a CKCS staff member will call you by telephone and ask you questions using the *Brief Child and Family Phone Interview*. The phone interview takes about 30 minutes and asks questions about common emotional and behavioral problems experienced by teenagers. You do not have to answer any questions that you don't want to.

(continued)

Box 15.2 (continued)

- You will be asked to come to CKCS four times (see the picture) over the next 20 weeks and will be invited to answer questions from four other questionnaires (*Client Engagement in Child Protective Services, Barriers to Adolescents Seeking Help, Barriers to Engagement in Treatment Survey,* and the *General Help Seeking Questionnaire*). You will be invited to answer these questions at the CKCS computer lab using a special computer program. Sitting at your own computer and wearing headphones, you will see each question appear on the computer screen one at a time, and you will hear the question being read through the headphones. You will be invited to answer the questions by using the click of the computer mouse. Each session of computer questions should take 30 to 40 minutes to complete. You do not have to answer any questions that you don't want to.
- You will be given a cash (or equivalent) incentive for your participation. The first time you answer the questions, you will receive $10, the second time (5 weeks later) will be $15, the third time (at 10 weeks) will be $20, and the fourth time (at 20 weeks) will be $30 (see the picture). In addition, food snacks will be provided at each meeting, and help with transportation to CKCS will also be available if you need it.

In addition to the above testing, your participation in this project also means that a project staff member will look at your CKCS case file to get the following information: the type of placement you live in now, how long you have lived at your current placement, the number of placements you have had before this one, the reason you entered care, the services that you receive during the 20 weeks of the project, whether you had contact with your birth family during the project, whether you moved from your placement during the project, and the number of times you contacted a CKCS worker during the time of the project.

Finally, half of the youth who participate in the project will invited to participate in a special 2 to 3 hour workshop that will include 6 youth at a time. The workshop will take place at CKCS, and it be run by a CKCS mental health worker. The main purpose of the workshop is to give you additional information about how you can best get help for your personal or emotional problems while living in the care of CKCS.

There is no way of knowing, at this time, whether you will be chosen to participate in the workshop. The decision will be made by chance. But if it turns out that the workshop is helpful to the youth that received it, then it will be made available to all other youth in CKCS after the project has ended.

Who Will Take Part in Our Project?

Up to 120 youth will take part in our project. All youth ages 12 years and older and living in care at CKCS are eligible to participate.

Would CKCS Ever Ask You to Stop Participating?

If you leave CKCS care within 5 weeks of the start of the project (or before you get a chance to participate in the

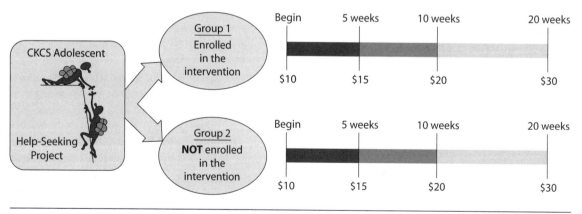

Figure 1 CKCS Adolescent Help-Seeking Project.

intervention), then your participation in the project will automatically end at that time. If you leave CKCS care after the intervention point, then we will invite you back to complete the additional questionnaires.

How Will Your Privacy (or Confidentiality) Be Protected?

Confidentiality means that we will do all we can to keep information gathered about you completely private. In order to protect your privacy in this project,

- We use numbers instead of names (or other identifiers) on all of the information we get so that no one can tell who the information came from.
- The information collected for this project will be sent to two professors at Western Michigan University. The information will not include anything that would identify you as an individual. The Western Michigan University professors and any research assistants they have working on this project will have been trained in confidentiality protection.
- Only a small number of CKCS staff members assigned to this project will have access to the information that you provide as part of this project. Your individual information will not be shared with your Children's Service Worker, your foster parent or caregiver, or any other workers at CKCS. Your information will only be used for this project.
- CKCS staff members assigned to this project will be trained by the Western Michigan Univesity researchers to protect your privacy.
- All information is stored in a safe locked area. The computers for this project are protected by a firewall system, and all users are required to use passwords.
- All of your answers will be kept private unless a staff member thinks you might be in danger of hurting yourself. If you tell us that you are using illegal drugs, or are thinking of harming yourself or someone else, project staff are obligated to inform your CKCS Children's Service Worker.
- The information from the project will be used to write papers, make presentations, and work with other education or research centers using the information from the project for scientific purposes only. Please remember that your name or information that could identify you will never be used. We study the data "as a group" and not for any one individual. You or your family will not be identified (for example, by name or social insurance number) in any reports or publications of this project.

Are There Any Times When Your Information Might Be Shared With Others?

Yes. These are called "exceptions to confidentiality." If we know or think we know that a child is being abused, we are obligated, under law, to take action to protect that child. We will inform your CKCS Children's Service Worker if this is the case. We will also report when we hear that someone plans to hurt themselves or someone else. We will tell your Children's Service Worker if we think a child is in immediate danger of trying to hurt or kill themselves.

What Are Your Rights as a Participant in Our Project?

As a participant in our project, you have certain rights that help protect you:

- It is up to you to decide if you want to be in our project. That means your participation is completely voluntary.
- You have the right to change your mind at any time about being in the project. If you decide to quit the project, there will be no penalty of any kind.
- You have the right to refuse to answer any question(s). Some questions might be personal or sensitive to you. These questions are important to our project, and we would like you to answer them honestly. However, if there are some questions you do not want to answer, you may skip them and move on to other questions.
- You will be given copies of this Project Description as well as the Consent Form.
- This Project Description and Consent Form will also be explained verbally to you. If you have any difficulty in reading these forms a staff person will read them to you.
- At any time you can ask any staff member questions about our project. You may also call collect Mike Stephens (1-877-XXX-XXXX, extension 4110), the Chief Executive Officer at CKCS.

(continued)

Box 15.2 (continued)

- If you would like to contact someone outside the project staff with questions or concerns, please feel free to call Yvonne Unrau at 269-387-3185 or Rick Grinnell at 269-387-3189, who are the two Western Michigan Univesity researchers involved with the project. You may also contact the Chair, Human Subjects Institutional Review Board (269-387-8293) or the Vice President for Research (269-387-8298) at Western Michigan Univesity if questions or problems arise during the course of the study. You may call collect.

What Are the Possible Risks to You as a Participant in the Project?

As a participant, there are very few risks to you. You may, however, feel a little embarrassed or uncomfortable because of the personal nature of some of the questions on the questionnaires or due to certain things we ask you to do, such as role play in the workshop or being asked questions about how you have asked for help in the past. Remember, you are free to say "No" to any questions or activities. If you feel uncomfortable or you want to talk to someone about any of these risks, please let us know.

What Are the Benefits to You as a Participant?

Many people find it helpful to have a chance to think and talk about personal information about themselves and their families. Being in the project gives you a chance to do this.

CKCS is interested in finding ways to better serve teenagers in out-of-home placement care. The project will improve our knowledge about how youth in care can get better seek help when they need it. The information gained might help us understand more about how parents, foster parents, and CKCS can work together to help teenagers that are placed in foster or group care. This information might be used to prevent problems for teenagers in the future and to help those that might be having trouble. As a participant, you will be part of a valuable project that might help other people in the future.

What Are Ways CKCS Will Try to Make It Easy for You to Participate?

- Pizza or other food, pop, and money (or gift certificates) each time you complete the questionnaires.
- Free transportation to and from CKCS to participate in the study.
- Flexible appointment schedule during daytime, evenings, and weekends if you cannot make it to CKCS to complete the questionnaires at the time assigned for your group.
- If you have difficulty reading any of the forms or questionnaires, project staff will be glad to assist or read the forms to you.

Please sign below to show that you have reviewed this Project Description and that you have had all your questions answered.

_____   _____

Participant Signature   Date

_____   _____

Project Staff Signature   Date

Principle 1: Evaluation and Service Delivery Activities Should Be Integrated

Evaluation and service delivery activities should be integrated to the extent possible. When evaluation is regarded as part of the service delivery process, it is much more likely that data collection will be focused on relevant issues and carried out conscientiously. As well, it is much more likely that the resulting information will be used

Box 15.3 Example of an Assent Form

To be signed after they have gone over it with a social worker (Box 15.2).

Assent Form—Youth in CKCS Care

I have been invited to be part of an evaluation study entitled "Chatham-Kent Children's Services (CKCS) Help-Seeking Project for Adolescents in Out-of-Home Placement." The main purpose of the study is to see if a workshop and additional support given to youth living in out-of-home placement at CKCS will make youth more skilled at asking for help with their personal or emotional problems.

- I will be phoned by a CKCS staff member twice over 20 weeks and be invited to answer questions from the *Brief Child and Family Phone Interview (BCFPI).*
- I will be invited to come to CKCS four times over the next 20 weeks to answer questions from four other questionnaires (*Client Engagement in Child Protective Services, Barriers to Adolescents Seeking Help, Barriers to Engagement in Treatment Survey,* and the *General Help Seeking Questionnaire*). I will answer these questionnaires using a special computer program at CKCS. After the first testing, CKCS will pay me $10 (or equivalent). After the second testing point, CKCS will pay me $15 (or equivalent). After the third testing point, CKCS will pay me $20 (or equivalent). After the fourth (and final) time, CKCS will pay me $30 (or equivalent). CKCS will also provide food snacks at each testing time.
- A project staff member will look at my case file to get the following information about me without recording my name: the type of placement I live in now, how long I have lived at my current placement, the number of placements I have had before this one, the reason I entered care, the services that I got during the 20 weeks of the project, whether I had contact with my birth family during the project, whether I moved from my placement during the project, and the number of times I contacted a CKCS worker during the project. Instead of recording my name, this information will be recorded using a number code.
- I may also be invited to participate in a 2 to 3 hour workshop with a small group of about five other youth in care. The workshop will take place at CKCS and be run by a CKCS mental health worker, and possibly someone who formerly lived in out-of-home placement. At the workshop I will get information and ideas about asking for help related to personal or emotional problems that are common with teenagers.

If I don't want to participate, there will be no effect on the service I receive from CKCS.

Even if I agree today to participate by signing this form, I can change my mind at any time when testing begins or at any time during testing, or at any time when the workshop begins or during the workshop.

If I choose to complete any or all of the questionnaires for the study, then my scores will be sent to researchers at Western Michigan Univesity in Kalamazoo, Michigan.

My name will not be on any of the questionnaires that get sent to Kalamazoo, Michigan. The researchers will use a code number instead. The researchers will keep a list of names and code numbers that will be destroyed once the researchers have looked at all of the questionnaires completed by about 120 youth participating in this project.

All of my answers will be kept private, which means even my Children's Service Worker or caregivers won't know what I say unless project staff members think I might be in danger of hurting myself or others or someone else might be in danger. Then project staff will need to tell my Children's Service Worker.

Your signature below indicates that you agree to be tested using the:

- The Brief Child and Family Phone Interview (BCFPI)
- Client Engagement in Child Protective Services (CECPS)
- Barriers to Adolescents Seeking Help (BASH)
- Barriers to Engagement in Treatment Survey (BETS)

(continued)

Box 15.3 (continued)

- General Help Seeking Questionnaire (GHSQ)

  Your signature also indicates that you agree:

- to have your case file reviewed for the following information: the type of placement I live in now, how long I have lived at my current placement, the number of placements I have had before this one, the services that I got during the project, whether I have contact with my birth family, and the number of times I contacted a CKCS worker during the project.
- to be eligible to be assigned to participate in a special help-seeking workshop for this project.

- for CKCS to give the researchers my test scores and case file information only. (Your name will not be sent to the researchers.)

  _____

  Print your name here

  _____

  Sign your name here, and write today's date

  Assent obtained by: _____

as feedback for development rather than as evidence for judgment. Integrating evaluation with service delivery tends to ground evaluation activities and lessens the chance that evaluation will become a political tool or weapon.

While the idea that "evaluation and service delivery go hand in hand" is easy enough to grasp intellectually, it is practiced far too rarely. Evaluators must make a special effort to advocate this position and help administrators and workers alike to see the benefits of it. There are a number of things an evaluator can do to increase the likelihood that the concept of evaluation as an integral part of the service delivery structure is accepted.

First, the "evaluation–practice integration" message may need to be sent repeatedly. Successfully incorporating evaluation activities into the client service delivery process involves educating staff members at all levels, from line-level social workers up to management. The message needs to be included in training and repeated as necessary. Second, helping administrators and staff use evaluation products effectively is a powerful strategy; once they see the how data from an evaluation can help inform decision making, support for integrating evaluation activities is sure to increase. Finally, data collection protocols should ensure that only those data that are truly needed are collected, and in a manner that imposes as little burden on staff members as is possible. Data collection has costs associated with it; the benefits of collecting any data should clearly outweigh the costs of collecting them, and should be perceived to do so by staff.

Principle 2: Involve From the Beginning as Many Stakeholder Groups as Possible

Because of the different points of view represented by various stakeholder groups, and because of the possibility that some group or groups may wish to use an evaluation to promote their agenda—hidden or open—it is important to involve members from relevant stakeholder groups early in the evaluation process. The benefit of including as many stakeholder groups as possible is that the evaluation plan will be open to scrutiny from a diverse range of perspectives and therefore the interests of the different groups are likely to be balanced.

The downside, of course, is that "too many cooks spoil the broth." Thus, while it is important to include as many stakeholder groups as possible, it is not necessary to involve everyone in all aspects of the evaluation effort. Stakeholder groups could be invited to periodic review meetings where updates are provided and the main interests and concerns of stakeholder groups are aired and discussed. Between formal meetings, stakeholder groups can be kept involved in other ways. Written information, perhaps in the form of an insert to the program newsletter, could be circulated about the status of the evaluation, describing current evaluation activities, results, and decisions. Responses can be invited, thereby ensuring ongoing stakeholder feedback.

Principle 3: Involve All Levels of Staff in the Evaluation Process

A constructive environment is one in which all levels of staff are involved in the evaluation process. A frequent mistake is to make the assumption that only senior-level staff members need to be involved in planning the evaluation and that only they should receive the findings derived from an evaluation. In well-functioning programs, decisions are made at all levels. Consequently, it is important that the evaluation system serves the needs of staff members at all levels, providing information for high-quality decision making throughout the program. Making decisions on the basis of an evaluation's findings is, as we have seen, a matter of making effective use of feedback. Depending on the extent to which a program's objectives are being achieved, decisions can be made to continue existing activities, modify them, or switch to new ones.

When staff members at any level in the organization are required to operate without adequate feedback, the effectiveness of their contributions will be decreased. In the process, the entire organizational performance suffers.

Principle 4: Make Explicit the Purpose of the Evaluation

The purpose of an evaluation should be clearly spelled out to all those who are asked to participate as well as to those who will be affected by its findings and recommendations. Purpose includes information about who initiated and is funding the evaluation as well as the types of decisions to be based on the findings. This is a time for clarity and frankness. If the purpose of an evaluation is to develop information (via reliable and valid data) that can help in making decisions about funding, this should be clearly spelled out. If specific aspects of program functioning are the primary concern and it is hoped that evaluation results will shed light on relevant procedures and practices, this, too, should be explicitly stated.

Although this guideline may seem obvious, it is sometimes violated. For example, it is sometimes claimed that the purpose of an evaluation is to obtain data for program development, but it subsequently turns out that it was actually commissioned to provide data for a funding decision. It is clearly unethical for evaluators to knowingly engage in evaluations with hidden agendas; if evaluators discover such a situation in the course of the work, they have a responsibility to make known their concerns and find appropriate remedies. These remedies may include discussions to resolve the concern, formal dissent in the form of a cover letter, refusal to sign the report, or resignation (American Evaluation Association, 1994).

Principle 5: Provide a Balanced Report and Disseminate Early and Regularly

The manner in which findings are reported and disseminated is an important matter of evaluation practice. The need to tailor reports to the audience and to report in a clear, comprehensible manner has already been discussed in this chapter. The contents of reports is another matter for attention; it is important that reports be balanced and fair. It may be tempting, for example, to give great weight to positive findings while playing down or ignoring disappointing findings. Positive findings tend to be more enthusiastically received, but it is obviously just as important to know when results fall short of expectations. Moreover, all evaluations have limitations, and thus it is important to describe such limitations in a way that lets decision makers understand what the limitations imply.

Sometimes, the dissemination of reports will become controversial. Because information is a source of power in our world, some stakeholders may seek to further their political ambitions by manipulating the dissemination of an evaluation's results and findings—withholding, delaying, or selectively circulating reports. Such manipulative tactics can be short-circuited if evaluators pay attention to establishing procedures for dissemination early in the process, well before results are in. The most equitable practices are those that provide for dissemination to all stakeholder groups through regularly scheduled reports in the case of a monitoring evaluation, and through early dissemination in a project-type evaluation.

SUMMING UP AND LOOKING AHEAD

This chapter presented various considerations that should be taken into account when evaluating a social service program. Because programs take place in the real world, politics and political influence are often unavoidable. As well, because they are complex entities, technical decisions can often influence the course of the evaluation as well as its results. Evaluators have a responsibility to ensure that their work provides accurate, fair, and complete information to decision makers and that it is used in an open, constructive decision-making process.

Professional standards, ethical guidelines for conducting research, and evaluation practice principles provide guidance to evaluation practitioners that will help them to ensure that their evaluations are constructive, ethical, and of the highest quality. The following chapter builds on the ethical and professional issues discussed in this chapter, in that it presents diversity issues that must be addressed in an evaluation.

RECAP AND ONLINE MATERIALS

In this chapter, you learned how to make sense out of the politics and ethics that surround social work evaluation endeavors.

You should also recall the concept of ethics from your foundational research course. If not, go online to take a free crash course in ethics.

You can also find the following materials online to help you master the concepts you just learned:

- Chapter Outline
- Learning Objectives
- Key Terms and Concepts
- Flash Cards
- Practice Multiple-Choice Tests
- Essay Questions with Answers
- Links

www.oup.com/us/swevaluation

STUDY QUESTIONS

1. Select one outcome evaluation that was published in a professional social work journal. Assess the evaluation procedures of the case study according to the standards for evaluation practice in the areas of utility, feasibility, fairness, and accuracy. Explain your answer in detail.

2. In your own words, list the factors that can influence evaluation outcomes. What strategies can you offer to minimize the bias that these factors may introduce into evaluation outcomes? See appendix that is at the end of this book, then discuss the process of obtaining informed consent from a client.. What level of detail would you use to explain the client's participation in the evaluation? Would your approach to receiving informed consent from a client be formal or informal? Explain your answer in detail.

3. Discuss the differences between internal and external uses of evaluation data. Provide a specific example of each. Many workers fear and resist program evaluation as a formal part of client service. What strategies can you suggest to increase their level of comfort with the notions of accountability and evaluation? What strategies can you suggest to minimize the misuse of program evaluation in social service agencies? Explain your answer in detail.

4. In groups of four, create a code of ethics to guide social workers in conducting evaluations. Develop brief guidelines focused on the following themes: purpose of evaluation, informed consent, evaluation design, and dissemination of results.

5. In groups of five, choose a program-level social work intervention. Clearly identify a purpose, or reason, for evaluating the intervention. How does defining the purpose of the evaluation affect the choice of evaluation design, sampling procedures, data collection, data analysis, and dissemination of results? What other purposes of evaluation can you identify? How do different purposes influence the design and procedure of the evaluation?

6. A coworker maintains that evaluation of interventions and programs always produce the same result. You will comment on that. You argue that the selection of objectives affects the outcome of an evaluation at the case and program levels. Outline the main points of your argument. You also maintain that the timing of data collection may also affect evaluation outcomes. How do you support your position? You argue that sample selection and interpretation of results affect evaluation outcomes. Why?

7. Given that evaluation is a social activity, why is ethical evaluation practice so important? Ethical guidelines and principles for social workers indicate that the purpose of the evaluation should be clearly spelled out for all those who participate. Why is this important?

8. Ethical guidelines also require informed consent for participation in evaluations. Why? How is confidentiality a paramount component of ethical evaluation? How can the confidentiality of participants be ensured? Discuss in detail. Provide a social service example throughout your discussion.

9. How do ethical considerations affect the selection of evaluation designs at the case and program level? Discuss in detail. Provide a social service example throughout your discussion. How do ethical considerations affect the dissemination of results at the case and program level? Discuss in detail. Provide a social service example throughout your discussion.

10. In a county agency, an evaluation has been commissioned to justify decisions about budget cuts that have already been made. In what ways is this an inappropriate use of evaluation? Discuss in detail. Provide a social service example throughout your discussion. How can an evaluation be used to distract attention from negative publicity? Discuss in detail. Provide a social service example throughout your discussion. How can evaluation data be used appropriately to guide internal decision making? Discuss in detail. Provide a social service example throughout your discussion. How can evaluation data be used appropriately to guide external decision making? Discuss in detail. Provide a social service example throughout your discussion. The establishment of a constructive context for evaluation begins with making a commitment to internal, continuous, self-directed evaluation. What practices must be adopted to accomplish this? Discuss in detail. Provide a social service example throughout your discussion.

References, Further Reading, and Resources

Abramson, M. (1985). The autonomy-paternalism dilemma in social work practice. *Social Casework, 66,* 387–393.

American Evaluation Association. (2004, July). *Guiding principles for evaluators.* Retrieved February 20, 2006, from http://www.eval.org/Publications/GuidingPrinciples.asp

Berliner, A. K. (1989). Misconduct in social work practice. *Social Work, 34,* 69–72.

Besharov, D.S. (1985). *The vulnerable social worker.* Silver Spring, MD: National Association of Social Workers.

Besharov, D. S., & Besharov, S. H. (1987). Teaching about liability. *Social Work, 32,* 517–522.

Billups, J. O. (1992). The moral basis for a radical reconstruction of social work. In P. N. Reid, & P. R. Popple (Eds.), *The moral purposes of social work* (pp. 100–119). Chicago: Nelson-Hall.

Black, P. N., Hartley, E. K., Whelley, J., & KirkSharp, C. (1989). Ethics curricula: A national survey of graduate schools of social work. *Social Thought, 15*(3/4), 141–148.

Conrad, A. P. (1989). Developing an ethics review process in a social service agency. *Social Thought, 15*(3/4), 102–115.

Dickson, D. T. (1998). *Confidentiality and privacy in social work.* New York: Free Press.

Gambrill, E., & Pruger, R. (Eds.). (1997). *Controversial issues in social work: Ethics, values, and obligations.* Needham Heights, MA: Allyn & Bacon.

Gilchrest, L., & Schinke, S. (2001). Research ethics. In R. M. Grinnell, Jr. (Ed.), *Social work research and evaluation: Quantitative and qualitative approaches* (6th ed., pp. 55–69). Itasca, IL: F. E. Peacock.

Goldberg, J. E. (1989). AIDS: Confidentiality and the social worker. *Social Thought, 15*(3/4), 116–127.

Goldmeier, J. (1984). Ethical styles and ethical decisions in health settings. *Social Work in Health Care, 10*(1), 45–60.

Goldstein, H. (1987). The neglected moral link in social work practice. *Social Work, 32,* 181–186.

Jayaratne, S., Croxton, T., & Mattison, D. (1997). Social work professional standards: An exploratory study. *Social Work, 42,* 187–198.

Joint Committee on Standards for Educational Evaluation (1994). *Program evaluation standards* (2nd ed.) Thousand Oaks, CA: Sage.

Joseph, M. V. (1989). Social work ethics: Historical and contemporary perspectives. *Social Thought, 15*(3/4), 4–17.

Kagle, J. D., & Giebelhausen, P. N. (1994). Dual relationships and professional boundaries. *Social Work, 39,* 213–220.

Keith-Lucas, A. (1977). Ethics in social work. In J. Turner (Series Ed.), *Encyclopedia of social work* (17th ed., Vol. 1, pp. 350–355). Silver Spring, MD: National Association of Social Workers.

Keith-Lucas, A. (1992). A socially sanctioned profession? In P. N. Reid, & P. R. Popple (Eds.), *The moral purposes of social work* (pp. 51–70). Chicago: Nelson-Hall.

Kopels, S., & Kagle, J. D. (1993). Do social workers have a duty to warn? *Social Service Review, 67,* 101–126.

Kurzman, P. A. (1983). Ethical issues in industrial social work practice. *Social Casework, 64,* 105–111.

Levy, C. S. (1982). *Guide to ethical decisions and actions for social service administrators.* New York: Haworth Press.

Loewenberg, F., & Dolgoff, R. (1996). *Ethical decisions for social work practice* (5th ed.). Itasca, IL: F. E. Peacock.

McGowan, B. G. (1995). Values and ethics. In C. H. Meyer, & M. A. Mattaini (Eds.), *The foundations of social work practice* (pp. 28–41). Washington, DC: NASW Press.

National Association of Social Workers. (1996). *Code of ethics.* Washington, DC: Author.

Popple, P. R. (1992). Social work: Social function and moral purpose. In P. N. Reid, & P. R. Popple (Eds.), *The moral purposes of social work* (pp. 141–154). Chicago: Nelson-Hall.

Reamer, F. G. (1987). Informed consent in social work. *Social Work, 32,* 425–429.

Reamer, F. G. (1987). Values and ethics. In A. Minahan (Series Ed.), *Encyclopedia of social work* (18th ed., Vol. 2, pp. 801–809). Silver Spring, MD: National Association of Social Workers.

Reamer, F. G. (1988). Social workers and unions: Ethical dilemmas. In H. J. Karger (Ed.), *Social workers and labor unions* (pp. 131–143). Westport, CT: Greenwood Press.

Reamer, F. G. (1989). Liability issues in social work supervision. *Social Work, 34,* 445–448.

Reamer, F. G. (1990). *Ethical dilemmas in social service* (2nd ed.). New York: Columbia University Press.

Reamer, F. G. (1995). Ethics consultation in social work. *Social Thought, 18*(1), 3–16.

Reamer, F. G. (1997). Ethical standards in social work: The NASW Code of Ethics. In R. L. Edwards (Series Ed.), *Encyclopedia of social work* (19th ed., Suppl., pp. 113–123). Washington, DC: NASW Press.

Reamer, F. G. (1998). *Ethical standards in social work: A critical review of the NASW Code of Ethics.* Washington, DC: NASW Press.

Reamer, F. G. (2005). Research ethics. In R. M. Grinnell, Jr., & Y. A. Unrau (Eds.), *Social work research and evaluation: Quantitative and qualitative approaches* (7th ed., pp. 33–43). New York: Oxford University Press.

Summers, A. B. (1989). The meaning of informed consent in social work. *Social Thought, 15*(3/4), 128–140.

Timms, N. (1983). *Social work values: An enquiry.* London: Routledge & Kegan Paul.

VandeCreek, L., Knapp, S., & Herzog, C. (1988). Privileged communication for social workers. *Social Casework, 69,* 28–34.

Weinbach, R. W. (2005). Research contexts. In R. M. Grinnell, Jr., & Y. A. Unrau (Eds.), *Social work research and evaluation: Quantitative and qualitative approaches* (7th ed., pp. 23–32). New York: Oxford University Press.

On Informed Consent

Anderman, C., Cheadle, A., Curry, S., Diehr, P., Shultz, L., & Wagner, E. (1995). Selection bias related to parental consent in school-based survey research. *Evaluation Review, 19,* 663–674.

Baker, J. R., Yardley, J. K., & McCaul, K. (2001). Characteristics of responding-, nonresponding-, and refusing-parents in an adolescent lifestyle choice study. *Evaluation Review, 25,* 605–618.

Dent, C. W., Sussman, S. Y., & Stacy, A. (1997). The impact of a written parental consent policy on estimates from a school-based drug use survey. *Evaluation Review, 21,* 698–712.

Ellickson, P. L., & Hawes, J. A. (1989). An assessment of active versus passive methods for obtaining parental consent. *Evaluation Review, 13,* 45–55.

Esbensen, F. A., Deschenes, E. P., Vogel, R. E., West, J., Arboit, K., & Harris, L. (1996). Active parental consent in school-based research. *Evaluation Review, 20,* 737–753.

Esbensen, F. A., Miller, M. H., Taylor, T. J., He, N., & Freng, A. (1999). Differential attrition rates and active parental consent. *Evaluation Review, 23,* 316–335.

Hollmann, C. M., & McNamara, J. R. (1999). Considerations in the use of active and passive parental consent procedures. *Journal of Psychology, 133,* 141–156.

Iverson, A. M., & Cook, G. L. (1994). Guardian consent for children's participation in sociometric research. *Psychology in the Schools, 31,* 108–112.

Jason, L. A., Pokorny, S., & Katz, R. (2001). Passive versus active consent: A case study in school settings. *Journal of Community Psychology, 29,* 53–68.

Johnson, K., Bryant, D., Rockwell, E., Moore, M., Straub, B. W., Cummings, P., et al. (1999). Obtaining active parental consent for evaluation research: A case study. *American Journal of Evaluation, 20,* 239–249.

Kearney, K. A., Hopkins, R. H., Mauss, A. L., & Weisheit, R. A. (1983). Sample bias resulting from a requirement for written parental consent. *Public Opinion Quarterly, 47,* 96–102.

Korn, J. H., & Bram, D. R. (1988). What is missing in the method section of APA journal articles? *American Psychologist, 43,* 1091–1092.

Levine, R. J. (1995). Adolescents as research subjects without permission of their parents or guardians: Ethical considerations. *Journal of Adolescent Health, 17,* 287–297.

Mammel, K. A., & Kaplan, D. W. (1995). Research consent by adolescent minors and institutional review boards. *Journal of Adolescent Health, 17,* 323–330.

Miller, F. G., & Rosenstein, D. L. (2002). Reporting of ethical issues in publications of medical research. *The Lancet, 360,* 1326–1328.

Moolchan, E. T., & Mermelstein, R. (2002). Research on tobacco use among teenagers: Ethical challenges. *Journal of Adolescent Health, 30,* 409–417.

Noll, R. B., Zeller, M. H., Vannatta, K., Bukowski, W. M., & Davies, W. H. (1997). Potential bias in classroom research: Comparison of children with permission and those who do not receive permission to participate. *Journal of Clinical Child Psychology, 26,* 36–42.

Oakes, J. M. (2002). Risks and wrongs in social science research. An evaluator's guide to the IRB. *Evaluation Review, 26,* 443–479.

O'Donnell, L. N., Duran, R. H., Doval, A. S., Breslin, M. J., Juhn, G. M., & Stueve, A. (1997). Obtaining written parent permission for school-based health surveys of urban young adolescents. *Journal of Adolescent Health, 21,* 376–383.

Pokorny, S. B., Jason, L. A., Schoeny, M. E., Townsend, S. M., & Curie, C. J. (2001). Do participation rates change when active consent procedures replace passive consent? *Evaluation Review, 25,* 567–580.

Renger, R., Gotkin, V., Crago, M., & Shisslak, C. (1998). Research and legal perspectives on the implications of the Family Privacy Protection Act for research and evaluation involving minors. *American Journal of Evaluation, 19,* 191–202.

Ross, J. G., Sundberg, E. C., & Flint, K. H. (1999). Informed consent in school health research: Why, how, and making it easy. *Journal of School Health, 69,* 171–176.

Severson, H. H., & Ary, D. V. (1983). Sampling bias due to consent procedures with adolescents. *Addictive Behaviors, 8,* 433–437.

Severson, H. H., & Biglan, A. (1989). Rationale for the use of passive consent in smoking prevention research: Politics, policy, and pragmatics. *Preventive Medicine, 18,* 267–279.

Thompson, T. L. (1984). A comparison of methods of increasing parental consent rates in social research. *Public Opinion Quarterly, 48,* 779–787.

Tigges, B. B. (2003). Parental consent and adolescent risk behavior research. *Journal of Nursing Scholarship, 35,* 283–289.

CULTURALLY APPROPRIATE EVALUATIONS

16

Carol Ing

Our village has grown to encompass the world. Faster means of transportation, the expansion of trade, and the human desire to seek a better life have created societies that no longer find their roots in one cultural tradition and their voice in one common language. Rather, migration trends and globalization activities have laid the foundations for complex, culturally diverse societies with representation from several racial, ethnic, and cultural groups. Diversity is reflected throughout society: in schools, in the workplace, and within all types of formal organizations. Social service organizations are no exception; there is increasing diversity both among staff and also among service recipients. Of course, diversity also has an impact on the field of evaluation; the challenge for evaluators is to work effectively in culturally diverse settings.

As is made clear throughout our book, evaluation is more than the technical practice of organizing and implementing data collection activities, analyzing data, and reporting findings. Although these are important evaluation activities, evaluation also involves working effectively with a variety of stakeholders in a wide range of organizations. The tasks include working with people to clarify expectations, identify interests, reconcile differences, and win cooperation.

Evaluators must therefore be adept in establishing interpersonal and working relationships in addition to bringing technical expertise to the evaluation process. When working with different cultural groups or in different cultural settings, evaluators must be culturally competent and also have the ability to adapt the technical processes of evaluation so that they are appropriate for the setting.

In this chapter, a brief overview of culture and cultural competence is provided, followed by a discussion of key issues in culturally competent evaluation practice. As the issues are discussed, we will make use of examples of worldview perceptions, communications, and behaviors that may be characteristic of particular cultures. These are intended only as examples of cultural patterns and not to suggest that any characteristics describe all members of the group. We fully recognize that cultures are not monolithic and that a variety of cultural patterns may exist within broadly defined cultural groups. The descriptions provided within this chapter are for illustrative purposes only and are not meant to be stereotypical of the members of any culture.

We also know that each individual is unique, and we recognize that within any culture a wide range of individual perceptions, communications, and behaviors may exist. In evaluation, as in any other human interactive process, there is no substitute for meeting each person with openness and acceptance—regardless of cultural background.

THE IMPACT OF CULTURE

Culture

The values, traditions, norms, customs, arts, history, folklore, and institutions that a group of people share, who are unified by race, ethnicity, language, nationality, or religion.

Tradition

Traditional cultural beliefs that we accept "without question" as true; one of the ways of knowing.

Culture is many things: a set of customs, **traditions**, and beliefs, and a world view. They are socially defined and passed on from generation to generation (Porter & Samovar, 1997). Culture is manifested in the perceptions through which we view our surroundings and the patterns of language and behaviors through which we interact with others. Culture exists at two levels: at the micro level and at the macro level. Micro-level culture is found with individuals and is reflected in their personal values, beliefs, communication styles, and behaviors. Macro-level culture exists at the level of organizations, institutions, and communities; it is manifested in mandates, policies, and practices.

Fundamentally, culture acts as a filter through which people view, perceive, and evaluate the world around them. At the same time, it also provides a framework within which people process information, think, communicate, and behave. Because different cultures establish different frameworks for perceiving and judging as well as for thinking and acting, misperceptions, miscommunications, and conflicts are not only possible but likely. Where people are unaware of how culture filters thinking, actions, perceptions, and judgments, the likelihood for misunderstanding is even greater.

The Japanese, for example have traditionally used bowing as a form of greeting, but in North America hand shakes are prevalent; in certain European countries, hugging and kissing are customary. It is easy to see that what is meant as a friendly gesture in one culture may be viewed as an intrusion in another. In a meeting, for example, a statement that is meant as a hypothetical example in one culture may be viewed as a firm commitment in another.

Moreover, what is valued in one culture may not be nearly as important in another. In North America, for example, there is considerable emphasis on the "bottom line," which translates to outcomes in evaluation. Thus, evaluations are often concerned with assessing the outcomes of a social service program (see Chapter 7). In some cultures, however, the fact that a program has been created and now operates and provides employment for community members (see Chapter 6) may be viewed as at least as important as the actual results of the services.

BRIDGING THE CULTURE GAP

Under the principle "respect for people" as set out by the American Evaluation Association (1994), evaluators are expected to be aware of and respect differences among people and to be mindful of the implications of cultural differences on the evaluation process. Evaluators thus need (1) a clear understanding of the impact of culture on human and social processes generally and on evaluation processes specifically, and (2) skills in cross-cultural communications to ensure that they can effectively interact with people from diverse backgrounds.

Cultural Awareness

As the previous discussion makes clear, culture provides a powerful organizing framework that filters perceptions and communications and also shapes behaviors and interactions. To practice effectively in different cultural settings, evaluators need a general awareness of the role that culture plays in shaping our perceptions, ideas, and behaviors. Further, evaluators need fundamental attitudes of respect for difference, a willingness to learn about other cultures, and a genuine belief that cultural differences are a source of strength and enrichment rather than an obstacle to be overcome. In particular, evaluators need **cultural awareness**: They need to be on guard that their perceptions, communications, and actions are not unduly influenced by ethnocentrism, enculturation, and stereotyping—processes that act as barriers to effective communications and relationships.

Because our own history is inevitably based in our own culture, and because we generally continue to be immersed in that culture, a natural human tendency is to judge others and other cultures by the standards of our own beliefs and values. This is known as ethnocentrism; it leads to defining the world in our own terms. Thus, we might tend to view as normal that which is typical in our own culture; different practices, structures, or patterns that may be typical in other cultures are likely then viewed as "abnormal" or even problematic (Neuliep, 2000).

Among some social groups, for example, child rearing is viewed as a community

> **Cultural awareness**
> Our understanding of and appreciation for the values, traditions, norms, customs, arts, history, folklore, and institutions that a group of people share, who are unified by race, ethnicity, language, nationality, or religion.

responsibility, with extended family and other community members taking an active role when necessary. This is seldom typical in urban North American culture, where high mobility often places families in communities without extended family or other support networks. Thus, in a large urban setting an appropriate outcome for family support programs may be that the family remains intact, but in communities located in rural or remote areas or on Native American reservations, a more appropriate outcome might be that suitable caregiving arrangements are identified within the family's kinship or community network. In short, an ethnocentric evaluator might, however unwittingly, apply mainstream North American values to a Native American family support program; this would clearly result in a distortion in the evaluation process.

Enculturation is a related process, which refers to the fact that, as children, we learn to behave in ways that are appropriate to our culture. We also come to adopt a variety of core beliefs about human nature, human experience, and human behavior. This process teaches us how to behave, interact, and even think. Of course, other cultural groups will have different ways of thinking, behaving, and interacting. In some Asian cultures, for example, people value discussion, negotiation, and relationship, whereas in North America, people tend to be more direct and task-oriented (Hall, 1983). Similarly, some cultures such as the Swiss and Germans emphasize promptness, whereas in some Southern cultures, a meeting is seldom expected to start at the appointed time, but only after everyone has arrived (Lewis, 1997).

The differences in behavior patterns and interactions are real; however, it is important for evaluators to recognize that others' patterns are as legitimate and appropriate as their own. When evaluators are unable to do this, stereotyping may occur, resulting in misunderstanding and misjudgment. For example, an evaluator may become frustrated because it is difficult to start meetings on time in a community or because it is not possible to keep to a tight schedule, and she may begin to stereotype the group she is working with as uninterested, noncooperative, and disorganized. Obviously, such stereotypes will have the effect of creating additional barriers to communications and interactions and will hinder the evaluation process.

Intercultural Communication

Awareness of the impact of culture is important, but effective relationships depend on the actual communications. Because evaluation is as much a relationship process as a technical matter, effective communication is always important, particularly so in communication across cultures.

There are many models of **intercultural communication**. One of the more useful ones is offered by Porter and Samovar (1997). In this model, perceptions are regarded as the gateway to communications; they are the means by which people select, evaluate, and organize information about the world around them. Perceptions, of course, depend in large part upon an individual's worldview, which is, in part, formed as a result of his

Intercultural communication

Means by which people select, evaluate, and organize information about the world around them.

or her cultural experiences. Perceptions help us select, organize, and interpret a variety of external stimuli, including the communications that others direct toward us.

After we process the communications that are directed toward us, we usually respond. Different cultures support different communication patterns and styles, and thus our response is also shaped and formed, at least in part, by our cultural background. Communications, then, are inextricably bound with culture. The opportunity for misunderstanding, ever present in any communication, is even greater when individuals from different cultural backgrounds interact.

Intercultural communication takes place at both the nonverbal and verbal levels. Anyone who interacts with members of another culture needs an understanding of both nonverbal and verbal communications patterns typical in that culture. We will briefly look at communications at each of these levels.

Nonverbal

An important part of human communications takes place nonverbally. Facial expressions, time, use of space, and gestures convey much information and are deeply based in culture. Without an understanding of the meaning of **nonverbal communication** symbols used by a culture, it is all too easy to misinterpret signs.

Nonverbal communication Non-language communication such as noises, gestures, or facial expressions.

For example, a hand gesture that has virtually no meaning in one culture may be a vulgar symbol in another culture. For example, the OK sign, widely used in North America, is a circle formed by the thumb and the first finger; this sign is considered to be offensive and unacceptable in Brazil, and to mean money in Japan (Morrison, Conway, & Borden, 1994).

Positioning oneself in relation to another may result in an inadvertent message of disinterest or aggression. North Americans usually feel comfortable standing at a distance of about two and half to four feet from others. However, members of some cultures, among them Arabic, prefer to stand much closer when engaged in a conversation (Hall, 1983). An evaluator who positions himself at a North American distance may be perceived as cold, aloof, and disinterested by members of such cultures.

Similarly, the use of eye contact carries culturally specific meaning. In European-based cultures, eye contact is used extensively to demonstrate interest and to confirm that one is listening. Many other cultures, however, do not use eye contact extensively and may perceive it as disrespectful and even threatening. For example, prolonged eye contact in cultures such as that of the Japanese is considered to be rude (Samovar, Porter, & Stefani, 1998).

Verbal

On the verbal level, words also derive much of their meaning through culture. As language is the primary means through which a culture communicates its values and beliefs, the same words may have different meanings within different cultures. For example, the Japanese use the word *hai*, meaning "yes," to indicate that they have heard what was said and are thinking about a response. Because, in many circumstances, it is considered impolite to openly express disagreement, *hai* is used even when the listener is actually in disagreement with what is being said (Koyama, 1992). Thus the meaning assigned to "yes" is quite different than that commonly understood by North Americans, who consider "yes" to mean that the listener is in agreement.

As the evaluation process involves extensive transmission of information through communications, it is obviously vital that **verbal communications** be accurate and effective. Without an understanding of intercultural communication generally and an ability to understand the specific patterns used by the group with whom the evaluator is dealing, communications problems may arise and derail the evaluation process.

Verbal communication
Language communication using words.

CULTURAL FRAMEWORKS

As we have seen, culture often defines a group's values and beliefs, and creates its communications patterns. In addition, culture also provides frameworks for other complex structures and processes. Different cultural groups, for example, have different methods of gathering information and of making decisions. An understanding of these patterns is essential to ensure that data collection and analytical processes are appropriate and reports are practical and relevant. This section briefly looks at cultural frameworks regarding data, decision making, individualism, tradition, the pace of life, and concepts of time.

Orientation to Information

Some cultures thrive on "hard" data and greatly value processes, such as research, that produce data which can then be considered and acted upon (Lewis, 1997). These cultures, which include the North American mainstream culture, are considered data oriented. On the other hand, some cultures such as Middle Eastern and Latin American cultures are viewed as "dialogue oriented," in that they pay more attention to relationships and process than to data (Lewis, 1997). These groups tend to view statistics and data with some suspicion and regard it as only part of a picture. Such cultures consider relationships and context as more important than numbers.

Decision Making

In many Western cultures, logic and rationality are highly valued and used extensively in making decisions about important matters (Hoefstede, 1997; Lewis, 1997). The research approaches upon which evaluation processes are based are examples of this style of "scientific" thinking. However, some cultures are less impressed by science and prefer intuition or more subjective, personal approaches to thinking and decision making. When evaluators prepare a report for people whose culture supports a scientific orientation to thinking, quantitative data with statistical analyses is quite appropriate; however, if the users are people who come from a culture that prefers more subjective and intuitive approaches to decision making, a report organized around the presentation of quantitative results will be less useful and comprehensible.

Individualism

Although most cultures support both individualistic and collectivistic tendencies, there is in every culture a bias toward one or the other (Hoefstede, 1997). In **individualistic cultures** such as the mainstream North American culture people work toward individual goals, and initiative, competition, and achievement are highly valued. In **collectivistic cultures,** people are group oriented; loyalty, relationships, and overall community development are valued while individual goals are downplayed. In such cultures, the family, organizations with which people are affiliated (including the workplace), and the community are particularly important.

Keeping in perspective an organizations' cultural view on individualism versus collectivism is important in understanding the behaviors, the interactions, the work processes, and the structures that may be found in the course of an evaluation. What may appear from an individualistic perspective to be an unwieldy work process involving too many people may, in fact, be explained by a culture-based desire not to leave anyone out and to create as wide a network of involvement as is possible.

Individualist cultures
Emphasizing personal achievement at the expense of group goals, resulting in a strong sense of competition, such as the cultures of the United States and Western Europe.

Collectivist cultures
Emphasizing family and workgroup goals, such the cultures of China, Korea, and Japan.

Tradition

Some cultures are more traditional and value the status quo and conformity while others encourage innovation and view change as necessary if progress is to be made (Dodd, 1998). Change-oriented cultures such as mainstream North American society encourage experimentation, risk taking, and innovation. They consider change to be an opportunity to improve. In other cultures, such as with some traditional Asian cultures, values are centered around tradition and continuity. The young are expected to give way to the wishes of the older generation, and new ideas are not encouraged because they might disrupt the structure of society.

The reader will readily recognize that evaluation, as a change and improvement oriented activity, is grounded in Western cultural values. As such, the concept of evaluation itself may seem alien to those steeped in more traditional cultures. After all, evaluation is concerned with identifying areas for improvement, which therefore implies change, but traditional cultures value stability and continuity. Inevitably, evaluators will sometimes work with organizations that are based in a tradition-oriented culture. In such circumstances, evaluators need to be sensitive to the fact that there may not exist a common understanding even about the basic premises of the evaluation process.

Pace of Life

In North America, especially in larger cities, we live our lives at an accelerated pace. Our schedules are jammed with many activities; agendas are overloaded, and there is an expectation that everything is a priority and must be done immediately. Time is viewed as linear and rigid; we live with the sense that if we miss an event it is forever gone. In such cultures, which are called monochronic, people tend to organize their lives by the clock (Hall, 1983). Clearly, in such cultures it is important to be on time for meetings to meet deadlines and to stay on schedule (Samovar, Porter, & Stefani, 1998). In a sense, time is so central that members of the culture are hardly aware of its importance, but all things, including personal relationships, take second place to successful time management.

On the other hand, in polychronic cultures life is lived at a slower pace; activities grind to a halt on weekends, during rest times, and during festivals and important celebrations. Slower-paced cultures—for example, those in Latin America, the Middle East, and Indonesia—tend to be less aware of time and hold less of a concept of it as a commodity that must be managed. Time is seen as circular and flexible; the Indonesians even refer to it as "rubber time" (Harris & Moran, 1996). Time is not nearly as important an organizing force in people's lives as it is in monochronic cultures; if the scheduled start time passes without the event taking place, people are not unduly disturbed as another appropriate start time can be set. "Time is money" could not have arisen as a central idea in these cultures, which focus on relationships and interactions. Time management and business come second (Hall, 1983). In such cultures, it is vital to establish a personal relationship before conducting business.

Obviously evaluators need to have a good understanding of the concept of time held within the setting where they conduct their work. Tight schedules that provide few opportunities for cementing working relationships and disregard widely observed rest periods, holidays, and celebrations are obviously unrealistic and will be unsuitable in polychronic cultures. Attempting to impose such a schedule will be regarded as thoughtless and will impede rather than facilitate the evaluation process.

Further, in assessing the achievement of milestones and other accomplishments, evaluations need to take into account the concept of time and the pace of life prevalent in the particular culture. In setting up a new social service program, for example, planning, procedure, policy development, initial staffing, and other preparatory activities may be accomplished in a much briefer period of time in one setting than in another. Both the concept of time and the pace of life might be, in fact, equally appropriate when cultural orientation toward time is taken into account.

PUTTING IT TOGETHER: THE PRACTICE OF CULTURALLY COMPETENT EVALUATION

Although some evaluators come from minority backgrounds, many do bring a mainstream North American cultural orientation to their work. This orientation will result in part from their own cultural background and in part from their formation and education as evaluators. The methods of evaluation are, to a large degree, based in a Western or North American cultural tradition. Inevitably, evaluators will bring their own culturally based beliefs, values, and perspectives as well as their culturally based toolkit to the work.

More and more evaluations are conducted in settings that are culturally different from mainstream North American culture. Evaluations are conducted on reservations, at women's shelters, in organizations serving immigrants, and at agencies that grew from the needs and aspirations of minority communities and reflect the cultures of those communities.

Evaluators who undertake work in culturally different settings or among people from different cultural backgrounds require the skills to effectively conduct their work and to make the evaluation process meaningful within those settings. The essential competencies are (1) cultural awareness, (2) intercultural communication skills, (3) specific knowledge about the culture in which they hope to work, and (4) an ability to appropriately adapt evaluation methods and processes.

Cultural Awareness

To be effective in intercultural work, evaluators need a degree of cultural awareness that will provide them with an understanding of the impact of culture on all human values, attitudes, and behaviors as well as interactions and processes. They need to understand how culture filters communications and how evaluation itself is a culture-based activity. Further, evaluators should have an understanding of concepts such as ethnocentrism, enculturation, and stereotyping—all of which may subtly, or not so subtly, raise barriers to effective communications and relationships.

In addition, evaluators need to bring attitudes of openness and acceptance to their work as well as a genuine belief that cultural differences need not pose barriers but can strengthen and enrich the evaluation process. Evaluators who wish to practice in diverse settings also need a high degree of self-awareness as well as understanding of their own cultural values and experiences, and the impact of these values and experiences on their communications patterns, relationships, and professional work.

Cultural awareness increases through contact with other cultures and through experiencing differences. Travel, work in culturally different settings, and living in diverse communities are ways in which evaluators can develop their awareness and attitudes.

Intercultural Communication Skills

The ability to approach others with openness and acceptance is foundational to the effective communications, regardless of setting; in intercultural communications it is particularly important. However, effective intercultural communication also requires specific knowledge of the other culture and its communication symbols. As we now know, the meaning of nonverbal or verbal symbols is culturally defined. It is, therefore, important to know the meaning of common nonverbal and verbal communications symbols to ensure accuracy in both the transmission as well as the reception of messages.

Evaluators can prepare for their work by reading novels set in the culture, watching high-quality movies, and perusing books and guides that describe prevailing communications patterns. The use of cultural guides, to be discussed in the following section, is also helpful in learning to understand the meaning of common communication symbols.

Developing Specific Knowledge About the Culture

In the previous section, the importance of developing specific understandings about prevailing communications patterns in a specific culture was discussed. However, more than communication patterns must be understood by an evaluator who wishes to be effective in a culturally different setting. Specific knowledge about various details of the culture are important to ensure that effective relationships can be established, the work is planned in a realistic manner, and the resulting products will have utility.

Among other things, it is important to have some sense of the history of the group who comprise the culture in which the evaluation will be conducted. On Native American reservations, for example, the history of oppression and dislocation is vitally important and helps to frame values, attitudes, and beliefs. Among certain immigrant groups, escape from oppression is a dominant theme, and newly found freedoms and opportunities help to frame a highly individualistic and achievement-oriented culture.

Beyond history, specific values, beliefs, and perspectives that shape individuals' and groups' perceptions and communications are vital to understand, as are the cultural structures, processes, and frameworks that are characteristic of the group. For example, in working with Native American groups on reservations, it is customary to include elders on advisory committees and listen with respect to the ideas and opinions that they express. Further, meetings begin with a prayer to the Creator and not with a review of the agenda, as is the case in most Western-oriented institutions. Concepts of time have been discussed previously; it is sufficient to say that the scheduled starting time for meetings may or may not be firmly fixed, depending on the setting.

There are a myriad of other details about culture, some of which may be important to understand to work successfully in the setting. For example, one of the authors of this book once conducted an evaluation on a reservation; the work included observing a restorative justice circle in action. The program had been conceived carefully with extensive use of traditional symbols. One of these symbols was the circle itself, which symbolized a teepee; a convention had developed over time that participants entered and left the circle in one particular place that symbolized the entry to the teepee. Entering or leaving in any other place was regarded as the equivalent of walking through the walls of the teepee.

Of course, an evaluator coming from the outside would not have been aware of this and would inevitably have committed a cultural *faux pas* at some point during the process. Happily, this was averted in this case because a member of the evaluation project, who was from the community itself, served as a cultural guide and had briefed the evaluator on the meaning of the cultural symbols involved as well as appropriate behaviors.

In general, specific cultural knowledge can be obtained through the same methods as suggested for understanding the specifics of communications patterns: travel, reading guidebooks and histories by writers from the culture, and watching movies. Engaging collaborators from within the cultural group, although not necessarily from within the organization itself is perhaps the most effective way of learning about values, beliefs, traditions, behavior patterns, and the detailed texture of another culture.

Adapting Evaluations

Developing cultural awareness, intercultural communications skills, and specific knowledge of the culture of the group with which an evaluator is involved are foundational to conducting effective evaluations. The final set of skills involves adapting the evaluation processes and methods so that they will be appropriate and meaningful within the culture of the organization where the evaluation is being conducted. Adapting evaluations involves (1) working with stakeholders, (2) ensuring that the work processes are appropriate, and (3) ensuring that the products are meaningful and useful.

Working With Stakeholders

As is discussed throughout this book, a variety of groups, including funders, staff members, program participants, and community members may have an interest in how a program performs and, consequently, in the evaluation results. Different groups of stakeholders are likely to have different interests, and this will particularly be true in the case of evaluations conducted in settings with culturally different stakeholders.

Generally, funders represent powerful institutions such as governments and foundations within mainstream society. They will therefore articulate their interests from a North American or Western cultural perspective. In practice, funders will likely be interested in data that shed light on the extent to which the program is delivering the services that had been contracted and with what effect.

Further, they will prefer to have the data packaged as a formal report, replete with quantitative data and statistics as well as specific recommendations for change and improvement. On the other hand, if the setting is based in a different culture, staff members, service recipients, and community members may be more interested in understanding the role that the program is playing within the community. If they come from a dialogue-oriented culture, they may be interested in descriptions of the service process, and service recipients' stories about their experiences with the service and its impact on their families. They will be looking not so much to receive data for the purpose of making changes but rather to develop broader and deeper understanding of the program and its place in the community.

Evaluators need to work at understanding each stakeholder group's perspectives, expectations, and interests and realize that these may be fundamentally different from one another. Therefore, a culturally competent evaluator must be committed to accommodating within the evaluation process the different perspectives and interests of diverse stakeholders.

Adapting Processes

Evaluation work always involves obtaining the cooperation of staff members and other stakeholder groups in carrying out the required evaluation procedures—particularly data collection. This is especially true when a monitoring system of quality improvement is put into place; the effectiveness of such a system depends on staff members carrying out their assigned roles in the evaluation process in a knowledgeable and consistent manner. It is therefore very important that the work processes be designed so that they are congruent with the culture within the organization.

For example, evaluators need to take into account the cultural meaning of time in the organization. If the organization is polychronic and operates at a relatively relaxed pace, the scheduling of evaluation events and activities must take this into account. A schedule that may be appropriate in an organization that operates from a monochronic cultural perspective may be totally unfeasible within a polychronic culture. Attempting to impose such a schedule will create tensions and stresses and is likely to result, at best, in very inconsistent implementation of evaluation activities. At worst, the entire evaluation enterprise may be discredited and collapse.

It is thus important that evaluators design work processes in a manner that is congruent with the cultural meaning of time. Scheduling should take into account the concept of time and orientation to time, not impose a burden that would be regarded by the culture as unduly stressful or inappropriate; it should ensure that holidays, community celebrations, and festivals are taken into account in the setting of schedules.

Similarly, data collection activities need to take into account the cultural orientation of the staff members who are likely to collect the data, and the service recipients who are likely to provide them. In dialogue-oriented cultures, the collection of highly quantitative data involving the use of standardized measures, rating scales, and structured surveys may be inappropriate and result in inconsistent data collection at best. At worst, service recipients and staff members will go through the motions of providing and collecting data without really understanding why the data are needed or how they are to be used. The reliability and validity of such data, of course, are likely to be low, compromising the entire evaluation effort.

Data collection protocols and procedures need to take into account whether evaluation participants are orientated to "data" or "dialogue" and should be designed to be as meaningful and culturally appropriate as is possible. In dialogue-oriented cultures it may not be entirely possible, or advisable, to avoid the collection of quantitative data, but such data collection methods should be used sparingly. Ample explanations and support should also be provided to evaluation participants so that they can find meaning in these tasks and carry them out effectively.

Providing Meaningful Products

Ultimately, evaluations are undertaken to generate information products that stakeholders will find useful. It is particularly important that evaluation products be appropriate to the culture of stakeholders. As discussed earlier, funders are likely to find reports useful when they address the extent to which the program meets its contractual obligations for providing services and describe the outcomes of those services. Further, funders will look for quantitative data and statistical analyses that support the findings of the report. Managers who regularly deal with funders may also favor reports of this type.

However, other stakeholder groups may not find such products useful or understandable. This will be especially the case if stakeholders come from cultural back grounds that are dialogue oriented. Reports with descriptions, stories, illustrations, and even pictures are likely to prove more meaningful to such stakeholders.

Culturally competent evaluators should accommodate all stakeholder groups who have a legitimate interest in an evaluation's results. Tailoring reports to funders' needs alone represents poor evaluation practice and is unlikely to result in meaningful program change. Program development necessarily comes from the inside and is based, primarily, on the initiative of the managers and staff. Evaluation products should support the efforts of managers and staff to develop the program by providing data that are meaningful, practical, and useful.

It is usually the case that quantitative and qualitative approaches can be combined within an evaluation. Although matters that interest funders are likely to be more suited to quantitative data collection and analyses, increased understanding can result from including descriptively oriented material that focuses on contextual matters. Statistics describing the demographic makeup of service recipients, for example, can be supplemented by providing more detailed descriptions of a few selected service recipients. Often this can be accomplished by providing people the opportunity to tell their stories in their words (see Chapter 13).

As described in Chapter 15, the Joint Committee on Standards for Educational Evaluation (1994) calls for the implementation of utility standards. These standards are intended to ensure that an evaluation will serve the information needs of intended users. Clearly, this underscores the responsibility of evaluators to understand the intended audience for evaluations and to ensure that evaluation products are culturally appropriate and therefore comprehensible, meaningful, and useful.

SUMMING UP AND LOOKING AHEAD

This chapter presented the challenges of applying evaluation methods in culturally diverse settings. Conducting evaluations is a complex endeavor, and undertaking evaluations that involve stakeholders from different cultural backgrounds adds considerable complexity. The next chapter presents how to write a grant to obtain funds for a social service program.

RECAP AND ONLINE MATERIALS

In this chapter, you learned how to do culturally appropriate social work evaluations.

You should also recall the concept of culture from your foundational research course. If not, go online to take a free crash course in culture.

You can also find the following materials online to help you master the concepts you just learned:

- Chapter Outline
- Learning Objectives
- Key Terms and Concepts
- Flash Cards
- Practice Multiple-Choice Tests
- Essay Questions with Answers
- Links

www.oup.com/us/swevaluation

STUDY QUESTIONS

1. Pick a social problem such as child abuse, domestic violence, homelessness, or teen pregnancy. Identify 10 value or belief statements that you have about the social problem that you picked. Share your statements with a person of a different culture than yours. Does the person agree or disagree with your views?
2. List the different cultural groups that are part of your local community. Identify what you know about the customs, traditions, beliefs, and worldview of each. Is what you believe about different cultures in your community based on cultural truths or stereotypes?
3. Which of the different cultural groups in your community are you least comfortable with? Identify patterns of communication in your culture and this other culture. Discuss how the differences in communication patterns might impact your understanding of service needs in this other culture.
4. "It is important that social workers are aware of their ethnocentric beliefs and behaviors." Discuss why you agree or disagree with this statement.
5. You are a social worker who has been hired to evaluate a family support program in a culture that is different from yours. Discuss steps that you could take to ensure that intercultural communications between you and program stakeholders are accurate.
6. Imagine that you are the lead evaluator of a social service program that serves people in a culture that values personal approaches to decision making over "scientific" data collected from a group. Identify strategies to measure the impact

of the program on clients served that are congruent with the values and beliefs of the program.

7. Discuss the ways in which different cultural orientations to information, individualism, tradition, and time can impact the planning of an evaluation for a social service program.

8. Discuss how reading a novel about a different culture might assist you with increasing intercultural awareness. What are the dangers of relying solely on novels to teach you about other cultures? Visit a social service agency that serves clients from a culture that is different from yours. Discuss with the worker the knowledge and skills needed to be successful with helping clients from that particular culture.

9. Discuss the advantages and disadvantages of adapting evaluation procedures to fit the unique characteristics of one particular culture.

10. Develop a plan for yourself that will protect you from judging others through your ethnocentric worldview. Specifically, identify names of people that could be your cultural guides and steps that you can take to reflect on your words and behaviors as you work with people from other cultural groups.

REFERENCES, FURTHER READING, AND RESOURCES

American Evaluation Association. (2004, July). *Guiding principles for evaluators.* Retrieved February 20, 2006, from http://www.eval.org/Publications/GuidingPrinciples.asp

Beach, M. C., Price, E. G., Gary, T. L., Robinson, K. A., Gozu, A., Palacio, A., et al. (2005). Cultural competence: A systematic review of health care provider interventions. *Medical Care, 43*(4), 356–373.

Beiser, M., Gill, K., & Edwards, R. (1993). Mental health care in Canada: Is it accessible and equal? *Canada's Mental Health, 41*(2), 2–7.

Berman, R. I. (1994). Staff development in mental health organizations. *Administration and Policy in Mental Health, 2*(1), 49–55.

Bhui, K., Stansfeld, S., Hull, S., Priebe, S., Mole, F., & Feder, G. (2003). Ethnic variations in pathways to and use of specialist mental health services in the UK. *British Journal of Psychiatry, 182*, 105–116.

Boerstler, H., & de Figueiredo, J. M. (2003). Pathways of low-income minority patients to outpatient psychiatric treatment. *American Journal of Psychiatry,160*(5), 1004–1007.

Bonder, B., Martin, L., & Miracle, A. (2001). Achieving cultural competence: The challenge for clients and healthcare workers in a multicultural society. *Generations: Journal of the American Society on Aging, 25*(1), 35–42.

Boyle, D. P., & Springer, A. (2001). Toward a cultural competence measure for social work with specific populations. *Journal of Ethnic and Cultural Diversity in Social Work, 9*(3/4), 53–71.

Byington, K., Fischer, J., Walker, L., & Freedman, E. (1997). Evaluating the effectiveness of a multicultural counseling ethics and assessment training. *Journal of Applied Rehabilitation Counseling, 28*(4), 15–19.

Cain, R. (1996). Heterosexism and self-disclosure in the social work classroom. *Journal of Social Work Education, 32*, 65–76.

Carlson, M. H., Brack, C., Laygo, R., Cohen, R., & Kirkscey, M. (1998). An exploratory study of multicultural competence of counselors in training: Support for experiential skills building. *Clinical Supervisor, 17*(2), 75–87.

Coleman, H. (1996). Portfolio assessment of multicultural counseling competency. *Counseling Psychologist, 24*(2), 216–229.

Constantine, M. G., Juby, H. L., & Liang, J. J. (2001). Examining multicultural counseling competence and race-related attitudes among White marital and family therapists. *Journal of Marital and Family Therapy, 27*(3), 353–362.

Constantine, M. G., & Ladany, N. (2000). Self-report multicultural counseling competence scales: Their relation to social desirability attitudes and multicultural case conceptualization ability. *Journal of Counseling Psychology, 47*(2), 155–164.

Corrigan, P. W., & McCracken, S. G. (1998). An interactive approach to training teams and developing programs. *New Directions for Mental Health Services, 79*, 3–12.

Cross, T. L., Bazron, B., Dennis, K. K., & Isaacs, M. R. (1989). *Towards a culturally competent system of care.* Washington, DC: Howard University Press.

Cummings, A. L. (1992). A model for teaching experiential counseling interventions to novice counselors. *Counselor Education and Supervision, 32*(1), 23–31.

Dean, R. G. (2001). The myth of cross-cultural competence. *Families in Society: The Journal of Contemporary Human Services, 82*(6), 623–630.

D'Andrea, M., & Daniels, J. (1997). Multicultural counseling supervision: Central issues, theoretical considerations, and practical strategies. In D. B. Pope-Davis, & H. Coleman (Eds.), *Multicultural counseling competencies: Assessment, education and training, and supervision* (Vol. 7, pp. 290–309). Thousand Oaks, CA: Sage.

D'Andrea, M., Daniels, J., & Heck, R. (1991). Evaluating the impact of multicultural counseling training. *Journal of Counseling and Development, 70*, 143–150.

Diaz Lazaro, C., & Cohen, B. B. (2001). Cross-cultural contact in counseling training. *Journal of Multicultural Counseling and Development, 29*(1), 41–56.

Dodd, C. (1998). *Dynamics of intercultural communication* (5th ed.). New York: McGraw-Hill.

El-Guebaly, N., Toews, J., Lockyer, J., Armstrong, S., & Hodgins, D. (2000). Medical education in substance-related disorders: Components and outcome. *Addiction, 95*(6), 949–957.

Fenwick, T. J. (2000). Putting meaning into workplace learning. In A. L. Wilson & E. R. Hayes (Eds.), *Handbook of adult and continuing education* (pp. 294–311). San Francisco: Jossey-Bass.

Fong, R. (2001). Culturally competent social work practice. Past and present. In R. Fong & S. Furuto (Eds.), *Culturally competent practice: Skills, interventions and evaluations* (pp. 1–9). Boston: Allyn & Bacon.

Ford, J. K., Smith, E. M., Weissbein, D. A., Gully, S. M., & Salas, E. (1998). Relationships of goal orientation, meta cognitive activity and practice strategies with learning outcomes and transfer. *Journal of Applied Psychology, 83*(2), 218–233.

Galambos, C. M. (2003). Moving cultural diversity toward cultural competence in health care. *Health & Social Work, 28*(1), 3–7.

Garcia, B., & Van Soest, D. (2000). Facilitating learning on diversity: Challenges to the professor. *Journal of Ethnic and Cultural Diversity in Social Work, 9*(1/2), 21–39.

Giffort, D. W. (1998). A systems approach to developing staff training. *New Directions for Mental Health Services, 79*, 25–33.

Hall, E. T. (1983). *The dance of life: Other dimensions of time.* New York: Doubleday.

Harris, P. R., & Moran, T. (1996). *Managing cultural differences: Leadership strategies for a new world business* (4th ed.). London: Gulf.

Hoefstede, G. (1997). *Cultures and organizations: Software of the mind.* New York: McGraw-Hill.

Holcomb-McCoy, C. C., & Myers, J. E. (1999). Multicultural competence and counselor training: A national survey. *Journal of Counseling and Development, 77*(3), 294–302.

Koyama, T. (1992). *Japan: A handbook in intercultural communication.* Sydney, NSW, Australia: National Center for English Language Teaching and Research.

Ladany, N., Inman, A. G., Constantine, M. G., & Hofheinz, E. W. (1997). Supervisee multicultural case conceptualization ability and self-reported multicultural competence as functions of supervisee racial identity and supervisor focus. *Journal of Counseling Psychology, 44*(3), 284–293.

Lewis, R. D. (1997). *When cultures collide: Managing successfully across cultures.* London: Nicholas Brealey.

Lum, D. (2003). *Culturally competent practice: A framework for understanding diverse groups and justice issues* (2nd ed.). Pacific Grove, CA: Brooks/Cole and Thomson Learning.

Manoleas, P. (1994). An outcome approach to assessing the cultural competence of MSW students. *Journal of Multicultural Social Work, 3*(1), 43–57.

Morrison, T., Conway, W. A., & Borden, G. A. (1994). *Kiss, bow, or shake hands: How to do business in six countries.* Holbrook, MA: Adams Media Corporation.

Morrison Van Vooris, R. (1998). Culturally relevant practice: A framework for teaching the psychosocial dynamics of oppression. *Journal of Social Work Education, 34*(1), 121–133.

Neuliep, J. W. (2000). *Communication: A contextual approach.* New York: Houghton-Mifflin.

Oles, T. P., Black, B. M., & Cramer, E. P. (1999). From attitude change to effective practice: Exploring the relationship. *Journal of Social Work Education, 35*(1), 87–100.

Ottavi, T. M., Pope-Davis, D. B., & Dings, J. G. (1994). Relationship between white racial identity attitudes and self-reported multicultural counseling competencies. *Journal of Counseling Psychology, 41*(2), 149–154.

Pearlsmutter, S. (1998). Self-efficacy and organizational change leadership. *Administration in Social Work, 22*(3), 23–38.

Ponteretto, J. G., Rieger, B. P., Barrett, A., Sparks, R., Sanchez, C. M.,& Magidis, D. M. (1996). Development and initial validation of the Multicultural Counseling Awareness Scale. In G. R. Sodowsky, & J. C. Impara (Eds.), *Multicultural assessment in counseling and clinical psychology* (pp. 247–282). Lincoln: University of Nebraska–Lincoln, Buros Institute of Mental Measurements.

Poole, D. L. (1998). Politically correct or culturally competent? *Health and Social Work, 23*(3), 163–166.

Pope-Davis, D. B., & Dings, J. G. (1995). The assessment of multicultural counseling competencies. In J. G. Ponterotto, J. M. Casa, L. A. Suzuki & C. M. Alexander (Eds.), *Handbook of multicultural counseling* (pp. 287–311). Thousand Oaks, CA: Sage.

Pope-Davis, D. B., & Nielson, D. (1996). Assessing multicultural counseling competencies using the Multicultural Counseling Inventory: A review of the research. In G. R. Sodowsky & J. C. Impara (Eds.), *Multicultural assessment in counseling and clinical psychology* (pp. 325–343). Lincoln: University of Nebraska–Lincoln, Buros Institute of Mental Measurements.

Pope-Davis, D. B., Reynolds, A. L., Dings, J. G., & Nielson, D. (1995). Examining multicultural counseling competencies of graduate students in psychology. *Professional Psychology: Research and Practice, 26*, 322–329.

Porter, R. E., & Samovar, L. A. (1997). An introduction to intercultural communication. In L. A. Samovar, & R. E. Porter, *Intercultural communication: A reader* (8th ed., pp. 5–26) Belmont, CA: Wadsworth.

Price, E. G., Beach, M. C., Gary, T. L., Robinson, K. A., Gozu, A., Palacio, A., et al. (2005). A systematic review of the methodological rigor of studies evaluating cultural competence training of health professionals. *Academic Medicine, 80*(6), 578–586.

Ridley, C. R., Espelage, D. L., & Rubinstein, K. J. (1997). Course development in multicultural counseling. In D. B. Pope-Davis & H. Coleman (Eds.), *Multicultural counseling competencies: Assessment, education and training, and supervision* (Vol. 7, pp. 131–158). Thousand Oaks, CA: Sage.

Ridley, C. R., Mendoza, D. W., & Kanitz, B. E. (1994). Multicultural training: Reexamination, operationalization, and integration. *The Counseling Psychologist, 22*(2), 227–289.

Rittner, B., Nakanishi, M., Nackerud, L., & Hammons, K. (1999). How MSW graduates apply what they learned about diversity to their work with small groups. *Journal of Social Work Education, 35*(3), 421–431.

Ronnau, J. P. (1994). Teaching cultural competence: practical ideas for social work educators. *Journal of Multicultural Social Work, 3*(1), 29–42.

Samovar, L. A., & Porter, R. E. (1997). *Intercultural communication: A reader* (8th ed.). New York: Wadsworth.

Samovar, L. A., Porter, R. E., & Stefani, L. A. (1998). *Communication between cultures*. Belmont, CA: Wadsworth.

Sandelands, E. (1998). Emerging issues in continuing professional development. *Continuing Professional Development, 1,* 74–84.

Sodowsky, G. R., Kuo-Jackson, P. Y., Richardson, M. F., & Corey, A. T. (1998). Correlates of self-reported multicultural competencies: Counselor multicultural social desirability, race, social inadequacy, locus of control racial ideology, and multicultural training. *Journal of Counseling Psychology, 45*(3), 256–264.

Sodowsky, G. R., Taffe, R. C., Gutkin, T. B., & Wise, S. L. (1994). Development of the Multicultural Counseling Inventory: A self-report measure of multicultural competencies. *Journal of Counseling Psychology, 41*(2), 137–148.

Tsang, A. K. T., & Bogo, M. (1997). Engaging with clients cross-culturally: Towards developing research-based practice. *Journal of Multicultural Social Work, 6*(3/4), 73–91.

Williams, C. C. (2002). A rationale for an anti-racist entry point to anti-oppressive social work in mental health services. *Critical Social Work, 2*(2), 20–31.

Writing Grant Proposals

17

The Foundation Center

The subject of this chapter is **proposal** writing. It introduces you to the process of how to go about writing a grant to obtain funds so that you can create your own social service program. But your proposal does not stand alone. It must be part of a process of planning and of research on, outreach to, and cultivation of potential foundation and corporate donors.

This process is grounded in the conviction that a partnership should develop between you and the donor. When you spend a great deal of your time seeking money, it is hard to remember that it can also be difficult to give money away. In fact, the dollars contributed by a foundation or corporation (the **donor**) have no value until they are attached to solid social work agencies (the **donees**).

This truly is an ideal partnership. Social work agencies have the ideas and the capacity to solve problems, but no dollars with which to implement them. The foundations and corporations have the financial resources but not the other resources needed to create programs. Bringing the two together effectively results in a dynamic collaboration.

You need to follow a step by step process in the search for private and public dollars. It takes time and persistence to succeed. After you have written a proposal, it could take as long as a year to obtain the funds needed to carry it out. And even a perfectly written proposal submitted to the right prospect (the donor) can be rejected for any number of reasons.

Proposal
A written application asking for money, often accompanied by supporting documents, submitted to a foundation or corporation who provides the funds.

Donor
An individual or organization who makes a grant or contribution to a donee.

Donee
The recipient of a grant.

Raising funds is an investment in the future. Your aim should be to build a network of foundation and corporate funders, many of whom give small gifts on a fairly steady basis and a few of whom give large periodic grants. By tenaciously pursuing the various steps of the process, each year you can retain most of your regular supporters and strike a balance with the comings and goings of larger donors.

Our recommended process is not a formula to be rigidly adhered to. It is a suggested approach that can be adapted to fit the needs of any social work agency and the peculiarities of each situation. Fundraising is an art as well as a science. You must bring your own creativity to it and remain flexible.

GATHERING BACKGROUND INFORMATION

The first thing you will need to do in writing the proposal is to gather the documentation for it. You will require background documentation in three areas: (1) the program concept, (2) the program itself, and (3) program expenses.

If all of this information is not readily available to you, determine who will help you gather each type of information. If you are part of a small social work agency with no staff, a knowledgeable board member will be the logical choice. If you are in a larger agency, there should be program and financial support staff who can help you. Once you know with whom to talk, identify the questions to ask. This data-gathering process makes the actual writing much easier. And by involving other stakeholders in the process, it also helps key people within your agency seriously consider the program's value to the organization.

Program Concept

It is important that you have a good sense of how your proposed program fits into the philosophy and mission of your agency. The social need that the proposal is addressing must also be documented. These concepts must be well articulated in the proposal. Funders want to know that a program reinforces the overall direction of an organization, and they may need to be convinced that the case for your proposed program is compelling. You should collect background data on your organization and on the social need to be addressed so that your arguments are well documented.

Your Program

Here is a checklist of the program information you will require:

- The nature of the program and how it will be conducted.
- The timetable for the program.

- The anticipated outcomes and how best to evaluate the results.
- The staffing and volunteer needs, including deployment of existing staff and new hires.

Program Expenses

You will not be able to pin down all the expenses associated with your program until the program details and timing have been worked out. Thus, the main financial data gathering takes place after the narrative part of the master proposal has been written. However, at this stage you do need to sketch out the broad outlines of the **budget** to be sure that the costs are in reasonable proportion to the outcomes you anticipate. If it appears that the costs will be prohibitive even with a foundation grant, you should then scale back your plans or adjust them to remove the least cost-effective expenditures.

Budget
A financial plan for saving and spending money.

COMPONENTS OF A PROPOSAL

Executive Summary: An umbrella statement of your case and summary of the entire proposal (1 page).

Statement of Need: Why this program is necessary (2 pages).

Program Description: Nuts and bolts of how the program will be implemented and evaluated (3 pages).

Budget: Financial description of the program plus explanatory notes (1 page).

Organization Information: History and governing structure of the social work agency; its primary activities, audiences, and services (1 page).

Conclusion: Summary of the proposal's main points (2 paragraphs).

Executive Summary

The first page of your proposal, the **executive summary**, is the most important section of the entire document. Here you will provide the reader with a snapshot of what is to follow. Specifically, it is a sales document that summarizes all of the key information and is designed to convince the reader that this program should be considered for financial support. Be certain to include these points:

Executive summary
A nontechnical summary statement designed to provide a quick overview of the full-length report on which it is based.

- *Problem.* A brief statement of the social problem or need your agency has recognized and is prepared to address (one or two paragraphs).
- *Solution.* A short description of your proposed program, including what will take place and how many people will benefit from the program, how and where it will operate, for how long, and who will staff it (one or two paragraphs).

- *Funding Requirements.* An explanation of the amount of grant money required for your program and what your plans are for funding it in the future (one paragraph).
- *Organization and Its Expertise.* A brief statement of the name, history, purpose, and activities of your agency, emphasizing its capacity to carry out this proposal (one paragraph).

Statement of Need

If funders read beyond the executive summary, you have successfully piqued their interest. Your next task is to build on this initial interest in your proposed program by enabling the funder to understand the social problem that your proposed program hopes to remedy.

The statement of need will enable the reader to learn more about the issues. It presents the facts and evidence that support the need for your program and establishes that your social work agency understands the problems and therefore can reasonably address them.

The information used to support your case can come from authorities in the field as well as from your agency's own experience. You want the need section of your proposal to be succinct yet persuasive. Like a good debater, you must assemble all the arguments then present them in a logical sequence that will readily convince the reader of their importance. As you marshal your arguments, consider the following six points.

1. *Decide which facts or statistics best support your proposed program.* Be sure the data you present are accurate. There are few things more embarrassing than to have the funder tell you that your information is out of date or incorrect. Information that is too generic or broad will not help you develop a winning argument for your program. Information that does not relate to your organization or the proposed program you are presenting will cause the funder to question the entire proposal. There also should be a balance between the information presented and the scale of your program.

2. *Give the reader hope.* The picture you paint should not be so grim that the solution appears hopeless. The funder will wonder whether an investment in a solution is worthwhile. Here's an example of a solid statement of need: "Breast cancer kills. But statistics prove that regular check-ups catch most breast cancer in the early stages, reducing the likelihood of death. Hence, a program to encourage preventive check-ups will reduce the risk of death due to breast cancer." Avoid overstatement and overly emotional appeals.

3. *Decide if you want to put your program forward as a model.* This could expand the base of potential funders, but serving as a model works only for certain types of programs. Don't try to make this argument if it doesn't really fit. Funders may well expect your agency to follow through with a replication plan if you present your program as a model.

If the decision about a model is affirmative, you should document how the social problem you are addressing occurs in other communities. Be sure to explain how your solution could be a solution for others as well.

4. *Determine whether it is reasonable to portray the need as acute.* You are asking the funder to pay more attention to your proposal because either the social problem you address is worse than others or the solution you propose makes more sense than others. Here is an example of a balanced but weighty statement: "Drug abuse is a national problem. Each day, children all over the country die from drug overdoses. In the South Bronx the problem is worse. More children die here than anyplace else. It is an epidemic. Hence, our drug prevention program is needed more in the South Bronx than in any other part of the city."

5. *Decide whether you can demonstrate that your program addresses the need differently or better than other programs that preceded it.* It is often difficult to describe the need for your program without being critical of the competition. But you must be careful not to do so. Being critical of other social work programs will not be well received by the funder. It may cause the funder to look more carefully at your program to see why you felt you had to build your case by demeaning others. Additionally, the funder already may have invested in these other programs or may begin to consider investing in them now that you have brought them to the funder's attention.

If possible, you should make it clear that you are cognizant of, and on good terms with, others doing work in your field. Keep in mind that today's funders are very interested in collaboration. They may even ask why you are not collaborating with those you view as key competitors. So at the least you need to describe how your work complements, but does not duplicate, the work of others.

6. *Avoid circular reasoning.* In circular reasoning, you present the absence of your solution as the actual problem. Then your solution is offered as the way to solve the problem. For example, the circular reasoning for building a community swimming pool might go like this: "The problem is that we have no pool in our community. Building a pool will solve the problem." A more persuasive case would cite what a pool has meant to a neighboring community, permitting it to offer recreation, exercise, and physical therapy programs. The statement might refer to a survey that underscores the target audience's planned usage of the facility and conclude with the connection between the proposed usage and potential benefits that enhance life in the community.

The statement of need does not have to be long and involved. Short, concise information captures the reader's attention.

Program Description

The program definition section of your proposal should have five subsections: (1) objectives, (2) methods, (3) staffing/administration, (4) evaluation, and (5) sustainability. Together, objectives and methods dictate staffing and administrative requirements, and they then become the focus of the evaluation to assess the results of the program. The program's sustainability flows directly from its success, hence its ability to attract other financial support. Taken together, the five subsections present an interlocking picture of the total program.

Objectives

Objectives are the measurable outcomes of the program. They define your methods. Your objectives must be tangible, specific, concrete, measurable, and achievable in a specified time period. Grant seekers often confuse objectives with goals, which are conceptual and more abstract. For the purpose of illustration, here is the goal of a program with a subsidiary objective:

Goal

Our afterschool program will help children read better.

Objective

Our afterschool remedial education program will assist 50 children in improving their reading scores by one grade level as demonstrated on standardized reading tests that will be administered after they have participated in the program for six months.

The goal in this case is abstract: improving reading. The objective is much more specific, and it is achievable in the short term (six months) and is measurable (improving 50 children's reading scores by one grade level).

With competition for dollars so great, well-articulated objectives are increasingly critical to a proposal's success. Using a different example, there are at least four types of objectives:

1. *Behavioral*—A human action is anticipated. Example: Fifty of the 70 children participating will learn to swim.
2. *Performance*—A specific time frame within which a behavior will occur, at an expected proficiency level, is expected. Example: Fifty of the 70 children will learn to swim within six months and will pass a basic swimming proficiency test administered by a Red Cross–certified lifeguard.
3. *Process*—The manner in which something occurs is an end in itself. Example: We will document the teaching methods used and identify those with the greatest success.
4. *Product*—A tangible item results. Example: A manual will be created to be used in teaching swimming to this age and proficiency group in the future.

In any given proposal, you will find yourself setting forth one or more of these types of objectives, depending on the nature of your proposed program. Be certain to present the objectives very clearly. Make sure that they stand out on the page and do not become lost in verbiage. You might, for example, use numbers, bullets, or indentations to denote the objectives in the text. Above all, be realistic in setting objectives: Don't promise what you can't deliver. Remember, the funder will want to be told in the final report that the program actually accomplished these objectives.

Methods, or Interventions

By means of the objectives, you have explained to the funder what will be achieved by the program. The methods section describes the specific activities that will take place to achieve the objectives. It enables the reader to visualize the implementation of the program. It should convince the reader that your agency knows what it is doing, thereby establishing its credibility. It might be helpful to divide your discussion of methods into the following: how, when, and why.

How. This is the detailed description of what will occur from the time the program begins until it is completed. Your methods should match the previously stated objectives.

When. The methods section should present the order and timing for the tasks. It might make sense to provide a timetable so that the reader does not have to map out the sequencing on his or her own. The timetable tells the reader "when" and provides another summary of the program that supports the rest of the methods section.

Why. You may need to defend your chosen methods, or interventions, especially if they are new or unorthodox. Why will the planned work lead to the outcomes you anticipate? You can answer this question in a number of ways, including using expert testimony and examples of other programs that work.

Staffing/Administration

In describing the methods, you will have already mentioned staffing for the program. You now need to devote a few sentences to discussing the number of staff, their qualifications, and specific assignments. Details about individual staff members involved in the program can be included either as part of this section or in an appendix, depending on the length and importance of this information.

"Staffing" may refer to volunteers or consultants as well as paid staff. Most proposal writers do not develop staffing sections for programs that are primarily run by volunteers. Describing tasks that volunteers will undertake, however, can be most helpful to the proposal reader. Such information underscores the value added by the volunteers as well as the cost-effectiveness of the program.

For a program with paid staff, be certain to describe which staff will work full time and which will work part time on the program. Identify staff already employed by your social work agency and those to be recruited specifically for the program. How will you free up the time of an already fully deployed individual?

Salary and program costs are affected by the qualifications of the staff. Delineate the practical experience you require for key staff as well as the level of expertise and educational background. If an individual has already been selected to direct the program, summarize his or her credentials and include a brief biographical sketch in the appendix. A strong program director can help influence a grant decision.

Describe for the reader your plans for administering the program. This is especially important in a large operation and if more than one agency is collaborating on your proposed program. State who will be the fiscal agent. It needs to be crystal clear who is responsible for financial management, program outcomes, and reporting.

Evaluation

An evaluation plan should not be considered only after the program is over; it should be built into the program. Including an evaluation plan in your proposal indicates that you take your objectives seriously and want to know how well you have achieved them. Evaluation is also a sound management tool. Like strategic planning, it helps a social work agency refine and improve its programs. An evaluation can often be the best means for others to learn from your experience in conducting the program.

There are two general types of evaluations. One measures the product; the other analyzes the process. Either or both might be appropriate to your program. The approach you choose will depend on the nature of your program and its objectives. For either type, you will need to describe the manner in which evaluation information will be collected and how the data will be analyzed. You should present your plan for how the evaluation and its results will be reported and the audience to whom it will be directed. For example, it might be used internally or be shared with the funder, or it might deserve a wider audience. A funder might even have an opinion about the scope of this dissemination.

Sustainability

A clear message from grantmakers today is that grant seekers will be expected to demonstrate in very concrete ways the long-term financial viability of the program to be funded and of the social work agency organization itself.

It stands to reason that most grantmakers will not want to take on a permanent funding commitment to a particular agency. Rather, funders will want you to prove that your program is finite (with start-up and ending dates); or that it is capacity building (that it will contribute to the future self-sufficiency of your agency and/or enable it to expand services that might be revenue generating); or that it will make your organization attractive to other funders in the future. With the new trend toward adopting some of the investment principles of venture capital groups to the practice of philanthropy, evidence of fiscal sustainability becomes a highly sought-after characteristic of the successful grant proposal.

It behooves you to be very specific about current and programed funding streams, both earned income and fundraised, and about the base of financial support for your social work agency. This is an area where it is important to have backup figures and prognostications at the ready in case a prospective funder asks for these, even though you are unlikely to include this information in the actual grant proposal. Some grantmakers, of course, will want to know who else will be receiving a copy of this same proposal. You should not be shy about sharing this information with your potential funder.

Budget

The budget for your proposal may be as simple as a one-page statement of program expenses. Or your proposal may require a more complex presentation, perhaps including a page on program support and revenue and notes explaining various items of expense or revenue.

Expense Budget

As you prepare to assemble the budget, go back through the proposal narrative and make a list of all personnel and nonpersonnel items related to the operation of your proposed program. Be sure that you list not only new costs that will be incurred if your program is funded but also any ongoing expenses. Then get the relevant costs from the person in your agency who is responsible for keeping the books. You may need to estimate the proportions of your agency's ongoing expenses that should be charged to the program and any new costs, such as salaries for program personnel not yet hired. Put the costs you have identified next to each item on your list.

Your list of budget items and the calculations you have done to arrive at a dollar figure for each item should be summarized on worksheets. You should keep these to remind yourself how the numbers were developed. These worksheets can be useful as you continue to develop the proposal and discuss it with funders; they are also a valuable tool for monitoring the program once it is under way and for reporting after completion of the grant.

A portion of a worksheet for a year-long program might look like Table 17.1. With your worksheets in hand, you are ready to prepare the expense budget. For most programs, costs should be grouped into subcategories, selected to reflect the critical areas of expense. All significant costs should be broken out within the subcategories,

Table 17.1 Sample Worksheet for a Year-Long Program

Item	Description	Costs
Executive Director	Supervision	10% of salary = $10,000 25% benefits = $2,500
Program Director	Hired in month one	11 months at $35,000 = $32,083 25% benefits = $8,025
Tutors	12 working 10 hours per week for three months	12 × 10 × 13 × $ 4.50 = $7,020
Office Space	Requires 25% of current space	25% × $20,000 = $5,000
Overhead	20% of program cost	20% × $64,628 = $12,926

but small ones can be combined on one line. You might divide your expense budget into personnel and nonpersonnel costs; your personnel subcategories might include salaries, benefits, and consultants. Subcategories under nonpersonnel costs might include travel, equipment, and printing, for example, with a dollar figure attached to each line.

Support and Revenue and Statement

For the typical program, no support and revenue statement is necessary. The expense budget represents the amount of grant support required. But if grant support has already been awarded to the program, or if you expect program activities to generate income, a support and revenue statement is the place to provide this information.

In itemizing grant support, make note of any earmarked grants; this will suggest how new grants may be allocated. The total grant support already committed should then be deducted from the "Total Expenses" line on the expense budget to give you the "Amount to Be Raised" or the "Balance Requested."

Budget Narrative

A narrative portion of the budget is used to explain any unusual line items in the budget and is not always needed. If costs are straightforward and the numbers tell the story clearly, explanations are redundant. If you decide a budget narrative is needed, you can structure it in one of two ways. You can create "Notes to the Budget," with footnote-style numbers on the line items in the budget keyed to numbered explanations. If an extensive or more general explanation is required, you can structure the budget narrative as straight text. Remember that the basic narrative about the program and your organization belongs elsewhere in the proposal, not in the budget narrative.

Organizational Information

Normally a resume of your social work agency organization should come at the end of your proposal. Your natural inclination may be to put this information up front in the document. But it is usually better to sell the need for your proposed program and then your agency's ability to carry it out.

It is not necessary to overwhelm the reader with facts about your organization. This information can be conveyed easily by attaching a brochure or other prepared statement. In two pages or less, tell the reader when your social work agency came into existence; state its mission, being certain to demonstrate how the subject of the proposal fits within or extends that mission; and describe the organization's structure, programs, and special expertise.

Discuss the size of the board, how board members are recruited, and their level of participation. Give the reader a feel for the makeup of the board. (You should include a list of all the board members as an appendix.) If your agency is composed of volunteers or has an active volunteer group, describe the function that the volunteers fill. Provide details on the staff, including the numbers of full and part-time staff, and their levels of expertise.

Describe the kinds of activities in which your staff engage. Explain briefly the assistance you provide. Describe the audience you serve, any special or unusual needs they face, and why they rely on your agency. Cite the number of people who are reached through your programs.

Conclusion

Every proposal should have a concluding paragraph or two. This is a good place to call attention to the future, after the grant is completed. If appropriate, you should outline some of the follow-up activities that might be undertaken to begin to prepare your funders for your next request. Alternatively, you should state how your proposed program might carry on without further grant support.

This section is also the place to make a final appeal for your proposed program. Briefly reiterate what your social work agency wants to do and why it is important. Underscore why your agency needs funding to created a new program. Don't be afraid at this stage to use a bit of emotion to solidify your case.

LETTER PROPOSAL

Sometimes the scale of a proposed social service program might suggest a small-scale letter format proposal, or the type of request might not require all of the proposal components or the components in the sequence recommended here. The guidelines and policies of individual funders will be your ultimate guide. Many funders today state that they prefer a brief letter proposal; others require that you complete an application form. In any case, you will want to refer to the basic proposal components as provided here to be sure that you have not omitted an element that will support your case.

As noted, the scale of the program will often determine whether it requires a letter or the longer proposal format. For example, a request to purchase a $1,000 fax machine for your program simply does not lend itself to a lengthy narrative. A small contribution to your program's annual operating budget, particularly if it is a renewal of past support, might also warrant a letter rather than a full-scale proposal.

What are the elements of a letter request? For the most part, they should follow the format of a full proposal, except with regard to length. The letter should be no more than three pages. You will need to call upon your writing skills because it can be very hard to get all of the necessary details into a concise, well-articulated letter.

As to the flow of information, follow these steps while keeping in mind that you are writing a letter to someone. It should not be as formal in style as a longer proposal would be. It may be necessary to change the sequence of the text to achieve the correct tone and the right flow of information.

Here are the components of a good letter proposal:

- *Ask for the gift:* The letter should begin with a reference to your prior contact with the funder, if any. State why you are writing and how much funding is required from the particular foundation.
- *Describe the need:* In a very abbreviated manner, tell the funder why there is a need for this program, piece of equipment, etc.
- *Explain what you will do:* Just as you would in a fuller proposal, provide enough detail to intrigue the funder's interest. Describe precisely what will take place as a result of the grant.
- *Provide agency data:* Help the funder know a bit more about your organization by including your mission statement, brief description of programs offered, number of people served, and staff, volunteer, and board data, if appropriate.
- *Include appropriate budget data:* Even a letter request may have a budget that is a half page long. Decide if this information should be incorporated into the letter or in a separate attachment. Whichever course you choose, be sure to indicate the total cost of the program. Discuss future funding only if the absence of this information will raise questions.
- *Close:* As with the longer proposal, a letter proposal needs a strong concluding statement.
- *Attach any additional information required:* The funder may need much of the same information to back up a small request as a large one: a board list, a copy of your IRS determination letter, financial documentation, and brief resumes of key staff.

It may take as much thought and data gathering to write a good letter request as it does to prepare a full proposal (and sometimes even more). Don't assume that because it is only a letter, it isn't a time-consuming and challenging task. Every document you put in front of a funder says something about your agency. Each step you take with a funder should build a relationship for the future.

What Happens Next?

Submitting your proposal is nowhere near the end of your involvement in the grant-making process. Grant review procedures vary widely, and the decision-making process can take anywhere from a few weeks to six months or more. During the review process, the funder may ask for additional information either directly from you or from outside consultants or professional references. Invariably, this is a difficult time for the grantseeker. You need to be patient but persistent. Some grantmakers outline their review procedures in annual reports or application guidelines. If you are unclear about the process, don't hesitate to ask.

If your hard work results in a grant, take a few moments to acknowledge the funder's support with a letter of thanks. You also need to find out whether the funder has specific forms, procedures, and deadlines for reporting the progress of your proposed program. Clarifying your responsibilities as a grantee at the outset, particularly with respect to financial reporting, will prevent misunderstandings and more serious problems later.

Nor is rejection necessarily the end of the process. If you're unsure why your proposal was rejected, ask. Did the funder need additional information? Would they be interested in considering the proposal at a future date? Now might also be the time to begin cultivation of a prospective funder. Put them on your mailing list so that they can become further acquainted with your organization. Remember, there's always next year.

Summing Up

This chapter briefly described how to go about obtaining funds to create a new social service program. All of the contents in the previous chapters of this book will have to be used to write a successful grant proposal. If you have a well-thought out program, via a program logic model, and you can write clearly and succinctly, getting funds to help your program get going is an easy task.

RECAP AND ONLINE MATERIALS

In this chapter, you learned how to write grant proposals in order to obtain funds to create a social work program.

You should also recall the concept of research proposals from your foundational research course. If not, go online to take a free crash course in proposal writing.

You can also find the following materials online to help you master the concepts you just learned:

- Chapter Outline
- Learning Objectives
- Key Terms and Concepts
- Flash Cards
- Practice Multiple-Choice Tests
- Essay Questions with Answers
- Links

www.oup.com/us/swevaluation

STUDY QUESTIONS

1. List and discuss the three types of background information you will need before you can write a proposal to fund a social service program. Provide a social work example throughout your discussion.
2. Discuss the purpose and the need to include an executive summary in a proposal. Provide a social work example throughout your discussion.
3. Discuss the purpose and need to include a statement of need in a proposal. Provide a social work example throughout your discussion.
4. Discuss the purpose and need to include a program description in a proposal. Provide a social work example throughout your discussion.
5. Discuss the purpose and need to include a methods, or intervention section in a proposal. Provide a social work example throughout your discussion.
6. Discuss the purpose and need to include a staffing/administration section in a proposal. Provide a social work example throughout your discussion.
7. Discuss the purpose and need to include an evaluation section in a proposal. Provide a social work example throughout your discussion.
8. Discuss the purpose and need to include a sustainability section in a proposal. Provide a social work example throughout your discussion.
9. Discuss the purpose and need to include a budget in a proposal. Provide a social work example throughout your discussion.
10. Discuss the purpose and need to include organizational information in a pro-

posal. List and discuss in detail the components of a proposal. Provide a social work example throughout your discussion.

References, Further Reading, and Resources

Bauer, D. G. (1999). *The "how to" grants manual*. Phoenix, AZ: Oryx Press.

Bauer, D. G. (2001). *How to evaluate and improve your grants effort*. Westport, CT: Oryx Press.

Boss, R. W. (1980). *Grant money and how to get it*. New York: Bowker.

Coley, S., & Scheinberg, C. (1990). *Proposal writing*. Thousand Oaks, CA: Sage.

Foundation Center [Web site]. (2006). Retrieved February 20, 2006, from http://www.fdncenter.org

Golden, L. (1997). *Successful grantsmanship*. San Francisco: Jossey-Bass.

National Science Foundation (2005). *A guide to proposal writing*. Arlington, VA: Author.

Williams, M., Tutty, L., & Grinnell, R. M., Jr. (2005). Writing quantitative proposals and reports. In R. M. Grinnell, Jr., & Y. A. Unrau (Eds.), *Social work research and evaluation: Quantitative and qualitative approaches* (7th ed., pp. 371–384). New York: Oxford University Press.

Williams, M., Unrau, Y.A., & Grinnell, R.M., Jr. (2005). Writing qualitative proposals and reports. In R. M. Grinnell, Jr., & Y. A. Unrau (Eds.), *Social work research and evaluation: Quantitative and qualitative approaches* (7th ed., pp. 421–435). New York: Oxford University Press.

Yuen, F. K., & Terao, K. L. (2003). *Practical grant writing and program evaluation*. Pacific Grove, CA: Brooks/Cole.

CREDITS

Figures

Figure 1.4 Mulroy, E.A. (2004). Theoretical perspectives on the social environment to guide management and community practice: An organization-in-environment approach. *Administration in Social Work, 28*(1), 77–96.

Figure 2.2 Various versions of the generic program evaluation process can be found at:
http://www.evaluationtools.org/planning.asp;
http://www.socialresearchmethods.net/kb/pecycle.htm;
http://www.cdc.gov/eval/steps.htm;
http://www.wkkf.org/default.aspx;
http://www.urban.org

Figure 4.8 Ellen Taylor-Powell, Ph.D., Evaluation Specialist, University of Wisconsin-Extension-Cooperative Extension. Retrieved from "Logic Models: A Framework for Program Planning and Evaluation" on May 12, 2006, from http://www.uwex.edu/ces/pdande/evaluation/powerpt/nutritionconf05.ppt#256

Figure 5.4 Adapted from "Designing measuring instruments," by C. Mindel, in R. M. Grinnell, Jr. (Ed.), *Social work research and evaluation: Quantitative and qualitative approaches* (6th ed.). Copyright © 2001 by F.E. Peacock Publishers.

Figure 9.1 Steven L. McMurtry. Copyright © 1994 by WALMAR Publishing Company and Steven L. McMurtry. Scale can be obtained from WALMYR Publishing Co., P.O., Box 12317, Tallahassee, FL 12317-2217. Reprinted with permission.

Figure 9.2 Adapted from P. N. Reid, and J. H. Gundlach, "A scale for the measurement of consumer satisfaction with social services," *Journal of Social Service Research, 7*, 37–54. Copyright © 1983 by P. N. Reid and J. H. Gundlach. Reprinted with permission.

Tables

Table 2.1 Dawn C. Koger, Ph.D., Early Childhood Consultant, Oakland Schools, 2111 Pontiac Lake Road, Waterford, MI 48328. Used with permission.

Table 6.1 Carol T. Mowbray, Mark C. Holter, Gregory B. Teague, & Deborah Bybee. *American Journal of Evaluation, 24*(3), 315–340, copyright 2003 by Sage Publications. Reprinted by permission of Sage Publications.

Table 9.1 Adapted from "Integrating data-gathering techniques and practice activities," by Deborah H. Siegel, in *Social Work Research and Evaluation* (3rd ed.), edited by Richard M. Grinnell, Jr. Copyright © 1988 by F. E. Peacock Publishers.

Table 10.1 Lampkin, L. M., & Hatry, H. P. (2003). *Key steps in outcome management.* Washington, DC: Urban Institute. Reprinted with permission.

Table 10.2 W. K. Kellogg Foundation Toolkit. Retrieved on May 12, 2006, from www.wkkf.org. Reprinted with permission.

Table 10.3 "But Does It Work? Improving Evaluations of Sexuality Education," by Debra W. Haffner and Eva S. Goldfarb, *SIECUS Report*, Vol. 25, No. 6 (August/September, 1997). Reprinted with permission.

Boxes

Box 1.1 National Association of Social Workers (1996). *Code of ethics.* Silver Spring, MD: Author.

Box 1.2 Council on Social Work Education (2005). *Curriculum policy statement.* Washington, DC: Author.

Box 1.3 "What Is Stakeholder Involvement?" Retrieved on November 1, 2005, from Stephen T. Russell, Nicole Polen, and Sherry Betts, http://cals-cf.calsnet.arizona.edu/fcs/content.cfm?content=stakeholder. Reprinted with permission.

Box 1.4 California's Child Welfare Stakeholder's Group. Retrieved on December 11, 2005, from www.dss.cahwnet.gov/cdssweb/ChildWelfa_285.htm

Box 2.1 National Educational Research Laboratory. Retrieved December 11, 2005, from http://www.nwrel.org/evaluation/planning.shtml

Box 2.2 W.K. Kellogg Foundation Toolkit. Retrieved on October 24, 2005, from www.wkkf.org/Programming/Extra.aspx?CID=281&ID=27. Reprinted with permission.

Box 2.3 Paul F. McCawley, Ph.D., Associate Director and Professor, University of Idaho Extension, Ag Science Building, Room 58, Moscow, Idaho 83844-2338. Reprinted with permission.

Box 3.2 W.K. Kellogg Foundation. (2004). *Logic model development guide.* Battle Creek, MI: Author. Reprinted with permission.

Box 4.1 W.K. Kellogg Foundation Toolkit. Retrieved on October 24, 2005, from www.wkkf.org. Reprinted with permission.

Box 4.2 W.K. Kellogg Foundation Toolkit. Retrieved on October 24, 2005, from www.wkkf.org. Reprinted with permission.

Box 4.3 CSAP's Prevention Pathways. Retrieved on May 12, 2006, from http://pathways courses.samhsa.gov/eval101/eval101_supps_pg4.htm

Box 5.2 Lampkin, L.M., & Hatry, H.P. (2003). *Key steps in outcome management.* Washington, DC: Urban Institute. Reprinted with permission.

Box 5.3 Sally L. Bond, Sally E. Boyd, Kathleen A. Rapp, Jacqueline B. Raphael, and Beverly A. Sizemore. *Taking stock: A practical guide to evaluating your own program.* Copyright © 1997 by Horizon-Research, Inc. Reprinted with permission.

Box 7.1 Freeman, W. (January 2005). Common myths regarding outcome measures. *National Resource Center E-Newsletter: The Best of the Best.* Retrieved on May 12, 2006 from http://www.ccfbest.org/outcomemeasurements/commonmyths.htm

Box 7.2 Hatry, H. P., Cowan, J., Weiner, K., & Lampkin, L.M. (2003). *Developing community-wide outcome indicators for specific services.* Washington, DC: Urban Institute. Reprinted with permission.

Box 7.3 W. K. Kellogg Foundation (1998). *Evaluation handbook.* Battle Creek, MI: Author. Reprinted with permission.

Box 8.2 National Institute of Drug Abuse. Retrieved on May 12, 2006, from http://www.nida.nih.gov/IMPCOST/IMPCOST2.html

Box 8.3 National Institute of Drug Abuse. Retrieved on May 12, 2006, from http://www.nida .nih.gov/IMPCOST/IMPCOST2.html

Box 9.1 Steven L. McMurtry. Copyright © 1994 by WALMAR Publishing Company and Steven L. McMurtry. Scale can be obtained from WALMYR Publishing Co., P.O., Box 12317, Tallahasee, FL 12317-2217. Reprinted with permission.

Box 9.2 Hatry, H. P., Cowan, J., Weiner, K., & Lampkin, L. M. (2003). *Developing community-wide outcome indicators for specific services.* Washington, DC: Urban Institute. Reprinted with permission.

Box 9.3 Reprint of the article "A Catalog of Family Process Measures," by Margaret Caspe, in *The Evaluation Exchange*, vol. 10, no. 4, pp 8–9, published by Harvard Family Research Project. Reprinted with permission.

Box 10.3 Lampkin, L. M., & Hatry, H. P. (2003). *Key steps in outcome management.* Washington, DC: Urban Institute. Reprinted with permission.

Box 10.5 Lampkin, L. M., & Hatry, H. P. (2003). *Key steps in outcome management.* Washington, DC: Urban Institute. Reprinted with permission.

Box 13.1 Sally L. Bond, Sally E. Boyd, Kathleen A. Rapp, Jacqueline B. Raphael, and Beverly A. Sizemore. *Taking stock: A practical guide to evaluating your own program.* Copyright © 1997 by Horizon-Research, Inc. Reprinted with permission.

Box 15.1 The Joint Committee on Standards for Educational Evaluation, Inc. (1994). *The program evaluation standards* (2nd ed.). Thousand Oaks, CA: Sage. Reprinted with permission.

Chapters

Chapter 12 Minter, E., & Michaud, M. (2003). *Using graphics to report evaluation results.* Madison, WI: University of Wisconsin Extension. Reprinted with permission.

Chapter 13 Taylor-Powell, E., & Renner, M. (2003). *Analyzing qualitative data.* Madison, WI: University of Wisconsin Extension. Reprinted with permission.

Chapter 17 "Proposal Writing Short Course." Available at www.fdncenter.org/learn/short course/prop1.html. Copyright © 2006 The Foundation Center, 79 Fifth Avenue, New York, NY 10003, 212-620-4230, www.fdncenter.org. Used by permission.

Index

Page numbers in italics indicate graphics; page numbers followed by *b* or *t* indicate boxes and tables.

decision making affected by, 422–423

definition of, 418

dialogue-oriented, 429–430

enculturation, 420

ethnocentrism, 419

evaluation adapted for, 427–430

impact of, 418–419

individualist, 423

information and, 422

intercultural communication, 420–422, 426

knowledge about, 426–427

macro-level, 418

meaningful products based on, 429–430

micro-level, 418

overview of, 417–418

pace of life based on, 424–425

polychronic, 424, 429

time as viewed by, 424, 428–429

tradition and, 423–424

data

in aggregate forms, 215, 217

archival, 288*t*

budget, 448

case-level evaluation, 9–10

census, 136, 290–291

client, 136, 291

client contact, 314–317

client satisfaction

description of, 177, 311

nonstandardized, 311

social desirability of, 178

standardized, 311

connections among, 352

cultural influences on, 422

definition of, 9, 32, 130, 248, 305, 361

demographics, 107

existing. *See* existing data

external users of, 393

follow-up, 211, 397

historical, 288*t*

identifying needs, 105–106

information vs., 9–10

intake forms for, 176

interview, 137

narrative. *See* narrative data

new. *See* new data

objective, 361–362

original. *See* original data

for outcome evaluation, 210–212

outcomes-related, 114

precision of, 361

presentation of, 357*b*

process evaluation, 157

program, 136–137, 291

program-level evaluation, 9–10

qualitative. *See* qualitative data

quantitative

analysis of, 400*b*

description of, 143–145, 147–150

reliability of, 175, 300

reporting of, 323

scoring of, 179–180

service statistics, 109–110

sorting of, 351

subjective, 362–363

validity of, 175, 300

data analyses

definition of, 134, 322

indications for, 310

in needs assessment, 143–146

in outcome evaluation, 212–214

in process evaluation, 179–180

recurring themes found during, 355*b*

secondary, 136–137

data collection

about families, 160

case-level, 308–310

computer-assisted, 322

costs of, 105

cultural considerations, 429

decision making and, 307

definition of, 44

Department of Social Services case study

client contact data, 314–317

feedback data, 318–321

intake data, 311–314

termination data, 317–318

forms, 321

by front-line workers, 397

integration of, 105–106, 355*b*

persons responsible for, 212, 397

practice objectives, 318

program-level, 310–321, 376

protocols, 408

purposes of, 309

social problem's effect on, 130

timing of, 177–178, 397

training for, 300

data collection instruments

client intake form, 174

description of, 173

ease of use, 173–174

functions of, 299

program's operations and, 174–175, 299

user input, 175, 299

data collection methods

archival data, 288*t*

characteristics of, 298–299

definition of, 134, 283, 397

description of, 178–179, 212

document analysis, 287*t*

ease of use, 298

factors that influence, 135

functions of, 299

group interviews

focus groups, 138–139, 139*b*, 285*t*, 294–295, 295*b*, 397

nominal groups technique, 140–141, 295–296

public forums, 141, 294, 295*b*

individual interviews, 137–138, 284*t*–285*t*

information value affected by, 179

key informants, 137–138

mail surveys, 141–142, 293–294

for outcome evaluation, 212

participant observation, 286*t*–287*t*

political influences on, 397–398

program's operations and, 174–175, 299

questionnaire, 284*t*

results affected by, 397

reviewing existing reports, 135–136

secondary data analyses, 136–137

surveys, 141–142

telephone surveys, 141–142

usefulness of, 298

user input, 299

data collection monitoring system

data collection methods, 178–179

definition of, 208

description of, 175

development of, 299–300

as feedback system, 300

number of cases to include in, 176–177

times to collect data, 177–178

data collection plan

definition of, 134

needs addressed in, 307

data entry, 324

data information system

administrators' role in, 306

costs of, 306–307

evaluation questions
    amount of, 106
    asking of, 91–93
    changing of, 93
    data used to answer, 283
    development of, 90b–91b
    example of, 92
    formulation of, 44
    identifying of, 105
    implementation time for, 94t
    phrasing of, 283
    types of, 93
evaluation report, 215. *See also* report(s)
evaluation research, 29t
evaluator
    credibility of, 399b
    culturally competent, 430
    diversity of, 101
    responsibilities of, 102b
    role of, 37
evidence-based practice
    contributions to, 10–11
    definition of, 10
executive summary, of proposal, 439–440
existing data
    census data, 290–291
    client data, 291
    in data sets, 290
    definition of, 143, 276
    in documents, 289–290
    limitations of, 291
    narrative, 289
    obtaining of, 289–291
    program data, 291
    in reports, 289–290
    statistical, 289–290
expense budget, 445–446
expenses, 439
expert consultants, 90b
expressed needs, 127
external evaluation, 32
external project approach
    changes, 34
    characteristics of, 32
    difficulty to incorporate in practice
        settings, 35
    externally driven nature of, 32
    feedback, 34
    impracticality in applied settings, 35
    intrusiveness, 34
    resistant social workers, 34

external validity, 215
eye contact, 421

face-to-face interviews, 284t–285t, 292
Family Adaptability and Cohesion
    Evaluation Scales, 266b
family context measures, 265b–266b
Family Environment Scale, 265b
family outcomes, 203b–204b
family process measures, 265b–267b
Family Relationship Scale, 265b
family-focused questions, 131
feasibility standards, 399b, 401
feedback
    benchmarks for, 111–112, 112t
    continuous, 38, 42
    data collection for obtaining, 300, 318–
        321, 392
    decision making based on, 409
    definition of, 111
    formative evaluation for providing, 33
    from internal monitoring approach,
        40–41
    lack of, 34
    ongoing, 38
    in outcome evaluation, 214–215
    in process evaluation, 180, 182
    program-level, 182
    relevant, 40
    system for, 180, 182, 300
    timeliness of, 41
findings. *See also* results
    decision making based on, 409
    disclosure of, 399b
    interpretation of, 398
    valuation of, 398
firsthand data sources, 277–278
fiscal accountability, 18
fiscal responsibility, 400b
fixed conditions of employment, 164
flowchart, 308, *308*
focus groups
    data collection using, 138–139, 139b,
        285t, 294–295, 295b
    participation in, 397
focusing
    of evaluation, 93
    of qualitative data analysis, 343
follow-up data, 211, 397
follow-up phase, of case-level evaluation,
    372–375
formal agreements, 399b

formative evaluation
    definition of, 27, 33, 155, 157. *See also*
        process evaluation
    recurring themes in, 355b
funders
    cultural considerations, 428–429
    description of, 15, 108–109, 391
funding
    of agencies, 53–54, 437
    cost-benefit evaluation and, 227
    description of, 392
    importance of, 437–438
    proposal description of, 444–445

Gantt chart, 101, 103, *103*
general public, 14
generalizing of results, 353–354
goal attainment scale
    data generation, 257–258
    definition of, 254
    sample, 257t
goal-free evaluation, 29t
goals-based evaluation, 30t
grant proposal
    background information for, 438–439
    budget listed in, 439, 445–446
    definition of, 437
    executive summary of, 439–440
    organizational information in, 447
    program concept, information, and
        expenses listed in, 438–439
    program description in
        administration, 444
        evaluation, 444
        interventions, 443
        methods, 443
        objectives, 442–443
        overview of, 441–442
        staffing, 443–444
        sustainability, 444–445
    statement of need in, 440–441
graphic rating scales, 251
graphics
    bar charts, 332t, 334
    characteristics of, 333
    checklist about, 337–338
    definition of, 331
    illustrations, 332t, 335–336, *336*
    line graphs, 332t, 334, *335*
    photographs, 332t, 336–337, *337*
    pie charts, 332t, 334, *335*
    when to use, 332t

objectives
    description of, in grant proposal, 442–443
    performance, 442
    process. *See* process objectives
    product, 442
    program. *See* program objectives
objectivity, 249
observation
    participant, 297–298
    structured, 296–297
observer
    complete, 298
    definition of, 296
    participant, 297
open forums, 294, 295*b*
open-ended questions, 148, 341
organizational learning, 42
organization-in-environment perspective, 21
original data
    definition of, 143, 276
    from group interviews
        focus groups, 285*t*, 294–295, 295*b*
        nominal groups technique, 295–296
        public forums, 294, 295*b*
    from individual interviews, 292
    from observation
        participant, 297–298
        structured, 296–297
    obtaining of, 291–298
    from surveys, 292–294
outcome evaluation
    accountability through, 193
    collaborative effort of, 196
    data for
        analysis and display of, 212–214
        collection of, 205*b*
        description of, 210–212
        monitoring system, 201, 208–212
        preset expectations, 213–214
    decision making affected by, 195
    definition of, 27, 155, 191
    description of, 30*t*
    design of, 194
    development of, 204*b*–206*b*
    before efficiency-focused evaluation, 224
    examples of, 216*b*
    follow-up data, 211
    implementation of, 94*t*, 204*b*–206*b*
    myths regarding, 192*b*
    performance targets, 205*b*–206*b*

process evaluation and, 155
purpose of, 193–194
results of
    acceptable, 380
    inadequate, 381
    mixed, 380–381
sampling used in, 279
steps involved in
    data analysis and display, 212–214
    data monitoring system, 201, 208–212
    dissemination and communication of results, 215, 217
    feedback system, 214–215
    measurements, 199–201
    operationalizing program objectives, 196, 199
    outcomes, 199–201
    unit of analysis, 208–210
    uses of, 194–196, 202*b*
outcomes
    achievement of, 204*b*
    benchmarks for, 113
    client, 112–114
    community, 203*b*–204*b*
    description of, 48
    in efficiency-focused evaluation, 224–225
    examples of, 197*b*–198*b*, 259*b*–262*b*
    family, 203*b*–204*b*
    indicators and, 49, 205*b*, 259*b*–262*b*, 277*t*
    individual, client-focused, 202*b*–203*b*
    initial, 259*b*–260*b*
    interim, 206*b*
    intermediate, 259*b*–260*b*
    long-term, 260*b*–262*b*
    measurement of, 114, 200, 204*b*–205*b*
    needs assessment, 148–149
    nonmonetary, 231
    organization effects, 204*b*
    program, 203*b*
    program-level evaluation, 376–379
    of prospective efficiency-focused evaluations, 223
    stating of, 199–201
    system-level, 203*b*
    types of, 202*b*–204*b*, 231
outcomes-based logic model, 78*b*
outputs, in social services programs, 48
outside funders
    cultural considerations, 428–429
    description of, 391

pace of life, 424–425
Parent as a Teacher Inventory, 266*b*
Parent–Child Affective Quality, 266*b*
Parent–Child Interaction Task, 266*b*
parent–child relationship measures, 266*b*
Parent–Teacher Involvement Questionnaire, 267*b*
parenting practices, 266*b*
Parenting Practices Questionnaire, 266*b*
Parenting Practices Scale, 266*b*
Parenting Stress Index, 265*b*
participant observation, 286*t*–287*t*, 297–298
participant observer, 297
perceived needs, 126
perceptions, 420–421
performance appraisals, 391–392
performance evaluation, 31*t*
performance objectives, 442
performance targets, 205*b*–206*b*
person-in-environment perspective, 19–20
phone interviews, 286*t*
photographs, 332*t*, 336–337, *337*
physiological needs, 125, *126*
pie charts, 332*t*, 334, *335*
pilot study, 179
planning
    documentation production, 103–104
    elements of, 46–47
    importance of, 89–90
    process of, 45–46, 75
    with stakeholders, 89–104
    strategies for
        concept mapping, 94–96, *96*
        evaluation questions, 91–93
        literature review, 96–97
        schedules. *See* schedules
    volunteers, 100–101
policy-level decision making, 393
policymakers
    description of, 13–14
    public monies allocated by, 14
political influences
    data collection methods, 397–398
    interpretation of findings, 398
    manipulation, 394–395
    misdirection, 395–398
    program objectives, 395–396
    sample selection, 396–397
political viability, 399*b*, 401
politics, 389–390
polychronic culture, 424, 429

population
  census data about, 290–291
  definition of, 213
practice objectives
  changes in, 367–372
  data collection about, 318
  definition of, 250
  description of, 69–71
  operationalization of, 256
  program objectives vs., 69–71, 256–258
  setting of, 365–367
  weighting of, 256
practitioners
  description of, 15–16
  internal monitoring approach effects
    on, 41
  satisfaction of, 41
precision, 249
present value of benefits
  adjusting for, 233–235
  description of, 225b
preset categories, for narrative data, 344
prevalence, 144
probability sampling, 280, 281b
problem solving
  client-centered changes for, 37
  operationalization of, 199
  program's intentions for, 61
process evaluation
  cost efficiency estimations using, 158–
    159
  data collected from, 157, 177
  definition of, 27, 155, 444
  description of, 31t
  implementation time for, 94t
  outcome evaluation and, 155
  profession knowledge generated from,
    158
  program operations improved by, 157
  purposes of, 156–159
  questions asked during
    activities, 162, 164
    administrative supports in place to
      support client service delivery,
      164, 171
    background of program, 159–160
    client profile of program, 160
    efficiency of program, 173
    interventions, 162, 164
    service provided to clients, 161–162
    staff profile of program, 160–161
    stakeholder satisfaction, 171–172
  sampling used in, 279

steps involved in
  asking of questions. *See* process
    evaluation questions asked during
  data analysis and scoring, 179–180
  data collection instruments, 173–
    175
  data collection monitoring system,
    175–179
  dissemination and communication
    of results, 182
  feedback system, 180, 182
  summary of, 182
process objectives, 375, 442
product evaluation, 444
product objectives, 442
professional accountability, 18
professional jargon, 250
professional standards
  accuracy, 400b, 402
  feasibility, 399b, 401
  Joint Committee on Standards of
    Educational Evaluation, 398,
    399b–400b, 430
  propriety, 399b, 401–402
  utility, 399b, 400–401
professionalism, 41
program(s)
  accountability of, 393
  activities, 71, 357b
  agencies vs., 61
  background of, 159–160, 173
  boundaries of, 88–89
  change intended from, 66
  client capacity, 89
  communication in, 75
  complexity of, 89
  conceptualization of, 62, 63b
  context of, 356b–357b, 400b
  data collection, 310–321. *See also* data
    collection
  definition of, 8, 56, 87, 361, 378
  description of, 42, 88
  design of, 61–69
  duration of, 89
  efficiency of, 173
  evaluations integrated into, 42
  examples of, 57–58
  extension of, 211
  history of, 160
  internal monitoring approach effects
    on, 39–40
  language used to describe, 156
  monitoring in, 38

  naming of, 60
  organizational structure of, 57
  outcomes of, 48
  philosophy of, 160
  quality improvement in, 8–10
  relationship among, 57
  scope of, 88–89
  staff of. *See* staff
  stages of, 180
  structure of, 268b
  theory of, 64, 73b
  timing of effect, 89
  understanding of, 39–40
program data, 136–137, 291
program fidelity
  checking on, 162, 164
  criteria, 165t–170t
  definition of, 162
  monitoring of, 163
  research studies about, 165t–170t
program goals
  agency goals vs., 62, 64–66
  characteristics of, 63
  development of, 159
  purpose of, 64
  unintended results, 64
program logic model
  activities, 77b–78b, 80b, 207b
  application of, 73b–74b
  basics of, 76b–77b
  components of, 72b
  definition of, 71, 72b–73b, 106
  description of, 71
  development of, 207
  evaluation planning, 49
  examples of, 73b–74b, 77b–80b
  external influences, 48–49
  group process and, 76b
  if . . . then assumptions used in, 76b
  illustration of, 107
  impacts, 72, 77b
  impacts measured through, 206b–207b
  indicators, 49
  inputs, 47
  intended results, 72b–73b
  outcomes, 48, 72, 77b
  outcomes-based, 78b
  outputs, 48, 72, 77b
  planned work, 72b
  planning elements, 46–47
  planning process, 45–46, 75
  program investment and, 76b
  program success and, 75b–76b

recurring themes, 355*b*
referrals, 308–309
Reid-Gundlach Social Service Satisfaction Scale, *255*
relational databases, 323
relative needs, 127
reliability
    of data, 175, 300
    definition of, 14, 200
    of information, 400*b*
    interrater, 178
    of measuring instruments, 200, 262
    of objective data, 367
report(s)
    balanced, 410
    clarity of, 399*b*
    content of, 410
    dissemination of, 410
    existing data in, 289–290
    timeliness of, 399*b*
reporting
    of data, 323
    impartial, 400*b*
    of results, 356*b*
representation, 88, 402
research
    description of, 29*t*
    ethical standards for, 5
    example of, 403*b*–408*b*
responsive evaluation, 31*t*
results
    acceptable, 380
    data collection method effects on, 397
    generalizing of, 353–354
    inadequate, 381
    interpretation of, 398
    mixed, 380–381
    outcome evaluation, 380–381
    of outcome evaluation, 215, 217
    of process evaluation, 182
    reporting of, 356*b*
    valuation of, 398
retrospective efficiency-focused evaluation, 224–226
return on investment, 225*b*
reviewing existing reports, 135–136

sample
    definition of, 396
    selection of, 396–397
sampling
    availability, 282*b*
    cluster, 281*b*

convenience, 282*b*
definition of, 133
indicators for, 282–283
intervention targets obtained through, 133
nonprobability, 280, 282*b*
probability, 280, 281*b*
purposive, 282*b*
quota, 282*b*
simple random, 281*b*
snowball, 282*b*
stratified random, 281*b*
systematic random, 281*b*
sampling frame, 279–280, 282
satisfactory change, 370–372
schedules and scheduling
    function of, 98–99
    roles, 99–101
    tasks, 99
    timeliness, 101, 103
scientific thinking, 422–423
scope, 88–89
secondary data analyses, 136–137
secondhand data sources, 278
security needs, 125, *126*
self-actualization, 125, *126*
self-anchored rating scales, 251–252
Self-Perceptions of the Parental Role scale, 266*b*
self-protection, 41
self-report measuring instruments, 200–201
sensitivity analyses, 224
service delivery
    accountability integrated with, 17–18
    evaluation activities integrated with, 406, 408
service orientation, 399*b*
service statistics, 109–110
services
    amount of, 161–162
    intensity of, 161
simple random sampling, 281*b*
situation statement, 47
snowball sampling, 282*b*
social acceptability, 123
social desirability, 178
social injustices, 6
social needs
    definition of, 124
    expressed needs, 127
    Maslow's hierarchy of needs, 125–126, *126*

normative needs, 126–127
perceived needs, 126
relative needs, 127
for social problems, 125
solutions to, 127–128
Social Network Questionnaire, 265*b*
social problems
    data collection based on, 130
    defining of, 130
    definition of, 122
    line of acceptability for, 123
    rate comparisons, 144
    solutions to, 127–128
    visibility of, 123, 124*t*
social services
    agencies. *See* agencies
    programs. *See* program(s)
    shared understanding in, 248
social workers
    bias of, 249
    cooperative, 37
    influential role of, 6–8
    objectivity of, 249
    professionalism of, 41
    resistant, 34
    responsibilities of, 8
solutions
    description of, 127–128
    direct, 132
    indirect, 132
specific program objective, 68
staff
    data information system development by, 306–307
    description of, in grant proposal, 443–444
    involvement of, 409
    profile of, 160–161
    retraining of, 175
stakeholder(s)
    collaboration with, 11–12
    concept map building with, 95
    cultural considerations, 428
    definition of, 12, 88, 394
    in evaluation process, 43, 105
    feedback system for, 300
    identification of, 399*b*
    involvement by, 12
    manipulation by, 394–395
    planning with, 89–104
    satisfaction of, 171–172
stakeholder groups
    clients. *See* client(s)